Risky Behavior among Youths

A National Bureau
of Economic Research
Conference Report

Risky Behavior among Youths
An Economic Analysis

Edited by   **Jonathan Gruber**

The University of Chicago Press

Chicago and London

JONATHAN GRUBER is professor of economics at the Massachusetts Institute of Technology and a research associate of and director of the Program on Children at the National Bureau of Economic Research.

The University of Chicago Press, Chicago 60637
The University of Chicago Press, Ltd., London
© 2001 by the National Bureau of Economic Research
All rights reserved. Published 2001
Printed in the United States of America
10 09 08 07 06 05 04 03 02 01   1 2 3 4 5
ISBN: 0-226-31013-2 (cloth)

Library of Congress Cataloging-in-Publication Data

Risky behavior among youths : an economic analysis / edited by
    Jonathan Gruber.
        p.   cm.—(A National Bureau of Economic Research
    conference report)
    "Papers presented at a conference held at the South Seas
    Plantation, in December 1999"—Ack.
    Includes bibliographical references and index.
    ISBN 0-226-31013-2 (cloth : alk. paper)
    1. Youth—Psychology—Economic aspects—Congresses.
    2. Risk taking (Psychology) in adolescence—Economic aspects—
    Congresses. 3. Decision making in adolescence—Economic
    aspects—Congresses. I. Gruber, Jonathan. II. Conference report
    (National Bureau of Economic Research)
    HQ796.R554   2001
    305.235—dc21   00-047973

To my wife, Andrea, whose constant support was very helpful in making this project a reality, and to my children, Ava, Jack, and Sam

Contents

Acknowledgments

This project is part of the National Bureau of Economic Research's Program on Children, which seeks to bring economists together to study the range of issues related to child well-being. I am grateful to Martin Feldstein, president of the NBER, for having the vision to put together this general program and for his support for this project in particular. The idea for this project grew out of work I did at the U.S. Treasury Department and in particular out of conversations with Larry Summers, for which I am also grateful.

The project was supported by generous funding from the Smith Richardson Foundation and the Robert Wood Johnson Foundation. I am very grateful to Phoebe Cottingham at Smith Richardson and Tracy Orleans at RWJ for guiding the proposal through the funding process.

The papers in this volume were presented at a conference at the South Seas Plantation in December 1999. The NBER conference department staff, and in particular Kirsten Foss Davis and Joel Whalen, worked tirelessly to make this a terrific experience for everyone involved. Helena Fitz-Patrick patiently guided us through the difficult terrain of the review process and was instrumental in turning this project into an actual volume.

Introduction

Jonathan Gruber

There are a host of potentially risky behaviors in which youths engage, all of which have important implications for both their well-being and their life prospects. Activities such as smoking, drinking, having sex, and taking drugs are generally first encountered before age nineteen, yet they have important ramifications for the remainder of these youths' lives. For example, roughly one-third of high schoolers have smoked in the past thirty days, and over three-quarters of smokers start before they turn nineteen (Gruber and Zinman, chap. 2 in this volume). Over half of individuals first have sexual intercourse in high school, and almost 10 percent have been pregnant in high school (CDC 1998). And 80 percent of high schoolers have imbibed alcoholic beverages, and 63 percent of high school seniors have been drunk (University of Michigan 1998).

Moreover, the past decade has seen dramatic shifts in the intensity with which youths pursue these risky activities. The youth homicide rate fell 40 percent from 1993 to 1997, and teen births declined by 20 percent from 1991 to 1998. At the same time, youth smoking rose by one-third from 1991 to 1997, and marijuana use virtually doubled over this same period.

Despite the significance of these youth risky behaviors and the resulting ramifications for adult well-being, economists have paid relatively little attention to modeling the youth pursuit of risky behaviors, particularly

Jonathan Gruber is professor of economics at the Massachusetts Institute of Technology and a research associate of and director of the Program on Children at the National Bureau of Economic Research.

The author is grateful to James Berry, Cristian Gonzales, and Jon Zinman for research assistance; to the Smith Richardson Foundation and the Robert Wood Johnson Foundation for research support; and to two referees for helpful comments.

when compared with the attention paid the subject in other disciplines, such as developmental psychology. The purpose of this volume is to take a first step toward remedying this deficiency. Two recent developments suggest that it is an auspicious time to consider such a perspective. First, there is some preliminary evidence that youths are very responsive to economic factors, such as prices, when deciding whether to undertake risky behaviors. These findings were part of the motivation for the recent legislative activity that substantially raised the price of tobacco products. In contrast to just a few years earlier, when nonprice regulatory barriers were perceived as the most appropriate impediment to youth smoking, the Clinton administration claimed, during the recent policy debate, that "the most reliable method for reducing teen smoking is to increase the price of cigarettes" (U.S. Department of the Treasury 1998, 1).

Second, there has been a recent growth in both the quantity and the quality of data available for studying youth risky behavior. Analysis has traditionally been limited to either the cross-sectional data on high school seniors from the Monitoring the Future (MTF) study or sporadic questions in the National Longitudinal Study of Youth (NLSY). But, in the 1990s, the MTF added cohorts of eighth and tenth graders, and, in the Youth Risk Behavior Survey (YRBS), the Centers for Disease Control (CDC) provided new cross-sectional data on ninth to twelfth graders to complement the MTF; the CDC made available for this project, and for all future work, state identifiers for the YRBS that are not generally available for the MTF. There was also the introduction of the Adolescent Health Survey (AddHealth), a rich new cross-sectional/longitudinal data source on a wide variety of risky behaviors.

These developments, along with the development of a group of first-class economists who are specifically interested in youth behavior, suggested that the time was right for an analysis of youth risky behavior from an economics perspective. This volume provides such an analysis. It incorporates studies from nine teams of leading empirical economists on a variety of behaviors: smoking (Jonathan Gruber and Jonathan Zinman); driving (Thomas S. Dee and William N. Evans); sex and pregnancy (Phillip B. Levine); suicide (David M. Cutler, Edward L. Glaeser, and Karen E. Norberg); marijuana use (Rosalie Liccardo Pacula, Michael Grossman, Frank J. Chaloupka, Patrick M. O'Malley, Lloyd D. Johnston, and Matthew C. Farrelly); crime (Steven D. Levitt and Lance Lochner); drinking (Philip J. Cook and Michael J. Moore); dropping out of school (David Card and Thomas Lemieux); and misnutrition (Jay Bhattacharya and Janet Currie). In addition, the first chapter in the volume, by Ted O'Donoghue and Matthew Rabin, provides a theoretical overview of a set of issues from behavioral economics that are relevant for thinking about the modeling of risky behavior among youths.

In this introductory chapter, I endeavor both to set the stage for the analyses that follow and to distill their key lessons. I begin, in the first section, by providing some theoretical structure for thinking about these issues, drawing on mainstream economic analysis, developmental psychology, and new developments in behavioral economics. I also discuss the existing evidence from developmental psychology for the differences (or the lack thereof) between the behaviors of youths and those of adults. In the next section, I provide some facts on both the incidence of and the time-series trends in youth risky behaviors and draw some comparisons to time trends in adult behaviors. The third section then discusses the lessons for both policy and future research to be learned from these analyses. The last section concludes.

Theoretical Background

In this section, I review the theoretical perspectives on youth risk taking, first from traditional economic analysis, then from developmental psychology, and, finally, from new developments in behavioral economics. In each case, the discussion will focus on what is "special" about youths. To what extent can the standard framework that is applied to adult decision makers be applied to youths as well, and to what extent are special features required to adapt the model to the youth decision-making process?

Traditional Economic Analysis

The traditional economic approach to modeling decisions over risky activities is expected utility maximization with exponential (time-consistent) preferences. Individuals face some risky choice with benefits (e.g., personal enjoyment or social respect) and costs (e.g., current or future health risks), and they incorporate both into a utility-maximization problem. If the net benefits of pursuing the activity exceed the costs, it is pursued; if there is uncertainty about costs and/or benefits, then the comparison is made over expected utilities.

Perhaps the best-developed example of this approach is the "rational-addiction" model of Becker and Murphy (1988). In their model of the decision to pursue such addictive activities as smoking, forward-looking individuals trade off the benefits from the activity today against its costs, which include both the monetary costs of the activity and the costs in terms of increasing the stock of addiction to the activity. That is, rational addicts recognize the long-run negative implications of pursuing risky activities, but they may pursue them anyway if the benefits outweigh the costs.

In this framework, there is nothing particularly "special" about youths relative to adults; the same utility-maximization calculus is followed independent of age. Nevertheless, there are a number of reasons why, in practice, youths may behave differently than adults. For example, youths may be more sensitive to the prices of addictive goods because they have lower incomes or because they have built up a lower stock of the addiction.

Developmental Psychology

The standard economics framework is not necessarily at odds with the perspective of the field that has focused the most on youth risk taking, developmental psychology. But developmental psychology provides a much more detailed framework, one that considers a wider variety of factors that might affect youth decisions to take risks, albeit at the cost of much less modeling precision than is provided by the parsimonious economics model. The developmental perspective on risk taking is nicely summarized in Fischoff (1992).

As noted by Fischoff, the most general definition of *risk taking* is any action having at least one uncertain outcome. The decision to undertake these types of activities will be determined by *cognitive* development (how people think about the world), *affective* development (how people feel about the world), and *social* development (the roles that others play in people's choices). Cognitive development consists of three components: capacity for thinking through problems; knowledge of alternatives and their implications; and skill in carrying out analyses of the alternatives. Affective development consists of *hot affect,* the deep states of arousal (fear, anger, passion) that can drive people to action or inaction, and *cold affect,* the more dispassionate cognitive representations of those desires (what might be labeled *values*). Social development consists of incorporating society's attitudes toward risky behaviors into one's own decision-making process.

Developmental psychologists have provided a range of evidence that allows one to compare the decision-making capacities of youths and adults, and this evidence suggests both important commonalities and important differences. Chapter 1 by O'Donoghue and Rabin, emphasizes the commonalities between decision making by youths and decision making by adults. For example, Beyth-Marom et al. (1993) asked both teens and adults about the perceived consequences of youth risk taking along a number of dimensions, such as drinking, smoking, drug use, etc. They found substantial homogeneity in the perceived consequences of these activities.[1] Similarly, Jacobs-Quadrel, Fischoff, and Davis (1993) found that, while youths appear to consider themselves somewhat invulnerable to the consequences of risk taking, their perceived invulnerability was no stronger than was adults'.

---

1. It is worth noting, however, that, while Jacobs-Quadrel (1990) found that youths and adults drawn from the same middle-class distribution performed similarly when asked to think about the consequences of risk taking, a group of at-risk youths performed much more poorly, demonstrating less knowledge and exhibiting more overconfidence about risky decisions than did middle-class youths.

Other evidence suggests more important differences between how youths and adults make decisions. A recent study by Halpern-Felsher and Cauffman (2000) asked youths and adults about the short- and long-run costs and benefits of different interventions, such as cosmetic surgery or whether to participate in an experimental medical study, and found that adults generally outperformed youths on measures of decision-making competence, such as considering all options, risks, and long-term consequences. The differences were particularly striking between adults and younger adolescents (those in the sixth and eighth grades).

Most important among the differences between youths and adults appears to be the role of social reactions. For example, Beyth-Marom et al. (1993) found that consequences of risky activities involving social reactions are considered more heavily by youths than by adults. Studies of susceptibility to peer influence, as opposed to self-reliance, tend to find an inverted-U relation, with susceptibility increasing between childhood and early adolescence, peaking sometime around age fourteen, and declining during the high school years (e.g., Steinberg and Cauffman 1996).

Fischoff (1992) found that youths have problems with emotional control when hard thought does not produce clear-cut answers to important decision problems. That is, since youths do not understand that some questions in life have no simple answers, they may overreact by allowing transient emotional states to resolve uncertainties. And existing studies suggest that moodiness (volatility of mood) may be more characteristic of adolescents than of adults. In a particularly interesting study of emotional experiences, Larson, Csikszentmihalyi, and Graef (1980) obtained direct data by having adolescents and adults carry electronic pagers and signaling subjects to report on their mood and its intensity at various points in the day. The results indicated that adolescents have more rapid and more extreme mood swings (both positive and negative) than do adults. Moreover, some evidence suggests that adolescents have a harder time controlling their impulses than do adults; the few comparisons of adults and adolescents that exist suggest that thrill seeking and disinhibition are higher during adolescence than during adulthood (Steinberg and Cauffman 1996).

Finally, a number of articles suggest an increase in future orientation with age. Lewis (1981) finds that older adolescents are more likely than younger adolescents to recognize the risks and future consequences of decisions. Greene (1986) and Nurmi (1991) find gains in future orientation both between childhood and adolescence and between adolescence and young adulthood.

Of course, an important limitation with all this evidence is that it relies on responses by youths and adults to hypothetical scenarios rather than on observations of risk taking in reality. As highlighted by Steinberg and Cauffman (1996), given the important potential role of emotional and social influences, more substantial differences between youths and adults may emerge in the field than in the laboratory. In particular, there is little evidence elucidating the relation between self-reliance or future orientation and the quality of judgments made by teens.

Behavioral Economics

The models of developmental psychologists suggest a number of dimensions along which the economics model of youth decision making might be enriched. Some of these, such as evolving time preferences with age or the role of peer pressure, can be incorporated in a straightforward manner into standard models (e.g., Becker and Mulligan 1997). But others suggest the value of extending the standard framework. This is the goal of recent work in behavioral economics that is nicely summarized here by O'Donoghue and Rabin (chap. 1). They point in particular to three ways in which modeling these decisions by youths could potentially be improved by augmenting the standard model.

The first is to consider alternatives to the way in which economists typically model the trade-off between activities that have short-run benefits and long-run costs. This is a central feature of virtually all the risky activities considered in this volume. O'Donoghue and Rabin point out that there are two problems with the simple standard of exponentially discounted utility for considering these types of decisions by youths. The first problem is simple excessive myopia; that is, from the perspective of a paternalistic adult, youths may simply discount the future too much. The second problem is that, even if the long-run discount rate is "appropriate," youths may have preferences that are *time inconsistent.* Virtually every laboratory experiment that has been run demonstrates that individuals do not use a constant discount rate in considering decisions in the near term and in more distant periods. This suggests that time discounting may be better represented by *hyperbolic* models, which allow the discount rate to be higher in the short run than in the long run. These models have the important feature that there may be intrapersonal conflict between "selves" in different periods; the decision made by today's self for tomorrow is not necessarily the one that tomorrow's self would make. And, from the perspective of either a patient social planner or even today's self, there is "too much" pursuit of activities with short-run benefits and long-run costs in these models, even though long-run discounting is appropriate (Gruber and Koszegi 2000).

The second is to introduce *projection bias,* or the notion that youths may inappropriately project the current moment's preferences onto their future tastes. Once again, there is substantial laboratory evidence that, across identical individuals, random changes to current states affect long-run decision making. This has important implications for youths because they may not appreciate the extent to which their preferences may adapt as they age. For example, high school seniors considering dropping out of school may not appreciate the fact that, when they are older, they will care about the quality of their job; given today's preferences, all jobs seem equally unappealing. This underestimation of the value later in life of having a high school degree can raise odds of dropping out of school today. O'Donoghue and Rabin point out a variety of other arenas in which this type of projection bias could lead to poor decision making by youths.

The third is to recognize that risky decisions are made in an uncertain environment and are made repeatedly and that it is therefore possible that increases in riskiness can actually *increase* risk-taking behavior. This is because, for many risky activities, the cost is onetime and permanent (e.g., getting AIDS from having unprotected sex). As a result, once the activity has been engaged in to some extent, the marginal risk from additional engagements is lower. Thus, if the activity is highly enjoyed by youths and they find out that the risk is higher than they thought, then they will engage more because they are likely to have already borne the cost. That is, in the limit, if having sex once causes AIDS for sure, then the marginal risk of a second sexual encounter is 0, and raising the risk of AIDS to 1 will increase sexual activity among those already having sex. This is an important point because it can generate significant "multiplier" effects on mistakes made in the past.

Summary

Developing a comprehensive model of how youths make risky decisions is a daunting task. Economists and developmental psychologists have taken very different routes in approaching this task. Economists have used the standard, powerful tools of utility maximization to provide modeling precision and generate sharp, testable predictions. Developmental psychologists have raised a much richer list of considerations that may ultimately be impossible to integrate in one comprehensive model. Recent work in behavioral economics is trying to carve out a middle ground between these two paths, enriching standard models along the lines suggested by the psychological evidence but retaining the rigorous mathematical structure that allows for prediction, welfare analysis, and hypothesis testing.

The analyses presented in this volume will not resolve the question of the "correct" way in which to model youth risk taking. There is clear evidence from a number of studies that the costs and benefits of risky activities are incorporated in youth decision making, which rejects extreme forms of irrationality or purely emotional decision making. But, as emphasized by O'Donoghue and Rabin (chap. 1), these findings are consistent with a broad set of models from economics and psychology. Thus, these analyses are best viewed as generating important facts and empirical relation that can help guide the formulation of future theories rather than as definitively favoring one approach over another.

Facts about Risk Taking by Youths and Adults

The Incidence of Risky Behaviors among Youths

As noted earlier, a host of data sets are now available that provide information about different risky behaviors pursued by youths. For this analysis, I rely on the Youth Risk Behavior Survey (YRBS) from the CDC, which provides recent (1997) data for a large number of different risky activities. Before perusing the numbers, however, it is worth noting that the estimates of the incidence of risky behaviors are sensitive to the survey used; for example, the teen-smoking rate is roughly 20 percent higher in the YRBS than it is in the MTF survey. However, the time trends across these surveys appear comparable for the 1990s, as noted in the chapter on smoking (chap. 2, Gruber and Zinman).

These data can be used to highlight three stylized patterns of behavior. First, we can examine the incidence of risky behaviors by age. One theory of the evolution of preferences for risky behavior might be that younger teens are both more impatient (supported by the evidence from Lewis [1981] cited above) and more subject to peer pressure, which could increase risk taking by younger teens relative to older teens. Of course, countervailing this are three factors; biology, which may make some risky activities (e.g., sexual intercourse) more desirable with age; income, as older teens may have more of their own income that can be used to finance risky activities; and the law, in that some risky activities are illegal for younger teens but legal for older teens.

Perhaps reflecting these countervailing influences, figure 1 illustrates that there is no clear age pattern to be found for risk taking. This figure shows the incidence of eight risky behaviors for the four grades represented in the YRBS data. The behaviors considered are smoking regularly in the past month, having five or more drinks in a row in the past month, carrying a weapon in the past month, attempting suicide in the past year, smoking marijuana in the past month, using other illegal drugs in the past year, driving while drunk in the past month, and having sex without using birth control at some point in life.

Some of these activities show a clear increase with age, particularly the activities related to drinking (having five or more drinks in a row; drinking and driving). Smoking shows a rise with age, but that rise is much more modest (although it is important to note that the MTF data used in the smoking chapter show a much steeper rise with age). Marijuana and other drug use shows a rise from the ninth to the eleventh grade and then a falloff in the senior year; once again, the MTF data show a steeper rise with age. But carrying a weapon, having unprotected sex, and attempting suicide actually show declining risk taking with age.

While it is difficult to draw firm conclusions from these types of data,

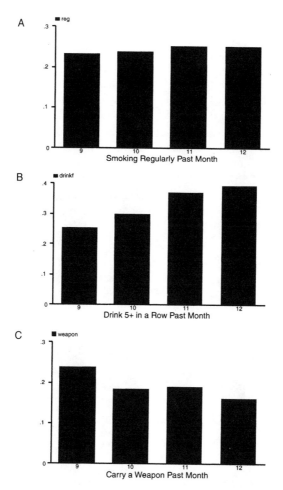

Fig. 1   Distribution of risky behaviors by grade: *A*, **smoking regularly in the past month;** *B*, **having 5 or more drinks in a row in the past month;** *C*, **carrying a weapon in the past month;** *D*, **attempting suicide in the past year;** *E*, **smoking marijuana in the past 30 days;** *F*, **using other illegal drugs in the past year;** *G*, **driving while drunk in the past 30 days;** *H*, **having unprotected sex ever**

these findings do suggest the power that two important economic variables have in determining behavior: age-specific legal penalties and income. Drinking and driving—both regulated by clear-cut age-specific laws— show the strongest pattern of risk taking rising with age. Smoking, which is not illegal per se at younger ages—only the purchase of cigarettes is so regulated—also shows a slight rise with age. But drug use—illegal for anyone of any age—shows a less pronounced age pattern and actually declines for high school seniors in the YRBS data. The age pattern for carrying a

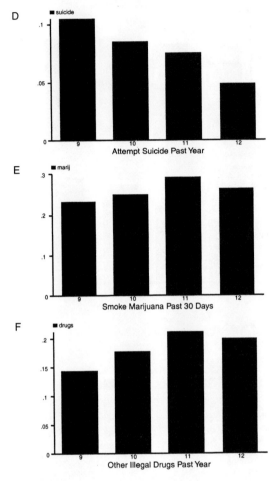

Fig. 1   (cont.)

weapon—again illegal for anyone of any age—is reversed. And attempted suicide and having unprotected sex—which are not illegal at any age— actually show a declining age pattern. These patterns are also consistent with pure income effects in that the activities that cost money (such as purchasing substances) are more likely to rise with age than are activities that are free (sex and suicide).

These facts suggest that economic incentives do matter for risk taking in that the risks for which there are age-specific penalties or likely income effects show the strongest patterns with age. This is also consistent with the finding in the chapter on crime (chap. 7, Levitt and Lochner) that the age pattern of crime follows very precisely the relative penalties imposed on youths and adults for criminal activity. These facts, therefore, also sug-

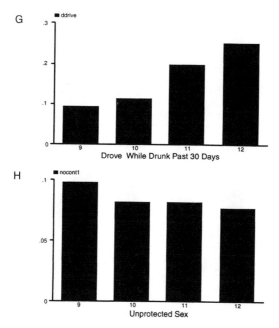

Fig. 1   (cont.)

gest the potential deterrent power that government intervention can have on risky behavior through both penalty and pricing policies.

A second feature of the data is that there is substantial heterogeneity in the intensity with which risky activities are carried out. Figure 2 shows histograms of number of days on which cigarettes were smoked in the past month, number of days on which a drink was had in the past month, number of times marijuana was smoked in the past month, and number of times sex was had in the past three months (where "never had sex" is one option). In every case, while there is a substantial number of youths who have never engaged in the activity in question, there is also a wide distribution among those youths who have. Indeed, only for drinking is there a clear pattern of continual decline; for smoking, there is actually a greater incidence at thirty days per month than at any other nonzero value, and teens are almost as likely to have had six or more sex partners as they are to have had three.

These facts would appear to support the importance of the third theoretical observation discussed in the section on behavioral economics above, that, once risky behaviors are undertaken, there may be low marginal costs to additional risk taking. This also raises an important question for analysis: how does one weight reduced incidence of any activity against the intensity with which that activity is pursued? This is important because some policy tools may be found to reduce either the extensive margin or

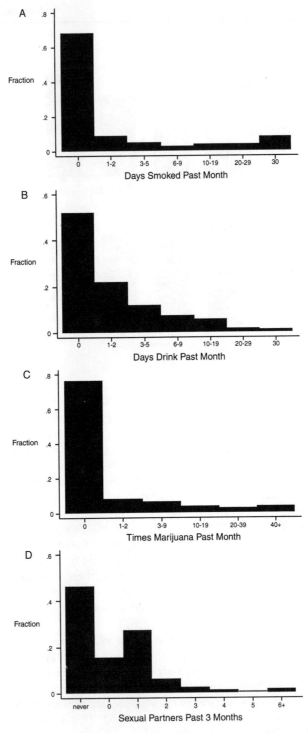

Fig. 2 Distribution of frequencies of risky activities: *A*, number of days on which cigarettes were smoked in the past month; *B*, number of days on which a drink was had in the past month; *C*, number of times marijuana was smoked in the past month; *D*, number of times sex was had in the past 3 months

the intensive margin, but not both. For example, the chapter on smoking (chap. 2, Gruber and Zinman) finds that restrictions on youth cigarette purchase reduce the intensity of smoking but not smoking participation while price increases seem to have a greater effect on participation than on conditional intensity.

Finally, the data suggest that no simple model can describe how youths make decisions across the range of risky activities. Two natural alternatives might be labeled the *bad-seed model* and the *conservation-of-risk model*. The bad-seed model would suggest that a certain segment of the youth population is predisposed toward risky activities and that the remainder is not. The conservation-of-risk model, on the other hand, would suggest that most youths have a tendency to take some risks and that, if they reduce risky activity in one area, they will increase it in another. These two models obviously have very different implications for policy: the bad-seed model would suggest that targeted efforts to reduce the youth pursuit of risky activities can be effective, whereas the conservation-of-risk model would suggest that efforts to reduce one kind of risk taking will simply induce substitution into another mode. They also have very different implications for the distribution of risk taking: the bad-seed model would suggest that the pursuit of risky activities is concentrated in a segment of the youth population that undertakes many of these activities; the conservation-of-risk model would suggest that risk taking is spread more broadly, with most youths taking some risk.

As figure 3 shows, however, neither model is supported in the extreme. This figure plots the histogram for the number of risky activities under-

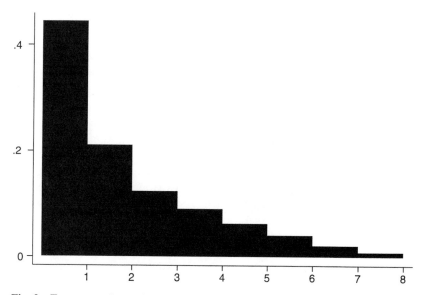

Fig. 3   Frequency of pursuit of risky activities

taken by youths in the YRBS data, drawing from the list of eight activities used for figure 1 above. Almost half of teenagers did not engage in any of these risky activities, but only 22 percent engaged in three or more of them. This appears to suggest neither purely a segment of the youth population that takes many risks nor a model in which every youth takes some risks. Moreover, it is striking to note that this exact pattern emerges within each grade as well and therefore does not reflect compositional effects across grades.

Time Trends in Risky Behaviors among Youths

The changes in the incidence of risky behaviors among youths over the past twenty years are also striking. This is illustrated in two ways in figures 4 and 5. Figure 4 plots the time-series patterns for eight of the risky behaviors discussed in this volume over the period 1976–97; there are no comparable data on nutrition, so this is not included. The eight time series depicted are the percentage of high school seniors who smoked in the past thirty days; fatal auto accidents per 100,000 sixteen- to nineteen-year-olds; the percentage of fifteen- to nineteen-year-old girls giving birth; the number of suicides per 100,000 fifteen- to nineteen-year-olds; the percentage of high school seniors who smoked marijuana in the past thirty days; the number of homicides in the fourteen- to seventeen-year-old age group per 100,000 persons; the percentage of high school seniors who had a drink in the past thirty days; and the percentage of fourteen- to seventeen-year-olds not enrolled in school.

The commonalities as well as the contrasts among these series are quite interesting. The first feature to note is the general reduction in teen risk taking from the beginning of the sample period (1976) over the next decade (to 1985). For some behaviors, such as smoking cigarettes or marijuana or being involved in a fatal car crash, the declines are dramatic. For the others—drinking, teen pregnancy, crime, and dropping out of school—the gains are more modest but still clear. Only for suicides is there an adverse trend over this period, and, even in this case, the trend is relatively modest. This is not a period on which the studies in this volume focus, but it is a particularly interesting one because of the reduction in risk taking across the board. Clearly, an important priority for future work is to understand what factors drove the general decline in this period.

The remainder of the period is usefully divided into two eras, the first running from 1985 through the early 1990s (roughly 1992), the second from the early 1990s through 1997 (the last year for which data are available). The trends in risky behaviors are much more heterogeneous over these periods. Over the middle period (1985–92), there is a continued decline in drinking, smoking, marijuana use, and dropping out of school. But there is a very sharp rise in the rate of youth homicide, teen pregnancy, and suicide. Both these trends are reversed over the last period, with teen

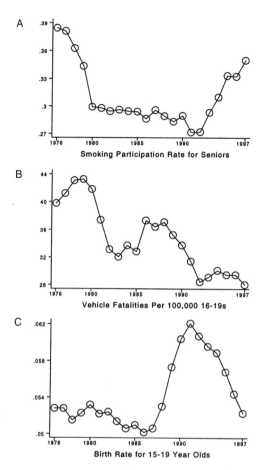

Fig. 4 Time-series trends in youth risky behaviors: *A*, smoking participation rate among high school seniors; *B*, vehicle fatalities per 100,000 16–19-year-olds; *C*, birthrate for 15–19-year-olds; *D*, suicides per 100,000 15–19-year-olds; *E*, percentage of high school seniors who smoked marijuana in the past 30 days; *F*, homicides per 100,000 14–17-year-olds; *G*, the percentage of high school seniors who had a drink in the past 30 days; *H*, the percentage of 14–17-year-olds not enrolled in school

homicides, pregnancies, and suicides plummeting, teen smoking and marijuana use skyrocketing, and drinking and traffic fatalities either flattening or rising modestly.

The patterns over time are particularly interesting, and highly correlated, for two pairs of behaviors: smoking and marijuana use; crime and teen pregnancy. These patterns are illustrated more closely in figure 5, which is drawn "scale free" so that movements in the four series can be viewed along the same scale. Both these pairs of series trend closely to-

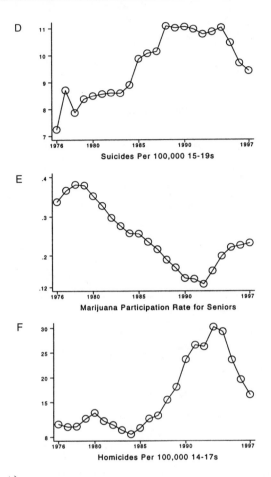

Fig. 4   (cont.)

gether, even moving together through very volatile rises and falls; the only exception is the gradual decline in marijuana use over the period 1976–91, while smoking falls quickly to 1980 and then declines more slowly after that. The time trend for teen suicide also matches fairly well, but not as closely, with the series for pregnancy and homicide.

For smoking and marijuana, the correlation is perhaps not surprising and provides some credence to the notion of complementarities between the use of these substances. But the parallel movements in crime and teen pregnancy are more surprising. There is no direct link between these behaviors, one of which is almost exclusively the purview of males and the other by definition exclusively the purview of females. But there is an implicit link as these are the two most "deviant" activities that males and females can pursue as teens. The fact that they move so closely together

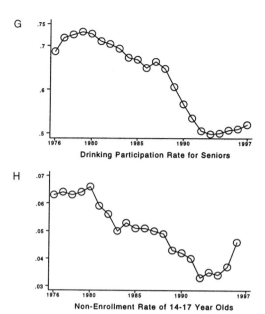

Fig. 4 (cont.)

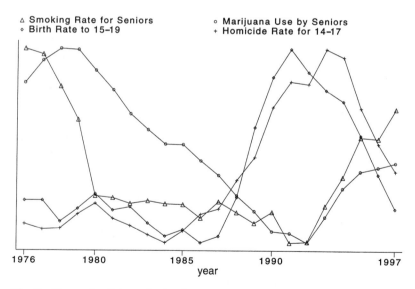

Fig. 5   Comparing time-series trends

suggests that there are clear taste shifts among teens regarding the pursuit of very risky activities and that these tastes can shift quite quickly over very short periods of time; the youth homicide rate almost tripled, and then halved, over a period of only a decade.

Time Trends among Adults

In terms of thinking about what is "special" about youths, it is instructive to contrast these time trends with the trends that we have seen over this same period in the adult pursuit of risky behaviors. Figure 6 compiles data on time-series trends in adult participation in risky behaviors, paralleling the data for youths (except for dropping out of school, for which there is no comparable adult behavior). The adult data are less consistent and more variable in quality than are the youth data since they come from a wider variety of sources and generally not the same sources from which the youth data are drawn. But the basic patterns should reflect general trends in adult behavior.[2]

Comparing this figure to figure 5 above, there are in general substantial differences between the time trends for adults and youths. The only strong exception is vehicle fatalities, where the series are quite similar; the series are also fairly similar for drinking, with a substantial decline from the mid-1980s to the early 1990s, then a modest rise to 1997.[3] On the other hand, adult smoking has declined steadily since the late 1970s, flattening in the mid-1990s, while youth smoking declined precipitously, remained flat, and then rose. Teen fertility rose precipitously in the late 1980s but has declined steadily throughout the 1990s; adult fertility rose slightly in the late 1980s, then declined in the early 1990s, but has started to rise again. Teen suicides rose throughout the 1980s while adult suicides were declining; both series show some decline in the 1990s, although it is much steeper for teens. Marijuana use by both teens and adults rose in the late 1970s and declined throughout the 1980s, but, while use has been roughly flat for adults in the 1990s, it has risen sharply for youths. In the late 1980s, homicides rose sharply among teens while they were flat among adults, although both series show a decline in the 1990s.

These strong differences in time-series trends stand somewhat in contrast to the subset of psychological studies that does not document important differences in the decision-making processes of youths and adults. Of

2. Smoking data were obtained from the CDC website (www.cdc.gov), tabulated from National Health Interview Surveys over time. Data on vehicle fatalities, birthrates, suicides, and homicides were obtained from the same sources used for youths in chapters on these topics. Marijuana and alcohol data were kindly tabulated by Matthew Farrelly from the National Household Survey on Drug Abuse.

3. As Cook and Moore (chap. 8 in this volume) note, there is a very tight correspondence between the time series for youth drinking incidence and per capita total consumption of alcohol.

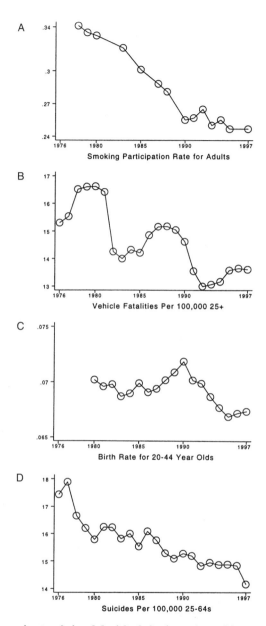

Fig. 6   Time-series trends in adult risky behaviors: *A*, smoking participation rate, age 18 and older; *B*, vehicle fatalities per 100,000 age 25 and older; *C*, birthrate for 20–44-year-olds; *D*, suicides per 100,000 25–64-year-olds; *E*, marijuana use, age 26 and older; *F*, homicides per 100,000 25–34-year-olds; *G*, drinking participation rate, age 26 and older

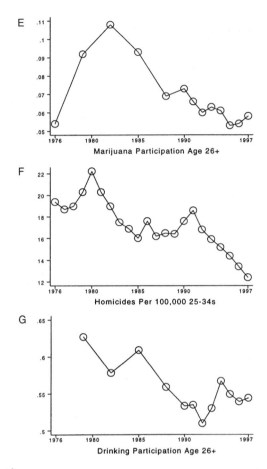

Fig. 6 (cont.)

course, from these figures it is impossible to tell whether it is differences in decision-making processes per se or differences in the underlying context in which these decisions are made that drive these differing time-series patterns. But one interesting feature of the comparison is that the youth series appear much more variable than do the adult series over any given time interval, particularly with reference to the activities that were the focus of figure 5 above. This extreme variability for youths would be consistent with either more "emotional" (hot-affective) decision making by youths or multiplier effects through peer influence. These contrasting time-series patterns therefore suggest that there may be important differences in how youths and adults make decisions about risky activities in practice, even if these differences are muted in interviews.

Implications and Directions for Future Work

Risk taking has always been an important feature of the teen years and undoubtably will continue to be so. But the interesting time-series patterns that we have seen over the past decade suggest that risk taking is not a static or a monolithic process. And the chapters in this volume suggest that risk taking is responsive to a variety of factors that influence a teen's environment.

Lessons to Be Learned from This Volume

While the studies in this volume have been carried out in very different ways, four clear lessons emerge. First, incentives matter. The notion that teens are "pathological" risk takers who are not responsive to economic incentives is strongly rejected by virtually every chapter in this volume. Almost every study finds that either prices or other economic/regulatory incentives matter significantly for youth risk taking:[4] (1) Teen smoking decisions are found to be very sensitive to cigarette prices, with an estimated elasticity of smoking participation with respect to price of −0.67 for high school seniors. (2) Mandatory seat-belt laws reduced vehicle fatalities among youths by 8–10 percent, and there were significant declines as well associated with higher minimum legal drinking ages. (3) Teen pregnancy risk falls as the incidence of AIDS rises (raising the risk of unprotected sex) and as welfare benefits fall (lowering the potential value of support for an out-of-wedlock child).[5] (4) Teen marijuana use is also very sensitive to price, with central price elasticities of annual participation of roughly −0.24. (5) A central determinant of the criminality of youths relative to that of adults is the relative stringency of the legal system with respect to youth and adult crime. (6) While the evidence for the effect of alcohol taxes on drinking is mixed, there is very clear evidence that the age-specific legality of drinking is a key determinant of the age pattern of drinking and particularly of binge drinking. (7) State college tuition policy is an important determinant of the decision to drop out of high school: when state tuition is low, individuals are more likely to complete high school as the cost of continuing education is reduced. (8) Access to free school meals improves the quality of the diet of youths.

Second, the economic environment in which youths make risky decisions matters, and even policies not directly aimed at youth risk taking

---

4. The one exception is the chapter on suicide, where there is no obvious price or regulatory variable to be studied in this context.

5. The latter conclusion, from Levine (chap. 4 in this volume), is somewhat tenuous because of a wrong-signed coefficient on the welfare-reform variable (more restrictive welfare reforms appear to raise pregnancy risk); on net, these welfare coefficients appear roughly to offset each other.

can therefore have important effects on these activities: (1) A 1 percentage point rise in the teen employment-population ratio, which raises the opportunity cost for teenage girls of having children, is estimated to lower the risk of teenage girls becoming pregnant by 0.2 percentage points. (2) Teen suicide rates fall significantly as median incomes rise. (3) The share of children in poverty and that of adults without a high school diploma are significant determinants of homicide rates across Chicago census tracts. (4) The dropout rate is significantly higher when unemployment rates are low and the opportunity costs of schooling are therefore highest.

Third, despite the powerful role that economic incentives play in driving these behaviors, many of the studies find that neither changes in background factors nor changes in incentives or prices can explain much of the dramatic time-series shifts that we have seen over the past decade: (1) The downward trend in cigarette prices in the early 1990s appears to explain at most about one-quarter of the upward trend in smoking by high school seniors. Moreover, smoking by younger teens appears not to be price sensitive, yet the upward trend in smoking in the 1990s is similar. (2) Less than 20 percent of the downward trend in youth motor-vehicle fatalities can be explained by mandatory seat-belt laws or higher minimum drinking ages. (3) Less than 20 percent of the fall in pregnancies among black teens can be explained by rising teen-employment ratios. (4) The rise in youth homicides across Chicago census tracts between 1980 and 1990 cannot at all be explained by changes in youth poverty or adult education; on the other hand, the relative stringency of legal systems toward youth criminals does appear to explain over half the relative rise in youth crime over the period 1978–93. (5) Neither trends in prices nor changes in background characteristics can explain any of the trends in youth drinking behavior. (6) The decrease in college attendance by recent cohorts of youths cannot be very well explained by changes in family background characteristics, tuition costs, unemployment rates, or cohort size (the latter factor explaining at most a fifth of the trend).

On the other hand, two of the studies do suggest that much of the time-series trend can be explained. Two-thirds of the trend in teen suicide can be explained by rising divorce rates, given the powerful correspondence between divorce rates and suicide in both micro data on suicide attempts and county-level data on suicides. And more than two-thirds of the time trends in marijuana use may be explained by trends in marijuana price and potency.[6]

Finally, several papers in this volume have explored the critical issue of the intertemporal linkage between youth and adult risky behaviors and

6. The results here are somewhat tenuous because the estimated models in Pacula et al. (chap. 6 in this volume) are fairly sensitive to the form of time trends; the fact cited here is from models that include linear time trends.

have found these links to be strong. Simple correlations between youth and adult risk taking, of course, are difficult to interpret, as they may reflect, not habit formation through youth participation, but rather heterogeneity across individuals that causes some persons to participate in risky activities at all ages and other persons never to participate at any age (Cook and Moore, chap. 8 in this volume). But several of these studies use exogenous variation in the underlying environment facing youths to examine the habit component, and the findings suggest important intertemporal correlations: (1) Women who grew up in states with lower cigarette taxes smoke more as adults, even conditional on the cigarette tax that they currently face. (2) Young adults who faced younger legal drinking ages at age fourteen were more likely to be binge drinking later in life. (3) Shifts in the environment that increase dropping out of school (e.g., reductions in the unemployment rate) have roughly comparable effects on completed education years later as well; youths do not reenroll later to make up for this reduction in education.

Thus, the overall lessons to be learned from this volume are mixed. On the one hand, incentives and the economic environment in which risky decisions are made clearly matter for this decision-making process. Clearly, youths are not purely irrational or emotional decision makers, and the standard calculus of cost-benefit comparison that has served economics so well in other contexts can help in this one as well. Moreover, these incentives have not only transitory effects on decision making by youths but long-run implications for decision making by adults as well. On the other hand, however, these "price" variables cannot take us very far in explaining the dramatic trends that we have documented in youth risk-taking behavior. This suggests that the empirical work needs to be enriched, ideally in ways informed by the theory, if our goal is to model youth risk taking fully.

Implications for Policy

These findings have important implications for government policy. The government is not powerless to affect youth risk taking. The types of incentives that are under government control, such as excise taxes or penalties for illegal behavior by teens, make important differences in the level of risk taking. Moreover, the casual evidence presented earlier, as well as more rigorous studies by Farrelly et al. (1999) and Dee (1999), suggest that tougher government regulation of one behavior will not cause youths to substitute other risky behaviors; if anything, these behaviors appear to be complements, not substitutes. So government restrictions on risky behavior can have positive spillover effects in mitigating other risky activities. On the other hand, government regulation is not a panacea. Most of what is driving these decisions is not captured by even the types of rich models estimated by the papers in this volume.

But the third major finding implies that government can have indirect influences on youth risk taking that are very important as well. This suggests that government decisions on economic policy should consider, not just the intended effects, but the unintended consequences for these types of risk taking as well. While these implications may seem modest relative to the direct effects of, say, macroeconomic policy, they may not be. For example, the chapter on dropping out of school finds that youths who drop out in order to take advantage of economic booms are unlikely ever to return. These decisions can therefore have long-run consequences that may be sizable relative to the short-run policy goals of the government.

Unanswered Questions and Directions for Future Work

The most important implications of the findings in this volume are for future work on this array of fascinating topics. The papers contained here are all innovative explorations of topics that are, with some exceptions, relatively new to economists. As such, the papers have been designed to lay out some basic issues but not to try definitely to resolve all the important questions. The simple fact that we are able to explain so little of the time-series trends over the past decade highlights the importance of future investigations of risky behaviors.

There are, in particular, five obvious directions for future work. The first is to try to disentangle the role of youths, their parents, and their peers in driving risky decision making. The papers in this volume have focused largely on incentives for youths per se. But parents and peers are clearly important influences on how these decisions are made. The influence of parents does not seem, at a minimum, to be able to explain the dramatic time-series shifts over relatively short time periods that we have documented in this volume. But, over the long run, parents establish the environment in which many of these decisions are made. Peers may be playing a bigger role in sharp time-series movements since, in peer models, even small shifts in the environment can spread rapidly through the entire population (through "peer multiplier" effects).

Unfortunately, disentangling the roles of these other factors is a daunting challenge. Modeling the influence of parents is conceivable, using some of the rich new data sources (such as the NLSY or AddHealth data) that contain information on both parents and children. But even these sources do not have much information on parents' histories of risky behaviors, histories that might influence how children's decisions are made. Peer influences are even harder to model as there are well-known econometric difficulties with disentangling group effects from omitted factors that might be influencing the individual's decisions. For example, if smoking rises among my peers and I also smoke more, is this the result of peer influence or some omitted environmental change that is simultaneously affecting both me and my peers? While these challenges are daunting, this is clearly the direction in which work in this area must head if we hope to develop better explanations of how these decisions are made.

The second direction for future work is to think about the *benefits* of risky activities. The studies in this volume are very much written from the perspective of the *costs* of these activities, but youths must be perceiving some benefits from these actions, or they would not be undertaking them. The evidence available in this model, such as the effect of low unemployment on dropping out of high school, suggests that benefits are important in the calculus of risk taking.

Understanding, and ultimately modeling, these benefits is important for two reasons. First, it will help explain better how these decisions are made. But, second, it will assist in normative conclusions about "optimal" levels of intervention in these types of decisions. It is likely, and even probable, that the optimal level of risk taking along the lines described in this volume is not zero (with the possible exception of suicide). If youths' preferences are such that they really enjoy smoking or having unprotected sex, the utility gained from engaging in these activities must be accounted for in the calculation of how tightly to regulate these activities. But economics has very little to say at this point about the gains to risk taking among this population, and a clear priority for future work is to build this into the analysis as well.

The third direction is to consider how these risk-taking decisions fit together. As I have mentioned, the available evidence suggests that many of these risk-taking activities are complements. But this work has explored only a few of the natural links (e.g., between drinking and smoking), and many of the others that may be important (e.g., between drinking, using drugs, and having unprotected sex) have not been explored. Only through modeling the full systemwide implications of economic incentives and other factors can we completely understand how these incentives will affect youth risk taking. The growing availability of data sets with information on a variety of risk-taking behaviors should make it feasible to explore these interactions further.

Fourth, there should be much more work done on the long-run implications of risk taking by youths. For many of the activities considered in this volume (particularly substance use), we care less about the implications for the youths themselves than about the implications for long-term behavior. Several of the papers in this volume provide some initial evidence on the intertemporal correlation of risk taking as a youth and as an adult, but this type of analysis could, and should, be pursued for all these risk-taking activities. Moreover, these activities have implications not only for future risk taking but for other elements of future well-being as well, such as long-run health, education, earnings, and family structure. Thus, a significant determinant of the well-being of many older persons will be the risky decisions that they made as youths. This implies that understanding both what drives these decisions and how they affect later well-being is a critical priority for future work.

Finally, and perhaps most important, there should be a greater attempt to integrate the theoretical insights discussed above with the types of empirical analyses conducted in the various papers presented in this volume. All of these papers, with the obvious exception of the first chapter, were purposely designed to be purely empirical analyses in order to lay down a set of facts and hypothesis tests that could inform future work on these topics. But integrating these types of empirical analyses and the theoretical insights of standard economic models, developmental psychology, and behavioral economics can lead to a much richer understanding of the underlying processes by which these decisions are made. This integration should be a two-way street: theoretical models can inform the hypotheses that are tested by future empirical work, and the facts documented here can inform the construction of such models. But, ultimately, it is the integration of the two that can most fruitfully advance the economic modeling of these behaviors.

Conclusions

Youth risk taking is an area that has received far too little attention among economists. Dramatic changes in the nature of youth risk taking over the past decade, suggestions that economic incentives matter in important ways for these decisions, and the potentially enormous long-run implications of risk taking for well-being all suggest the value of increased economic analysis of youth risky decision making. Moreover, the advent of excellent new data sources suggests that the time is ripe for work in this area.

This volume provides a rich and exciting set of new analyses of this area that substantially advance our understanding of the role, and limitations, of economic incentives in driving risk taking. Each of these high-quality papers can provide a natural springboard to future work, and the set of conclusions, summarized in this introduction, can be helpful for thinking more generally about theories of risk taking among youths. In the future, economists can and should play a more central role in the debate over the positive and normative implications of youth risk taking in the United States.

References

Becker, Gary, and Casey Mulligan. 1997. The endogenous determination of time preference. *Quarterly Journal of Economics* 112:729–58.
Becker, Gary, and Kevin M. Murphy. 1988. A theory of rational addiction. *Journal of Political Economy* 96:675–700.

Beyth-Marom, Ruth, Laurel Austin, Baruch Fischoff, Claire Palmgren, and Marilyn Jacobs-Quadrel. 1993. Perceived consequences of risky behaviors: Adults and adolescents. *Developmental Psychology* 29:549–63.

Centers for Disease Control (CDC). 1998. *Youth risk behavior survey 1995–CD-ROM.* Atlanta.

Dee, Thomas. 1999. The complementarity of teen smoking and drinking. *Journal of Health Economics* 18:769–93.

Farrelly, Matthew, Jeremy Bray, Matthew Zarkin, and Brett Wendling. 1999. The joint demand for cigarettes and marijuana: Evidence from the National Household Surveys on Drug Abuse. Working paper. Research Triangle Park, N.C.: Research Triangle Institute.

Fischoff, Baruch. 1992. Risk taking: A developmental perspective. In *Risk taking,* ed. J. F. Yates. New York: Wiley.

Greene, A. 1986. Future time perspective in adolescence: The present of things future revisited. *Journal of Youth and Adolescence* 15:99–113.

Gruber, Jonathan, and Botond Koszegi. 2000. Is addiction "rational"? Theory and evidence. Working Paper no. 7507. Cambridge, Mass.: National Bureau of Economic Research.

Halpern-Felsher, Bonnie, and Elizabeth Cauffman. 2000. Costs and benefits of a decision: Decision-making competence in adolescents and adults. University of California, San Francisco. Mimeo.

Jacobs-Quadrel, Marilyn. 1990. Elicitation of adolescents' risk perceptions: Qualitative and quantitative dimensions. Ph.D. diss., Carnegie-Mellon University.

Jacobs-Quadrel, Marilyn, Baruch Fischoff, and Wendy Davis. 1993. Adolescent (in)vulnerability. *American Psychologist* 48:102–16.

Larson, M., M. Csikszentmihalyi, and R. Graef. 1980. Mood variability and the psychosocial adjustment of adolescents. *Journal of Youth and Adolescence* 9: 469–90.

Lewis, C. C. 1981. How adolescents approach decisions: Changes over grades seven to twelve and policy implications. *Child Development* 52:538–44.

Nurmi, J. 1991. How do adolescents see their future? A review of the development of future orientation and planning. *Developmental Review* 11:1–59.

Steinberg, Laurence, and Elizabeth Cauffman. 1996. Maturity of judgment in adolescence: Psychosocial factors in adolescent decision making. *Law and Human Behavior* 20:249–72.

University of Michigan. 1998. *1997 Monitoring the Future survey data tables and figures.* Ann Arbor, Mich.

U.S. Department of the Treasury. 1998. *A comprehensive approach to reducing youth smoking.* Washington, D.C.

1

Risky Behavior among Youths
Some Issues from
Behavioral Economics

Ted O'Donoghue and Matthew Rabin

The goal of this volume is to provide an economic analysis of *risky behavior among youths,* loosely defined to be behavior by people under age nineteen that might have important future ramifications. Examples of such behaviors include smoking, drinking, having unprotected sex, and engaging in crime. The traditional approach used by economists would seem to have important shortcomings in this realm. The rational-choice model provides a powerful tool for understanding behavior and has yielded an array of insights across a broad range of human activities. But a growing number of economists have come to recognize that the rational-choice model is inaccurate in some systematic and important ways, and that to take full advantage of the economic insights and methodology, economists must embrace insights from psychology and other social sciences so as to make our models more relevant and realistic.

While the shortcomings of the rational-choice model are relevant for people of all ages, they seem particularly acute for youths. In this chapter, we discuss how recent efforts combining psychology and economics can be used to help understand risky behavior by adolescents. We are not (in the least) experts in youthful risky behavior and do not provide a very broad perspective on all the psychology relevant to this topic. Our goal here is less ambitious and more specific: to explore what some of the main

Ted O'Donoghue is assistant professor of economics at Cornell University. Matthew Rabin is professor of economics at the University of California, Berkeley, and a member of the Russell Sage Foundation Behavioral Economics Roundtable.

The authors thank George Loewenstein and Ken Train for useful conversations and Jon Gruber and participants in the NBER conference for useful feedback. For financial support, the authors thank the National Science Foundation (award 9709485) and the NBER project; Rabin thanks the Russell Sage, Alfred P. Sloan, and MacArthur Foundations.

insights and issues raised by recent research in behavioral economics suggest about risky behavior by adolescents.[1] Our focus is on the potential for applying formal behavioral-economic models to theoretical and empirical research on youthful behavior.

Why should economists be motivated to study risky behavior among youths? It could be that we have only a "positive" interest—we are interested merely because we would like to understand society better and estimate or predict drug use, criminal behavior, suicide, and so forth. For most people, however, the interest in youths' behavior is motivated by "normative" considerations. Parents, citizens, policy makers, and even many economists are interested not merely in predicting whether sixteen-year-olds start smoking, use cocaine, get pregnant, or kill themselves, but also in understanding the welfare consequences of these behaviors.

One important normative question is whether risky behavior among youths creates negative externalities that affect other members of society. Negative externalities are obviously an important facet of many of the behaviors studied in this volume—for example, crime, or such behaviors as alcohol and drug use that can lead to crime and automobile accidents, or any behavior that leads to increased dependence on the state. Similarly, a major concern in preventing early pregnancy among girls is the harm done to society (and to the children born). A reasonable guess is that youths have a higher preference than adults for activities that create negative externalities and that society may therefore be especially keen to curtail these activities.

But, clearly, most of us are concerned about risky adolescent behavior in large part because we believe that adolescents are not behaving in their own best interests and because we feel that something should be done to help them. This concern is warranted by the clear evidence that even adults often do not behave in their own best interests. Of course, even if this concern motivates our research, we could help study suicide, drug use, sex, and so forth without taking an explicit stand on whether these behaviors are good or bad and then let policy makers and other audiences use our behavioral conclusions to further their normative concerns. We intend that this chapter help in this way. We believe, however, that behavioral economics provides some valuable insights into the precise nature of the harm that youths may cause themselves, and, hence, the most central contribution of behavioral economics may be helping policy makers understand the connection between behavior and welfare. This will be our main emphasis.

Our welfare emphasis may be controversial. Over the years, economists have developed an aggressive agnosticism with regard to welfare analysis for individual choice, refusing to make any judgments that people are not

---

1. For a general overview of some of the topics studied by behavioral economics, see Thaler (1992), Camerer (1995), and Rabin (1998).

behaving in their own best interests. Caution is, of course, warranted because, more often than not, people probably have a better idea of what is in their own best interests than do economists, other social scientists, and policy makers. But this caution has largely transformed itself into an a priori presumption that people always behave in their own best interest. There are some realms where common sense, compassion, and intellectual curiosity all tell us that we should consider the possibility that people may not be behaving in their own best interests. Risky behavior by youths is one of those realms.[2]

Of course, we should not replace welfare agnosticism with a "promiscuous paternalism" that provides undisciplined assertions that others' behaviors are not good for them and that we know better what they should do. Rather, we need a principled way in which to study when and how people make errors, what types of interventions might help mitigate these errors, and when we can have some confidence that these interventions help more than they harm. When considering risky behavior among youths, it is important to avoid both opinionated moralism as to what is the right behavior and naive faith that sixteen-year-olds make no predictable mistakes in their choices. By identifying systematic patterns in errors that people make, behavioral economics provides just such an approach.

The development of behavioral economics has not been targeted at analyzing the behavior of adolescents. The literature has developed with a belief that people make errors at all ages. It is, indeed, worth stressing the similarities in the mistakes made at different ages. A fifty-year-old may sacrifice too much for sexual gratification just as a fifteen-year-old may, or a thirty-six-year-old may drive too soon after drinking just as a sixteen-year-old may. Errors associated in the common imagination with one's youth are often made throughout life, and bad decisions attributed to youth may not be as strongly associated with age as is often claimed.[3]

That said, there are likely broad differences between adolescents and adults in many of the realms that we discuss. Young people almost surely make more mistakes. In section 1.1, we briefly discuss psychological evidence on how youths make decisions and how youths differ from adults. As we proceed, we shall relate some of our theoretical analysis back to

---

2. Given our focus on welfare, we shall not devote this essay to proving beyond (an economist's) doubt that behavior predicted outside the rational-choice framework is fundamentally inconsistent with rational choice. We doubt the general usefulness of the widespread methodology of employing post hoc attempts to fit behavior into the rational-choice framework without any inquiry as to whether it is the correct explanation. In making welfare assessments, this approach is clearly inappropriate.

3. This interpretation has been endorsed by some of the leading political figures of our day. As many of those attacking Bill Clinton for lying about his extramarital affairs were exposed for their own misbehavior, *youthful indiscretion* became something of a catchphrase for bad behavior at virtually any age. This is, e.g., precisely the term that seventy-four-year-old Congressman Henry Hyde used to describe the extramarital affair he had had at age forty-one.

this evidence, but more often we speculate on how some of the obvious but little-researched differences between youths and adults relate to the behavioral phenomena that we consider.

Before proceeding to this evidence, however, we briefly outline the other sections of this chapter. We focus on three types of questions that can all be usefully thought of in terms of their relation to a rational-choice base model. Throughout the chapter, we assume that a person's overall well-being is determined by adding up her well-being at each moment. We refer to a person's well-being in period t as her *instantaneous utility* in period t, which we denote by u_t. To allow for the possibility that the person's instantaneous utility in period t is stochastic, let S_t be the set of possible states for period t, and for $s \in S_t$, let $p_t(\cdot, s)$ and $u_t(\cdot, s)$ be the probability of state s and instantaneous utility function in state s, respectively. The person's expected instantaneous utility in period t is therefore $\Sigma_{s \in S_t} p_t(\cdot, s) u_t(\cdot, s)$. Finally, we assume that the person's overall well-being from the perspective of period t, which we denote by W^t, is given by

$$W^t \equiv \sum_{\tau=t}^{T} \left[\sum_{s \in S_\tau} p_\tau(\cdot, s) u_\tau(\cdot, s) \right].$$

Section 1.2 is devoted to discounting. The reader will notice that our base model assumes no discounting: the expected instantaneous utilities for all periods are weighted equally. We begin our discussion in section 1.2 by arguing that, from a normative perspective, there should be no discounting. Just because an adolescent cares very little for her thirty-five-year-old self, it does not follow that *we* should care very little for her thirty-five-year-old self. We then discuss some recent approaches that formalize the ways in which people underweight the future consequences of their actions and the lessons that such approaches have for youthful behavior. We discuss excessive myopia per se (pure underweighting of the future) and the tendency to have a time-inconsistent preference for immediate gratification (pursuing immediate gratification on a moment-by-moment basis in a way that does not match the person's own long-run best interests). We also discuss the closely related error of overoptimism about future self-control problems, which implies an underestimate of future misbehavior.

Section 1.3 discusses ways in which people incorrectly predict future instantaneous utilities. Hence, while section 1.2 explores ways in which people pay too little attention to the future consequences of their actions, section 1.3 explores ways in which people incorrectly predict how they will feel in the future about those consequences. We describe some systematic ways in which youths may underestimate the future harm caused by their current behavior because they do not fully recognize the extent of day-to-day fluctuations in tastes, or the extent to which peer pressure will temporarily influence their preferences, or just how much their preferences when older will differ from their youthful preferences.

In section 1.4, we discuss some issues with respect to the probability function p_τ, focusing on the logic of repeated risky choices. Since both past and future risky behavior may change the consequences of current risky behavior—in particular, behaving in a risky way at other times may affect the marginal risk accrued by behaving in a risky way now—certain types of risky behavior can be understood only in an intertemporal context. We flesh out the logic of repeated risky choices largely in a rational-choice setting but then explore how those implications might differ when people make errors in assessing risks, have self-control problems, or incorrectly predict their own future preferences.

We conclude in section 1.5 with a more general discussion of the issues raised and lessons learned from the analysis in this chapter.

1.1 Evidence on Adolescent Decision Making

In this section, we review some evidence from psychology and related fields concerning how youths make decisions and how youths differ from adults.

The paradigm of psychological research most closely related to the economic approach is behavioral decision theory, which examines people's actual decision-making processes and how these compare to "normative" (Bayesian) decision making. Behavioral decision theory often breaks down decision making into a sequence of steps so that performance on individual steps can be analyzed in isolation. There are extensive literatures that identify weaknesses in the ways in which adults perform these steps (see, e.g., Camerer 1995; and Fischhoff 1988).

There is a smaller literature that attempts to analyze the decision-making performance of adolescents and how adolescents differ from adults. The general themes in this literature seem to be that there is little evidence, particularly evidence that makes direct comparisons between adolescents and adults, that much of the evidence is, as assessed by researchers whose analysis most resembles the perspective of economists, weak owing to methodological problems, and that, while what little evidence there is suggests a few differences between adolescents and adults, on the whole they are remarkably similar. Indeed, a review article by Furby and Beyth-Marom (1992) emphasizes that many common conceptions of how youths differ from adults do not seem to be borne out by the evidence.[4]

Many studies ask subjects to formulate lists of potential consequences of various behaviors. Beyth-Marom et al. (1993) is one of the few studies

---

4. For reviews in this vein, see also Fischhoff (1992) and Beyth-Marom and Fischhoff (1997).

of this type that directly compares adolescents and adults. Teens and parents were asked to generate possible consequences of several decisions (e.g., you were [your child was] at a party where marijuana was passed around and decided to smoke). Although there were a few differences— for instance, on average, adults generated slightly more consequences, and adolescents were slightly more likely to mention consequences involving social reactions—overall the most striking conclusion was the similarity between adults and adolescents.

Some list-the-consequences studies focus on the question of how future-oriented youths are. Lewis (1981) conducted a study that compares adolescents in three grade categories (grades 7–8, 10, and 12). In simulated peer-counseling sessions, subjects were presented hypothetical dilemmas and asked what advice they would give to a peer who faced these dilemmas. One of the main results was a significant increase with grade level in the mention of the potential risks and future consequences of decisions, which supports the hypothesis that there is an increase in future orientation through adolescence.[5] Further evidence of this hypothesis is reviewed in Greene (1986), who concludes that "adolescents, as compared to younger children: (1) demonstrate greater depth and extension of temporal perspective . . . ; (2) project a more complex, differentiated set of future expectations . . . ; and (3) describe future aspirations with greater planfulness, organization, and realism" (p. 100).[6]

Comparisons have been conducted between adolescents and adults not only in awareness of consequences but also in perceptions of the likelihood of those consequences. Quadrel, Fischhoff, and Davis (1993) test the conventional wisdom that youths are prone to feelings of invulnerability by asking subjects to assess the likelihood that various negative events would occur to themselves, an acquaintance, a close friend, and their parent or child. Subjects typically assessed similar likelihoods for themselves and for others. There was some evidence for feelings of invulnerability—conditional on assessing different likelihoods, subjects were twice as likely to assess lower likelihoods for themselves—but this invulnerability was not stronger for adolescents than for adults.[7]

In fact, there is evidence that youths are in some ways overly pessimistic about their future. Fischhoff et al. (2000) survey youths about personal probabilities of dying young. For a representative sample of fifteen- and sixteen-year-olds, the mean response to how likely it is that they would die

5. A contrary result, however, was that there seemed to be no difference across grade levels in recommendations as to whether peers or parents should be consulted for advice.

6. Greene conducts an experiment to determine whether such changes are correlated with the emergence of Piaget's formal-operations reasoning and finds at best very weak evidence.

7. In fact, the invulnerability was stronger among adults than among adolescents, but this seemed merely to reflect the plausible consensus among youths and adults that the adults *were* less vulnerable to many of the risks under consideration.

in the next year was 18.6 percent, whereas the statistical estimate is 0.08 percent. The mean response to how likely it is that they would die by age twenty was 20.3 percent, whereas the statistical estimate is 0.4 percent.

Researchers have also asked whether adolescents are competent decision makers. For instance, Weithorn and Campbell (1982) presented adolescents with hypothetical medical- and psychological-treatment decisions, finding that fourteen-year-olds scored as well as eighteen- and twenty-one-year-olds in competency, and Lewis (1987) concludes that, in terms of pregnancy and contraceptive decisions, adolescents may equal adults in their competence to reason.

While the studies discussed above examine hypothetical decisions, another literature examines how adolescents' perceptions of consequences, the likelihood of consequences, and the importance of consequences predict their own behavior. For instance, Bauman (1980) presented seventh graders with fifty-four potential consequences that might occur if they used marijuana and asked them to rate on a five-point scale both the likelihood and the importance of those consequences to themselves. These ratings were then found to be predictive of self-reported marijuana use by the same individuals one year later. A similar technique has been used by a variety of researchers to study cigarette smoking, drinking, and sexual intercourse. Furby and Beyth-Marom (1992) summarize (and criticize) these studies and conclude that, "in sum, what little evidence there is (with all its mentioned weaknesses) suggests that to at least some small extent teens choose to engage in behaviors which are more likely to bring consequences they perceive as positive and less likely to bring consequences they perceive as negative" (pp. 16–17).

Many of the studies in this volume also support this conclusion. For instance, Gruber and Zinman (chap. 2) find that youth smoking depends negatively on price, at least for older teens; Pacula et al. (chap. 6) find that youth marijuana use depends negatively on both price and the perceived risk of future harm; and Levine (chap. 4) finds that teenage women are less likely to have sex and more likely to use contraceptives when labor market conditions are good and when the perceived risk of HIV infection is high. These findings that adolescents react to costs and benefits suggest that youths are to some degree rational in pursuing their well-being. But, since all behavioral-economics models with which we are familiar assume that people respond to costs and benefits, such findings say nothing about the validity of the extreme rational-choice model.

The evidence reviewed above suggests that adolescents are similar to adults in terms of their ability to carry out the decision-making process. Youths seem to differ more from adults in how they value the consequences of decisions. In fact, research in developmental psychology that studies adolescent behavior focuses not on the decision-making process, but rather on what considerations matter most to adolescents. Much of this research focuses on adolescent concerns with such things as identity formation, sexual-identity formation, and establishing autonomy and independence. This research suggests that adolescents may make decisions based primarily on these considerations, not on "objective" consequences. For instance, an adolescent male may drive fast so as to confirm his masculine identity, virtually ignoring the potential negative consequences. Baumrind (1987) even argues that many risk-taking behaviors by adolescents play an integral role in identity formation and making the transition to adulthood.[8]

There are, of course, other reasons why youths and adults might value consequences differently. Over the years, many studies have found that youths tend to score higher than adults on sensation-seeking and risk-taking behavior (e.g., Zuckerman, Eysenck, and Eysenck 1978; and Arnett 1994). And, presumably, youths are more concerned than adults are with how their peers will react to their behavior.

Differences in how youths and adults value consequences reflect differences in preferences, which in our model means differences in the instantaneous utility functions. If a young male engages in some risky behavior because it satisfies a need to confirm his masculine identity, or because it yields desirable sensations, or because it will provoke positive reactions from his peers, it seems natural to conclude that he has positive marginal instantaneous utility from engaging in the behavior.

The theoretical analysis developed below does not focus per se on how adolescent preferences differ from adult preferences. Instead, we focus on the ways in which youths fail to behave in their own best interests and for the most part remain agnostic about what those best interests are. But the fact that youths care a lot about such things as identity formation, sensation seeking, and peer reactions that tend to increase short-term benefits in a highly variable way may imply that the errors that we discuss are particularly problematic for youths, even if youths and adults do not differ in their inherent propensity for these errors.

The evidence on risk perceptions and differential preferences discussed above suggests some ways in which our analysis in section 1.3 of incorrectly predicting preferences and in section 1.4 of repeated risky choices may be especially applicable to youths. While the evidence discussed above comparing the future orientation of adolescents and that of adults is relevant to our analysis of self-control problems in section 1.2, we discuss more direct evidence on the relation between age and self-control problems when we discuss evidence on self-control problems more generally.

8. For recent research by economists that explores the role of identity, see Akerlof and Kranton (2000).

1.2   Trading Off Present versus Future Consequences

Most of the risky behaviors addressed in this volume involve a trade-off between short-term benefits and long-term costs. The decision whether to have sex involves a trade-off between the short-term benefit of sexual pleasure and the long-term cost of possibly getting pregnant or acquiring a sexually transmitted disease. The decision whether to commit a crime involves a trade-off between the short-term thrill or material benefits of the crime and the long-term costs of possibly going to jail. The decision whether to drink alcohol, smoke cigarettes, or use other drugs involves a trade-off between the short-term benefits of consumption and the long-term costs to future health, job prospects, and personal satisfaction. Each of these domains is quite rich, and, clearly, no single factor can explain the misbehavior of youths in these domains. But there is a simple error that plays a significant role across all these domains: excessive myopia in trading off present versus future consequences.

In order to discuss errors in trading off present versus future consequences, we must begin with a normative standard of how a person *should* trade off present versus future consequences to maximize her true well-being, which requires a discussion of the appropriateness of discounting. Economists use the notion *discounting* in a variety of ways.[9] Most common and most literal is to assume that discounting is part of a person's preferences. However, given the fundamental disposition toward revealed-preference theory and the assumption that whatever informed people do must be optimal for them, economists often take the view that, if such discounting is merely a matter of preference, then it is not to be questioned. We take a different view, one that we think is more in accord with the intuition that everybody—including most economists when we let our methodological guard down—views as a more sensible welfare criterion: that we should wish on ourselves, our children, our neighbors, and society the equal weighting of the expected hedonic well-being at different moments.

Most of us would find it morally repugnant if, controlling for uncertainties, personality, physical differences, etc., a parent admitted openly that he cares about the well-being of his five-year-old son ten times more than he cares about the well-being of his ten-year-old daughter. We would similarly be repulsed if he admitted that, again controlling for uncertainties, he cares ten times more about his five-year-old's current well-being than he cares about the same child's well-being five years from now, when he becomes a ten-year-old. For a parent to apply such differential weights

---

9. We ignore the "financial discounting" of money owing to interest earned, which has nothing to do with issues of hedonic discounting of the sort that we consider here.

to the hedonic well-being of his different children or to the hedonic well-being of one of his children at different ages is morally insane.

We believe that people should be just as repulsed if a fifteen-year-old says that he cares ten times more about his own current well-being than he cares about his own well-being five years from now, when he becomes a twenty-year-old. That is, we ought to be willing to make the same sort of normative judgments that we make about how a parent weights the hedonic well-being of his children about how an individual weights his hedonic well-being at different times in his life. Just as we must at times make reasoned judgments about whether a particular thirty-five-year-old is a fit guardian for a particular fifteen-year-old, so, too, we must at times make reasoned judgments about whether the fifteen-year-old is a fit guardian for her thirty-five-year-old self.

This argument for no hedonic discounting provides the basis for not including a discount function in our base model. But, as most economists (implicitly or explicitly) recognize, a discount function often serves as a useful reduced form to capture unmodeled uncertainties such as the probability of death or severe illness. As a simple illustration, suppose that the only uncertainty that matters is whether a person is alive or dead and that the person's utility is a function of consumption if living and a constant if dead. If the probability of dying between periods τ and $\tau + 1$ is q, then, from the perspective of period t, the probability of being alive in period τ is $(1 - q)^{\tau - t}$—that is, $p_\tau(\text{alive}) = (1 - q)^{\tau - t}$. Normalizing $u_\tau(\cdot, \text{dead}) = 0$, we can then usefully conceptualize the person's true well-being as being given by $W^t = \sum_{\tau = t}^{T} \delta^{\tau - t} u_\tau(\cdot, \text{alive})$, where $\delta \equiv 1 - q$.

In a variety of settings, therefore, a discount factor ought to be incorporated into the model as a sort of heuristic used by the people we are modeling, or as a heuristic being used by the modelers, to capture unmodeled contingencies. People should discount the future in the same sense that they discount a rumor of a coming appearance by (say) Johnny Depp—because they doubt whether it will happen. Our claim is that, from a normative perspective, such "heuristic discounting" is the only proper source of discounting.

Of course, when one looks at the choices that people make, substantial discounting beyond plausible uncertainties seems to be a fundamental behavioral reality—that is, people are excessively myopic relative to what would maximize their true well-being.[10] To model excessive myopia, we begin with the simple exponential-discounting formulation that is commonly used by economists. Suppose that a person makes choices that affect her well-being in periods $1, 2, \ldots, T$, and let u_τ denote her instanta-

---

10. For an overview of how to go about separating assessment of hedonic return to activities from revealed-preference theory, see Kahneman, Diener, and Schwartz (1999).

neous utility in period τ. Suppose further that the person's true overall well-being from the perspective of period t is given by

$$W^t \equiv \sum_{\tau=t}^{T} \hat{\delta}^{\tau-t} u_\tau .$$

In this formulation, $\hat{\delta}$ is the person's heuristic discount factor, capturing unmodeled uncertainties as discussed above.

As a simple form of inappropriate discounting, we suppose that, in period t, the person chooses her behavior to maximize period t intertemporal preferences

$$U^t \equiv \sum_{\tau=t}^{T} \delta^{\tau-t} u_\tau ,$$

where δ is the discount factor that she uses when making decisions. Simple excessive myopia says that the discount factor that the person uses when making decisions is smaller than her true heuristic discount factor—that is, $\delta < \hat{\delta}$. As a result, at each moment, the person gives too little weight to her future well-being.

Because the risky behaviors studied in this volume tend to generate positive short-term benefits and negative long-term consequences, simple excessive myopia makes people overly likely to engage in risky behaviors relative to the normative standard. Suppose, for instance, that a young person must decide whether to engage in sexual intercourse. In making this decision, she takes into account both the sexual pleasure that she would derive from the act and the expected costs that she might bear later in life. Formally, suppose that there are two periods, youth and adulthood, and that engaging in sexual intercourse in period 1 yields immediate pleasure $u_1 = 10$ but causes an expected future cost of 15, so $u_2 = -15$. Abstinence yields $u_1 = u_2 = 0$. If the person's true heuristic discount factor is $\hat{\delta} = 1$, the youth should choose abstinence, but if to make decisions the youth uses any discount factor $\delta \leq 2/3$, she would choose sex.

It is instructive to explore calibrationwise what magnitudes of discounting are consistent with heuristic discounting of the sort that we discuss above. Suppose, for instance, that a fifteen-year-old has a 50 percent chance of being alive and well at age thirty-five (which is obviously conservative). Then, under the simple formulation with $W^t = \sum_{\tau=t}^{T} \hat{\delta}^{\tau-t} u_\tau$, the person's yearly $\hat{\delta}$ should be something on the order of 0.966 (i.e., $0.966^{20} = 0.5$). Hence, even yearly discount factors of 0.95 should perhaps be considered excessive myopia.

The discussion presented above suggests that youths might engage in too much risky behavior because they attach too little weight to their well-being as adults. A related question arises: In terms of the discount factor that they use in making decisions, are youths more impatient than adults?

Indeed, researchers sometimes claim that youths discount the future at a higher rate than do adults and that this difference might explain certain differences in behavior between youths and adults (e.g., Becker and Murphy 1988).[11] We think that there is truth to this but that there are some subtleties involved of which researchers are not fully aware. In particular, people seem to have in mind using the exponential-discounting formulation combined with an assumption that δ gets larger as a person gets older—for example, a sixteen-year-old has preferences $\Sigma_{\tau=16}^{T} (0.8)^{\tau-16} u_\tau$, whereas a thirty-year-old has preferences $\Sigma_{\tau=30}^{T} (0.9)^{\tau-30} u_\tau$. But this formalization would imply that preferences are time inconsistent, and, moreover, the form of the time inconsistency seems intuitively wrong: it would imply, for instance, that people systematically plan to be indulgent in their distant future and then change their minds when the moment arrives. As we discuss below, people tend to exhibit exactly the opposite behavior.[12]

Realistically, youths are more impatient than adults. But it is probably best to model such differences by assuming date-specific per period discount factors. That is, for each k, there exists a discount factor δ_k between periods k and $k + 1$, and in period t the person chooses her behavior, to maximize the intertemporal preferences represented by

$$U^t \equiv \sum_{\tau=t}^{T} \left(\prod_{k=t}^{\tau-1} \delta_k \right) u_\tau.$$

Unfortunately, this formulation is not very easy to work with. Both empirical research and theoretical research become more difficult when there are multiple discount parameters to consider.

While the formulation presented above assumes time-consistent discounting, evidence is clear that people tend to have a time-inconsistent preference for immediate gratification. That is, when people make decisions that have both short-run and long-run consequences, they tend to satisfy their immediate wants in ways that they do not like from a long-run perspective.[13] Such preferences imply that people have self-control problems wherein they are unable on a moment-by-moment basis to behave in their own long-run best interests.

While the phenomenon is more general, there is a particularly simple

11. An alternative explanation is that youths "look" more impatient than adults because their perceived instantaneous utilities differ. We discuss this possibility in sec. 1.3 below.

12. Another subtlety goes hand in hand with the time inconsistency: Is the person aware of how her preferences will change? We discuss this issue below in the context of a preference for immediate gratification.

13. See, e.g., Ainslie (1975, 1991, 1992), Ainslie and Haslam (1992a, 1992b), Loewenstein and Prelec (1992), Thaler (1991), and Thaler and Loewenstein (1992). While the rubric *hyperbolic discounting* is often used to describe such preferences, the qualitative feature of the time inconsistency is more general (and more generally supported by empirical evidence) than the specific hyperbolic functional form.

model of preferences that captures the notion of a time-inconsistent taste for immediate gratification:[14]

$$U^t \equiv u_t + \beta \sum_{\tau=t+1}^{T} \delta^{\tau-t} u_\tau,$$

where $\beta < 1$. This formulation is a simple modification of the standard model of exponential discounting, where the parameter β represents the time-inconsistent preference for immediate gratification—at any given moment, the person has an extra bias for the present over the future.

The assumption that people have a preference for immediate gratification accords with introspection, folk wisdom, and the psychological evidence. The most prevalent form of psychological evidence is evidence of declining discount rates. As an illustration, consider the findings in Green, Fry, and Myerson (1994). As part of their study (we shall return to other parts), twelve undergraduates at Washington University in St. Louis (averaging twenty years of age) were asked to make a series of choices between a delayed reward of $1,000 and an immediate reward ranging between $1 and $1,000. The length of the delay and the amount of the immediate reward were varied.[15] From this procedure, and from the relatively consistent behavior observed, discount functions can be inferred by comparing the "immediate equivalent" of $1,000 delayed by different durations.

Green, Fry, and Myerson do not report the raw data but visually present the median immediate equivalents. By our own visual inspection of this picture (their fig. 1), the immediate equivalent of $1,000 in one year was $625, the immediate equivalent of $1,000 in five years was $350, and the immediate equivalent of $1,000 in twenty-five years was $100. These numbers correspond to discount rates of 60 percent per year for year 1, but only 16 percent per year for years 2–5, and only 6 percent per year for years 6–25.[16] While the specific discount rates are not closely matched with other discount rates reported in the same study—for example, discounting was less severe for a $10,000 delayed reward—or in other studies, the general feature of declining discount rates is universal.[17]

14. These preferences were originally developed by Phelps and Pollak (1968) in the context of intergenerational altruism and later used by Laibson (1994) to model time inconsistency within an individual. This model has since been used by Laibson (1996, 1997), Laibson, Repetto, and Tobacman (1998), O'Donoghue and Rabin (1999a, 1999b, 1999c, 1999d, in press), Fischer (1997), and others.

15. Delays of one week, one month, six months, one year, three years, five years, ten years, and twenty-five years were used. Thirty different values between $1 and $1,000 were used for the immediate rewards.

16. For example, $625(1.6) = $1,000, and $350(1.6)(1.16)^4 = $1,000.

17. Extreme caution should be used in making too much of these results. In addition to having a small sample size, this study infers discount functions from trade-offs involving money amounts, which should not logically serve as proxies for utility discounting. Even so, there have been dozens of studies over the years that find that variants of hyperbolic discounting fit human and nonhuman choice better than exponential discounting (for additional

A time-inconsistent taste for immediate gratification implies that people might want to engage in some indulgent behavior at the present moment while at the same time they would prefer not to engage in the same indulgent behavior in the future. Hence, when people think about having sex, drinking alcohol, taking drugs, and so forth, their desire to do the activity now is greater than their current desire to do it in the future. This, in turn, implies that a person is more likely to engage in an indulgent activity at the moment of action than she would have preferred at some prior moment.

To illustrate, consider a modification of our earlier sex example. Suppose that having sex yields immediate benefits of 10 but has expected long-term costs of 15, and suppose that a person has the (β, δ) preferences described above with $\beta = 1/2$ and $\delta = 1$. Consider how a person feels in period t about having sex now, in period t, versus having sex in the future, in some period $t' > t$. Because having sex now yields utility $10 - (1/2)15 > 0$, the person would like to have sex now; and, because having sex in the future yields utility $(1/2)10 - (1/2)15 < 0$, the person in period t would prefer not to have sex in period t'. But, when period t' arrives, the person will then view having sex as yielding utility $10 - (1/2)15 > 0$ and will therefore then prefer to have sex.

The implications of having a preference for immediate gratification often depend on the person's beliefs about her own future behavior. Most research has focused on two extreme assumptions about beliefs. *Sophisticated* people are fully aware of their future self-control problems and therefore correctly predict how their future selves will behave, and *naive* people are fully unaware of their future self-control problems and therefore believe that their future selves will behave exactly as they currently would like them to behave.[18] But, clearly, this is a continuum; O'Donoghue and Rabin (1999d, in press) model a person who is *partially naive*—she is aware that she has future self-control problems, but she underestimates their magnitude.

A simple way in which to formalize these different beliefs is to suppose that a person is characterized not only by her true preference for immediate gratification, as reflected by β, but also by her beliefs as to what her future preference for immediate gratification will be, which we denote by $\hat{\beta}$. A sophisticated person, who knows exactly her future preference for immediate gratification, has perceptions $\hat{\beta} = \beta$. A naive person, who believes that she will not have a preference for immediate gratification in the

examples with human subjects, see Solnick et al. [1980], Myerson and Green [1995], and Kirby and Marakovic [1995]). To the best of our knowledge, there have been no studies in which behavior was found that fits exponential discounting better than hyperbolic discounting.

18. Strotz (1956) and Pollak (1968) carefully lay out these two assumptions (and develop the labels) but do not much consider the implications of assuming one versus the other. Fischer (1997) and Laibson (1994, 1996, 1997) assume sophisticated beliefs. O'Donoghue and Rabin (1999c) consider both and explicitly contrast the two.

future, has perceptions $\hat{\beta} = 1$. A partially naive person has perceptions $\hat{\beta} > \beta$ but $\hat{\beta} < 1$.

To illustrate the importance of beliefs, consider yet another version of our sex example. We again suppose that having sex yields immediate benefits of 10 but long-term costs of 15 and that a person has (β, δ) preferences with $\beta = 1/2$ and $\delta = 1$. But, instead of analyzing a person who is deciding whether to have sex now, we analyze a person who is planning to go on a date tonight (which we think of as the next period), during which she might have sex. Our discussion above implies that the person would prefer not to have sex tonight, and, hence, if she predicts that she would have sex, she may make some "commitment" so as to prevent herself from having sex—for example, she might cancel the date, ask a friend or parent to come along as a chaperone, etc. What is her prediction? Given beliefs $\hat{\beta}$, the person believes that this evening she will feel that having sex yields utility $10 - \hat{\beta}(15)$, and, thus, she predicts that she will have sex this evening if $\hat{\beta} < 2/3$. We can conclude that if $\hat{\beta} < 2/3$, she would avoid having unwanted sex, whereas if $\hat{\beta} > 2/3$, she would not make a commitment and end up having unwanted sex.

Beliefs about one's future preference for immediate gratification need not influence behavior. There is a class of situations in which beliefs do not affect behavior, namely, when decisions are disconnected in the sense that both the short-term and the long-term consequences of any specific decision are unrelated to those of any other decision. But, when one decision constitutes a commitment that changes later choice sets, or when the benefits or costs of decisions in different periods are tied together in some way, beliefs typically matter. This is likely the case for many of the behaviors examined in this volume. For instance, there may be decreasing returns to the number of times a person has sex in a week, or the expected future costs of having sex may be nonlinear in the number of times a person has sex. The very essence of addictive behaviors such as smoking cigarettes, drinking alcohol, and taking other drugs is that the utility from both consumption and nonconsumption depends on how much a person has consumed in the past.

To further illustrate the implications of sophistication versus naïveté, we return once again to our sex example. Suppose that a person has multiple opportunities to have sex and that the expected future cost of having sex is a nonlinear function of the number of sexual encounters. For any individual encounter, the perceived future cost of having sex on this particular occasion depends on both how often the person has had sex in the past and how often she expects to have sex in the future. Suppose, for simplicity, that the person has two opportunities to have sex, in periods 1 and 2, and then possibly experiences some cost in period 3. The benefits from having sex in periods 1 and 2 are V_1 and V_2, respectively. Let C_n be the expected period 3 cost if the person has sex n times, in which case the expected future cost is nonlinear if $C_2 - C_1 \neq C_1$. Finally, we assume that $\delta = 1$ and $V_2 < \min\{C_1, C_2 - C_1\}$, which implies that, from a long-run perspective, the person should not have sex in period 2.

Consider the period 1 decision when $V_2 > \max\{\beta C_1, \beta(C_2 - C_1)\}$, which implies that in period 2 the person will have sex regardless of what she did in period 1. A sophisticated person in period 1 recognizes that she will have sex in period 2 and therefore views her decision in period 1 as having sex twice versus having sex once. Hence, she chooses to have sex in period 1 if $V_1 > \beta(C_2 - C_1)$. In contrast, a naive person in period 1 believes that she will not have sex in period 2 and therefore views her decision in period 1 as having sex once versus not having sex at all. Hence, she chooses to have sex in period 1 if $V_1 > \beta C_1$. Whether a naive person is more or less likely than a sophisticated person to indulge in period 1 depends on whether the costs are convex or concave. With convex costs, pessimism about the future makes a sophisticated person perceive the cost of current indulgence to be larger than does a naive person, and, hence, a sophisticated person is less likely to indulge. With concave costs, pessimism about the future makes a sophisticated person perceive the cost of current indulgence to be smaller than does a naive person, and, hence, a sophisticated person is more likely to indulge.

In fact, more matters than just the effects of pessimism. Let us reconsider this example when $\beta C_1 > V_2 > \beta(C_2 - C_1)$, which implies that in period 2 the person will have sex only if she had sex in period 1. The mindset of a naive person is the same as before: she expects not to have sex in period 2 no matter what she does now and therefore chooses to have sex in period 1 if $V_1 > \beta C_1$. A sophisticated person, in contrast, recognizes in period 1 that her decision is effectively between having sex twice versus not having sex at all and therefore chooses to have sex in period 1 if $V_1 > \beta[C_1 + (C_2 - C_1) - V_2]$. Inspection reveals that, for this case, a naive person is unambiguously more likely to choose to have sex in period 1.

The two cases in this example illustrate two effects of sophistication. On one hand, there is a *pessimism effect:* a sophisticated person is more pessimistic than a naive person about her future behavior, and this pessimism may affect the perceived future consequences of current indulgence. As the example illustrates, this effect can go in either direction. Second, there is an *incentive effect:* a sophisticated person might recognize that to avoid future indulgence, she must restrain herself now.[19]

Although, in theory, sophistication about future self-control problems can mitigate or exacerbate misbehavior, we suspect that for realistic environments, sophistication more often than not mitigates the harm caused

---

19. These two effects are first identified (and named) in O'Donoghue and Rabin (1999a, 1999b) for the realm of addiction. Those papers show that, for addictive goods, the pessimism effect leads a sophisticated person to indulge more than a naive person while the incentive effect leads a sophisticated person to indulge less.

by a preference for immediate gratification. This suspicion is somewhat impressionistic, but it is based on a conjecture that, in real-world environments, the incentive effect is likely quite important. Naive people are hurt not just because optimism about the future leads them to perceive small costs of current misbehavior, but also because they fail at self-management—they do things in the present that lead them to do more indulgent things in the future.

In what ways might self-control problems be particularly relevant for youths? There are two immediate points of comparison between youths and adults. First, do youths have a larger preference for immediate gratification than do adults—that is, do youths have a smaller β? Second, are youths less good at predicting their future preference for immediate gratification—that is, do youths have a larger $\hat{\beta}$? While the answers to these questions are both intuitively yes, there is limited evidence. We know of no experimental evidence on how adolescents compare to other age groups in terms of awareness of self-control problems, but the Green, Fry, and Myerson (1994) study cited above provides some suggestive evidence in terms of the magnitude of the preference for immediate gratification. In addition to gathering evidence on twenty-year-old college students, Green, Fry, and Myerson also report data on sixth graders (averaging twelve years old) from private religious schools and elderly subjects (averaging sixty-eight years old) from a subject pool maintained by the Washington University Psychology Department for the study of aging. Using the same methods that we used above to derive the discount rates for college students of 60, 16, and 6 percent per year for horizons of one year, one to five years, and five to twenty-five years, the comparable numbers are 111, 21, and 2 percent for sixth graders and 14, 8, and 8 percent for elderly subjects. We are highly skeptical of the external validity of the precise estimates, but they suggest that near-term discounting becomes less severe through adolescence (comparing the twenty-year-olds and the twelve-year-olds) and even less severe through adulthood.[20]

Of course, even if youths were no different from adults in terms of both their preference for immediate gratification and their awareness, the implications of these errors could still be quite different in youths and in adults. A preference for immediate gratification is relevant only to the extent that the person faces temptations, and youths and adults may differ on this dimension in a number of ways. First, there may be differences in inherent preferences—in the types of activities that youths and adults actually enjoy. Second, even for activities that yield equal intrinsic benefits for youths and adults, youths may perceive even larger immediate benefits from en-

20. Again, extreme caution should be used in making too much of these results. In addition to our earlier reservations, here the money amounts likely mean different things to the different age groups.

gaging in the activity owing to secondary considerations unique to adolescents, such as peer pressure, identity formation, or establishing autonomy. As a result, such activities become even more tempting for youths. Third, youths and adults face different opportunity sets that affect the types of tempting situations with which they are faced. Given the professional and personal constraints that adults face, many activities that might be tempting are so costly as not to pose a problem. Youths may be tempted to use illicit drugs, for instance, when the costs are too high for adults.

1.3 Mispredicting Future Utility

Section 1.2 above discusses errors in intertemporal trade-offs owing to excessive discounting. This section discusses a second way in which people make errors in weighing intertemporal trade-offs: they misperceive how they will feel about the future consequences of their actions.

The source of such errors is changing preferences, changes due to such factors as past behavior, temporary fluctuations in tastes, and changes in the environment. The notion that "states"—factors other than contemporaneous consumption—can affect preferences is not new to economics. For instance, many models over the years posit that people become accustomed to past consumption levels (see, e.g., Duesenberry 1952; Ryder and Heal 1973; and Bowman, Minehart, and Rabin 1999), Becker and Murphy (1988) build a model of addiction based on earlier research on habit formation (e.g., Pollak 1970, 1978) wherein the utility from consuming an addictive product depends on past consumption, and Laibson (in press) studies how changes in exogenous states, which he calls *cues,* can affect well-being.

Most models of state-dependent utility assume that a person can perfectly predict how changes in future states will affect her future preferences. For example, if a person must make summer vacation plans during the winter, it is assumed that she can predict how she will feel in the summer; and, if a person must decide whether to try crack cocaine for the first time, it is assumed that she can correctly predict how this consumption will influence her future enjoyment of activities, including consuming more crack cocaine. In a recent paper, Loewenstein, O'Donoghue, and Rabin (1999) formalize and explore the implications of a general bias in such predictions, which they label *projection bias:* people tend to underappreciate the effects of changes in their states and hence falsely project their current consumption preferences onto their future preferences. In this section, we review the evidence in support of such projection bias, present a simplified version of their model, and discuss its implications both in general and for youths in particular.

Research shows that people underappreciate short-term, transient changes in preferences, such as those induced by fluctuations in hunger or the presence of environmental cues, and slowly developed but longer-lasting changes, such as those induced by addiction or changes in one's accustomed standard of living. Moreover, people underappreciate endogenous changes in preferences that depend on prior choices, such as drug addiction, and exogenous changes in preferences that do not depend on prior choices, such as those associated with aging. We discuss here a few representative studies.[21]

The prototypical example of incorrectly predicting short-term fluctuations in tastes is underappreciating the effects of hunger. Read and van Leeuwen (1998), for instance, asked office workers to choose between healthy snacks and unhealthy snacks that they would receive in one week, at a time when they should expect to be either hungry (late in the afternoon) or satiated (immediately after lunch). Subjects were approached to make the choice either when they were hungry (late in the afternoon) or when they were satiated (immediately after lunch). In general, people who expected to be hungry the next week were more likely to opt for unhealthy snacks than were those who expected to be satiated. But the key finding was that people who were hungry when they made the choice were also more likely to opt for unhealthy snacks than were those who were satiated, suggesting that people were projecting their current preferences onto their future selves.

Loewenstein, Nagin, and Paternoster (1997) provide evidence of projection bias with regard to sexual arousal. Male undergraduates were randomly assigned to view sexually arousing or nonarousing photographs. Subjects were then exposed to a vivid first-person date scenario in which "their date" suddenly requested a termination of physical intimacy, and asked to report their likelihood of behaving in a sexually aggressive fashion in this situation. Aroused subjects reported substantially higher likelihoods (70 percent) than did nonaroused subjects (50 percent), suggesting again that people's current preferences affect their predictions of future preferences.

The prototypical example of projection bias in predicting long-term changes in tastes is the underappreciation of adaptation. There is a plethora of evidence that adaptation is a central component of human well-being (see Helson [1964]; and for a recent review, see Frederick and Loewenstein [1999]). This literature consistently shows that people adapt to major changes in life circumstances. But there is also a great deal of evidence that people underestimate the extent to which they will adapt to new circumstances and hence overestimate the effect of major changes in circumstances on their long-run level of happiness. For instance, Loewenstein and Frederick (1997) compared the predictions by survey respon-

---

21. For a more extensive review of the evidence, see Loewenstein, O'Donoghue, and Rabin (1999).

dents of how changes in various environmental (e.g., a decline in sport fishing), social (e.g., increases in coffee shops), and personal (e.g., increases in body weight or income) factors would affect their well-being over the next decade to the reports of others about how actual changes in the last decade had affected their well-being. A clear pattern of underprediction of adaptation emerged in the data: people expected future changes to affect their well-being much more than others believed that matched changes in the past had affected their well-being.

To model such incorrect predictions, suppose that a person's true instantaneous utility in period t is given by $u(c_t, s_t)$. The vector c_t is the person's period t consumption vector, which includes all period t behavior relevant for current or future instantaneous utilities. The vector s_t is the person's "state" in period t. An individual state could be determined by past consumption (e.g., a person's addiction level) or by exogenous factors that might be internal (e.g., depression) or environmental (e.g., peer pressure). In addition, calendar time could be a state variable; we suspect that projection bias over states associated with aging may be quite important for youths.

Let $\tilde{u}(c_\tau, s_\tau | s_t)$ denote the prediction of a person currently in state s_t of what her instantaneous utility would be from consuming c_τ in state s_τ in period $\tau > t$. If a person were fully rational, her prediction would be correct—that is, $\tilde{u}(c_\tau, s_\tau | s_t) = u(c_\tau, s_\tau)$. But the evidence presented above suggests that people tend to exhibit *projection bias*, which, roughly speaking, means that predicted utility $\tilde{u}(c_\tau, s_\tau | s_t)$ lies "in between" true utility $u(c_\tau, s_\tau)$ and utility in the current state $u(c_\tau, s_t)$. For the purposes of the discussion here, we shall consider a particularly simple formulation of projection bias:[22]

DEFINITION. *Predicted utility exhibits* simple projection bias *if there exists* $\alpha \in [0, 1]$ *such that, for all* c, s_τ, *and* s_t, $\tilde{u}(c_\tau, s_\tau | s_t) = (1 - \alpha)u(c, s_\tau) + \alpha u(c, s_t)$.

If $\alpha = 0$, the person predicts her future instantaneous utility correctly and therefore has no projection bias. If $\alpha > 0$, the person has projection bias, where the bigger is α, the stronger is the bias.

For any period t and initial state s_t, a fully rational person would choose a path of consumption $(c_t, c_{t+1}, \ldots, c_T)$ to maximize true intertemporal utility $U^t = \sum_{\tau=t}^{T} \delta^{\tau-t} u(c_\tau, s_\tau)$, taking into account how the consumption path affects the evolution of future states. A person with projection bias attempts to maximize her intertemporal utility: for any period t and initial state s_t, a person with projection bias chooses a path of consumption $(c_t, c_{t+1}, \ldots, c_T)$ to maximize her perceived intertemporal utility $\tilde{U}^t =$

---

22. This simple formulation incorporates two key features. First, the person understands the qualitative nature of changes in her preferences but underestimates the magnitude of these changes. Second, the more the person's future preferences differ from her current preferences, the further her prediction is from her true future utility. For a more general formulation that incorporates these two features, see Loewenstein, O'Donoghue, and Rabin (1999).

$\sum_{\tau=t}^{T} \delta^{\tau-t} \tilde{u}(c_{\tau}, s_{\tau}|s_t)$, taking into account how the consumption path affects the evolution of future states. In other words, she behaves exactly as a fully rational person would except that she attempts to maximize $\tilde{U}^t \neq U^t$.

Projection bias can have important implications in a broad array of environments. There are three categories of errors to which projection bias can lead, which we illustrate with some simple examples along the lines of the behaviors discussed in this volume.

The first category of projection-bias errors involves choosing a suboptimal behavior owing simply to incorrect predictions of the future utility consequences of the behavior. To illustrate this type of error, suppose that a person is contemplating suicide owing to extreme depression. Suppose that the person is currently depressed and that the depression is sufficiently painful that, if it were to last a long time, it would be optimal for the person to commit suicide. Because projection bias can lead a person to underestimate the true utility of happy times, it can lead a depressed person to conclude incorrectly that suicide is optimal even when it is not.

We formalize this situation with a two-period model in which the person is "depressed" in period 1 and "happy" in period 2—that is, no matter what her behavior, the person's state will be D in period 1 and H in period 2. At the start of period 1, the person decides whether to commit suicide, where we normalize the utility from committing suicide to be 0. If the person chooses to live, then she receives utility $u(\text{life}, D) = -2$ in period 1 and utility $u(\text{life}, H) = 3$ in period 2. Assuming no discounting, the person's optimal choice is clearly to live because the eventual happy times are sufficiently happy to make it worth enduring the depression. But, with simple projection bias α, at the time she is deciding whether to commit suicide the person perceives her period 2 payoff from life to be $\tilde{u}(\text{life}, H \mid D) = (1 - \alpha)(3) + \alpha(-2)$. If her projection bias is big enough ($\alpha > 3/5$), then the person makes the incorrect choice to commit suicide.[23]

In the example given above, the person's state in each period is independent of her behavior; she chooses suboptimally only because her state at the time she makes the decision clouds her evaluation of the available options. Projection bias has more complicated and more damaging effects when the person's future state depends on her current behavior. In particular, if engaging in some activity causes future preferences to change in a deleterious way, then projection bias leads to overindulgence in that activity. For instance, if becoming addicted to cigarettes decreases a person's overall well-being, a person with projection bias will overindulge in cigarettes.

The first category of projection-bias errors is driven by incorrect predic-

---

23. A simple extension of this example shows the benefits of cooling-off periods for potential suicide victims. If the person delays until the depression at least partially subsides, she will perceive the utility of happy times to be closer to its true value and therefore will be less likely to commit suicide when she should not. This theme is discussed further in Loewenstein, O'Donoghue, and Rabin (1999).

tions of the future utility consequences of today's behavior. Incorrectly predicting future preferences can also cause a person to incorrectly predict future behavior, and—just as we saw for a preference for immediate gratification—incorrect predictions of future behavior can lead to bad decisions today. The second and third categories of projection-bias errors both revolve around how incorrect predictions of future behavior can lead to suboptimal decisions now.

The second category of projection-bias errors occurs when incorrect predictions of future behavior cause incorrect predictions about the future consequences of current choices. For instance, if projection bias leads a person to underestimate how often she will have sex in the future, then she may have an incorrect prediction about the future cost of having sex now. This logic is similar to that behind the pessimism effect in the realm of self-control problems and, just as for the pessimism effect, can lead to more or less current indulgence depending on the specifics of the environment. For instance, if a person who is not pregnant incorrectly predicts that, if she were pregnant, she would not get an abortion, then she would perceive the potential costs of having sex to be larger than they truly are and hence might be prone toward having too little sex (of course, this effect might be offset by other errors which we discuss that lead to having too much sex).

The third category of projection-bias errors involves *state mismanagement*. Because a person's future behavior depends on her future state, avoiding certain behaviors may require avoiding certain states.[24] But, since projection bias can lead a person not to recognize how a certain state would influence behavior, the person might end up engaging in unanticipated indulgent behavior. This failure to avoid situations in which indulgence is irresistible is similar to the lack of the incentive effect in people who are naive about self-control, and both errors tend to cause overindulgence.

To illustrate this type of error, suppose that, in the early evening, a person who is not sexually aroused must decide whether to go to a bar. If she decides not to go to the bar, then she remains at home and sexually unaroused for the entire night. If, instead, she goes to the bar, she meets someone, becomes sexually aroused, and then chooses whether to have sex. Suppose that optimal state management involves not going to the bar because she would choose to have sex if she did go to the bar, whereas, from an ex ante perspective, she would prefer to stay at home all night than go out and have sex.

To formalize this situation, consider a model with two periods, early

24. Although his model assumes exogenous states, Laibson (in press) discusses how in a more general model it is important to manage cues so as to avoid some undesirable behaviors. He refers to this phenomenon as *cue management*, which motivates our term *state management*.

evening and later that night. In period 1, the person decides either to go to the bar or stay home, and her state is sexually unaroused, which we denote by N. If she decides to stay home in period 1, then she remains at home and sexually unaroused for period 2. If she decides to go to the bar, in contrast, then her period 2 state is sexually aroused, which we denote by A, and in this state she must make the decision whether to have sex or to go home. We assume the instantaneous utilities to be as follows:

In Unaroused State	In Aroused State
$u(\text{home}, N) = 0$	$u(\text{home}, A) = -2$
$u(\text{bar}, N) = 1$	$u(\text{sex}, A) = -1.5$
$u(\text{sex}, N) = -3$	

The person is better off in period 1 if she goes to the bar rather than staying home. But going to the bar can lead to undesirable period 2 behavior, and, indeed, for this example, going to the bar will lead to having sex. Optimal behavior is to stay home for the entire night because $u(\text{bar}, N) + u(\text{sex}, A) < u(\text{home}, N) + u(\text{home}, N)$. Now suppose that the person has simple projection bias α. First note that, no matter what is α, the person would prefer to stay home for the entire evening if she thought she would have sex in period 2. But, since she perceives $\tilde{u}(\text{sex}, A|N) = (1 - \alpha)(-1.5) + \alpha(-3)$ and $\tilde{u}(\text{home}, A|N) = (1 - \alpha)(-2) + \alpha(0)$, for $\alpha > 1/7$ the person perceives that she would choose not to have sex in the event that she goes to the bar, and, moreover, for $\alpha > 1/2$ she would choose to go to the bar.

Such state mismanagement owing to projection bias can arise in a variety of other domains. For instance, if having one beer creates an increased desire for additional beers, then optimal state management may require avoiding bars altogether, whereas projection bias might lead the person to go to a bar expecting to have only one beer and end up drinking too many. Similarly, if being in a smoke-filled room provokes a strong desire to smoke, then optimal state management may require avoiding smoke-filled rooms, whereas projection bias might undermine this decision.

This third category of projection-bias error includes errors that are not state mismanagement per se; it might also involve a person failing properly to prepare for some behavior because she did not expect to engage in that behavior. To return to the sex example, for instance, if the person goes to the bar expecting not to have sex, she might not bother to bring a condom. As a result, even if optimal behavior were to have sex with a condom, the person might have sex without a condom because she planned not to have sex.

How might projection bias be particularly relevant for youths? The first question to ask is whether youths are more susceptible to projection bias than are adults. While the answer is almost certainly yes, we know of no good evidence on this issue. Suggestive evidence is that people are clearly aware of projection-bias problems and develop rules to help overcome them over the course of their lives—for example, the common wisdom "never shop on an empty stomach." At the same time, the evidence cited earlier and in Loewenstein, O'Donoghue, and Rabin (1999) makes it clear that adults do not fully appreciate changes in their preferences even on dimensions such as hunger where they have accumulated a great deal of experience. Hence, much as for self-control problems, our impression is that the major differences between adults and adolescents in terms of projection bias are driven not so much by different degrees of the bias, but by how a given degree of bias operates on the different preferences and situations that confront youths and adults.

As discussed in section 1.1 above, youths differ from adults in their concern for identity formation, establishing autonomy, and maintaining the regard of peers. The natural way to incorporate such concerns into a decision-making framework is in the utility function; if a person suddenly feels pressure from his peers to smoke marijuana, then his perceived marginal utility of smoking marijuana increases. Similarly, if a young person is driving and suddenly feels a drive to confirm his masculine identity, then his perceived marginal utility from driving fast increases.

Because such forces influence utilities, they are subject to projection bias. For instance, while youths likely recognize that their friends will influence their desire to engage in various activities, they likely underestimate the magnitude of these forces when they are not with their friends and, as a result, end up engaging in unwanted behaviors. State mismanagement becomes an important problem. A young person may go out with his friends expecting to resist peer pressure but then fail to do so. He may, for instance, go to a bar expecting to have one beer but then be pressured by his friends to drink many more. Giving in to peer pressure or drives to confirm identity and autonomy may also, in turn, affect the management of other states. For instance, a college student might choose to give in to peer pressure and drink alcohol every weekend, planning to quit when the peer pressure subsides, but not realizing how much more she will crave alcohol after she has become addicted.

Projection bias over the states associated with aging may be quite important for youths. To evaluate the long-term consequences of many risky behaviors, adolescents must predict how they will feel as adults. But youths and adults clearly have different preferences, and projection bias predicts that youths will underestimate how much their preferences will change as they age.

To illustrate the importance of this youth-to-adult projection bias, consider a young man who is debating whether to drop out of school, a decision that will affect whether he has a good job or a bad job as an adult.

Suppose that when he becomes an adult, he will care a lot about having a good job, but as a youth, he does not care at all. If the young man has projection bias with respect to differences between his youthful and his adult preferences, he will underestimate the long-run costs of dropping out of school and will therefore be too likely to drop out of school. An analogous conclusion would hold for any risky behavior, such as taking drugs, that might influence his future job prospects.

This youth-to-adult projection bias is perhaps even more important in the light of changing constraints. For instance, while youths have significant free time, adults must work five days a week. If youths are aware of these changing constraints, and if, because of projection bias, they predict that their utility function will not change very much, then they may predict that their actual utilities will change a lot. If youths currently think that working five days a week would be horrible and project this preference onto their adult selves, they might think that adulthood is going to be one, long miserable existence and may therefore care very little about imposing additional costs on their adult selves.

An implicit theme throughout the discussion presented above is that youths may exhibit behaviors that appear to be extremely myopic when in fact they are not. Consider a person who gives in to peer pressure or a drive to confirm his masculine identity. At first glance, we might be inclined to interpret this behavior as a sudden increase in myopia—to assume that peer pressure made the person neglect the future. We feel that this interpretation is incorrect. An alternative, projection-bias interpretation is that, when the pressure to conform is aroused, projection bias causes the person to exaggerate the persistence of this pressure. Hence, while he acts as if he cares only about his current well-being, he thinks that pursuing his immediate well-being is also what he must do for his long-run well-being.[25]

1.4 Repeated Risky Choices

Sections 1.2 and 1.3 above abstract away from the probabilistic nature of the long-term consequences of risky behavior. We now focus on riskiness per se, examining situations in which a person repeatedly chooses while young whether to engage in some behavior that might cause a future

---

25. Some actions in pursuit of immediate gratification may well be usefully thought of not in terms of either extreme discounting or projection bias but rather in terms of something more akin to the "visceral" model of choice discussed in Loewenstein (1996). If, e.g., a teenage boy makes Meatlovian promises with lifelong consequences in the pursuit of immediate sexual gratification, this is perhaps not to be thought of in terms of either an active belief that his current state of sexual frustration will last a lifetime or a conscious decision that his near-term gratification is more important to him than an entire lifetime of consequences; rather, he may simply not be attending to these future consequences at all.

bad outcome and does not learn while young whether his behavior thus far has assured the bad outcome. Many risky behaviors match this abstract description to some degree. Even when a young person is aware that smoking can lead to lung cancer or emphysema, he must repeatedly choose whether to smoke without knowing how much future harm he has already caused himself. Or a young person might face decisions whether to have sex on multiple occasions before knowing whether past sexual experiences have led to pregnancy or AIDS.

We begin our analysis within the rational-choice framework. While the rational-choice analysis is of interest in its own right, we also use it as a template to study the implications of the errors discussed in sections 1.2 and 1.3 above in the context of repeated risky choices, and to study the role that incorrect perceptions of risk can play in risky behavior.

Suppose that a fully rational person chooses up front the number of times, n, in which to engage in an activity. Let $V(n)$ be the total pleasure received from engaging in the activity n times, where V is increasing and concave. We interpret concavity as a proxy for the fact that enjoyment of the activity varies over time and the person indulges only at the n most enjoyable times. But we emphasize that, while concavity is convenient, it is not necessarily a good assumption here.[26]

Engaging in the activity carries with it the probabilistic cost of some bad outcome that might occur in the future. We assume that the bad outcome either occurs or does not occur, and if it occurs, then the person incurs a cost $\Gamma > 0$. In other words, the risk of harm accumulates, but the extent of harm does not. This feature is central to our results. While unrealistic in its extreme, it captures well the qualitative nature of many of the risky activities examined in this volume.

Formally, we assume that each time the person engages in the activity, there is an independent probability p that doing so causes the bad outcome to occur (had it not already been caused). Hence, if the person engages in the activity once, then the bad outcome occurs with probability p; if the person engages in the activity twice, then the bad outcome occurs with probability $p + (1 - p)p$; and, if the person engages in the activity n times, then the bad outcome occurs with probability $\pi(n; p) \equiv 1 - (1 - p)^n$. The expected cost of engaging in the activity is therefore

$$C(n; p) \equiv \pi(n; p)\Gamma \equiv [1 - (1 - p)^n]\Gamma.$$

Assuming for simplicity that there is no discounting, and assuming for analytic ease that n is a continuous variable, the person chooses n to maximize his net payoff $V(n) - C(n; p)$. Let $n^*(p, \Gamma)$ denote the person's opti-

---

26. In particular, convexity might be a better assumption for the consumption of addictive products; consuming moderate amounts of the product can be a horrible mix that yields many moments of the pain of withdrawal.

mal choice as a function of his perception of the risk p and the severity of the bad outcome Γ.

The perceived severity of the bad outcome has a simple and straightforward effect on the person's behavior: the more costly is the bad outcome— the larger is Γ—the less the person will engage in the activity. For instance, the worse a person perceives pregnancy or acquiring HIV to be, the less unprotected sex the person will have.

Owing to some interesting features of the cost function $C(n; p)$, however, the perceived riskiness p has considerably more complicated effects on the person's behavior. Because $C(n; p)$ is concave in n, $V(n) - C(n; p)$ can be convex, which gives rise to possible "corner solutions." For some parameter values, it can be that the person wants to engage in either none of the activity or a lot of the activity, never in between. But the more notable feature of $C(n; p)$ is that increasing the riskiness p can decrease the marginal cost of engaging in the activity—that is, can decrease $\partial C(n; p)/\partial n$. Formally, define $\pi_{np} \equiv \partial^2\pi/(\partial n\partial p)$, which is the cross-partial of π. It is straightforward to derive $\pi_{np} = (1 - p)^{n-1}[1 + \ln(1 - p)]$ so that $\pi_{np} = 0$ for $n = 1/[-\ln(1 - p)] \equiv \hat{n}(p)$. Moreover, $\pi_{np} > 0$ for $n < \hat{n}(p)$, in which case increasing p increases the marginal cost of engaging in the activity, and $\pi_{np} < 0$ for $n > \hat{n}(p)$, in which case increasing p decreases the marginal cost of engaging in the activity. Figure 1.1 illustrates how the total cost and marginal cost depend on n and p.

As indicated by panel A of figure 1.1, the larger is the perceived riskiness, the higher is the expected total cost for any given n. Hence, there is one straightforward prediction: if, for a given p, the person would not engage in the activity at all, then, for any larger riskiness, the person also would not engage in the activity at all. If a teenager is refraining entirely from unprotected sex or drug use and then comes to believe that the bad consequences of that activity are even more likely than she had earlier thought, she clearly will not start engaging in the activity.

But, if, for a given p, the person would engage in at least some of the

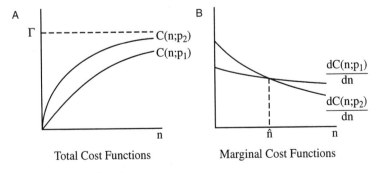

Total Cost Functions   Marginal Cost Functions

Fig. 1.1   Cost functions for $p_2 > p_1$

activity, an increase in the riskiness might either decrease or increase her level of that activity. To illustrate, consider the following special functional form for the benefits $V(n)$:

$$
V(n) = \begin{cases}
rn & \text{if } n \leq n_L, \\
rn_L + s(n - n_L) & \text{if } n \in [n_L, n_H], \\
rn_L + s(n_H - n_L) & \text{if } n \geq n_H,
\end{cases}
$$

where $r > s$. This function implies that the marginal utility of engaging in the activity is given by

$$
V'(n) = \begin{cases}
r & \text{if } n \leq n_L, \\
s & \text{if } n \in [n_L, n_H], \\
0 & \text{if } n \geq n_H.
\end{cases}
$$

This contrived functional form is useful because, given the concavity of costs, the person chooses $n \in \{0, n_L, n_H\}$. In other words, the person chooses either abstinence, low indulgence n_L, or high indulgence n_H. Because we are interested in whether an increase in riskiness leads to more or less indulgence, we consider the case where initially the person chooses low indulgence, or $n^*(p, \Gamma) = n_L$.

If $n_H < \hat{n}(p)$, then an increase in riskiness raises the marginal cost of changing from n_L to n_H and therefore will not lead to increased indulgence. If, however, $\hat{n}(p) < n_L$, then an increase in riskiness lowers the marginal cost of changing from n_L to n_H, and therefore the person may now prefer high indulgence to low indulgence. Of course, the increase in riskiness also raises the total cost of engaging in the activity at levels n_L and n_H, so now abstinence may be optimal. But, if r is sufficiently high, the person will not respond to greater risk by switching to abstinence, and, if s is sufficiently high—for instance, if initially the person was just indifferent between engaging in the activity n_L versus n_H times—then the increase in riskiness will lead the person to switch from low indulgence to high indulgence.

This example illustrates the more general point that there are two possible reactions that a person might have to an increase in perceived riskiness. First, there is the intuitive reaction wherein the person reduces his indulgence so as to avoid the bad outcome whose likelihood has increased. But, second, there is a fatalistic reaction: the person instead might decide that, because he is not willing to choose very low indulgence, the bad outcome is now essentially unavoidable, and therefore he might as well increase indulgence. If a young person is sufficiently committed to some level of sexual activity, then, if he comes to believe that the risk is greater, he may increase his activity. If an adolescent perceives that, once she uses drugs, she will surely become an addict, then she is likely to use drugs a great deal if she uses them at all. More generally, for any activity in which a person will engage to some degree no matter what, an increase in the perceived riskiness can potentially lead to increased indulgence.

This fatalistic reaction relies on two key assumptions. First, it must be that, given the amount in which the person might plausibly want to indulge, the probability of harm done is not negligible. Second, as we assume throughout, the eventuality being risked must be all or nothing rather than cumulative—that is, if the bad thing happens once, then it either cannot happen again or will not cause much further harm if it does occur.

We do not have a strong empirical sense of whether, for realistic benefits and risk levels, the fatalistic reaction identified above is likely to be important within the rational-choice setting. As we shall discuss shortly, however, such fatalism is more likely to be important when a person suffers from an overly strong taste for immediate gratification or from projection bias. Moreover, even within the rational-choice framework, a similar logic applies on a more realistic level when adolescents choose among alternative activities, where the more pleasurable activities are also riskier. To illustrate, suppose that an adolescent can engage in activities 1 and 2, at levels n_1 and n_2, and suppose that the benefits are

$$V(n_1, n_2) = \begin{cases} r \min\{n_1, \bar{n}\} & \text{if } n_1 > n_2, \\ s \min\{n_2, \bar{n}\} & \text{if } n_1 \leq n_2. \end{cases}$$

This contrived functional form implies that the activities are substitutes for each other. In addition, again because of concave costs, the person will do one of three things: engage in neither activity, engage in level $\bar{n}$ of activity 1, or engage in level $\bar{n}$ of activity 2. Suppose that the risks associated with the two activities are p_1 and p_2 and that the expected cost to the person is given by $C(n_1, n_2; p_1, p_2) = [1 - (1 - p_1)^{n_1}(1 - p_2)^{n_2}]\Gamma$. Hence, these activities are substitutes not only in terms of the benefits that they supply, but also in terms of the risks that they carry. Finally, assume that $s > r$ but that $p_2 > p_1$ so that activity 2 is both more enjoyable and riskier.

Suppose that, given some initial risks (p_1, p_2), the person chooses to engage in level $\bar{n}$ of activity 1, and consider what happens when p_1 increases. If initially the person strictly prefers no activity to level $\bar{n}$ of activity 2, then the only possible change following an increase in the riskiness of activity 1 is to no activity. But, if initially the person prefers level $\bar{n}$ of activity 2 to no activity, then the only possible change following an increase in the riskiness of activity 1 is to level $\bar{n}$ of activity 2.

This example illustrates the more general point that an increase in the perceived riskiness of less risky behaviors can lead people not to abstain, but rather to engage in riskier substitute behaviors. For instance, if young gay men suddenly perceive oral sex to carry a larger risk of HIV infection than they had thought, they may start engaging in riskier activities, such as anal sex. Similarly, if young heterosexuals suddenly learn that even condoms do not protect fully against the risk of pregnancy, they may start having unprotected sex.

While the rational-choice analysis of repeated risky choices yields some important implications, additional insights are yielded by relaxing the assumptions that people rationally perceive the probability consequences of their actions and that people react optimally to such perceptions. We now discuss these additional insights in general intuitive terms rather than with a formal analysis.

Consider first the case where people rationally foresee the probability consequences of their actions but, along the lines discussed in sections 1.2 and 1.3 above, do not react optimally to these beliefs. When people make repeated risky choices, overindulgence due to self-control problems and projection bias becomes more pronounced. More precisely, when self-control problems and projection bias cause overindulgence, the concavity of $C(n; p)$ exacerbates this overindulgence because the person perceives further indulgence as less costly.

This basic idea can play itself out in a couple of ways. Sections 1.2 and 1.3 emphasize how naïveté about self-control problems and projection bias can lead to failures of self-management: people fail to avoid situations in which they will not be able to resist indulgence. Because each choice to indulge in a series of risky choices reduces the costs of future indulgences, each failure at self-management is potentially more harmful than if the choice were made in isolation. For instance, while initially there might be only a few situations in which adolescents cannot resist having sex, once they have succumbed in such episodes, they will realize that having further sex is less costly and will therefore succumb in even more situations. Hence, naive self-control problems and projection bias can lead to an eventual fatalism and therefore high levels of indulgence.

Sophistication about self-control problems overcomes such descents into fatalistic consumption due to failures at self-management. But sophistication can lead to overconsumption due to an up-front feeling of fatalism. A person who is worried about future self-control problems may expect not to behave optimally in the future. Hence, even when the person does not want to indulge moderately, he may pessimistically (but correctly) predict that there will be a number of future occasions on which he will not be able to control himself. Given the concavity of $C(n; p)$, such pessimism reduces the perceived cost of indulgence at any given moment and hence makes indulgence more likely.[27]

We next consider the possibility that people have irrational beliefs about the probability consequences of their actions. Suppose that, given some level of an activity n, the true likelihood of the bad outcome is $\pi(n; p)$ but

---

27. As in our analysis in sec. 1.2 above, whether awareness of self-control problems helps or hurts a person here depends on the specifics of the environment.

that a young person perceives the likelihood to be $\hat{\pi}(n) \neq \pi(n; p)$. We initially focus on errors induced by the incorrect perception of risk per se and therefore assume that the person does not depart in any other way from full rationality.

The simplest form of incorrect risk perceptions is that adolescents may incorrectly perceive the riskiness, p, of each episode of the activity. If they believe that each indulgence carries with it probability $\hat{p} \neq p$ of incurring the bad outcome, then their perceived risk function will be $\hat{\pi}(n) = \pi(n; \hat{p})$. For instance, the folk wisdom that adolescents have a false sense of invulnerability might be conceptualized as perceiving $\hat{p} < p$.[28] For an otherwise fully rational person, this error would cause the same effects on behavior as a decrease in the true riskiness. Hence, following the logic outlined above, while feelings of invulnerability might have the intuitive effect of causing the person to engage in more of the activity, it can in fact decrease how often he engages in the activity if he becomes (falsely) convinced that he has not doomed himself by engaging in moderate amounts of the activity.

Unfortunately, there is evidence that people, especially youths, have a more extreme form of irrational belief: quite apart from incorrectly perceiving the true risk per episode of an activity, adolescents think that the probability function is more concave in n than it actually is—in our notation, $\hat{\pi}(n)$ is more concave than $\pi(n; p)$. For instance, Linville, Fischer, and Fischhoff (1993) find that college students wildly exaggerate the chance of acquiring HIV from one sexual encounter but then think that the chance of acquiring it from ten sexual encounters is not much higher. In reality, for the levels of heterosexual activity that are most common, the probability of contracting HIV is approximately proportional to the number of sexual encounters. This finding that people form probabilistic beliefs that are too insensitive to the number of times in which they engage in an activity accords well with the more general psychological phenomenon of diminishing sensitivity and what Kahneman (1994) has called *extension neglect*. In a variety of domains, people are much less sensitive to the magnitude of variables than they rationally ought to be. For instance, in deciding ahead of time how burdensome having to walk to a hotel with suitcases will be, people are more sensitive to having to walk three blocks versus two blocks than they are to having to walk twenty blocks versus nineteen blocks. This heuristic that the difference between nineteen and twenty is smaller than the difference between two and three may be correct in most environments, but in some environments—such as walking with suitcases—it is quite inappropriate. In the context of risky choice, diminishing

---

28. We remind the reader that, while such feelings of invulnerability are commonly associated with youths, there is very little evidence supporting this conventional wisdom, and there are some ways in which youths seem to overestimate the risks.

sensitivity, taken literally and to its extreme, suggests that people are likely vastly to underestimate the risk of all but the first time they engage in some activity.

This error can be expected to have the same general effect that overestimating p has. Because people overestimate the perceived risk from engaging in the activity a few times, it may induce abstinence. But, if people cannot resist indulging to some degree, an undersensitivity to the number of times that they indulge may lead them to indulge a great deal. Taking the results in Linville, Fischer, and Fischhoff (1993) literally, for instance, and assuming that acquiring HIV is the only risk from sex, then we would expect their subjects to have unsafe sex quite a lot or not at all.

Because the discussion presented above of irrational beliefs assumes that people react optimally to these beliefs, our conclusions about behavior represent departures from what would be optimal given the true risk $\pi(n; p)$. In other words, if we let $W[\hat{\pi}(n)|\pi(n; p)]$ be the true well-being of a person who optimizes with respect to beliefs $\hat{\pi}(n)$ when the true risk is $\pi(n; p)$, then $W[\hat{\pi}(n)|\pi(n; p)] \leq W[\pi(n; p)|\pi(n; p)]$. If, however, a person suffers from other psychological errors, false risk beliefs can interact with these other errors. While the behavioral implications of the false beliefs discussed above do not change, these effects can exacerbate or counteract other errors that people make. Indeed, a common theme in psychological research is that irrational beliefs can help rather than hurt a person in many situations. Along these lines, we believe that it is important to understand how false beliefs interact with self-control problems and projection bias.

Because self-control problems and projection bias generally lead to overindulgence, false beliefs help when they lead to less indulgence and hurt when they lead to more indulgence. Whether falsely believing that the risk function is more concave than it really is (because people exaggerate the riskiness of the activity or suffer from extension neglect) helps or hurts depends crucially on the degree to which the person is enticed by the activity. Exaggerated beliefs about risk may help if they make it so that the person is able to resist even the strongest temptations. If, for instance, the perceived risk of a single sexual encounter is sufficiently exaggerated, it may help a person with self-control problems refrain altogether. But, if there are likely to be a number of occasions on which the person cannot resist, then false beliefs in the direction of more concavity can exacerbate overindulgence.

1.5   General Discussion

In this section, we attempt to tie together our analysis by briefly discussing some empirical and policy implications.

Our focus in this chapter has been the potential for applying formal behavioral-economic models to theoretical and empirical research on youthful behavior. While there is a broad range of issues from both psychology and economics that are relevant to the behavior of adolescents, we discuss only a few specific topics. Nonetheless, we believe that the errors that we discuss may go a long way toward understanding excessive risk taking by adolescents.

Behavioral-economic models abandon those features of the classical economic model that psychological evidence indicates are wrong, such as the assumption that discounting is time consistent. But behavioral-economic models incorporate the features of the rational-choice model that are realistic, such as the assumption that people generally pursue satisfying rather than unsatisfying activities. Indeed, almost all the qualitative empirical results that are lauded as support for the rational-choice model—such as prices affecting consumption of addictive goods—are consistent with the behavioral models that we discuss and with all other behavioral models with which we are familiar.[29]

Although in many instances the rational-choice model and behavioral models both make correct *qualitative* predictions, in those same instances behavioral models make sounder *quantitative* predictions and can better explain observed behaviors with reasonable parameter values. For example, while the rational-choice model can explain certain observed patterns of consumption of addictive products, this explanation often seems to require absurd levels of impatience. Because even small departures from the rational-choice model can lead to significant quantitative changes in behavior, the same observed patterns of consumption that require absurd levels of impatience when viewed through the lens of rational choice can be explained, for instance, by reasonable levels of impatience and a small self-control problem.

There is, however, an important qualitative implication of our models that is different from the rational-choice model: systematic incorrect predictions of future behavior. The rational-choice model permits incorrect predictions due to uncertainty but rules out any systematic bias in these incorrect predictions. By contrast, the behavioral models that we discuss above suggest systematic incorrect predictions. Naïveté about self-control problems yields a systematic underestimation of future indulgence. Projec-

---

29. Research proposing behavioral alternatives to the classical economic model is often designed to persuade the audience of the truth and usefulness of the behavioral alternatives and therefore typically emphasizes how the behavioral alternatives make distinct comparative-static predictions from the classical economic model. Since such persuasion is one of our goals, we, too, discuss comparisons. But we also emphasize that there is overwhelming support for the assumption that people have a time-inconsistent preference for immediate gratification and strong support for the assumption that people suffer from projection bias. Hence, we do not limit ourselves solely to comparisons of comparative-static predictions but instead focus more on the direct goal of understanding the implications of these true behavioral assumptions.

tion bias also yields systematic incorrect predictions, although the direction is more environment specific. Consider, for example, projection bias over the addictiveness of cigarettes. An unaddicted person projects her current low craving onto her future preferences and therefore tends to underestimate future consumption. An addicted person, on the other hand, projects her current high craving onto her future preferences, which moves her toward overestimation of future consumption.

Evidence of systematic incorrect predictions therefore provides some support for these models. A direct approach to investigating such incorrect predictions is to ask people to predict future behavior and then later compare predictions to actual behavior. This approach is commonly used in psychological research, and, in fact, systematic incorrect predictions are often found; much of the evidence for projection bias was exactly such evidence.

For economists unwilling to infer anything from self-reported predictions, however, a second approach is to look for situations in which a person's behavior provides information about her predictions of future behavior. As a contrived example, consider how a fifteen-year-old might react differently to two different changes in the pricing scheme for cigarettes:

PLAN A. *The price of cigarettes is permanently increased by fifty cents per pack.*

PLAN B. *There is no change in the price of cigarettes, but to buy cigarettes, a person must purchase an access card for an up-front fee of $500.*

If the fifteen-year-old were asked which of these plans she would prefer, her answer would reveal her beliefs about how much she expects to smoke. In particular, since $500 is less than three years of fifty cents per day, preferring option A suggests that the fifteen-year-old does not plan to be smoking for more than three years, and preferring option B suggests that she does not plan to be smoking for fewer than three years.

Suppose that there are two types of states, those that implement plan A and those that implement plan B, and consider how the behavior of fifteen-year-olds would differ across the two types of states. In particular, consider what the rational-choice model has to say about the states in which we would expect to see more fifteen-year-olds become long-term smokers. Rational actors facing little uncertainty plan to be either nonsmokers, short-term smokers, or long-term smokers and then stick to their plans. Because the price of long-term smoking is lower and the price of short-term smoking is higher in plan B states, the rational-choice model predicts that more fifteen-year-olds become long-term smokers in plan B states.

In contrast, if people underestimate future consumption owing either to naïveté about self-control problems or to projection bias, then we could expect to see fewer fifteen-year-olds become long-term smokers in plan B states. In addition to people who carry out their plans to be nonsmokers, short-term smokers, or long-term smokers, our models suggest that there will also be people who plan to be short-term smokers but end up being long-term smokers. Although, just as in the rational-choice model, there is a tendency for more people to plan long-term smoking in plan B states, the higher cost of short-term smoking in plan B states deters people from planning short-term smoking and ending up as long-term smokers. This latter effect could dominate when underestimation is large.

More realistic empirical tests comparing our models to rational-choice models revolve around how people react both to changes in short-term costs and benefits and to changes in long-term costs and benefits. For instance, suppose that there is an improvement in detox programs that reduces the long-term cost of becoming addicted. According to the rational-choice model, such a change should lead to many people becoming addicted because many prospective addicts should now be enticed by the lower cost of addiction. When people underestimate their likelihood of becoming addicted, however, such a change would have less effect because the marginal consumer who ends up in the detox program is unlikely to have been planning to get addicted.

We conclude with some brief and speculative discussion of the policy implications of our analysis. While the simplified nature of our analysis prevents its confident use for specific policy prescriptions, some general themes emerge for each of the two approaches that society often considers for combating excessive risk taking by adolescents, regulation and education.

The main theme of our analysis is that youths do not react optimally to the intrinsic costs and benefits that they face. Because so many of the risky behaviors studied in this volume involve short-term benefits and long-term costs, providing short-term rewards for good behavior may be quite important. Policy can be designed to manipulate incentives to better align their perceived immediate incentives with their actual long-term goals.

Our analysis also suggests that one of the major problems that youths have is that they fail to recognize when current indulgence will lead to future indulgence. Hence, policy makers should perhaps create incentives that encourage youths to take into account the linkages between decisions. By making youths pay a large sum up front for the right to begin smoking, for instance, plan B discussed above may provide an alternative tax-incentive scheme that will force adolescent smokers to decide whether they want to be smokers when they begin their habit rather than paying incrementally as in plan A. While there are, of course, some practical limits to this approach, an appealing feature of such incentives is that they would presumably do relatively little harm to those youths who are rationally taking up the career of smoking—who correctly realize that $500 up front is worth the lifetime of pleasure—while preventing smoking among those who might be developing the smoking habit unintentionally.

The second category of efforts to reduce risky behavior is education. If adolescents were fully rational and caused no harm to others by their risky behavior, then the optimal education policy would be to provide them with as much accurate information as possible. If youths make errors, in contrast, there may be a role for "propaganda" aimed at misleading adolescents about the true risks involved in their activities. There are many reasons that society and government might wish only to tell the truth, from moral disposition to worries about loss of credibility. But, even under the constraints of only telling the truth, there is usually scope for what to emphasize. Our analysis can provide some insights into the types of truthful or untruthful education campaigns that might be most useful.

Raising perceptions of the severity of bad outcomes is likely to have a direct and desired effect. Exaggerating the costs of being pregnant, acquiring AIDS, being jailed for committing a crime, or being addicted is likely to diminish risky behaviors and, hence, improve the welfare of adolescents. In a real-world example of this approach, a recent poster used by the state of California to discourage young men from smoking shows a cigarette drooping, connoting a high risk of sexual dysfunction from smoking. Presumably, the state of California believed that sexual dysfunction will register to the target audience as a more salient cost than (say) lung cancer.

Whereas raising perceptions of the severity of bad outcomes is likely to have the desired effects, our analysis in section 1.4 above suggests that raising perceptions of the likelihood of bad outcomes is not guaranteed to reduce risk-taking behavior. A wariness of exaggerating dangers as a means of discouraging risky behavior is especially warranted in situations in which an adolescent is choosing among substitute risky behaviors. Preaching the dangers of marijuana use can cause more harm than good if it induces young people who use marijuana to exaggerate the degree to which their lives are ruined already and hence to underestimate the additional harm of cocaine or, worse yet, if it leads them to substitute cocaine for marijuana to begin with. This issue is very much on the minds of at least some of those working to discourage risky behavior. There is frequent debate in the gay press, for instance, about whether to emphasize the dangers of acquiring HIV through unprotected oral sex. Some have argued that even truthful emphasis on the dangers of oral sex might lead gay men to engage in unprotected anal sex under the premise that they are at great risk unless they refrain from sexual activity altogether, which they are unwilling to do.

Our policy prescriptions are not very specific or concrete because our analysis draws out general principles rather than specific implications. Research aimed at developing practical policies to combat risky behaviors must be based on analyses that are far more context specific and empirically grounded than ours has been. We hope, however, that by discussing some important lessons from behavioral economics and their potential implications for risky behavior, we have helped lay the groundwork for such research.

References

Ainslie, G. 1975. Specious reward: A behavioral theory of impulsiveness and impulse control. *Psychological Bulletin* 82, no. 4:463–96.

———. 1991. Derivation of "rational" economic behavior from hyperbolic discount curves. *American Economic Review* 81, no. 2:334–40.

———. 1992. *Picoeconomics: The strategic interaction of successive motivational states within the person.* New York: Cambridge University Press.

Ainslie, G., and N. Haslam. 1992a. Hyperbolic discounting. In *Choice over time,* ed. G. Loewenstein and J. Elster. New York: Russell Sage.

———. 1992b. Self-control. In *Choice over time,* ed. G. Loewenstein and J. Elster. New York: Russell Sage.

Akerlof, G., and R. Kranton. 2000. Economics and identity. *Quarterly Journal of Economics* 115:715–53.

Arnett, J. 1994. Sensation seeking: A new conceptualization and a new scale. *Personality and Individual Differences* 16:289–96.

Bauman, K. E. 1980. *Predicting adolescent drug use: Utility structure and marijuana.* New York: Praeger.

Baumrind, D. 1987. A developmental perspective on adolescent risk taking in contemporary America. In *Adolescent social behavior and health* (New Directions for Child Development, no. 37), ed. C. E. Irwin Jr. San Francisco: Jossey-Bass.

Becker, G., and K. Murphy. 1988. A theory of rational addiction. *Journal of Political Economy* 96:675–700.

Beyth-Marom, R., L. Austin, B. Fischhoff, C. Palmgren, and M. J. Quadrel. 1993. Perceived consequences of risky behaviors: Adults and adolescents. *Developmental Psychology* 29:549–63.

Beyth-Marom, R., and B. Fischhoff. 1997. Adolescents' decisions about risks: A cognitive perspective. In *Health risks and developmental transitions during adolescence,* ed. J. Schulenberg, J. L. Mags, and K. Hurrelmann. New York: Cambridge University Press.

Bowman, D., D. Minehart, and M. Rabin. 1999. Loss aversion in a consumption-savings model. *Journal of Economic Behavior and Organization* 38:155–78.

Camerer, C. 1995. Individual decision making. In *Handbook of experimental economics,* ed. J. Kagel and A. E. Roth. Princeton, N.J.: Princeton University Press.

Duesenberry, J. S. 1952. *Income, saving, and the theory of consumer behavior.* Cambridge, Mass.: Harvard University Press.

Fischer, C. 1997. Read this paper even later: Procrastination with time-inconsistent preferences. Ph.D. diss., University of Michigan.

Fischhoff, B. 1988. Judgment and decision making. In *The psychology of human thought,* ed. R. J. Sternberg and E. E. Smith. Cambridge: Cambridge University Press.

———. 1992. Risk taking: A developmental perspective. In *Risk taking,* ed. J. F. Yates. New York: Wiley.

Fischhoff, B., A. M. Parker, W. Bruine de Bruin, J. Downs, C. Palmgren, R. Dawes, and C. F. Manski. 2000. Teen expectations for significant life events. Carnegie-Mellon University. Mimeo.

Frederick, S., and G. Loewenstein. 1999. Hedonic adaptation. In *Well-being: The foundations of hedonic psychology*, ed. D. Kahneman, E. Diener, and N. Schwarz. New York: Russell Sage.

Furby, L., and R. Beyth-Marom. 1992. Risk taking in adolescence: A decision-making perspective. *Developmental Review* 12:1–44.

Green, L., A. Fry, and J. Myerson. 1994. Discounting of delayed rewards: A life-span comparison. *Psychological Science* 5, no. 1:33–36.

Greene, A. L. 1986. Future-time perspective in adolescence: The present of things future revisited. *Journal of Youth and Adolescence* 15:99–113.

Helson, H. 1964. *Adaptation-level theory: An experimental and systematic approach to behavior.* New York: Harper & Row.

Kahneman, D. 1994. New challenges to the rationality assumption. *Journal of Institutional and Theoretical Economics* 150:18–36.

Kahneman, D., E. Diener, and N. Schwartz, eds. 1999. *Well-being: The foundations of hedonic psychology.* New York: Russell Sage.

Kirby, K., and N. Marakovic. 1995. Modeling myopic decisions: Evidence for hyperbolic delay-discounting within subjects and amounts. *Organizational Behavior and Human Decision Processes* 64, no. 1:22–30.

Laibson, D. 1994. Essays in hyperbolic discounting. Ph.D. diss., Massachusetts Institute of Technology.

———. 1996. Hyperbolic discount functions, undersaving, and savings policy. Working Paper no. 5635. Cambridge, Mass.: National Bureau of Economic Research.

———. 1997. Hyperbolic discounting and golden eggs. *Quarterly Journal of Economics* 112, no. 2:443–77.

———. In press. A cue-theory of consumption. *Quarterly Journal of Economics.*

Laibson, D., A. Repetto, and J. Tobacman. 1998. Self-control and saving for retirement. *Brookings Papers on Economic Activity,* no. 1:91–196.

Lewis, C. C. 1981. How adolescents approach decisions: Changes over grades seven to twelve and policy implications. *Child Development* 52:538–44.

———. 1987. Minors' competence to consent to abortion. *American Psychologist* 42:84–88.

Linville, P. W., G. W. Fischer, and B. Fischhoff. 1993. AIDS risk perceptions and decision biases. In *The social psychology of HIV infection,* ed. J. B. Pryor and G. D. Reeder. Hillsdale, N.J.: Erlbaum.

Loewenstein, G. 1996. Out of control: Visceral influences on behavior. *Organizational Behavior and Human Decision Processes* 65:272–92.

Loewenstein, G., and S. Frederick. 1997. Predicting reactions to environmental change. In *Environment, ethics, and behavior,* ed. M. Bazerman, D. Messick, A. Tenbrunsel, and K. Wade-Benzoni. San Francisco: New Lexington.

Loewenstein, G., D. Nagin, and R. Paternoster. 1997. The effect of sexual arousal on predictions of sexual forcefulness. *Journal of Crime and Delinquency* 34: 443–73.

Loewenstein, G., T. O'Donoghue, and M. Rabin. 1999. Projection bias in predicting future utility. Mimeo.

Loewenstein, G., and D. Prelec. 1992. Anomalies in intertemporal choice: Evidence and an interpretation. *Quarterly Journal of Economics* 107, no. 2:573–97.

Myerson, J., and L. Green. 1995. Discounting of delayed rewards: Models of individual choice. *Journal of Experimental Analysis of Behavior* 64, no. 3:263–76.

O'Donoghue, T., and M. Rabin. 1999a. Addiction and present biased preferences. Mimeo.

———. 1999b. Addiction and self-control. In *Addiction: Entries and exits,* ed. J. Elster. New York: Russell Sage.

————. 1999c. Doing it now or later. *American Economic Review* 89, no. 1:103–24.

————. 1999d. Procrastination in preparing for retirement. In *Behavioral dimensions of retirement economics,* ed. H. Aaron. Washington, D.C.: Brookings; New York: Russell Sage.

————. In press. Choice and procrastination. *Quarterly Journal of Economics.*

Phelps, E. S., and R. A. Pollak. 1968. On second-best national saving and game-equilibrium growth. *Review of Economic Studies* 35:185–99.

Pollak, R. A. 1968. Consistent planning. *Review of Economic Studies* 35:201–8.

————. 1970. Habit formation and dynamic demand functions. *Journal of Political Economy* 78, no. 4:745–63.

————. 1978. Endogenous tastes in demand and welfare analysis. *American Economic Review* 68, no. 2:374–79.

Quadrel, M. J., B. Fischhoff, and W. Davis. 1993. Adolescent (in)vulnerability. *American Psychologist* 48:102–16.

Rabin, M. 1998. Psychology and economics. *Journal of Economic Literature* 36, no. 1:11–46.

Read, D., and B. van Leeuwen. 1998. Predicting hunger: The effects of appetite and delay on choice. *Organizational Behavior and Human Decision Processes* 76:189–205.

Ryder, H. E., and G. M. Heal. 1973. Optimal growth with intertemporally dependent preferences. *Review of Economic Studies* 40:1–33.

Solnick, J., C. Kannenberg, D. Eckerman, and M. Waller. 1980. An experimental analysis of impulsivity and impulse control in humans. *Learning and Motivation* 11:61–77.

Strotz, R. H. 1956. Myopia and inconsistency in dynamic utility maximization. *Review of Economic Studies* 23, no. 3:165–80.

Thaler, R. H. 1991. Some empirical evidence on dynamic inconsistency. In *Quasi rational economics.* New York: Russell Sage.

————, ed. 1992. *The winner's curse: Paradoxes and anomalies of economic life.* New York: Free Press.

Thaler, R., and G. Loewenstein. 1992. Intertemporal Choice. In *The winner's curse: Paradoxes and anomalies of economic life,* ed. R. Thaler. New York: Free Press.

Weithorn, L. A., and S. B. Campbell. 1982. The competency of children and adolescents to make informed treatment decisions. *Child Development* 53:1589–98.

Zuckerman, M., S. Eysenck, and H. J. Eysenck. 1978. Sensation seeking in England and America: Cross-cultural, age, and sex comparisons. *Journal of Consulting and Clinical Psychology* 46:139–49.

2

Youth Smoking in the United States
Evidence and Implications

Jonathan Gruber and Jonathan Zinman

One of the most striking trends in the behavior of youths in the United States during the 1990s has been the increased incidence of smoking. After steadily declining over the previous fifteen years, youth smoking began to rise precipitously in 1992. By 1997, smoking by teenagers in the United States had risen by one-third from its 1991 trough. This trend is particularly striking in the light of the continuing steady decline in adult smoking in the United States. Indeed, today we are in the alarming position of having a youth-smoking rate that is roughly 50 percent greater than the smoking rate of adults.

This striking time trend has motivated substantial public-policy interest in youth smoking, highlighted by the recent unsuccessful attempt of the Clinton administration to pass a comprehensive tobacco regulation bill that had the ostensible main purpose of reducing youth smoking. This public-policy interest arises out of concern that youths are not appropriately recognizing the long-run implications of their smoking decisions. Indeed, young smokers clearly underestimate the likelihood that they will still be smoking in their early twenties and beyond. For example, among

Jonathan Gruber is professor of economics at the Massachusetts Institute of Technology and a research associate of and director of the Program on Children at the National Bureau of Economic Research. Jonathan Zinman is a graduate student in economics at the Massachusetts Institute of Technology.

The authors are grateful to James Berry, Cristian Gonzalez, Jeffrey Hoffner, and Choonsiang Tan for outstanding research assistance, and to seminar participants at the NBER, the University of Pennsylvania, and the University of Chicago for helpful comments. Gruber acknowledges financial support from the National Institute on Aging and the National Science Foundation; Zinman acknowledges support from MIT's John Castle Fellowship, the Harry S. Truman Scholarship Foundation and the Social Science Research Council's Program in Applied Economics.

high school seniors who smoke, 56 percent say that they will not be smoking five years later, but only 31 percent of them have in fact quit five years hence. Moreover, among those who smoke more than one pack per day, the smoking rate five years later among those who stated that they would not be smoking (74 percent) is actually *higher* than the smoking rate among those who stated that they would be smoking (72 percent) (DHHS 1994).

If youth smoking leads to adult smoking, particularly in a manner that is underappreciated by the young smokers themselves, it can have drastic implications for the health of the U.S. population. Smoking-related illness is the leading preventable cause of death in the United States, and smokers on average live 6.5 (males) to 5.7 (females) fewer years than those who never smoked (Cutler et al. 1999). Thus, it is critical to understand the role that public policy can play in deterring youth smoking.

Yet, despite this interest and concern, we do not very well understand either the determinants or the implications of youth-smoking behavior. This paper attempts to remedy these deficiencies in our understanding by providing new evidence on four aspects of youth smoking.

The first is the correlation between background characteristics such as race, sex, education, family structure, and work behavior and the decision to smoke (or how much to smoke conditional on smoking). We explore how well smoking behavior can be explained both by clearly exogenous background characteristics and by potentially endogenous attitudine variables. And we assess how these relations have changed over time as youth smoking has risen. Our key findings here are that background characteristics explain only a small share of the decision to smoke and that smoking participation is not simply concentrated among the most disadvantaged youths; indeed, increasingly over time, youth smoking is taking place among white, suburban youths with college-educated parents and good grades.

The second is an assessment of the extent to which changes in background characteristics or changes in attitudes toward smoking can explain the precipitous recent rise in youth smoking. In short, we find that neither plays an important role in explaining this rise; background characteristics can explain at most 10 percent of it.

The third is an understanding of the role that public policy can play in deterring youth smoking. We provide a comprehensive analysis of the effect of prices and other public policies on youth smoking in the 1990s, using three different data sets with information on youth smoking to assess the robustness of our findings.

We find that the most important policy determinant of youth smoking, particularly among older teens, is price. There is a statistically significant and quantitatively large response of smoking by older teens to prices in all three data sets, although the estimated price elasticity varies significantly. On the other hand, price does not appear to be an important determinant of smoking by younger teens. There is little consistent evidence of other public policies meant to reduce youth smoking having a robust effect, although there is some suggestion that restrictions on youth purchase of cigarettes reduce the quantity of cigarettes smoked. And we find that black youths and youths with less-educated parents are much more responsive to price than are white teens and teens with more-educated parents, suggesting a strong correlation between price sensitivity and socioeconomic status.

The final part of this paper then builds on these findings to assess the long-run implications of youth smoking and in particular to forecast what the recent rise in youth smoking bodes for future smoking in the United States. We do so in two ways. First, we pursue a cohort analysis, examining what the historical record tells us about the implications of higher rates of youth smoking for the adult smoking of those same cohorts as they age. Second, we use the Vital Statistics Natality data to examine the extent to which policy interventions when individuals are young determine their smoking decisions later in life. Both approaches yield similar results: there are significant intertemporal linkages between youth smoking and adult smoking, with each percentage point of additional smoking by youths translating into only 0.25–0.5 percentage points more smoking by those youths as adults. This finding suggests that there will be a significant rise in future adult smoking because of the 1990s experience. Rough calculations suggest that, even if this rise in youth smoking is transitory (owing to significant recent price increases), the adult-smoking rate for this cohort will rise by 8–16 percent and that at least 1.6 million total life years will be lost by this cohort.

The paper proceeds as follows. Section 2.1 provides background on trends in youth smoking and on previous work in this area. Section 2.2 presents our cross-sectional analysis of demographic determinants of smoking decisions and what this analysis implies for explaining time trends. Section 2.3 explores the role of price and other public policies. Section 2.4 then turns to the intertemporal implications of youth smoking. Section 2.5 concludes.

2.1 Background

2.1.1 Youth Smoking: Where It Has Been, Where It Is Going, and Why We Should Care

The time-series trends in youth smoking are depicted in figures 2.1 and 2.2. Figure 2.1 shows the trend since the 1970s for the three available surveys of seniors: the Monitoring the Future (MTF) survey, which has surveyed high school seniors since 1976 but eighth and tenth graders only since 1991; the National Health Interview Survey (NHIS); and the Na-

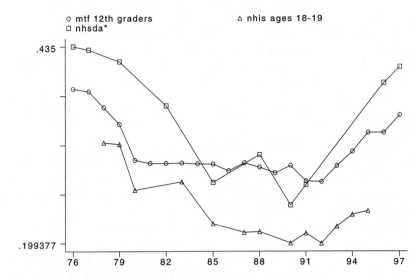

Fig. 2.1   Smoking participation: Older youths time series
Note: NHSDA data are for persons age 17–19 through 1991 and age 18–20 in 1996–97.

tional Household Survey of Drug Abuse (NHSDA). The latter two surveys are household surveys; from them we use data on older teens.[1] There is considerable uncertainty over the relative value of in-school versus household surveys for collecting smoking information; the latter have the advantage of collecting information on dropouts but the disadvantage that youths may be less willing to give honest answers when their parents may overhear. Despite these differences in sources, however, all three surveys show the same basic trend: large declines over the late 1970s, flattening and slow declines in the 1980s, and a steep rise in the 1990s.

Figure 2.2 focuses on the trend for the 1990s for all high school youths, using data from the MTF survey and the Youth Risk Behavior Survey (YRBS), which collected data for 1991, 1993, 1995, and 1997 on a large sample of ninth to twelfth graders. For both data sets, there are dramatic increases in the 1990s. In the MTF data, there is an increase of 7.2 percentage points, or 35 percent; in the YRBS, the increase starts from a higher base, but the increase is larger, at 8.7 percentage points, so that the percentage increase is also about one-third.

This dramatic upswing in youth smoking is a concern because smoking as a youth has been strongly correlated with smoking as an adult. Table 2.1 shows tabulations from the 1992 NHIS and the 1995 NHIS on the age of initiation of smoking by current or former adult smokers. This table reveals that 42 percent of current or former adult smokers started before

---

1. In particular, from the NHIS, we use eighteen- to nineteen-year-olds, and, from the NHSDA, we use seventeen- to nineteen-year-olds through 1991 and eighteen- to twenty-year-olds for 1996–97.

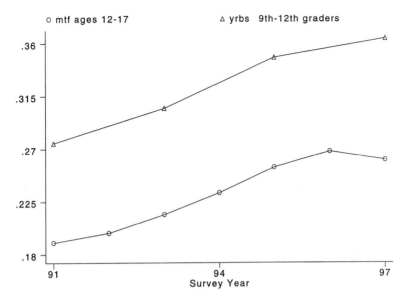

Fig. 2.2   Youth-smoking participation in the 1990s

Table 2.1   **Percentage of Those Who Ever Smoked Who Began Smoking at Each Age**

Age	% Starting at Age	Cumulative %	Age	% Starting at Age	Cumulative %
6	.47	.47	19	4.47	79.35
7	.79	1.26	20	5.48	84.82
8	1.05	2.31	21	3.21	88.03
9	1.24	3.55	22	1.76	89.79
10	2.67	6.22	23	1.05	90.83
11	1.85	8.08	24	.85	91.68
12	6.50	14.57	25	1.47	93.16
13	6.63	21.21	26	.39	93.54
14	8.81	30.01	27	.42	93.97
15	11.52	41.53	28	.40	94.37
16	13.53	55.06	29	.19	94.56
17	8.73	63.79	30	.98	95.53
18	11.09	74.88			

Source: NHIS smoking supplements, 1992 and 1995.

their sixteenth birthday and that 75 percent started before their nineteenth birthday. Conversely, of those smoking a pack a day as high school seniors in the MTF survey, 87 percent are smoking five years later. Even among those smoking one to five cigarettes per day, 70 percent are smoking five years later.

If youth smoking is a strong determinant of adult smoking, then the long-run secular decline in adult smoking may be reversed. Of course, these facts do not prove that the current upswing in youth smoking will lead to higher long-run adult-smoking rates, for two reasons. First, it is difficult to distinguish causality from these intertemporal correlations; smoking later in life may not be a consequence of youth smoking for adults in the past, but, rather, smoking at both points in life may simply arise from intertemporal correlation in tastes for this activity. This suggests a natural test for the causality of this relation between youth smoking and adult smoking, which is to assess whether exogenous shifts in youth smoking affect the smoking of those same individuals later in life. This is the exercise that we will take up in section 2.4 below.

Second, however, there may also have been a structural shift in the nature of youth smoking. New young smokers today may be different from new young smokers in the past—in particular, with a greater resolve to quit—and therefore this intertemporal correlation may be broken. We do find some evidence for this view (which we present below) in that there is a relative rise in the smoking rates of more advantaged youths in the 1990s. But these changes are modest relative to the enormous rise in smoking within virtually every identifiable subgroup in our data.

2.1.2   Previous Literature on Youth Smoking

There is a substantial literature on the background characteristics of youths that are most closely correlated with smoking decisions. This literature is reviewed in DHHS (1994), which provides a comprehensive overview of the state of knowledge to that point. Many of the conclusions in that chapter are echoed and updated in the discussion presented below as they draw on the same data that we use.

One interesting additional piece of data that does not come from the data that we use below is the brand preferences of youths relative to those of adults. In 1993 (the latest year for which data are available for adults and teens), smoking among adults was relatively dispersed across many brands, with the top three brands (Marlboro, 24 percent; Winston, 6.7 percent; Newport, 4.8 percent) accounting for only 35 percent of the total cigarettes smoked. But smoking among youths was much more concentrated, with the top three brands (Marlboro, 60 percent; Camel, 13.3 percent; Newport, 12.7 percent) accounting for 85 percent of cigarettes smoked.

There is also a sizable literature on the responsiveness of youth smoking to prices and other public policies. The early work on the price elasticity of youth smoking was cross-sectional in nature. This work generally found quite strong effects of prices on youth smoking. While there is some variation, a representative estimate that is frequently cited is Chaloupka and Grossman's (1996) estimate of a participation elasticity of -0.675 and a total smoking elasticity of -1.313. Similar estimates are found in Lewitt, Coate, and Grossman (1981) and Lewitt and Coate (1982), although the result is disputed by Wasserman et al. (1991).

This literature has been strongly criticized, however, by DeCicca, Kenkel, Mathios (1998) and Evans and Huang (1998), who point out that, in cross-sectional data, it is impossible to disentangle price and policy effects from other underlying long-run determinants of smoking attitudes. For example, as they note, taxes are traditionally the lowest in the tobacco-producing states, where smoking is also the highest, and it is difficult to disentangle causality in that relation. These two papers take different approaches to solving this problem. DeCicca, Kenkel, and Mathios pursue a strategy of focusing on smoking initiation, which compares changes in smoking rates to changes in price within a cohort, and they find no significant price effect. Evans and Huang, on the other hand, use repeated cross sections of youths and include state fixed effects to control for fixed-state tastes toward smoking, and they find a significant participation price elasticity of -0.5 over the period 1985–92 (using repeated cross sections of the restricted MTF data discussed below).

Both these approaches have weaknesses. The DeCicca, Kenkel, and Mathios (1998) methodology excludes the responsiveness of quitting to price increases; ultimately, it is the level of youth smoking that is the concern, not just initiation. Evans and Huang do consider the overall level of smoking, but they do not include the other controls for state smoking regulations that are deemed quite important by DeCicca, Kenkel, and Mathios. Moreover, neither paper focuses on the period of most interest, the 1990s.

A smaller literature has studied the effect of other antismoking policies on youth smoking. DeCicca, Kenkel, and Mathios (1998) include in their model measures of state access restrictions on youth tobacco purchase and of restrictions on smoking in public places and find no effect on smoking. Chaloupka and Grossman (1996) include a variety of measures of access restrictions and clean-air regulations; they find no (actually wrong-signed) effects of the former but fairly strong negative effects of the latter in their cross-sectional study. Another cross-sectional study by Chaloupka and Pacula (1998) focusing on youth-access-restriction enforcement does find some evidence that more tightly enforced youth-access restrictions lower youth smoking. But these cross-sectional studies once again suffer from the fact that the legislation and enforcement of youth-access restrictions may be correlated with fixed underlying attitudes toward smoking. Two interesting case studies of communities that implemented tough youth-access restrictions found mixed results, with Jason et al. (1991) finding substantial (50 percent) declines in youth smoking in Woodridge, Illinois, and Rigotti et al. (1997) finding very limited effects on sales to youths and on youth smoking in several Massachusetts communities.

To summarize, the literature on both prices and policies has produced somewhat mixed conclusions, particularly the limited literature that has attempted to control for unobserved state characteristics. Moreover, another limitation of most of the work on price responsiveness is that it has focused on either only one cohort or only one age group of teens. In fact, as we document at length below, there is considerable heterogeneity among the teen population in terms of responsiveness to policy variables.

2.2   Determinants of Youth Smoking

2.2.1   Data and Empirical Strategy

For this part of the analysis, we will be using the public-use data set from the Monitoring the Future (MTF) survey, a large, nationally representative cross section of high school seniors. This survey contains information on a rich set of background characteristics and attitudinal variables, making it an excellent source for trying to model the determinants of youth smoking comprehensively. These public-use data do have two drawbacks, however. First, they are only for high school seniors, which means that we cannot explore how these background characteristics affect smoking decisions by younger teens. Second, they do not contain very detailed location information, which means that we cannot explore the role of state-level policies. We address both these issues in our policy analysis below. We use data from the MTF surveys over the period 1976–97.

We will estimate simple cross-sectional models of smoking, using two different dependent variables: a dummy for smoking participation (defined as smoking any cigarettes over the previous month) and the number of cigarettes smoked conditional on smoking at all. For the former, we will estimate linear-probability models for ease of coefficient interpretation; our results are very similar if we use probit or logit models instead. For the latter, the results are somewhat difficult to interpret since factors that affect the participation decision can have composition effects on the conditional number of cigarettes smoked.

2.2.2   Cross-Sectional Results for 1997

We begin by estimating cross-sectional models for 1997, the last year in our sample. We include a broad set of variables in our base specification that are plausibly exogenous to the smoking decision. Our basic results for 1997 are presented in tables 2.2 (participation) and 2.3 (conditional intensity). There are a number of findings of interest: The single most important determinant of smoking is race: blacks and those of "unknown race" (likely other nonwhites) smoke much less. Those living with fewer than two parents are more likely to smoke. Males are less likely to smoke (but smoke more when they do smoke); in the raw data, males are more likely

Table 2.2   **1997 MTF Public-Use Regression Results: Participation**

Covariate	Coeff.	Covariate	Coeff.
SMSA	−.0276	Age < 18	.0126
	(.0102)		(.00746)
Number of siblings	−.0015	GPA (normalized by regional	−.265
	(.00403)	annual average)	(.0197)
Race (1 = black)	−.30	Married (omitted =	−.0368
	(.0118)	unmarried	(.0274)
Race unknown (captures	−.141	Engaged (omitted =	.0689
Latino etc. + no response)	(.00891)	unmarried	(.016)
Parents < 2 (omitted = two-	.0209	Separated/divorced (omitted	.045
parent household)	(.00862)	= unmarried)	(.0414)
Sex (1 = male)	−.0122	College-prep program	−.0233
	(.00769)	(omitted = general high	(.0091)
Grew up in rural area	−.0357	school program)	
(omitted = 'grew up	(.0139)	Vocational-prep program	.0269
mostly in suburbs')		(omitted = general high	(.014)
Grew up in a town	.0178	school program)	
(omitted = grew up mostly	(.0116)	No plan to attend college	.0741
in suburbs)		(omitted = plan to attend	(.0142)
Grew up in city (omitted =	−.0307	college)	
grew up mostly in suburbs)	(.0109)	Probably will not attend	.0418
Father's education < high	−.0082	college (omitted = plan to	(.0139)
school (omitted = high	(.0133)	attend college)	
school education)		Probably will attend college	.0175
Mother's education < high	−.0318	(omitted = plan to attend	(.0101)
school (omitted = high	(.0136)	college)	
education)		Mom worked (omitted =	.00753
Father has some college	.0076	mom never worked when	(.0101)
(omitted = high school	(.0117)	growing up)	
education		Works (1 = yes, 0 = no)	−.0177
Mother has some college	.0232		(.0124)
(omitted = high school	(.011)	Job hours per week	.00224
education)			(.000559)
Father college graduate	.0248	$/week from job	.000458
(omitted = high school	(.0108)		(.000109)
education)		$/week from other sources	.000665
Mother college graduate	.0373		(.000131)
(omitted = high school	(.0103)	Religion important	−.00545
education)			(.00451)
Northeast region (omitted	.0134	Attend religious services	.000242
= Midwest region)	(.0108)	regularly	(.00439)
South region (omitted =	−.0263	Days missed school	.0161
Midwest region)	(.0099)		(.001)
West region (omitted =	−.0546	N	15,525
Midwest region)	(.0127)		
Adjusted R^2	.1125		

Note: Regressions estimated using 1997 cross section of MTF data by linear-probability model; mean of dependent variable is 0.353. Standard errors are given in parentheses. SMSA = standard metropolitan statistical area.

Table 2.3　　　　**1997 MTF Public-Use Regression Results: Conditional Intensity**

Covariate	Coeff.	Covariate	Coeff.
SMSA	−.143	Age < 18	.318
	(.303)		(.234)
Number of siblings	−.0114	GPA (normalized by regional	−4.35
	(.127)	annual average)	(.595)
Race (1 = black)	−5.61	Married (omitted =	1.55
	(.492)	unmarried	(.944)
Race unknown (captures	−2.57	Engaged (omitted =	1.55
Latino etc. + no response)	(.33)	unmarried	(.443)
Parents < 2 (omitted = two-	1.1	Separated/divorced (omitted	5.29
parent household)	(.265)	= unmarried)	(1.19)
Sex (1 = male)	.867	College-prep program	−1.02
	(.244)	(omitted = general high	(.285)
Grew up in rural area	−.394	school program)	
(omitted = 'grew up	(.418)	Vocational-prep program	.915
mostly in suburbs')		(omitted = general high	(.409)
Grew up in a town	.761	school program)	
(omitted = grew up mostly	(.359)	No plan to attend college	1.77
in suburbs)		(omitted = plan to attend	(.419)
Grew up in city (omitted =	−.994	college)	
grew up mostly in suburbs)	(.341)	Probably will not attend	.776
Father's education < high	−.569	college (omitted = plan to	(.416)
school (omitted = high	(.417)	attend college)	
school education)		Probably will attend college	−.279
Mother's education < high	−.059	(omitted = plan to attend	(.321)
school (omitted = high	(.441)	college)	
education)		Mom worked (omitted =	−.0113
Father has some college	−.312	mom never worked when	(.321)
(omitted = high school	(.367)	growing up)	
education		Works (1 = yes, 0 = no)	−2.2
Mother has some college	.25		(.419)
(omitted = high school	(.342)	Job hours per week	.0837
education)			(.0177)
Father college graduate	−.188	$/week from job	.0135
(omitted = high school	(.334)		(.00347)
education)		$/week from other sources	.0209
Mother college graduate	−.042		(.00394)
(omitted = high school	(.321)	Religion important	.2
education)			(.142)
Northeast region (omitted	.205	Attend religious services	−.419
= Midwest region)	(.322)	regularly	(.138)
South region (omitted =	−1.06	Days missed school	.187
Midwest region)	(.312)		(.028)
West region (omitted =	−2.48	N	5,450
Midwest region)	(.405)		
Adjusted R^2	.139		

Note: Regressions estimated using 1997 cross section of MTF data by linear-probability model; mean of dependent variable is 7.329. Standard errors are given in parentheses. SMSA = standard metropolitan statistical area.

to smoke, but this appears to be reversed by the inclusion of variables such as work status and family structure. Those living in suburbs (the omitted location group) are likely to smoke more. Those with more highly educated parents are *more* likely to smoke, with no clear pattern for the intensity of smoking. There are lower smoking rates in the West. Academic performance and trajectory appear to be very significant. Current GPA (relative to year/region normalization) has huge significant effects (with better students smoking less), and students in college-preparatory programs and those planning on attending college smoke significantly less across the board. Those who are married are less likely to smoke, but those who are engaged or divorced/separated are more likely to smoke. Those who work are less likely to smoke, but smoking rises quite strongly with hours worked and with income. Those who are absent from school more frequently are more likely to smoke. Overall, the model has modest explanatory power, with an R^2 of 0.11, which is fairly high for a linear-probability model.

The key findings of these regressions are that smoking is not as purely concentrated in disadvantaged youths as it is concentrated in low-socioeconomic-status adults: smoking is much lower among minorities than among whites; it is more likely in the suburbs than in either the city or rural areas; and it is positively correlated with parents' education. On the other hand, youth smoking is much more likely among those with worse academic performance, those who miss more school, and those who do not plan to go to college. There also appear to be strong income effects on smoking: more hours worked and more income lead to more smoking among high school seniors. An interesting question is whether the positive association with indicators of advantage such as suburban dwelling or college-educated parents are also picking up unmeasured aspects of income.

2.2.3   Can We Explain the Time Series?

In trying to explain the dramatic increase in smoking in the 1990s, the first step is to assess whether there were changes in background characteristics that might play an important role. We do this by taking our cross-sectional models and using the estimated relations to predict smoking in each year, given the values of the X's in each year. If changes in background characteristics are explaining the time-series pattern, then this predicted series should mimic actual smoking behavior.

We present the results from doing so in figure 2.3. We use here a cross-sectional model estimated in 1985–86 to predict smoking in each year so that we can do out of sample predictions on both the steep decline in the 1970s and the steep increase in the 1990s; we come to the issue of coefficient stability next. In fact, we find that this model can predict very little of either the decline in the 1970s or the rise in the 1990s. The predicted series

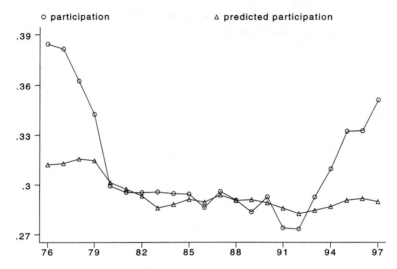

Fig. 2.3   Smoking participation: predicted vs. actual
Note: p-values were generated using 1985–86 coefficients.

does rise very slightly in the 1990s, by 0.7 percentage points, but this is less than 10 percent of the 7.8 percentage point rise in smoking by high school seniors over this period. Thus, the steep increase in smoking participation of the 1990s is not explained by changes in background characteristics.

Figure 2.4 shows the same exercise for smoking intensity. Here, the model predicts somewhat better the changes over time, but this is perhaps not surprising since the changes are much more modest.

2.2.4   Changes in the Estimated Relations

One issue of importance is whether it is very inappropriate to apply constant coefficients to the estimated relations between smoking and background characteristics because the relations are changing over time. This is a particularly interesting question owing to our inability to find the expected negative relation between socioeconomic status and smoking in the recent cross section. Is this because over the 1990s smoking has become more of a "yuppie phenomenon"?

We investigate this by examining the changes in the coefficients in our cross-sectional model over time. Table 2.4 shows changes in these coefficients for smoking participation, first from 1976 to 1986, then from 1986 to 1997. The second column shows the coefficients for 1976, the third column for 1986, and the fourth column for 1997; the fifth column shows the change from 1976 to 1986 (the 1986 coefficient minus the 1976 coefficient) and a *t*-statistic on that difference; the next column does the same for 1986–97; and the final column does the same for the entire period 1976–97.

The results show substantial stability in the characteristics of smokers

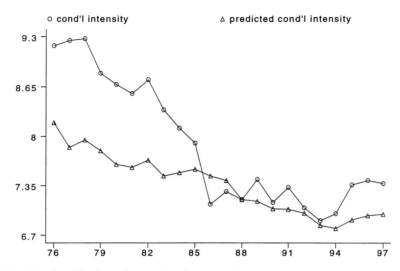

Fig. 2.4   Smoking intensity: predicted vs. actual
Note: p-values were generated using 1985–86 coefficients.

over this twenty-one-year period; only eleven of the thirty-five coefficients change significantly. But there is a striking and consistent story from the coefficients that do change: smoking is rising much more among "advantaged" youths, particularly in the 1990s. There is a significant rise in smoking among whites relative to nonwhites, among those students who do not work relative to those students who do, among those students who live in suburban settings relative to those who live in town or urban settings, among those whose mothers are college educated relative to those whose mothers are not, and among religious students. Perhaps the most striking pattern is the association of high relative GPA and smoking: while smoking fell significantly for high-GPA students relative to low-GPA students between 1976 and 1986, it then rose even more over the next decade for the high-GPA strata.

Thus, smoking is indeed rising significantly among advantaged youths relative to their disadvantaged counterparts. But it is worth noting that these relative changes are completely swamped by the secular increases among all groups. To confirm this point, in figure 2.5 we graph smoking rates over time for four comparison groups: men and women; whites and blacks; suburban and urban dwellers; and high- (top 25 percent) and low- (bottom 25 percent) GPA students. For every group, smoking rates rise precipitously in the 1990s; the only group for which this rise appears modest is low-GPA students. Thus, we conclude that, while there was a shift toward more smoking by advantaged students over the past ten to twenty years, that shift was swamped in the past decade by other factors that are affecting all students.

Table 2.4   Smoking-Participation Coefficient Stability, MTF Public-Use Data

Covariate	1976 (1)	1986 (2)	1997 (3)	1986–76 (4)	1997–86 (5)	1997–76 (6)
SMSA	−.041	−.034	−.028	.007	.006	.013
	(.01)	(.01)	(.01)	(.014)	(.014)	(.014)
Age[a]	.017	−.003	.013	−.02	.016	−.004
	(.009)	(.008)	(.007)	(.012)	(.011)[a]	(.011)[a]
Black	.025	−.2	−.31	−.226	−.1	−.326
	(.013)	(.012)	(.012)	(.018)	(.017)	(.018)
Other nonwhite	−.011	−.075	−.134	−.065	−.059	−.124
	(.013)	(.011)	(.01)	(.017)	(.015)	(.016)
Works 1/0	.009	.001	−.018	−.008	−.019	−.027
	(.012)	(.012)	(.012)	(.017)	(.017)	(.017)
Job hours per week	.003	.002	.002	−.0009	.0004	−.0004
	(.0004)	(.001)	(.001)	(.0007)	(.0008)	(.0007)
Job income per week (/100)	.04	.03	.05	−.01	.02	.00
	(.001)	(.01)	(.01)	(.01)	(.02)	(.02)
Other income per week (/100)	.00	.04	.07	.04	.02	.07
	(.01)	(.02)	(.01)	(.02)	(.02)	(.02)
Male	−.063	−.067	−.012	−.004	.055	.051
	(.008)	(.007)	(.008)	(.011)	(.011)	(.011)
Grew up in rural area	−.028	−.039	−.036	−.011	.003	−.008
	(.013)	(.013)	(.014)	(.019)	(.019)	(.019)
Grew up in a town	.001	−.035	−.018	−.036	.017	−.02
	(.011)	(.011)	(.012)	(.016)	(.016)	(.016)
Grew up in a city	.024	−.012	−.031	−.035	−.019	−.055
	(.011)	(.01)	(.011)	(.015)	(.015)	(.015)

	(1)	(2)	(3)	(4)	(5)	(6)
Father's education < high school	.01	−.019	−.008	−.029	.011	−.018
	(.011)	(.011)	(.013)	(.016)	(.017)	(.017)
Mother's education < high school	−.023	.001	−.032	.023	−.033	−.009
	(.011)	(.011)	(.014)	(.016)	(.018)	(.018)
Father has some college	−.007	.003	.008	.009	.005	.014
	(.014)	(.011)	(.012)	(.018)	(.016)	(.018)
Mother has some college	.007	.002	.023	−.004	.021	.017
	(.013)	(.01)	(.011)	(.016)	(.015)	(.017)
Father college graduate	.021	.013	.025	−.009	.012	.003
	(.012)	(.01)	(.011)	(.016)	(.015)	(.016)
Mother college graduate	−.02	.009	.037	.028	.029	.057
	(.013)	(.01)	(.01)	(.016)	(.014)	(.016)
GPA	−.282	−.203	−.265	.08	−.063	.017
	(.02)	(.018)	(.02)	(.027)	(.027)	(.028)
Northeast	.022	.009	.014	−.013	.005	−.008
	(.01)	(.01)	(.011)	(.014)	(.015)	(.015)
South	−.007	−.029	−.026	−.022	.003	−.019
	(.01)	(.009)	(.01)	(.014)	(.014)	(.014)
West	−.11	−.106	−.055	.004	.051	.056
	(.011)	(.011)	(.013)	(.015)	(.017)	(.017)
Mother ever worked	.007	.016	.008	.005	−.008	−.004
	(.008)	(.008)	(.01)	(.012)	(.013)	(.013)
Fewer than 2 parents	−.001	.022	.021	.022	−.001	.022
	(.01)	(.008)	(.009)	(.013)	(.012)	(.013)
Married	.039	−.095	−.037	−.134	.058	−.077
	(.025)	(.025)	(.027)	(.036)	(.037)	(.037)
Engaged	.054	.053	.069	−.001	.016	.015
	(.015)	(.015)	(.016)	(.021)	(.022)	(.022)

(continued)

Table 2.4   (continued)

Covariate	1976 (1)	1986 (2)	1997 (3)	1986–76 (4)	1997–86 (5)	1997–76 (6)
Separated/divorced	.066 (.058)	.004 (.042)	.045 (.041)	−.062 (.071)	.042 (.059)	−.022 (.071)
College-prep program	−.038 (.01)	−.061 (.009)	−.023 (.009)	−.023 (.013)	.038 (.013)	.015 (.013)
Vocational-prep program	.032 (.011)	.023 (.012)	.027 (.014)	−.009 (.016)	.004 (.018)	−.005 (.018)
No plan to attend college	.093 (.012)	.073 (.012)	.074 (.014)	−.02 (.017)	.001 (.019)	−.019 (.019)
Probably will not attend college	.044 (.012)	.042 (.012)	.042 (.014)	−.003 (.017)	0 (.018)	−.003 (.019)
Probably will attend college	.025 (.011)	.004 (.01)	.017 (.01)	−.021 (.014)	.013 (.014)	−.008 (.015)
Days missed school	.019 (.001)	.016 (.001)	.016 (.001)	−.003 (.001)	0 (.001)	−.003 (.001)
Attend religious services regularly	−.035 (.004)	−.029 (.004)	0 (.004)	.006 (.006)	.029 (.006)	.036 (.006)
Religion important	−.029 (.005)	−.014 (.004)	−.005 (.005)	.016 (.006)	.008 (.006)	.024 (.006)
Adjusted R^2	.123	.112	.113	.127	.117	.119
N	16,078	15,310	15,525	31,388	30,835	31,603
Joint F-test of stability interactions				[b]	[b]	[b]

[a] The MTF data provide only whether younger than 18 or 18 and older in 1997, year of birth in 1976 and 1986. We construct a measure to make this consistent across the 1976 and 1986 data, but the mean and distribution differ substantially from 1997. Accordingly, the stability tests for age in cols. 5 and 6 are probably inaccurate.

[b] Probability $> F = 0$.

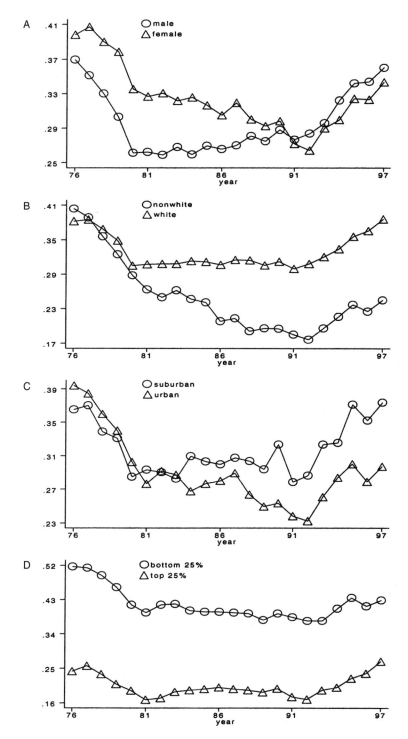

Fig. 2.5 Smoking participation by subgroup: *A*, gender; *B*, race; *C*, urban vs. suburban; *D*, GPA

2.2.5   Adding Attitude Variables

The MTF data have a variety of other attitude variables that may potentially be correlated with smoking decisions but are also potentially endogenous to the same external factors that are causing smoking to increase. While we have excluded these variables from our basic model, given the failure of changes in background characteristics to explain the time trend in smoking participation, it is of interest to know whether changes in attitudes can explain this trend. We have therefore augmented our basic models by including the host of attitude variables that may be relevant for smoking decisions: Do you disapprove of those who smoke one or more packs per day? How often do you see antismoking ads? Does smoking make a guy/girl your age look cool, insecure, independent, conforming, mature, or trying to look mature and sophisticated? Do you prefer to date a nonsmoker? Has the harm from smoking been exaggerated? Does smoking reflect bad judgment? Do you mind being around others who smoke? Is smoking a dirty habit? How much of a physical risk does smoking pose? How severe are the consequences of smoking for students in your school?

The full set of these variables is available only since 1989, so, for this exercise, we focus on the period from 1989 to 1997. Over this period, somewhat surprisingly, there do not appear to be any clear trends in attitude variables. There is a slight rise in the share of teens exposed to counteradvertising in 1996–97, although this variable has no effect on smoking decisions in our cross-sectional models.

Perhaps reflecting this lack of trends, adding these variables to our model does not improve its predictive performance. Indeed, as figure 2.6 shows, the model with attitude variables actually predicts declining smoking in 1996 and 1997, when smoking continues to rise. So changing attitudes, at least as reported in the MTF survey, do not appear to explain the rise in smoking in the 1990s either.

2.2.6   The Role of Other Substances

One interesting question is what role other risky behaviors, and in particular, the use of other substances, are playing in this time-series pattern. We explore this issue in figure 2.7, which shows, along with smoking participation, the use of alcohol, marijuana, and other drugs; in each case, *participation* is defined as any use over the past thirty days, analogously to smoking. In fact, in all three cases, the time trend looks very much like that for smoking, with declines until 1991 and increases thereafter. The correspondence is particularly striking for marijuana, although use drops off some in 1997.

Interpreting these correlated trends is difficult as there are at least three possibilities. The least likely is that there have been exogenous shifts in the use of these other substances that have led to increased smoking; although

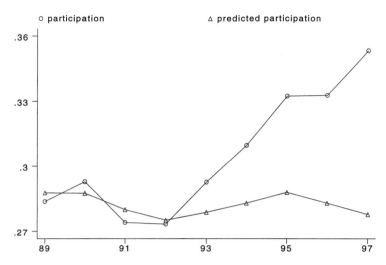

Fig. 2.6 Predicted vs. actual participation with attitude variables
Note: p-values were generated using 1989–90 coefficients.

there is no statistically convincing evidence, most work on pathways of substance use suggests that smoking is a pathway to the use of other substances, not the reverse. A second possibility is, therefore, the reverse: that the rise in smoking in the 1990s led to more use of these other substances. We present evidence below that falling cigarette prices in the 1990s can explain 30 percent or more of the trend in smoking by highschool seniors over this time period. And there are a number of studies that suggest that smoking is complementary with the use of these other substances (Chaloupka et al. 1998; Dee 1999). Thus, at least part of these trends in other substances may have been driven by falling cigarette prices.

But it seems unlikely that this can explain all these strong trends, particularly for marijuana. A third alternative is, therefore, that there were other shifts in tastes that led to greater use of all these substances. One piece of suggestive evidence for this view is the lack of correspondence between the time trends in the use of cigarettes and the use of these other substances in the 1980s: the use of other substances fell much more than did smoking. These trends cast some doubt on either of the two alternatives suggested above and favor instead a shift in taste toward all substance use in the 1990s.

2.3   Prices and Other Public Policies

Given the failure of background characteristics to explain the trend in youth smoking in the 1990s, a particularly important question is whether price movements can explain this upsurge. In fact, as figure 2.8 documents,

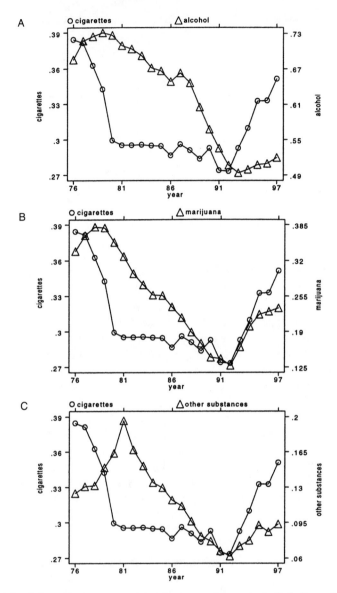

Fig. 2.7   Other substances, participation vs. smoking: *A*, alcohol; *B*, marijuana; *C*, other drugs

there was a substantial decline in prices in the early 1990s, corresponding precisely to the timing of the increase in youth smoking. Of course, youth smoking continued to increase even after prices began to rise again, but the most precipitous increases in youth smoking were over the period 1992–94, when prices were falling. Moreover, recently released data for

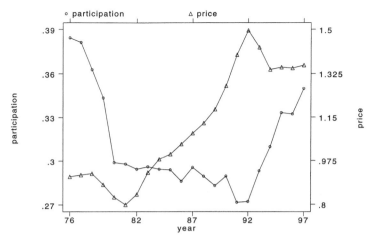

Fig. 2.8   Smoking participation vs. cigarette price

1998 reveal both a sharp increase in prices (by 10 percent) and the first decline in youth smoking of the decade, as smoking among high school seniors fell by 1.4 percentage points (3.8 percent). So the question naturally arises, Can price movements explain the time-series trend?

This ties into a more general question of the role that public policy can play in determining youth-smoking behavior. A primary determinant of price movements for cigarettes is excise-tax policy. Moreover, there are a variety of other policy tools that state and federal policy makers can pursue in an attempt to reduce youth smoking. Are these successful, and what do they suggest for future policy directions? We address these questions below.

2.3.1   Data

The public-use data from the MTF survey are not suitable for this exercise because they do not contain information on state of residence and they are not available for teens other than high school seniors. We therefore searched for data sets that had available data on smoking for repeated cross sections of teens of all ages over the 1990s as well as state identifiers so that cigarette prices and taxes could be matched to the youths. Three data sources meet this criterion, and all three are used.[2] The first, and best,

---

2. A fourth data set that could have been used here is the National Household Survey of Drug Abuse (NHSDA), but this was excluded for two reasons. First, the quality of these data before the mid-1990s is quite suspect owing to the use of in-home surveys without computer assistance that could suffer from bias owing to observation by parents; indeed, these data do not appear to show an increase in smoking among teens through the mid-1990s, while the more respected MTF and YRBS surveys both do. Second, there is no public-use or even private-use version of the NHSDA data available with state identifiers; only selected researchers can access these data.

source for our purposes is a restricted-use sample of the MTF data that includes information on smoking behavior, race, age, sex, and state of residence for eighth, tenth, and twelfth graders, from 1991 through 1997. We focus on 1991 as the starting point for the analysis for three reasons: this is the last year before teen smoking began to rise; this is the year in which the eighth- and tenth-grade MTF data become available; and this is the year in which the YRBS data (described next) became available.

The second data source is the YRBS data graphed earlier. These data provide information on smoking and a limited set of background characteristics for 1991, 1993, 1995, and 1997 for a sample of ninth to twelfth graders. The MTF and YRBS data are comparable in that they provide nationally representative, in-school surveys of youths. As noted earlier with reference to figure 2.2 above, they suggest different levels of smoking among teens but similar trends. The sample sizes of these surveys are also comparable. But the MTF data have the strong advantage of being a more complete survey over this sample period; the survey includes data on thirty-five states in every year from 1991 to 1997 and a total of 277 state-year pairs over this time period. On the other hand, the YRBS is a survey that is phasing into coverage of the entire nation, with only ten states in the survey in every year and only 102 state-year pairs over this time period.[3] As a result, while from 1991 to 1997 there are fifty-nine tax changes to be studied in the MTF data, there are only fourteen in the YRBS data. Thus, the results that we obtain with the MTF data are more robust to the specification check pursued below, and we will rely on them as our primary estimates.

The third data source is the Vital Statistics Natality detail files. These data are a census of birth certificates for the United States, with approximately 4 million observations per year. The data contain information, since 1989, on the smoking behavior of the mother during pregnancy, and they are available for virtually every state in every year from 1991 on, providing even more variation than the MTF survey (seventy-three tax changes over this time period).[4] But these have the disadvantage of being focused solely on one particularly select group of teens, those having children before their nineteenth birthday. Owing to the enormous size of the Natality database (over 300,000 teen mothers per year for our seven years of analysis), we do not analyze micro data on smoking rates by mothers. Rather, we group these data into state $\times$ year $\times$ age cells and analyze cell mean rates of smoking and conditional smoking intensity where the regressions are weighted by cell size.

3. All our YRBS means and estimates are weighted using weights designed to reproduce national representativeness.

4. Smoking data are not available for California, Indiana, and South Dakota for any year and for New York for 1991–93; smoking data for New York City, but not the remainder of the state, are available beginning in 1994.

Table 2.5   **Means of MTF, YRBS, and Natality Price-Regression Samples**

	Any Smoking	Cigarettes/ Day When Smoking	Real Price	Real Excise Tax
MTF Data, 1991–97:				
12th grade ($N = 91,567$)	.309	7.21	1.39	.21
	(.462)	(8.87)	(.17)	(.10)
8th–10th grade ($N = 213,527$)	.217	5.42	1.38	.21
	(.412)	(8.38)	(.17)	(.10)
8th–12th grade ($N = 336,665$)	.246	6.13	1.39	.21
	(.431)	(8.63)	(.17)	(.10)
YRBS data, 1991, 1993, 1995, 1997:				
12th grade ($N = 14,346$)	.358	6.06	1.28	.21
	(.479)	(6.13)	(.15)	(.10)
9th–11th grade ($N = 38,932$)	.315	5.15	1.28	.21
	(.464)	(5.70)	(.15)	(.10)
9th–12th grade ($N = 53,278$)	.326	5.42	1.28	.21
	(.469)	(5.85)	(.15)	(.10)
Natality data, 1991–97:				
17–18 years old ($N = 666$)	.180	10.23	1.23	.19
	(.075)	(1.31)	(.14)	(.10)
13–16 years old ($N = 1,319$)	.127	9.21	1.22	.19
	(.071)	(1.70)	(.14)	(.10)
13–18 years old ($N = 1,985$)	.164	9.93	1.22	.19
	(.078)	(1.51)	(.14)	(.10)

Note: Authors' tabulations of MTF, YRBS, and Natality data. All prices and taxes in 1982 dollars. Micro data for MTF and YRBS; cell-level data for Natality, as described in the text, with means weighted by cell count. "Cigarettes per day when smoking" is cigarettes per day smoked on days when smoking. Standard deviations are given in parentheses.

The means for all three data sets are presented in table 2.5. We consider two measures of smoking: *participation,* defined as any smoking over the past month, and *conditional intensity.*[5] The latter measure has the difficulty as a dependent variable that, if there are policy effects on participation, there could be sample-selection bias to the effects on conditional intensity; for example, if higher prices reduce smoking participation and those who quit are low-intensity smokers, then higher prices could be associated with higher intensity among those who remain smokers through this composition effect.

As noted above, smoking rates are somewhat higher in the YRBS than in the MTF data sets; for high school seniors over this time period, participation rates are 31 percent in the MTF and 36 percent in the YRBS. Smoking rates are much lower for teen mothers; for seventeen- to eighteen-

5. In the MTF and YRBS data, conditional intensity is measured in intervals, and we use the midpoint of each interval for intensity. In the Natality data, the intensity question is continuous.

year-old teen mothers, the smoking rate is only 18 percent. However, smoking intensity for high school seniors is higher in the MTF survey, averaging 7.2 cigarettes per day, compared to 6.1 cigarettes per day in the YRBS. Intensity is even higher for teen mothers, averaging over 10 cigarettes per day for seventeen- to eighteen-year-old mothers. Thus, smoking among teen mothers appears less frequent but more intense when these women are participating. Note that this is not just a male/female difference; smoking participation among males and females is very similar in the YRBS and MTF surveys, and intensity is actually somewhat higher for males.

Smoking is less frequent, and smoking intensity lower, for younger teens in all three surveys. In the MTF and YRBS surveys, the full sample results are weighted more closely to the results for younger teens since the samples of younger teens are much larger; in the Natality data, they are weighted toward older teens since there are so many more births to older teens in the data.

The key independent variables to be used in the analysis are state-level measures of prices, taxes, and other policies. Prices as of November of each year for each state are provided in Tobacco Institute (1998), and a monthly series can be constructed from information on taxes given in that volume as well. The MTF and YRBS surveys are both conducted in the spring, so we use an average of the prices from November of year $t-1$ and November of year t as our price measure and the tax rate as of February as our tax measure. For the Natality data, we know the actual month of the birth, so we use the tax rate from that month of birth.

The two dimensions of antismoking policy that we explore are clean-air regulations and youth-access restrictions. Clean-air regulations, which are described in substantial detail in Jacobson and Wasserman (1997), are laws that restrict smoking in certain public areas. We constructed a comprehensive database of such laws using information from the state legislative records, Coalition on Smoking OR Health (various years), and the Centers for Disease Control website (http://www2.cdc.gov/nccdphp/osh/state/). While there are a large number of such laws, we categorize them into five categories: restrictions on private workplaces, public (e.g., state and local government) workplaces, restaurants, schools, and other public places (e.g., elevators, public transportation, theaters).

Youth-access restrictions are laws designed to limit youth purchases of tobacco products since, while youth smoking is legal, selling cigarettes to youths is not. As reviewed in Jacobson and Wasserman (1997), states have therefore endeavored to implement barriers to youth access to cigarette purchase along various dimensions. Categorizing these state efforts is difficult as there are a large number of different regulatory tools, and states enforce them with varying degrees of rigor. We therefore rely on the expert opinion of a panel convened by the National Cancer Institute (NCI) to evaluate state laws limiting youth access to cigarettes (Alciati et al. 1998). This panel reviewed a wide variety of state laws in this area and formed an index to capture their overall "bite" in limiting youth access. Its members considered nine categories of state regulation and provided a score within each, which is aggregated into a total index. Their index is available for 1993–96; we have followed their rules, in consultation with them, to use state laws to extend the data back to 1991 and forward to 1997. We did augment their index by adding some finer disaggregation of categories and by correcting some inconsistencies with actual legislation. We also added three additional categories that they did not consider: advertising restrictions; licensing of retailers; and penalties on minors themselves for tobacco purchase. The index also reflects state efforts to comply with the recent Synar amendments proposed by the Food and Drug Administration.

We describe in more detail how this index was created in the appendix. Appendix table 2A.1 also shows means for the MTF data of the clean-air and youth-access-index variable. The average value of our access index is roughly 12 (where the maximum possible value is 26); about half of students were subject to restrictions on smoking in private workplaces, whereas restrictions in restaurants, government work sites, schools, and other sites were more common.

The other frequently discussed public-policy intervention meant to reduce youth smoking is counteradvertising. While this is a major focus of very recent discussions, over the time period studied in this paper (ending in 1997) there was very little counteradvertising in most states.[6]

2.3.2   Empirical Strategy

For all three data sets, we pursue a similar estimation strategy, considering the effect of prices and public policies on smoking in the following regression framework:

$$(1) \quad \text{SMOK}_{ijt} = \alpha + \beta \text{PRICE}_{jt} + \delta \text{ACCESS}_{jt} + \gamma \text{CLNAIR}_{jt}$$
$$+ \eta X_{ijt} + \lambda S_j + \nu T_t + \varepsilon_{ijt},$$

where i indexes individuals, j indexes states, t indexes years, SMOK is a measure of smoking (participation or conditional intensity), PRICE is the price per pack of cigarettes (inclusive of taxation), ACCESS is the index of access restrictions, CLNAIR is a set of dummy variables for clean-air regulations, X is a set of individual control variables (which varies by data set), S is a set of state dummies, and T is a set of year dummies.

---

6. Based on conversations with experts at the Office on Smoking and Health at the Centers for Disease Control. The available data suggest that only a few states had major programs in place by 1997 and that the spending on those programs was fairly constant over our time period.

By including a complete set of state fixed effects, this regression surmounts any problems with fixed differences across states in both the level of prices and the propensity to smoke, for example, owing to tobacco-production intensity. However, two potential concerns remain with the interpretation of the price coefficient in this specification. First, if tobacco companies are doing any state-specific pricing, then prices may be endogenous to smoking levels. While 80 percent of the variation in prices within states over time is driven by tax changes (Gruber and Koszegi 2000), there remains 20 percent that is possibly demand driven. We therefore instrument prices with the tax rate in the state to provide identification solely from tax-induced price movements. All estimates presented below are from such instrumental-variables models.

Second, the identifying assumption of this estimator is that within-state changes in taxation (and other public policies) are not themselves determined by youth-smoking behavior. It is plausible that tax policy is set as a function of smoking in a state, with revenue-maximizing legislators and an inelastically demanded good. Since youths smoke only about 2 percent of the total number of cigarette packs smoked annually, it is doubtful that youth smoking per se is driving tax policy. But it is possible that youth smoking is correlated with some of the same factors that drive adult smoking and possibly therefore with tax setting. With this short panel it is difficult to address this concern definitively, but we discuss an attempt to do so below.

Another important estimation issue is that we are using a large number of observations in each of these data sets but really have variation in our key variables only across state and year cells. As a result, all regressions are estimated with the standard errors corrected for within-state-year-cell correlations in the error terms.

2.3.3   Results—MTF Data

We begin the analysis by focusing on the MTF data, the MTF being, as discussed above, the highest-quality source of nationally representative data. We also start with high school seniors, to parallel most previous work in this area.

The results of estimating equation (1) for high school seniors are presented in the first two columns of table 2.6. The most important finding is that there is a negative and statistically significant effect of prices on smoking participation. The implied elasticity at the sample mean is -0.67. The effect on conditional intensity is negative but insignificant, implying a small elasticity of conditional intensity of -0.06. As noted earlier, it is difficult to interpret these estimates as the pool of smokers is changing. In particular, it seems likely that those who quit smoking as the price rises have the lowest ex ante intensity, which would lead to a positive composition bias to the estimates.

Table 2.6 Effect of Price and Regulations on Youth Smoking in the MTF Data

	12th Graders		8th & 10th Graders		8th–12th Grader	
	Participation	Cigarettes/Day	Participation	Cigarettes/Day	Participation	Cigarettes/Day
Price	−.148	−.310	−.033	−.013	−.055	−.129
	(.078)	(2.388)	(.035)	(1.243)	(.034)	(1.132)
	[−.666]	[−.059]	[−.21]	[−.003]	[−.311]	[−.029]
Access index/100	.084	−3.48	.033	−5.520	.066	−5.22
	(.106)	(2.76)	(.060)	(1.640)	(.056)	(1.49)
Private workplace	−.041	.462	−.006	1.464	−.021	1.045
	(.028)	(.589)	(.017)	(.489)	(.017)	(.348)
Government workplace	.022	−1.128	−.019	−.813	−.001	−.834
	(.026)	(.517)	(.015)	(.394)	(.013)	(.251)
Restaurant	.032	2.166	.012	.868	.016	1.318
	(.030)	(.783)	(.017)	(.615)	(.015)	(.483)
Schools	.050	.931	.044	.788	.040	.645
	(.030)	(.915)	(.018)	(.553)	(.015)	(.392)
Other	−.080	−2.791	−.032	−1.424	−.038	−1.617
	(.041)	(1.234)	(.020)	(.775)	(.019)	(.621)
Male	.016	1.235	−.009	.926	−.001	1.041
	(.004)	(.115)	(.003)	(.085)	(.003)	(.069)
Nonwhite	−.153	−1.908	−.076	−.436	−.1	−.962
	(.007)	(.171)	(.004)	(.119)	(.005)	(.115)
Grade 8			−.088	−2.746	−.185	−3.815
			(.018)	(.576)	(.014)	(.538)

(continued)

Table 2.6   (continued)

	12th Graders		8th & 10th Graders		8th–12th Grader	
	Participation	Cigarettes/Day	Participation	Cigarettes/Day	Participation	Cigarettes/Day
Grade 10					−.098	−1.055
					(.019)	(.632)
Grade 8, age ≤ 13			−.027	.217	.03	.181
			(.018)	(.573)	(.014)	(.519)
Grade 8, age ≥ 14			.026	1.829	.083	1.8
			(.018)	(.572)	(.014)	(.515)
Grade 10, age ≤ 15			−.037	−1.211	.019	−1.334
			(.003)	(.104)	(.019)	(.625)
Grade 10, age ≥ 16					.055	−.119
					(.019)	(.627)
Grade 12, age ≤ 17	−.013	−.546			−.012	−.512
	(.003)	(.113)			(.003)	(.112)
No. of observations	106,539	32,868	230,126	49,927	336,665	82,795

Note: Standard errors (corrected for state/year clustering) are given in parentheses, standard errors in square brackets. All regressions also include the full set of state and year fixed effects.

We obtain much less convincing evidence for the role of other policies, however. There is a negative effect of access restrictions on the quantity of cigarettes smoked, but the coefficient is not significant. The only clean-air restrictions for which there are significant negative effects are for restrictions on government workplaces (in terms of conditional quantity smoked) and for restrictions on other sites (for both participation and quantity smoked). It seems highly unlikely that there is a true causal effect of restrictions in government work sites on youths; it is perhaps more plausible that restrictions on other sites, such as public transportation, might matter.

Does this significant price effect suggest that we can explain the time-series movements by the price decline of the early 1990s? From 1991 through 1997, the price of cigarettes fell by fourteen cents. At our estimated coefficient on participation, this explains 26 percent of the 8 percentage point rise in smoking for high school seniors over this time period. Thus, price is playing an important role but not the dominant one.

The next four columns of table 2.6 investigate the effect of prices and policies on younger smokers (eighth and tenth graders). Interestingly, there is little effect of price on the smoking of younger teens. The coefficients on both participation and intensity are insignificant for eighth to tenth graders and, as a result, for the full sample of eighth to twelfth graders. Over the full sample, the price elasticity for participation is only −0.31, with a conditional-intensity elasticity of −0.03. This casts further doubt on the role of price as the primary determinant of the time-series trend since the trends in smoking are quite similar for eighth to tenth graders and for high school seniors. On the other hand, even though younger smokers are less price sensitive, their estimated price sensitivity is still nontrivial; it is similar, for example, to the elasticity of smoking participation estimated for adults by Evans, Ringel, and Stech (1999).

The effects of other policies on the smoking of eighth to tenth graders are more interesting than are their effects on the smoking of high school seniors. We now estimate a highly significant effect of youth-access restrictions on the conditional quantity of cigarettes consumed by younger teens, which is not subject to selection bias owing to the insignificant effects on participation. This coefficient suggests that moving from the lowest to the highest value of this index would lower smoking intensity by 1.38 cigarettes per day, or 25 percent. This is interesting because it is indeed possible that, by raising the hassle costs of obtaining cigarettes, access restrictions do not deter youths from smoking at all but rather limit the extent to which they do smoke. We also again obtain negative effects of government-work-site restrictions on smoking intensity and negative effects of other clean-air restrictions on both intensity and participation.

There is a paucity of control variables available in these restricted MTF data. We do find that smoking rises with grade. The age variables are defined only conditional on grade (owing to restrictions in the MTF data), but they have the expected pattern: older children within each grade smoke more. Nonwhite youths are much less likely to smoke, and there is a positive effect of being male among high school seniors but a negative effect among eighth and tenth graders, with the result that, for the full sample, the effect is insignificant. As we showed above, the positive effect for high school seniors of being male becomes negative when other covariates available in the public-use data are included.

2.3.4   YRBS and Natality Data

As emphasized above, a key advantage of our analytic strategy is that we have brought several data sets to bear on this question in order to analyze the most consistent patterns of effects of public policy on smoking. In this spirit, tables 2.7 and 2.8 replicate the results for the MTF data in the YRBS and Natality data, once again for older teens (seniors in the YRBS, seventeen- to eighteen-year-olds in the Natality data), younger teens (ninth to eleventh graders in the YRBS, thirteen- to sixteen-year-olds in the Natality data), and overall.

The most strikingly consistent finding across all three data sets is the negative effect of prices on smoking by older teens. In the YRBS, the elasticities are enormous: there is an elasticity of -1.5 on participation *and* an elasticity of -1.5 on conditional intensity. In the Natality data, the elasticities are more modest, with an elasticity of participation of -0.38 and an elasticity of conditional intensity of -0.15. It is perhaps not surprising that the elasticity is smaller for teen mothers than for other groups given that the very fact that these women are smoking reveals their insensitivity to information about the hazards posed by smoking to newborns. This smaller elasticity is not due to the gender composition of the sample. In both the MTF and the YRBS data, we estimate very similar elasticities for males and females; the elasticities are somewhat higher for males in the MTF and somewhat higher for females in the YRBS.

Moreover, there is a consistent finding of a much smaller effect of prices on young smokers. In the YRBS data, the elasticity of participation is wrong signed, and the elasticity of conditional intensity insignificant, for ninth to eleventh graders. In the Natality data, both coefficients are right signed but insignificant.

Why might we be finding that older teens are more price sensitive? There are several possible explanations. One is that smoking means different things at different ages. Younger teens may view participation as pure experimentation, which is less well described by economists' models of addictive behavior (e.g., Becker and Murphy 1988) and which is as a result less sensitive to such economic factors as price. But, by the time these youths have become high school seniors, they have completed their experimentation phase, and smoking follows expected relations with price and other economic factors. This type of story is consistent with the fact that

Table 2.7   Effect of Price and Regulations on Youth Smoking in the YRBS Data

	12th Graders		9th–11th Graders		9th–12th Graders	
	Participation	Cigarettes/Day	Participation	Cigarettes/Day	Participation	Cigarettes/Day
Price	-.429 (.200) [-1.534]	-7.462 (3.461) [-1.576]	.103 (.134) [.419]	-.912 (1.847) [-.227]	-.032 (.103) [-.126]	-2.228 (1.937) [-.526]
Access index/100	-.060 (.169)	.461 (3.985)	-.098 (.092)	-.804 (2.223)	-.098 (.088)	-.316 (2.308)
Private workplace	.006 (.047)	-2.723 (1.742)	.064 (.046)	1.146 (.552)	.051 (.042)	.905 (.476)
Government workplace	-.075 (.032)	-.168 (1.459)	-.088 (.037)	-1.800 (.473)	-.087 (.034)	-1.971 (.396)
Restaurant	-.162 (.028)	-1.435 (1.466)	-.006 (.025)	.383 (.627)	-.050 (.025)	-.447 (.783)
Schools	.006 (.060)	-.578 (1.161)	.008 (.045)	.517 (.567)	.008 (.034)	.578 (.533)
Other	.012 (.065)	6.164 (2.260)	-.015 (.054)	.775 (.813)	.002 (.048)	1.842 (.950)
Male	.002 (.014)	1.283 (.268)	-.001 (.010)	.846 (.164)	.000 (.008)	.984 (.146)
White	.048 (.028)	.585 (.634)	.046 (.014)	-.148 (.506)	.044 (.012)	.071 (.382)
Black	-.206 (.033)	-3.16 (.621)	-.128 (.018)	-2.69 (.541)	-.149 (.015)	-2.73 (.417)
Hispanic	-.013 (.030)	-2.10 (.627)	.003 (.016)	-2.09 (.448)	-.002 (.014)	-2.02 (.354)
Grade 10			-.055 (.010)	.261 (.366)	-.055 (.011)	.266 (.363)

(*continued*)

Table 2.7   (continued)

	12th Graders		9th–11th Graders		9th–12th Graders	
	Participation	Cigarettes/Day	Participation	Cigarettes/Day	Participation	Cigarettes/Day
Grade 11			-.076	.289	-.075	.379
			(.017)	(.455)	(.017)	(.452)
Grade 12					-.092	.103
					(.022)	(.551)
Age 15	-.052	12.28	.079	1.04	.079	1.00
	(.211)	(6.70)	(.013)	(.369)	(.013)	(.370)
Age 16	-.044	-14.86	.146	1.39	.146	1.36
	(.161)	(4.93)	(.016)	(.443)	(.016)	(.444)
Age 17	-.106	-15.50	.191	2.28	.191	2.13
	(.145)	(4.62)	(.020)	(.542)	(.020)	(.544)
Age 18	-.086	-14.95	.244	2.71	.218	2.53
	(.144)	(4.66)	(.035)	(.772)	(.023)	(.618)
Father a high school graduate	.014	-.349	-.007	-.384	-.002	-.362
	(.022)	(.431)	(.015)	(.252)	(.012)	(.215)
Father has some college	.008	-1.07	-.035	-.488	-.025	-.660
	(.027)	(.549)	(.018)	(.410)	(.014)	(.332)
Father college graduate	-.004	-1.26	-.055	-.905	-.042	-.971
	(.024)	(.493)	(.019)	(.305)	(.015)	(.232)
Mother a high school graduate	-.058	-.701	-.014	-.640	-.027	-.686
	(.024)	(.403)	(.017)	(.416)	(.015)	(.339)
Mother has some college	-.031	-.382	-.030	-.935	-.030	-.751
	(.030)	(.508)	(.013)	(.429)	(.015)	(.326)
Mother college graduate	-.044	-.785	-.038	-.908	-.041	-.891
	(.027)	(.446)	(.017)	(.423)	(.015)	(.338)
No. of observations	14,346	4,429	38,932	11,368	53,278	15,797

Note: Standard errors (corrected for state/year clustering) are given in parentheses, standard errors in square brackets. All regressions also include the full set of state and year fixed effects.

Table 2.8   Effect of Price and Regulations on Youth Smoking in the Natality Data

	17–18-Year-Olds		13–16-Year-Olds		13–18-Year-Olds	
	Participation	Cigarettes/Day	Participation	Cigarettes/Day	Participation	Cigarettes/Day
Price	-.055	-1.209	-.025	-.436	-.047	-1.003
	(.018)	(.527)	(.018)	(.638)	(.016)	(.440)
	[-.376]	[-.145]	[-.240]	[-.058]	[-.353]	[-.124]
Access index/100	.023	-1.771	-.006	-1.010	.013	-1.485
	(.026)	(.718)	(.024)	(1.106)	(.023)	(.651)
Private workplace	.009	.037	.013	.555	.011	.134
	(.007)	(.329)	(.007)	(.466)	(.005)	(.254)
Government workplace	.000	.014	-.005	.180	-.002	.021
	(.003)	(.109)	(.004)	(.160)	(.003)	(.089)
Restaurant	-.012	-.493	.002	-.972	-.007	-.597
	(.004)	(.233)	(.005)	(.355)	(.004)	(.193)
Schools	.002	-.195	.006	-.613	.004	-.316
	(.004)	(.175)	(.005)	(.220)	(.004)	(.148)
Other	-.003	.231	-.011	.299	-.006	.300
	(.005)	(.238)	(.006)	(.327)	(.004)	(.205)
% white	.179	2.16	.131	-.839	.171	-.016
	(.093)	(2.67)	(.056)	(2.59)	(.046)	(1.61)
% black	-.263	2.09	-.139	-2.40	-.203	-2.42
	(.096)	(2.80)	(.052)	(2.39)	(.044)	(1.49)
% Hispanic	-.255	-1.90	-.238	.34	-.238	-1.15
	(.044)	(1.64)	(.028)	(1.13)	(.025)	(.896)

(continued)

Table 2.8   (continued)

	17–18-Year-Olds		13–16-Year-Olds		13–18-Year-Olds	
	Participation	Cigarettes/Day	Participation	Cigarettes/Day	Participation	Cigarettes/Day
Age 14			.017	−.158	.009	−.187
			(.004)	(.366)	(.004)	(.363)
Age 15			.024	.317	.009	.213
			(.005)	(.354)	(.005)	(.349)
Age 16			.033	.734	.011	.557
			(.007)	(.375)	(.006)	(.354)
Age 17					0.14	.912
					(.007)	(.368)
Age 18	.003	.502			.019	1.362
	(.002)	(.055)			(.007)	(.376)
No. of observations	1,319	1,189	666	666	1,985	1,855

Note: Standard errors (corrected for state/year clustering) are given in parentheses, standard errors in square brackets. All regressions also include the full set of state and year fixed effects.

younger teens who smoke consume a smaller quantity of cigarettes and with the evidence (presented below) that the demographic correlates of socioeconomic disadvantage (race and parents' education) lead to higher price sensitivity for high school seniors but not for younger teens.

Alternatively, younger teens may be pursuing smoking in order to be accepted by a peer group, and, by the time they are high school seniors, they have been accepted into the group. If smoking as a younger teen regardless of price is required to gain acceptance to a peer group but, once within the group, peer effects have their usual multiplier effect on price elasticities, then this would yield low price elasticities on younger teens and higher ones on older teens. Finally, it may simply be that teens using their own money are more price elastic than are those who rely on money from parents (obtained either complicitly or illicitly).

In contrast to the robust and significant effect of prices on youth smoking, however, we obtain much more mixed evidence on a role for other public policies. There is no public-policy variable other than price that is significant for either age group in all three data sets or even in both the data sets representing the full teen population (the MTF and the YRBS). The most robust finding appears to be for the effect of youth-access restrictions on the quantity of cigarettes smoked, which is negative for both younger teens and high school seniors and significant for the latter in the Natality data; the magnitudes of the effects for teen mothers are much smaller than for all teens in the MTF. We also find negative effects of clean-air regulations for restaurants (which are significant for participation by high school seniors in the Natality and YRBS data) and of clean-air regulations for other sites such as public transportation (which are highly significant in the MTF and are negative and marginally significant for younger teen participation in the Natality data).

The coefficients on the covariates in the YRBS generally conform to expectations. There is little effect of sex and an enormous negative effect of race on smoking rates. Smoking rates fall with grade (conditional on age) but rise strongly with age so that, on average, smoking is rising with grade as well. Echoing the findings presented above using MTF micro data, there is little effect of parents' education on smoking, at least for high school seniors; there is some evidence that having more-educated parents leads to less smoking for eighth and tenth graders.[7] There are very few covariates in the Natality data, but they do confirm that smoking rises with age and is much higher among whites.[8] One interesting difference between the Natality and the YRBS data sets is that smoking among Hispan-

---

7. Parents' education is not available in the 1991 YRBS and is missing for a number of respondents in other years, so the omitted category here is either parents who are high school dropouts or parents for whom education is missing.

8. Note that the covariates here are cell means, e.g., percentage white in the age-year-state cell.

ics is much lower in the Natality data but is only marginally lower in the YRBS. Unfortunately, owing to the restricted nature of the MTF data, we cannot bring that evidence to bear on racial distinctions; the data report only whether the youth is white or nonwhite.

In summary, there are four conclusions to be drawn from these basic results. First, there is a sizable and significant negative effect of price on smoking by high school seniors, particularly for the decision to participate. This finding is robust to all three data sets. We estimate elasticities that range from -0.38 (Natality) to -1.5 (YRBS), but the most reliable estimate is probably the elasticity of -0.66 from the MTF data. Second, however, we find that there is no effect of price on younger teens so that, in the aggregate, the price effects on teen smoking are weak, with overall price elasticities for teens ranging from -0.13 (YRBS) to -0.35 (Natality). Third, there is some suggestion that laws that restrict youth access to tobacco products reduce the intensity of youth smoking but not smoking participation. Finally, there is little consistent evidence that clean-air restrictions matter for youth-smoking decisions.

We have also considered specification tests to address two potential concerns about this exercise. The first is that, for two of our three data sets, we have data only on students, not on high school dropouts. This may lead to a biased estimate of the aggregate teen elasticity if dropouts are differentially price sensitive, but, since the quoted statistics on teen smoking come from the in-school surveys used here, these are the relevant data for trying to explain time trends. More perniciously, however, if high school dropout rates are somehow correlated with tobacco taxation, then there could be a sample-selection bias to our estimates. We have included in the regressions reported here data on dropout rates by state and year. In no case did including these control variables much change our coefficient on price, nor did the variables themselves enter significantly in our regressions. So this suggests no bias from selection on who remains in school as taxes change.

Another more serious concern, mentioned earlier, is that excise taxes may be endogenous, if not directly to youth smoking, then to aggregate cigarette consumption, which may in turn be correlated with youth-smoking decisions (either positively, through adult and peer effects, or negatively, through teen contrariness). This general endogeneity concern is impossible to address perfectly, in particular given the very short panel of data with which we are working. One approach to addressing the specific concern that our finding is driven by an omitted correlation of youth and adult smoking is to include directly in the regression a control for aggregate cigarette consumption in that state in the previous year. Once again, the results are very robust (with the exception of a decline in the participation elasticity estimate to -1.2 in the YRBS data), and the coefficients on lagged packs per capita themselves are generally insignificant. Thus, it appears that correlations between aggregate consumption and both tax setting and youth smoking cannot explain our findings.

2.3.5 Heterogeneity

The analysis thus far has considered youth smoking as a simple aggregate and has not explored the heterogeneity in policy effects across different groups of youths. But there are considerable differences across youths in their underlying propensity to smoke. Most noticeable are racial differences, and the YRBS suggests some differences by parents' education as well, at least for younger teens. In this section, we explore the heterogeneity in the price responsiveness of young smokers. In particular, we assess whether socioeconomically disadvantaged youths are more responsive to prices, suggesting a cross-elasticity between price and income.

The results for a racial decomposition of smoking responsiveness are presented in table 2.9. For the MTF sample, we can compare only white and nonwhite youths since this is the only racial distinction available in these restricted data. In the YRBS and Natality data, we can compare white and black youths more specifically. When we have estimated models for whites and all nonwhites in these other data sets, the results are similar but more muted than those for whites and blacks.

The results for the MTF and YRBS data for high school seniors are striking: there is much higher price responsiveness among blacks than among whites. In the MTF, the price elasticity of participation for white high school seniors is only -0.35 and is insignificant, and there is a positive coefficient on conditional intensity. But for black high school seniors the elasticity of participation is an enormous and statistically significant -2.32, and there is a significant elasticity of conditional intensity of -2.03 as well. In the YRBS, the results are even more extreme, with an elasticity of -0.63 for white smoking participation and an unreasonable elasticity of -9.3 for blacks; this implausibly large estimate likely reflects the effect of examining a small number of tax changes in only a subsample of the data. In the Natality data, on the other hand, the results are reversed: the price elasticity for whites is slightly larger than for the full sample, and there is no price responsiveness of participation among blacks (although there is a large negative effect on conditional intensity).

For younger teens, there is a much less clear racial pattern. There are no significant elasticities for either whites or blacks in the MTF or YRBS data. For the Natality data, the elasticities are once again significant for whites and wrong signed for blacks.

One explanation for this higher price sensitivity among black youths is lower income. A number of articles have found price elasticities for adult smokers that fall with income (e.g., Evans, Ringel, and Stech 1999). If the same is true for teens, then the lower incomes of black high school seniors may explain their increased responsiveness. Unfortunately, none of these

Table 2.9   Price-Coefficient Heterogeneity by Race

	Older Teens		Younger Teens		All Teens	
	Participation	Cigarettes/Day	Participation	Cigarettes/Day	Participation	Cigarettes/Day
MTF data:						
Whites	-.091	.721	-.054	-1.611	-.057	-.848
	(.010)	(2.637)	(.047)	(1.214)	(.041)	(1.225)
	[-.350]	[.130]	[-.300]	[-.393]	[-.277]	[-.181]
Nonwhites	-.323	-7.690	.025	4.962	-.039	2.417
	(.163)	(3.749)	(.050)	(2.843)	(.045)	(2.395)
	[-2.324]	[-2.03]	[.226]	[1.488]	[-.327]	[.691]
YRBS data:						
Whites	-.198	-13.70	.083	.470	.026	-3.563
	(.271)	(4.554)	(.177)	(2.326)	(.123)	(2.344)
	[-.628]	[-2.662]	[.303]	[.106]	[.092]	[-.775]
Blacks	-1.187	-22.78	-.132	12.48	-.369	11.24
	(.485)	(20.50)	(.372)	(12.44)	(.351)	(10.81)
	[-9.259]	[-8.248]	[-.874]	[4.958]	[-2.530]	[4.393]
Natality data:						
Whites	-.079	-.934	-.060	.307	-.079	-.639
	(.023)	(.556)	(.023)	(.682)	(.021)	(.453)
	[-.412]	[-.109]	[-.385]	[.040]	[-.433]	[-.076]
Blacks	.026	-3.357	.033	-2.809	.028	-3.256
	(.017)	(1.286)	(.019)	(2.113)	(.015)	(1.144)
	[.534]	[-.539]	[1.115]	[-.494]	[.671]	[-.539]
YRBS data, parents' education:						
Mother & father high school dropouts or graduates	-1.266	-2.036	.79	10.806	.207	4.464
	(.583)	(8.497)	(.369)	(5.889)	(.206)	(5.4)
	[-4.387]	[-.401]	[2.721]	[2.514]	[.715]	[.103]
Mother & father have some college or are college graduates	-.067	-10.068	.228	-1.432	.157	-3.285
	(.238)	(4.159)	(.231)	(3.144)	(.188)	(2.353)
	[-.236]	[-2.393]	[.956]	[-.390]	[.645]	[-.874]

Note: Coefficient on price from regressions in the MTF (first panel), YRBS (second and fourth panels), and Natality (third panel) data. Regressions include all the controls shown in tables 2.2–2.5 above, including the full set of state and year fixed effects. Standard errors (corrected for state/year clustering) are given in parentheses, price elasticity in square brackets.

data sets contain information on income. But the YRBS data do have an excellent proxy for permanent income: parents' education.

In the final panel of table 2.9, we therefore present results that divide the YRBS sample into those whose mother and father are high school dropouts or graduates and those whose mother and father have some college or are college graduates. There is a striking difference across these groups for high school seniors: the elasticity of participation is −4.4 for the low-education group and is only −0.2 for the high-education group (and is highly insignificant for the latter). This is offset to some extent by a very large conditional-intensity elasticity for the high-education group. But, overall, there is a clear negative correlation of price responsiveness and socioeconomic status measured this way. Once again, however, there is no clear relation for younger teens; the elasticity of participation is actually positive and significant for younger teens with less-educated parents and is positive and insignificant for younger teens with more highly educated parents.

Taken together, the results presented in table 2.9 suggest two important conclusions. First, for high school seniors, there is a strong cross-elasticity between price and income. Lower-income groups, whether measured racially or by parents' education, are much more price sensitive. Moreover, the fact that the results by race for teen mothers are reversed is consistent with the fact that, while white teens are much more advantaged than black teens as a whole, among teen mothers blacks actually have a higher median income.[9] Second, there continues to be evidence that the smoking decisions of younger teens are determined primarily by noneconomic factors. Not only are younger teens not price sensitive, but there is also no pattern of increased relative sensitivity with income, as proxied by either race or parents' education.

2.4   Intertemporal Correlation in Youth Smoking

While the previous discussion has suggested that seniors are responsive to the price of cigarettes, it does not resolve the more important question: the long-run intertemporal implications of youth smoking. That is, what does rising youth smoking today imply for the adult smoking rate in the future? If shifts in youth smoking imply long-run increases in adult smoking, then we are headed toward a substantial reversal in the downward trend in smoking in the United States.

There are two extreme possibilities for thinking about the linkage between youth smoking and adult smoking. At one extreme, which we label

---

9. Specifically, in 1997, median family income for white teens was $47,000, while it was only $25,000 for black teens. At the same time, median income was $3,000 among white teen mothers and $4,300 among black teen mothers.

Table 2.10 **Age of Initiation versus Current Smoking**

	Start at Age 12–14	Start at Age 15–17	Start at Age 18–20	Start at Age 21–25
Those age 28+:				
Smoke now?	.52	.49	.46	.52
Smoke every day?	.45	.41	.36	.42
Cigarettes per day	19.6	18.1	15.8	16.7
Those age 33+:				
Smoke now?	.49	.46	.43	.49
Smoke every day?	.42	.38	.35	.40
Cigarettes per day	20.4	18.6	16.3	16.8
Those age 38+:				
Smoke now?	.45	.43	.40	.46
Smoke every day?	.40	.36	.33	.38
Cigarettes per day	21.2	19.1	16.8	17.4

Note: Authors' tabulations of the 1992 NHIS and the 1995 NHIS. Each cell shows either the proportion smoking or cigarettes per day for the group indicated in the column heads at the age denoted for each panel.

the *public-health view,* all that matters for adult smoking are youth-smoking decisions. Since almost all smokers start as youths, if we could end youth smoking, we would end adult smoking. At the other extreme, which we label the *delayed-initiation view,* there is a fixed predisposition to experiment with cigarettes, and setting up barriers to youth smoking simply delays the period of experimentation until after the teen years. Under this view, reducing teen smoking has little effect on long-run adult smoking.

Some casual evidence on this issue is provided in table 2.10. This table presents cross-tabulations of the odds of smoking at older ages against the age of initiation, using data from the 1992 NHIS and the 1995 NHIS. We find that, as the public-health view would suggest, initiation at twelve to fourteen is worse than initiation in later teen years in terms of the subsequent likelihood of smoking. On the other hand, initiation at twenty-one to twenty-five appears to have similar implications for later smoking participation, if not intensity, as does initiation at twelve to fourteen. This is not simply an artifact of the feature of the data that, at any age past twenty-five, ages twenty-one to twenty-five are closer than are ages twelve to fourteen. As the age group used for this table ages, the relative relations persist; indeed, for those age thirty-eight and older, the odds of smoking participation are higher for those who started at ages twenty-one to twenty-five than they are for those who started at ages twelve to fourteen.

Of course, this evidence does not provide definitive evidence for either view described above since it may simply represent individual heterogeneity; the set of persons who begin smoking after age twenty may intend more to continue smoking at later ages. But it is nevertheless suggestive of the merit of the delayed-initiation view.

In this section, we take two approaches to trying to assess more rigorously the extent to which more youth smoking will translate into increased adult smoking. The first, and most direct, is to examine whether shifting patterns of smoking across cohorts of youths are reflected in the smoking rates of those cohorts as adults. This approach will yield an estimate of the relation between rising youth smoking and rising adult smoking that is free of individual heterogeneity bias; this is akin to using cohort dummies as instruments. But, while we attempt several approaches below, this method may not be able to disentangle general time-series effects from true cohort shifts in smoking propensities.

The second method is therefore to assess the implications for adult smoking of differential taxes on youths. That is, if there are two adults who face the same tax regime today but who faced different tax regimes as teens, by how much does their smoking differ? This approach has the advantage that it best approximates the experiment of interest, which is exogenously to induce some groups of teens to smoke and others not to smoke. But it has the disadvantage that one can infer the implications of our findings for the long-run implications of youth smoking only indirectly. To the extent that this indirect inference yields results similar to those yielded by the first method, then these provide two reinforcing approaches to estimating this important intertemporal correlation.

The only paper of which we are aware that attempts to carry out an exercise of this nature is Glied (1999), which examines the effect of cigarette taxes in the state where the smoker was fourteen on later smoking, using the National Longitudinal Survey of Youth (NLSY), and which finds no effect of youth taxes. But Glied's relatively small sample does not permit the inclusion of fixed effects for either state of birth or state of residence; also, the standard errors on her estimates are too large to rule out relatively sizable effects of youth taxes on later smoking.

2.4.1   Intertemporal Correlation across Cohorts

We first consider the extent of intertemporal correlation in smoking across cohorts, in two ways. First, we use data on smoking by high school seniors from the MTF data matched to the smoking of this same cohort ten years later, as twenty-seven- to twenty-eight-year-olds, from the Behavioral Risk Factor Surveillance System (BRFSS) data, which provide an annual survey of smoking rates for a large representative sample of the U.S. population. We match data from the period 1976–87 on smoking of high school seniors to data from 1986–97 on the smoking of this same cohort as twenty-seven-to twenty-eight-year-olds. We focus on young adults because this maximizes the number of cohort comparisons that we can make, given that the MTF data are not available before 1976.

The results of doing so are presented in the first panel of table 2.11. We first show a simple bivariate regression of the smoking of twenty-seven-to twenty-eight-year-olds on the smoking of this cohort as high school seniors

Table 2.11   **Intertemporal Correlations across Cohorts in Smoking Behavior**

	No Controls	Time Trends	Smoking among 42–43-Year-Olds	Time Trends & 42–43 Smoking
BRFSS 27–28-year-olds ($N = 12$, 1986–97):				
MTF high school senior smoking rate in year $t - 10$	.648 (.088)	.397 (.157)	.781 (.273)	.500 (.298)
Time trend		−.0030 (.0016)		−.0029 (.0017)
42–43-year-old smoking rate			−.202 (.389)	−.148 (.354)
NHIS 27–28-year-olds ($N = 36$, 1950–95):				
NHIS 17–18 smoking rate in year $t - 10$	.673 (.482)	1.185 (.131)	.067 (.179)	.350 (.127)
Time trend		−.0058 (.0002)		−.0044 (.0007)
42–43-year-old smoking rate			1.082 (.056)	.485 (.100)

Note: Standard errors are given in parentheses. Regressions in the first panel match data from the BRFSS on 27–28-year-olds and 42–43-year-old controls for 1986–97 to corresponding MTF data from 10 years earlier; second panel matches backcast data from the NHIS for 27–28- and 42–43-year-olds to data from 10 years earlier on 17–18-year-olds. First column is just bivariate regression of 27–28-year-old smoking rates on 17–18-year-old smoking rates; second column includes linear time trend; third column includes contemporaneous smoking rate of 42–43-year-olds; and final column includes both time trends and 42–43-year-olds.

ten years earlier. We find a very strong correlation, with a coefficient of 0.65. Of course, this finding may reflect simple secular trends in the data; if smoking is declining over time, even in the absence of any within-cohort correlation one will find that cohorts born later smoke less both as teens and as adults. We attempt to control for this in two ways in table 2.11. First, we include a linear time trend. This time trend is marginally significant, indicating a secular decline in smoking of 0.3 percentage points per year for this population over our twelve-year sample, and the coefficient on the lagged youth-smoking rate falls to 0.4. Second, we include the smoking rate in each year of forty-two to forty-three-year-olds as a proxy for trends in adult smoking that should not be determined by the smoking of high school seniors ten years earlier. This additional control is insignificant, and, when it is included with the time trend, the coefficient on lagged youth smoking actually rises to 0.5.

The disadvantage of this approach is its relatively narrow historical coverage. We therefore next turn to data from the NHIS, which in several years (1978, 1979, 1980, 1987, and 1988) asked current and former smokers the age at which they began smoking (as well as when they quit if they are former smokers). This allows us to calculate by cohort, not only their current smoking rate in the survey year, but their smoking rate when they were high school seniors (ages seventeen to eighteen) as well as when they were twenty-seven to twenty-eight and forty-two to forty-three.[10] We can then draw comparisons between the smoking rate of high school seniors and the smoking rate of those same youths as they age, but over a much larger historical range. We restrict the data to those persons age sixty and younger to minimize any bias to this exercise through the differential mortality of smokers. As a result, the earliest cohort comprises those who were sixty in 1978, or high school seniors in 1936 and forty-two- to forty-three-year-olds (our "control" group) in 1960. Data are available on adult smoking from these look-back surveys through 1988 and then from cross-sectional NHIS data sets through 1995. Thus, we can model the smoking of twenty-seven- to twenty-eight-year-olds on their smoking rates as seventeen- to eighteen-year-olds, and include forty-two- to forty-three-year-olds as a control, from 1960 through 1995 (thirty-six observations).

The results of doing so are shown in the next panel of table 2.11. Once again, when one simply examines the correspondence between the smoking of these cohorts as youths and their smoking as young adults, the correlation is quite strong, with a coefficient that is very similar to the first column of the top panel. But, once again, when we control for time trends, the coefficient falls, and here it falls farther when we control as well for the smoking of forty-two- to forty-three-year-olds (to capture general trends in taste for smoking). The final column reveals an intertemporal correlation of 0.35, a time trend of -0.44 percentage points per year over this period, and very significant positive effect of the smoking of older adults.

Thus, the findings from this first exercise suggest that higher smoking rates among youths translate in a significant way to the smoking rates of adults. The final estimates are similar across these data sets, suggesting an intertemporal correlation of 0.35 to 0.5. On the other hand, the fact that this estimate is significantly smaller than 1, even observing cohorts ten years later, suggests that the pure public-health view is not appropriate; there is more to reducing adult smoking than simply stopping youths from smoking.

2.4.2   Youth Taxes and Adult Smoking

The advantage of the cohort approach is that it yields relatively straightforward estimates of the intertemporal correlation across cohorts. The disadvantage is that it does not definitively prove that there is an important

---

10. For most years, we can backcast from more than one NHIS (e.g., for the cohort that was seventeen years old in 1940, we can use those who were fifty-five in 1978, fifty-six in 1979, and fifty-seven in 1980); in those cases, we average the smoking rates for each cohort that we obtain from the various years of the NHIS to reduce measurement error in the backcasted smoking rates. The NHIS also asks about age of initiation in 1992 and 1995 but not about age of quitting for former smokers, so this backcasting exercise is not possible in those years.

intertemporal correlation since there may be underlying time-series trends that cannot be captured by our controls. We therefore attempt the second approach laid out above, examining the effect of taxes on youths on their smoking as adults. Once again, the motivation is to use variation in taxes that individuals faced as youths, conditional on the tax environment in which they currently live, to provide exogenous variation in youth smoking for the purposes of assessing intertemporal correlations. There is significant variation in youth taxes, conditional on current taxes, even for nonmovers, owing to changes in state tax policy over time.

We use the Natality data used earlier—which, in addition to other strengths, also have information on the state of birth of these mothers— to assess the effect of the tax rate that teens faced on their smoking as adults. The regressor of interest here is the average tax rate in the teens' state of birth during the years when they were fourteen to seventeen years old. Of course, state of birth is not the ideal measure for this exercise since some individuals move between birth and the teen years. However, in the 1990 census, 74 percent of thirteen- to seventeen-year-olds lived in their state of birth, so this is a reasonable proxy for state of residence as a teen. Moreover, we (crudely) correct the estimates for mobility by using information on state of birth and state of residence. If the mother's state of birth is the same as her current state of residence, we assume that she was in that state as a teen. If not, we assume that she moved only from the state of birth to the state of residence (making no other moves) and assign her a weighted average of the tax rates in the two states when she was a teen. These weights come from tabulations from the NLSY, which was used to compute, for movers of a given age, at what age they moved; this provides a means of averaging the state of birth and the state of residence to reflect, given current age, the odds of moving before age fourteen.[11] In practice, this correction has little effect on the estimates; for the most reliable estimates, we will use nonmovers only to mitigate this measurement-error concern. We focus on women age twenty-four and older to allow for a sufficient lag to separate current and teen tax rates.

Since estimating this model on the 15 million observations in the micro data is impractical, we first convert the eight years of Natality data into a set of year of birth $\times$ year of survey $\times$ state of birth $\times$ state of residence cells. We then use the means of smoking rates in these cells to estimate models of smoking today on the tax rates in both the current state of residence and the state of birth, including fixed effects for each of these sets of states (residence and birth), for year of birth, for year of the survey, and for age. We also control for the racial composition of the cell and the share of the cell that are high school dropouts, are high school grad-

---

11. We are grateful to Phil Levine for providing us with these estimates from the NLSY.

uates, or have at least some college. All regressions are weighted by the cell counts.

The primary dependent variable is the average number of cigarettes smoked by women giving birth in the cell, incorporating zeros. We then decompose this effect into the effect on smoking participation and the effect on conditional smoking intensity. On average in the sample (as is shown in the bottom row of the regression in table 2.12), women who give birth smoke roughly 1.95 cigarettes per day. This consists of a participation rate of 15.8 percent and conditional cigarette consumption among those who do smoke of 12.85. These smoking rates can be compared to the full population of twenty-four- to forty-five-year-old females over this period, where smoking rates were 26 percent and conditional cigarettes per day were seventeen,[12] women giving birth smoke less than the typical adult, but smoking is still distressingly common in this population.

Table 2.12 shows the results that include both the contemporaneous tax and the teen tax along with the control variables described above. For total cigarettes smoked, we find an elasticity of −0.46.[13] This is almost identical to the overall elasticity of cigarettes smoked for adults estimated in either aggregate data (Becker, Grossman, and Murphy 1994) or micro data (Evans, Ringel, and Stech 1999). This effect is then decomposed into a large negative effect on participation, with an elasticity of −0.6, and a small positive effect on conditional intensity. As discussed earlier, this wrong-signed effect may be the result of sample selection into who remains a smoker as the tax changes. But the elasticity here is small in any case.

There is also a strong negative effect of the tax as a teen. The overall elasticity is −0.19, which is over 40 percent as large as the effect of current taxes. This arises from a participation elasticity of −0.06 and a negative conditional-intensity elasticity.

One problem noted above is that the tax rate is assigned with some error since we know only birthplace and not the state of residence as a teen. To mitigate this measurement error, in the second set of columns in table 2.12 we use only the sample of nonmovers, for whom we can presume that the state of both birth and current residence is the state in which the mother resided as a teen. For this sample, the effect of both current taxes and taxes as a teen is somewhat larger, and the effect of youth taxes is somewhat larger, with the result that the overall elasticity with respect to youth taxes is −0.22 and the participation elasticity −0.078.

These findings clearly provide evidence for the addictive nature of smoking: if one exogenously shifts women early in life to nonsmoking status with higher taxes, they will smoke less later in life as a result. But their

---

12. Authors' tabulations from the 1989–97 BRFSS data.

13. Even though we are using tax rates as the regressor here, we show price elasticities, assuming one for one pass-through of taxes to prices.

Table 2.12   The Effect of Current and Teen Taxes on the Smoking of Pregnant Women

	All			Nonmovers only		
	Cigarettes Smoked	Participation	Cigarettes/Day If Smoking	Cigarettes Smoked	Participation	Cigarettes/Day If Smoking
Current tax	-.810	-.080	.536	-.970	-.086	.327
	(.033)	(.002)	(.131)	(.064)	(.004)	(.186)
	[-.455]	[-.552]	[.046]	[-.513]	[-.559]	[.028]
Teen tax	-.480	-.013	-.678	-.598	-.017	-.500
	(.061)	(.004)	(.242)	(.111)	(.007)	(.324)
	[-.188]	[-.061]	[-.040]	[-.221]	[-.078]	[-.030]
% high school dropout	5.73	.390	4.66	3.98	.256	7.26
	(.038)	(.002)	(.134)	(.228)	(.017)	(.677)
% high school graduate	2.93	.214	1.90	3.59	.255	3.94
	(.018)	(.001)	(.079)	(.136)	(.010)	(.409)
% some college	1.56	.121	.797	2.84	.260	.902
	(.021)	(.001)	(.094)	(.166)	(.012)	(.512)
% white	.838	.022	2.58	2.31	.102	6.19
	(.045)	(.003)	(.189)	(.347)	(.026)	(1.14)
% black	-.047	.015	-1.87	2.72	.210	1.47
	(.049)	(.003)	(.205)	(.361)	(.027)	(1.18)
% Hispanic	-2.71	-.178	-3.17	-3.20	-.218	-6.11
	(.042)	(.003)	(.181)	(.258)	(.019)	(.844)
No. of observations	337,690	338,167	182,379	9,941	9,947	8,945
Mean of dependent variable	1.95	.158	12.85	2.07	.167	12.86

Note: Standard errors are given in parentheses, price elasticities in square brackets. Coefficients are those from regressions that also include the full set of dummy variables for state of birth, state of residence, year of birth, year of survey, and age.

magnitudes are difficult to interpret in a vacuum. To do so, we can compare the elasticity of adult smoking with respect to youth taxes to the earlier estimates of the elasticity of youth smoking with respect to youth taxes. Such a comparison is not fully direct since these women were youths during the period 1957–85 and our estimates pertain to the 1990s, but these youth elasticities nevertheless provide a sensible benchmark. In the MTF data, over all youths (since this exercise compares average youth taxes to adult smoking), the elasticity of smoking participation with respect to price is −0.31. We find here that the elasticity of participation as an adult with respect to youth taxes is −0.078, or 25 percent as large. Thus, these results imply that there is an intertemporal correlation coefficient of −0.25.

Thus, we conclude that there is evidence for both hypotheses about the potential effect of youth smoking. Youth smoking is clearly an important determinant of adult smoking, with an intertemporal correlation of from −0.25 to −0.5, and our second piece of evidence suggests in particular that the taxes that youths face clearly have an important effect on the decision to smoke many years later. But youth smoking is by no means the sole, or even the primary, determinant of smoking later in life; indeed, the taxes that smokers face as adults are significantly more important than the taxes that they faced as youths.

2.5   Conclusions

The 1990s is a decade that has produced a very mixed track record with respect to risky behaviors among youths. While teen births and crime rates are steeply down (Levine, chap. 4 in this volume; Levitt and Lochner, chap. 7 in this volume), we have shown here that rates of substance use, and particularly smoking rates, are rising. The increase in smoking rates is particularly vexing given the expected, widely postulated intertemporal correlation between the decisions of youths to smoke and their subsequent smoking as adults, with the corresponding costly effects on health.

We have attempted to investigate several aspects of the youth-smoking question in this paper in an effort to advance our understanding of what drives these important decisions. We report four findings of interest. First, smoking participation is not simply concentrated among the most disadvantaged youths; indeed, increasingly over time, youth smoking is taking place among white, suburban youths with college-educated parents and good grades. Second, we show that neither changes in demographic characteristics nor changes in attitudes toward smoking can explain the striking increase in smoking rates in the 1990s.

Third, we find that the single greatest policy determinant of youth smoking is the price of cigarettes. We consistently estimate across several data sets that older teens are very sensitive to the price of cigarettes, with a central price-elasticity estimate of -0.67. This estimate implies that the sharp reduction in cigarette prices in the early 1990s can explain roughly 26 percent of the increase in smoking over the subsequent six years. Moreover, this price sensitivity rises for more socioeconomically disadvantaged groups such as blacks or those with less-educated parents.

At the same time, we find that younger teens are not sensitive to prices on average, nor is there any relation between price sensitivity and socioeconomic status for younger teens. These findings suggest important heterogeneity in the teen population. Younger teens appear to be price-insensitive experimenters who evolve into more price-sensitive smokers by their older teen years. An important priority for future work in this area is to understand the evolution of smoking between the younger and the older teenage years.

These findings also hold out little hope for other policies as a means of reducing youth smoking. We do find some evidence that policies that restrict youth access to cigarettes reduce the quantity of cigarettes smoked by the youths so affected, but this finding is not nearly as robust as the price relation. There is no consistent evidence that restrictions on smoking in public places decrease smoking.

Finally, the results imply that this rise in youth smoking will have important implications for the long-run stock of smokers in the United States. Evidence from two different approaches, examining the intertemporal correlation across cohorts and modeling the effect of youth taxes on adult smoking, suggests that between 25 and 50 percent of the rise in youth smoking will persist into adulthood. Over this period, smoking rose by 8 percentage points for high school seniors in the MTF survey. This implies a long-run rise in the adult-smoking rate of 2–4 percentage points. Compared to the current adult-smoking rate of 25 percent, this is a rise of 8–16 percent, a nontrivial increase. Of course, whether this recent rise will persist into adulthood in the manner suggested by past cohort shifts is unclear. The technology for quitting smoking has improved dramatically in recent years, and these youths are moving into workplaces that almost universally ban smoking, raising significantly the hassle costs of maintaining a habit. But the historical record speaks clearly, which should indicate a very significant rise in adult smoking going forward.

On the other hand, the recent decline in youth smoking in the face of modest price increases suggests that this may cause, not a permanent upward shift in adult smoking, but perhaps a "bulge" in smoking rates across cohorts. The prices of cigarettes rose by roughly 30 percent over the course of 1999, as a result of a shifting forward by tobacco manufacturers of the costs of settling their state lawsuits. Using the estimates presented here, this price rise should cause a 20 percent decline in youth smoking, which would almost fully undo the rise from 1991 to 1997.

Even if the rise from 1991 to 1997 was a transitory one, however, the long-run health consequences could be substantial. A 2–4 percentage point rise in smoking for this seven-year cohort, along with a somewhat reduced increase for the 1998 cohort of high school seniors (as prices began to rise), implies 477,000–954,000 more adult smokers. Of course, some of these adults will then quit in their adult years, and those who quit sufficiently before the age of greatest medical risk from smoking (age sixty on) can substantially reduce their mortality risk. On the basis of the NHIS data for 1987–88 on age of initiation and age of quitting, we can estimate that, of those who started smoking as youths and are still smoking at age thirty-five, 45 percent will quit by age sixty. So a conservative estimate is that 263,000–525,000 additional persons will have their lives shortened owing to increased smoking.

As noted above, smoking throughout one's life shortens life expectancy by 6.5 years for men and 5.7 years for women. Taking a simple average across men and women, this implies that the rise in youth smoking will cause a reduction of 1.6–3.2 million life years, even if this rise is totally undone. At a value of $100,000 per life year (Cutler and Richardson 1997), and discounted at a real 3 percent rate from age sixty-nine (typical life expectancy for smokers) to age nineteen, this is a forgone value of life years in today's dollars of $36–$73 billion. Once again, this is a vast oversimplification as both quitting technologies and the mortality effects of smoking are evolving rapidly over time. But it suggests the importance of even a potentially transitory rise in youth smoking for the health of the U.S. population.

Overall, these results imply that policy makers should be concerned about rising youth smoking; even if there is not a one-for-one translation into higher adult-smoking rates, the health implications can be enormous. And this concern should lead policy makers to consider cigarette taxes as the most effective means of reducing youth smoking. Of course, with youths smoking only about 2 percent of cigarette packs, taxes are a very blunt instrument with which to address youth-smoking issues. Thus, there are a host of additional issues that must be considered in deriving the optimal cigarette tax beyond considerations of youth smoking; Chaloupka and Warner (in press), Evans, Ringel, and Stech (1999), and Gruber and Koszegi (2000) provide further discussions of these factors. But the results presented here suggest that consideration of optimal cigarette-tax policy must include the very strong effect that taxes have on teen smoking.

Appendix
Youth-Access Index

Our Youth-Access Index (YAI) is based on the National Cancer Institute's (NCI) decision criteria for rating state youth-access laws. The NCI's criteria include nine categories: minimum age of purchase; packaging; clerk intervention; photo identification; vending-machine availability; free distribution; graduated penalties; random inspections; and statewide enforcement. For each category, a score is granted on a scale of 1–4 or 1–5 as a function of the stringency of state regulation in that area. For example, states get a score of 0 if the minimum age is younger than eighteen; a score of 3 if the minimum age is eighteen but there is no requirement of signposting and/or there is no specific penalty for failure to post a sign; a score of 4 if the minimum age is eighteen with specific signposting requirements and penalties for failure to post; and a score of 5 if there is a minimum age older than eighteen and there are posting/penalty provisions. These scores are then summed across categories to get a total access index score. Then states' points are reduced by two points (to a minimum score of 0) if they allow their state regulation to preempt a stricter local ordinance.

While the general framework of the two indexes is the same, the YAI contains several variations in order to describe state tobacco laws in more detail. The largest difference is the inclusion of three categories in addition to the nine utilized by the NCI—advertising, licensing, and restrictions on minors. Points are awarded for advertising restrictions on a scale between 1 and 4. A state earns a score of 1 for minimal limitations (no advertising on school buses etc.) and a score of 4 for a ban on all tobacco advertisements. Including licensing in the YAI captures the extent to which retailers, vendors, and wholesalers are regulated by state agencies. Maximum licensing requirements (applicable to retailers, vendors, and wholesalers) received a score of 4, while states mandating only wholesale licenses received a score of 1. The restrictions-on-minors category encompasses laws relating to the underage purchase, possession, and use of tobacco. Those states outlawing these actions but implementing no penalties for violating the laws received a score between 0 and 1. The highest possible score, 4, is given to states outlawing the purchase, possession, and use and implementation of graduated penalties.

The YAI also allows for more point levels under each category than does the NCI index to create a finer gradation between the stringency of various laws. For example, one problem with the minimum-age categorization noted above is that some states mandate signage at the point of purchase while others mandate signage but not at the point of purchase; we awarded the latter group of states a score of 3.5 instead of 4. This affected twenty-one states overall. Similar half-point steps were added to the scoring of each of the nine original NCI categories. The purpose of this variation from the NCI index was to distinguish more clearly between the stringency of varying state requirements.

In several instances we also altered scoring decisions made by the NCI in the final computation of state scores. After extensive investigation of state laws and statutes, several inconsistencies were discovered between the laws and the NCI point allotment. For example, on consultation with NCI representatives, it was revealed that Connecticut received a score of 2 for the vending-machine category in 1996. The justification for this score was that a 1996 law added new restrictions. However, certain sections of the law did not take effect until after the time period of the NCI study. Since the law had already passed, however, the NCI awarded points to reflect that fact. For this project, however, this point assignment was inappropriate. Credit for laws was awarded only after those laws came into effect. Therefore, the YAI contains several modifications to the factual basis of the NCI index.

Table 2A.1   Means of Regulatory Variables in the MTF Survey

	12th Graders	8th & 10th Graders	8th–12th Graders
Access index	11.91	11.69	11.76
	(5.29)	(5.46)	(5.41)
Clean air:			
Private workplace	.44	.44	.44
	(.50)	(.50)	(.50)
Government workplace	.73	.71	.72
	(.44)	(.45)	(.45)
Restaurants	.64	.61	.62
	(.48)	(.49)	(.49)
Schools	.90	.85	.87
	(.30)	(.36)	(.34)
Other	.93	.91	.92
	(.25)	(.29)	(.28)
No. of observations	106,539	230,126	336,665

Note: From authors' tabulations of 1991–97 MTF restricted sample data described in the text. Standard deviations are given in parentheses.

References

Alciati, Marianne H., et al. 1998. State laws on youth access to tobacco in the United States: Measuring their extensiveness with a new rating system. *Tobacco Control* 7:345–52.

Becker, Gary S., Michael Grossman, and Kevin Murphy. 1994. An empirical analysis of cigarette addiction. *American Economic Review* 84:396–418.

Becker, Gary, and Kevin Murphy. 1988. A theory of rational addiction. *Journal of Political Economy* 96:675–700.

Chaloupka, Frank J., and Michael Grossman. 1996. Price, tobacco control policies, and youth smoking. Working Paper no. 5740. Cambridge, Mass.: National Bureau of Economic Research.

Chaloupka, Frank J., and Rosalie Pacula. 1998. Limiting youth access to tobacco: The early impact of the Synar amendment on youth smoking. University of Illinois at Chicago. Mimeo.

Chaloupka, Frank, Rosalie Pacula, Matthew Farrelly, Lloyd Johnston, and Patrick O'Malley. 1998. Do higher cigarette prices encourage youth to use marijuana? Working Paper no. 6939. Cambridge, Mass.: National Bureau of Economic Research.

Chaloupka, Frank J., and Kenneth Warner. In press. The economics of smoking. In *Handbook of health economics,* ed. Anthony Culyer and Joseph Newhouse. Amsterdam: North-Holland.

Coalition on Smoking OR Health. American Lung Association. Various years. *State legislated actions on tobacco issues.* Washington, D.C.

Cutler, David, and Elizabeth Richardson. 1997. Measuring the health of the U.S. population. *Brookings Papers on Economic Activity: Microeconomics,* 217–82.

Cutler, David, et al. 1999. The economic impacts of the tobacco settlement. Harvard University. Mimeo.

DeCicca, Philip, Donald Kenkel, and Alan Mathios. 1998. Putting out the fires: Will higher cigarette taxes reduce youth smoking? Cornell University. Mimeo.

Dee, Thomas. 1999. The complementarity of teen smoking and drinking. *Journal of Health Economics* 18, no. 6 (December): 769–93.

Department of Health and Human Services (DHHS). 1994. *Preventing tobacco use among young people: A report of the surgeon general.* Washington, D.C.: U.S. Government Printing Office.

Evans, William N., and Lynn Huang. 1998. Cigarette taxes and teen smoking: New evidence from panels of repeated cross-sections. Working paper. University of Maryland, Department of Economics.

Evans, William, Jeanne Ringel, and Diana Stech. 1999. Tobacco taxes and public policy to discourage smoking. In *Tax policy and the economy 13,* ed. James Poterba. Cambridge, Mass.: MIT Press.

Glied, Sherry. 1999. Youth tobacco policy: Reconciling theory and evidence. Columbia University. Mimeo.

Gruber, Jonathan, and Botond Koszegi. 2000. Is addiction rational? Theory and evidence. Working Paper no. 7507. Cambridge, Mass.: National Bureau of Economic Research, January.

Jacobson, Peter D., and Jeffrey Wasserman. 1997. *Tobacco control laws: Implementation and enforcement.* Santa Monica, Calif.: Rand.

Jason, Leonard A., Peter Ji, Michael Anes, and Scott Birkhead. 1991. Active enforcement of cigarette control laws in prevention of cigarette sales to minors. *Journal of the American Medical Association* 266:3159–61.

Lewitt, Eugene, and Douglas Coate. 1982. The potential for using excise taxes to reduce smoking. *Journal of Health Economics* 1:121–45.

Lewitt, Eugene, Douglas Coate, and Michael Grossman. 1981. The effects of government regulation on teenage smoking. *Journal of Law and Economics* 24: 545–69.

Rigotti, Nancy, et al. 1997. The effect of enforcing tobacco-sales laws on adolescents' access to tobacco and smoking behavior. *New England Journal of Medicine* 337:1044–51.

Tobacco Institute. 1998. *The tax burden on tobacco.* Richmond, Va.

Wasserman, Jeffrey, Willard Manning, Joseph Newhouse, and John Winkler. 1991. The effects of excise taxes and regulations on cigarette smoking. *Journal of Health Economics* 10:43–64.

3

Teens and Traffic Safety

Thomas S. Dee and William N. Evans

Hollywood has always portrayed teens and cars as a volatile mixture. Whether it was the game of chicken from *Rebel without a Cause,* the drag race in *American Graffiti,* or the misadventures with dad's car in *Risky Business* and *Ferris Bueller's Day Off,* a teen behind the wheel of a car has always moved the plot along to some calamitous event. Although movies are sometimes a poor barometer of what ails society, unfortunately in this case these depictions may not be too far from the truth. In 1997 alone, there were 10,208 motor-vehicle fatalities among young adults aged fifteen to twenty-four, accounting for roughly one-third of all deaths in this age group. Motor-vehicle fatalities are far and away the leading cause of death among young adults.

The large fraction of deaths among young adults attributed to car travel is not entirely unexpected. Driving is an inherently risky activity, and the young rarely die of other nonviolent causes.[1] Furthermore, teens are increasingly dependent on automobiles. In 1995, the average teen aged sixteen to nineteen traveled 11,500 miles in cars, many of them as the driver. This number is nearly double the value for 1983, when teens traveled an average of only 5,861 miles per year in cars.[2] However, although a certain

Thomas S. Dee is assistant professor of economics at Swarthmore College. William N. Evans is professor of economics at the University of Maryland, a research associate of the National Bureau of Economic Research, and a senior research associate for the Project HOPE Center for Health Affairs.

The authors thank Jon Gruber for a number of helpful comments and Diana Stech and Julie Topeleski for excellent research assistance.

1. In 1997, accidents of all forms, homicides and other legal interventions, and suicides accounted for 24,797 of the 31,544 deaths of young adults.

2. Authors' calculations based on data from the 1983 and 1995 National Personal Transportation Survey.

amount of traffic-related injury and death is to be expected, teens die at a rate far higher than do older drivers. The teen motor-vehicle-fatality rate (defined as deaths per 100,000 people) is nearly double the rate for adults aged twenty-five and up. When fatalities are denominated by miles of travel, this ratio is nearly 2.5. Part of this difference is almost surely due to the lack of driving experience among teens. For example, compared to older drivers, teens are much more likely to die as occupants in accidents where general driver error is the cause, such as single-vehicle crashes and vehicle rollovers. However, much of the difference in rates across age groups is due specifically to the fact that teens tend to take more risks than do older drivers. In a recent National Highway Traffic Safety Administration (NHTSA) telephone survey, 60 percent of teen drivers reported that they were more likely to pass other cars than to be passed, 16 percentage points higher than the number for twenty-five- to thirty-four-year-olds and more than twice the rate for adults thirty-five to forty-four.[3] In the same survey, 67 percent of teens said that they tended to keep up with faster cars when driving in heavy traffic, a slightly lower rate than that for twenty-one- to twenty-four-year-olds (69 percent) but substantially higher than the responses for twenty-five- to thirty-four- and thirty-five- to forty-four-year-olds (58 and 48 percent, respectively). Nearly all studies have found that young people, and males in particular, were the most likely to be involved in fall-asleep crashes (Pack et al. 1995; Horne and Reyner 1995). Teens are also less likely than adults are to use an important traffic-safety device, a seat belt. Data from the Centers for Disease Control (CDC) indicate that, nationally, belt-use rates are about 10 percentage points higher for adults than for teens aged eighteen and nineteen. Finally, nearly one-quarter of all teen car-occupant fatalities are alcohol related, with the vast majority of these cases being single-vehicle crashes. Interestingly, the fraction of alcohol involvement for adults aged twenty-five and older is only 4 percentage points higher than that for teens, although all states now have a minimum legal drinking age of twenty-one.

In this chapter, we examine four broad questions about teen traffic safety: How has teen traffic safety changed in the past twenty-five years, and what are the possible causes of these changes? Why are teen drivers worse than adults? Who are the bad teen drivers? Which government policies have influenced teen traffic safety? These are by no means an exhaustive set of questions, but, given the trends in travel patterns and government regulation, we believe that we have isolated a number of interesting results that shed light on this risky and highly costly aspect of teen behavior. Our task for this project was made simpler by the extraordinary number of data sets available that include information about teen traffic safety

---

3. Results of the NHTSA aggressive driving survey can be found at http://www.nhtsa.dot. gov/people/injury/aggressive/unsafe/att-beh/Chapt4.html#1.

and risk taking. Specifically, we used data from a variety of national data sets, including the Fatal Accident Reporting System, the National Personal Transportation Survey, the National Automotive Sampling Survey, the Behavioral Risk Factor Surveillance Survey, the Youth Risk Behavioral Surveillance Survey, and the NHTSA 19 City Survey. We supplemented these sources with demographic data at the state level about the size of the teen population as well as other basic demographic data. We also utilized a number of published sources to isolate the timing of several important state policy changes.

The paper has three main sections. In section 3.1, we summarize the traits and trends in teen traffic safety. In section 3.2, we identify the observed characteristics of risky teen drivers by examining self-reports of hazardous driving practices. Finally, in section 3.3, we look at a number of important state policies that have been adopted over the past twenty-five years that have important ramifications for teen traffic safety. This discussion focuses, in particular, on four classes of state-level policies: policies that influence youth access to alcohol; policies directed at the specific and general deterrence of drunk driving; mandatory seat-belt laws; and highway speed limits. In the final section, we summarize our findings on this important dimension of risky teen behavior.

3.1   Teen Traffic Fatalities—Traits, Trends, and Hypotheses

3.1.1   Teen Traffic Fatalities—Historical and Cross-Sectional Data

To help focus our discussion, we first present cross-sectional and time-series evidence of the demographics of teen traffic safety. Our goal is to provide some evidence about the characteristics of traffic accidents that involve teens, who gets into accidents, and how key factors have changed over time. In this section, we focus on one particular type of traffic accident, namely, that which produces fatalities. This decision will obviously capture only one dimension of teen driving, and, clearly, there are other types of costs generated by such accidents. More specifically, the morbidity and property damage generated by traffic accidents involving teens are not trivial. Our decision is, however, guided by the relative importance of traffic fatalities and by the availability of high-quality, nationally representative data on motor-vehicle fatalities over a long period of time.

The primary data set used to construct the numerator in a motor-vehicle-fatality rate is the Fatal Accident Reporting System (FARS). The FARS is a census of motor accidents resulting in an occupant or a nonmotorist fatality within thirty days of the accident. The FARS collects data that describe the accident, the vehicle, all the persons involved, and the drivers. The FARS is administered by the NHTSA, and data are collected at the state level by FARS analysts, who utilize such information as police

Table 3.1   Distribution of Motor-Vehicle Fatalities, 1998

Type of Fatality/Group	Count/% of Passenger-Vehicle-Occupant Fatalities		
	16–19	20–24	25+
Motor-vehicle fatalities	4,643	4,853	28,880
% motor-vehicle occupants	93.3	91.7	84.1
% car occupants	88.8	82.7	74.6
Among car occupants (%):			
Males	65.1	74.2	61.8
Used seat belt	28.7	26.4	38.2
In car with air bag	17.4	21.4	23.6
Driver	59.7	68.1	75.6
Alcohol was involved	25.8	48.9	29.8
Friday/Saturday accident	35.3	36.0	33.4
Nighttime accident	52.8	61.7	36.5
Accident on Friday/Saturday night	20.9	23.9	13.8
By type of incident:			
Multivehicle	41.6	39.1	57.5
Single vehicle	43.6	46.4	31.9
Noncollision	14.8	14.5	10.6

reports, driver's-license and vehicle-registration data, death certificates, and hospital and emergency-room reports as well as other sources. Data are available beginning in 1975.

We begin the analysis by presenting, in table 3.1, the distribution of motor-vehicle deaths in 1998 for three age groups: teens sixteen to nineteen; young adults twenty to twenty-four; and adults twenty-five and older. This table provides a useful backdrop for establishing important stylized facts and for exploring what might constitute meaningful measures of teen traffic-fatality rates. Of the 4,643 motor-vehicle fatalities among teens in 1998, the vast majority are vehicle occupants, with almost 89 percent being fatalities among car occupants.[4] Nonoccupant deaths in all age categories are predominately among pedestrians. Adults have a much smaller fraction of car-occupant deaths than do younger people because a larger fraction of adults deaths occur in commercial trucks. Given the preponderance of teen deaths in cars, we present in the bottom portion of the table the fraction of all car-occupant deaths in particular groups. In all groups, the majority of deaths are among males, but this gender differential is higher among younger populations. There are a number of other intriguing results that also signal the relative prevalence of risk taking among teen drivers. First, teens have low belt-use rates, and they are more likely to be

4. We define *car occupants* as people in cars, vans, minivans, sport-utility vehicles, and light trucks.

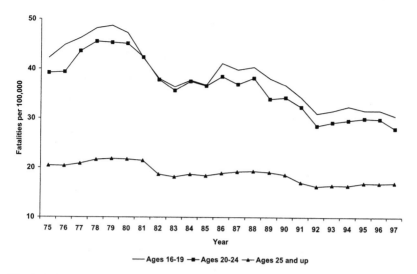

Fig. 3.1   Motor-vehicle-fatality rate

in a car without an air bag relative to the older adults. Second, one-quarter of all teen deaths are alcohol related.[5] This rate is surprisingly only 4 percentage points lower than the rate for adults even though all states have adopted minimum legal drinking ages of twenty-one. For adults, three-quarters of car-occupant deaths are drivers. However, among teens, fewer than 60 percent are drivers, indicating that teens are substantially more likely to be passengers in fatal accidents. In the case of teens, most passenger fatalities occur in cars driven by other teens. The fraction of fatalities that happen on a Friday or Saturday is similar across age groups. However, teen traffic fatalities are more concentrated during the nighttime. Likewise, one-fifth of teen car-occupant fatalities happen on a Friday or Saturday night, compared to roughly one-sixth of adult deaths. Certain types of vehicle accidents are more likely to be caused by driver error than are others. For example, it is easier to assign driver blame in single-vehicle crashes and noncollision accidents like vehicle rollovers. Teens are much more likely to be involved in these types of crashes than are adults. About 60 percent of teen occupant deaths are single-vehicle crashes or noncollision accidents like rollovers, compared to just over 40 percent for adults.

In figure 3.1, we report the time series of motor-vehicle-accident rates for the three age groups over the period 1975–97. A fatality rate should

5. The NHTSA defines a traffic-related fatality as alcohol involved if anyone involved in the accident has a blood-alcohol concentration (BAC) of 0.01 or more. BAC measures the weight of alcohol in a given volume of blood (grams per deciliter) and can be identified through an evaluation of breath, blood, urine, or saliva. Since BAC data are not available for all participants in fatal accidents, the NHTSA imputes some data.

control for the underlying exposure of the population to risk. In this case, we use a simple measure of exposure, namely, fatalities per 100,000 people in the given age group. Population is a coarse measure of exposure to risk since driving intensity may vary considerably across age groups. But, given the lack of data on miles of travel by time and age, we start with this admittedly restrictive measure. The numbers in figure 3.1 demonstrate that the teen vehicle-fatality rate is roughly comparable to that for adults aged twenty to twenty-four and that both are about twice as large as the rate for adults aged twenty-five and older. The time-series pattern in all three series is similar, showing a large increase in rates during the late 1970s, a rapid decline in fatalities during the 1980s recession, a slight increase in rates through 1986, then a steady decline in rates until 1992. After 1992, fatality rates have been relatively constant. The long-term decline in teen fatality rates since the peak value in 1979 is stunning. Between 1979 and 1997, traffic-fatality rates for teens fell by 37 percent. Much of the drop occurred over the period 1986–92, when rates fell 25 percent. The drop in teen fatality rates is much larger than the drop for adults aged twenty-five and older, where fatality rates fell by 22 percent in the period 1979–97 and by 13 percent between 1986 and 1992. In figure 3.2, we report single-age fatality rates for teens aged sixteen to nineteen over the same period. The general time-series pattern is very similar to that reported in figure 3.1 above, with rates declining for all age groups after 1986. In general, these rates are monotonically higher for older drivers. However, this difference has converged over time with particularly strong reductions in traffic fatalities among older teens.

The motor-vehicle-fatality rate includes many type of victims, including drivers, occupants, passengers on public transportation, pedestrians, bik-

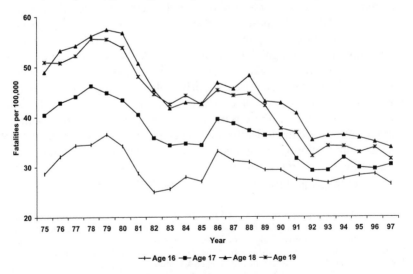

Fig. 3.2   Motor-vehicle-fatality rates for teens

ers, etc. The results shown in table 3.1 above illustrated that teen motor-
vehicle fatalities are primarily from accidents involving the family car, but,
in comparison to older adults, there are a higher fraction of nondriver-
occupant deaths among teens. Therefore, a measure that may more accu-
rately reflect risk taking by teens is the prevalence of fatalities in passenger
vehicles. Using data from the FARS for the years 1975–97, we construct
passenger-vehicle-fatality rates for each of the three age groups. In figures
3.3 and 3.4, we repeat the structure of the two previous graphs using

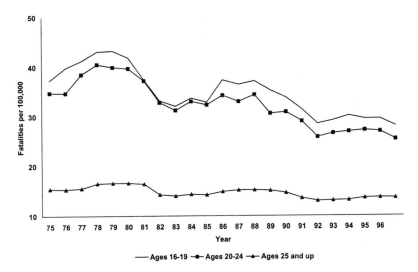

Fig. 3.3   Passenger-car-occupant-fatality rates

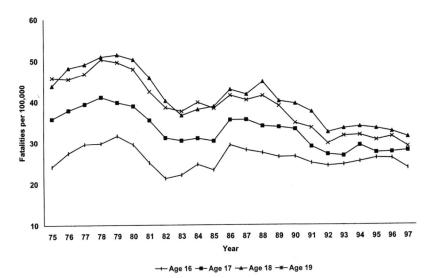

Fig. 3.4   Passenger-car-occupant-fatality rates among teens

passenger-vehicle-fatality rates as the outcome. Since teen fatalities are heavily concentrated among passenger-vehicle occupants, the trends and relative magnitudes of changes for this outcome are roughly comparable to the motor-vehicle deathrate numbers in figures 3.1 and 3.2 above. In contrast, the drop in occupant fatalities among adults twenty-five and older is less dramatic (17 percent) than that in the total vehicle fatality rate (22 percent).

As suggested earlier, denominating fatality rates with population is a coarse way in which to measure exposure to risks. The risks could vary considerably across groups if, for example, the types of roads, the types of travel, or the amount of travel varies across groups. Unfortunately, detailed data about these factors are sparse, and, therefore, we can view changes in fatality rates that are defined by different denominators only for particular years. More specifically, we can produce relatively detailed and age-specific estimates of car travel by relying on data from the National Personal Transportation Survey (NPTS).[6] The NPTS is a nationally representative survey of U.S. households. The NPTS is sponsored by the Federal Highway Administration and has been conducted in 1969, 1977, 1983, 1990, and 1995. In this chapter, we employ data from the three most recent surveys. Information is collected for all household members aged five and older. Data for children five to thirteen were reported by a household adult, and persons fourteen and older were interviewed directly. Information was collected about all trips taken by surveyed household members during a designated twenty-four-hour period (the "travel day" file) and about trips of seventy-five miles or more taken during the preceding fourteen-day period (the "travel period" file). The survey collected data on mode of transportation, trip purpose, distance, and time of trip. These values are used to construct aggregate estimates of annual travel. In 1995, data were collected from about forty-two thousand households. Roughly twenty-two thousand households were interviewed in 1990 and roughly sixty-four hundred in 1983.

From the day-trip data file, we calculated the distance of motor-vehicle trips in personal vehicles for all respondents. Using the sample weights, we then calculated the annual miles of car travel by age for the 1983, 1990, and 1995 surveys. We then constructed age-specific car-occupant-fatality rates for these years using vehicle miles of travel as the denominator. These results are reported in table 3.2. In the first columns, we report per capita vehicle miles of travel by age group for the three survey years. Notice that, for all three years of data, teens have much lower miles of car travel than do adults. In 1983, for example, adults twenty-five and older had 36 percent more per capita miles of travel than did teens. These results suggest

6. A detailed description of and data for the NPTS can be found at http://www.bts.gov/ntda/npts.

that conventional population-based fatality rates (e.g., fig. 3.3) vastly understate the difference in fatality risks across age groups. In 1983, for example, the ratio of age sixteen to nineteen to age twenty-five and older vehicle-occupant-fatality rates when rates are constructed using population is 2.2, but the ratio is just slightly over 3.0 when rates are constructed by vehicles of travel. The disparity in vehicle miles of travel across age groups fell considerably over the next twelve years. Between 1983 and 1995, per capita vehicle miles of travel increased from 5,861 to 11,498 for teens, a jump of 96 percent. In contrast, per capita miles of travel increased by only 69 percent for adults twenty-five and older. This implies that the population-denominated rates in figure 3.1 above understate the considerable gains in traffic safety among teens. To see this in more detail, in table 3.3 we report the change in fatality rates by age group for the periods 1983–95 and 1990–95. We report the change in rates for both the population- and the miles-denominated fatality rates. Notice that, using

Table 3.2   Passenger-Vehicle-Occupant-Fatality Rates, 1983, 1990, and 1995

Age Group	Annual per Person Car Miles of Travel	Fatalities per 100,000 People	Fatalities per Billion Car Miles of Travel
	1983		
16–19	5,861	32.06	54.22
20–24	9,773	31.21	31.62
25+	7,972	14.00	17.40
	1990		
16–19	8,218	33.78	40.74
20–24	10,177	30.85	30.01
25+	9,293	14.63	15.64
	1995		
16–19	11,498	29.48	25.43
20–24	12,656	27.20	21.29
25+	13,503	13.59	9.97

Sources: Fatalities are taken from the FARS. Occupant miles are taken from the 1983, 1990, and 1995 NPTS.

Table 3.3   Percentage Changes in Passenger-Vehicle-Occupant-Fatality Rates

Age Group	1983–95		1990–95	
	Fatalities per 100,000 People	Fatalities per Billion Car Miles of Travel	Fatalities per 100,000 People	Fatalities per Billion Car Miles of Travel
16–19	−8.0	−52.5	−12.7	−37.8
20–24	−12.8	−32.7	−11.8	−29.1
25+	−2.9	−42.7	−7.1	−36.3

population-denominated rates, there was only an 8 percent reduction in teen fatalities from 1983 to 1995 and a 12.7 percent reduction over the period 1990–95. Both these changes were substantially larger than the drop in rates for adults aged twenty-five and older. In contrast, the drop in rates is much more dramatic in both periods when one considers the large increase in vehicle miles traveled by teens. Over the period 1983–95, fatality rates denominated by miles fell by over 50 percent for teens and 43 percent for adults. Over the period 1990–95, the drop in fatality rates denominated by miles was similar for teens and older adults, in the 36–38 percent range. Because of the large increase in miles of travel over the period, the ratio of the teen miles-denominated fatality rate to the adult rate fell to 2.5 by 1995.

The trends in teen traffic fatalities also exhibit a distinctive heterogeneity with respect to gender, with most of the gains in traffic safety over this period concentrated among males. In figure 3.5, we report the percentage of car-occupant fatalities that are males by each age group. Notice that, for all age groups, we observe a large drop in the fraction male over the period 1982–97. For example, among teens, the fraction of fatalities that are male falls 11 percent between 1982 and 1997, from about three-quarters of all deaths to just over two-thirds. When we graph the male and female car-occupant-fatality rates by sex for teens (see fig. 3.6), we see that the drop is driven by a much larger reduction in the male deathrate. Between 1982 and 1997, male teen deathrates fell by 32 percent, about twice the rate for female teens.

There are a number of possible explanations for why teen car travel in-

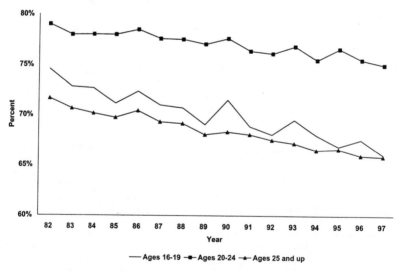

Fig. 3.5   Percentage of total motor-vehicle fatalities that are male

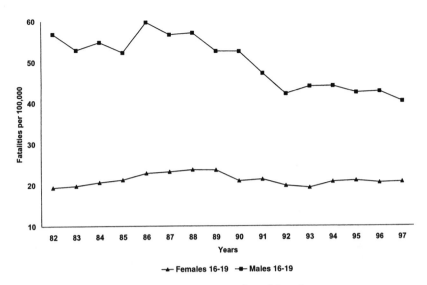

Fig. 3.6   Total motor-vehicle-fatality rates, male and female teens

creased so dramatically between 1983 and 1995. However, we should first note that car travel increased for all other age groups as well, so the increase among teens is part of a larger trend toward more car travel in society. Nonetheless, we can begin considering the increases in teen driving by first identifying a determinant that does not appear to explain the trends. There appears to have been no large change in the fraction of teens working or in teen labor income over this period. Using data from the 1984 and 1996 March Current Population Survey (CPS), we calculated a number of labor market variables for those aged seventeen to twenty. Since the March CPS provides labor market data for the previous year, these samples represent work for those aged sixteen to nineteen (roughly) in 1983 and 1995. Over these years, there was little change in teen work. The fraction of teens with labor income in these years was 68.3 and 68.2 percent, respectively. Likewise, real annual labor market earnings (in 1995 dollars) increased only slightly, from $3,910 in 1983 to $4,034 in 1995.

Part of the increase in car travel can potentially be explained by greater vehicle ownership in households with teens. Using data from the NPTS, we find that mean vehicles per household in households with teens increased from 2.28 in 1983 to 2.44 in 1995. More important, the fraction of households with more than one car increased from 69 to 79 percent, and the fraction with more than two cars increased from 42 to 48 percent. We should stress that, although these figures suggest that teens may have more opportunities to drive today, there is also the possibility that households may have increased vehicle ownership in response to the higher travel demands of other household members.

Some have suggested to us that the increased labor force participation of women may explain increased travel among teens. As women have entered the job market, driving patterns have changed, greatly increasing the number and composition of trips that women take (Spain 1997; McGuckin and Murakami 1999). Having a working mother may also influence the driving of teens, providing them with a greater need and/or more opportunity to drive. Data from the 1995 NPTS support the hypothesis that teens with working mothers drive more. From this survey, we constructed a sample of teens from the person data file. This file contains a composite measure of annual miles driven as well as detailed demographic information about respondents and their families. For teens who report that they are children of the household reference person, we merge into their observation an indicator that equals 1 when the mother works and 0 otherwise. Regressing annual miles driven on controls for household income, family size, age, race, ethnicity, sex, population size of the area where the household is located, and whether the mother works, we find that teens who have a working mother drive thirteen hundred miles more (t-statistic of 2.76) than other teens, which is about 20 percent of the sample mean of miles driven. Although the difference in annual driving miles across the two groups is large, the rise in labor force participation can explain only a small fraction of the increase in car travel. Data from the March CPS suggest that, among women aged thirty-five to sixty-five with school-age children in the family, the fraction with labor income increased by 10 percentage points, from 77 to 87 percent, between 1983 and 1995. This change in female labor force participation would explain only a 130-mile increase in driving over this period.

Another possible explanation for increased teen driving is the large drop in fuel prices over this period. Data from the Department of Energy indicate that nominal prices for a gallon of unleaded regular gasoline were $1.24 in 1983 and $1.15 in 1995.[7] Deflating these numbers by the consumer price index, the real price of a gallon of gasoline has fallen by almost 40 percent over this period. We suspect that the price elasticity of demand for gasoline is larger in absolute value for teens than for adults for two reasons. First, teens have lower incomes. More important, however, we suspect that teen car travel is more discretionary, and there is some evidence that discretionary car travel is more sensitive to price changes (Walls, Krupnick, and Hood 1993; Berkowitz et al. 1990).

3.1.2 Why Have Teen Traffic Fatality Rates Fallen since the 1980s?

The evidence presented here indicates that there have been substantive gains in teen traffic safety over the last two decades. When teen traffic fatalities are denominated by vehicle miles traveled, fatality rates have

---

7. See http://www.eia.doe.gov/pub/energy.overview/monthly.energy/mer9-4.

fallen by 50 percent since 1983, which exceeds the corresponding gain among adults over this period (table 3.3 above). This important trend could reflect two general influences: a reduction in the number of accidents and an increase in the survivability of crashes. This latter determinant can change for at least three reasons. First, the types of crashes may have changed if, for example, there are fewer high-speed crashes today than there were in previous years. Second, the crashworthiness of the automobiles driven by teens may have changed, enhancing the chances of crash survival. Finally, crash survivability can be enhanced through better medical care and the use of important occupant-safety devices such as seat belts and air bags. In this section, we present novel evidence suggesting that each of these factors has to varying degrees contributed to the downward trend in teen traffic fatalities.

Changing Crash Rates

Holding crash survivability constant, fatality rates should track the frequency of crashes. While there is some evidence that crash rates have declined, these changes may explain only part of the drop. More specifically, using data on the frequency of accidents from the National Automotive Sampling Survey (NASS), we find that crash rates have changed only modestly in recent years. The NASS is an annual sample of police accident reports that is sponsored by the NHTSA. The initial survey year for the NASS was 1988, so, unfortunately, we have a much smaller time series for accident rates than for fatalities. By 1998, the NASS reported data on about fifty thousand of the more than 6 million police-reported accidents. The structure of the NASS is similar to that of the FARS in that data are reported at the person, accident, and vehicle level.

In figure 3.7, we report the time series of accident rates for passenger-vehicle occupants by age groups for the period 1988–97. In this figure, accidents are per one thousand people. As with fatalities, teen rates are two to three times that of older adults. More important, accident rates follow a similar pattern as fatalities; that is, there was a sharp drop between 1988 and 1992, with a small increase in accidents since then. These results do suggest that some of the decline in fatalities can be attributed to a change in the frequency of accidents. However, crash rates have not fallen nearly as fast as fatalities. Between 1988 and 1992, for teens, fatality rates fell by 23 percent, but crash rates fell by only 11 percent.

The crashes represented by figure 3.7 are of various levels of severity, varying from simple "fender benders" to multivehicle accidents with fatalities. We would prefer to examine the time-series pattern for accident rates that are likely to produce injuries and fatalities. However, in this case, we cannot define severity on the basis of occupant injuries since vehicle crashworthiness may have changed over time. Instead, we can define accident rates on the basis of external damage to the vehicle. Specifically, we

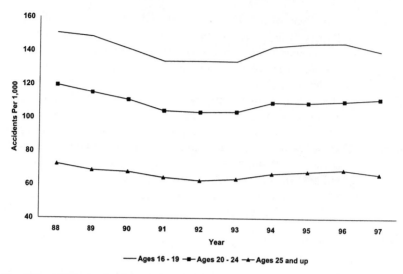

Fig. 3.7   Accident rates for passenger-car occupants

restrict our attention to accidents where the damage was great enough that the vehicle had to be towed from the accident scene.[8] In figure 3.8, we report the occupant crash rates for occupants who were in vehicles that were damaged enough to be towed away. The percentage drop in tow-away rates in the period 1988–92 is nearly identical to the drop in all crashes. Interestingly, however, there has been a large increase in tow-away crashes since 1992, with only a small increase in fatalities. The fact that the drop in accident and tow-away rates over the late 1980s and early 1990s is smaller than the drop in fatalities suggests that a change in crash rates can at best explain only part of the improvements in traffic safety. In the next section, we present evidence that crash survivability has also been enhanced.

These results do, however, beg the question why accident and fatality rates have fallen. Perhaps the most promising explanation involves the relation between teen alcohol use and traffic safety.[9] As is discussed in a later section, the widely recognized links between teen traffic accidents and alcohol use have motivated extensive policy making at the state and federal levels designed both to limit teens' access to alcohol and to deter drunk driving. There is a variety of direct medical evidence indicating that

8. Technically, we include all towed vehicles in the accident rate, including those that were towed for reasons other than drivability, such as the physical condition of the driver. These represent a small fraction of towed vehicles.

9. Changes in the prevalence of drunk driving may also have influenced crash rates as well as crash survivability through possible effects on crash severity and responsiveness to subsequent medical care.

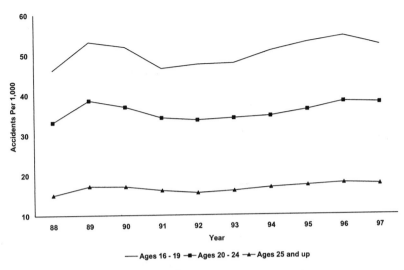

Fig. 3.8   Tow-away-accident rates for passenger-car occupants

alcohol use significantly impairs driver judgment as well as such critical motor skills as tracking, steering, and emergency responsiveness even at fairly low BACs (GAO 1999). Zador (1991) found, using FARS data, that the risk of fatal-crash involvement was substantially increased at BACs in the range of 0.05–0.09, particularly for young drivers.[10] More recently, Levitt and Porter (1999a) examined the fatality risk of drunk driving by adopting a unique empirical approach, one based on comparing the alcohol involvement of drivers in single-vehicle and two-car crashes. Their estimates suggest that drinking drivers are at least eight to nine times more likely than sober drivers to cause fatal crashes.[11]

However, Levitt and Porter (1999a) also recognized that the FARS data on BACs are not gathered for all participants in fatal crashes and that police reports of alcohol involvement may be incomplete.[12] Fortunately, we can construct a plausible proxy for alcohol-involved teen traffic fatalities by exploiting the distinct diurnal pattern in rates of alcohol involvement. The available data clearly indicate that alcohol involvement in fatal crashes is substantially higher at night. For example, using fatalities with identified BAC levels for teens over the period 1982–92, we graph in figure 3.9 the percentage of fatalities that have alcohol involvement by the time of day

10. In most states, it is "illegal per se" to drive with a BAC of 0.10 or more. Seventeen states have now set this limit at 0.08. Several other developed nations have also adopted regulations that make it illegal to drive with a BAC of 0.08 or lower.

11. Their estimates also point to the more limited fatality risk associated with young but sober drivers, which suggests the influence of other kinds of risk taking and/or inexperience.

12. They evaluate the robustness of their findings in part by replicating their results with data from states with high rates of BAC testing.

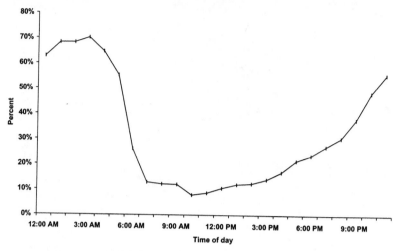

Fig. 3.9   Percentage alcohol involvement of motor-vehicle fatalities by time of day, FARS 1982–92, teens aged 15–19

when accidents happen. Notice that, for certain times of the day, alcohol-related fatalities represent as much as 70 percent of all motor-vehicle deaths. In contrast, between the hours of 6:00 A.M. and 6:00 P.M., alcohol is a cofactor in only about 15 percent of all crashes. Therefore, like other literature in this area, we use nighttime motor-vehicle fatalities as a proxy for the number of fatalities with alcohol involvement. Following the NHTSA's convention, we define *nighttime traffic fatalities* as those that occur between 6:00 P.M. and 5:59 A.M.

In figure 3.10, we present the nighttime motor-vehicle-fatality rate over the period 1975–97 for the three age groups. Notice that the drop in these alcohol-sensitive measures is fairly dramatic—between 1979 and 1997, this teen alcohol-sensitive fatality rate fell by almost 50 percent. In figure 3.11, we report age-specific nighttime fatality rates for teens. These figures suggest that the largest drop in fatality rates has been among eighteen- and nineteen-year-olds. The drop in alcohol-related fatalities can be traced in part to restricted access to alcohol and more aggressive drunk-driving legislation. Most notably, in 1977, thirty states had a minimum legal drinking age (MLDA) of eighteen. However, by the late 1980s, partly in response to federal pressure, all states had raised their MLDA to twenty-one. These legislative changes coincided with the large drop in fatalities during the 1980s (fig. 3.11). In the next section, we take a closer look at the effect that these and other alcohol and drunk-driving policies have had on teen motor-vehicle-fatality rates.

The effect that the drop in alcohol-related fatalities has had on aggregate fatality rates can be seen by looking at the time-series graph for daytime

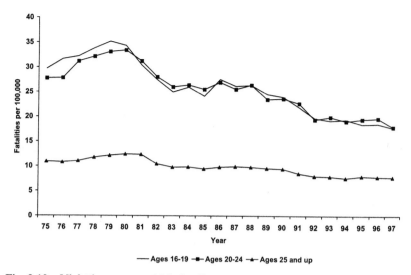

Fig. 3.10   **Nighttime motor-vehicle-fatality rate**

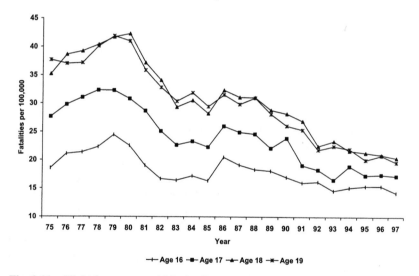

Fig. 3.11   **Nighttime motor-vehicle-fatality rates for teens**

fatality rates, shown in figure 3.12. Between 1979 and 1997, a time period when alcohol-related motor-vehicle fatalities are falling by 50 percent, daytime fatalities have stayed roughly constant. Since nighttime fatalities account for roughly 72 percent of all fatalities in 1979, these fatalities have fallen by 50 percent, and daytime fatalities have not fallen at all, it is not surprising that total motor-vehicle fatalities have fallen by almost (72 percent × 50 percent =) 36 percent over this period.

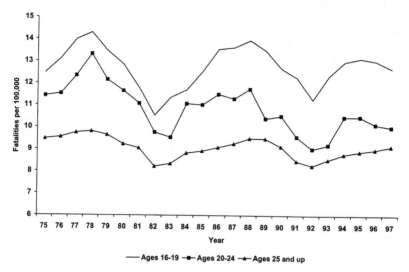

Fig. 3.12   Daytime motor-vehicle-fatality rate

Changes in Crash Survivability

It looks as though the drop in alcohol-related accidents may explain a large fraction of the long-run change in teen fatality rates. However, this important class of changes does not tell the whole story. In particular, note that alcohol-related fatalities, as measured by nighttime fatality rates, have fallen steadily since 1986. In contrast, aggregate fatality rates (both total and occupant, as measured in figs. 3.1 and 3.3 above) have been holding steady since 1992. Part of the reversal in the aggregate trend can be traced to an uptick in accidents. In figures 3.7 and 3.8 above, we saw that accident and tow-away-accident rates have actually increased by 5 and 10 percent, respectively, over the period 1992–97. However, part of the change in fatality rates may also have been driven by changes in crash survivability.

There have been four major trends that have altered the crashworthiness of automobiles. Between 1975 and 1985, new cars became much more fuel efficient, primarily by shedding vehicle weight. Over this time period, the curb weight of new cars sold fell by a thousand pounds (Kahane 1997). In a reversal of this trend, as real gas prices have fallen, the big automobile has returned, this time in the form of light trucks—pickups, sport-utility vehicles, and minivans. Between 1985 and 1993, the population of such light trucks increased by 50 percent (Kahane 1997). Today, light trucks represent one-third of registered vehicles (Gabler and Hollowell 1998). Light trucks are also 340 pounds heavier than the average new car. Larger vehicles, especially light trucks, are also much more crashworthy than lighter automobiles (Joksch, Massie, and Pichler 1998). In table 3.4, we present data from the NASS that identifies by age the fraction of occu-

Table 3.4   **Characteristics of Passenger-Vehicle Occupants in Accidents, NASS**

Category/Age Group	1988	1992	1997
% Belt Use among Occupants in Accidents			
16–19	41.6	68.8	67.9
20–24	43.1	71.4	66.0
25+	38.4	77.4	70.7
% of All Occupants in Accidents in Light Trucks/Minivans/SUVs			
16–19	12.2	16.1	20.0
20–24	14.3	17.1	19.7
25+	13.8	18.7	22.2

pants in accidents who were drivers or passengers in light trucks. This fraction has doubled since 1988.

Another factor leading to improved survivability is enhanced trauma care. Regional trauma centers were established nearly twenty years ago to reduce injury-related mortality. By 1995, twenty-two states had regional trauma systems (Nathans et al. 2000). Evaluations suggest that the presence of regional trauma centers has reduced mortality among crash victims. Mullins and Mann (1999) found a 15–20 percent improved survival rate among the seriously injured treated at trauma centers. Nathans et al. (2000) found that states with regional trauma centers had a 9 percent lower automobile-accident-mortality rate than did states without such centers. Quantifying the benefits of these centers is not the focus of this paper, but there is some evidence in the FARS that enhanced medical care has improved the probability of survival among those who make it to a hospital. Consider the following example. Let D represent whether a crash victim dies and H represent whether he or she went to the hospital. We suspect that improved medical care has enhanced survivability or reduced the conditional probability $\text{prob}(D|H)$. Because the FARS contains only those involved in fatal accidents, we cannot estimate this probability directly. However, we can use the data in FARS by recognizing that, by Bayes's theorem, $\text{prob}(D|H) = \text{prob}(H|D)\text{prob}(D)/\text{prob}(H)$. Notice that the probability of survival if a victim makes it to the hospital is proportional to the probability that we observed someone in a hospital given that he or she died. The intuition is straightforward. Suppose that, of a hundred crash victims, fifty die at the scene, and the remaining victims are transported to a hospital. If in-hospital-survival rates improve, then $\text{prob}(H|D)$ must fall. The 1980 FARS data indicate that 68 percent of fatalities were admitted to a hospital. This number fell considerably over the next eighteen years, dropping to 52 percent by 1997. These results are consistent with the hypothesis of improved medical care.

Another important trend that has clearly altered crash survivability substantively is the increased prevalence of seat-belt use (e.g., table 3.4).

Wearing a seat belt has been demonstrated to reduce significantly the fatality risk of crashes.[13] However, roadside and highway observations in the United States during the 1970s and early 1980s suggested that belt-use rates were only about 14 percent. Surprisingly, this rate had been relatively constant across prior years (Evans 1991). However, more recent observations suggest that belt use has risen nearly fivefold to 70 percent (NHTSA 1999a). As a later section demonstrates, a substantial proportion of these gains is directly due to the state-level adoption of mandatory seat-belt laws. At the beginning of 1984, no state required the use of a seat belt. However, since then, every state except New Hampshire has adopted some form of mandatory belt-use law (NHTSA 1999b). These laws were promoted in part by a federal regulation that would have delayed introduction of a proposed passive-restraint standard if two-thirds of the country were covered by mandatory belt-use laws. Since much of the surveillance data on belt use is based on direct roadside and highway observation, it is implausible to rely on that data to establish trends in youth-specific belt use. However, survey data do allow us to consider the age-specific trends in belt use. While any survey data are qualified by the potential biases inherent in self-reported health behaviors, they appear to track observed belt use as well as policy responses (Dee 1998).

The longest time series of belt use available is from the CDC's Behavioral Risk Factor Surveillance System (BRFSS). The BRFSS is an annual telephone-based survey designed to generate representative state-level data on the prevalence of important health behaviors among those aged eighteen or older (CDC 1998). The BRFSS began in 1984 by fielding surveys in fifteen states. By 1993, respondents in all fifty states were questioned. In figure 3.13, we plot the yearly belt-use rates for our three age groups. *Belt use* is defined as the percentage of BRFSS respondents who report always wearing a seat belt. In all years, teens have lower rates of belt use than do older drivers. However, all three age groups have dramatic increases in self-reported belt-use rates over this period. Use rates among teens increased by a factor of almost four, going from only 15 percent in 1984 to just under 57 percent in 1995. The percentage point increase in use was larger for adults, going from 23 to 68 percentage points, but this was only a threefold increase in use.

Unfortunately, the BRFSS surveys only adults eighteen and older. To obtain some evidence on belt use in a slightly younger population, we examine data from the Youth Risk Behavior Surveillance System (YRBSS), which is introduced in the next section. The YRBSS surveyed high school students in 1991, 1993, 1995, and 1997. Restricting our attention to the

13. Evidence on the technological efficacy of seat belts, the effects of mandatory seat-belt laws, and the possibility of compensating risk taking by drivers is discussed in detail in a later section.

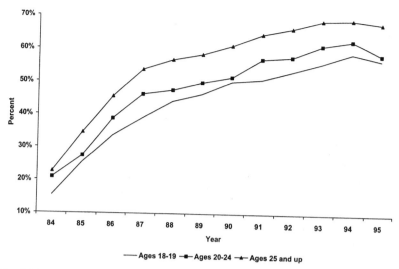

Fig. 3.13   Seat-belt use (all the time), BRFSS

driving-age population, we calculated belt-use rates (defined as the fraction who always wear a seat belt) for three age groups (sixteen, seventeen, and eighteen and older) for the four years of the survey. The use rates for sixteen-year-olds in the four survey years are 29.0, 31.9, 31.5, and 34.0 percent, respectively. The numbers for seventeen-year-olds (28.6, 34.8, 34.6, and 37.1 percent, respectively) and the eighteen and older group (27.2, 31.2, 35.2, and 34.5 percent, respectively) are similar to those for sixteen-year-olds. These data suggest that belt use is less common among these younger teens. However, during the 1990s, their belt use has been trending upward.

Another trend that is also likely to have improved crash survivability over this period is the increased installations of air bags. In 1984, the NHTSA required that automatic occupant-protection systems, such as air bags or automatic belts, be phased into passenger cars during 1987–90. All vehicles manufactured after 1 September 1993 were required to have automatic protection for the driver and right-front passenger. The Intermodal Surface Transportation Efficiency Act (ISTEA), passed by Congress in 1991, required all passenger cars manufactured after 1 September 1997 and light trucks manufactured after 1 September 1998 to have driver and passenger air bags plus manual lap-shoulder belts. However, since belt use has increased so sharply over this period and belts are substantially more effective at reducing fatality risk, it is unlikely that the adoption of air bags is as empirically relevant. Levitt and Porter (1999b) find that conventional estimates have overstated the efficacy of air bags. They estimate that air bags reduce fatality risk by between 9 percent (partial frontal collisions) and 16 percent (direct frontal collisions) but that seat belts reduce fatality risk by 60 percent. The Insurance Institute for Highway Safety estimates that roughly 46 percent of cars and light trucks on the road today have driver-side air bags and that one-third of these cars have passenger-side air bags.[14]

3.2 Who Are the Risky Teen Drivers?

The numbers given in table 3.1 above illustrate that the vast majority of teen motor-vehicle fatalities occur among males. Are there other observed characteristics that would allow one to predict who will be the risk takers? To address this question, we evaluated data from the national school-based YRBSS. The YRBSS is a nationally representative survey of roughly sixteen thousand high school students from 150 schools. The survey is sponsored by the CDC and has been fielded every two years since 1991. The purpose of the survey is to track priority health-risk behaviors of high schoolers over time. In our work, we present estimates from the 1997 YRBSS.[15]

From the YRBSS, we can construct three variables that indicate teen risk taking in the car. The first variable equals 1 for those who report always wearing a seat belt, the second equals 1 for those who drove after drinking in the past thirty days, and the third equals 1 for those who rode in a car in the past thirty days with a driver who had been drinking. With these variables, we estimate a simple probit that predicts a response of yes to these questions. For our analysis, we use data for sixteen- to eighteen-year-olds, deleting data for fifteen-year-olds since most cannot drive. Although the YRBSS contains detailed data on risky behavior, the data set has limited information on individual characteristics. We can include as covariates information on age, race, sex, parents' education, and urbanicity. Given the variation across states in traffic-safety laws, we also include in each model a full set of state dummy variables.

The results of these simple probits are included in table 3.5. The sample means for each outcome are reported in the final row of the table. We report the marginal effects, which represent the change in the probability of the event happening given a change in the covariate. So, for example, females are 10.3 percentage points more likely to wear a safety belt, which represents about a 35 percent higher use rate relative to the mean. Females are also much less likely to drive after drinking or to ride in a car with a drinking driver. Blacks and Hispanics are both less likely to wear seat belts but also less likely to be associated with drunk driving. The only strong effects of age are that younger drivers are less likely to drive drunk but also slightly less likely to wear a seat belt. Parents' education is a strong

14. See http://www.highwaysafety.org/safety_facts/airbags.htm.
15. Results from the three other YRBSS data sets were similar.

Table 3.5   **Probit Estimates of Traffic-Safety-Choice Models, 1997 YRBSS, 16–18-Year-Olds, Probit Marginal Effects**

	Traffic-Safety Choice (1 = yes, 0 = no)		
Covariate	Always Wear Seat Belt?	Drove after Drinking in Past 30 Days?	Rode in Car Driven by Someone Under the Influence in Past 30 Days?
Female	.103	−.113	−.078
	(.010)	(.008)	(.010)
Black	−.174	−.119	−.045
	(.018)	(.016)	(.017)
Hispanic	−.058	−.028	−.027
	(.019)	(.016)	(.018)
Other race	−.113	−.059	−.033
	(.014)	(.012)	(.014)
Age 16	−.038	−.104	−.043
	(.013)	(.011)	(.013)
Age 17	.006	.000	.031
	(.013)	(.010)	(.012)
Parents' education not reported	−.092	−.049	−.036
	(.024)	(.021)	(.023)
Highest parents' education is high school dropout	−.193	.028	.032
	(.022)	(.017)	(.020)
Highest parents' education is high school graduate	−.100	−.005	−.00
	(.015)	(.012)	(.014)
Highest parents' education is some college	−.043	−.030	−.018
	(.012)	(.011)	(.012)
Live in urban area	.109	−.135	−.121
	(.021)	(.017)	(.020)
Live in suburban area	.123	−.111	−.127
	(.021)	(.016)	(.020)
Mean of dependent variable	.352	.206	.385

Note: All models include state fixed effects. Standard errors are reported in parentheses.

predictor of belt use, with use monotonically increasing with parents' education. Interestingly, there is little correlation with parents' education and the two drinking-and-driving variables. Suburban and urban respondents look similar, and both are much more likely than rural residents to wear seat belts and not drink and drive.

One important characteristic that is strongly associated with teens' risk taking behind the wheel is their actions concerning other risky behaviors. Teens' decisions not to wear a seat belt or drive drunk appear to follow a pattern of risk taking along many dimensions—teens who take risks in the car appear to take risks in other aspects of life as well. In the first column of table 3.6, we report a number of questions from the 1997 YRBSS that measure, with a discrete yes-or-no variable, students' responses to ques-

Table 3.6   Difference in Means by Traffic-Safety Indicator (yes-no), 1997 YRBSS, 16–19-Year-Olds

Health Habit (1=yes, 0=no)	Males					Females				
	Obs.	Sample Mean	Always/ Mostly Wear Seat Belt?	Rode in Car with Drinking Driver?	Drove Car After Drinking?	Obs.	Sample Mean	Always/ Mostly Wear Seat Belt?	Rode in Car with Drinking Driver?	Drove Car after Drinking?
Smoked cigarette in past 30 days?	7,293	.378	-.227 (.011)	.351 (.011)	.434 (.013)	7,581	.347	-.144 (.012)	.318 (.011)	.514 (.016)
Use bicycle helmet?	5,889	.335	.030 (.013)	-.041 (.013)	-.134 (.016)	4,946	.114	-.033 (.010)	.007 (.010)	-.036 (.014)
Had at least 1 drink in past 30 days?	7,523	.340	-.212 (.011)	.457 (.010)	.648 (.011)	7,829	.248	-.088 (.010)	.354 (.009)	.641 (.013)
Had 5 or more drinks in a row in past 30 days?	7,690	.279	-.182 (.010)	.418 (.009)	.644 (.010)	8,007	.174	-.057 (.009)	.293 (.008)	.550 (.012)
In a physical fight in past year?	7,738	.455	-.159 (.011)	.197 (.011)	.204 (.014)	8,038	.258	-.171 (.010)	.147 (.010)	.127 (.015)
Smoked pot in last 30 days?	7,716	.302	-.205 (.010)	.318 (.010)	.374 (.012)	8,008	.215	-.083 (.010)	.264 (.009)	.376 (.013)
Used a condom last time had sex?	4,261	.647	.110 (.015)	-.086 (.015)	-.072 (.016)	3,956	.539	.020 (.016)	-.079 (.016)	-.089 (.020)
Ate fruit yesterday?	7,770	.666	.085 (.011)	.007 (.011)	-.035 (.013)	8,056	.614	.154 (.012)	-.038 (.011)	-.075 (.017)
Ate vegetables/salad yesterday?	7,771	.638	.100 (.011)	.022 (.011)	-.019 (.013)	8,061	.629	.074 (.012)	-.005 (.011)	.008 (.017)
Ate burger/hot dog/ sausage yesterday?	7,771	.482	-.103 (.011)	.130 (.012)	.083 (.014)	8,055	.332	-.036 (.011)	.028 (.011)	-.012 (.016)
Ate fries/potato chips yesterday?	7,769	.604	-.083 (.011)	.066 (.011)	.066 (.014)	8,054	.509	-.091 (.012)	.053 (.012)	.050 (.017)
Any aerobic exercise in past week?	7,754	.882	.046 (.007)	.001 (.008)	-.016 (.009)	8,046	.758	.105 (.010)	-.022 (.010)	.034 (.015)
Any strength exercise in past week?	7,760	.776	.013 (.010)	.019 (.010)	.005 (.012)	8,048	.671	.120 (.011)	-.025 (.011)	.025 (.016)

Note: Standard errors are reported in parentheses.

tions about a number of activities that pose health risks. For each health habit, we report the number of valid observations and the sample mean. We next report the difference in means for the particular health habit on the basis of whether a respondent reports always wearing a seat belt or riding in or driving a car after drinking. These numbers are reported for males and females. So, in the first row, 37.8 percent of males report smoking in the past thirty days. This smoking rate is 22.7 percentage points lower for those who always wear a seat belt, 35 percentage points higher among those who rode with a drinking driver, and 43 percentage points higher for those who drove after drinking. For males, knowing whether you are a risky driver indicates that you have twice the average chance of smoking!

The results in the rest of the table are striking. Risky drivers (those not wearing seat belts and those riding/driving after drinking) are less likely to wear a bicycle helmet, more likely to have been drinking in the past thirty days, more likely to have been in a fight in the past year, more likely to smoke marijuana, more likely to have had unprotected sex, more likely to have had fatty foods like burgers and fries, less likely to eat fruits and vegetables, and less likely to exercise! The differences in means are in most cases slightly smaller for females, but, for some of the variables (e.g., smoking), the estimates are comparable.

3.3   Which Policies Have Improved Teen Traffic Safety?

The evidence presented in the previous sections of this paper has underscored the dramatic level of lethal risk faced by teens in cars as well as important stylized facts about the character of these risks. However, this evidence also indicated that, over the past twenty years, there have been impressive gains in teen traffic safety, both in absolute terms and relative to adult traffic-related risks. This evidence also suggested that these gains have been driven both by a reduction in the number of accidents and by increases in the probability of surviving a crash. However, these striking conclusions beg further questions about what factors might constitute the root causes of these impressive improvements. The extensive literature on traffic safety has attributed much of these gains to the broad and aggressive new regulation over this period of key behaviors related to traffic safety. This section presents a critical overview of this evidence. First, we discuss the theoretical and empirical evidence linking the adoption and enforcement of mandatory seat-belt laws to the observed improvements in the prevalence of belt use among teens (fig. 3.13 above). Then we discuss the more general evidence on the efficacy of key traffic-safety regulations, in part, by presenting reduced-form evaluations of how state-level policies have influenced the number of teen traffic fatalities. This discussion focuses, in particular, on four classes of state-level policies: policies that influence youth access to alcohol, policies directed at the specific and general deterrence of drunk driving,[16] mandatory seat-belt laws, and highway speed limits.

3.3.1 Seat-Belt Use

Evidence from both technological evaluations and actual crashes suggests that seat belts are highly effective at reducing the fatality risk associated with a crash. Early estimates indicated that this risk reduction was roughly 50 percent (Evans 1986; NHTSA 1984). However, in a recent study, Levitt and Porter (1999b) conclude that such estimates may be biased downward because of sample selectivity and that the actual risk reduction associated with seat-belt use is 60 percent. Regardless, it was in part a growing awareness of such dramatic lifesaving benefits that motivated the widespread adoption of state laws mandating their use. Beginning with New York in late 1984, every state but New Hampshire has adopted a mandatory seat-belt law.[17] However, these laws were accompanied by differing levels of enforcement. More specifically, most states (currently thirty-eight) adopted "secondary" enforcement, which allows only a citation for a seat-belt violation if the driver has been stopped for another infraction. In the eleven states with "primary" enforcement, a seat-belt violation alone is sufficient cause for a citation.

The technological efficacy of seat belts suggests that the widespread adoption of mandatory seat-belt laws may have generated substantive gains in traffic safety. However, there are at least two reasons to suspect that these gains may have been sharply attenuated. One is the possibility of "selective recruitment"—a smaller response in belt use among those most likely to be involved in accidents (young drivers, males, those who drink). A second reason is the possibility of risk-compensating behavior. Peltzman (1975) argued that the lifesaving benefits of such safety requirements as seat-belt laws may be reduced if drivers subsequently increase their risk taking behind the wheel. A casual reading of the U.S. experience with seat-belt laws suggests that this may actually have occurred. More specifically, naive evaluations that compare belt-use rates before and after a seat-belt law suggest that such laws increased use by roughly 28 percentage points (Campbell and Campbell 1988). If seat belts reduce fatality risks by 50 percent, this increase in belt use should be accompanied by a decrease in traffic fatalities of roughly 14 percent in the absence of a compensating behavioral response. However, most studies suggest that fatalities fell by only about 8 percent (Evans and Graham 1991). Nonetheless, Dee (1998) argues that the U.S. experience with seat-belt laws did not

16. General deterrence is an attempt to reduce drunk driving in the general population. Specific deterrence is an attempt to punish known offenders so that they do not offend again.

17. Two states (Massachusetts and Nebraska) adopted, rescinded, and later reinstated such laws.

Table 3.7   **OLS and Probit Estimates of Impact of Mandatory Seat-Belt Laws on Seat-Belt Use**

| | | | | OLS Coefficient or Probit Marginal Effect | |
| | | | | Model (2) | |
Data Set and Sample	Sample Size	Mean Belt Usage	Model (1): Mandatory Seat-Belt Law	Mandatory Seat-Belt Law, Primary Enforcement	Mandatory Seat-Belt Law, Secondary Enforcement
NHTSA 19 City Survey (1985–91)	126	.422	.172 (.019)	.351 (.043)	.158 (.018)
1984–93 BRFSS:					
All respondents	577,422	.541	.183 (.003)	.260 (.006)	.172 (.003)
Balanced panel of 15 states	239,779	.504	.144 (.004)	.212 (.011)	.141 (.004)
25+	513,557	.549	.190 (.003)	.247 (.006)	.179 (.003)
20–24	47,244	.488	.137 (.010)	.233 (.023)	.126 (.010)
18–19	16,621	.438	.147 (.017)	.249 (.040)	.136 (.019)
18–19 males	7,953	.383	.105 (.024)	.209 (.058)	.091 (.027)
18–19 females	8,668	.489	.188 (.024)	.286 (.053)	.176 (.026)

Note: All models include year and state or city fixed effects. The BRFSS models also include covariates for gender, race/ethnicity, age, and age squared. Standard errors are reported in parentheses. For further details, see Dee (1998).

induce a dramatic increase in risk taking by drivers.[18] The flaw in the prior reasoning is that it does not seem that seat-belt laws actually increased belt use by 28 percentage points. Such estimates (which are typically based on interrupted time-series analysis) appear to confound the long-term trend toward increased belt use with the adoption of the state laws, overstating those laws' effects dramatically. Dee (1998) concludes that mandatory seat-belt laws increased belt use by only about 18 percent—a magnitude consistent with the observed reduction in fatalities and a number that suggests that compensating risk taking is of minor importance. However, Dee (1998) does find evidence of selective recruitment: a smaller response in belt use among the young and, in particular, young male drivers.

Table 3.7 summarizes this evidence by presenting estimates of how man-

18. Evans and Graham (1991) also present evidence consistent with this claim: the adoption of mandatory seat-belt laws was not associated with increases in pedestrian or cyclist deaths related to traffic accidents.

datory seat-belt laws and their enforcement levels influenced belt use. This evidence draws on two distinct data sources. The first source is pooled city-level data from the 1985–91 19 City Surveys, which employed observation techniques to gather information (e.g., NHTSA 1989). While these aggregate data do not allow us to address the selective-recruitment hypothesis by focusing on heterogeneous responses in particular subgroups, they do have the virtue of being observed as opposed to self-reported. Pooling seven years of data over eighteen cities leaves a data set with 126 observations.[19] With this data set, we estimate a simple analysis-of-covariance model in which we regress the fraction belt use on a series of city and year fixed effects and the belt-use intervention dummy variables, which equal 1 in years when the laws were in effect and 0 otherwise. These estimates, reported in the first row of table 3.7, suggest that mandatory seat-belt laws increased use by about 17 percentage points and that these effects were plausibly heterogeneous with regard to enforcement levels.[20] The importance of mandatory belt-use laws in explaining increased use rates is also illustrated by the experience in Massachusetts. A secondary-enforcement belt-use law went into effect in Massachusetts on 1 January 1986, but the law was repealed in a statewide referendum just eleven months later. Observation studies found that belt use increased from 20 percent before the law went into effect to 37 percent after. However, belt use quickly fell back down to 25 percent after the law was repealed (Hingson et al. 1988).

To examine the effect of belt-use laws on teen use of seat belts, we must move away from the observational data and utilize individual self-reports of belt use. For this exercise, we use the BRFSS data introduced above. We pool the BRFSS data over the period 1984–93, constructing a sample of 577,422 respondents (Dee 1998). *Belt use* was defined by a binary indicator equal to 1 for respondents who claimed to use a seat belt "always." For this sample, we estimate simple linear-probability models, controlling for basic demographic characteristics, state and year effects, plus the belt-use intervention indicator variables. The remaining results in table 3.7 present estimates of how mandatory seat-belt laws influenced this belt-use measure for all respondents as well as for specific age and gender groups. Overall, evaluations based on the BRFSS data are similar to those based on observation data. Mandatory seat-belt laws increased belt use by roughly 18 percentage points with a plausible heterogeneity with respect to the level of enforcement. As we noted above, the BRFSS contained data

19. The eighteen cities are Atlanta, Baltimore, Birmingham, Boston, Chicago, Dallas, Houston, Los Angeles, Miami, Minneapolis/St. Paul, New Orleans, New York, Phoenix, Pittsburgh, Providence, San Diego, San Francisco, and Seattle. Data from Fargo/Moorhead were excluded since this area crossed state lines.

20. However, since Houston and Dallas are the only represented cities with primary enforcement over this period, these results may not be fully generalizable to the experiences across the country (Dee 1998).

from only fifteen states in 1984 and expanded to include data for fifty states by 1993. We examined whether this change in sample composition is influencing our basic results. Evaluations based only on data from the fifteen states surveyed in all ten years return similar results. The evidence from evaluations based on subsets of the BRFSS respondents points to the existence of some selective recruitment. Younger respondents and young males in particular were less likely to increase their belt use in response to mandatory seat-belt laws and their enforcement levels sharply influenced belt use among teens and may, therefore, have been an important source of recent improvements in teen traffic safety. The reduced-form models presented in the next section provide more direct evidence on this question by evaluating the influence of these regulations on the number of traffic fatalities.

3.3.2   Traffic Fatalities

This section discusses the reduced-form evidence linking a variety of state policies to reductions in teen traffic fatalities.

Prior Literature

One widely recognized determinant of the recent reductions in teen traffic fatalities is the nationwide movement calling for an MLDA of twenty-one. In the late 1960s and 1970s, many states had lowered their MLDA in response to a general sentiment toward the enfranchisement of young adults as well as considerable doubt about the efficacy of prohibiting alcohol. By 1977, thirty states had an MLDA of only eighteen. However, there was a growing realization that relaxed access to alcohol may have increased the number of teen traffic fatalities. Partly in response to this realization as well as strong financial pressure by the federal government, all states increased their MLDA to twenty-one by the late 1980s. Several studies have established a clear link between the state-specific timing of movements to higher MLDAs and reductions in traffic fatalities (e.g., Cook and Tauchen 1984; Evans et al. 1991; Chaloupka et al. 1993; Ruhm 1996; Dee 1999). Similarly, some studies have also concluded that there are traffic-safety benefits of another regulation that can limit access to alcohol: excise taxes on beer (Chaloupka et al. 1993; Evans et al. 1991; Ruhm 1996). However, recent evidence, which is discussed in more detail here, has suggested that these links may be spurious (Dee 1999; Mast et al. 1999).

Another important set of policies that may have influenced the distinctive recent trends in youth traffic fatalities is those aimed at the deterrence of drunk driving. Policies designed to reduce drunk driving have proliferated over the last twenty years in response to increased public awareness and indignation. One important type of state-level drunk-driving law was the kind that made it "illegal per se" to drive with a specific BAC. All states except Massachusetts and South Carolina currently have such an explicit limit. Most states initially established their BAC limit at 0.10 or more. However, an increasing number of states (now nineteen) have established a stricter definition at a BAC of 0.08. Federal efforts to compel all states to adopt 0.08 BAC laws have foundered recently, in part because of controversies over the efficacy of such laws at the state level (GAO 1999; Dee, in press). Another major drunk-driving policy that has sometimes been adopted simultaneously with an explicit BAC level is a regulation allowing "administrative license revocations." This policy, which has been adopted in forty-one states, allows state licensing agencies to suspend or revoke the driver's license of an allegedly drunk driver prior to any court action.[21] All states have now also adopted "zero-tolerance" laws that make it illegal per se for underage drivers to have a positive BAC regardless of its value. Other drunk-driving policies include "dram-shop" statutes (or case law) that allow injured parties to sue the servers of alcohol and regulations that mandate jail time for first-time DUI offenders. Recent reviews of the efficacy of such drunk-driving policies (e.g., DeJong and Hingson 1998; Hingson 1996; Zador et al. 1989) uniformly conclude that all these policies have been highly effective. However, this evidence should be interpreted with some caution since the research methodologies vary widely across studies. Ruhm (1996) addresses the efficacy of several drunk-driving and alcohol-related policies and finds that inferences regarding their effects can be sensitive to the omission of state and year fixed effects that purge the unobserved and potentially confounding determinants that vary across states and over time. However, Ruhm (1996) does find that administrative license revocations were somewhat effective in reducing traffic fatalities among youths. This evidence is developed further here by examining evidence on the hypothesized interactive effects of administrative license revocations and other policies that establish specific BAC limits at which it is illegal to drive.

A third set of policies evaluated in this context is the mandatory seatbelt laws discussed earlier. Given the evidence that these laws substantially increased belt use among young drivers, we would expect to find significant fatality reductions in the absence of a compensatory increase in risk taking. Since the available evidence suggests that the enforcement level of these laws is relevant, those distinctions are allowed. The fourth set of policies evaluated here reflects the changes in each state's maximum speed limit. In response to the Arab oil embargo, a national maximum speed limit (NMSL) of fifty-five miles per hour (MPH) was established in the early 1970s. In 1987, these regulations were relaxed, and states were allowed to raise their speed limits to sixty-five MPH on portions of the rural interstate system (and in that year alone, thirty-eight states did so). In

---

21. The constitutionality of these regulations has been unsuccessfully challenged in several states.

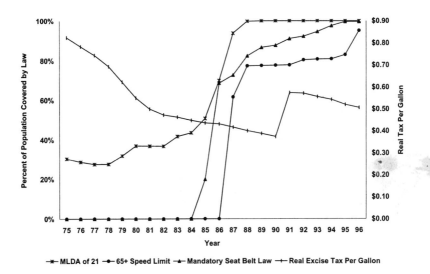

Fig. 3.14   Key state traffic-safety policies by year

1995, the federal regulation of speed limits was eliminated, and most states raised their maximum speed limit above sixty-five MPH.[22] The prior empirical evidence on the effects of higher speed limits is mixed. Lave and Elias (1994) suggest that the movement in the late 1980s to sixty-five-MPH speed limits actually reduced overall fatalities by redirecting traffic away from more dangerous secondary roads and influencing patterns of police enforcement. However, this conclusion has been challenged in recent studies (e.g., Farmer et al. 1999) that also considered the effects of more recent movements to speed limits above sixty-five MPH. The evaluations presented here provide further evidence on this question.

In figure 3.14, we report the time-series of the percentage of the population covered by four traffic-safety policies: mandatory belt-use laws, an MLDA of twenty-one, the beer tax, and a speed limit of sixty-five. Notice the steep increase in the fraction covered by belt use since 1984 and the sharp drop in those covered by an MLDA of eighteen. The beer tax is drifting downward until a federal tax hike in 1991; then it drifts downward slowly again. The time-series pattern for this variable is determined mainly by the changes in the price index. Over this period, few states are changing their nominal excise tax on beer, and inflation is eroding its real value over time.

In figure 3.15, we report for a shorter period the percentage of people covered by laws aimed at the specific and the general deterrence of drunk driving. Notice that, over this short period, coverage rates for most laws

22. During the day in portions of Montana, there is no posted speed limit for cars.

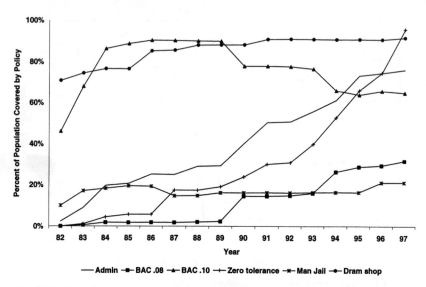

Fig. 3.15   Key alcohol-control policies by year

are increasing dramatically. The lone exception is the BAC 0.10 laws, which are declining somewhat as states shift to an "illegal per se" BAC limit of 0.08. In both figure 3.14 and figure 3.15, there are a significant number of laws that are coming into effect during our period of analysis. Subsequently, in any model that analyzes the within-state changes in fatality rates over time, we should be able to detect whether these programs reduced fatalities.

The models presented here also include controls for state-specific macroeconomic trends (unemployment rate, real state personal income per capita). Prior evidence (e.g., Evans and Graham 1988) has indicated that traffic fatalities are procyclic, possibly reflecting the increased risk associated with road congestion as well as the associated variation in patterns of alcohol use and drunk driving. To control for changes in safety that are common to all states (e.g., the crashworthiness of cars, declining drinking and driving owing to nonlegislative factors), we also include in all models a set of year effects.

Certain state policies that are omitted from these evaluations also deserve special mention. For example, several states require driver education as a condition for getting a license. Unfortunately, the available evidence (NHTSA 1994) suggests that these programs are not effective. However, a number of recent studies have emphasized the possible traffic-safety benefits of "graduated-licensing" systems for beginning drivers.[23] Such regula-

23. Foss and Evenson (1999) review the evaluation results from graduated-licensing systems in New Zealand and related studies on curfew restrictions and conclude that graduated licensing is likely to be successful.

tions require that new drivers acquire experience in low-risk settings before moving on to more complex driving environments. These systems vary in their details (e.g., supervision requirements, driving curfews) but generally consist of three distinct stages: a learning period, during which direct supervision is required; an intermediate period, which may allow for unsupervised driving in low-risk situations; and full licensure (IIHS 1999). In recent years, these regulations have been widely adopted in the United States. More specifically, since July 1996, twenty-four states have implemented some form of graduated licensing (IIHS 1999). Unfortunately, these experiences are too recent to evaluate with the currently available FARS data.

However, age-specific regulations like driver licensing and MLDAs raise more profound questions about their overall efficacy that have not been extensively explored in the current literature. Alcohol use and driving (while either drunk or sober) are both activities where experiential learning is likely to be important. The relevance of learning by doing to such activities raises the possibility that the lifetime efficacy of MLDAs and licensing-age policies may be attenuated. More specifically, policies that keep young adults away from alcohol and car travel may to some degree simply shift the attendant mortality risks to an older age, where learning by doing occurs. Both Males (1986) and Asch and Levy (1987) present some evidence in support of this view with regard to the MLDA. These studies can be criticized on methodological grounds.[24] Nonetheless, this issue suggests an important direction for future research on MLDAs and driver-licensing policies.

Data and Specifications

The evaluations presented here are based on state-level counts of teen traffic fatalities over the period 1977–97 that were drawn from FARS. In order to evaluate response heterogeneity as well as inform the plausibility of these inferences, ten distinct measures of teen traffic fatalities are employed. These ten measures are based on five different fatality types defined over two age groups: sixteen- to seventeen-year-olds and eighteen- to nineteen-year-olds. The five different fatality types are passenger-vehicle fatalities, total fatalities from nighttime accidents (6:00 P.M. to 5:59 A.M.), total fatalities from daytime accidents (6:00 A.M. to 5:59 P.M.), and total fatalities by gender. The unweighted state-year means for these counts are reported in table 3.8. The daytime measure is particularly useful in this context since it provides the basis for a compelling counterfactual that evaluates the reliability of conventional inferences regarding policies related to alcohol and drunk driving. More specifically, as stated earlier, alcohol involvement in fatal accidents is substantially higher at nighttime

---

24. For example, the Asch and Levy (1987) study is based on a single cross section of state-level data.

Table 3.8   State-Level Panel Data on Teen Traffic-Fatality Counts, 1977–97 FARS

	Mean		% Obs. ≤ 10 Fatalities		% Obs. ≤ 25 Fatalities	
Fatality Type	16–17	18–19	16–17	18–19	16–17	18–19
Passenger vehicles	46.3	64.0	15.5	9.1	34.9	27.1
Nighttime	29.2	44.1	24.9	16.5	55.9	39.1
Daytime	16.8	19.4	41.2	34.6	77.9	76.3
Male	31.1	47.4	23.8	15.0	54.1	36.5
Female	15.2	16.5	45.1	41.0	84.1	82.3

than during the day. Given this important stylized fact, we would expect the estimated effects of alcohol and drunk-driving policies to be sharply attenuated, if not nonexistent, in models for daytime counts. However, if such policies generate relatively large effects in daytime models, we could conclude that the model is generating specious inferences.[25]

Most reduced-form econometric specifications for panel data on traffic fatalities model the fatality rate denominated by population size or number of miles traveled. However, the evaluations presented here are based on an alternative approach. Specifically, since the fatality counts examined here are constructed relatively finely by age and other observed characteristics, employing a conventional fatality rate could substantially reduce the signal-to-noise ratio. Table 3.8 presents some limited information on the distribution of fatality counts that illustrates the nature of this concern. A substantial fraction of the state-year observations have fewer than ten or twenty-five fatalities in a year. This problem is particularly acute for modeling traffic fatalities among females as well as those that occur during the day. Because of this concern, the evaluation results presented here are based on count-data models that explicitly recognize that all the dependent variables are nonnegative integers. Within this framework, the natural log of the relevant population is treated instead as an additional regressor. However, since the prior literature has emphasized the need to control for unobserved state-specific effects, conventional count-data techniques cannot be employed. More specifically, conventional count-data models do not generate consistent estimates when cross-sectional fixed effects are introduced because of the "incidental-parameter" problem. Therefore, we adopt the conditional-maximum-likelihood approach for negative binomial models, which was developed Hausman, Hall, and Griliches (1984) to study the development of patents in a panel of firms.[26] The estimates

25. The power of this ad hoc counterfactual to identify specification error should not be overdrawn. We may find plausible results in daytime models despite the presence of specification error. And, even when this approach clearly suggests specification error, it provides at best limited guidance as to its nature.

26. The negative binomial model is less restrictive than a Poisson regression since it accommodates the presence of overdispersion in the counts.

generated by these models can be interpreted as the proportionate change in the given fatality count.

Results

The first set of results reported in table 3.9 presents evidence on how mandatory seat-belt laws, MLDAs, a sixty-five-MPH speed limit, and the macroeconomic variables influence passenger-vehicle fatalities. In this table, we report estimates for all fatalities by age and sex groupings. These models are based only on data from the period 1977–92. The sample is truncated in this fashion since nearly all the within-state variation in two key policies (mandatory seat-belt laws and the MLDA) had ended by the early 1990s.

In table 3.9, the estimated coefficients in the first row suggest that a seat-belt law with primary enforcement significantly reduced passenger-vehicle fatalities among sixteen- to seventeen-year-olds by nearly 8 percent and among eighteen- to nineteen-year-olds by almost 10 percent. In general, these effects are smaller in states that had only secondary enforcement for their seat-belt laws and substantially larger among female teens. These estimates are consistent with associated increases in belt use (table 3.7 above) and the technological efficacy of seat belts and suggest that risk-compensating behavior has not dramatically attenuated the lifesaving benefits of these laws. The coefficients on the MLDA variables suggest that a lower MLDA (i.e., easier access to alcohol) was associated with significantly higher counts of traffic fatalities among eighteen- to nineteen-year-olds. Males aged eighteen to nineteen are more affected by the MLDA than are females, which is to be expected given the higher alcohol use among males. These large and statistically significant increases were in most cases plausibly concentrated among nighttime as opposed to daytime fatalities and, interestingly, were also concentrated among male teens. In contrast, the evidence linking the MLDA variation to traffic fatalities among sixteen- to seventeen-year-olds is at best limited.[27] Other results in table 3.9 indicate that the initial movement to sixty-five-MPH speed limits did not significantly influence teen traffic fatalities but that these outcomes do consistently vary inversely with the state unemployment rate.

To provide some estimate of how much of the secular decline in per capita mortality rates can be attributed to these law changes, we conducted a simple simulation. To avoid the incidental-parameters problem, we estimated a conditional maximum-likelihood model in which we conditioned on the total number of deaths in a state over a fixed period of time. Because in our simulation we will want to examine how total fatalities change when regulations are changed, this econometric model does not lend itself well to these types of simulations. Therefore, we reestimated the basic

---

27. Cook and Tauchen (1984) reported similarly imprecise links between MLDA exposure and traffic fatalities among sixteen- to seventeen-year-olds.

Table 3.9   Conditional Maximum-Likelihood Estimates of Fixed-Effects Negative Binomial Models for Teen Motor-Vehicle Fatalities, 1977–92 FARS

Independent Variable	Mean	Fatality Counts—Passenger Vehicles					
		All		Male		Female	
		16–17	18–19	16–17	18–19	16–17	18–19
Mandatory seat-belt law, primary enforcement	.107	−.078	−.096	−.090	−.068	−.058	−.171
		(.031)	(.029)	(.037)	(.032)	(.055)	(.049)
Mandatory seat-belt law, secondary enforcement	.199	−.043	−.070	−.057	−.062	−.020	−.090
		(.029)	(.028)	(.034)	(.031)	(.050)	(.045)
MLDA of 18	.206	−.043	.046	−.049	.056	−.027	.024
		(.027)	(.025)	(.031)	(.028)	(.048)	(.042)
MLDA of 19	.156	.036	.052	.034	.063	.039	.025
		(.026)	(.024)	(.031)	(.027)	(.046)	(.040)
MLDA of 20	.051	.034	.033	−.007	.088	.122	−.147
		(.051)	(.048)	(.059)	(.052)	(.091)	(.087)
65-MPH speed limit	.306	.046	.025	.020	.018	.077	.041
		(.040)	(.036)	(.047)	(.039)	(.069)	(.061)
State unemployment rate	6.67	−.020	−.023	−.024	−.026	−.011	−.011
		(.006)	(.006)	(.007)	(.007)	(.011)	(.010)
Real per capita personal income (00,000)	1.23	−.029	−.272	−.059	−.189	.127	−.149
		(.141)	(.133)	(.166)	(.146)	(.252)	(.227)

Note: Standard errors are reported in parentheses. There are 768 observations in each model (48 states over 16 years). Each model includes state and year fixed effects and the natural log of the population for the given age and/or gender.

models from table 3.9 with a negative binomial maximum-likelihood model, inserting a complete set of dummies. The coefficients on the regulation dummy variables were nearly identical to the results from conditional maximum-likelihood estimations. We use this second set of negative binomial estimates in the simulations. Using these parameter values, we can estimate, for each state and year, the expected number of deaths given the state's observed characteristics and the set of regulations. Summing these predicted values in a given year and dividing by population will produce a predicted estimate of the national fatality rate, which in practice is a very accurate estimate. Next, we reconstruct this estimate for 1992, assuming that the laws present in 1979 never changed, that is, assuming that belt-use laws were never adopted and that those states with an MLDA under twenty-one stayed at these levels through 1992.

Results from this simulation for passenger-vehicle fatalities among eighteen- to nineteen-year-olds are presented in table 3.10. In the first row of the table, we report the actual percentage change in fatalities that we observe between 1979 and 1992. In the next row, we present the predicted change that would have happened had no belt-use laws been adopted. For eighteen- to nineteen-year-olds, without a belt-use law, fatalities would have fallen only 32.6 percent, meaning that ([38.4 − 32.6]/38.4 or) 15 percent of the drop can be attributed to belt-use laws. Had MLDA laws stayed at their 1980 values, the fatalities would have fallen by 36 percent, meaning that MLDA law changes can explain only 6.3 percent of the reduction in fatalities. Finally, the passage of belt-use laws and MLDA hikes can explain only 19.5 percent of the reduction in the fatality rate. The effect of the laws is not necessarily additive since this is a highly nonlinear model.

In table 3.11, we report model estimates for our alcohol-sensitive measure (nighttime fatalities) and daytime fatalities. In these models, we also add the real beer tax as an alcohol-specific intervention. The results presented in this table suggest that, as expected, the effect of MLDAs of eighteen and nineteen is larger in the alcohol-specific regressions compared

Table 3.10	Percentage of Drop in 18–19-Year-Old Passenger-Vehicle-Fatality Rate Explained by State Interventions		
	% Change in Fatality Rate, 1979–92	% of Change Explained by Law Changes
Actual change	−38.4	
Predicted change with no adoption of belt-use laws	−32.6	15.0
Predicted change with no increases to an MLDA of 21	−36.0	6.4
Predicted change with no adoption of belt-use laws and no increases to an MLDA of 21	−30.9	19.5

Table 3.11   Conditional Maximum-Likelihood Estimates of Fixed-Effects Negative Binomial
                    Models for Teen Motor-Vehicle Fatalities, 1977–92 FARS

| | | Passenger-Vehicle Fatalities | | | |
| | | Nighttime | | Daytime | |
Independent Variable	Mean	16–17	18–19	16–17	18–19
Mandatory seat-belt law, primary	.107	−.059	−.081	−.073	−.062
enforcement		(.038)	(.034)	(.049)	(.047)
Mandatory seat-belt law, secondary	.199	−.055	−.063	.015	−.037
enforcement		(.036)	(.032)	(.045)	(.044)
MLDA of 18	.206	.018	.113	−.078	.024
		(.034)	(.030)	(.045)	(.044)
MLDA of 19	.156	.034	.069	.069	.071
		(.032)	(.028)	(.042)	(.040)
MLDA of 20	.051	.031	.046	.059	.008
		(.031)	(.055)	(.082)	(.083)
Real state and federal excise taxes	.519	−.448	−.697	−.540	−.530
on beer		(.154)	(.141)	(.190)	(.186)
65-MPH speed limit	.306	−.010	−.006	.092	.002
		(.048)	(.041)	(.063)	(.060)
State unemployment rate	6.67	−.010	−.012	−.030	−.044
		(.008)	(.007)	(.010)	(.010)
Real per capita personal income	1.23	−.038	−.292	.227	.140
(00,000)		(.171)	(.152)	(.226)	(.223)

Note: Standard errors are reported in parentheses. There are 768 observations in each model (48 states over 16 years). Each model includes state and year fixed effects and the natural log of the population for the given age.

to the samples shown in table 3.9 above. This suggests that the daytime/ nighttime counterfactual does function properly. The beer-tax results in table 3.11 deserve special mention. Prior studies have documented strong links between beer taxes, abusive teen drinking, and traffic fatalities. The results presented in table 3.11 replicate this reduced-form evidence by implying that increases in beer taxes would significantly reduce the number of teen traffic fatalities. However, several recent studies have suggested that these links may be spurious (e.g., Dee, in press; Mast et al. 1999). In part, this is because the direct links between beer taxes and the prevalence of teen alcohol use have typically been based on cross-sectional identification strategies and are not robust to the inclusion of state fixed effects (Dee 1999). But the reduced-form link between beer taxes and teen traffic fatalities has proved robust even in two-way fixed-effects specifications (e.g., Ruhm 1996). However, there are at least two reasons to be skeptical about the validity of such inferences. One is that the estimated tax effects are implausibly large. For example, the estimated tax elasticity of nighttime traffic fatalities among sixteen- to seventeen-year-olds is roughly -0.23 (i.e., $-.448 \times .519$). However, since beer taxes are only a fraction (roughly 10 percent) of the price of beer, this tax elasticity implies a substantially and implausibly larger price elasticity (roughly -2.3).[28] A second and perhaps more compelling type of evidence of the validity is based on comparing the models of daytime and nighttime fatalities. The estimated tax effects are quite large and statistically significant in the models of daytime fatalities even though the rate of alcohol involvement in these fatalities is just a fraction of what it is at night. One explanation for why beer taxes appear implausibly effective in such models is that these tax variables proxy for the unobserved trends specific to each state. The within-state variation in nominal beer taxes is fairly limited, and the overall time-series profile in real taxes is smoothly declining in most states owing to price inflation.[29] Regardless, a conservative interpretation of this evidence is that we should be substantially less sanguine than most of the prior literature suggests about the possible lifesaving benefits of higher beer taxes. In part, this is because we simply have not had sufficient state-level experiences with such tax changes to allow us to evaluate their effects.

The remaining tables present evaluations of the key drunk-driving policies discussed earlier. These evaluations are based on data from the period 1982–97, when much of the relevant policy variation occurred.[30] These evaluations include regressors defined as the interaction of administrative license revocations with each of the three BAC variables: illegal per se at 0.08 BAC; illegal per se at 0.10 or higher BAC; and zero-tolerance laws. In the absence of these interaction terms, most drunk-driving policies appear ineffective (e.g., Ruhm 1996). However, the recent debate over 0.08 BAC laws has underscored the claim that such laws are effective largely through their interaction with administrative license revocations (GAO 1999).[31] Furthermore, as a practical matter, the sample variation is sometimes defined only for such interactions. In particular, in the case of 0.08 BAC laws, the timing of their adoption was typically quite close to that of a regulation allowing administrative license revocations (Dee, in press). Tables 3.12 and 3.13 present the results of these evaluations for all ten fatality counts. These results suggest that illegal per se laws may generate large reductions in traffic fatalities through their interaction with administrative license revocations. For example, these results imply that the combination of a 0.08

28. Another reason to be skeptical of the implied price elasticity is that not all teen traffic fatalities are alcohol related, implying that the effects of the tax on drunk driving by teens are even larger.

29. The beer-tax estimates are sensitive to including state-specific trends as regressors (e.g., Dee 1999). However, since this often removes much of the available sample variation, the implied sensitivity is not clearly as meaningful as the results of the counterfactual estimations.

30. Nonetheless, the MLDA, seat-belt law, and macroeconomic regressors are also included. The beer-tax variable is omitted.

31. Since 1970, the NHTSA has advocated this sort of "systems approach" to reducing drunk driving, one based on a combination of laws, enforcement, and public education.

Table 3.12   Conditional Maximum–Likelihood Estimates of Fixed-Effects Negative Binomial Models for Teen Motor-Vehicle Fatalities, 1982–97 FARS

| | | Fatality Counts—Passenger Vehicles | | | | | |
| | | All | | Nighttime | | Daytime | |
Independent Variable	Mean	16–17	18–19	16–17	18–19	16–17	18–19
Illegal per se at 0.08 BAC	.105	.025	.096	-.032	.118	.119	.103
		(.127)	(.112)	(.162)	(.129)	(.185)	(.181)
× administrative license revocation	.101	.164	-.254	.262	-.278	.006	-.292
		(.152)	(.134)	(.193)	(.158)	(.224)	(.217)
Illegal per se at 0.10 or higher BAC	.753	.030	-.047	-.037	-.054	.167	-.004
		(.040)	(.035)	(.049)	(.039)	(.064)	(.063)
× administrative license revocation	.376	.212	-.133	.233	-.136	.131	-.198
		(.088)	(.078)	(.111)	(.092)	(.135)	(.128)
Zero-tolerance law	.269	-.037	-.016	.001	-.026	-.088	-.004
		(.033)	(.030)	(.042)	(.035)	(.047)	(.049)
× administrative license revocation	.212	-.10	-.069	-.056	-.055	.051	-.104
		(.041)	(.038)	(.053)	(.045)	(.061)	(.061)
Administrative license revocation	.494	-.211	.136	-.196	.129	-.182	.229
		(.091)	(.081)	(.115)	(.096)	(.140)	(.133)
Dram-shop statute or case law	.764	.010	.041	.007	.051	.039	.033
		(.038)	(.035)	(.048)	(.039)	(.058)	(.059)
Mandatory jail time for first DUI offense	.284	-.011	.071	.010	.110	-.036	-.008
		(.038)	(.035)	(.048)	(.040)	(.055)	(.058)
65-MPH speed limit	.526	.031	.005	.033	-.021	.013	.061
		(.036)	(.032)	(.045)	(.037)	(.055)	(.055)
70+-MPH speed limit	.061	.135	.039	.106	-.008	.160	.134
		(.060)	(.056)	(.077)	(.067)	(.087)	(.092)

Note: Standard errors are reported in parentheses. There are 768 observations in each model (48 states over 16 years). Each model includes state and year fixed effects, the natural log of the population for the given age and/or gender, three MLDA variables, two seat-belt-law variables, the state unemployment rate, and the real state personal income per capita.

Table 3.13   **Conditional Maximum-Likelihood Estimates of Fixed-Effects Negative Binomial Models for Teen Motor-Vehicle Fatalities, 1982–97 FARS**

	Fatality Counts—Passenger Vehicles			
	Male		Female	
Independent Variable	16–17	18–19	16–17	18–19
Illegal per se at 0.08 BAC	.050	.050	−.036	.222
	(.156)	(.123)	(.210)	(.195)
× administrative license revocation	.109	−.204	.285	−.412
	(.187)	(.150)	(.252)	(.234)
Illegal per se at 0.10 or higher BAC	.066	−.056	−.039	−.009
	(.048)	(.039)	(.070)	(.064)
× administrative license revocation	.154	−.136	.320	−.181
	(.108)	(.089)	(.148)	(.138)
Zero-tolerance law	−.012	−.031	−.086	.013
	(.040)	(.034)	(.054)	(.052)
× administrative license revocation	−.051	−.105	.065	.030
	(.051)	(.043)	(.067)	(.065)
Administrative license revocation	−.108	.157	−.400	.134
	(.112)	(.092)	(.153)	(.143)
Dram-shop statute or case law	.018	.022	−.012	.096
	(.047)	(.039)	(.064)	(.061)
Mandatory jail time for first DUI offense	.040	.057	−.107	.093
	(.046)	(.039)	(.062)	(.060)
65-MPH speed limit	.012	−.017	.068	.075
	(.044)	(.036)	(.061)	(.058)
70+-MPH speed limit	.107	−.036	.187	.221
	(.075)	(.064)	(.099)	(.097)

Note: Standard errors are reported in parentheses. There are 768 observations in each model (48 states over 16 years). Each model includes state and year fixed effects, the natural log of the population for the given age and/or gender, two seat-belt-law variables, three MLDA variables, the state unemployment rate, and the real state personal income per capita.

BAC law and administrative license revocations reduced passenger-vehicle fatalities among eighteen- to nineteen-year-olds by 25 percent. It should be noted that, although these estimated effects are large, they are only marginally significant. However, these effects are plausibly concentrated in reductions of nighttime and not daytime fatalities. The results reported in table 3.13 also suggest that these interactions were relatively more effective for females than for males. The evidence from tables 3.12 and 3.13 also suggests that zero-tolerance laws were typically ineffective either alone or in concert with administrative license revocations. However, it should be noted that these results may reflect a relative lack of enforcement.[32]

The other results reported in tables 3.12 and 3.13 provide little support

32. GAO (1999) notes that, in California, more underage drivers were prosecuted under that state's 0.08 BAC law than under its zero-tolerance law.

for the hypothesis that either of the other drunk-driving policies (dramshop case law or statutes, mandatory jail time for DUI offenders) or sixty-five-MPH speed limits had any detectable effects. It is, however, not entirely surprising that the initial movement to a sixty-five-MPH speed limit had no detectable effect among teens since these limits were restricted to rural interstate roads, where such fatalities are rare. Interestingly, these evaluations do suggest that the movement to maximum speed limits above sixty-five MPH did significantly increase counts of some teen traffic fatalities. In particular, these large increases (12–20 percent) were concentrated among the younger (sixteen- to seventeen-year-old) teens and among females.

3.4   Conclusions

Unfortunately for most parents, life begins for many teenagers when they get their driver's license. Teenagers travel upward of ten thousand miles in an automobile per year, many of those behind the wheel as a driver. As we illustrated here, parents have good reason to be alarmed. Driving is an inherently risky activity, and teens' inexperience and risk taking make the problem even worse. Teen fatality rates are two to three times those for adults aged twenty-five and older.

Teens are, on average, more aggressive drivers, are less likely to use safety equipment such as seat belts, and are about as likely to drive drunk as adults—even though no teens can legally drink. It is hard to disentangle whether a high teen fatality rate is due to risk taking or inexperience because both variables change with age. Teen traffic fatalities are, however, more a function of such driver behaviors than are fatalities among other age groups. Teens have a high frequency of accidents where driver error or risk taking is the clear cause, such as single-vehicle crashes and vehicle rollovers. This pattern of potential risk taking is consistent with other behaviors that we see among teens. The teens who do not wear their seat belts or who drive after drinking are those teens who take other health risks, like smoking, drinking, using drugs, and fighting.

The situation has, however, improved considerably over the last twenty years. When denominated by population, teen traffic fatalities have fallen by about 37 percent since 1979. This decline is probably an underestimate of the true improvements in traffic safety since teens are driving much more today than they have in past years. Most of the decline seems to be due to large reductions in alcohol-related fatalities. However, there have also been substantive increases in occupant protection, owing primarily to an increase in belt use and a move to heavier, more crashworthy automobiles.

Even with these important gains, traffic fatalities are still the leading cause of mortality among teens and, by implication, a major concern for health policy. However, there is cause for optimism. The U.S. experience over the past twenty years has clearly demonstrated that traffic safety is one area where government regulations can change important behaviors. For example, the state-specific movement away from MLDAs of eighteen has been associated with a drop in teen occupant fatalities of at least 5 percent. Furthermore, the widespread adoption of mandatory seat-belt laws at the state level has substantially increased belt use among teens, resulting in a 7–10 percent drop in teen occupant fatalities. More aggressive enforcement of seat-belt laws could possibly generate further gains. Additionally, these results suggest that drunk-driving policies like administrative license revocations may work in tandem with illegal per se laws that establish explicit BAC limits to reduce alcohol-related fatalities among teens. However, there is one possible and largely unexplored caveat to this evidence of the lifesaving benefits of certain government regulations. These benefits may be somewhat attenuated over the life cycle if traffic-safety policies simply shift to older teens and young adults the experiential learning that occurs in risky settings. These benefits may also be somewhat limited because teens who take driving risks are substantially more likely to be risk takers in other contexts as well.

References

Asch, P., and D. T. Levy. 1987. Does the minimum drinking age affect traffic fatalities? *Journal of Policy Analysis and Management* 6, no. 2:180–92.

Berkowitz, M. K., et al. 1990. Disaggregate analysis of the demand for gasoline. *Canadian Journal of Economics* 23, no. 2:253–75.

Campbell, B. J., and F. Campbell. 1988. Injury reduction and belt use associated with occupant restraint laws. In *Preventing automobile injury: New findings from evaluation research,* ed. J. D. Graham. Dover, Mass.: Auburn House.

Centers for Disease Control (CDC). 1998. *Behavioral risk factor surveillance system's user guide.* Atlanta: U.S. Department of Health and Human Services.

Chaloupka, F. J., et al. 1993. Alcohol-control policies and motor-vehicle fatalities. *Journal of Legal Studies* 22, no. 1:161–86.

Cook, P. J., and G. Tauchen. 1984. The effect of minimum drinking age legislation on youthful auto fatalities, 1970–1977. *Journal of Legal Studies* 13:169–90.

Dee, T. S. 1998. Reconsidering the effects of seat belt laws and their enforcement status. *Accident Analysis and Prevention* 30, no. 1:1–10.

———. 1999. State alcohol policies, teen drinking, and traffic fatalities. *Journal of Public Economics* 72, no. 2:289–315.

———. In press. Does setting limits save lives? The case of 0.08 BAC laws. *Journal of Policy Analysis and Management.*

DeJong, W., and R. Hingson. 1998. Strategies to reduce driving under the influence of alcohol. *Annual Review of Public Health* 19:359–78.

Evans, L. 1986. The effectiveness of safety belts in preventing fatalities. *Accident Analysis and Prevention* 18, no. 3:229–41.

———. 1991. *Traffic safety and the driver.* New York: Van Nostrand Reinhold.

Evans, W. N., and J. D. Graham. 1988. Traffic safety and the business cycle. *Alcohol, Drugs, and Driving* 4, no. 1:31–38.

———. 1991. Risk reduction or risk compensation? The case of mandatory safety-belt use laws. *Journal of Risk and Uncertainty* 4, no. 1:61–73.

Evans, W. N., et al. 1991. General deterrence of drunk driving: Evaluation of recent American policies. *Risk Analysis* 11, no. 2:279–89.

Farmer, C. M., et al. 1999. Changes in motor vehicle occupant fatalities after repeal of the national maximum speed limit. *Accident Analysis and Prevention* 31, no. 5:537–43.

Foss, R. D., and K. R. Evenson. 1999. Effectiveness of graduated driver licensing in reducing motor vehicle crashes. *American Journal of Preventive Medicine* 16, no. 18:47–56.

Gabler, H. C., and W. T. Hollowell. 1998. The aggressivity of light trucks and vans in traffic crashes. Paper no. 980908. Warrendale: Society of Automotive Engineers, February. Paper available at http://www-nrd.nhtsa.dot.gov/include/nrd10/aggressivity/documents/980908/980908.htm.

General Accounting Office (GAO). 1999. Highway safety: Effectiveness of state .08 blood alcohol laws. Washington, D.C.

Hausman, J., B. H. Hall, and Z. Griliches. 1984. Econometric models for count data with an application to the patents-R&D relationship. *Econometrica* 52, no. 4:909–38.

Hingson, R. 1996. Prevention of drinking and driving. *Alcohol Health and Research World* 20, no. 4:219–26.

Hingson, R., S. Moelock Levenson, T. Heeren, T. Nagione, C. Rodgers, T. Schiavone, and R. P. Hertz. 1988. Repeal of the Massachusetts seat belt law. *American Journal of Public Health* 78, no. 5:548–52.

Horne, J., and L. Reyner. 1995. Sleep related vehicle accidents. *British Medical Journal* 310, no. 6979:565–67.

Insurance Institute for Highway Safety (IIHS). 1999. *Graduated licensing: A blueprint for North America.* Arlington, Va.

Joksch, H., D. Massie, R. Pichler. 1998. *Vehicle aggressivity: Fleet characteristics using traffic collision data.* Washington, D.C.: National Highway Traffic Safety Administration, U.S. Department of Transportation.

Kahane, C. J. 1997. Relationships between vehicle size and fatality risk in model year 1985–93 passenger cars and light trucks. Report no. DOT HS 808 570. Washington, D.C.: National Highway and Traffic Safety Administration, January.

Lave, C., and P. Elias. 1994. Did the 65-MPH speed limit save lives? *Accident Analysis and Prevention* 26, no. 1:49–62.

Levitt, S. D., and J. Porter. 1999a. Estimating the effect of alcohol on driver risk using only fatal accident statistics. Working Paper no. 6944. Cambridge, Mass.: National Bureau of Economic Research.

———. 1999b. Sample selection in the estimation of air bags and seat belt effectiveness. Working Paper no. 7210. Cambridge, Mass.: National Bureau of Economic Research.

Males, M. A. 1986. The minimum purchase age for alcohol and young-driver fatal crashes: A long-term view. *Journal of Legal Studies* 15:181–211.

Mast, B. D., et al. 1999. Beer taxation and alcohol-related traffic fatalities. *Southern Economic Journal* 66, no. 2:214–49.

McGuckin, N., and E. Murakami. 1999. Examining trip-chaining behavior: A comparison of travel by men and women. Washington, D.C.: Federal Highway Administration, U.S. Department of Transportation.

Mullins, R. J., and N. C. Mann. 1999. Population-based research assessing the effectiveness of trauma systems. *Journal of Trauma* 47, no. 3, suppl.:559–566.

Nathans, A. B., G. J. Jurkovich, F. P. Rivara, and R. V. Maier. 2000. Effectiveness of state trauma systems in reducing injury-related mortality: A national evaluation. *Journal of Trauma* 48, no. 1:25–30.

National Highway Traffic Safety Administration (NHTSA). 1984. *Regulatory impact analysis of FMVSS 208: Occupant crash protection.* Washington, D.C.: U.S. Department of Transportation.

———. 1989. *Restraint usage in the traffic population: 1988 report.* Washington, D.C.: U.S. Department of Transportation.

———. 1994. *Research agenda for an improved novice driver education program.* Washington, D.C.: U.S. Department of Transportation.

———. 1999a. *Observed belt use in 1998.* Washington, D.C.: U.S. Department of Transportation.

———. 1999b. *Traffic safety facts, 1998.* Washington, D.C.: U.S. Department of Transportation.

Pack, A., et al. 1995. Characteristics of crashes attributed to the driver having fallen asleep. *Accident Analysis and Prevention* 27, no. 6:769–75.

Peltzman, S. 1975. The effects of automobile safety regulation. *Journal of Political Economy* 83, no. 4 (August): 677–726.

Ruhm, C. J. 1996. Alcohol policies and highway vehicle fatalities. *Journal of Health Economics* 14, no. 5:583–603.

Spain, D. 1997. Societal trends: The aging baby boom and women's increased independence. Washington, D.C.: Federal Highway Administration, U.S. Department of Transportation.

Walls, M. A., A. J. Krupnick, and H. C. Hood. 1993. Estimating the demands for vehicle-miles-traveled using household survey data: Results from the 1990 Nationwide Personal Transportation Survey. Discussion Paper no. ENR93-25. Washington, D.C.: Resources for the Future, Energy and Natural Resources Division.

Zador, P. L. 1991. Alcohol-related relative risk of fatal driver injuries in relation to driver age and sex. *Journal of Studies on Alcohol* 52, no. 4:302–10.

Zador, P. L., et al. 1989. Fatal crash involvement and laws against alcohol-impaired driving. *Journal of Public Health Policy* 10, no. 4:467–84.

4

The Sexual Activity and Birth-Control Use of American Teenagers

Phillip B. Levine

Pregnancies among America's teenagers have caught our attention as one of the nation's greatest troubles. A Gallup poll conducted on 23 and 24 May 1999 found that 7 percent of those surveyed reported that youth/teen pregnancy was "the most important problem facing this country today" (Gallup Organization 1999). It was the fifth most common specific problem reported. The concern about teen pregnancy has even led to national goals regarding its reduction. The first family planning objective stated in *Healthy People 2000,* written in 1990, is to "reduce pregnancies among females aged 15–17," and additional goals include increased abstinence along with reduced activity and increased contraceptive use among those adolescents who do engage in intercourse (U.S. DHHS 1999a). Similar goals have been proposed for the next decade in *Healthy People 2010* (U.S. DHHS 1999b).

In fact, statistics regarding teen pregnancy are quite startling. Each year, roughly 10 percent of women between the ages of fifteen and nineteen and 6 percent of women between the ages of fifteen and seventeen get pregnant (Henshaw 1999). Approximately half these pregnancies result in a live birth. The share of teen women who become pregnant each year is considerably higher in the United States than it is in other developed countries. Rates in England and Canada are half the level and rates in Japan one-tenth the level of those in the United States (Alan Guttmacher Institute 1998). The high rate of teen pregnancy is a particularly American prob-

Phillip B. Levine is associate professor of economics at Wellesley College and a research associate of the National Bureau of Economic Research.

The author thanks Marcellus Andrews, Jon Gruber, Ann Velenchik, and conference and preconference participants for their helpful suggestions and Joyce Abma, Gil Crouse, Bob Schoeni, Sharon Terman, and Tori Velkoff for their assistance in acquiring and using the data.

lem, which rules out the possibility that teens are simply too young to control their sexual activity and/or too shortsighted to use contraception. Social factors must come into play.

Researchers from many academic disciplines, including anthropology, demography, developmental psychology, and sociology, have contributed to the literature attempting to identify the factors that lead to teen pregnancy. From these perspectives, teens' sexual activity and use of contraceptives is governed by their stage of development, which is dependent on a complicated array of factors influencing them since birth (and potentially even before that). Within this framework, particular acts are viewed as spontaneous and irrational, and teen pregnancies are viewed as "mistakes." Economists have rarely contributed to the study of teen sexual activity and birth-control use directly but have examined the determinants of teen fertility. The contribution of economic analysis in that context is that it provides a focus on the costs and benefits of particular decisions and applies more sophisticated statistical techniques to the study of the topic.

The purpose of this paper is to review the theory and empirical evidence regarding teens' sexual activity and birth-control use with an emphasis on the contribution that economic analysis can make. In section 4.1, I present a series of descriptive statistics designed to document recent trends in these activities for the population as a whole and for racial/ethnic subgroups. Section 4.2 will present a review of prior research, including both theoretical contributions across disciplines and previous empirical work that has estimated models of the determinants of sexual activity and birth-control use. Section 4.3 will report an analysis of two data sets that are designed to accomplish two different goals. First, examination of cross-sectional data can provide correlational evidence regarding who engages in sexual activity and uses birth control. Second, I use state-level data over time attempting to identify whether changes in "prices" affect these activities, where prices are measured by economic conditions, AIDS incidence, welfare generosity, and the restrictiveness of abortion policy. The results of this analysis indicate that some prices do indeed matter; if engaging in sexual activity is "more expensive" through, say, an improved labor market or an increased probability of contracting AIDS, then teenagers are less likely to have sex and/or more likely to use contraception. Section 4.4 will review the evidence on the effect of teen childbearing on the subsequent well-being of women. Section 4.5 concludes by discussing the implications of this analysis for public policy.

4.1   Recent Trends

4.1.1   Pregnancies, Abortions, and Births

Perhaps part of the recent public attention paid to the sexual activity of teens can be attributed to the rather unusual trends that have occurred over the past decade or so in birth-, abortion, and pregnancy rates. As reported in figure 4.1*A*, after years of slowly declining teen birthrates, the late 1980s saw a sudden reversal in which the rate of births to women aged fifteen to nineteen jumped from about fifty per thousand women in this age group to sixty-two by 1991. Just as suddenly, that trend reversed, and teen birthrates have fallen back to about the level observed before the increase, at fifty-one births per thousand women aged fifteen to nineteen

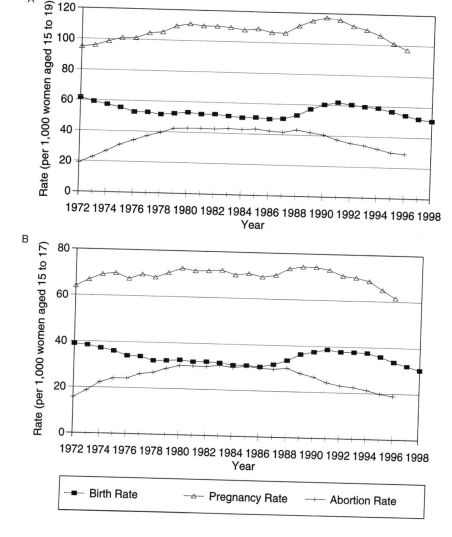

Fig. 4.1   Birth-, pregnancy, and abortion rates for women: *A*, aged 15–19; *B*, aged 15–17

Sources: Henshaw (1999); Ventura, Matthews, and Curtin (1999).

in 1998. The use of abortion, on the other hand, used to follow inversely the trend in births; decreases in teen birthrates through the late 1980s were matched by increases in the use of abortion services by these women. Over the last decade or so, however, abortions have become less and less common among teens, indicating that, since 1991, both abortions and births have fallen simultaneously. If fewer women are aborting and fewer women are giving birth, then it must be the case that pregnancies are falling even more rapidly. In fact, a constructed pregnancy rate (one that simply adds the birth- and abortion rate and factors in a fixed rate of miscarriages) for teens shows a dramatic decline, falling from 115 pregnancies per thousand teenage women in 1991 to ninety-seven in 1996, a 16 percent decline over only five years. Figure 4.1*B*, shows that similar trends are observed among fifteen- to seventeen-year-old women.

These data can be used to decompose the decline in births into one component attributable to risky sexual activity and one attributable to abortion behavior if we assume that the probability of becoming pregnant if one engages in risky sexual activity and the probability of a miscarriage are assumed to be constant. Between 1991 and 1996, the birthrate fell from 62.1 to 54.4, a 12 percent decline. If the abortion rate remained unchanged, one would have expected the birthrate to have fallen by 16 percent, or 133 percent of the decline, on the basis of a reduction in risky sexual activity. The fact that abortion became less prevalent offset this effect, increasing the odds of giving birth conditional on a pregnancy by 4 percent. A similar decomposition can be conducted for the rise in birthrates between 1986 and 1991, when the birthrate rose by 24 percent from 50.2 to 62.1. About two-thirds of this increase can be attributed to a reduction in abortion and one-third to an increase in risky sexual activity.

Although data on abortions are not available by race/ethnicity, patterns in birthrates are quite different across different groups. Figure 4.2 shows birthrates for fifteen- to nineteen- and fifteen- to seventeen-year-old women by race and ethnicity. Any trends in these figures within groups are overshadowed by the huge disparity in teen birthrates across groups. In the peak years of the early 1990s, black, non-Hispanic teens were three times as likely to give birth as were white, non-Hispanic teens. Since then, birthrates for all groups have fallen, but the decline for black, non-Hispanic teens has been precipitous. In 1991, 119 teen births per thousand women in this group were recorded; in just six years, that level had fallen to ninety-one in 1997, a 24 percent decline. An even greater relative decline occurred for younger black, non-Hispanic teens. In 1990, there were eighty-seven births per thousand fifteen- to seventeen-year-old women in this group, and this level fell by 28 percent to sixty-three births. Declines are also observed for Hispanic and white, non-Hispanic teen women over the last few years, but nothing as dramatic as that witnessed for black, non-Hispanic teens. The decline for black, non-Hispanic teens is so large that, even though they make up only about 15 percent of all female teens,

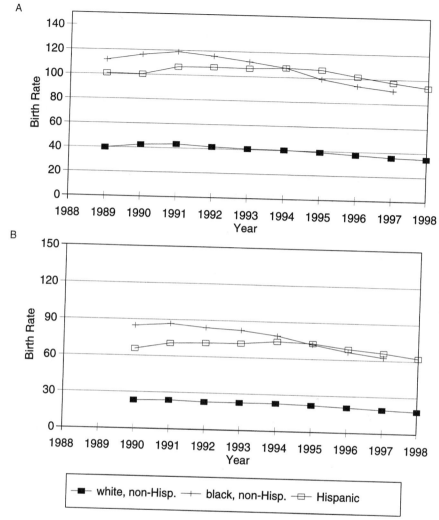

Fig. 4.2   Birthrates for women by race/ethnicity: *A*, aged 15–19; *B*, aged 15–17
Sources: Ventura, Martin, et al. (1999); Ventura, Matthews, and Curtin (1999).

they account for about 45 percent of the decline in the overall teen birth-rate between 1991 and 1997.[1]

The public concern about the level of teen pregnancies and births can perhaps be attributed to the fact that the share of teen births that take place outside marriage has skyrocketed over the past several decades. Figure 4.3*A* shows that the fraction of births to unmarried mothers has increased for all women but particularly so for teens. For nonteens, few

1. This estimate is based on data presented in Ventura et al. (1995) and Ventura, Martin, et al. (1999a).

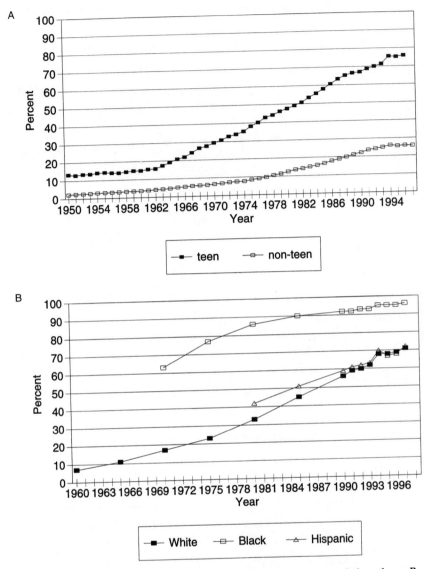

Fig. 4.3 *A*, The percentage of teen and nonteen births to unmarried mothers; *B*, the percentage of teen births to unmarried mothers by race/ethnicity

Sources: A, DHHS (1995, 1998); Ventura et al. (1996); Ventura et al. (1997, 1998); Ventura, Martin, et al. (1999); and author's calculations; *B*, DHHS (1995, 1998); Ventura, Martin, et al. (1999).

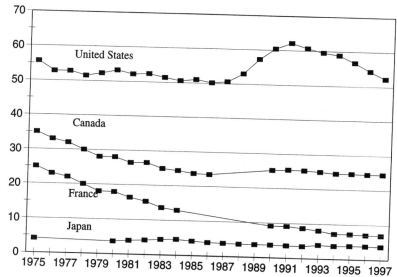

Fig. 4.4   Teen fertility rates in the United States and other industrialized countries
Source: U.S. Bureau of the Census, International Data Base.

births to unmarried mothers occurred until the 1960s, and then the fraction grew slowly before leveling off at about one-quarter by the 1990s. For teens, on the other hand, 15 percent of births in 1960 were to unmarried mothers, but that rate rose to 78 percent by 1997. Moreover, racial differences in teen births are dramatic, as shown in figure 4.3*B*. Currently, virtually all births to black teens are outside marriage.[2]

These statistics on teen pregnancies, abortions, and fertility stand in stark contrast to the experiences of other developed countries. Figure 4.4 reports trends in teen (age fifteen to nineteen) fertility rates for the United States, Canada, France, and Japan going back to 1975. Clearly, a high birthrate for teenage women is a particularly American phenomenon. Even in 1975, the teen birthrate in the United States was high—at over fifty-five births per thousand teenage women—relative to the other countries. Canada was the next highest, with a rate of only thirty-five, and, in Japan, there were only four births per thousand teenage women. Over the next two decades, however, downward trends are apparent in Canada and France, while Japan remained at a very low level.[3] By 1997, the teen birth-

2. Statistics for whites and blacks are inclusive of Hispanics. Data for white and black non-Hispanics are available only for the last decade or so and are not reported in order to provide a longer time series.

3. An analysis of the determinants of the decline in Canada and France is beyond the scope of this paper. One potential explanation for the decline, that a greater use of abortion has reduced teen fertility, can be ruled out at least for Canada, however. In Canada throughout most of the 1970s and 1980s, the teen abortion rate was roughly constant—at about

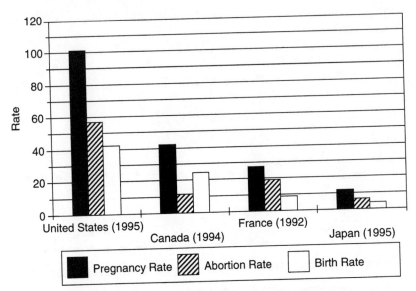

Fig. 4.5   Birth-, abortion, and pregnancy rates in the United States and other developed countries

Source: UN Department of Economic and Social Affairs (various years).

rate in the United States still stood at about fifty-two, while Canada's rate had fallen to less than half that, at twenty-five. Teen births in France became as uncommon as they were in Japan over the period. Consistent with these trends, abortions and pregnancies are considerably lower in these other developed countries compared to the United States. Figure 4.5 shows that pregnancies among teens in the United States are more than twice as common as in Canada and ten times more likely than in Japan. The abortion rate is also three times or more greater than that observed in these other countries, but births still remain considerably higher.

4.1.2   Sexual Activity and Birth-Control Use

These trends in births and pregnancies among teens suggest that changes must be occurring in levels of sexual activity and/or birth-control use over time. In fact, public pronouncements of such patterns have been put forth by the U.S. Department of Health and Human Services over the last few years. In 1997, Donna Shalala, the secretary of this department, proclaimed: "The long-term increase in teenage sexual activity may finally have stopped" (NCHS Press Office 1997). In 1998, she went further, stat-

---

fifteen per thousand teen women—until a Canadian Supreme Court ruling in 1988 increased the availability of abortion (Miller, Wadhera, and Henshaw 1997). Thereafter, the abortion rate rose to 21.5 by 1993. The timing of this trend is inconsistent with the reduction in teen births displayed in fig. 4.4.

ing: "For the first time in two decades, fewer young people are engaging in sexual behavior. . . . It is truly good news for all of us involved in the lives of America's teenagers" (CDC Press Office 1998). Both press releases also cite evidence of increased contraceptive use.

Although evidence of such trends does exist, it is not quite as transparent as one would expect given these assessments. Two main sources of data are used to track trends in sexual activity and birth-control use for American teens. The National Survey of Family Growth (NSFG) is administered to women of childbearing age (fifteen to forty-four) but is large enough that a separate analysis of teens (fifteen to nineteen as well as fifteen to seventeen) to track national trends is feasible. Comparable surveys were conducted in 1982, 1988, and 1995.[4] The second source of data is the Youth Risk Behavior Survey (YRBS), which has been administered biannually starting in 1991 to a nationally representative sample of roughly fifteen thousand ninth- through twelfth-grade boys and girls. The estimates reported will pertain only to the girls in the YRBS.[5] All the statistics displayed in the figures presented below can be found in table 4.1.

These data, however, do not show widespread trends toward decreased sexual activity and greater birth-control use.[6] Figure 4.6*A* displays the available evidence on the percentage of teens who have engaged in sexual activity in the preceding three months. Although Secretary Shalala's assessment that "fewer young people are engaging in sexual behavior"—is technically correct, the evidence is not particularly strong. Among those fifteen to nineteen in the NSFG data (the evidence used to support her assertion), a large decline was observed between 1988 and 1995, which followed a large increase between 1982 and 1988. But the 1995 level is only 0.2 percentage points lower than the 1982 level. Moreover, evidence from the same source showed virtually no recent change among those fifteen to seventeen; between 1988 and 1995, the percentage who engaged in sexual activity fell by 0.2 percentage points. Estimates from the YRBS data show that girls in high school became more sexually active through 1995 before decreasing their sexual activity between 1995 and 1997.

Broad evidence of general declines in sexual activity is also weak when one considers whether teens have ever engaged in sexual activity. Figure 4.6*B* shows that the YRBS data do indicate a decrease between 1995 and 1997 and that the 1997 level is lower than that observed in any of the previous years. The NSFG data show a very slight decrease in the percent-

4. NSFG surveys conducted in the 1970s are not comparable because they were administered only to married women.

5. For purposes of comparability with the NSFG data, the estimates from the YRBS reported here will be restricted to those for girls. In subsequent analyses of the YRBS reported below, however, I will take advantage of the availability of information on both boys and girls from that survey.

6. All the estimates reported here have been computed by the author, but those reported by Abma and Sonenstein (1998) and Terry and Manlove (1999) are comparable.

Table 4.1 Sexual Activity and Contraceptive Use by Race/Ethnicity

	NSFG: Ages 15–19			NSFG: Ages 15–17			YRBS			
	1982	1988	1995	1982	1988	1995	1991	1993	1995	1997
Sexual Activity Ever										
All	46.9	52.5	51.1	32.2	37.7	38.0	50.8	50.1	52.1	47.7
White	44.4	52.2	59.0	29.7	35.5	35.3	47.1	47.4	49.0	44.0
Black	58.9	61.0	60.0	44.1	50.5	48.3	75.9	70.4	67.0	65.6
Hispanic	49.9	46.9	56.5	34.4	34.1	50.4	43.3	48.3	53.3	45.7
Sexual Activity in Past 3 Months										
All	40.0	46.1	39.8	26.8	30.9	27.7	38.2	37.5	40.4	36.5
White	37.1	43.1	39.3	25.2	27.8	25.9	35.9	35.2	38.5	35.1
Black	53.6	50.8	45.8	38.8	39.5	33.9	55.3	53.2	50.6	47.3
Hispanic	42.2	31.5	45.2	22.0	20.4	39.0	32.8	37.9	39.3	33.2
No Contraceptive Use during First Intercourse										
All	51.8	34.9	24.6	59.8	31.8	24.1	N.A.	N.A.	N.A.	N.A.
White	44.1	30.6	18.9	51.8	25.7	19.0	N.A.	N.A.	N.A.	N.A.
Black	64.1	46.6	31.7	68.8	45.0	28.0	N.A.	N.A.	N.A.	N.A.
Hispanic	77.1	44.5	42.7	87.7	39.0	38.5	N.A.	N.A.	N.A.	N.A.
No Contraceptive Use during Last Intercourse in Past Three Months										
All	N.A.	22.9	30.6	N.A.	26.8	33.2	18.1	16.2	17.3	14.9
White	N.A.	20.2	28.2	N.A.	22.7	29.6	13.6	13.7	13.1	12.9
Black	N.A.	32.0	29.7	N.A.	41.4	27.1	26.9	22.7	18.3	17.8
Hispanic	N.A.	32.1	44.4	N.A.	30.9	53.7	29.0	23.1	34.9	30.3
Pregnancy Risk[a]										
All	N.A.	9.8	12.2	N.A.	7.7	9.2	6.9	6.0	6.9	5.4
White	N.A.	8.7	11.1	N.A.	6.3	7.7	4.9	4.8	5.0	4.5
Black	N.A.	16.3	13.6	N.A.	16.3	9.2	14.7	12.0	9.1	8.4
Hispanic	N.A.	10.1	20.1	N.A.	6.3	21.0	9.5	8.7	13.7	10.0

Source: Author's calculations from the 1982, 1988, and 1995 NSFG and the 1991, 1993, 1995, and 1997 YRBS.

Note: Race/ethnic groups are mutually exclusive. Sample weights were used in estimation so that all statistics are representative for the particular subgroup of the nation's population. Owing to sample-size limitations, some estimates (particularly those for birth-control use for Hispanics and for the younger age category) are somewhat imprecise. N.A. = not available.

[a] Sexually active in past three months and no contraceptive use during last intercourse.

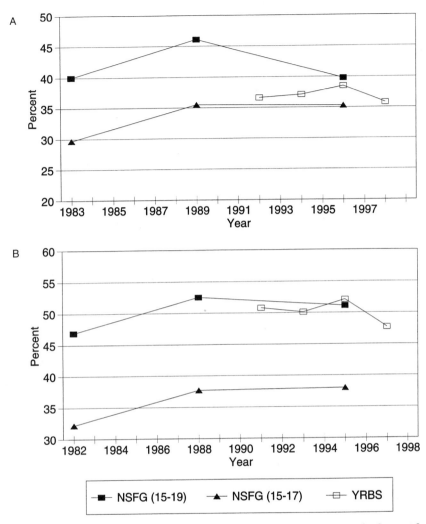

Fig. 4.6 *A*, **The percentage of teens who have had sexual intercourse in the past 3 months;** *B*, **the percentage of teens who have ever had sexual intercourse**
Source: Author's calculations from the NSFG and the YRBS.

age of ever sexually active women among fifteen- to nineteen-year-olds between 1988 and 1995, but the rate in 1995 is still almost 5 percentage points higher than that observed in 1982. Moreover, younger teens continue to be increasingly likely to have ever engaged in sexual activity through 1995.

Estimates of the use of birth control also provide mixed findings for the population as a whole. All statistics regarding birth-control use are reported here as the fraction who did *not* use contraception at a particular incident rather than the more traditionally reported figures of those who did use contraception. This decision was made because it is the failure to use contraception that places the woman at risk of becoming pregnant and that is the focus of this paper. Figure 4.7A displays the available evidence on the likelihood of failing to use contraception during the last intercourse in the past three months.[7] Data from the YRBS show decreases through the 1990s. On the contrary, the NSFG data show an increase between 1988 and 1995 (this information is not available from the NSFG for 1982). A reconciliation is perhaps possible if a dramatic upward trend in the late 1980s followed a sharp rebound in the early 1990s; neither data set provides sufficient information to test this hypothesis.[8]

The reported increase in the failure to use birth control based on the NSFG data is particularly surprising in the light of recent advances in contraceptive technology. Highly effective, longer-term contraceptive methods, including Norplant and Depo Provera, have recently become available.[9] Although these new methods have been adopted by a significant number of teens, their use has largely been among those who might have used the Pill otherwise. Figure 4.7B shows the methods used during last intercourse by women fifteen to nineteen who have engaged in sexual activity in the past three months. It indicates that 7.7 percent of these women used either Norplant or Depo Provera in 1995 (these methods were not listed as options in 1988). Most other forms of contraception were used at roughly the same rate, with the important exception of the Pill. In 1988, 41.5 percent of teenage women used this effective form of contraception, but that level fell to 23.3 percent in 1995. This fall was not compensated for by the increased use of new contraceptive methods; the difference is made up by those not using any method at all (on the basis of these data).

7. It is evident that estimates from the YRBS data are substantially lower rate than those from the NSFG samples. A potential explanation for this finding rests in the particular questions asked in the two surveys. The YRBS appears quite specific in indicating that some form of birth control should have been used by asking, "The last time you had sexual intercourse, what one method did you or your partner use to prevent pregnancy?" Estimates from the NSFG are derived from a less-directed approach (where respondents are asked whether they used a series of types of contraception), one that may have been better able to illicit a response that no form was used. Another potential explanation is that the YRBS is conducted in school while the NSFG is conducted in home and that that difference may affect the reporting of sensitive behaviors. Regardless of the differences in levels, estimates over time should still provide trends that can legitimately be compared.

8. I have spoken with representatives of the Centers for Disease Control (CDC) about this apparent contradiction. Although they have confirmed finding similar patterns in their own analyses, they too have been unable to resolve the apparent inconsistency across data sources.

9. This discussion ignores the introduction of the *morning-after pill*, otherwise known as *emergency contraception*, because such methods were not approved for use by the U.S. Food and Drug Administration until February 1997, after the date for which statistics are being reported in this paper. Nevertheless, the use of emergency contraception is still uncommon. A recent survey found that only 1 percent of all women of reproductive age have ever used it and that only 11 percent even know that it exists and is available for use (Kaiser Family Foundation 1997).

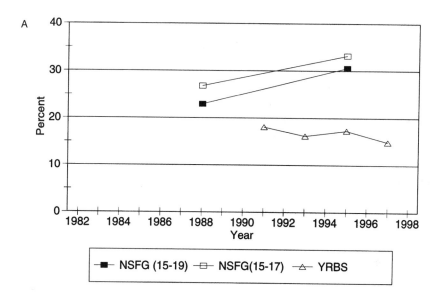

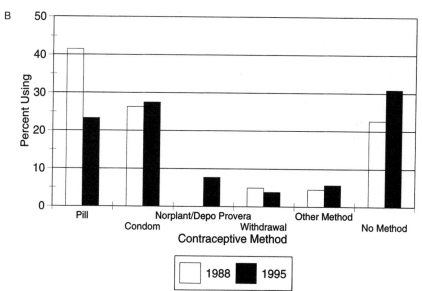

Fig. 4.7 *A*, The percentage of teens who failed to use contraception during last intercourse in the past 3 months; *B*, contraceptive methods used during last intercourse by 15–19-year-old women; *C*, the percentage of teens who failed to use contraception during first intercourse

Source: A, Author's calculations from the NSFG and the YRBS; *B*, Terry and Manlove (1999); *C*, author's calculations from the NSFG.

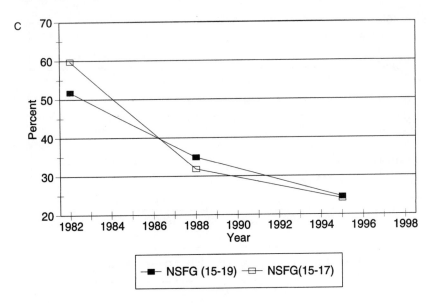

Fig. 4.7   (cont.)

On the other hand, fewer and fewer teens appear to undertake their first sexual encounter without using contraception. Figure 4.7C reports these data for both age groups of the NSFG data (no comparable data are available in the YRBS); the reduction has been dramatic. In 1982, more than half of teens in both age groups did not use any contraception during first intercourse. In 1995, however, only about one-quarter failed to do so. Although this trend is important, it is probably not as good a predictor of the risk of becoming pregnant as is birth-control use at last intercourse since the latter is probably a better gauge of typical practices for a larger proportion of sexual activity.

To approximate the risk of pregnancy that a typical teen faces at a point in time, the data on sexual activity in the past three months along with the failure to use contraception during the last intercourse in the past three months are combined to create a statistic representing the joint probability of the two behaviors. This statistic, to which I refer as the *pregnancy risk,* constitutes the probability that in the past three months a teenage girl had sex and did not use contraception, placing her at risk of becoming pregnant. It is a useful statistic because it incorporates abstinence as a form of contraception. On the other hand, because it captures only failure to use contraception during the last intercourse, it is likely to understate the fraction of teens who are truly at risk of getting pregnant.[10] Nevertheless,

10. Moreover, the three-month window that it uses is shorter than the annual window with which births, abortions, and pregnancies are typically measured. For both these reasons, a comparison of pregnancy risk to the pregnancy rate will incorrectly make it appear that a huge fraction of teens are at risk of becoming pregnant.

trends in this statistic would seem to be strongly correlated with the true fraction at risk.

The estimated pregnancy risk across samples over time is reported in figure 4.8. As one would expect on the basis of the earlier patterns of sexual activity in the past three months and contraceptive use during the last intercourse over that period, trends in pregnancy risk between the two surveys conflict. The NSFG data indicate an increase in pregnancy risk between 1988 and 1995, but the YRBS shows a decline between 1991 and 1997. Again, these findings may not be inconsistent if an upward trend in the late 1980s reversed in the early 1990s. Nevertheless, they do not present a clear picture regarding changes over time in the risk that teens face of becoming pregnant.

These results for sexual activity, birth-control use, and pregnancy risk do not appear to coincide with the evidence on pregnancies and births presented earlier. The rapid decline in these outcomes through the 1990s would certainly suggest that a reduction in sexual activity and an increase in contraceptive use should be readily apparent in these data, but they are not.

To reconcile these findings, one must recall that the trends in births were considerably stronger for blacks than for whites and Hispanics. In fact, evidence consistent with these trends by race/ethnicity is observed, as reported in table 4.1 above. Several measures of sexual activity for black, non-Hispanic women have decreased rather dramatically, while similar statistics for white, non-Hispanic and Hispanic teenage women show no such patterns. For instance, estimates from the NSFG indicate that the

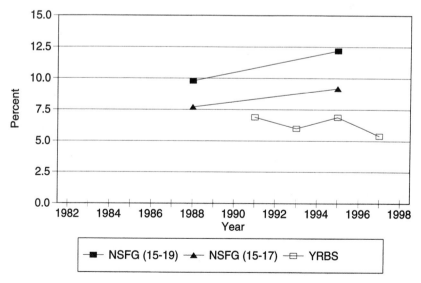

Fig. 4.8 The percentage of teens who are at risk for pregnancy
Source: Author's calculations from the NSFG and the YRBS.

share of black, non-Hispanic women aged fifteen to nineteen who have been sexually active in the past three months fell from 53.6 percent in 1982, to 50.8 percent in 1988, to 45.8 percent in 1995. Similar findings are observed for those fifteen to seventeen in the NSFG and for school-age girls from the YRBS. Results are less supportive of this trend when considering whether women have ever engaged in sexual activity, but that measure is probably less indicative of the risk of pregnancy than is sexual activity in the past three months. On the other hand, little evidence of decreased sexual activity among white, non-Hispanic and Hispanic women is observed in any of the data (if anything, there is evidence of an increase in activity for Hispanics).

Moreover, fewer black, non-Hispanic women engage in sexual activity without using contraceptives. During first intercourse, rates of use have jumped significantly for all demographic groups. But contraceptive use during the last intercourse in the past three months has risen strongly only for black, non-Hispanic women. In the YRBS, for instance, one-quarter of school-age girls in this group failed to use birth control during their last intercourse in 1991, but that rate fell continuously to 18 percent by 1997. Perhaps most striking is the evidence on the constructed pregnancy-risk measure. For both the younger teens from the NSFG between 1988 and 1995 and the school-age teens in the YRBS between 1991 and 1997, the risk of pregnancy was cut almost in half. On the basis of all the findings reported above, one can see that the national trend toward lower teen birthrates is largely driven by a reduction in births to black, non-Hispanic women and that the trend for that group is consistent with those women's reduction in sexual activity and increased reliance on contraception, reducing their risk of becoming pregnant.

4.2   Review of the Literature on Teen Sexuality

The models of the determinants of teen sexuality and use of contraception that economists have put forward are considerably different from those introduced in the other social sciences. This section will provide a brief overview of these perspectives and offer a framework for characterizing their differences. I will then describe recent advances in the field of behavioral economics that can provide something of a synthesis of the two contrasting approaches. Finally, I will briefly review the empirical literature that attempts to identify those factors that are related to sexual activity and contraceptive use.

4.2.1   Alternative Theoretical Perspectives

The models to which noneconomists subscribe tend to be very intricate and factor in the effect of a multitude of potential components that affect developmental outcomes, including teen sexuality, and may well affect each other (see Brooks-Gunn and Furstenberg 1989; Hardy and Zabin

1991; Brooks-Gunn and Paikoff 1997). For instance, Hardy and Zabin (1991) present a life-course model in which these factors are broadly decomposed into those that are biological or health related and those that pertain to one's environment or family. Each of these categories contains a large number of factors. Within biological/health factors, indicators of the child's health go back from before birth (i.e., mother's nutrition status, drug use, etc.), through infancy and childhood (i.e., congenital deficits, accidents, nutrition, etc.), and into adolescence (i.e., sexual maturation, mental health, etc.). Family and environmental factors include characteristics of the individual's parents and family (i.e., parents' education, parenting skills, family composition, etc.), available resources (i.e., economic resources, support networks, etc.), community characteristics (i.e., crime, education quality, family patterns, etc.), and peers and the media (i.e., friends' characteristics, exposure to movies/television, etc.). These factors are allowed to interact with each other. Beyond this extensive set of characteristics, other factors, such as stressful life events, are also included in the model. All these components contribute to a complex process by which developmental outcomes of children, such as teen sexual activity, are determined.

Economic models, in contrast, rely on the rationality of the individual decision maker; decisions are made on the basis of a comparison of the benefits and costs of the alternatives (see Leibowitz, Eisen, and Chow 1986; Lundberg and Plotnick 1995; and Kane and Staiger 1996).[11] Interestingly, specific models of sexual activity and birth-control use are rarely provided. The literature on fertility in general, and teen fertility in particular, traditionally includes models that begin with the decision to become pregnant, simply treating abstinence from sex as the ultimate means of avoiding an undesirable pregnancy. Within this framework, women "choose" to become pregnant if the benefits of a pregnancy are greater than its costs. These costs typically involve what one gives up by becoming pregnant, costs that are lower if, for instance, welfare benefits are higher or labor market conditions are weaker. A similar approach of comparing costs and benefits may be applied to the specific decision to engage in sexual activity or to use contraception among those who are sexually active.

This framework is best represented in the form of a "game tree," as shown in figure 4.9. Women are presented with a set of decisions that must be made, and each decision leads to a new "branch" of the tree where additional decisions are required. In the context of fertility behavior, women must choose whether to engage in sexual activity. Those who do so must decide whether to use contraception. Their decision at this stage leads to varying probabilities of becoming pregnant (defined here to be p_1 if they

---

11. Akerlof, Yellen, and Katz (1996) provide an alternative type of economic model that describes bargaining power between men and women within relationships to propose an explanation for the growth in out-of-wedlock births over the past few decades.

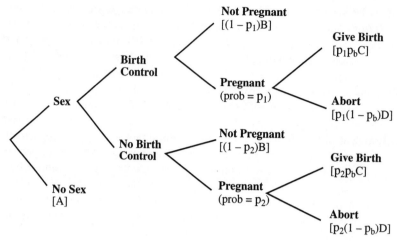

Fig. 4.9   Teen sexuality decision tree

use contraception and p_2 if they do not, where p_2 is greater than p_1), but, in both cases, it is possible that a pregnancy would result.[12] If pregnant, the woman must decide whether to abort her pregnancy or carry it to term and chooses to give birth with probability p_t. A more complicated version could also include the decision to get married, which enters the decision tree at various points (e.g., before the decision to engage in sexual activity or after a pregnancy results).

This representation of the decision-making process is not exclusive to economics since the diagram itself may be thought of as a simple sequencing of events. The difference between economics and other disciplines is that economists associate with each outcome a particular cost/benefit that individuals take into consideration in their decision making. In fact, the costs and benefits incurred at the later stages are assumed to be taken into consideration when decisions are made at the earlier stages of the game tree. For example, if abortion policy becomes more restrictive and, hence, more expensive for teens, then these costs should be incorporated into the decision regarding whether to engage in sexual activity.

4.2.2   Comparison and Synthesis of Models

An important distinction between the economic and the noneconomic models involves the degree to which an adolescent girl has the ability to make rational decisions (Lowenstein and Furstenberg 1991). Develop-

---

12. In the decision tree represented in fig. 4.9, the actual payoff if one engages in sexual activity and becomes pregnant is the same regardless of whether or not contraception is used (equal to B). One could argue that psychic costs would be greater if birth control is used, but this simplification does not affect the analytic framework and is maintained here. Similar arguments could be made regarding the actual payoffs to giving birth or aborting (equal to C or D).

mental models of sexuality describe a series of stages in which girls age through puberty, adolescence, and their later teenage years with a greater ability to make such decisions. According to these models, this ability is limited in the earlier teenage years for most girls, and sexual encounters tend to be spontaneous. These beliefs are expressed by Moore et al. (1995), who write: "There is abundant evidence . . . that sex is irrational, in the sense that it is often not planned, but impulsive. This is especially true for first sexual experience. Another way that the data seem to support a 'sex as irrational' premise is the pattern of time inconsistency, in which teens (and others) often plan to 'just say no' but end up saying 'yes,' and most teens think the best age to begin having sex is later than the age when they began" (p. 11). Within this framework, teen pregnancies are viewed as unavoidable mistakes. The economics literature may express concern regarding teens' abilities to make rational decisions but typically circumvents the problem by arguing that the difference between teens and adults is that teens have a "higher rate of time preference," through which the benefits incurred at the moment are valued more highly than the (potentially) high costs that may be incurred some time in the future (see Leibowitz, Eisen, and Chow 1986).

Recent advances in the field of behavioral economics may provide an appropriate middle ground on which the two sets of models may be reconciled. For instance, O'Donoghue and Rabin (1999) present a model of behavior in which rational individuals make decisions on the basis of the relevant benefits and costs but may still choose to act in ways that appear to be spontaneous. In their model, the benefits and costs that are incurred in the future are discounted in the same way as they would be in standard economic models, but individuals place heightened value on those rewards received right at the moment. On the basis of such a model, engaging in unprotected sexual activity today would be more likely since today's benefit is disproportionately weighted even in the face of potentially large future costs. On the other hand, teens may still state a preference not to engage in sexual activity at some future point because the heavy weight placed on immediate gratification would be absent. This sort of model maintains the assumption of rationality in that individuals are maximizing their utility, but it also allows for a form of spontaneity. In fact, such a model would yield additional predictions that are consistent with those from other fields. One would expect that, as teens get older and gain experience regarding their sexuality, they may be able to make more forward-looking decisions (like acquiring birth control) so that they are not placed in a position in which immediate desires overrule longer-term costs.

4.2.3 Empirical Correlates

An extensive review of the literature on teen sexual activity, contraceptive use, and fertility is available in Moore et al. (1995). That review uncovers a multitude of factors that have been found to be correlated with the initiation of sexual activity, including older age, age at menarche, pubertal status, frequent church attendance, supportive family relationships, educated parents, school performance, living in a single-parent household, using alcohol or other drugs, dating young, and having sexually active siblings and friends. Similar characteristics are related to contraceptive use during first intercourse. The emphasis on factors such as these is consistent with noneconomists' models of teen sexual activity in that a complex array of interrelated factors that affect a child's development should also be related to their sexual behavior.

Unfortunately, statistical difficulties plague the interpretation of many of the results. In particular, many of the variables considered are either jointly determined with sexual activity and contraceptive use or correlated with other unobservable factors that may also be related to these behaviors, preventing a causal interpretation. For example, the factors that influence drug and alcohol use are also likely to influence decisions to engage in sexual activity and use birth control.[13] Therefore, finding a positive relation between drug or alcohol use and, say, sexual activity does not imply that drinking may lead to having sex. Alternatively, children raised in families that invest less in them (in the form of time or other resources) may be more likely to become sexually active and to perform worse in school. Such a relation would invalidate a causal interpretation of the effect of school performance on sexual activity.

Economists have rarely conducted empirical studies regarding sexual activity and contraceptive use; they have more commonly studied the determinants of fertility with a particular emphasis on the effect of policies that alter the costs of having children. This emphasis is consistent with an economic model that emphasizes rationality and the fact that one might expect to observe behavioral responses to changes in the incentives facing individuals. I will focus this review on those costs that can be considered as determinants of sexual activity and contraceptive use, including labor market conditions, AIDS incidence, abortion access, and welfare policies.

Regarding labor market conditions, Butz and Ward (1979) and Macunovich (1995) estimated the relation between the gains from work for women and their level of fertility, although neither of these papers focuses specifically on teenage women. Although Butz and Ward report evidence supporting the proposition that the timing of childbearing is negatively correlated with changes in earnings, Macunovich disputes that finding because of data and econometric problems. In particular, she argues that wage changes bring about both income and substitution effects that make it difficult to predict the optimal response to a change in wage. A higher wage increases the return to work (the substitution effect) but also pro-

13. Recent work by Dee (1999), however, has specifically dealt with the econometric problems in this particular example.

vides additional income that can enable one to "consume" more (the income effect). Below, I will evaluate the responsiveness of fertility to changes in job availability (through the employment-to-population ratio), not the wage. Since the effect of labor market conditions on the decision to bear children for those without jobs is solely a function of the substitution effect, one might predict that an improved labor market would lower the teen fertility rate.

The effect of the AIDS epidemic on sexual behavior was not considered to be within the domain of economics until the work of Philipson and Posner (1993) and Ahituv, Hotz, and Philipson (1996). These papers argue quite forcefully that economics studies the response of individuals to incentives and that AIDS provides a strong incentive for those potentially at risk of AIDS to alter their sexual practices in response. They also find empirical evidence supporting the position that those most at risk of contracting AIDS have indeed become more likely to engage in safe sex. Although these papers do not focus on teens, the fact that most teen sexual activity occurs outside marriage and potentially with multiple partners implies that one could extend their analysis to indicate that teens should either become more likely to practice abstinence or become more likely to use condoms should they be sexually active.

Research on the effects of abortion access on fertility behavior has grown considerably over the past few years (see Levine, Trainor, and Zimmerman 1996; Kane and Staiger 1996; and Matthews, Ribar, and Wilhelm 1997). Earlier research on abortion access had restricted its focus to the effect on abortion demand, and the results generally supported the notion that the demand curve for abortion services is downward sloping; an increase in the cost reduces the demand (see Blank, George, and London 1996; and Haas-Wilson 1996). The major advance is that more recent work provides empirical tests of the proposition that changes in abortion access could also affect the likelihood of pregnancy. Results typically confirmed that restricted abortion access lowered the demand for abortion services but found no evidence of an increase in births, which must mean that pregnancies declined. One could then infer that sexual activity and/or contraceptive use was affected, but no direct test of these behaviors was provided owing to data limitations.

Economists have long been contributors to the research on the effects of welfare generosity on nonmarital fertility. That literature is reviewed by Moffitt (1998), who states that the conventional wisdom based on the evidence existing earlier in the decade was that welfare receipt had no effect on fertility behavior but that more recent work suggests that a relation may indeed exist. Little of this work is directed specifically at teenagers, but a disproportionate share of welfare recipients began their spells by giving birth as teens, suggesting that we may expect to see some effect for teens as well. To date, relatively little research has examined the effect of welfare reform on teen fertility. Most of the recent work that has been conducted has focused on the results of one particular provision, the family cap, among many reforms instituted simultaneously. The family cap eliminates the benefit increase that would otherwise result if a woman on welfare had an additional child. Research on the family cap has also provided mixed evidence regarding its effect (Argys, Averett, and Rees, in press; Fairlie and London 1997; O'Neill 1994; and Camasso et al. 1999). The only work of which I am aware that has examined the effect of a wide-ranging set of welfare reforms is that by Horvath and Peters (1999), who find that the introduction of reforms led to declines in nonmarital fertility among teens. Additional research supporting this finding would be required, however, before one could make strong conclusions regarding the effect of welfare reform on teen fertility.

An important implication of these findings is that evidence does seem to support the position that changes in the costs of childbearing affect teen fertility behavior. This has obvious implications for teen sexual activity and birth-control use, but direct evidence of such effects is largely unavailable at present. Part of the subsequent empirical analysis will address this omission in the literature.

4.3 Empirical Analysis

4.3.1 Analysis of Demographic Correlates

This section of the paper will employ cross-sectional data to analyze the individual factors that are related to sexual activity and use of contraception among those who have engaged in sexual activity. The data to be employed here are the first wave of the National Longitudinal Survey of Adolescent Health (AddHealth), which was conducted in 1994–95. The public-release version of these data contains information on 6,504 boys and girls in grades 7–12. Tremendous detail is available on these individuals, including demographics, scores on a test of cognitive ability (the Peabody Picture Vocabulary Test [PPVT]), grades in school, characteristics of the child's mother and household, and extensive attitudine variables, which will be used here to determine the correlates of teen sexual activity and contraceptive use.[14]

Results of this analysis are reported separately for girls and boys in tables 4.2 and 4.3, respectively. The first row of these tables provides estimates of the percentage of students who engaged in sexual activities that

---

14. Characteristics of mothers were obtained from a separate questionnaire. Interviewers were clearly instructed to attempt to gather information from the respondent's mother (or other mother-type figure), not the father, and the vast majority of parents responding to this part of the survey were mothers. The sample is limited to those students between the ages of twelve and eighteen.

Table 4.2   Correlates of Teen Sexual Activity and Contraception for Girls, Probit Derivatives (standard errors in parentheses)

Variable	Sexual Intercourse Ever		Sexual Intercourse in Past Three Months		No Contraception during First Intercourse		No Contraception during Last Intercourse		Pregnancy Risk	
	Full Sample	Age 15+	Full Sample	Age 15+	Full Sample	Age 15+	Full Sample	Age 15+		
Weighted percentage engaging in activity	37.6	50.9	35.0	47.7	32.4	32.5	35.7	34.6	12.5	16.5
Student's characteristics										
Age	.079	.063	.076	.056	-.022	.032	-.014	.003	.026	.019
	(.017)	(.026)	(.016)	(.026)	(.026)	(.030)	(.027)	(.031)	(.009)	(.014)
Black non-Hispanic	.098	.066	.098	.044	-.114	-.073	-.058	-.018	.019	.016
	(.032)	(.043)	(.031)	(.043)	(.039)	(.044)	(.043)	(.050)	(.018)	(.025)
Hispanic	-.012	-.044	-.021	-.053	.092	-.019	.103	.092	.029	.027
	(.039)	(.051)	(.038)	(.049)	(.062)	(.063)	(.063)	(.067)	(.025)	(.031)
Grade in school	.071	.074	.061	.070	-.019	-.041	-.010	-.018	.007	.005
	(.017)	(.024)	(.017)	(.024)	(.026)	(.029)	(.027)	(.029)	(.009)	(.013)
PPVT, standardized score ($\times$ 10)	-.001	-.002	.013	.003	-.055	-.033	-.052	-.024	-.007	-.004
	(.009)	(.013)	(.009)	(.012)	(.015)	(.017)	(.015)	(.017)	(.005)	(.007)
GPA (if computable)	-.118	-.135	-.105	-.120	-.040	-.014	-.037	-.014	-.042	-.035
	(.016)	(.023)	(.015)	(.022)	(.024)	(.027)	(.025)	(.028)	(.008)	(.012)
Catholic	-.069	-.049	-.060	-.061	-.067	-.059	-.071	-.085	-.037	-.050
	(.027)	(.036)	(.026)	(.035)	(.042)	(.043)	(.044)	(.044)	(.013)	(.018)
No religion reported	-.042	-.046	-.027	-.040	.120	.145	.127	.122	.031	.048
	(.033)	(.055)	(.033)	(.054)	(.055)	(.064)	(.056)	(.063)	(.023)	(.036)
Attends religious services at least once per week	-.138	-.062	-.130	-.060	.056	.023	.083	.048	-.016	.005
	(.022)	(.032)	(.022)	(.032)	(.039)	(.042)	(.040)	(.044)	(.012)	(.019)

(continued)

Table 4.2 (continued)

Variable	Sexual Intercourse Ever		Sexual Intercourse in Past Three Months		No Contraception during First Intercourse		No Contraception during Last Intercourse		Pregnancy Risk	
	Full Sample	Age 15+	Full Sample	Age 15+	Full Sample	Age 15+	Full Sample	Age 15+		
Family background										
Mother's age ($\times$ 10)	−.004	.013	−.003	.016	−.006	−.044	−.007	−.017	−.002	−.009
	(.020)	(.028)	(.020)	(.027)	(.030)	(.039)	(.030)	(.035)	(.012)	(.017)
Mother high school graduate	−.009	.007	−.018	−.016	.079	.098	.133	.147	.037	.054
	(.039)	(.052)	(.037)	(.051)	(.059)	(.066)	(.061)	(.066)	(.022)	(.033)
Mother attended some college	.019	.082	.017	.079	.032	.020	.142	.130	.044	.068
	(.045)	(.059)	(.044)	(.058)	(.068)	(.074)	(.072)	(.078)	(.030)	(.043)
Mother college graduate	−.018	.039	−.043	.017	.042	.068	.090	.126	.015	.057
	(.045)	(.062)	(.043)	(.061)	(.074)	(.082)	(.076)	(.084)	(.027)	(.043)
Mother worked in past year	.037	.038	.064	.055	.030	−.031	.044	−.006	.033	.011
	(.032)	(.044)	(.029)	(.044)	(.052)	(.058)	(.053)	(.057)	(.016)	(.026)
Mother married	−.047	−.078	−.049	−.063	.003	−.046	−.003	−.014	−.011	−.011
	(.031)	(.043)	(.031)	(.042)	(.045)	(.048)	(.046)	(.049)	(.018)	(.025)
Mother's age at first marriage	−.003	−.006	−.004	−.005	−.002	−.004	−.001	−.002	−.001	−.001
	(.021)	(.003)	(.002)	(.003)	(.003)	(.003)	(.003)	(.003)	(.001)	(.002)
Mother receiving public assistance	.030	.048	.034	.089	.059	−.020	.179	.095	.069	.083
	(.051)	(.067)	(.050)	(.065)	(.071)	(.071)	(.076)	(.081)	(.036)	(.051)
Household income less than $10,000	.033	.027	.044	.004	−.028	−.077	−.087	−.143	−.009	−.061
	(.057)	(.078)	(.056)	(.077)	(.074)	(.073)	(.073)	(.071)	(.027)	(.031)
Household income between $10,000 and $30,000	−.031	−.081	−.023	−.062	.033	−.025	−.017	.015	−.012	−.011
	(.035)	(.049)	(.035)	(.048)	(.055)	(.058)	(.056)	(.062)	(.019)	(.027)
Household income between $50,000 and $100,000	−.046	−.048	−.028	−.031	−.040	−.059	−.074	−.086	−.031	−.040
	(.032)	(.045)	(.031)	(.044)	(.052)	(.052)	(.050)	(.053)	(.016)	(.023)
Household income greater than $100,000	−.071	−.105	−.057	−.107	−.077	−.105	−.166	−.165	−.055	−.085
	(.049)	(.072)	(.049)	(.069)	(.086)	(.080)	(.077)	(.078)	(.020)	(.023)

	(1)	(2)	(3)	(4)	(5)
Own attitudes/expectations/knowledge					
Friends respect you more if you have sexual intercourse	−.012 (.074)	.007 (.072)	.106 (.070)	−.035 (.091)	−.024 (.039)
Partner loses respect for you if you have sexual intercourse	−.139 (.038)	−.159 (.037)	.082 (.060)	.087 (.063)	−.021 (.022)
Getting pregnant would be one of the worst things	−.195 (.039)	−.170 (.040)	−.032 (.044)	−.208 (.047)	−.147 (.031)
Likely to go to college	−.064 (.041)	−.060 (.040)	−.062 (.047)	−.042 (.048)	−.033 (.025)
Percentage correct on knowledge quiz	.004 (.001)	.005 (.001)	−.001 (.001)	−.003 (.001)	.0001 (.001)
Parents' attitudes					
Mother disapproves of having sex at this time	−.227 (.039)	−.201 (.039)	−.020 (.040)	−.084 (.041)	−.080 (.026)
Mother disapproves of birth-control use at this time	−.202 (.031)	−.186 (.031)	.150 (.050)	.091 (.050)	−.025 (.019)
Risk perceptions					
Little or no probability of pregnancy in single incident	−.003 (.042)	−.009 (.041)	.177 (.055)	.125 (.056)	.049 (.028)
Little or no probability of pregnancy over entire month	.132 (.041)	.102 (.042)	.029 (.048)	.007 (.050)	.028 (.027)
Sample size	3,023	3,050	1,107	1,049	3,050
Sample size	1,830	1,836	874	831	1,836

Source: Author's calculations from Wave I of AddHealth.

Note: The models estimated also include dummy variables indicating whether grade data were available to compute GPA, whether household income was reported, and whether mother's characteristics are available. In cols. 7–9, the universe is restricted to those girls who have ever engaged in sexual intercourse. In cols. 10–12, the universe is restricted to those girls who have had intercourse in the past three months.

Table 4.3   Correlates of Teen Sexual Activity and Contraception for Boys, Probit Derivatives (standard errors in parentheses)

Variable	Sexual Intercourse Ever		Sexual Intercourse in Past Three Months		No Contraception during First Intercourse		No Contraception during Last Intercourse		Pregnancy Risk	
	Full Sample	Age 15+	Full Sample	Age 15+	Full Sample	Age 15+	Full Sample	Age 15+	Full Sample	Age 15+
Weighted percentage engaging in activity	38.9	50.3	34.0	44.7	34.0	33.0	30.2	30.3	10.3	13.5
Student's characteristics										
Age	.083	.067	.080	.068	-.022	.002	.022	.010	.028	.018
	(.168)	(.025)	(.015)	(.024)	(.023)	(.027)	(.022)	(.029)	(.008)	(.014)
Black non-Hispanic	.257	.169	.218	.116	.015	.031	-.036	-.019	.034	.015
	(.033)	(.042)	(.032)	(.042)	(.042)	(.048)	(.042)	(.050)	(.017)	(.025)
Hispanic	.043	-.006	.071	.046	.135	.037	.034	-.007	.027	.005
	(.040)	(.052)	(.038)	(.050)	(.058)	(.064)	(.057)	(.062)	(.022)	(.028)
Grade in school	.033	-.002	.028	-.004	.013	.008	-.016	.005	-.000	.000
	(.017)	(.022)	(.016)	(.022)	(.023)	(.025)	(.023)	(.026)	(.008)	(.012)
PPVT, standardized score (× 10)	-.017	-.016	-.003	-.006	-.002	-.000	-.001	-.002	-.004	-.007
	(.009)	(.013)	(.008)	(.013)	(.014)	(.016)	(.001)	(.002)	(.004)	(.007)
GPA (if computable)	-.108	-.090	-.101	-.088	-.009	.010	-.037	-.029	-.036	-.033
	(.015)	(.021)	(.014)	(.021)	(.023)	(.026)	(.023)	(0.027)	(.008)	(.012)
Catholic	-.032	-.050	-.030	-.063	-.008	.041	.012	-.007	-.005	-.020
	(.029)	(.037)	(.027)	(.036)	(.045)	(.052)	(.047)	(.051)	(.014)	(.020)
No religion reported	.062	.020	.080	.048	.071	.070	.064	.037	.040	.021
	(.037)	(.051)	(.035)	(.049)	(.050)	(.059)	(.052)	(.059)	(.022)	(.029)
Attends religious services at least once per week	-.099	-.050	-.075	-.028	.021	.071	.024	.040	-.014	.005
	(.024)	(.034)	(.022)	(.033)	(.039)	(.046)	(.041)	(.047)	(.012)	(.020)

Family background

	(1)	(2)	(3)	(4)	(5)	(6)	(7)	(8)	(9)	(10)
Mother's age (× 10)	.005 (.021)	.018 (.028)	.000 (.020)	.005 (.028)	.009 (.029)	−.023 (.031)	−.011 (.031)	−.034 (.034)	−.001 (.010)	−.009 (.016)
Mother high school graduate	−.013 (.039)	−.035 (.052)	.028 (.037)	−.000 (.051)	.036 (.055)	.059 (.062)	.026 (.058)	.027 (.062)	.014 (.021)	.004 (.029)
Mother attended some college	−.031 (.043)	.012 (.059)	.015 (.042)	.050 (.058)	.038 (.065)	.096 (.074)	−.028 (.065)	.016 (.074)	−.006 (.023)	.013 (.035)
Mother college graduate	−.093 (.045)	−.036 (.062)	−.052 (.043)	−.009 (.060)	−.040 (.070)	.015 (.081)	.071 (.080)	.102 (.087)	−.006 (.023)	.040 (.041)
Mother worked in past year	.012 (.032)	.015 (.045)	.006 (.029)	.003 (.043)	.015 (.049)	.039 (.054)	−.024 (.052)	−.043 (.058)	−.007 (.016)	−.016 (.024)
Mother married	−.113 (.033)	−.047 (.044)	−.093 (.031)	−.030 (.043)	.002 (.045)	−.019 (.050)	−.017 (.046)	−.030 (.051)	−.028 (.017)	−.021 (.024)
Mother's age at first marriage	−.002 (.002)	−.011 (.004)	−.004 (.002)	−.010 (.003)	−.006 (.003)	−.008 (.004)	−.004 (.003)	−.007 (.036)	−.002 (.001)	−.005 (.002)
Mother receiving public assistance	.019 (.052)	−.017 (.076)	.002 (.047)	−.010 (.071)	−.070 (.057)	−.097 (.061)	.006 (.067)	−.025 (.076)	.000 (.023)	−.015 (.033)
Household income less than $10,000	−.043 (.053)	−.075 (.078)	−.069 (.048)	−.124 (.069)	.097 (.085)	.125 (.107)	−.037 (.079)	−.067 (.091)	−.023 (.022)	−.048 (.030)
Household income between $10,000 and $30,000	.010 (.035)	−.022 (.047)	.016 (.033)	.022 (.047)	.008 (.052)	−.020 (.057)	−.020 (.051)	−.104 (.053)	.002 (.018)	−.036 (.022)
Household income between $50,000 and $100,000	−.012 (.034)	−.010 (.044)	−.007 (.032)	−.008 (.043)	.010 (.057)	−.009 (.060)	−.060 (.053)	−.123 (.052)	−.016 (.016)	−.051 (.021)
Household income greater than $100,000	−.090 (.054)	−.170 (.064)	−.058 (.051)	−.152 (.060)	−.057 (.095)	−.026 (.108)	−.099 (.085)	−.109 (.092)	−.044 (.019)	−.073 (.024)

Own attitudes/expectations/knowledge

	(1)	(2)	(3)	(4)	(5)	(6)	(7)	(8)	(9)	(10)
Friends respect you more if you have sexual intercourse		.101 (.038)		.107 (.038)		.101 (.045)		.099 (.047)		.072 (.026)
Partner loses respect for you if you have sexual intercourse		−.146 (.043)		−.137 (.042)		.115 (.074)		−.009 (.075)		−.029 (.024)

(*continued*)

Table 4.3 (continued)

Variable	Sexual Intercourse Ever		Sexual Intercourse in Past Three Months		No Contraception during First Intercourse		No Contraception during Last Intercourse		Pregnancy Risk	
	Full Sample	Age 15+	Full Sample	Age 15+	Full Sample	Age 15+	Full Sample	Age 15+	Full Sample	Age 15+
Getting pregnant would be one of the worst things		−.011 (.045)		−.144 (.044)		−.121 (.051)		−.115 (.052)		−.087 (.031)
Likely to go to college		−.122 (.036)		−.068 (.035)		−.076 (.041)		−.050 (.043)		−.039 (.021)
Percentage correct on knowledge quiz		.003 (.001)		.003 (.001)		−.001 (.001)		.000 (.001)		.001 (.0004)
Parents' attitudes										
Mother disapproves of having sex at this time		−.199 (.034)		−.171 (.035)		.062 (.040)		.012 (.042)		−.029 (.022)
Mother disapproves of birth-control use at this time		−.091 (.036)		−.098 (.035)		.065 (.055)		.075 (.056)		−.007 (.022)
Risk perceptions										
Little or no probability of pregnancy in single incident		.024 (.037)		.045 (.036)		.113 (.045)		.050 (.045)		.036 (.021)
Little or no probability of pregnancy over entire month		.054 (.035)		.052 (.034)		.032 (.042)				
Sample size	2,795	1,734	2,832	1,747	1,135	866	1,021	792	2,831	1,746

Source: Author's calculations from Wave I of AddHealth.

Note: The models estimated also include dummy variables indicating whether grade data were available to compute GPA, whether household income was reported, and whether mother's characteristics are available. In cols. 7–9, the universe is restricted to those boys who have ever engaged in sexual intercourse. In cols. 10–12, the universe is restricted to those boys who have had intercourse in the past three months.

may lead to a pregnancy. Responses for boys and girls are generally similar.[15] For the full sample, 37.6 percent of girls and 38.9 percent of boys have ever had sexual intercourse, and 35 percent of the girls and 34 percent of the boys have done so in the past three months. Roughly one-third of sexually active girls and boys failed to use contraception during first intercourse as well as during their last sexual encounter in the past three months. On the basis of the behaviors of girls in the past three months, the risk of pregnancy is estimated to be 12.4 percent. For boys, the risk of a partner's pregnancy is 10.3 percent. Among just those boys and girls aged fifteen and over, sexual activity is somewhat more common, but contraceptive use is not.

The remainder of tables 4.2 and 4.3 presents probit estimates of the relation between each of these outcomes and a series of characteristics of teens and their families. Two separate models are estimated here for each of the five different outcomes. The first includes the full sample of girls and boys and includes just demographics and mother's/household characteristics, which are more likely to be exogenous to the behaviors being studied. Responses to attitudine/expectations questions are also considered in the second model, but the sample is restricted to those between the ages of fifteen and eighteen since many of these questions were asked only of this older group.[16] These variables are examined separately because teens' responses to these questions may be influenced by their behavior (i.e., they are endogenous).

For girls (table 4.2), estimates from models of sexual activity are quite similar regardless of whether the activity relates to the past three months or ever. Many of the girls' characteristics are significantly related to sexual activity, which is more likely among those who are older, in a higher grade, perform worse in school, are a religion other than Catholic, and do not attend religious services on a weekly basis. An additional year of age and of schooling increases the likelihood of having sex by 6–8 percentage points, depending on the measure of sexual activity and the age composition of the sample. Every additional tenth of a point in a girl's GPA reduces her likelihood of sexual activity by 11–14 percent. On the other hand, once one controls for the girl's own characteristics, few of the attributes of her mother or her household are significantly related to sexual activity.

In models that include potentially endogenous variables representing attitudes, expectations, and risk perceptions, these variables are also observed to be significantly related to the likelihood of sexual activity. Girls

15. One reason why this finding may not be obvious is that about one-third of the partners of sexually active women aged fifteen to seventeen are two or more years older than the women themselves are (Darroch, Landry, and Oslak 1999).

16. For purposes of comparison with the first set of models in tables 4.2 and 4.3, I have also estimated models for those aged fifteen to eighteen excluding the attitudine/expectations variables and obtained similar results.

who report that getting pregnant would be one of the worst things to happen to them are roughly 20 percentage points less likely to engage in sexual activity. Both measures of parents' disapproval yield similar estimates. On the other hand, those who view little or no risk of pregnancy from sexual activity over an entire month are 13 percentage points more likely to have sex. Of course, the concern regarding interpretation of these relations as being causal is that, for instance, girls who regularly engage in sex may downplay their concerns regarding pregnancy, the level of their parents' disapproval, or their perceived risk of pregnancy to be consistent with their own behavior.

Compared to models of sexual activity recently or ever, results from models of contraceptive use indicate some differences in the factors that are correlated with a girl's behavior. In fact, in a multivariate context, very little is significantly related to contraceptive use during first intercourse. Black, non-Hispanic girls are less likely to fail to use contraception, as are those who score higher on the available aptitude test. Those who report no religion are significantly less likely to have failed to use contraception. In models that include attitudine/expectations measures, girls who reported that their mothers disapproved of birth-control use and those who perceived there to be little or no probability of getting pregnant after a single act were more likely to have failed to use contraception as well. Among the multitude of other characteristics reported, none of the others are found to be significantly related to contraceptive use during first intercourse. Ironically, girls who report that getting pregnant would be one of the worst things that could happen to them were no more likely to use contraception than others.

Models of failure to use contraception during last intercourse, on the other hand, find that many personal and family-background characteristics are important correlates. Test scores, religion, mother's education, receipt of public assistance, and family income are all found to contribute to the failure to use contraception during last intercourse. Many of the attitudine/expectations variables are significant as well. In fact, those women who report that getting pregnant would be the worst thing that could happen to them are 20 percentage points less likely to have failed to use contraception (i.e., more likely to use contraception) during their last intercourse.

A potential explanation that would be consistent with the divergent findings between the two measures of contraceptive use could involve the spontaneity of the act. If first intercourse is more likely to be an unplanned event, then contraception would be more likely to be used randomly. On the other hand, once girls begin having sex more frequently, the activity becomes more planned, and appropriate precautions may be more likely to be used by those who want to take them. Such an interpretation is consistent with the earlier discussion of the contribution of economics to modeling sexual activity in that spontaneity need not be ruled out but, once the activity becomes repeated, one would expect a greater degree of rationality.

The final set of models reported in table 4.2 reports the factors related to a teenage girl's *pregnancy risk,* which I have defined as the likelihood that a girl has had sexual intercourse in the past three months and did not use contraception during her last intercourse in that period. Econometric models of pregnancy risk have important advantages compared to the more traditional approach of separately examining sexual intercourse and the use of birth control. First, estimates of the relation between a personal characteristic and sexual activity may contradict the estimated relation between that characteristic and the use of contraception, making it more difficult to determine whether a girl with that trait is more or less likely to be at risk of becoming pregnant. For instance, among the full sample of AddHealth respondents, those who attend religious services at least once per week are less likely to have engaged in sexual activity in the past three months (reducing their pregnancy risk), but those who did have sex were less likely to use contraception (increasing their pregnancy risk). Estimates from the pregnancy-risk models can indicate which of the two effects dominates or whether the two are perfectly offsetting.[17]

Moreover, estimates from models of contraceptive use among the sample of respondents engaging in sexual activity are subject to sample-selection bias. For instance, suppose that the AIDS epidemic led many risk-averse individuals to choose abstinence over sexual activity with some form of contraception. If the less risk averse did not change their behavior, the sample of sexually active girls would contain a larger fraction of those who do *not* use contraception, and one might inappropriately conclude that AIDS reduces the use of birth control. A model of pregnancy risk for which the target population is all teenage girls avoids this selection problem.

Results from these models are reported in the final two columns of table

---

17. Of course, one could also derive the effect of the two separate effects on the pregnancy risk. To see this, define the share of respondents who have had sexual intercourse during the last three months to be $P(\text{sex}) = S/N$, where S is the number having sex, and N is the sample size. Then define the probability of failing to use contraception conditional on having sex as $P(\text{fail}) = F/S$, where F is the number failing to use contraception. Then the risk of pregnancy $P(\text{preg}) = P(\text{sex}) \times P(\text{fail}) = F/N$. The derivative of $P(\text{preg})$ with respect to any variable, X, is obtained by the product rule

$$\frac{\partial[P(\text{preg})]}{\partial X} = P(\text{fail}) * \frac{\partial[P(\text{sex})]}{\partial X} + p(\text{sex}) * \frac{\partial[P(\text{fail})]}{\partial X}.$$

Standard errors for these estimates would have to be calculated using the delta method. Defining a pregnancy rate, then estimating models of its determinants directly, is much simpler. Estimates from these pregnancy-risk models may differ slightly from the formula just derived because probit derivatives are estimated at the value of the sample mean for each variable rather than estimating separate derivatives for each person and then taking the mean.

4.2. For the full sample, they indicate that pregnancy risk increases with age, having a working mother, and having a mother who receives public assistance and falls with school performance, being Catholic, and being at the top of the income distribution. In the model of older teens that includes potentially endogenous variables, the results further indicate that pregnancy risk is lower for those who view a pregnancy as one of the worst things that could happen to them and whose mothers disapprove of them having sex at this time. The perception that pregnancy is unlikely is positively associated with pregnancy risk, but the estimate is not statistically significant.

Estimates from comparable models for boys are presented in table 4.3. Regarding sexual activity, a few relevant distinctions in the results between boys and girls are noteworthy. First, racial differences are far more pronounced among the boys than among the girls. For instance, black, non-Hispanic boys are 25 percent more likely to report having engaged in sexual activity ever relative to white, non-Hispanic boys. The comparable gap for girls is only 10 percent. Second, in models that include attitudes and expectations, boys who report that their friends will respect them more if they have sexual intercourse are 10 percentage points more likely to have engaged in sexual activity. No such effect is observed for girls. Here, in particular, it is important to raise the caveat of endogeneity in attitudes. Regarding contraceptive use during last intercourse, the main difference between boys and girls is the influence of mother's characteristics. In particular, mother's level of education and welfare receipt are important determinants of contraceptive use during last intercourse for girls but not for boys.

4.3.2 Analysis of "Prices"

This section of the paper will examine the effect of increases in costs associated with becoming pregnant and giving birth on teenagers' patterns of sexual activity, contraceptive use, and pregnancy risk. These costs can be thought of as an increase in the price of having sex and/or failing to use contraception and can be monetary or otherwise in nature. The hypothesis that is being examined here is that increases in the cost will reduce the likelihood of having sex and increase the likelihood of using contraception.

The specific costs that I will use in this analysis include labor market conditions, the incidence of AIDS, the generosity of the welfare system, and abortion restrictions in place in a teenager's state of residence.[18] Labor

18. Another potential policy variable that could be important in determining sexual activity and contraceptive use is sex education in schools, which could reduce information deficiencies for teens making these decisions. For instance, Oettinger (1999) uses data on individual enrollment in sex-education classes and finds that taking such classes increases the likelihood of becoming sexually active earlier but has only a weak effect on the likelihood of

market conditions represent a price in the form of an opportunity cost. In periods when job opportunities are limited, the cost of becoming pregnant is lower because the opportunity cost associated with a reduced ability/willingness to work is lower at that time. The incidence of AIDS represents a clear cost since greater levels of sexual activity without the use of condoms can impose substantial health risks. If welfare benefits are more generous and/or easier to get, the cost of a pregnancy is lower because the government will pay some modest living expense in that event. Finally, restricted abortion access may reduce one's ability to abort an unwanted pregnancy, making it more costly to become pregnant in the first place. The estimated effect of these costs on fertility behavior based on past research was reviewed earlier. To the extent that they are related to fertility, they may also be related to sexual activity and birth-control use, yet no previous research of which I am aware examines these relations.

In the subsequent analyses, for purposes of completeness all models will be estimated separately for boys and girls.[19] Although most of the costs considered would affect girls more than boys (with AIDS being a possible exception), it is unclear how these costs would be related to boys' sexual activity. On the one hand, one might consider boys as acting something like a control group. If costs that are imposed only on girls have an estimated effect on the sexual activity of both boys and girls, then perhaps the finding is spurious. Alternatively, because high school boys are the likely (but not exclusive) sex partners of high school girls, one may expect to see spillovers in the sense that, if something affects girls' likelihood of engaging in sexual activity, it will also affect boys' likelihood.

To determine whether sexual activity and birth-control use are related to their costs, I use 1991, 1993, 1995, and 1997 YRBS data, described previously. Although personal characteristics of the respondents in these data are quite limited, their particular advantage for the present purpose is the availability of state-of-residence identifiers for each respondent. This information allows me to link state-level data for the relevant year to the costs examined. I obtained state-level employment-to-population ratios for teenagers directly from the U.S. Bureau of Labor Statistics.[20] The data on

---

an earlier pregnancy. I have chosen not to consider sex education in the present analysis for two reasons. First, I am unable to identify enrollment in sex-education classes for individuals in the YRBS data, and I have been unable to piece together state-level data for sex-education requirements for all the survey years available. Second, as described below, geographic identification using the YRBS data is limited because of the number of states repeatedly covered by the survey, suggesting that a more parsimonious specification may be preferable.

19. Obviously, boys face no pregnancy risk themselves but do face the risk of getting a girl pregnant. For ease of exposition, in the remainder of the discussion I will discuss pregnancy risk symmetrically with the implication that, for boys, it should be interpreted in the appropriate way.

20. These data reflect unpublished estimates from the Current Population Survey (CPS) and were provided directly from the Local Area Unemployment Statistics division of the Bureau of Labor Statistics.

AIDS incidence come from the CDC and measure the number of AIDS cases per 100,000 population in the state (see U.S. DHHS, *HIV/AIDS Surveillance Report,* various issues).[21]

Data on welfare generosity take two forms. First, I use the maximum welfare benefit for a family of two under the Aid to Families with Dependent Children (AFDC) or the Temporary Assistance for Needy Families (TANF) program, depending on which was in place in each year; these data were obtained from the *Green Book* (U.S. House of Representatives, various years). Second, I create an indicator variable that identifies whether a state has a "reformed" welfare system. These reforms could have come about either through waivers requested by states and granted by the federal government before national welfare reform in 1996 or through the state implementing a valid TANF plan after national welfare reform.[22] These data were obtained from the Council of Economic Advisers (1999).

The final set of variables is a series of three indicator variables that represent whether a particular type of abortion restriction was in place in a particular state and year. The three specific restrictions that I consider are Medicaid funding restrictions (which largely prohibit the use of public funds for abortions), parent consent/notification laws (which require a minor either to notify or to obtain consent from a parent before obtaining an abortion), and mandatory-waiting-period laws (which require a woman seeking an abortion to wait, typically, twenty-four or forty-eight hours after notifying a provider of her intent to abort before having the abortion performed). These data were obtained from NARAL Foundation, *Who Decides?* (various years).

Using these data, I estimate probit models with state and year fixed effects where the dependent variables are the sexual-activity/contraceptive-use measures described earlier and the explanatory variables include a vector of prices along with the limited personal characteristics available for each respondent. In such a model, price effects are identified by comparing changes between states over time. All reported results from the probit model represent the value of the derivatives estimated at the sample mean of the independent variables.

Although the YRBS is the data set best suited to estimate such a model because of its multiple survey years and available state identifiers, it does have some limitations. In particular, the survey is school based, and, al-

---

21. The definition of *AIDS* changed beginning in 1993, leading to a large increase in the number of cases counted. In the data used for this paper, I have adjusted the 1991 data by estimating a cubic trend in AIDS incidence rates and using the discrete jump between 1992 and 1993 as the scaling factor. The results presented are generally similar to (although less precise than) that obtained when I use only data from the period 1993–97.

22. The determination of whether a waiver was in place is based on the waiver's implementation date, not the date on which the waiver was requested. For those years in which a waiver or a TANF plan was implemented in the middle of the year, I use the fraction of the year in which the reform was in place.

though the sample is relatively large (between about eleven and sixteen thousand teens per year) and is chosen to be nationally representative, its school-based nature leads the respondents to be more concentrated geographically. In fact, in any given year only about half the states are represented. Of course, the larger states like California and New York are represented in each survey; some of the smaller states appear much less frequently, if at all. For instance, over the four survey years, only forty-one states (including the District of Columbia) are included at all, and thirteen states are represented only once. In a model with state fixed effects, this latter group of states offers no additional identification because no change can be observed within the state over time. In fact, only eleven states are represented in each survey year.[23]

Moreover, a model with state fixed effects is identified only on the basis of changes within states over time. For those policy variables that are discrete in nature, such as abortion restrictions, the power of the analysis may be limited because so few changes have taken place over the sample period within these states.[24] Although continuous price measures like the employment-to-population ratio and AIDS incidence provide greater variation, the power of an analysis of welfare generosity may also be limited in that very few states substantially changed the nominal value of their benefits over the sample period in the available states. This caveat should be kept in mind in interpreting the results reported subsequently.

The results of this analysis are reported in table 4.4. The first row of this table indicates the percentage of respondents who are engaging in each of the specified outcomes. Differences do emerge when comparing these estimates to those found from the AddHealth data. Some, but not all, of these differences can be attributed to the fact that the YRBS sample (high school students) is slightly older than the AddHealth sample (grades 7–12). After adjusting for age by focusing on the older AddHealth respondents, those in the YRBS appear less likely to report that they engaged in sexual activity in the last three months and that they failed to use contraception during last intercourse in the past three months and are at less risk of pregnancy. These differences may be due to differences in survey procedures.

The remainder of table 4.4 presents estimates of probit models where the outcomes represent indicator variables of sexual activity, birth-control

---

23. These states are California, Colorado, Florida, Georgia, Michigan, Mississippi, New York, Ohio, Pennsylvania, Texas, and Washington. To examine the effect on the findings of using an unbalanced sample, I have also estimated all reported models separately for just the eleven states that are represented in each survey year. Except where discussed below, all results from this subset of the data are qualitatively similar to those reported for the full sample.

24. In only three, seven, and six states are changes observed between the first and the last available survey years in Medicaid funding restrictions, parent consent/notification laws, and mandatory waiting periods, respectively.

Table 4.4 The Relation between Geographic Factors and Teen Sexual Activity, Contraception, and Pregnancy, Probit Derivatives (standard errors in parentheses)

Variable	Sexual Intercourse Ever		Sexual Intercourse in Past Three Months		No Contraception Used during Last Intercourse in Past 3 Months		Pregnancy Risk	
	Girls (1)	Boys (2)	Girls (3)	Boys (4)	Girls (5)	Boys (6)	Girls (7)	Boys (for partners) (8)
Weighted % engaging in activity	49.6	53.0	37.6	35.2	16.5	14.7	6.2	5.2
Student's characteristics								
Age	.100	.105	.086	.081	.028	.006	.023	.013
	(.008)	(.009)	(.008)	(.008)	(.009)	(.009)	(.003)	(.003)
Black non-Hispanic	.213	.365	.138	.307	.075	.018	.053	.051
	(.018)	(.012)	(.016)	(.018)	(.012)	(.018)	(.007)	(.011)
Hispanic	.031	.153	.028	.103	.140	.106	.054	.058
	(.016)	(.019)	(.014)	(.021)	(.022)	(.027)	(.010)	(.013)
Other race	.002	.010	-.006	.011	.021	.023	.005	.009
	(.023)	(.029)	(.024)	(.026)	(.031)	(.027)	(.011)	(.011)
Grade in school	.020	-.008	.023	.008	-.042	-.022	-.013	-.007
	(.011)	(.008)	(.011)	(.009)	(.010)	(.008)	(.004)	(.003)

Geographic variables

Teen employment-to-population ratio (× 10)	−.112	−.081	−.106	−.068	−.011	.016	−.022	−.002
	(.031)	(.029)	(.024)	(.024)	(.024)	(.027)	(.010)	(.009)
Log maximum AFDC/TANF benefit for a family of 2	.282	−.021	.073	.296	.301	.081	.121	.072
	(.098)	(.133)	(.090)	(.118)	(.086)	(.108)	(.039)	(.039)
Reformed welfare system	.104	.059	.078	.037	.013	−.048	.017	−.012
	(.028)	(.024)	(.021)	(.019)	(.020)	(.021)	(.008)	(.076)
AIDS rate per 100,000 population (× 100)	−.259	−.052	−.072	−.064	−.007	−.061	−.025	−.024
	(.103)	(.091)	(.087)	(.070)	(.080)	(.083)	(.031)	(.031)
Medicaid funding restrictions	−.013	.023	−.011	−.008	−.066	.015	−.017	.006
	(.101)	(.044)	(.084)	(.017)	(.055)	(.026)	(.026)	(.009)
Parent consent/notification required for abortion	−.023	.065	−.004	.027	.043	−.016	.015	−.001
	(.047)	(.031)	(.032)	(.030)	(.023)	(.035)	(.011)	(.014)
Mandatory waiting period for abortion	.014	−.062	.019	−.027	−.021	−.021	−.005	−.011
	(.054)	(.051)	(.040)	(.042)	(.032)	(.029)	(.014)	(.010)
Sample size	27,137	25,623	27,137	25,623	10,610	10,508	27,137	25,623

Source: Author's calculations from the 1991, 1993, 1995, and 1997 YRBS.

use, and pregnancy risk. Estimated coefficients for the demographic variables are generally consistent with those obtained in the analysis of Add-
Health data. For girls, for the geographic variables representing differences
in prices, estimated effects of differences in the employment-to-population
ratio provide support for the hypothesis that prices matter. A 1 percentage
point rise in this ratio (which represents an increase in the cost of a pregnancy) is predicted to reduce the likelihood of sexual activity ever or in
the past three months by about 1 percentage point (cols. 1 and 3). The
likelihood of failing to use contraception is estimated to fall by 1.1 percentage points (col. 5). Combining these two effects, the risk of pregnancy is
estimated to fall by 0.2 percentage point (col. 7). To put these numbers in
perspective, the teen employment-to-population ratio rose from an annual
average of 41.9 to 43.5 from 1991 to 1996 and would be predicted to have
reduced the risk of pregnancy by 0.3 percentage point, or 5 percent using
the average risk of pregnancy of 6.2 percent as a base. In comparison,
pregnancies are estimated to have fallen by 16 percent from 1991 to 1996,
as reported earlier.

For boys, a stronger labor market is estimated to lead to less frequent
sexual activity but not failure to use contraception during the last intercourse in the past three months. Point estimates indicate that the effect on
sexual activity is smaller for boys than it is for girls, which is consistent
with the notion that some, but not complete, spillover might be expected
in the behavior of high school boys and girls.

Some support for a price effect is also found in the estimates of the effect
of AIDS incidence. Here, results indicate that AIDS is negatively and significantly related to a girl's likelihood of ever having sexual intercourse
(i.e., positively related to abstinence). Abstinence is the strongest response
one could have to the fear of contracting AIDS. For those who are sexually
experienced, I find estimated effects on sexual activity in the past three
months and contraceptive use that are not statistically significant. One
might suspect these effects to be weaker than that regarding abstinence
since, having once decided to engage in sexual activity in the presence of
AIDS, one may be less likely substantially to reduce that activity. Moreover, those using contraception may have been more likely to switch to
condoms, but this does not represent an increase in the use of contraception and would not be captured by this model. In terms of pregnancy risk,
estimates in table 4.4 suggest that greater AIDS incidence in a girl's state
reduces her risk, but not significantly.[25]

---

25. On the other hand, when the sample is restricted to the eleven states for which data
are available for all four survey years, estimates indicate that a ten case per 100,000 increase
in AIDS incidence reduces the probability of pregnancy risk for girls by 0.9 percentage point,
which is significantly different from 0 (results available on request). Since this analysis is
based on eleven of the largest states, this sample may be more representative of the locations
where AIDS is a greater threat.

Regarding welfare generosity, results provide mixed support for the role of prices. Welfare benefits do appear to be positively related to the likelihood of sexual activity and the failure to use birth control for both boys and girls. A 10 percent increase in welfare generosity is estimated to raise the risk of pregnancy by 1.2 percent for girls and 0.7 percent for boys. On the other hand, some of the results regarding the effect of welfare reform are counterintuitive. For instance, teens residing in states that reformed their welfare system were *more* likely to engage in sexual activity than girls in other states. Almost universally, welfare reform in a state meant that women faced increased difficulty collecting benefits, which would have been predicted to reduce sexual activity. Taking into account birth-control use, the results indicate that the effect of welfare reform is positive and marginally statistically significant for girls. One potential explanation for these findings is that the reform initiatives may have been endogenous in that the states that were experiencing the biggest increases in teen sexuality were the ones most concerned about the potential caseload growth in the future and, therefore, were more likely to crack down sooner on welfare receipt.

The results regarding abortion restrictions find little evidence that the imposition of a restriction has any effect on teens' sexual activity, use of birth control, or pregnancy risk. A potential explanation for this finding is the lack of power inherent in the statistical methodology, as described earlier. This problem can be attributed to the limited sample of states and the pattern of changes of abortion restrictions across states. Of the three types of restrictions considered, relatively few changes were made over the sample period, and those changes were more likely to occur in smaller states that were not in the sample each possible year. Therefore, the ability to obtain precise before-and-after differences to compare to other states is limited and may have contributed to the general weakness in the findings along this dimension.

I have also estimated a model analogous to the probit models described above that includes interaction terms between each price variable and the race/ethnicity of each respondent. Since trends in sexual activity and contraceptive use differed so dramatically by race/ethnicity (and particularly for black non-Hispanics), one might expect these price effects to have differential effects as well. Table 4.5 reports the results of this analysis when all observations are used in the analysis separately for boys and girls. Identification in these models is weakened by the fact that sample sizes within states/years by race/ethnicity begin to get small, so imprecision plagues many of the results.

Nevertheless, some important differences emerge. In particular, the effect of labor market conditions is found to be greater for black non-Hispanics than for white non-Hispanics. For girls, an improvement in the employment-to-population ratio is found to have a significantly stronger

Table 4.5 The Relation between Geographic Factors and Teen Sexual Activity, Contraception, and Pregnancy by Race and Ethnicity, Probit Derivatives (standard errors in parentheses)

Geographic Variables	Sexual Intercourse Ever		Sexual Intercourse in Past Three Months		No Contraception Used during Last Intercourse in Past 3 Months		Pregnancy Risk	
	Girls (1)	Boys (2)	Girls (3)	Boys (4)	Girls (5)	Boys (6)	Girls (7)	Boys (8)
Employment-to-population ratio ($\times$ 10)	-.123	-.088	-.114	-.082	.006	.049	-.015	.005
	(.033)	(.029)	(.026)	(.025)	(.027)	(.029)	(.011)	(.010)
Black non-Hispanic	.035	.022	.021	.026	-.049	-.099	-.015	-.029
	(.038)	(.035)	(.033)	(.028)	(.020)	(.027)	(.009)	(.009)
Hispanic	-.004	.031	.018	.004	-.057	-.086	-.020	-.020
	(.028)	(.047)	(.026)	(.036)	(.038)	(.040)	(.013)	(.013)
Log maximum AFDC/TANF benefit for a family of 2	.281	-.016	.068	.312	.317	.078	.121	.068
	(.106)	(.137)	(.094)	(.119)	(.090)	(.104)	(.037)	(.038)
Black non-Hispanic	.049	-.040	-.010	.019	.057	.080	.024	.033
	(.058)	(.063)	(.047)	(.054)	(.028)	(.047)	(.013)	(.018)
Hispanic	.053	-.008	.019	-.019	.038	.032	.015	.012
	(.056)	(.074)	(.048)	(.053)	(.051)	(.077)	(.020)	(.026)
Reformed welfare system	.102	.059	.079	.033	.005	-.070	.014	-.019
	(.030)	(.027)	(.024)	(.022)	(.021)	(.027)	(.009)	(.009)
Black non-Hispanic	-.019	-.003	-.032	.041	.038	.035	.010	.016
	(.030)	(.043)	(.030)	(.036)	(.025)	(.036)	(.011)	(.013)
Hispanic	.012	-.045	.009	-.077	-.007	.035	.013	.002
	(.028)	(.052)	(.027)	(.038)	(.035)	(.048)	(.012)	(.017)

	(1)	(2)	(3)	(4)	(5)	(6)	(7)	(8)
AIDS rate per 100,000 population (× 100)	−.224	−.044	−.049	−.056	.015	−.026	−.006	−.017
	(.106)	(.093)	(.087)	(.081)	(.083)	(.093)	(.031)	(.035)
Black non-Hispanic (× 100)	−.061	.097	.003	.006	.015	−.108	.012	−.036
	(.086)	(.101)	(.087)	(.085)	(.083)	(.067)	(.024)	(.028)
Hispanic (× 100)	−.012	−.008	.000	−.057	−.257	−.033	−.083	−.011
	(.091)	(.101)	(.086)	(.075)	(.070)	(.094)	(.028)	(.033)
Medicaid funding restrictions	−.013	.026	.007	−.007	−.109	−.026	−.029	−.007
	(.104)	(.046)	(.084)	(.020)	(.062)	(.028)	(.030)	(.010)
Black non-Hispanic	.014	.020	−.052	−.003	.158	.159	.055	.062
	(.061)	(.066)	(.046)	(.056)	(.048)	(.070)	(.024)	(.032)
Hispanic	−.008	−.115	−.035	−.078	−.015	.082	−.009	.012
	(.059)	(.078)	(.047)	(.050)	(.054)	(.102)	(.019)	(.028)
Parent consent/notification required for abortion	−.031	.061	−.011	.020	.048	−.007	.016	.002
	(.049)	(.031)	(.036)	(.031)	(.025)	(.038)	(.013)	(.014)
Black non-Hispanic	.038	.031	.028	.023	−.008	−.001	.001	−.003
	(.044)	(.048)	(.042)	(.041)	(.024)	(.036)	(.011)	(.014)
Hispanic	−.027	−.023	−.004	−.002	−.070	.110	−.024	.024
	(.044)	(.083)	(.041)	(.062)	(.044)	(.095)	(.015)	(.032)
Mandatory waiting period for abortion	.049	−.075	.029	−.036	−.006	−.023	.002	−.014
	(.059)	(.052)	(.046)	(.043)	(.037)	(.039)	(.019)	(.010)
Black non-Hispanic	−.091	−.004	−.050	−.016	−.064	−.046	−.026	−.014
	(.050)	(.073)	(.039)	(.056)	(.020)	(.052)	(.009)	(.015)
Hispanic	−.063	.271	−.054	.269	.231	.173	.062	.132
	(.052)	(.110)	(.066)	(.148)	(.180)	(.161)	(.075)	(.119)

Source: Author's calculations from the 1991, 1993, 1995, and 1997 YRBS.

Note: All specifications include the same additional control variables as those reported in table 4.4.

effect on the likelihood of using contraception. The magnitude of the effect of labor market conditions on pregnancy risk is twice as great for blacks as it is for whites; the difference is significant at the 10 percent level. Racial differences for boys are even more dramatic; pregnancy risk is found to be roughly unaffected by labor market conditions for white, non-Hispanic boys, but a strong negative effect is observed for black, non-Hispanic boys. Some evidence also supports the position that the generosity of welfare benefits has a larger effect on black non-Hispanics than on white non-Hispanics. Again, the effect on failure to use contraception and pregnancy risk is significantly greater for blacks than it is for whites.

What can these results tell us about the potential determinants of recent trends in teens' sexual activity and contraceptive use? Recall that these trends are most clearly evident for black non-Hispanics. For these teens, the pregnancy risk fell by nearly half, from 14.7 to 8.4 percent between 1991 and 1997 (on the basis of YRBS data). The main potential predictor of a decline in that level given the results presented above would be labor market conditions. Between 1991 and 1997, the teen employment-to-population ratio rose from 41.9 to 43.4. The results presented in table 4.5 indicate that, for this demographic group, a 1.5 percentage point increase in the teen employment-to-population ratio would be predicted to lower the risk of becoming pregnant by 0.5 percentage points, a relatively small share of the decline.[26]

Other price-related factors offer little additional help in explaining the decline in pregnancy risk for black teen girls. Even if the estimated effect of AIDS was stronger, AIDS cases grew only through 1993 and have fallen back since then, with the result that the 1997 level is not much higher than that in 1991. Welfare-benefit generosity is found to be related to greater pregnancy risk, and more so for blacks, and real benefit levels have fallen by about 19 percent over the period 1991–97.[27] On the basis of the estimates given in table 4.4, this decline is predicted to reduce teen pregnancy risk by 2.8 percentage points, or about 44 percent of the overall decline. One should be cautious about providing such an interpretation of these results, however, given the counterintuitive estimates regarding the effect of welfare reform. Taking the welfare-reform estimates at face value, and given the fact that the entire country experienced welfare reform between 1991 and 1997, one would predict black teen pregnancy risk to rise by 2.4 percentage points on the basis of these estimates. This effect would almost

26. This calculation is based on the increase in the teen employment-to-population ratio for all races, not just black non-Hispanics, because the overall rates were used at the state level in the probit models. But the black, non-Hispanic employment-to-population ratio rose by even more between 1991 and 1997, increasing 3.6 points, from 22.6 to 26.2. Even if this larger increase were used, however, it would still explain a very small share of the decline in pregnancy risk over the period.

27. This decline represents a national average across states using the population weights in the YRBS data.

completely offset the effect of falling benefit generosity. It would also be difficult to attribute any causal effect of changes in abortion rules given the weakness of the evidence provided earlier regarding these policies. Taken as a whole, it would appear that a great deal of the decline in pregnancy risk among black non-Hispanics, which may have contributed to the dramatic decline in teen fertility among this group, cannot be explained by these factors.

4.4 Teen Motherhood and Subsequent Outcomes

The previous analysis considered the factors related to the risk of becoming pregnant, but the risk itself has not yet been defined. In particular, if a teen becomes pregnant and goes on to have a child, what cost does that impose on her during the remainder of her life? This section will evaluate the literature examining the effect of becoming a teen mother on the women's labor market outcomes and receipt of public assistance.

Earlier research on this topic is well summarized by Hofferth (1987). Results from this work identify some important life-cycle patterns in the labor market activity of teen mothers. Soon after giving birth, teen mothers face significant disadvantages compared to women who have delayed childbirth but are similar in some other dimensions. Teen mothers have significantly lower rates of labor force participation in the years immediately following teen childbirth. This difference is eliminated or even reversed by the time the women are in their late twenties, when those women who delayed childbearing are more likely to be caring for very young children. Little research has compared teen mothers with those who delayed childbearing until even later in life, and, while the available evidence suggests that teen mothers are somewhat less likely to work after their childbearing years, that difference is small.

Regardless of the point that they have reached in the life cycle, teen mothers earn less and have lower incomes than women who delay childbirth, even after controlling for several background characteristics. The fact that teen mothers also acquire significantly less education is strongly related to their lower earnings. Lower earnings also contribute to the higher rate of welfare receipt through the childbearing years, although some evidence indicates that the greater relative rate of welfare receipt diminishes over time as well.

The focus of more recent research has been to introduce alternative methodologies intended to compare teen mothers with other women who are identical on all relevant characteristics. For instance, even women who grew up in low-income, inner-city households may have been raised in very different family circumstances. One woman may have had parents who placed a heavy emphasis on education; another woman may have grown up in a household in which domestic violence occurred often. Ethnographic studies that track the lives of a relatively small number of women might be able to identify such differences. But this research can seldom be generalized to larger groups of women. Statistical analysis that relies on large samples of individuals cannot hope to control for these "unobservable" characteristics. More recent research in this area has applied innovative methods of identifying comparison groups across which even these differences are more likely to be held constant.

Geronimus and Korenman (1992) provide one example of this type of research. They compared the outcomes (including income, employment, and welfare receipt) of sisters, one who gave birth as a teen and one who did not. Of course, sisters differ in many ways, and Geronimus and Korenman control for differences between them in many of the same types of characteristics considered in first-generation studies. Since sisters generally share a common family background, however, differences in outcomes between them probably cannot be attributed to these characteristics, which would otherwise be unobservable in this type of study. The results of this study provide little evidence of a substantial detrimental effect of teen motherhood once these other factors are controlled for. Although the authors acknowledge that small sample sizes lead to imprecision in their estimates and limit the power of their analysis, they conclude that their results should lead one to be more cautious in finding a causal relation between teen motherhood and subsequent outcomes.

This research has led to a healthy exchange of papers, including replication exercises and alternative interpretations of the findings (Hoffman, Foster, and Furstenberg 1993a; Geronimus and Korenman 1993; and Hoffman, Foster, and Furstenberg 1993b), and the controversy has led to subsequent analysis by others. For instance, Hotz, McElroy, and Sanders (1996) provide another attempt to identify a sample of women who differ only by their status as teen mothers. These authors compare women who gave birth as teenagers to teens who became pregnant but miscarried. They report that roughly 10 percent of first teen pregnancies result in a miscarriage and that those who miscarry postpone subsequent childbearing three to four years, on average. If a miscarriage can be thought of as occurring "by chance," then it acts as a means of random assignment that separates pregnant teenagers into pseudo–control and –treatment groups, which can be compared using techniques similar to those of a controlled experiment.[28] Within their quasi-experimental framework, these authors find few negative labor market consequences or greater welfare receipt brought about by a teen birth.

Angrist and Evans (1996) introduce another quasi-experimental technique, using the legislative history of abortion liberalization to identify

---

28. Hotz, McElroy, and Sanders (1996) recognize that this assumption is not perfectly accurate and control for observable differences between the two groups in their analysis.

groups of women who are similar except for their status as teen mothers. They use the fact that the timing of abortion legalization in the early 1970s differed across states. In those states where abortion was legalized earlier, women—and teens in particular—may have responded by having relatively fewer children than women in states where abortion was not legalized until the 1973 *Roe v. Wade* Supreme Court decision. If a teen birth leads to differences in subsequent outcomes, the teenage women in those states that legalized abortion early should have had different outcomes within this window compared to teenage women living in states that did not liberalize their abortion laws until 1973. Angrist and Evans show few effects, if any, from differences in abortion laws. They identify a reduction in the probability of work among adult black but not white women who gave birth as teens. Moreover, even for blacks, the estimated effect is very imprecise, so it is difficult conclusively to determine whether the effect is large or small.

One last paper, by Grogger and Bronars (1993), uses a quasi-experimental design to identify relevant comparison groups. In this paper, women who have a first birth as teens are differentiated by whether they gave birth to twins or to a single child. Viewing the occurrence of twins as a "chance" event, having twins acts as a means of random assignment where women in a pseudo–control group have one child and women in a pseudo–treatment group have two. Comparing these groups can identify the independent effect of having an additional teen birth on the subsequent outcomes of these women.[29] Results indicate that having an additional child out of wedlock has no significant negative effect on employment but a small positive effect on welfare receipt for white women. For black women, the effect is larger.

It is clear that differences in outcomes between teen mothers and women who delay childbearing cannot be entirely attributed to the birth of the child. Given the evidence provided by recent research, it may even be an open question whether any economic disadvantage is "caused" by teen motherhood (except, perhaps, for blacks). Given the narrow categories of women on which the estimates from this research are based and the general imprecision in estimated effects, however, it would be premature definitively to draw such a conclusion.

4.5   Discussion

The prevalence of teen sexual activity without the use of contraception is clearly a concern of the American public (despite the fact that empirical

---

29. It is important to recognize that this exercise is not completely analogous to that conducted in the previous papers discussed, which attempted to estimate the effect of becoming a teen mother (with, most likely, one child) compared to delaying childbirth.

research has been unable to provide convincing evidence that the cost of a teen birth is large). This paper has documented that the level of such behavior is high by international standards and that little evidence indicates that it is declining rapidly (except, perhaps, among blacks). I have provided a discussion of alternative frameworks for thinking about this problem, with an emphasis on the contribution of economic analysis. The results of the empirical evidence provided in this paper provide some support for the conclusion that economic factors do affect individuals' decisions regarding sexuality and contraceptive use, although these factors cannot explain much of the recent trends.

The analysis presented in this paper can potentially provide a mechanism to help evaluate possible policy responses. The policies most commonly advocated to reduce the level of unprotected sexual activity by teens generally differ by political persuasion. From the Right, the advocacy of abstinence ("just say no") is the proposed response. From the Left, the expansion of sex education and increased funding for family planning are typically proposed. Within the framework of the analysis provided here, neither approach is likely to be particularly effective.

First, consider the calls for greater use of sex education and additional funding for family planning. If teen sexual activity is dictated by the developmental process and specific acts occur spontaneously, then the benefit of providing more information about contraception and the availability of low-cost family-planning services may be quite small. As teens age and reach a developmental level at which they are able to respond on the basis of perceived risks or an economic model in which costs are always weighed against benefits, greater information and lower costs are potentially useful tools. Their usefulness depends on the extent of misinformation and the extent to which these costs are altered by policy. On this basis, their effectiveness may be limited.

Evidence from a recent survey of high school students conducted by the Kaiser Family Foundation (1999) may be brought to bear on this question. The survey indicates that 95 percent of teenage girls know that they can become pregnant during first intercourse, 80 percent know that they can buy condoms in drugstores without their parents' permission, and 80 percent know that they qualify for free or low-cost contraception at family-planning clinics. Although relatively high percentages report wanting even more information, the vast majority seem to know the minimum required to avoid getting pregnant.[30] Although increased information may certainly

---

30. For instance, survey results indicate that 61 percent of girls mistakenly believe that they need their parents' permission to get birth-control pills and that 51 percent would like to have more information about birth control. These results suggest that increased sex education and family planning would still provide benefits for teens through greater choices and a more thorough understanding of their decisions. Nevertheless, most appear to have sufficient knowledge to make decisions that would prevent them from getting pregnant should they so desire.

result in some gains, it seems unlikely to provide a substantial reduction in teen pregnancy. Moreover, if the cost of teen pregnancy is as high as is often claimed, small changes in the price of birth control (such as providing free condoms) also seem unlikely significantly to shift the balance and cause people to use contraception who otherwise would not.

Promoting abstinence has similar problems. If younger teens have not developed sufficiently to make rational decisions, then they will be unable to respond to such calls. If they are making rational decisions on the basis of the relative costs and benefits of the activity, then just-say-no policies will be ineffective without any reference to either part of this comparison.

If none of the conventional proposals seem likely to have a significant effect on the sexual behavior of teens, what sorts of policies are likely to be effective? From a rational decision-making framework, only one set of alternatives is really possible. Since it would be difficult to alter the perceived benefits of sexual activity, one would have to focus on the costs. To yield a significant reduction, the perceived cost would have to be elevated considerably. This could take many forms. For instance, perhaps sex education should amend its focus away from health-related issues and add to the curriculum the economic risks that teen pregnancy poses. A thorough understanding of the potentially lifelong implications of one's decision as a teen to accept the risk of becoming pregnant could shift the balance. However, this would require teens to place sufficient weight on future costs compared to present benefits; models of such activity by behavioral economists in which tremendous weight may be placed on activity today would work against a large effect. Moreover, in the light of the recent empirical evidence reviewed above, it is unclear whether a teen birth does impose a large cost.

Other policies that actually do change the cost (as opposed to the perceived cost) of giving birth may also be effective. Given the evidence provided earlier, strengthening labor market opportunities for teens may increase the opportunity cost of childbearing and reduce its incidence. Improving those opportunities over the long term (rather than relying strictly on cyclic fluctuations), however, is a difficult task. The analysis provided earlier also suggests that AIDS incidence played some role in reducing risky sexual behavior, but, given its enormous cost to teens and others, no one could conceivably propose limiting the fight against AIDS solely for this purpose. More stringent welfare policies, such as those embedded in welfare reform, could also provide such costs through a greatly diminished value of benefits, provisions that limit benefit increases resulting from additional births, forcing teen mothers to live with their parents, and the like.[31] Yet the evidence presented earlier regarding the effect of welfare policies on sexual activity is mixed. Beyond options such as

---

31. Welfare-reform legislation also provided incentives to states to reduce the level of teen births, but it allows states to introduce their own specific policies.

these, it becomes clear that lowering the level of risky sexual practices among teens, and therefore lowering birthrates, is a very difficult exercise. In fact, if one takes the perspective that sexual activity is largely spontaneous and irrational, it would be virtually impossible for any intervention to have much of an effect.

One additional avenue that should be considered, one that has been given less attention in the literature and ignored here, is the behavior of men. Although the empirical analysis reported above estimated analogous models for school-age boys and girls, the costs considered were largely associated with the behavior of girls. The risk for teenage men associated with unprotected sexual activity is quite low and may be limited to the risk of contracting a sexually transmitted disease.[32] If men are rational decision makers, then the positive benefit combined with very little cost means that they should be willing to undertake such behavior regardless of its potential outcome. In fact, Akerlof, Yellen, and Katz (1996) argue that the changes in the availability of contraception and the legalization of abortion in the late 1960s and early 1970s are responsible for the current trend toward increasing out-of-wedlock births because the cost to men of engaging in sexual activity became so low. To the extent that policies could be designed that hold teenage men more accountable for their actions in this regard, they might be effective in helping reduce the rate of risky sexual behavior.

References

Abma, Joyce, and Freya L. Sonenstein. 1998. Teenage sexual behavior and contraceptive use: An update. Hyattsville, Md.: National Center for Health Statistics, Centers for Disease Control, 28 April.

Ahituv, Avner, V. Joseph Hotz, and Tomas Philipson. 1996. The responsiveness of the demand for condoms to the local prevalence of AIDS. *Journal of Human Resources* 31, no. 4 (fall): 869–97.

Akerlof, George A., Janet L. Yellen, and Michael L. Katz. 1996. An analysis of out-of-wedlock childbearing in the United States. *Quarterly Journal of Economics* 111, no. 2 (May): 277–318.

Alan Guttmacher Institute. 1998. *Facts in brief: Teen sex and pregnancy, 1998.* New York.

Angrist, Joshua D., and William N. Evans. 1996. Schooling and labor market consequences of the 1970 state abortion reforms. Working Paper no. 5406. Cambridge, Mass.: National Bureau of Economic Research, January.

32. One could argue that an additional cost for a teenage man is the probability that a woman gets pregnant and successfully identifies him as the father, potentially leaving him liable for child-support payments. Given the low earnings capacity at that stage of life, however, even this cost is likely to be quite small. This also works against the effectiveness of a policy strengthening the enforcement of child-support awards.

Argys, Laura, Susan Averett, and Daniel Rees. In press. Welfare generosity, pregnancies, and abortions among unmarried AFDC recipients. *Journal of Population Economics.*

Blank, Rebecca, Christine George, and Rebecca London. 1996. State abortion rates: The impact of policies, providers, politics, demographics, and economic environment. *Journal of Health Economics* 15, no. 5 (October): 513–53.

Brooks-Gunn, Jeanne, and Frank F. Furstenberg Jr. 1989. Adolescent sexual behavior. *American Psychologist* 44, no. 2 (February): 249–57.

Brooks-Gunn, Jeanne, and Roberta Paikoff. 1997. Sexuality and developmental transitions during adolescence. In *Health risks and developmental transitions during adolescence,* ed. John Schulenberg, Jennifer L. Maggs, and Klaus Hurrelmann. Cambridge: Cambridge University Press.

Butz, William P., and Michael P. Ward. 1979. The emergence of countercyclical U.S. fertility. *American Economic Review* 69, no. 3 (June): 318–28.

Camasso, Michael, Carol Harvey, Mark Killingsworth, and Radha Jagannathan. 1999. New Jersey's family cap and family size decisions: Some findings from a 5-year evaluation. Rutgers University, 8 April. Typescript.

Centers for Disease Control (CDC) Press Office. 1998. New CDC report cites drop in sexual risk behaviors among teens. Atlanta, 17 September. Press release.

Council of Economic Advisers. 1999. The effects of welfare policy and the economic expansion on welfare caseloads: An update. Washington, D.C., 3 August.

Darroch, Jacqueline E., David J. Landry, and Selene Oslak. 1999. Age differences between sexual partners in the United States. *Family Planning Perspectives* 31, no. 4 (July/August): 160–67.

Dee, Thomas S. 1999. The effects of alcohol use and availability on teen childbearing. Swarthmore College, February. Typescript.

Fairlie, Robert W., and Rebecca A. London. 1997. The effect of incremental benefit levels on births to AFDC recipients. *Journal of Policy Analysis and Management* 16, no. 4:575–97.

Gallup Organization. 1999. Gallup social and economic indicators—most important problem. 3 September 1999. *www.gallup.com/poll/indicators/indmip.asp.*

Geronimus, Arline T., and Sanders Korenman. 1992. The socioeconomic consequences of teen childbearing reconsidered. *Quarterly Journal of Economics* 107, no. 4 (November): 1187–1214.

———. 1993. The socioeconomic costs of teenage childbearing: Evidence and interpretation. *Demography* 30, no. 2 (May): 281–90.

Grogger, Jeff, and Stepen Bronars. 1993. The socioeconomic consequences of teenage childbearing: Findings from a natural experiment. *Family Planning Perspectives* 25, no. 3 (July/August): 156–62.

Haas-Wilson, Deborah. 1996. The impact of state abortion restrictions on minors' demand for abortions. *Journal of Human Resources* 31, no. 1 (winter): 140–58.

Hardy, Janet B., and Laurie Schwab Zabin. 1991. *Adolescent pregnancy in an urban environment.* Washington, D.C.: Urban Institute Press.

Henshaw, Stanley K. 1999. *Special report: U.S. teenage pregnancy statistics, with comparative statistics for women aged 20–24.* New York: Alan Guttmacher Institute, 1 June.

Hofferth, Sandra L. 1987. Social and economic consequences of teenage childbearing. In *Risking the future: Adolescent sexuality, pregnancy, and childbearing,* ed. Cheryl D. Hayes. Washington, D.C.: National Academy Press.

Hoffman, Saul D., E. Michael Foster, and Frank F. Furstenberg Jr. 1993a. Reevaluating the costs of teenage childbearing. *Demography* 30, no. 1 (February): 1–13.

———. 1993b. Reevaluating the costs of teenage childbearing: Response to Geronimus and Korenman. *Demography* 30, no. 2 (May): 291–96.

Horvath, Ann, and H. Elizabeth Peters. 1999. Welfare waivers and non-marital childbearing. Working Paper no. 109. Chicago: Joint Center for Poverty Research, September.

Hotz, V. Joseph, Susan Williams McElroy, and Seth G. Sanders. 1996. The impacts of teenage childbearing on the mothers and the consequences of those impacts for government. In *Kids having kids: Economic costs and social consequences of teen pregnancy,* ed. Rebecca A. Maynard. Washington, D.C.: Urban Institute Press.

Kaiser Family Foundation. 1997. *Is the secret getting out? 1997 national surveys of Americans and health care providers on emergency contraception.* Menlo Park, Calif.

———. 1999. *1999 national survey of 9th–12th grade public school students about sexual health issues and services.* Menlo Park, Calif.

Kane, Thomas J., and Douglas Staiger. 1996. Teen motherhood and abortion access. *Quarterly Journal of Economics* 111, no. 2 (May): 467–506.

Leibowitz, Arleen, Marvin Eisen, and Winston K. Chow. 1986. An economic model of teenage pregnancy decision-making. *Demography* 23, no. 1 (February): 67–77.

Levine, Phillip B., Amy B. Trainor, and David J. Zimmerman. 1996. The effects of Medicaid abortion funding restrictions on abortions, pregnancies, and births. *Journal of Health Economics* 15:555–78.

Lowenstein, George, and Frank Furstenberg. 1991. Is teenage sexual behavior rational? *Journal of Applied Social Psychology* 21, no. 12 (1991): 957–86.

Lundberg, Shelly, and Robert D. Plotnick. 1995. Adolescent premarital childbearing: Do economic incentives matter? *Journal of Labor Economics* 13, no. 2 (April): 177–200.

Mancunovich, Diane J. 1995. The Butz-Ward fertility model in the light of more recent data. *Journal of Human Resources* 30, no. 2 (spring): 229–55.

Matthews, Stephen, David Ribar, and Mark Wilhelm. 1997. The effects of economic conditions and access to reproductive health services on state abortion and birthrates. *Family Planning Perspectives* 29, no. 2 (March/April): 52–60.

Miller, Wayne J., Sirinder Wadhera, and Stanley K. Henshaw. 1997. Repeat abortions in Canada, 1975–1993. *Family Planning Perspectives* 29, no. 1 (January/February): 20–24.

Moffitt, Robert. 1998. The effect of welfare on marriage and the family. In *Welfare, the family, and reproductive behavior,* ed. Robert A. Moffitt. Washington, D.C.: National Academy Press.

Moore, Kristin A., Brent C. Miller, Dana Glei, and Donna Ruane Morrison. 1995. *Adolescent sex, contraception, and childbearing: A review of recent research.* Washington, D.C.: Child Trends, June.

National Abortion and Reproductive Rights Action League (NARAL) Foundation. Various years. *Who decides? A state-by-state review of abortion and reproductive rights.* Washington, D.C.

National Center for Health Statistics (NCHS) Press Office. 1997. Teen sex down, new study shows. Hyattsville, Md., 1 May. Press release.

O'Donoghue, Ted, and Matthew Rabin. 1999. Doing it now or later. *American Economic Review* 89, no. 1 (March): 103–24.

Oettinger, Gerald S. 1999. The effects of sex education on teen sexual activity and teen pregnancy. *Journal of Political Economy* 107, no. 3 (June): 606–44.

O'Neill, June. 1994. Report concerning New Jersey's Family Development Program. Baruch College. Typescript.

Philipson, Tomas J., and Richard A. Posner. 1993. *The AIDS epidemic in an economic perspective.* Cambridge, Mass.: Harvard University Press.

Terry, Elizabeth, and Jennifer Manlove. 1999. Trends in sexual activity and contraceptive use among teens. Paper presented at the Child Trends conference "Messengers and Methods for the New Millennium: A Round Table on Adolescents and Contraception," Washington, D.C., February.

UN Department of Economic and Social Affairs. Statistical Office. Various years. *Demographic yearbook.* New York.

———. Centers for Disease Control. National Center for Health Statistics. 1999a. *Healthy people 2000 review, 1998–99.* Hyattsville, Md., June.

———. Office of Disease Prevention and Health Promotion. 1999b. *Healthy people 2010—draft.* 20 August. *http://web.health.gov/healthypeople/default.htm.*

———. Office of the Assistant Secretary for Planning and Evaluation. 1998. *Trends in the well-being of America's children and youth: 1998.* Washington, D.C.: U.S. Government Printing Office.

———. Public Health Service. Centers for Disease Control. National Center for Health Statistics. 1995. *Report to Congress on out-of-wedlock childbearing.* Hyattsville, Md., September.

———. Public Health Service. Centers for Disease Control. National Center for Infectious Diseases. Division of HIV/AIDS. Various issues. *HIV/AIDS surveillance report.* Atlanta.

U.S. House of Representatives. Various years. *The green book.* Washington, D.C.

Ventura, Stephanie J., Joyce A. Martin, Sally C. Curtin, and T. J. Matthews. 1997. Report of final natality statistics, 1995. *Monthly Vital Statistics Report,* vol. 45, no. 11, suppl. (10 June).

———. 1998. Report of final natality statistics, 1996. *Monthly Vital Statistics,* vol. 46, no. 11, suppl. (30 June).

———. 1999. Births: Final data for 1997. *Monthly Vital Statistics Report,* vol. 27, no. 18 (29 April).

Ventura, Stephanie J., Joyce A. Martin, T. J. Mathews, and Sally C. Clarke. 1996. Advance report of final natality statistics, 1994. *Monthly Vital Statistics Report,* 44, no. 11, suppl. (24 June).

Ventura, Stephanie J., T. J. Matthews, and Sally C. Curtin. 1999. Declines in teenage birth rates, 1991–1998: Update of national and state trends. *National Vital Statistics Reports,* vol. 47, no. 26 (25 October).

Ventura, Stephanie J., Selma M. Taffel, William D. Mosher, Jacqueline B. Wilson, and Stanley Henshaw. 1995. Trends in pregnancies and pregnancy rates: Estimates for the United States, 1980–92. *Monthly Vital Statistics Report,* vol. 43, no. 11(S) (25 May).

5

Explaining the Rise
in Youth Suicide

David M. Cutler, Edward L. Glaeser,
and Karen E. Norberg

Emile Durkheim's *Suicide* documented a monotonically increasing relation between age and suicide. Such a relation has been observed repeatedly since the beginning of the nineteenth century, making it one of the most robust facts about suicide. The differences in suicide rates by age are very large. In the United States in 1950, for example, suicide rates were four times higher for adults (ages twenty-five to sixty-four) than for youths (ages fifteen to twenty-four) and eight times higher for the elderly (sixty-five and older) than for youths.[1] Economic theory explained this relation naturally, with the young having the most life to lose and also having the least information about what their life will be like (Hamermesh and Soss 1974).

In recent decades, however, the monotonic relation between age and suicide has disappeared. Figure 5.1 shows suicide rates by age in 1950 and 1990. Between 1950 and 1990, youth-suicide rates tripled (particularly among young men), while suicide rates for adults fell by 7 percent, and suicide rates for the elderly fell by 30 percent. In 1990, suicide rates for young adults (ages twenty to twenty-four) were equal to those for prime-age adults and were only 25 percent below suicide rates for the elderly.

David M. Cutler is professor of economics at Harvard University and a research associate of the National Bureau of Economic Research. Edward L. Glaeser is professor of economics at Harvard University and a faculty research fellow of the National Bureau of Economic Research. Karen E. Norberg is assistant professor of psychiatry at Boston University Medical School and a clinical associate of the National Bureau of Economic Research.

The authors are grateful to Srikanth Kadiyala for expert research assistance, to Jonathan Gruber and Senhil Mullainathan for comments, and to the National Institute on Aging for research support.

1. Throughout the paper, we refer to the fifteen- to twenty-four-year-old age group as *youths*. We sometimes divide this into *teens* (ages fifteen to nineteen) and *young adults* (ages twenty to twenty-four).

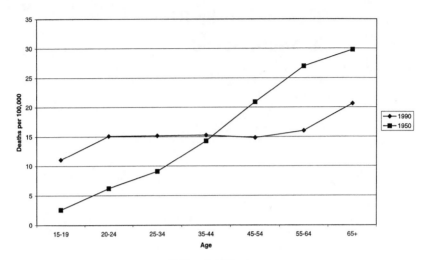

Fig. 5.1   Suicide rates by age, 1950 and 1990

Suicide is now the second or third leading cause of death for youths in the United States, Canada, Australia, New Zealand, and many countries of Western Europe.

If youth suicide is an epidemic, attempted suicide is even more so. For every teen who commits suicide (0.01 percent each year), four hundred teens report attempting suicide (4 percent per year), one hundred report requiring medical attention for a suicide attempt (1 percent per year), and thirty are hospitalized for a suicide attempt (0.3 percent per year).

Why have youth-suicide rates increased so much even as suicide among adults and the elderly has fallen? Why are there so many suicide attempts? It is easier to say what suicide is *not* than what it is. The U.S. rise in youth suicide has not been centered in America's troubled inner cities. The states with the largest increase in youth suicides between 1950 and 1990 are predominantly rural: Wyoming, South Dakota, Montana, New Mexico, and Idaho. The states with the most troubled inner cities in fact have the smallest increases: The District of Columbia, New Jersey, Delaware, Massachusetts, and New York. Indeed, when Durkheim wrote, suicide was primarily an urban phenomenon, but today youth suicides are 15 percent more prevalent in rural areas than in urban areas.[2]

This paper examines some of the economic and social roots of youth suicide and suicide attempts. Two stories illustrate our results. The first is reported by Rene Diekstra (1989, 16):

2. Durkheim ([1897] 1966) suggested that urban suicide was evidence for the role that traditional agrarian (and particularly Catholic) society plays in creating a well-functioning social environment.

It was around noon on 12 August 1969 that 19-year old Jurgen Peters climbed the ladder on the outside of the water tower in the German city of Kassel. By the time he reached the top, a number of people were already gathering where the young man was at.

It soon became clear that he intended to jump all the way down in an attempt to take his own life. Earlier that morning, Jurgen had been fired by his boss, a local garage owner for whom he worked as an apprentice mechanic. The reason had been that, upon being asked to test drive a client's car, he instead had gone joy riding and in the process had severely damaged that car as well as two others. Bystanders called the police, who in turn called the fire department for assistance. A fire ladder was put out to the top of the tower, and one of the firemen tried to talk Jurgen out of his plan, without success, however. Then a girl he had been dating and liked very much was asked to talk with him. She succeeded in persuading him to give up his attempt.

While stepping from the water tower onto the fire ladder and starting his descent, a couple of young men watching the scene began yelling: "Hey, coward, you don't even have the guts to jump, do you?" and similar provocative remarks. One could observe Jurgen hesitating, interrupting his descent. Then all of a sudden he climbed up the ladder, hopped on the top of the tower and almost in one movement jumped off it. He died on the spot.

The second was witnessed by one of the authors (see Norberg 1999). Between 30 December 1996 and 22 July 1997, there was a suicide epidemic in the white, predominantly low-income community of South Boston, Massachusetts. The area affected is an economically mixed and historically embattled community of about thirty thousand, somewhat physically isolated from the rest of the city. Although the community had been well represented in the city's and the state's political leadership for many years, its political influence seemed to be declining. The community was perceived by many observers, both insiders and outsiders, as having been deeply stressed and demoralized by recent and rapid social changes. Political and economic factors that have affected the community over the last generation include high rates of poverty, organized crime, and substance abuse and a history of political conflict with the rest of the city over school busing and public-housing integration. Within the previous three years, there had been new social stresses, including welfare reform, changes in the local political leadership, a major crackdown on the organized crime leadership in the community, and the privatization of city and state services, with a loss of public-sector jobs that had been the economic base for the community.

In addition to these general social stresses, there had been a concurrent drug epidemic that may have been intimately related to the suicide epidemic. A nationwide decrease in the price of heroin had resulted in an increase in heroin use by even very young adolescents in South Boston in 1995 and 1996. Other adolescents, not drug users themselves, reported an increased feeling of anxiety in the face of the community's manifest inability to stop this increase in serious adolescent drug use. In early 1996, a fifteen-year-old boy died of an accidental drug overdose in one of the housing projects in the community. Just before this overdose, he had made a name for himself by stabbing a man who was accused of raping his sister. By report, more than a thousand people attended this boy's wake and funeral; teenagers tattooed his name on their bodies, and the project hallways are still full of graffiti recording his name. He seems to have been memorialized, in part, because his death was seen as symbolic of a general crisis in the community. The first suicide of the epidemic occurred in the same housing project, close to the one-year anniversary of his death.

By the end of the epidemic, there had been six hanging deaths, all young white males, along with forty-eight serious but nonlethal suicide attempts, including five nearly fatal hanging attempts resulting in medical intensive-care-unit hospitalizations (all young white males aged fifteen to seventeen), eight intentional overdoses serious enough to require medical hospitalization in addition to psychiatric care, at least thirty-five other hanging, overdose, and other self-injury attempts, and seventy-eight other crisis evaluations resulting in psychiatric hospitalizations among adolescents primarily aged fifteen to seventeen in this community. The affected adolescents were more likely to be white and male and more likely to be between the ages of fifteen and seventeen than children and youths receiving emergency psychiatric screenings in baseline years. Given an estimated population of about thirteen hundred teenagers in this community between the ages of fourteen and seventeen, this represents a thirty-eight-fold higher suicide rate in the community than the teen suicide rate for the country as a whole, at least a fivefold increase in cases requiring medical hospitalization, and a psychiatric hospitalization rate of almost 10 percent of the adolescents in the community in a single narrow age group. Nearly all the persons making suicide attempts during this time cited the completed suicides as one of the stressors affecting them. Thirty-six of the forty-eight serious attempters reported being close to at least one of the teens who died.

These two stories foreshadow several questions that we address in this paper: What social stressors (such as the lost job for Jurgen and the heroin epidemic in Boston) are associated with the rise in youth suicide? What is the role of other high-risk behavior (the joyride, stabbing a community violator) in prompting crises leading to suicide? What is the role of peer pressure or social contagion in youth suicide?

We examine these issues of suicide and suicide attempts using two sources of data. The first is Vital Statistics data on youth suicides. These data are available at the aggregate level since the turn of the century and at the micro level since 1968. We briefly describe national time trends since

1900 and examine state-level cross-sectional data for 1950 and 1990 and county-level cross-sectional data for 1990. National data record all deaths, but the attribution of deaths by cause is somewhat problematic. This is most important in distinguishing between suicides and accidental deaths. For example, a youth who dies of a self-inflicted gunshot wound may be considered either a suicide or the victim of an accidental death; many single-vehicle motor-vehicle fatalities are thought to be probable suicides, although they are usually classified as accidents. In prior years, when there was more stigma associated with suicide, the share of deaths coded as accidents was higher and the share coded as suicides lower. As we discuss below, we do not think that reporting changes materially affect our conclusions about the reasons for increasing suicide over time.

National data on attempted suicide by youths are not available. Instead, to study suicide attempts, we turn to the National Longitudinal Survey of Adolescent Health (AddHealth). The AddHealth study surveys a nationally representative sample of about twenty thousand teenagers, their parents, and their social peers. We examine data from the first wave of this study, which took place in 1996. The AddHealth survey asks youths about suicidal thoughts, suicide attempts, and whether the attempt required medical treatment. It also gathers a broad range of demographic and social information.

Our empirical analysis leads us to three conclusions. First, we argue that there is a fundamental distinction between suicide attempts and suicide completions. While successful suicide is usually the result of a strongly held intent to end one's life, most suicide attempts are probably not. Instead, many suicide attempts can best be seen as a strategic action on the part of youths to resolve conflicts within themselves, with parents, or with others. Youths have little direct economic or familial power, and, in such a situation, self-injury can act as a powerful distress signal. It can also serve to punish other persons (playing off others' empathetic or altruistic inclinations) or to embarrass or "blackmail" persons who "should" be altruistically inclined toward the victim, if the gesture draws the attention of outside authorities or other persons whose opinion matters to the reluctant altruist.

Many factors suggest that the bulk of suicide attempts are strategic. For example, women attempt suicide 50 percent more often than men but complete suicide six times less frequently. Attempted suicides peak for fifteen-year-olds, while rates of completed suicides climb sharply between ages fifteen and twenty. Finally, suicide attempts by youths are greater in families where youths may have more to gain from a shift in resources.

Second, we find strong evidence that social interactions are important in teen suicide. Teenagers are much more likely to attempt suicide when they know someone else who has attempted suicide, and suicides are "clumped" across areas in a way suggesting local spillovers. Spillovers may occur in several ways: an attempt by one person may be more credible if it follows attempts by others; authorities may take a second suicide attempt more seriously than the first; people might learn about effective techniques from others (e.g., exactly how much medication it takes to get sick but not die); or youths may provoke other youths to attempt suicide if the alternative is bringing shame to one's group by a public display of stress. The presence of social interactions means that small differences in aggregate fundamentals can trigger large shifts in the number of youth suicides.

The importance of peer interaction in youth suicides was noted by Durkheim ([1897] 1966) a century ago and has been supported by other investigators in the current era (Gould et al. 1994). Contagion effects are far less evident for adults and the elderly, suggesting that social interactions are less important for these groups.

Third, we find that, to the extent that we can explain the rise in youth suicide over time, the most important aggregate variable explaining this change seems to be the increased share of youths living in homes with a divorced parent. To a lesser extent, higher female labor force participation rates also explain increased rates among males. Divorce rates at the county, state, and national levels are highly correlated with youth-suicide rates. The divorce rate is more highly correlated with youth suicides than is the share of children living with stepparents or the share of children in single-parent families (both divorced and never-married parents). Female labor force participation is another potential factor. Higher female labor force participation predicts higher rates of suicide, particularly for males. At the individual level, we find that family structure and parents' time budgets also seem to matter for youths' suicide attempts, albeit to a much less important degree than at the aggregate level for youth suicide. Both these factors predict youth suicide more strongly than they predict adult suicide.

We begin by presenting basic facts about youth suicides and suicide attempts. The second section discusses different theories about teen suicides. The third section presents data on suicide attempts from a nationally representative survey in 1996, and the fourth section examines county, state, and national data on completed suicides. The last section concludes.

5.1 Facts about Suicide

We begin with some basic facts about suicide to set the stage for our later analysis. While some of the facts are well-known, others are not.

5.1.1 Since 1950, Suicide Has Tripled among Youths and Fallen among Older Adults and the Elderly

Figure 5.1 above shows the change in suicide rates by age from 1950 to 1990. Suicide rates for youths tripled between 1950 and 1990, rising from

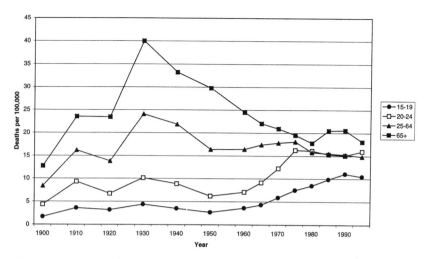

Fig. 5.2   Suicide rates by age over time

4.5 per 100,000 to 13.8 per 100,000. In contrast, suicide among adults has fallen by 10 percent and suicide among the elderly by half.

To highlight the differing trends by age, figure 5.2 shows suicide rates by age at decadal intervals over the twentieth century. Suicide rates first peaked about 1910. Suicide rates for adults and particularly the elderly rose again in the Great Depression and have fallen substantially since then. Total suicide rates in 1997 are the same as they were in 1950. Suicide rates for youths, in contrast, declined by 2.5 percent per year from their peak in 1908 through their trough in 1955 and since then have risen by 2.4 percent per year.

There is an increase in the youth-suicide rate for every single year of age, as shown in figure 5.3. Between 1970 and 1980, the percentage increase was roughly the same for all ages. Since 1980, suicide rates increased most rapidly among teenagers aged fifteen to nineteen.

One possible explanation for the rise in teen suicides is that teen deaths might have been coded as accidents in previous years. While this is certainly true to some extent, it does not change our findings materially. Figure 5.4 shows the suicide rate, the gun-accident deathrate, and the combined suicide and gun-accident rate for youths over time. Unfortunately, we cannot include motor-vehicle fatalities since motor-vehicle deaths change for so many other reasons over time (such as changes in car safety and legal driving speeds). The gun-accident rate declined over time but by nowhere near as much as the suicide rate increased. Thus, the rise in suicides and gun-accident deaths mirrors the rise in suicides alone.

The fact that suicide rates trend differently for young adults, older adults, and the elderly suggests that different factors may be at work for

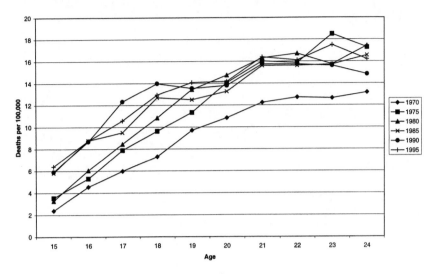

Fig. 5.3   Rates of teen suicide by year and age

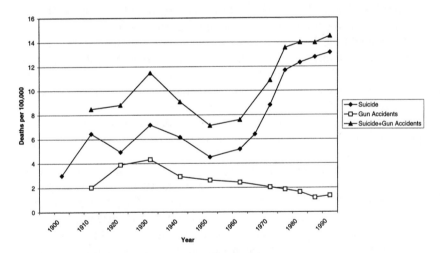

Fig. 5.4   Suicide and gun accidents among youths

the three groups in the population. This is true cross-sectionally as well. The correlation across states between youth- and adult- (elderly) suicide rates is only 0.46 (0.49), while the correlation between adult- and elderly suicide rates is 0.89.

5.1.2   Suicide Is the Third Leading Cause of Death among Youths

U.S. Vital Statistics records indicate that the annual suicide rate for youths (fifteen to twenty-four) is about thirteen per 100,000, or 0.01 percent per year. Over the course of ten years, therefore, about 0.1 percent of youths will commit suicide. The leading cause of death for youths is accidents (an annual rate of 38.5 per 100,000 in 1995), followed by homicide (an annual rate of 20.3 per 100,000).

5.1.3   There Are about Two to Four Hundred Suicide Attempts among Youths for Every Completed Suicide

There are no national surveillance figures in the United States for suicide attempts; estimates therefore come from a few national surveys and from local surveillance. As with suicide deaths, there is ambiguity in measuring suicide attempts. There is wide variation in the lethality of intent; thus, the definition of *suicide attempt* varies considerably from one study to another. The term *parasuicide* is sometimes used to refer to self-injury with low likelihood of lethal outcome (e.g., superficial cutting, minor overdoses), and *deliberate self-harm* is sometimes used to refer collectively to self-injuries across the full spectrum of lethality of intent.

Our data on suicide attempts come from AddHealth. Suicide attempts in AddHealth (described in more detail below) are based on self-reports and leave the definition of *suicide attempt* open to the responding interviewee. Table 5.1 shows data from AddHealth on suicide thoughts and attempts and from Vital Statistics on successful suicides.

About 14 percent of youths report thinking of suicide in the past year, and 4 percent report attempting suicide. About 1 percent of youths reported being seen medically for a suicide attempt. Other data from the National Hospital Discharge Survey indicate that about 0.2 percent of youths are hospitalized for self-injury each year. As shown in the last column, these numbers are substantially greater than the rate of the suicides.

Table 5.1	Suicide Thoughts, Attempts, and Completions among Youths, 1995 (%)			
	Thought About	Attempted	Seen Medically	Suicide Rate
All	14.2	4.0	1.0	.013
Male	11.8	2.5	.5	.022
Female	16.7	5.6	1.5	.004
White	14.7	4.3	1.0	.014
Black	11.4	3.4	1.0	.009
Other	14.5	3.7	.9	.013
Urban	14.5	5.0	1.3	.012
Rural	14.1	3.7	.9	.014
Above median income	14.4	3.7	.9	.011
Below median income	14.0	4.4	1.1	.015

Note: Figures in the first three columns are taken from AddHealth. Figures in the last column are taken from Vital Statistics.

There are about three hundred self-reported suicide attempts, about one hundred "medically seen" suicide attempts, and about sixteen medically hospitalized suicide attempts for every completed suicide.

These numbers in themselves suggest that not all teen suicide attempts are made by youths who truly wish to die. Many youths may instead be engaged in "strategic" suicide attempts—suicide attempts of varying severity, designed to get attention, to punish parents or other role models for perceived mistreatment, or to embarrass parents or other family members. Indeed, common sense suggests that succeeding at suicide is not all that difficult. After all, either a tall building or rope is often available, half of all households own a gun, and medications such as aspirin or acetomenophen are even easier to find and less frightening to use. As such, unsuccessful attempts must usually be thought of as actions that are, for the most part, designed to elicit a response other than one's own death. Successful attempts, on the contrary, most probably reflect a desire actually to end one's life. As such, we will discuss the theories of successful suicides and suicide attempts separately.

5.1.4   Girls Attempt Suicide More Often Than Boys; Boys Commit Suicide More Often Than Girls

Table 5.1 shows suicide rates for various demographic groups. The rate of suicide attempts is twice as high for girls as it is for boys, but the rate of successful suicides is six times higher for boys than it is for girls. Differences in suicide rates are evident throughout the life cycle. Figure 5.5 shows suicide rates by age and gender. Male suicide rates are roughly three

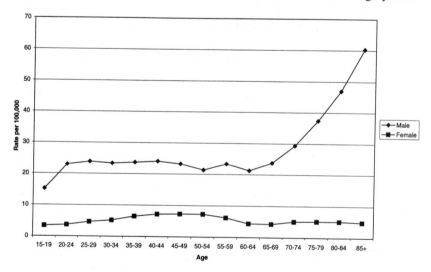

Fig. 5.5   Suicide rates by age and sex, 1997

Table 5.2   Incidence of Suicide Thoughts in Past Year by Age (%)

Age	AddHealth, 1995	Crosby, Cheltenham, and Sacks (1999), 1994
12	8.6	. . .
13	10.6	. . .
14	12.8	. . .
15	15.1	. . .
16	13.7	. . .
17	14.9	. . .
18	12.8	. . .
18–24	. . .	12.8
25–34	. . .	6.9
35–44	. . .	6.2
44–54	. . .	4.1
55–64	. . .	1.8
65+	. . .	1.0

times female rates for adults, before increasing dramatically after age sixty-five. Female rates, in contrast, have a relative peak in late middle age.

5.1.5   Suicide Attempts Decrease with Age after Adolescence

Table 5.2 shows suicide attempts by single year of age for youths (from AddHealth) and adults (from Crosby, Cheltenham, and Sacks 1999).[3] The peak age for suicide attempts is fifteen; attempt rates for eighteen-year-olds are 15 percent below the rate for fifteen-year-olds.[4] Suicidal thoughts decline in frequency from middle adolescence into adulthood and older years.

5.1.6   Rates of Suicide and Homicide Are Positively
Correlated in the National Data

Figure 5.6 shows suicide and homicide rates over time. There is a clear positive correlation between the two. Both rates rose substantially from 1910 through 1930 and then fell through 1960. In both cases, rates rose again through 1975. Total suicide rates began to fall again in the mid-1980s, while homicide rates fell in the early 1980s, rose in the late 1980s and early 1990s, and then have again fallen since 1994. The association between suicide and homicide is even stronger for youths, as shown in figure 5.7. Both rates rose from 1910 through 1933, fell over the next twenty to thirty years, and then began a prolonged increase, with a recent fall in both beginning in 1994.

3. These data are from a recent telephone survey of a nationally representative sample of adults.
4. A peak at around age fifteen is also found for suicide attempts among girls in Oregon.

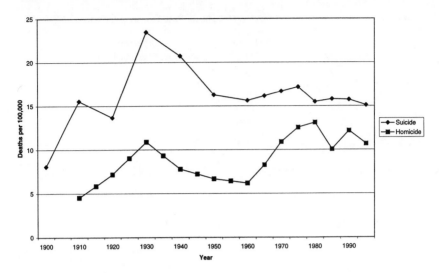

Fig. 5.6   Suicide and homicide rates

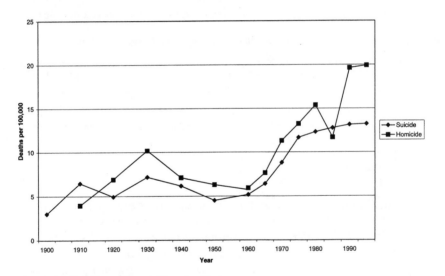

Fig. 5.7   Suicide and homicide rates for teens

5.1.7   Rural, Western States Have the Highest Youth-Suicide Rates and the Fastest Rate of Increase

Figure 5.8 shows the geographic dispersion in youth-suicide rates in 1950 and 1990. Table 5.3 shows the states with the highest and lowest suicide rates. Because Alaska and Hawaii were not states in 1950, they are not included in the figure. Suicide rates in 1990 are above those in 1950

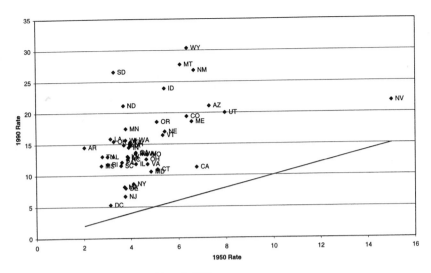

Fig. 5.8   Suicide rates in 1950 and 1990

Table 5.3   Suicide Rates for People 15–24 by State, 1950 and 1990

1950	Rate	1990	Rate
Nevada	15.0	Alaska	34.87
Utah	7.96	Wyoming	30.35
Arizona	7.25	Montana	27.73
California	6.77	New Mexico	26.82
New Mexico	6.67	South Dakota	26.57
. . .		. . .	
Rhode Island	3.03	New York	8.63
Alabama	3.02	Massachusetts	8.16
Tennessee	2.80	Delaware	7.94
Mississippi	2.75	New Jersey	6.65
Arkansas	2.03	District of Columbia	5.28

Source: Vital Statistics.

for all states. But there is substantial dispersion in changes in suicide rates over time. In 1950, suicide rates averaged 4.6 per 100,000, with a standard deviation of 2.0 (1.3 without Nevada). In 1990, the average rate was 15.3, with a standard deviation of 5.4.

Most surprisingly, suicide rates in 1990 are highest in rural, Mountain states and lowest in urban, Northeastern and Mid-Atlantic states. The highest suicide rates in 1990 are in Alaska, Wyoming, Montana, New Mexico, and South Dakota. This pattern became particularly pronounced between 1950 and 1990. Rates in Montana, New Mexico, and Wyoming were high in 1950 but not as far above average, those in South Dakota actually below average. These states replaced states that were relatively rural in 1950 but became more urban over the time period: California, Utah, and Arizona.

The states with the lowest suicide rates also changed. In 1950, the lowest suicide rates were generally in Southern states (Alabama, Tennessee, Mississippi, and Arkansas). By 1990, the states with the lowest suicide rates were the District of Columbia, New Jersey, Delaware, Massachusetts, and New York.

The high rate of suicide in Mountain states does not appear to result from coding differences between accidents and suicides. The correlation between suicide rates and accidental deathrates for teens in 1990 is 0.50.

5.1.8 Blacks Attempt and Complete Fewer Suicides than Whites

Table 5.1 above shows racial differences in suicide attempts and suicide completions. Blacks attempt suicide about one-quarter less frequently than do whites and complete suicides about one-third less. The lower rate of suicide for blacks than for whites suggests that youth suicides are not just a result of poor economic prospects. By any measure, whites have much greater economic prospects than do blacks. This ethnic difference also argues against some family-composition explanations, such as the hypothesis that the lack of a father in the household leads to more youth suicides. However, during the 1980s, suicide rates increased most rapidly among young black males, so some changing factors are clearly important in this relation.

5.1.9 Economic Differences Are Moderately Correlated with Suicide Rates

The last rows of table 5.1 above show suicide thoughts and completions in urban and rural areas and between richer and poorer families.[5] Suicide thoughts are moderately higher in urban areas, although suicide rates are higher in rural areas. Youths in poorer families are more likely to attempt and complete suicide than youths in richer families. These economic differences are not overwhelmingly large; the difference between rich and poor areas, for example, is much smaller than the difference in suicide between blacks and whites and between boys and girls.

5.1.10 Teen Suicide Is Primarily Accomplished with Guns

Table 5.4 shows the methods that youths used to commit suicides in 1950 and 1990. In both years, the overwhelmingly large share of deaths results from guns. Guns were used in 50 percent of deaths in 1950 and 64 percent in 1990. Hanging is second most important in 1990, followed by

---

5. In the last rows, the suicide rate is based on whether the county had median income above or below average.

Table 5.4	Method Used for Youth Suicides and Attempts (%)		
	Suicides		Attempts
Method	1950	1990	1988
Guns	50	64	.6
Hanging	14	19	1.6
Poison	27	6	82.0
Other	9	11	15.8

Source: Suicides are from U.S. Vital Statistics. Suicide attempt rates are from Andrus et al. (1991).

poison. Suicide rates by all methods except poison have increased over time. The increase is particularly pronounced for gun deaths.

The predominance of guns in teen suicides and the association between rural, mountainous states and suicide initially incline one toward a means theory of higher suicide rates: the availability of guns has increased youth suicides. The cross-state evidence suggests otherwise, however: if anything, we would expect that guns were relatively more available in rural, mountainous states in 1950 than in 1990.

In contrast to successful suicides, suicide attempters almost never use guns. Poison is used in over 80 percent of suicide attempts (e.g., drug overdoses).

5.2   Suicide among Youths: Theory

In explaining youth-suicide attempts and completions, we start off with two basic facts. The first fact is that people have variable feelings. Everyone has high and low moments. For youths, the variability of emotions is particularly great. Evidence suggests that the highs are higher and the lows lower for youths than for adults. The second fact is that youths do not have financial resources that they can use to influence others. Youths are still at the point in life where their consumption exceeds their net income.

These two facts suggest a number of different explanations for youth suicide. We group the alternative explanations into four categories. The first explanation is the *strategic suicide* theory: youths attempt suicide to signal others that they are unhappy or to punish others for their unhappiness. In this theory, suicide attempts are not primarily designed to result in death. Rather, they are a way for youths to influence others in nonfinancial ways. The second theory is the *depression theory:* at various points, youths become sufficiently unhappy that they "rationally" take their life. The third theory is the *contagion theory;* it is really an extension of the first two theories, suggesting that a "social multiplier" may amplify the effects of stressors leading to depression or may amplify the effects of factors leading to suicidal signaling as a method of conflict resolution among youths. The fourth theory has less to do with events that produce suicide thoughts and more to do with the ability to carry out suicide plans. We term this the *instrumentality theory:* when youths become particularly unhappy, they commit suicide if the means to do so is readily available. Thus, youths with access to guns will, for the same level of unhappiness, have higher suicide rates than will youths without access to guns. We illustrate each of these potential effects in turn.

5.2.1   The Rational-Suicide Theory

Our first theory is the most conventional one: suicide is a means of "rationally" ending one's life when the expected value of the future utility of being alive is below the value of death. The rational-suicide theory was developed by Hamermesh and Soss (1974) as a way of explaining why suicide seemed to increase monotonically with age. We have already seen that this monotonic increase with age is no longer true generally. Indeed, it was not even true for women at the time that Hamermesh and Soss's original paper was written. We further show in the appendix that the simple prediction of rising suicide rates with age does not necessarily follow from a rational-suicide model. But the intuition holds. Suicide is more likely when the variability of happiness is high, when unhappiness is correlated over time, and when people have high discount rates. If there is hyperbolic discounting, then individuals may want to precommit not to kill themselves.

Suicide and depression are clearly correlated for youths, as we show below. The difficult question is how the rational-suicide theory can explain the increase in youth suicide over time. It is possible that discount rates have risen over time for the young; changes in such an enduring individual characteristic could be the result of important changes in family structure or social environment that determine the individual's development of the capacity to regulate impulse. It is also possible that mean utility levels in youths have declined over time. If this is the driving factor, however, it must concern goods that are not usually purchased in the market economy since the average purchasing power of families has not declined.[6] A particularly plausible explanation is that the variance of the utility distribution has increased. If the variance of utility is greater, more youths will fall below the utility level at which suicide is a rational action.

We examine this by considering the factors that lead to depression among youths. Work on happiness suggests that family connections tend to be particularly important in promoting happiness; for adolescents, the family may be an important buffer for the variability of emotions. Changes

---

6. Hamermesh and Soss (1974) find that suicide and income are correlated at the occupation level, but this relation is not that strong. Moreover, Durkheim's ([1897] 1966) earlier evidence suggests a negative relation between suicide and income.

in family relations may have decreased this buffering role. Thus, one candidate explanation for the rise in teenage suicides is the increase in single-parent families. Alternatively, divorce, the partial absence of a known father, and remarriage might be more important in producing teenage unhappiness than the absence of a parent entirely because of conflict between ex-partners, conflict with a stepparent, or conflict with a nonresident parent who may not be as available as the child desires. The child may experience greater feelings of rejection and unhappiness when certain parental resources appear to exist but are not being devoted to the child than when it is clear that parental resources have been exhausted. This may explain why youth suicides are lower among blacks than among whites and why the suicide rates among black youths have been rising.

The events that cause depression need not be rationally undertaken for the suicide itself to be rational. A youth who discounts hyperbolically may take actions that bring short-term pleasure but long-term costs—stealing a car, for example, and getting caught, or taking illegal drugs, or engaging in premarital sex and getting pregnant. The youth who was caught might prefer ex post not to have stolen the car, but, conditional on being caught, the teen then faces the prospect of coping with an acute, painful state in the present in which the magnitude of the present pain (negative utility) exceeds the (discounted) present value of the possibly brighter future once the acute pain is past. The hyperbolic discounter has even more trouble than the "ordinary" discounter in moderating present pain with the hope for future pleasure—just as he has trouble moderating present exuberance with the anticipation of future pain.

Much unhappiness in teens may be related to romantic issues. In the same way that divorce is closely linked with suicide among adults, increasingly early sexual intimacy may contribute to intense turbulence in the relationships between adolescent sex partners; disappointments, conflict, and rejection in these physically intimate relationships among immature partners may lead to acute despair. It is possible that increased sexual activity among teenagers, stimulated by a number of factors since the 1960s, including the increased availability of safer and more effective contraception, has been a cause of youth unhappiness and increased suicide.

Families may be important in preventing youths from undertaking these types of actions, and the decline of the traditional family type may thus have led to increased suicide through the resulting influence on impulsive, long-term detrimental behavior. It is important to note that engaging in these activities may increase happiness among youths on average but may still lead to more variance in happiness, resulting in more youth suicides.

Beyond the immediate family, membership in social organizations is also a strong correlate with happiness. The decline in social capital discussed by Putnam (2000) and Putnam, Leonardi, and Nanetti (1994) may have created a rise in teenage unhappiness; indeed, Durkheim ([1897]

1966) argued that traditional societies with tight social connections had lower suicide rates.

5.2.2 The Strategic-Suicide Theory

A second explanation for youth suicide may be that suicidal behavior is designed, not to produce death, but merely to signal unhappiness and thus change the distribution of family resources. We think of this theory as applying to attempted suicides more than to successful suicides. The value of suicide as a signal may be direct or indirect. In some cases, the signal will convince adults that children are truly unhappy, and, thus, parents will devote more monetary or time resources to the child. Such a signal may be particularly credible in a repeated interaction. In other cases, the parent might not want to distribute more resources to the child, but the internal or external psychic cost (perhaps embarrassment) at having a child attempt suicide will induce the parent to do so anyway. If parents are sufficiently powerful in all respects, then self-harm may offer the only means available to the child of punishing the parents.

To formalize this, we consider a child with utility function $V(T, Z)$, where T is the amount of time or money that the parent transfers to the child, and Z is a vector of other factors that influence child happiness. Parents derive utility from their own consumption $[U(Y - T)]$ and the happiness of their child $[aV(T, Z)]$. The child's happiness, Z, is known to the child but not to the parent.

Children who are unhappy may want more parental input.[7] If child utility cannot be observed by the parent, children need to signal this unhappiness. Suicide attempts are a credible signal if there is some probability that they succeed and if the utility loss from death is smaller for unhappy children. The appendix shows that, if parents have no observable information about child happiness, the equilibrium is where children with $Z < Z^*$ attempt suicide and children with $Z > Z^*$ do not. The appendix also shows that suicide attempts are more common where Y is higher and thus there are more resources that suicide can help transfer.

The intuition for these results is simple. Children will want to communicate their unhappiness to parents so that they can get more resources. Suicide is a signal of this because a child who is less happy values future life less than one who is happier. As a result, children know that attempting suicide will convince their parents that they are not happy. But, for the signal to be transmitted, it must be the case that sometimes the event happens—on occasion, the child must die.

This prediction that suicide attempts will be more common when parental resources are greater—because there is more to redistribute—is the

---

7. Formally, this is a statement that $d^2V/dTdz < 0$—the value of parental resources is greater when the child is exogenously less happy.

central prediction for the strategic-suicide theory. This is opposite to the pure-depression theory, according to which a lack of parental resources induces child unhappiness and thus increased suicide attempts. We test for strategic suicide by examining how suicide attempts are related to family structure and income.

5.2.3   The Contagion Theory

Durkheim argued that suicides are imitative. He gives the example of fifteen prisoners who hung themselves from exactly the same hook in a Parisian prison and argues that this shows the power of social imitation. Several epidemiological studies (e.g., Gould et al. 1994) suggest that social contagion is a stronger factor in teen suicides and suicide attempts than in those by adults. It is not surprising to find that adolescents seem to be particularly influenced by their peer group in this form of high-risk behavior.

Contagion may operate in several ways. A member of a group who commits suicide may cause grief and stress within the group; this stress may decrease the ability of the group to buffer the problems faced by other members of the group or make suicide among other members more rational. People may also learn from the suicidal behavior of others: they may gain more exact information about the pain or discomfort involved in a particular action, and they may gain information about its probable effectiveness in accomplishing some end.

An important mechanism may involve the increase in the signal value of a suicide if some aspects become stylized. If a fifteen-year-old boy commits suicide, then other fifteen-year-old boys may draw more than the usual amount of attention for similar behaviors. If one person attempts or completes suicide using a particular method, then others may draw more than the usual attention by using a similar method, within the time frame during which the environment is sensitized to respond. As the signal becomes more stylized, the "receiver" can become more sensitive in detecting the signal. As the signal reception increases in sensitivity, the minimum effective signal can become less intense: social contagion may therefore lead to an increase in frequency, but a decrease in severity, of suicide attempts. Since bad news is more often reported than good news, an increase in the effective group size to which adolescents are exposed (which could have occurred, e.g., through the growth of the role of television [e.g., Phillips and Carstensen 1986]) could directly contribute to a rise in the rate of suicide.

At a certain point, the environment may "catch on" to the changing significance of the stylized attempt and react to less severe attempts with less attention. This may reduce suicide attempts on the part of those with only a small desire to attempt suicide. But a more sinister form of social contagion may also be set in motion. Members of a group may collude (covertly) to provoke an *escalation* of tactics leading to the martyrdom of at least one member of the group. One successful suicide (especially if widely advertised) may greatly refresh the credibility of the less lethal threats made by other members.

This may have been the basis for the provocations described in the case of Jurgen Peters. It is not so much that the other young men in the crowd were acutely suicidal—presumably they were a more or less random draw of young men who happened to be nearby, with no more than the average share of despair typical for young men in that community at that time—but they may have identified with Jurgen's age and gender, and each young man in the crowd might have expected his own reputation for possible dangerous action to rise with Jurgen's violent death. In fact, if they did not know him, his death may have been no loss to them at all—only an emblematic event that enhanced their own strategic position in the community.

The South Boston story also highlights many of these potential effects. The first teen's accidental death made him a martyr whom other teens wanted to imitate. And, as the seriousness of the epidemic grew, even hints of suicide thoughts would be taken more seriously.

5.2.4 The Instrumentality Hypothesis

The final theory is the instrumentality hypothesis—that access to lethal means increases suicides. This theory stresses the immediate costs and benefits of suicide, not the long-term forward-thinking behavior of the other models. In this theory, suicide is impulsive, and access to the appropriate method at the right time can determine whether a suicide occurs.

The instrumentality explanation is most commonly applied to access to guns. As we saw above, teenagers overwhelmingly commit suicides using guns. Brent et al. (1991) and Brent et al. (1993) show that adolescents who committed suicide were about four times as likely to live in a home with any gun than were a matched group of community or psychiatric controls and were thirty-two times more likely to have lived in a home where a gun was kept loaded. The availability of guns differs greatly over space and thus could explain some of the geographic distribution of youth suicide. Beyond firearms, there is some evidence that differences in access to lethal methods—tall buildings in Manhattan (Marzuk et al. 1992), coal gas in the United Kingdom—may be associated with differences in rates of completed suicide.

The counterhypothesis is that lethal means of one kind or another—for example, hanging or jumping from a height—are so widely available that a suicidal person will simply substitute one method for another, depending on which one is more accessible. A classic example is bridge barriers: if one bridge is fenced, the suicidal person may simply find another nearby bridge to use instead (O'Carroll and Silverman 1993).

The strongest evidence against the instrumentality theory is noted above: youth-suicide rates have increased the most in areas where guns have historically been the most plentiful—rural, Western states. The instrumentality theory would predict the opposite, that suicide rates would rise most in urban areas with high poverty, where guns have become increasingly common in more recent years.

There could be another, more subtle role for instrumentality, linked to the social-contagion models described above. Perhaps there has been an increase in nonlethal suicide attempts, driven by an increase in the availability of dangerous but usually nonlethal methods: for example, prescription psychotropic medications, which came into more common use starting in the 1960s.

5.3   Evidence on Suicide Attempts

We start our empirical analysis by looking at suicide attempts. We examine attempts with an eye to which of our four theories appears to offer the best prediction of adolescent self-injury.

The data that we use are from AddHealth. AddHealth is a nationally representative stratified random sample of U.S. high school students in the ninth to the twelfth grades; the survey is based on direct interviews with the adolescents themselves, their parents, and school administrators and covers a wide range of topics concerning risk and protective factors for high-risk adolescent behavior. Our sample consists of 17,004 adolescents between the ages of twelve and eighteen in 1996 for whom we have the necessary observations from the first wave of the AddHealth survey. The key features of the results presented here can also be observed when we consider outcomes in wave 2, but the 25 percent sample attrition between waves makes these results less statistically significant.

Our primary dependent variable is whether the youth reported a medically screened suicide attempt. We focus on medically screened attempts to get some measure of severity of attempt. Reporting issues may also influence whether some youths report less severe suicide attempts. We also examine reports of suicide attempts whether or not they were treated medically. Our results are very consistent across these two samples. We note one obvious feature of this sample: youths who successfully committed suicide are not in the sample. Thus, these data tell us about the determinants of "unsuccessful" suicide attempts only. Four percent of teens reported making a suicide attempt in wave 1, and 1 percent reported a suicide attempt that resulted in some kind of medical contact.[8]

We relate the probability that the teen has made a suicide attempt to a variety of factors reflecting the different theories outlined above. Table 5.5

8. In wave 2, 0.7 percent of teens reported making a medically screened attempt.

Table 5.5 **Summary Statistics for Individual Data**

Category	Variable Name	Mean	S.D.	Minimum	Maximum
Attempted suicide	Medically treated	1.0%		0	1
	Any attempt	4.0%		0	1
Demographics	Female	50.7%		0	1
	Black	22.3%		0	1
	Asian	7.8%		0	1
	Native American	3.5%		0	1
	Urban	31.5%		0	1
Age dummies	12	2.6%		0	1
	13	11.1%		0	1
	14	13.6%		0	1
	16	20.0%		0	1
	17	19.8%		0	1
	18	14.8%		0	1
Employment and income	Family receives public support	27.3%		0	1
	Annual family income (normalized)	.0	.9	−.88	18.47
	Mother's labor force participation	70.7%		0	1
Family structure	How often mother not home in evening	1.5	1.1	1	5
	How often father not home in evening	2.5	1.7	1	5
	Never knew father	4.0%		0	1
	Knew father, father not now in home	34.0%		0	1
	Stepfather in home	8.0%		0	1
Interaction with parents	Relationship with mother	1.5	1.1	0	5
	Relationship with resident father	.9	1.1	0	5
	Relationship with nonresident father	.2	.8	0	5
Sexual activity	Ever had intercourse	39.2%		0	1
	Ever raped (females only)	3.7%		0	1
Violence and delinquency	Delinquency score (normalized)	.0	1.0	−.75	7.97
	Violence: used weapon	.3	1.0	0	11
	Violence: got hurt	.2	.5	0	5
Drugs and alcohol	Ever use hard drug	7.4%		0	1
	Any problem with alcohol	35.0%		0	1
Participation	Total clubs	1.7	2.4	0	33
	Belongs to honor society	7.6%		0	1
	Participates in weekly sports	30.8%		0	1
	Hours/week watching television	2.3	.9	0	3
Contagion	Friend has attempted suicide	17.4%		0	1
	Friend has died by suicide	2.9%		0	1

Table 5.5   (continued)

Category	Variable Name	Mean	S.D.	Minimum	Maximum
	Relative has attempted suicide	4.4%		0	1
	Relative has died by suicide	.9%		0	1
Depression	Depression score (normalized)	.0	1.0	−2.41	5.85

Note: Data are from AddHealth. Sample size is approximately 18,000.

describes these variables and shows the means and (where appropriate) standard deviations. Our first measures are demographic controls: age (in single years), gender, ethnicity, and urban residence.

To capture family resources, we include family-income and employment variables. The strategic-suicide theory argues that more family resources should increase suicide attempts. The rational-suicide explanation argues that more family resources should decrease suicide attempts if lower levels of resources are associated with decreased happiness among youths.

We also include measures of family structure and interactions with parents: how often the mother and father are home in the evening; whether there is a father present physically or in the life of the teen; and the teen's relationship with the mother, with a resident father, and with a nonresident father. The relationship variables are measured on a five-point scale aggregating questions about the frequency of specific activities and interactions between the teen and the parent. The strategic-suicide theory suggests that having a father present but not around should increase suicide attempts, as should a worse relationship with parents. The depression theory suggests that being without a father entirely should be worse than having a parent around but not in the household.

We include a variety of measures of activities of the teen, including measures of sexual activity (a dummy variable for whether the teen has ever had sexual intercourse; a dummy for whether the teen has been raped), measures of violence and delinquency (a normalized delinquency score; whether the teen has ever used a weapon; and whether the teen was hurt by violence), measures of drug and alcohol use (dummies for hard drug use or alcohol problems), and participation in various clubs (the total number of clubs; membership in an honor society; whether the child participates in sports; and the number of hours per week spent watching television). These partly measure happiness and partly measure the potential for conflict. The happiness theory suggests that teens who engage in these activities but have bad outcomes should attempt suicide more.

A clear issue with these variables is the endogeneity problem: children who take drugs more, for example, may be more likely to attempt suicide for other reasons. Without instruments for these teen activities, we cannot resolve the causality question.[9] We thus primarily think of these regressions as correlations more than a strict theory of causation. Some inferences can be made, however, by comparing the effect of different activities on suicide rates. The happiness explanation argues that teens who engage in these activities but suffer adverse outcomes (e.g., being arrested for drug use) would be more likely to commit suicide. Teens who engage in these activities but do not suffer adverse outcomes, however, would be no more likely to commit suicide.

We also include measures of social contagion: whether a relative or friend has attempted suicide and whether a relative or friend has successfully committed suicide. These variables permit particularly valuable tests of the social-contagion theory.[10]

Table 5.6 shows our regression results. We report OLS estimates for ease of interpretation; logit and probit models had very similar qualitative and quantitative results (when expressed as changes in probabilities). Recall that the dependent-variable mean is 1 percent, so small coefficients are to be expected. The first column of the table includes the basic demographic variables (which are included in all regressions) and the variables for family income and employment. The first row shows that girls are 0.8 percentage points, or 56 percent, more likely to report a relatively serious suicide attempt than are boys. This is consistent with the raw data described above: boys complete suicides more than girls, but girls attempt suicide more than boys. The next set of variables indicates ethnicity; Native American teens have 67 percent higher rates, Asian American teens have 23 percent higher rates, and African American teens have 10 percent lower suicide-attempt rates than white teens. These rates are not statistically significant, although they are statistically significant predictors of having attempted a suicide (whether or not it was medically treated).

There is a nonlinear relation between suicide attempts and age. Attempted suicides rise from age twelve to age fifteen (the omitted age dummy) and then decline. This stands in stark contrast to successful suicides, which rise sharply over these ages. One possible explanation for these results is that teenage independence increases at age sixteen, for example, the ability to drive. As such, the need either to signal parents or to punish them through self-damage may decrease with increasing age.

The next variables in the first column are for family economic status.

---

9. While AddHealth has a longitudinal component, even longitudinal data would not solve the endogeneity problem. It would still be necessary to know why teens start to engage in these activities.

10. One might worry somewhat about depression running in families and thus there being a common genetic component to suicide. Our results are similar for friends and relatives, however. One might also be worried about the self-selection of friends. Without instruments for one's friends (and it is not clear what such instruments might be), we do not have a way of addressing this issue.

Table 5.6   Explaining Suicide Attempts among Youths (dependent variable: medically treated suicide attempt)

Category	Variable Name	(1)	(2)	(3)	(4)	(5)	(6)
Demographics	Female	.008**	.008**	.010**	.005**	.008**	.008**
		(.001)	(.001)	(.001)	(.001)	(.001)	(.001)
	Black	-.002	-.002	-.001	-.0002	-.001	-.001
		(.002)	(.002)	(.002)	(.002)	(.002)	(.002)
	Asian	.002	.004	.005*	.003	.006**	.004
		(.003)	(.003)	(.003)	(.003)	(.003)	(.003)
	Native American	.006	.005	.002	.004	.002	.001
		(.004)	(.004)	(.004)	(.004)	(.004)	(.004)
	Urban	-.001	-.001	-.001	-.0004	-.002	-.002
		(.002)	(.002)	(.002)	(.002)	(.002)	(.002)
Age dummies	12	-.006	-.005	.000	-.003	.001	.002
		(.005)	(.005)	(.005)	(.005)	(.005)	(.004)
	13	-.001	-.001	.002	-.0004	.002	.003
		(.003)	(.003)	(.003)	(.003)	(.003)	(.003)
	14	-.001	-.001	.001	-.0003	.0003	.001
		(.003)	(.003)	(.003)	(.003)	(.003)	(.003)
	16	.000	-.002	-.001	.0006	-.002	-.002
		(.002)	(.002)	(.002)	(.002)	(.002)	(.002)
	17	.001	-.001	.000	.001	-.0006	-.001
		(.002)	(.002)	(.002)	(.002)	(.002)	(.002)
	18	-.000	-.003	-.002	.000	-.0008	-.001
		(.003)	(.003)	(.003)	(.003)	(.003)	(.003)

(continued)

Table 5.6 (continued)

Category	Variable Name	(1)	(2)	(3)	(4)	(5)	(6)
Employment and income	Family receives public support	.004** (.002)	⋮	⋮	⋮	-.001 (.002)	-.002 (.002)
	Annual family income (normalized)	-.002** (.001)	⋮	⋮	⋮	-.001 (.001)	-.0008 (.0008)
	Mother's labor force participation	.005 (.002)	⋮	⋮	⋮	.001 (.001)	.001 (.002)
Family structure	How often mother not home in evening	⋮	.0002 (.0007)	⋮	⋮	-.0006 (.001)	-.001 (.001)
	How often father not home in evening	⋮	-.0000 (.007)	⋮	⋮	-.0000 (.001)	-.0001 (.001)
	Never knew father	⋮	.009** (.004)	⋮	⋮	.007 (.004)	.006 (.009)
	Knew father, father not now in home	⋮	.007** (.003)	⋮	⋮	.005* (.0025)	.005** (.0025)
	Stepfather in home	⋮	.002 (.003)	⋮	⋮	.0007 (.003)	.0000 (.003)
Interaction with parents	Relationship with mother	⋮	-.002** (.001)	⋮	⋮	-.0015** (.0007)	.001 (.0008)
	Relationship with resident father	⋮	.000 (.001)	⋮	⋮	.0006 (.001)	.001 (.001)
	Relationship with nonresident father	⋮	-.003** (.001)	⋮	⋮	-.002** (.001)	-.002 (.001)
Sexual activity	Ever had intercourse	⋮	⋮	.002 (.002)	⋮	.001 (.002)	.0007 (.003)
	Ever raped (females only)	⋮	⋮	.029** (.004)	⋮	.027** (.004)	.025** (.004)
Violence and delinquency	Delinquency score (normalized)	⋮	⋮	.005** (.001)	⋮	.005** (.001)	.003** (.004)
	Violence: used weapon	⋮	⋮	.004** (.001)	⋮	.001 (.001)	.001 (.001)

		(1)	(2)	(3)	(4)	(5)	(6)
	Violence: got hurt	…	…	.015** (.002)	…	.014** (.002)	.013** (.002)
Drugs and alcohol	Ever use hard drug	…	…	.024** (.003)	…	.024** (.003)	.022** (.003)
	Any problem with alcohol	…	…	.003 (.002)	…	.002 (.002)	.001 (.002)
Participation	Total clubs	…	…	.0000 (.0004)	…	−.000 (.001)	.0000 (.0004)
	Belongs to honor society	…	…	−.002 (.003)	…	−.0005 (.003)	−.0004 (.003)
	Participates in weekly sports	…	…	−.0006 (.002)	…	−.0004 (.001)	.0005 (.002)
	Hours/week watching television	…	…	−.0003 (.001)	…	−.0005 (.0008)	−.0005 (.0008)
Contagion	Friend has attempted suicide	…	…	…	.012** (.002)	.006** (.002)	.004** (.002)
	Friend has died by suicide	…	…	…	.039** (.004)	.030** (.004)	.029** (.005)
	Relative has attempted suicide	…	…	…	.022** (.004)	.016** (.004)	.014** (.004)
	Relative has died by suicide	…	…	…	.057** (.008)	.039** (.008)	.039** (.008)
Depression	Depression score (normalized)	…	…	…	…	…	.007** (.0007)
Missing data dummies	Parent questionnaire missing	.0008 (.002)	.0008 (.002)	−.0006 (.002)	.001 (.002)	.0005 (.002)	.0000 (.002)
	In-school questionnaire missing	.005** (.002)	.005** (.002)	.002 (.002)	.005** (.002)	.003 (.002)	.003** (.002)
Summary statistics							
	N	18,085	17,267	18,260	18,169	17,002	17,001
	Adjusted R^2	.003	.0284	.034	.022	.044	.047

Note: Data are from AddHealth. Numbers in parentheses are standard errors.

*Statistically significant at the 10 percent level.

**Statistically significant at the 5 percent level.

Increased income reduces suicide attempts. A one-standard-deviation increase in family income decreases the risk of suicide attempt by almost 40 percent. Similarly, individuals whose families receive welfare are 30 percent more likely to attempt suicide.[11] It is unclear whether the welfare variable is picking up an income effect or a stigma effect; 1996 (the year of the first wave of AddHealth) was the year in which welfare reform was enacted into law, and thus discussion of welfare in a negative context was prominent. The income variables generally support the happiness explanation over the strategic explanation.

The second regression replaces the economic variables with family-structure variables. Teens who live with a single parent have about twice the rate of suicide attempts of those in two-parent families, even when one of the parents is a stepparent. Most surprisingly, we find that teens who know their father but whose father is not now in the home are just as likely to attempt suicide as teens who never knew their father. This is suggestive evidence of the strategic theory: suicide attempts may be a means to get an absent father to pay more attention to his children.

As the next rows show, teens who engage in more activities with their mother and nonresident father are less likely to attempt suicide. There is no such effect for relationship with a resident father. A one-standard-deviation increase in time spent with a mother decreases the risk of suicide attempt by about 27 percent. This is a very substantial effect. The effect of time with the nonresident father but not the resident father again suggests a strategic motive.

The third regression considers the relation between adolescent suicide attempts and other kinds of adolescent behavior. Sexual activity, rape, drug use, alcohol problems, and being hurt in a fight are among the strongest behavioral predictors of suicide attempts. Girls who report being raped are much more likely to attempt suicide than are other girls. Hard drug use more than doubles the risk of suicide attempt. A one-standard-deviation increase in minor delinquency increases the risk of suicide attempt by 25 percent.

Teens who have hurt others are more likely to have attempted suicide, as are teens who have been hurt in conflicts. The latter effect is particularly large; teens who have been hurt in conflicts are 75 percent more likely to attempt suicide.[12] Perhaps self-injurious impulses lead to getting hurt in a fight. Alternatively, being fearful and bullied may precipitate self-injurious impulses.

Membership in an honor society or engaging in weekly sports provided protection from the risk of making a suicide attempt, although not statistically significantly so.

11. In regressions that separate effects by gender, the welfare effect was particularly important for girls.

12. In regressions by gender, boys who have been injured during a fight are two times as likely to attempt suicide.

The evidence is clearly consistent with the happiness theory; unhappiness may cause both suicide attempts and other high-risk behavior. However, the evidence is also consistent with a strategic model: high-risk behavior may lead to negative consequences; suicide attempts may mitigate negative consequences by enlisting a response from the social environment. The evidence could also reflect other factors—perhaps individual biological vulnerability, early development, or present environmental conditions—that jointly influence happiness, suicide attempts, and other high-risk behavior.

The next regression considers the possible effects of social contagion. Teens who know friends or family members who have attempted suicide are about three times more likely to attempt suicide than are teens who do not know someone who attempted suicide. As best we can tell, this finding is causal. When we examine wave 2 data, teens who had not already made a suicide attempt in wave 1 are more likely to attempt suicide if they have a friend or relative who attempted suicide. We also find that teens who have had a family member commit suicide are more likely to report a suicide attempt in wave 1, but only half as likely to make an attempt in wave 2, as other teens. This suggests a complex model of contagion, consistent with our strategic-suicide hypothesis: teens who have experienced the suicide of an intimate may be sufficiently aware of the pain that this causes that they are less likely to engage in a merely symbolic attempt.

There are also significant gender differences in the pattern of social contagion. In separate regressions for girls and boys, girls are more likely to make a suicide attempt if they know someone else who has made an *attempt;* boys are less affected by attempts of other people but more affected by knowing someone who *completed* suicide. This suggests a social mechanism for the difference in completed suicide rates for boys and for girls. Groups of boys may dare and shame each other into maintaining the group's reputation for courage or dangerousness. Girls may be more willing to imitate a "failed" suicide attempt because they do not require the same level of reputation for daring.

The fifth column includes all these different variables together. The results are generally consistent with the regressions including the variables separately. The factors most strongly related to suicide attempts are the interaction-with-parents variables, the teen-activities variables, and the contagion variables.

In the final regression of the table, we add a measure of depression to the regression. The "feelings" scale used in the AddHealth survey is a modification of the Center for Epidemiological Studies Depression Scale (CESD) (Radloff 1977). The CESD is one of the most widely used measures in mental health epidemiology; it has been used in thousands of studies, and its psychometric properties are well-known. The AddHealth measure has dropped two items from the original twenty, rephrased two items, and added one. In the present study, we have standardized the Add-

Health feelings scale with a mean of 0 and a standard deviation of 1. The effect is large; a one-standard-deviation increase in reported depression nearly doubles the suicide risk. More surprisingly, the other variables in the regression generally still affect suicide attempts, even when the depression variable is included. Most of the variables are smaller in magnitude in column 6 than in column 5, but they generally still predict suicide attempts. Thus, not all the effect of these variables on suicides is through their influence on happiness.

Table 5.7 presents estimates of similar models for the broader measure of whether the teen reported attempting suicide, independent of whether it was medically treated. For ease of interpretation, we report only the results including all the variables together (equivalent to col. 5 of table 5.6 above) and that regression including the measure of depression (equivalent to col. 6 of table 5.6).

The results are similar to, and perhaps even stronger than, the results for medically treated suicide attempts. The signs of the coefficients are generally similar, but, because the dependent variable has a much higher mean (4 percent), the coefficients are larger, and more of them are statistically significant. The most important variables predicting this measure of suicide attempts are interaction with the mother and particularly a nonresident father, teen variables such as drug use and having been raped, and the social-contagion variables. The age effects are also pronounced. Suicide attempts peak at age fourteen and then decline through age eighteen. Depression is clearly related to suicide attempts, but it does not fully explain this pattern of results.

5.3.1   The Roots of Depression

To understand the role of happiness in explaining suicide among youths, we consider the determinants of depression among teens. We have already seen the relation between the teen variables and attempted suicides, both with and without depression as a control. These auxiliary regressions will help us determine which of these variables influence suicide through their effect on depression. These variables are also useful as a test of our previous results. Since suicide attempts are relatively rare, it may be that these depression results are more reliable than our results for suicide attempts.

Table 5.8 relates the depression scale to the independent variables included in table 5.6 above. The first regression in table 5.8 shows the relation between our demographic characteristics and depression (recall that the index has a mean of 0 and a standard deviation of 1). The age effects are sizable and different than those for suicide attempts. Younger teens are much less likely to be depressed than are older teens, by about one-third of a standard deviation. Girls are more depressed than are boys. Again the effect is large—nearly one-quarter of a standard deviation. All the racial and ethnic minorities have higher rates of depression than do whites. Living in an urban area also increases depression.

Table 5.7   **Explaining Suicide Attempts among Youths (dependent variable: any suicide attempt)**

Category	Variable Name	(1)	(2)
Demographics	Female	.027**	.033**
		(.003)	(.015)
	Black	−.003	−.005
		(.004)	(.004)
	Asian	.016**	.007
		(.005)	(.005)
	Native American	.010	.006
		(.007)	(.008)
	Urban	.003	.001
		(.003)	(.003)
Age dummies	12	.001	.004
		(.009)	(.009)
	13	.003	.007
		(.005)	(.005)
	14	.009*	.011**
		(.005)	(.005)
	16	−.006	−.007
		(.005)	(.005)
	17	−.002	−.003
		(.005)	(.005)
	18	−.008	−.009*
		(.005)	(.005)
Employment and income	Family receives public support	.003	−.001
		(.004)	(.003)
	Annual family income (normalized)	−.0028*	−.0016
		(.0016)	(.0016)
	Mother's labor force participation	−.001	.001
		(.003)	(.003)
Family structure	How often mother not home in evening	−.0007	−.0017
		(.0015)	(.0014)
	How often father not home in evening	.001	.001
		(.001)	(.001)
	Never knew father	−.008	−.011
		(.008)	(.008)
	Knew father, father not now in home	.006	.007
		(.005)	(.005)
	Stepfather in home	.005	.001
		(.006)	(.006)
Interaction with parents	Relationship with mother	−.0029*	−.0011
		(.0015)	(.0015)
	Relationship with resident father	.001	.002
		(.002)	(.002)
	Relationship with nonresident father	−.006**	−.005**
		(.002)	(.002)
Sexual activity	Ever had intercourse	.000	−.002
		(.003)	(.003)
	Ever raped (females only)	.076**	.065**
		(.008)	(.008)

(*continued*)

Table 5.7   (continued)

Category	Variable Name	(1)	(2)
Violence and delinquency	Delinquency score (normalized)	.016**	.011**
		(.002)	(.002)
	Violence: used weapon	.009**	.009**
		(.002)	(.002)
	Violence: got hurt	.009**	.005
		(.003)	(.003)
Drugs and alcohol	Ever use hard drug	.067**	.062**
		(.006)	(.006)
	Any problem with alcohol	.013**	.009**
		(.003)	(.003)
Participation	Total clubs	.000	.001
		(.001)	(.001)
	Belongs to honor society	−.014**	−.010*
		(.006)	(.006)
	Participates in weekly sports	−.0062*	−.0059
		(.0038)	(.0037)
	Hours/week watching television	−.0032**	−.0028*
		(.0016)	(.0016)
Contagion	Friend has attempted suicide	.042**	.035**
		(.004)	(.004)
	Friend has died by suicide	.028**	.027**
		(.009)	(.009)
	Relative has attempted suicide	.041**	.034**
		(.008)	(.008)
	Relative has died by suicide	.023	.022
		(.017)	(.017)
Depression	Depression score (normalized)	. . .	.033**
			(.002)
Missing data dummies	Parent questionnaire missing	−.001	−.003
		(.004)	(.004)
	In-school questionnaire missing	−.001	−.002
		(.004)	(.004)
Summary statistics			
N		17,003	17,002
Adjusted R^2		.081	.106

Note: Data are from AddHealth. Numbers in parentheses are standard errors.
*Statistically significant at the 10 percent level.
**Statistically significant at the 5 percent level.

Income is positively and strongly associated with happiness. Higher income reduces depression, and being on welfare increases depression. There is no effect of mother's labor force participation on depression. Economists may be surprised that the coefficient for income is not all that large. Absent fathers and mothers appear to be more important than income in predicting depression among teenagers.

Table 5.8   **Explaining Depression among Youths**

Category	Variable Name	(1)	(2)	(3)	(4)	(5)
Demographics	Female	.258**	.251**	.308**	.223**	.270**
		(.014)	(.014)	(.014)	(.014)	(.015)
	Black	.043**	.032**	.090**	.107**	.063**
		(.017)	(.018)	(.017)	(.017)	(.018)
	Asian	.228**	.234**	.269**	.228**	.294**
		(.027)	(.027)	(.026)	(.027)	(.026)
	Native American	.232**	.232**	.179**	.216**	.138**
		(.038)	(.039)	(.037)	(.038)	(.038)
	Urban	.074**	.070**	.077**	.096**	.042**
		(.015)	(.016)	(.015)	(.015)	(.015)
Age dummies	12	-.268**	-.203**	-.114**	-.224**	-.076**
		(.046)	(.047)	(.045)	(.046)	(.045)
	13	-.243**	-.191**	-.135**	-.232**	-.120**
		(.025)	(.027)	(.026)	(.027)	(.026)
	14	-.108**	-.082**	-.052**	-.097**	-.055**
		(.025)	(.026)	(.024)	(.025)	(.024)
	16	.054**	.027	.027	.062**	.029
		(.023)	(.023)	(.022)	(.023)	(.022)
	17	.072**	.023	.040*	.080**	.032
		(.023)	(.023)	(.022)	(.023)	(.023)
	18	.057**	-.009	.030	.078**	.029
		(.025)	(.025)	(.025)	(.025)	(.025)
Employment and income	Family receives public support	.196**	…	…	…	.106**
		(.017)				(.017)
	Annual family income (normalized)	-.051**	…	…	…	-.035**
		(.008)				(.007)
	Mother's employment status	-.074**	…	…	…	-.052**
		(.016)				(.016)

(continued)

Table 5.8 (continued)

Category	Variable Name	(1)	(2)	(3)	(4)	(5)
Family structure	How often mother not home in evening		.046**	...	...	.017**
			(.007)			(.006)
	How often father not home in evening		.021**	...	...	.030**
			(.006)			(.007)
	Never knew father	...	.189**	...	...	.103**
			(.042)			(.040)
	Knew father, father not now in home	...	.042*	...	...	−.024
			(.026)			(.025)
	Stepfather in home	...	.112**	...	...	−.093**
			(.030)			(.029)
Relationships with parents	Relationship with mother	...	−.087**	...	...	−.053**
			(.007)			(.007)
	Relationship with resident father	...	−.066**	...	...	−.050**
			(.008)			(.007)
	Relationship with nonresident father	...	−.039**	...	...	−.023**
			(.010)			(.010)
Sexual activity	Ever had intercourse	...	...	.091**	...	.049**
				(.016)		(.017)
	Ever raped	...	...	.401**	...	.326**
				(.037)		(.039)
Violence and delinquency	Delinquency score (normalized)	...	...	.188**	...	.166**
				(.008)		(.009)
	Violence: used weapon	...	...	−.003	...	−.015**
				(.007)		(.008)
	Violence: got hurt	...	...	.138**	...	.122**
				(.016)		(.016)

		(1)	(2)	(3)	(4)	(5)
Drugs and alcohol	Ever use hard drugs	…	…	.199**	…	.160**
				(.027)		(.028)
	Ever had problems related to alcohol	…	…	.113**	…	.098**
				(.016)		(.016)
Participation	Total clubs	…	…	-.018**	…	-.014**
				(.003)		(.003)
	Belongs to honor society	…	…	-.165**	…	-.124**
				(.028)		(.028)
	Participates in weekly sports	…	…	-.043**	…	-.008
				(.018)		(.018)
	Hours/week watching television	…	…	-.018**	…	-.012
				(.007)		(.008)
Contagion	Friend has attempted suicide	…	.325**	…	…	.203**
			(.020)			(.020)
	Friend has died by suicide	…	.165**	…	…	.042
			(.045)			(.045)
	Relative has attempted suicide	…	.381**	…	…	.206**
			(.039)			(.038)
	Relative has died by suicide	…	.079	…	…	.033
			(.084)			(.082)
Missing-data dummies	Parent questionnaire missing	.084**	.076**	.049**	.035*	.062**
		(.019)	(.019)	(.018)	(.020)	(.019)
	In-school questionnaire missing	.124**	.138**	.024	.119**	.026
		(.017)	(.016)	(.018)	(.017)	(.018)
Summary statistics						
N		17,245	18,283	17,467	17,428	16,293
Adjusted R^2		.056	.073	.136	.078	.164

Note: Data are from AddHealth. Numbers in parentheses are standard errors.

*Statistically significant at the 10 percent level.

**Statistically significant at the 5 percent level.

The second regression shows that the relationship with one's parents is a very strong determinant of teenage depression. Individuals who never knew their fathers are particularly likely to be depressed, even more so than those who know their father but whose father is not home. Note that these coefficients were about the same in the regressions for attempting suicide. Teens who report more interactions with their parents are much less likely to be depressed. This effect is large and supports the idea that parents' behavior can make a large difference to the happiness of teenagers.

The third regression shows that sexual activity predicts depression. One explanation for this is that romantic turmoil may increase the volatility of emotions, but there are certainly other explanations. Possibly, individuals who have not had sex live in more socially protective environments that fight depression in other ways. Use of drugs and alcohol is also related (not surprisingly) to depression. Again, the direction of causality for these variables is not completely clear. Delinquency is also correlated with depression. Having been hurt is a particularly strong positive predictor of depression, which may partially explain its earlier correlation with suicide attempts. Indeed, in table 5.5 above, the coefficient on having been hurt falls nearly by half when the depression variable is included. These variables may again reflect either direction of causality. It may be, for example, that delinquency leads people to be unhappy or that unhappiness makes delinquency seem relatively more attractive.

There is a significant relation between social interactions and depression. Teens who watch more television are more depressed than are teens that watch less television, and club membership is negatively related to depression. This corresponds well to the well-known correlation between organization membership and happiness in adult surveys. Honors society membership, sports participation, and religion all strongly reduce depression.

It is interesting that the maximum R^2 in our depression model is only 16 percent. The factors that we identify are related to depression, but, detailed as they are, there is substantial variance beyond these factors, and they work through other dimensions as well.

5.3.2 Summary

Our analysis of suicide attempts and teen depression leads us to three conclusions. First, we find clear evidence for the happiness theory. More depressed teens or teens with other problems leading to poor life prospects are more likely to attempt suicide than are other teens. This finding is not surprising. Second, there is strong evidence of social contagion; having a friend or relative attempt or commit suicide increases the risk that a given teen does as well. Third, there is suggestive evidence that the strategic theory is true as well. The age pattern of suicide attempts matches the predictions of the strategic theory—particularly in the light of opposite findings for depression—as do factors such as the characteristics of an absent father.

5.4 Completed Suicides

Suicide attempts are only part of our interest. We are also interested in the determinants of youth suicide itself. In this section, we examine the factors that predict youth suicide.

As with suicide attempts, we face data problems when attempting to measure suicide completions. In the case of suicide completions, there are very few data on the characteristics of individuals who commit suicide. Death records contain some information but generally nothing about the individual's mood, relations with others, activities, etc. Some psychological-autopsy studies have been performed, but these, too, have problems: the samples are small and the information often sketchy.

Accordingly, we address the problem of suicide completions using a different tack. We examine suicide rates at the national, state, and county level and consider what factors explain differing levels of suicide at a point in time and differing changes in suicide rates over time. Our primary analysis is based on county-level average suicide rates for the period 1989–91. Individual counties are identified only if they have more than 100,000 people. We thus form a sample of all counties identified individually and group the remaining counties into one observation for each state. The result is a sample of 516 county groups. Analysis of county groups is necessarily less convincing than having individual data, but, in this circumstance, individual data are simply not available.

As noted above, suicide completions are very different from suicide attempts. The two behaviors involve different methods and demographic groups. Most psychological-audit studies find that people who successfully commit suicide intend to die, whereas most people who attempt suicide probably do not. Equivalently, we suspect that people who do not strongly want to die but do constitute a small share of total suicides. Accordingly, we move away from considerations of strategic suicide attempts in our analysis of completed suicides. We instead consider the factors that would lead to more people truly wishing to end their lives.

This leaves us with three principal theories of suicide to test: the rational theory; the contagion theory; and the instrumentality theory. We examine the evidence for each of these theories in this section.

5.4.1   A First Test of Contagion

We start by considering possible evidence of contagion in suicide rates. To do this, we borrow a technique from Glaeser, Sacerdote, and Scheinkman (1996) and examine the excess variance of suicide rates across areas. The idea is simple. If each individual has a probability p of committing suicide, different areas will on average have a share p of people commit suicide, with some variance around that. Because p is a binomial variable, the variance of the theoretical suicide rate across areas is known. Contagion in suicide will make some counties have a higher suicide rate and other areas have a lower suicide rate. This would show up as an excess variance of the suicide rate across counties, even if the mean suicide rate is unaffected. Thus, a nonparametric test of suicide contagion is to compare the theoretical variance of suicide rates across counties with the actual variance of suicide rates across counties.

Formally, the test is the following. The social interaction index is defined as follows:

$$(1) \qquad \text{social interactions index} = \frac{\text{var}\left[(p_j - p_{US})\sqrt{N_j}\right]}{p_{US}(1 - p_{US})},$$

where N_j refers to the population of county j, p_j is the suicide rate in county j, and p_{US} is the suicide rate in the United States as a whole. If there are no social interactions, the index should take on a value of 1.

In evaluating youth suicides, the index value is 156—substantially above the expected value. For adult suicide, the index value is 50—still high but much smaller than that for youths. By comparison, comparable numbers for robbery and murder are 400 and 10, respectively. The implication is that teen suicide has significant social interactions, at least relative to adult suicide.

5.4.2 Explaining Suicide Rates across Counties

In the light of this result, we now look at several predictors of the youth-suicide rate across counties designed to proxy for our different theories. Variable descriptions and means are reported in table 5.9. We include basic demographic controls for urbanicity (dummy variables for large urban area, small urban area, farm) and the share of the area that is black, Native American, and Asian American. Our primarily explanatory variables are grouped into three categories. The first variable is the logarithm of median income in 1989, taken from the 1990 census. In our regressions for suicide attempts, income was significantly negatively associated with attempted suicide. The rational theory suggests that income should be negatively associated with completed suicides as well.

Our second variables are measures of family characteristics—the share of women in the county who are divorced, the share of children who are stepchildren, and the share of female-headed families. These variables are similar to the family-structure variables in our models for attempted suicide. It is important to note that these variables refer to current living status as of the time of the 1990 census. For example, the female divorce

Table 5.9   **Summary Statistics for County Data**

Variable	Mean
Youth-suicide rate (%)	12.6
Urbanicity:	
Large urban area (%)	64
Small urban area (%)	11
Farm (%)	1
Demographics:	
Black (%)	10
Native American (%)	1
Asian (%)	2
Economic:	
ln(median income) ($)	10.31
Family structure:	
% females currently divorced	9
% children living with stepparent	5
% households with female head	18
Means:	
Share who own guns (%)	44
Share who hunt (%)	8

Note: All observations are for 516 county groups, with the exception of gun ownership, which is present for 494 county groups.

rate is the share of women who are divorced and have not remarried. If the woman were remarried, she would report herself as married in the census. These measures are not ideal for our purpose—we would prefer to know the share of women who have ever been divorced, but this information is not available. About 9 percent of women are divorced, 5 percent of children live with a stepparent, and 18 percent of households are female headed.

Finally, to test the instrumentality theory, we include the share of people who own guns and the share of people who hunt. Gun ownership is measured at the state level in the National Opinion Research Center's General Social Survey (GSS) between 1972 and 1994. We aggregate these years to get precision; still, the variable is somewhat suspect because, while the GSS is designed to be representative at the national level, it is not representative at the state level. The share of people who hunt is measured at the county level by the U.S. Department of the Interior. Close to half of all people own a gun, while only 8 percent hunt.

Table 5.10 shows regressions relating these variables to youth-suicide rates. The first regression includes just urbanicity and demographic controls. The racial variables enter as expected. Percentage black is (insignificantly) negative, and percentage Native American is significantly positive. Percentage Asian is also positive. This corresponds with the basic ethnic patterns described above. We find no particular relation between

Table 5.10   Explaining County Suicide Rates

				Youths				Adults
Variable	(1)	(2)	(3)	(4)	(5)	(6)	(7)	(8)
Urbanicity:								
Large urban	2.51	3.30	-2.23	.77	-1.61	-.19	-.83	-2.00
	(2.31)	(2.30)	(2.38)	(2.40)	(2.47)	(2.69)	(2.21)	(2.43)
Small urban	1.70	1.57	-4.60	-.89	-2.88	-2.99	-2.07	-5.24
	(4.51)	(4.46)	(4.50)	(4.54)	(4.53)	(5.69)	(4.03)	(4.34)
Farm	45.17**	23.98	57.11**	45.74**	19.98	45.63*	24.98	-14.83
	(23.46)	(23.97)	(22.81)	(23.27)	(24.95)	(24.65)	(23.47)	(18.8)
Population > 1,000,000	-1.01	-.75	-1.09	-.78	-.75	-.29	-.58	-.56
	(1.47)	(1.45)	(1.42)	(1.47)	(1.44)	(.75)	(1.27)	(.56)
Demographics:								
Black	-3.82	-7.67**	-4.67	-13.37**	2.55	-3.49	2.21	-5.97
	(3.03)	(3.19)	(2.93)	(4.49)	(5.11)	(5.13)	(4.86)	(3.96)
Native American	75.47**	69.86**	64.11**	68.60**	59.22**	56.47*	54.12**	25.50
	(13.72)	(13.67)	(13.43)	(13.77)	(13.35)	(30.45)	(11.83)	(15.53)
Asian	10.62*	13.63**	11.68**	13.27**	8.92	-37.83**	-19.17**	9.21
	(6.16)	(6.15)	(5.97)	(6.28)	(6.10)	(10.56)	(13.61)	(8.21)
Economic:								
ln(median income)	...	-5.72**	...	...	-10.19**	-1.84	-.054	-5.87*
		(1.63)			(2.62)	(3.38)	(2.77)	(3.55)

Social characteristics:								
% females now divorced	...	...	111.46**	...	162.22*	157.31**	170.31**	121.18**
			(19.01)		(30.80)	(24.99)	(28.51)	(28.58)
Female employment rate	...	...	...	6.56	10.69	-3.05	-10.16	.86
				(5.77)	(7.66)	(7.63)	(7.28)	(7.56)
Share stepchildren	...	...	...	63.58**	-108.77**	-107.77**	-63.33*	-21.52
				(25.76)	(37.46)	(39.54)	(34.02)	(39.74)
Share female head	...	...	...	27.40**	-36.74**	-15.95	-20.10	5.88
				(9.58)	(13.68)	(10.66)	(13.02)	(9.04)
Gun ownership:								
Share owning	...	...	...	...	...	6.14*	-6.61	-1.61
						(3.76)	(3.77)	(3.79)
Share hunting	...	...	...	...	...	...	58.41*	18.40*
							(10.39)	(10.50)
Summary statistics:								
N	516	516	516	516	516	494	494	494
R^2	.078	.100	.137	.101	.168	.188	.234	.217

Note: Data are at the county level. Adults are aged 25–64. Numbers in parentheses are standard errors.

*Statistically significant at the 10 percent level.

**Statistically significant at the 5 percent level.

urbanization and teen suicide across counties, but the percentage of the population living on farms positively predicts suicide.

As the second column shows, there is a negative effect of median income on suicide rates, just as the economic model of suicide predicts. As income increases by 25 percent (roughly one standard deviation), the suicide rate drops by nearly 1.4 per 100,000, 11 percent of the mean amount. This is a reasonably large effect. Controlling for income causes the coefficients on race and urban status to become significant.

The third regression shows the effect of the divorce rate in the county on suicide rates. The divorce rate is strongly positive and quantitatively important. As the divorce rate increases by 2 percent (one standard deviation), the suicide rate rises by two per 100,000, 18 percent of the baseline amount. The connection between divorce and suicide at the aggregate level is well-known; Durkheim makes much of it. The usual explanation for this relation is that divorced individuals are more likely to commit suicide. Clearly, this is not the explanation for teen suicides.

There are several possible explanations for the divorce variable. One hypothesis is that more women work when the divorce rate increases and that having mothers who work is bad for teens because it reduces the amount of attention that they receive from parents. The difference in female employment rates in the United States and Europe has been cited by some as a reason for higher suicide rates among teens in the United States compared to Europe. A second theory is that there are more female-headed families in areas where there are more divorces and that children in female-headed families are more likely to commit suicide. From the AddHealth data, we know that the relation between single-parent families and suicide attempts is not particularly strong, so we are somewhat skeptical of this theory. A second explanation is that there are more stepchildren when divorce rates are higher and that conflict between stepchildren and their stepparents increases suicide rates. Again, we saw in AddHealth that there was little effect of a relation with a resident father on suicide, so we are somewhat skeptical of this theory. A third explanation is that, when more families divorce, teens have poorer relationships—but some relationship—with their fathers, and this increases the risk of suicide. In the AddHealth data, the relationship with a nonresident father was strongly predictive of suicidal behavior. Glaeser and Glendon (1998) report that the persons who are most likely to own guns are adult males, especially in the age range of fathers of teenage children. The strategic-suicide theory predicts that access to some parental resources (in this case, access to the father's time or income) predicts higher rates of self-injury than access to the least parental resources. Strategic conflict with parents, or a combination of strategic conflict and access to a gun owned by an adult male, may explain the association between divorce and youth suicide. A final explanation is that the divorce rate proxies for other factors in a community—social disorder, community conflict, general unhappiness, etc.—that influence youth-suicide rates.

To test these theories, we include measures of female labor force participation rates, the share of children who are stepchildren, and the share of families that are female headed. The fourth regression shows that the latter two variables are both related to suicide but that female labor force participation is not. The fifth column includes these three variables with the female divorce rate. Controlling for female divorce rates, the share of stepchildren and the share of female-headed families have a negative effect on youth suicides. Having a father who was once in the household appears to be more important for suicide than being without a father at all. Unfortunately, we do not have information at the county level on contact between children and absent fathers, so we cannot differentiate between that and other explanations of community factors. As such, the relation between the divorce rate and the youth-suicide rate remains something of a puzzle.

The next two columns show the relation between guns and youth suicide. There is mild evidence for the instrumentality theory. In areas where there is more hunting, suicide rates are higher. But this is not true of gun ownership in general, which we expect would be more closely related to youth suicide. Further, the increase in suicide in rural areas—despite the much more rapid increase in gun ownership in urban areas—casts doubt on the instrumentality theory.

The last column reports results for the suicide rate among adults. The same factors may, or may not, predict adult- and youth-suicide rates. We present the models primarily for comparison purposes. For adults, we find that income is a more significant predictor of suicide than it is for children. Comparing the seventh and eighth columns, the coefficient on income is small and statistically insignificant for youths but negative and statistically significant at the 10 percent level for adults. The greater income effect for adults matches the time-series evidence presented above. Female divorce rates are also related to suicide rates for adults, but the magnitude is one-third smaller than that for youths. This is again consistent with our theories and casual time-series evidence. Finally, we find no evidence that the other social characteristics affect adult-suicide rates and only weak evidence for the instrumentality theory.

5.4.3   Changes in Suicide Rates across States

A second test of these theories is to see whether they predict changes in suicide rates over time. The suicide rate started to increase in about 1950, so we consider data from 1950 to 1990. Data on suicide rates at the county level are not available prior to 1970. Accordingly, we focus on analysis at the state level. Such analysis is less than ideal; there were only forty-nine states in 1950 (including Washington, D.C.), so our standard errors are large. We thus consider the state-level analysis to be more suggestive than definitive.

Table 5.11 reports regression results for changes in state suicide rates between 1950 and 1990. The first column reports results for youths, and the second column reports results for total suicides. The regressions do not include data on gun ownership or hunting; such information is not available over time. The specification is thus equivalent to column 5 of table 5.10 above. The income effects are consistent for youth suicides but not total suicides. In states where income increased least, the youth suicide rate rose more. Further, the magnitude of the coefficient on income is very similar in the two models of youth suicide. In contrast, income has no

Table 5.11   Explaining Changes in State Suicide Rates, 1950–90

Variable	Mean	Youth	Total	Youths Male	Youths Female
Urbanicity:					
Change in % farm	−.145	−13.48	−.99	−25.09	−6.15
		(11.18)	(9.58)	(20.62)	(6.80)
% annual population growth	.338	−13.02	−16.99	7.14	−16.01
		(26.4)	(22.6)	(48.74)	(16.07)
Change in % urban	.098	−2.35	19.10**	−4.97	3.21
		(9.1)	(7.8)	(16.74)	(5.52)
Demographics:					
Change in % black	.014	−20.22*	−24.26**	−17.64	−5.93
		(10.75)	(9.22)	(19.83)	(6.54)
Change in % Native	.007	59.02	18.25	95.11	16.59
American		(49.93)	(37.64)	(81.04)	(26.72)
Change in % other	.035	9.01	−5.38	16.16	5.02
		(14.73)	(12.63)	(27.18)	(8.97)
Economic:					
Change in log(median family	.763	−12.74**	1.58	−11.96*	−3.45
income)		(3.78)	(3.24)	(6.98)	(2.30)
Social characteristics:					
Change in % women	.075	46.84	46.91	41.10	17.85
currently divorced/widowed		(42.46)	(36.38)	(78.33)	(25.83)
Change in female labor force	.301	34.86**	−15.20	47.96**	3.65
participation		(12.83)	(11.00)	(23.68)	(7.81)
Mean of dependent variable		10.6	1.5	18.1	1.5
Summary statistics:					
N	49	49	49	49	49
R²		.68	.58	.49	.37

Note: Data are at the state level; Alaska and Hawaii are not included. Numbers in parentheses are standard errors.

*Statistically significant at the 10 percent level.

**Statistically significant at the 5 percent level.

effect on total suicides in the state model but is associated with suicide for adults in the cross-county model (the coefficient from the regression for adults equivalent to col. 5 is -11.60 [2.35]).

The coefficient on the female divorce rate is positive but not statistically significant. Compared to table 5.10, the magnitude is less than one-third as large. Increased female divorce rates are also positively related to overall suicides but not statistically significantly so. In contrast, the female labor force participation rate is significantly related to increases in youth-suicide rates. A 7 percent increase in female labor force participation rates (roughly one standard deviation in the cross section) raises youth-suicide rates by two per 100,000. This effect is not found for total suicides, only for youth suicides. This finding is different from the cross-county evidence, where female labor force participation is not related to youth suicide.

The last two columns differentiate between male and female youth suicides. The coefficients on income, divorce rates, and especially female labor force participation are greater for male suicides than for female suicides. Since male suicide rates have increased more than female suicide rates, this suggests that these results may contribute to the true explanation for rising suicide among youths.

5.4.4   Explaining the Rise in Youth Suicide

The natural question is which of these factors (if any) can explain the increase in youth suicide over time. We use our cross-county regressions to address this since we have more observations and controls with these data. This estimate also allows us to see how well a cross-sectional analysis can predict a time-series change, a valuable exercise in itself.

To address this question, we consider a simple decomposition. Knowing that $\text{pr(suicide)}_j = \Sigma_i \beta_j X_j^i$ where i indexes all the factors that determine suicide, then $\Delta \text{ pr(suicide)} = \Sigma_i \beta_i \Delta X_i$. Thus, using our estimate of the importance of factors from the previous section, we will ask whether the change in observable variables is large enough to justify the observed overall change in suicide.

The AddHealth data suggested four variables that might seem to be robustly correlated with suicidal behavior at magnitudes that could explain the general rise in suicide: depression; delinquency; relationships with parents; and drug use. The cross-country analysis suggests that cross-sectional differences in teen suicide rates may be related to divorce rates, and both the AddHealth data and the cross-county data suggest that peer pressure or social contagion may amplify the effects of particular social stressors, with the result that adolescents may be affected by such community factors as the divorce rate even if their own individual families are not directly involved.

Since there are no really convincing data on teen depression over time, we know of no direct way to evaluate whether the rising suicide rates have

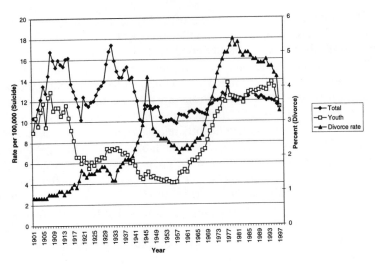

Fig. 5.9   Correlates of suicide rates

resulted from rising levels of teen depression. Indeed, Blanchflower and Oswald (2000) examine data from social surveys in the United States and Western Europe and conclude that mean "happiness" among youths has been increasing, not decreasing, over the last few decades. Of course, this is a statement about the median of the distribution, not the lower tail.

Delinquency and drug use have both risen significantly across this time period. We do not have good data on drug-use increase, and the importance of drugs cannot therefore be estimated. As shown above, there is a relation between the time-series movements of teen homicide and teen suicide. However, we cannot think about the changes in drug use, delinquency, and homicide as exogenous variation, so we leave this issue for further study.

Finally, although we have no national measures of the relationship between parents and children, we can measure the divorce rate. Between 1950 and 1990, the divorce rate rose from 2.3 percent to 8.8 percent. If we use the coefficient estimate from the third column of table 5.10, this suggests that there should have been an increase of 7.22 teenage suicides per 100,000 owing to the increase in the divorce rate. The actual increase was 10.5 suicides. Thus, if we believe this coefficient estimate, and if we treat the increase in the divorce rate as an exogenous variable, the rise in the divorce rate can explain more than two-thirds of the rise in teenage suicide.

Some confirmation of this theory is provided by aggregate time-series evidence. Figure 5.9 shows divorce rates and suicide rates in the twentieth century. In the first half of the century, the two do not seem to be highly correlated. Divorce rates were very low and rose only modestly (from 1 to

2 percent, exclusive of the post–World War II spike), while youth-suicide rates had a general downward trend. Since 1950, however, divorce rates and suicide rates track each other closely. Both were flat in the 1950s, rose in the late 1960s, and plateaued in the mid-1990s. It may be that, when divorce rates were high enough to be a significant factor in community life, trends in divorce rates became a significant driving factor for youths.

Clearly, these regressions and calculations should be taken with numerous shakers of salt, but they suggest that there is at least one coherent theory that can explain the basic facts. At a minimum, this theory deserves much further exploration.

5.5 Conclusion

Youth-suicide rates have tripled in the past three decades, and there are as many as four hundred suicide attempts for every suicide completion. Why the epidemic in youth suicide?

Our analysis of youth-suicide attempts and completions leads us to three conclusions. First, we find that suicide attempts are quite different from actual suicides and lend themselves to a strategic-suicide model. We interpret many youth-suicide attempts as signals of need or as ways to punish parents or other adults. Other suicide attempts are a result of bad things that happen to youths; the link between delinquency, drug use, sexual activity, victimization, and suicide is clear and strong. Some of these reflect the bad outcomes of risks that youths take, while others may be simply a product of the environments in which youths are raised.

It is harder to determine empirically whether completed suicides are the result of what we might consider to be strategic motivations. But we have found evidence for certain common factors that may have influenced the dramatic rise in youth suicide and what has probably been a rise in suicide attempts. The most important of these variables is the female divorce rate. In areas where more women are divorced, youth suicides are greater. This effect is large; if one takes the increase in divorce rates over time in consideration, one can explain as much as two-thirds of the increase in youth suicide.

Social contagion also plays a particularly important role in teen suicide and parasuicide. We find individual-level evidence of contagion in the Add-Health data and statistical evidence of nonrandom clustering in the county-level Vital Statistics. Contagion may involve the direct influence of one teen's suicidal behavior on another, or it may involve more indirect social and cultural processes, but, in either case, these "neighborhood effects" may multiply the effects of government policies or other exogenous shocks.

Economic opportunity plays a mixed role. The strategic-suicide model predicts that suicidal behavior may increase under circumstances where there are greater resources to be accessed. On the other hand, rising labor force participation may have had a protective effect for young women, and higher income is associated with reductions in suicide at the county level.

The factors that we have identified all deserve more research, but we are reasonably certain that the final answer to this question will have to encompass the data and explanations that we put forth here.

Appendix

The Strategic-Suicide Theory

We show in this appendix that, if parents have no knowledge about child utility, and if transfers substitute for innate happiness, a signaling equilibrium can exist where all children with $Z < Z^*$ engage in a suicide attempt and all children with $Z > Z^*$ do not.

Consider a case where Z^* is the cutoff point for attempting suicide. In this equilibrium, the transfers conditional on attempting suicide solve $U'(Y - T) = aE[V'(T, Z)|Z < Z^*]$, and the transfers conditional on not attempting suicide solve $U'(Y - T) = aE[V'(T, Z)|Z > Z^*]$. We will denote the transfers conditional on attempting suicide as $\overline{T}(Z^*)$ and the transfers conditional on not attempting suicide as $\underline{T}(Z^*)$ for the same Z^*.

Then Z^* must be found so that individuals with that level of innate unhappiness (Z^*) are indifferent between attempting suicide and not, that is, $(1 - d) V[\overline{T}(Z^*), Z^*] = V[\underline{T}(Z^*), Z^*]$. From the assumption $d^2V/dTdZ < 0$, everyone with $Z > Z^*$ strictly prefers no suicide attempt, and everyone with $Z < Z^*$ strictly prefers a suicide attempt. In fact, because the prospect of loss of life becomes less important as the teen becomes more unhappy, even with some (bounded) positive values of $d^2V/dTdZ < 0$, it will still be the case that there is a single crossing property where the more unhappy gravitate toward suicide.

Finally, we must prove that there exists a level of Z^* where this signaling equilibrium occurs. In principle, this requires proving that there exists a level of Z^* where $(1 - d) V[\overline{T}(Z^*), Z^*] - V[\underline{T}(Z^*), Z^*]$ equals 0. We specifically assume that $V(T, 0) < 0$, so that the most unhappy teenagers would actually commit suicide for nonstrategic reasons, and that $dV(T, 1) > V_1(0, 1) \times Y$, so that the happiest person would never commit suicide. Furthermore, we assume that all the derivatives of $V(T, Z)$ are finite. From the concavity of $V(\cdot, \cdot)$, it follows that

$$(A1) \quad V_1[\underline{T}(Z^*), Z^*][\overline{T}(Z^*) - \underline{T}(Z^*)] - dV[\overline{T}(Z^*), Z^*]$$
$$> (1 - d)V[\overline{T}(Z^*), Z^*] - V[\underline{T}(Z^*), Z^*] > V_1[\overline{T}(Z^*), Z^*]$$
$$[\overline{T}(Z^*) - \underline{T}(Z^*)] - dV[\overline{T}(Z^*), Z^*].$$

At $Z^* = 0$, the third term is clearly positive since $V(T, Z) < 0$. At $Z^* = 1$, the first term is clearly negative from $dV(T, 1) > V_1(0, 1) \times Y$. As such, $(1 - d) V[\overline{T}(Z^*), Z^*] - V[\underline{T}(Z^*), Z^*]$ goes from negative to positive as Z^* rises. The function is always continuous, so there must be at least one fixed point, from standard arguments. As such, as long as the happiest teenager will never attempt suicide and the least happy will always attempt suicide, there will exist an equilibrium where suicide serves as a signal. (In fact, there may exist multiple equilibria in this case if the function $[1 - d]$ $V\{\overline{T}[Z^*], Z^*\} - V\{\underline{T}[Z^*], Z^*\}$ is not monotonic.)

The Rational-Suicide Model

To formalize the rational-suicide model, we assume that individuals live three periods (youth, midlife, and old age). In each period, individuals receive a utility level equal to μ_t. Individuals learn the utility that they will receive at the start of each period and at that point decide whether to commit suicide. Utility is assumed to follow a random walk: $\mu_t = \mu_{t-1} + \varepsilon_t$. For simplicity, consider the possibility that ε_t is a binary random variable that takes on values of ε and $-\varepsilon$ with equal probability. Individuals discount the future with a discount factor β (which includes the probability of death from other causes). The expected utility from death is normalized to 0.

In the last period, the individual commits suicide if $\mu_3 < 0$. In the second period, the individual's decision whether to commit suicide takes into account both current utility and the option value of living for a third period. Thus, this individual will commit suicide if second-period utility (if the individual does not commit suicide) is $\mu_2 < -\beta\varepsilon/(2 + \beta)$. In the first period, the individual will commit suicide if $\mu_1 < -(2\beta + \beta^2)\varepsilon/(4 + 2\beta + \beta^2)$.

Thus, the first-period suicide rate will be highest when random shocks are large or when discounting is very high. Obviously, anything that raises the mean level of unhappiness in the first period will also increase suicide.

Just as the basic model predicts, the cutoff for suicide becomes progressively less stringent as people age. The option value of living makes individuals less likely to respond to current happiness. But this does not mean that individuals will be more likely to commit suicide as they age. If $F(\cdot)$ describes the cumulative distribution of μ_1, then the number of suicides in the first period will be $F[-(2\beta + \beta^2)\varepsilon/(4 + 2\beta + \beta^2)]$. The number of suicides in the second period will be $0.5\{F[2\varepsilon/(2 + \beta)] - F[-(2\beta + \beta^2)\varepsilon/(4 + 2\beta + \beta^2)]\}$. There is no reason to think that the number of suicides will increase over time. In the first period, individuals first learn their unhappiness, and the optimal suicide strategy suggests that many of them should be expected to commit suicide initially, as long as there is significant persistence in happiness levels. Further algebra also shows that it is quite possible that the suicide rate declines between youth and middle age and then rises again in old age.

It is worth emphasizing that, in the rational-actor model, individuals in the future will be grateful if the marginal suicide is prevented. The marginal suicide is sacrificing a positive future expected utility to alleviate current unhappiness. Thus, the intertemporal intrapersonal conflict that is most associated with suicide occurs with exponential discounting.

With hyperbolic discounting, it will be the case that individuals would like to commit themselves not to commit suicide at some point in the future. For example, in the model outlined above, if discounting is hyperbolic and individuals discount one period ahead by a factor $\beta\delta$, then the suicide cutoff in the second period will be $\mu_2 < -\beta\delta\varepsilon/(2 + \beta\delta)$. However, with hyperbolic discounting, individuals in period 1 discount periods 2 and 3 by β, so, in period 1, individuals would like to ensure that they will commit suicide only if $\mu_2 < -\beta\varepsilon/(2 + \beta)$. As such, in period 1, individuals would like to prevent themselves from committing suicide in the future in some cases.

References

Andrus, J., D. Fleming, M. Heumann, J. Wassell, D. Hopkins, and J. Gordon. 1991. Surveillance of attempted suicide among adolescents in Oregon. *American Journal of Public Health* 81, no. 8:1067–69.

Blanchflower, D., and A. Oswald. 2000. The rising well-being of the young. In *Youth employment and joblessness in advanced countries,* ed. D. Blanchflower and R. Freeman, 289–328. Chicago: University of Chicago Press.

Brent, D. A., J. A. Perper, C. J. Allman, G. M. Moritz, M. E. Wartella, and J. P. Zelenak. 1991. The presence and accessibility of firearms in the homes of adolescent suicides. *Journal of the American Medical Association* 266, no. 21: 2989–95.

Brent, D. A., J. A. Perper, G. Moritz, M. Baugher, J. Schweers, and C. Roth. 1993. Firearms and adolescent suicide: A community case-control study. *American Journal of Diseases of the Child* 147, no. 10:1066–71.

Crosby, A., B. Cheltenham, and J. Sacks. 1999. Incidence of suicidal ideation and behavior in the United States, 1994. *Suicide and Life Threatening Behavior* 29, no. 2:131–40.

Diekstra, R. F. W. 1989. Suicidal behavior in adolescents and young adults: The international picture. *Crisis* 10, no. 1:16–35.

Durkheim, E. [1897] 1966. *Suicide.* New York: Macmillan.

Glaeser, E., and S. Glendon. 1998. Who owns guns? Criminals, victims, and the culture of violence. *American Economic Review* 88, no. 2:458–62.

Glaeser, E., B. Sacerdote, and J. Scheinkman. 1996. Crime and social interactions. *Quarterly Journal of Economics* 111:507–48.

Gould, M., K. Petrie, M. H. Kleinman, and S. Wallenstein. 1994. Clustering of attempted suicide: New Zealand national data. *International Journal of Epidemiology* 23, no. 6:1185–89.

Hamermesh, D., and N. Soss. 1974. An economic theory of suicide. *Journal of Political Economy* 82, no. 1:83–98.

Marzuk, P. M., A. C. Leon, K. Tardiff, E. B. Morgan, M. Stajic, and J. J. Mann. 1992. The effect of access to lethal methods of injury on suicide rates. *Archives of General Psychiatry* 49:451–58.

Norberg, K. 1999. Preliminary report of the South Boston suicide epidemic. Presentation to the Massachusetts Department of Mental Health, February. Available through K. Norberg, Boston University, Department of Psychiatry.

O'Carroll, P. W., and M. M. Silverman. 1993. Case consultation: Community suicide prevention: The effectiveness of bridge barriers. Edited by A. L. Berman. *Suicide and Life Threatening Behavior* 24, no. 1:89–99.

Phillips, D., and L. Carstensen. 1986. Clustering of teenage suicides after television news stories about suicides. *New England Journal of Medicine* 315:685–89.

Putnam, R. D. 2000. *Bowling alone: The collapse and revival of American community.* New York: Simon & Schuster.

Putnam, R. D., R. Leonardi, and R. Y. Nanetti. 1994. *Making democracy work: Civic traditions in modern Italy.* Princeton, N.J.: Princeton University Press.

Radloff, L. S. 1977. The CES-D scale: A self-report depression scale for research in the general population. *Applied Psychological Measurement* 3:385–401.

6

Marijuana and Youth

Rosalie Liccardo Pacula, Michael Grossman,
Frank J. Chaloupka, Patrick M. O'Malley,
Lloyd D. Johnston, and Matthew C. Farrelly

A recent report sponsored by the National Institute on Drug Abuse and the National Institute on Alcohol Abuse and Alcoholism suggests that illicit drug use in America costs society approximately $98 billion each year (NIDA/NIAAA 1998). Adults alone do not generate these costs. Statistics from the National Household Survey on Drug Abuse (NHSDA) show that current use of illicit drugs among youths (twelve to seventeen years of age) doubled from a historic low in 1992 of 5.3 percent to 11.4 percent in 1997 before falling to 9.9 percent in 1998 (SAMHSA 1999). Data from the Monitoring the Future (MTF) study yielded even higher estimates of use and a similar sharp increase in that period (Johnston, O'Malley, and Bachman 1999). Even more disturbing, however, is the finding that, of an estimated 4.1 million people who met DSM-IV diagnostic criteria (APA

Rosalie Liccardo Pacula is an associate economist at the RAND Corp. and a faculty research fellow of the National Bureau of Economic Research. Michael Grossman is distinguished professor of economics at the City University of New York Graduate Center and director of the Health Economics Program at and a research associate of the National Bureau of Economic Research. Frank J. Chaloupka is professor of economics at the University of Illinois at Chicago (UIC), director of ImpacTeen: A Policy Research Partnership to Reduce Youth Substance Abuse at the UIC Health Research and Policy Centers, and a research associate of the National Bureau of Economic Research. Patrick M. O'Malley is senior research scientist in the University of Michigan's Institute for Social Research. Lloyd D. Johnston is distinguished research scientist and principal investigator of the Monitoring the Future study at the University of Michigan's Institute for Social Research. Matthew C. Farrelly is senior economist at the Center for Economics Research at the Research Triangle Institute.

This paper was presented at the Fourth Biennial Pacific Rim Allied Economic Organization Conference in Sydney, Australia, 11–16 January 2000, and at seminars at Vanderbilt University and the City University of New York Graduate School. The authors are extremely grateful to John DiNardo, Jonathan Gruber, Robert Kaestner, John F. P. Bridges, and conference and seminar participants for helpful comments and suggestions. They are indebted to John F. P. Bridges, Dhaval Dave, and especially Deborah D. Kloska for research assistance.

1994) for dependence on illicit drugs in 1998, 1.1 million (26.8 percent) are youths between the ages of twelve and seventeen (SAMHSA 1999).

Marijuana is by far the most commonly used illicit substance among adolescents and has been so for the past twenty-five years.[1] Figure 6.1 shows historical data on annual alcohol, marijuana, and other illicit drug use from the MTF survey of high school seniors, one of the main national studies used to track youth substance use and abuse. The prevalence of marijuana has consistently been about half that of alcohol, far greater than the overall proportion using any of the other illicit drugs (Johnston, O'Malley, and Bachman 1999). When the other illicit drugs are broken down by type of substance (fig. 6.2), it is easy to see that no other single substance has been even half as prevalent as marijuana during the period 1975–98.

The sheer popularity of marijuana among youths makes it an interesting illicit substance to examine. However, there are other factors that motivate a closer examination of the demand for marijuana by youths. First, early marijuana use has been associated with a wide range of antisocial and dangerous behaviors, including driving under the influence, dropping out of school, engaging in crime, and destruction of property (Brook, Balka, and Whiteman 1999; SAMHSA 1998a, 1998b; Yamada, Kendix, and Yamada 1996; Spunt et al. 1994; Osgood et al. 1988). Second, there is increasing evidence that marijuana is an addictive substance and that regular use can result in dependence (DeFonseca et al. 1997; SAMHSA 1998a). Third, regular marijuana use has been associated with a number of health problems, particularly among youths, including upper-respiratory problems (Polen et al. 1993; Tashkin et al. 1990) and reproductive-system problems (Nahas and Latour 1992; Tommasello 1982). Finally, it is widely believed that marijuana is a gateway substance or that early involvement with marijuana can increase the likelihood of later use of "harder drugs." Although there is no clear evidence of a causal link between early marijuana use and subsequent illicit drug use, there is significant evidence of a strong correlation and that early marijuana use is an antecedent (Kandel

They thank Nick Mastrocinque and Mark Redding of the Drug Enforcement Administration Intelligence Division for providing data from the *Illegal Drug Price/Purity Report* and for answering a variety of questions concerning these data. They also thank Steven D. Levitt for providing data on the per capita number of juveniles in custody. Research for this paper was supported by grants from the Robert Wood Johnson Foundation to the University of Illinois at Chicago and the University of Michigan, as part of the foundation's Bridging the Gap initiative, and a grant from the National Institute on Drug Abuse to the RAND Corp. (R01 DA12724-01). Monitoring the Future data were collected under a research grant from the National Institute on Drug Abuse (R01 DA01411). Any opinions expressed are those of the authors and not necessarily those of the Robert Wood Johnson Foundation or the NBER.

1. Although alcohol is an illegal substance for teenagers, we use the term *illicit substance* to refer to those substances that are illegal for persons of all ages.

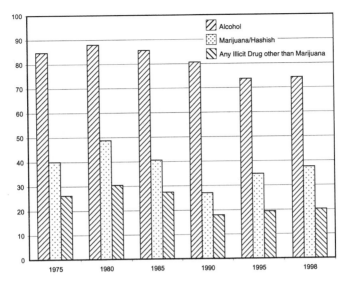

Fig. 6.1   Annual marijuana use relative to other substance use, MTF

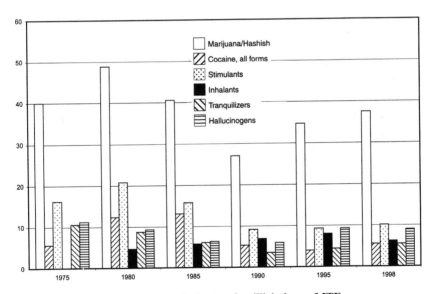

Fig. 6.2   Annual marijuana use relative to other illicit drugs, MTF

1975; Kandel, Kessler, and Margulies 1978; Ellickson, Hays, and Bell 1992; Brook, Balka, and Whiteman 1999; Ellickson and Morton, in press). In this chapter, we explore the demand for marijuana among a nationally representative sample of American high school seniors from the MTF survey. Our main contribution is to present the first set of estimates of the price sensitivity of the prevalence of youth marijuana use. A related contribution is to assess the extent to which trends in price predict the reduction in marijuana use in the 1980s and early 1990s and the increase in use since 1992. In section 6.1, we discuss in greater detail the magnitude of the problem, presenting summary statistics of the prevalence of marijuana use and how it has changed over time. We also discuss what is currently known about the short- and long-run implications of regular and heavy marijuana use. In section 6.2, we provide a brief summary of the literature on the contemporaneous and intertemporal demand for marijuana. In section 6.3, we present findings from a new time-series analysis of the demand for marijuana by youths using data from the 1982–98 MTF survey of high school seniors. The purpose of this section is to identify factors that are significantly correlated with the trend in marijuana use over time. In section 6.4, we reexamine the importance of these factors in repeated cross-sectional analyses of the 1985–96 Monitoring the Future surveys.

6.1   Youth Marijuana Use: The Scope of the Problem

As is indicated in figure 6.2 above, marijuana is the most popular illicit substance among youths and has been for at least the past twenty-five years. Its use, however, has fluctuated quite a bit. Figure 6.3 shows lifetime, annual, and thirty-day prevalence of marijuana use among high school seniors in the MTF study from 1975 to 1998. In the late 1970s and early 1980s, marijuana use was at its peak. In 1978, 37.1 percent of American high school seniors reported using marijuana in the previous thirty days. Annual prevalence of marijuana use was 50.2 percent, and lifetime prevalence was 59.2 percent. Annual and lifetime prevalence continued to climb over the next year, although thirty-day prevalence started to decline. From 1981 to 1992, marijuana use among high school seniors was declining across all measures of use. By 1992, youth marijuana use was at an all-time record low, with 11.9 percent of high school seniors reporting use of marijuana in the previous thirty days, 21.9 percent reporting use in the past year, and 32.6 percent reporting use in their lifetime. After 1992, the trend changed, and marijuana use again began to rise. By 1997, thirty-day prevalence rates were back up to 23.7 percent, and annual and lifetime prevalence rates were 38.5 percent and 49.6 percent, respectively. The 1998 data from the MTF survey suggest that the upward trend may be leveling off. In that year, 22.8 percent of high school seniors reported use of marijuana in the past thirty days, while 37.5 percent reported using in the past year, and 49.1 percent reported using in their lifetime.

Although current prevalence estimates are still well below their peak in the late 1970s, the recent upward trend in marijuana use among youths is disturbing for a number of reasons. First, the increase can be seen across

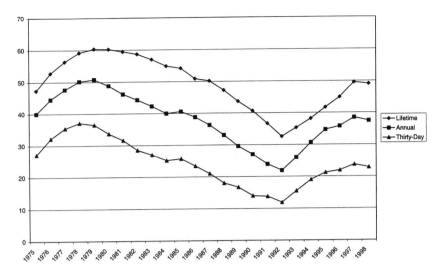

Fig. 6.3   Lifetime, annual, and thirty-day marijuana prevalence, MTF high school seniors

both genders and all ethnic groups, suggesting that this is not a trend being driven by a small subgroup of the youth population (Johnston et al. 1999; SAMHSA 1996). Second, the average age of first marijuana use has been declining during this period, with an average age of initiation of 17.7 in 1992 and 16.4 in 1996 (ONDCP 1999).

Finally, we may not yet really understand all the factors that led to the recent increase in marijuana use or, for that matter, the decline that occurred during the 1980s. Some factors, such as perceived harm, disapproval, and availability of marijuana, have been shown to be significantly correlated with marijuana use over time (Bachman, Johnston, and O'Malley 1998; Caulkins 1999; Johnston et al. 1999). Johnston and his colleagues (Johnston et al. 1999; Johnston 1991) have offered several explanations for why perceived harm, in particular, may have changed in the ways in which it did. These include increased media attention to the consequences of marijuana use beginning in the late 1970s; the large number of heavy users found in most schools by the late 1970s, affording peers the opportunity to directly observe the consequences of their drug use; and the active containment efforts by many sectors of society during the 1980s that included the antidrug advertising campaigns of the mid- to late 1980s. Similarly, for the upturn in the 1990s, Johnston and his colleagues hypothesize that several of the factors that may have contributed to the decline in the 1980s were reversed, including reduced attention from the national media beginning with the buildup to the Gulf War in 1991 and continuing afterward, reduced rates of use among peers providing fewer opportunities for vicarious learning in the immediate social environment, sizable cuts in federal funding for drug-prevention programs in schools in the early 1990s, and the substantial decline in the media placement of the national antidrug advertising campaign of the Partnership for a Drug Free America. In addition, they point to the increased glamorization of drug use in the lyrics, performances, and offstage behavior of many rock, grunge, and rap groups as a factor likely to have contributed to the rise in youth drug use in the 1990s.

To the extent that there is some degree of covariation among the various substances in their intertemporal trends (see fig. 6.4), there may be some common determinants of their use. This covariation was perhaps most apparent during the 1990s, when nearly all forms of licit and illicit drug use rose to some degree among high school seniors. However, there are enough differences among their cross-time usage profiles to conclude that there are also unique factors influencing their use (Johnston et al. 1999). Price, for example, is a logical candidate.

Unlike alcohol, cigarettes, or cocaine, for which the harmful consequences of youth use have been clearly established, there is tremendous uncertainty regarding the short- and long-term consequences of youth marijuana use. This uncertainty has led some to question why we should even be concerned that marijuana use is on the rise. Most regular or heavy marijuana users also use alcohol or other substances regularly, so it is difficult to identify a causal link between particular negative consequences and regular marijuana use. Nonetheless, two reports commissioned by the National Institute on Drug Abuse in the United States and the National Task

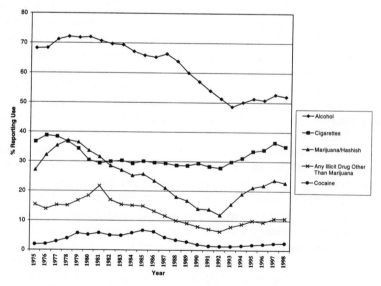

Fig. 6.4   Trends in thirty-day prevalence, MTF

Force on Cannabis in Australia review the existing scientific literature and identify several psychological and health effects that can be generally attributed to regular and/or chronic marijuana use and that can lead to negative outcomes, particularly among youths (NIDA 1995; Hall, Solowij, and Lemmon 1994). These areas include diminished cognitive functioning, diminished psychomotor performance, increased health-services utilization, and the development of dependence. In addition, both reviews cite the significant correlation between early marijuana use and subsequent harder drug use as a further reason to be concerned about the use of marijuana among youths.

6.1.1   Diminished Cognitive Functioning

One of the major reasons for the widespread recreational use of marijuana is that it produces a high associated with mild euphoria, relaxation, and perceptual alterations. Cognitive changes also occur during the high, including impaired short-term memory and a loosening of associations, which makes it possible for the user to become lost in pleasant reverie and fantasy. Recent studies have identified that this diminished cognitive functioning can be attributed to the presence of cannabinoid receptor sites in the areas of the brain that control memory (Matsuda, Bonner, and Lolait 1993; Heyser, Hampson, and Deadwyler 1993). Activation of these receptors interrupts normal brain motor and cognitive function, thus affecting attention, concentration, and short-term memory during the period of intoxication.

It is this negative effect on concentration, attention, and short-term memory that has led many to conclude that marijuana use diminishes human-capital formation for youths. Indeed, research shows that there is a significant contemporaneous correlation between marijuana use and poor grades and dropping out of school (Bachman, Johnston, and O'Malley 1998; Mensch and Kandel 1988; Yamada, Kendix, and Yamada 1996). However, findings from longitudinal studies suggest that these negative associations disappear when other factors, such as lower education aspirations, academic performance, and problem behavior, are controlled for (Ellickson et al. 1998; Newcombe and Bentler 1988; Kandel et al. 1986). One longitudinal study found the negative association to persist after controls were included for motivational factors, but it persisted for only one population subgroup: Latinos (Ellickson et al. 1998). Marijuana use remained insignificant for the general sample of young adults and for the other ethnic subgroups.

There are several shortcomings in these studies that make the interpretation of their findings suspect. In particular, early use of alcohol, cigarettes, and marijuana is consistently treated as an exogenous variable. Only one study to date explicitly tests this assumption, but it does so using a different measure of marijuana use than that typically examined by other studies. In a longitudinal analysis of the relation between marijuana initiation and dropping out of high school, Bray et al. (2000) examine the effect of initiating marijuana use by ages sixteen, seventeen, and eighteen on the likelihood of dropping out of school. They find that marijuana initiation is positively related to dropping out of high school, although the magnitude and significance of the relation varies with the age at which the individual drops out and with the other substances used. They test the possible endogeneity of marijuana initiation and find that they cannot reject exogeneity. However, because their measure does not distinguish new experimenters from regular or long-time users, their finding of exogeneity should not be generalized.

6.1.2   Diminished Psychomotor Performance

It is clear that marijuana use impairs judgment and motor skills by distorting perceptions of space and time. The extent of the impairment, of course, is largely determined by the inhaled or ingested dose, as in the case of alcohol. The question then becomes to what extent the impaired performance translates into accidental injury to the users or those around them. Much of the research in this area has focused on automobile accidents and fatalities. Epidemiological studies that try to identify an association between THC level and crashes and/or fatalities are problematic for two reasons. First, the vast majority of individuals involved in accidents test positive for alcohol use as well. One recent review of the epidemiology literature showed that, although 4–12 percent of drivers who sustained injury or death in crashes tested positive for THC, at least 50 percent, and in some cases 90 percent, of the drivers also tested positive for alcohol (Robbe and O'Hanlon 1999).[2] There have been relatively few studies that contain large enough samples of non-alcohol-impaired drivers to examine this issue. One study of drivers arrested for reckless driving who were not alcohol impaired did find that half these individuals tested positive for marijuana (Brookoff et al. 1994). A second problem with these studies, however, is that a positive test for marijuana does not necessarily mean that the individual was under the influence at the time of the accident. THC stays in the bloodstream much longer than other intoxicants, so a positive test may simply indicate recent use.

Experimental studies that use driving simulators and closed-course driving environments try to overcome these problems. In a review of this literature, Smiley (1986) concludes that, although drivers under the influence of marijuana are more likely to make errors (such as leaving their lane), they also drive more slowly than sober drivers and keep a greater distance from the car in front of them. Drunk drivers, on the other hand, are more likely

---

2. The authors note that higher values have been found among certain high-risk populations, such as young men and people living in large cities.

to increase their speed, which perhaps explains the comparatively smaller number of marijuana-related accidents on the road.

The preceding conclusion continues to be supported in more recent studies (e.g., Robbe and O'Hanlon 1993) and is consistent with findings from a recent econometric study using reduced-form equations to examine the relation between alcohol and marijuana use and the probability of nonfatal and fatal accidents among youths (Chaloupka and Laixuthai 1997). Using self-reported information on nonfatal accidents in the MTF survey, Chaloupka and Laixuthai (1997) find that a reduction in marijuana prices (which they show reduces youth drinking and presumably increases youth marijuana use) leads to a significant drop in the probability of a nonfatal motor-vehicle accident. They interpret this net negative effect as evidence that the substitution of marijuana for alcohol generates an increase in the probability of a nonfatal accident that is smaller than the decrease associated with the decline in drinking and driving. They draw a similar conclusion, using data from the Fatal Accident Reporting System, when examining the effects of marijuana decriminalization on the probability of a fatal motor-vehicle accident among youths. So, although there is significant evidence suggesting that marijuana intoxication leads to an increased risk of motor-vehicle accidents, the risk is not believed to be anywhere near as large as the risk associated with drinking and driving.

6.1.3   Increased Health-Services Utilization

There is increasing, albeit controversial, evidence that regular marijuana use is associated with upper-respiratory problems, such as chronic bronchitis, inflamed sinuses, and frequent chest colds (Nahas and Latour 1992; Tashkin et al. 1990), and reproductive-system problems, such as reduced sperm production and delay of puberty (Nahas and Latour 1992; Tommasello 1982). A significant problem in identifying the health effects associated with marijuana use is that the vast majority of marijuana users also use other substances, particularly alcohol and cigarettes. It is difficult, therefore, to identify whether particular substances or certain combinations generate specific health outcomes. Two approaches have been generally used to try to tease out the relation. The first approach relies on individual-level data where there is a high incidence of marijuana users who do not use other substances. For example, Polen et al. (1993) were able to identify 452 Kaiser Permanente enrollees who were daily marijuana smokers who never smoked tobacco. They compared the health-service utilization among these daily marijuana-only smokers to nonsmokers with similar demographics screened at Kaiser Permanente medical centers between July 1979 and December 1985. They examined medical-care utilization for a number of health-specific outcomes over a one- to two-year follow-up and found that marijuana smokers have a 19 percent increased risk of outpatient visits for respiratory illnesses, a 32 percent increased risk of injury, and a 9 percent increased risk of other illnesses and were 50 percent more likely to be admitted to the hospital than were nonsmokers. These results were adjusted for sex, age, race, education, marital status, and alcohol consumption.

The second approach to understanding the relation between marijuana use and health has focused on examining the correlation between general consumption rates and health-care utilization. For example, Model (1993) examined the effect of marijuana decriminalization status on the incidence of marijuana-related hospital-emergency-room episodes using data from the 1975–78 Drug Abuse Warning Network (DAWN). During the mid-1970s, several states chose to decriminalize possession of small amounts of marijuana, thus reducing the penalties associated with using it. Model (1993) found that states that had chosen to decriminalize experienced significantly higher rates of marijuana-related emergency-room episodes.

Although both approaches clearly establish a positive association between marijuana use and health-service utilization, they have yet to demonstrate a direct link between marijuana use and particular health outcomes or illnesses.

6.1.4   Development of Dependence

Until the late 1970s and early 1980s, the general-consensus opinion regarding marijuana was that it was not a drug of dependence because marijuana users did not exhibit tolerance and withdrawal symptoms analogous to those seen in alcohol and opiate dependence. In the late 1970s, however, expert opinion regarding marijuana dependence began to change as a new, more liberal definition of *drug dependence,* embodied in Edwards and Gross's (1976) alcohol-dependence syndrome, was extended to all psychoactive drugs (Edwards, Arif, and Hadgson 1981). This new definition reduced the emphasis on tolerance and withdrawal and attached greater emphasis on the continued use of the drug in the face of its adverse effects. It is this new conception of dependence that is reflected in DSM-III-R and DSM-IV, the third revised and fourth editions of the *Diagnostic and Statistical Manual* of the American Psychiatric Association (APA 1987, 1994). A diagnosis of psychoactive-substance dependence is made if any three of nine criteria are present for a month or longer. It is therefore not necessary that a person exhibit physical dependence on a drug for her to be diagnosed as dependent (Hall, Solowij, and Lemmon 1994).

Studies employing these new criteria for marijuana dependence have determined that marijuana-dependence syndrome occurs much more frequently than previously believed. According to data from the 1993 National Comorbidity Study, 9 percent of those who reported trying marijuana reported dependence at some stage (Anthony, Warner, and Kessler 1994). Data from the Epidemiologic Catchment Area study found that half those classified as having experienced drug dependence in their lifetime reported using only marijuana, suggesting that marijuana users constitute a substantial fraction of all those dependent on illicit drugs (Anthony and Helzer 1991).

Although tolerance and withdrawal symptoms are not required within the DSM-III-R and DSM-IV definitions, there is evidence that both can occur for chronic heavy cannabis users (Jones and Benowitz 1976; Georgotas and Zeidenberg 1979; Weller and Halikas 1982). There is also clinical and epidemiological evidence that some heavy marijuana users experience problems controlling their use despite the experience of adverse personal consequences (Stephens and Roffman 1993; Kandel and Davies 1992; Jones 1984). However, many researchers note that the physical withdrawal symptoms for those suffering from a physical dependence on marijuana are minor and typically pass within a few days if they are experienced at all (Jones 1987, 1992; Compton, Dewey, and Martin 1990).

Given that the predominant social pattern of marijuana use is recreational and/or the intermittent use of relatively low doses of THC, the actual risk of developing a dependence syndrome is relatively small for most individuals using marijuana. Further, assuming that the physical-withdrawal symptoms are truly minor, marijuana dependence would be fairly easy to treat. However, the addictive nature of marijuana is clearly underestimated by most individuals who decide to use the drug.

6.1.5   Marijuana as a Gateway Drug

The importance of marijuana as a gateway drug remains highly controversial, despite tremendous evidence of a correlation between early marijuana use and later hard drug use. The finding that marijuana use precedes harder drug use and that this sequencing persists across youths of different gender, race, and ethnicity is well established (Kandel 1975; Kandel, Kessler, and Margulies 1978; Ellickson, Hays, and Bell 1992; Kandel, Yamaguchi, and Chen 1992; Ellickson and Morton, in press). However, the proper interpretation of this consistent finding remains debatable. Temporal precedence and statistical correlation are only necessary conditions for establishing causality, not sufficient conditions. It might very well be the case that this consistent finding in the literature is the result of a spurious correlation driven by other individual factors or problem behaviors, such as truancy, poor grades, and delinquency. Debate ensues regarding the plausibility of alternative proposed causal mechanisms. These mechanisms can be grouped into two general categories: physiological and sociological factors.

The physiological arguments are based on findings from two recent papers in *Science* that demonstrate that cannabis activates neurochemical processes in rats that respond in a qualitatively similar way to cocaine, heroin, tobacco, and alcohol (DeFonseca et al. 1997; Tanda, Pontieri, and DiChiara 1997). These findings support the argument that favorable experimentation with and regular consumption of marijuana will make youths more receptive to experimenting with other types of intoxicants, particularly those that offer similar psychological effects. However, neither study actually examined the relation between rats' cannabis consumption and their consumption of harder drugs or their motivation to use these drugs, so their findings cannot be interpreted as definitive proof of causality.

Sociological arguments generally tend to focus on the information that is learned when experimenting with marijuana (Kaplan 1970; MacCoun, Reuter, and Schelling 1996). For example, it may be the case that seemingly safe experiences with marijuana might reduce the adolescent's perceptions regarding the perceived harmfulness, in terms of both legal risks and health risks, of using harder drugs. Alternatively, exposure to the marijuana marketplace may bring casual marijuana users into contact with hard-drug sellers, again influencing their perceptions regarding the legal risks of using illicit drugs. It was this latter argument that persuaded the Dutch to separate the soft- and hard-drug markets by permitting low-level cannabis sales in coffee shops and nightclubs (Ministry of Foreign Affairs 1995).

Despite the numerous theories that propose specific causal mechanisms for this observed sequencing, very little empirical work has been done trying to verify the existence of a causal mechanism. At least one published study reports a structural relation between prior marijuana use and current demand for cocaine, although it does not attempt to identify the causal mechanism (DeSimone 1998). Using data from the 1988 National Longitudinal Survey of Youth (NLSY), DeSimone (1998) estimates the current demand for cocaine as a function of past marijuana use (use reported in the 1984 survey) and current values of other correlates of cocaine demand using a sample of individuals who had not previously used cocaine. A two-stage instrumental-variables approach is used to account for the potential correlation between past marijuana use and the current-period error term. Instruments for the past use of marijuana included two measures of state-level penalties for marijuana possession, the beer tax, and an indicator of parents' alcoholism or problem drinking. Estimates from this model suggest that prior use of marijuana increases the probability of using cocaine by more than 29 percent, even after one controls for unobserved individual characteristics, providing the strongest evidence that the observed sequencing in use is not being driven by a spurious correlation between demand equations.

As the discussion above demonstrates, regular and/or heavy marijuana use is associated with a number of negative short- and long-term consequences, including reduced education attainment, increased risk of accidents, increased use of health-care services, increased risk of dependence, and a possible increased risk of the use of harder substances. The problem is that the literature exploring a causal link between marijuana and these potential consequences is still relatively sparse and much remains to be explored.

6.2 The Demand for Marijuana by Youths: Key Insights from the Literature

Few economic studies analyzing the determinants of marijuana demand were conducted prior to the 1990s because of the limited information available on the price of marijuana. Nonetheless, a significant literature developed thanks to the work of epidemiologists and other social scientists who were interested in exploring other correlates and causes of marijuana use. Most of these studies examine how individual and environmental characteristics, lifestyle factors (grades, truancy, religious commitment, evenings out for recreation), and proximate factors (perceptions and attitudes about marijuana) correlate with current use of marijuana among adolescents.

It is not surprising that a key finding from this literature is that the same general background and lifestyle factors that are significantly correlated with the early use of alcohol and other drugs are also correlated with marijuana use. Although gender and ethnicity are consistently significantly correlated with marijuana use, with men being significantly more likely to use marijuana than women and blacks being much less likely to use marijuana than whites, they are not viewed as leading determinants of marijuana use. Instead, truancy, frequent evenings away from home for recreation, low religiosity, and low perceived harmfulness or disapproval (Bachman et al. 1988; Bachman, Johnston, and O'Malley 1981; Jessor, Chase, and Donovan 1980) are considered to be the most significant correlates of marijuana use. Part-time employment and income are considered to be more moderate correlates, with youths who report working more hours per week and higher incomes being more likely to use marijuana (Bachman et al. 1988; Bachman, Johnston, and O'Malley 1981). Social factors, such as use by peers or family members and reduced family attachment, are also significantly correlated with marijuana use (Brook, Cohen, and Jaeger 1998; Kandel 1985; Jessor, Chase, and Donovan 1980).

Nisbet and Vakil (1972) contributed the first economic study to this literature. They used a self-administered survey of 926 University of California, Los Angeles, students in an effort to obtain information on the price of marijuana in addition to the quantity of marijuana consumed. Students were asked how many ounces of marijuana they purchased at current prices as well as how much they would buy if faced with alternative hypothetical price changes. Two alternative functional forms of very basic demand curves were estimated that included measures of the quantity of marijuana consumed in a month, the price per ounce, mean monthly total expenditures, and an expenditure-dispersion measure. Price was found to be a significant determinant of quantity consumed. Estimates of the price elasticity of demand ranged from -0.40 to -1.51 when information on hypothetical prices was included. When the data were restricted to just actual purchase data, the price elasticity of demand fell into a narrower range of -1.01 to -1.51.

The Nisbet and Vakil (1972) study provides us with the only published price elasticity of demand for marijuana. However, the findings from this study cannot be generalized because they are based on a very small convenience sample of college students, do not account for other important demand factors, and employ data that are almost thirty years old. In addition, the estimated price elasticities are likely to be overstated in absolute value because students who consume relatively large amounts of marijuana have incentives to search for lower prices.[3]

More recent studies by economists and other researchers that use nationally representative samples and include other demand factors lack information on the money price of marijuana. Most try to overcome this data shortcoming by focusing on other aspects of the full price of this substance. For example, several studies use cross-state variation in marijuana decriminalization status to examine the effect of reduced legal sanctions on the demand for marijuana. The findings with respect to the effect of decriminalization on the use of marijuana by youths and young adults are generally mixed. Early studies focusing on youth populations generally found that decriminalization had no significant effect on demand. For example, Johnston, O'Malley, and Bachman (1981) compared changes in marijuana use in decriminalized states to that in nondecriminalized states using data from the MTF survey of high school seniors and found no significant difference.

DiNardo and Lemieux (1992) came to a similar conclusion using state-level aggregated data from the 1980–89 MTF survey. They estimated log-linear and bivariate probit models of the likelihood of using alcohol and marijuana. In addition to including marijuana-decriminalization status, they included a regional price of alcohol and the minimum legal purchase age for beer in all specifications. They found that the marijuana-decriminalization variable had no significant effect on marijuana use. Thies and Register (1993) similarly found no significant effect of marijuana decriminalization on the demand for marijuana among a sample of young adults from the 1984 and 1988 NLSY. They estimated logit and tobit specifications of the demand for marijuana, binge drinking, and cocaine and included cross-price effects in all the regressions. Pacula (1998b) also found no significant effect of marijuana decriminalization in her two-part

---

3. The estimated price elasticities reported in secs. 6.3 and 6.4 below are not subject to this bias because they employ prevailing market prices rather than prices paid by individual consumers.

model specification of the demand for marijuana using data from the 1984 NLSY.

Two recent studies using youth samples from the MTF study and including information on the median fines imposed for possession of marijuana have found a positive effect of decriminalization on marijuana use. Chaloupka, Grossman, and Tauras (1999) used data from the 1982 and 1989 MTF to estimate annual and thirty-day prevalence of marijuana and cocaine use among high school seniors. Their models included measures of the median fines for possession of marijuana and showed that individuals living in decriminalized states were significantly more likely to report use of marijuana in the past year. They found no significant effect on thirty-day prevalence, however. In a separate study examining the relation between the demand for cigarettes and the demand for marijuana, Chaloupka, Pacula, et al. (1999) used data from the 1992–94 eighth-, tenth-, and twelfth-grade surveys to estimate a two-part model of the current demand for cigarettes and marijuana. They found that marijuana decriminalization had a positive and significant effect on both the prevalence and the quantity consumed of marijuana when median jail terms and fines were also included in the model.

Studies employing data on the overall population have generated more consistent findings with respect to the effects of marijuana decriminalization on the consumption of marijuana. For example, Model (1993) analyzed the effect of marijuana decriminalization on drug mentions in hospital-emergency-room episodes using data from the 1975–78 DAWN. Although she did not directly estimate demand functions for marijuana, results from multiple variants of her model consistently showed that cities in states that had decriminalized marijuana experienced higher marijuana emergency-room mentions and lower other drug mentions than nondecriminalized cities. Saffer and Chaloupka (1999) estimated individual-level prevalence equations for past-year and past-month use of marijuana, alcohol, cocaine, and heroin using data from the 1988, 1990, and 1991 NHSDA. They found that marijuana decriminalization had a positive and significant effect on marijuana prevalence, supporting the conclusion made by Model that individuals in the general population are responsive to changes in the legal treatment of illicit drugs.

Studies examining other components of the legal risk of using marijuana, such as fines for possession and marijuana arrest rates, have generated similarly mixed findings in terms of youth responsiveness. For example, using different samples from the MTF, Chaloupka, Grossman, and Tauras (1999) and Chaloupka, Pacula, et al. (1999) both found that youths were responsive to median fines for possession of marijuana. However, using individual-level data from the 1990–96 NHSDA to estimate state fixed-effects models of the prevalence of marijuana and cigarette use, Farrelly et al. (1999) found that higher median fines for possession of marijuana had no significant effect on youths between the ages of twelve and twenty. They did find a statistically significant effect on young adults between the ages of twenty-one and thirty. They further found that young adults, but not youths, were responsive to marijuana arrest rates. Individuals living in areas where marijuana arrests were a higher fraction of total arrests were significantly less likely to use marijuana.

Pacula (1998a) provided further evidence that young adults are sensitive to general enforcement risk, using data from the 1983 and 1984 NLSY. In her models of the intertemporal demand for alcohol and marijuana, she used a measure comparing common crime to the number of police officers at the SMSA (standard metropolitan statistical area) level as an indicator of the enforcement risk of using marijuana. She found that higher crime-per-officer ratios were associated with increased use of marijuana for young adults.

Unlike the economic literature on the demand for other intoxicating substances, in which the focus of the research has been on estimating the own-price elasticity of demand, much of the economic literature on the demand for marijuana has focused on analyzing cross-price effects because of the unavailability of marijuana-price data. The goal of this research has been to determine whether marijuana is an economic substitute for or complement to other substances that are believed to have more harmful consequences associated with use. The findings with respect to the relation between marijuana and cigarettes have been consistent so far. Higher cigarette prices lead to lower cigarette and marijuana use among youths and young adults (Chaloupka, Pacula, et al. 1999; Farrelly et al. 1999).

Findings are mixed, however, when it comes to other substances. Initial research on the relation between the demand for alcohol and the demand for marijuana suggested that these two goods were economic substitutes for youths. Using aggregated data from the MTF, DiNardo and Lemieux (1992) found that higher minimum legal purchase ages reduced alcohol consumption and increased marijuana consumption over time. They further found that individuals living in decriminalized states were significantly less likely to use alcohol, which they interpreted as evidence of a substitution effect even though decriminalization did not statistically influence marijuana consumption. Using individual-level data from the 1982 and 1989 MTF, Chaloupka and Laixuthai (1997) similarly found evidence of a substitution effect between alcohol and marijuana. They estimated ordered and dichotomous probits of drinking frequency and found that marijuana decriminalization had a consistent negative effect. In restricted models that incorporated information on marijuana prices, they further found that higher marijuana prices were generally associated with an increased likelihood of drinking and drinking heavily.

Subsequent research that analyzes individual-level demand equations for marijuana has raised some doubt of a substitution effect. In both her contemporaneous and her intertemporal demand models using the 1984 NLSY, Pacula (1998a, 1998b) finds that higher beer prices are associated with reduced levels of drinking and marijuana use. She interprets this as evidence of a complementary relation between alcohol and marijuana. Farrelly et al. (1999) similarly find that higher beer taxes reduce the probability of currently using marijuana among their sample of twelve- to twenty-year-olds from the 1990–96 NHSDA. However, they also find that higher beer taxes have no significant effect on the demand for marijuana among their young-adult sample (ages twenty-one to thirty). The finding of no significant effect among older populations is consistent with what was found by Saffer and Chaloupka (1999) when they estimated annual and thirty-day prevalence of marijuana use using the 1988, 1990, and 1991 NHSDA.

Although Model's (1993) research examining emergency-room episodes suggests that marijuana is an economic substitute for other illicit substances in general, studies that actually estimate individual-level demand equations generate mixed findings with respect to cross-price effects for specific substances. Saffer and Chaloupka (1999) find that higher cocaine prices are associated with reduced marijuana participation in the past month and the past year while marijuana decriminalization is generally associated with increased cocaine consumption, suggesting that these two goods are economic complements. The findings regarding marijuana and heroin, however, are more mixed. Higher heroin prices are found generally to reduce marijuana participation, although the findings are sensitive to other prices included in the model. Marijuana decriminalization, on the other hand, has no significant effect on heroin participation.

Of course, a major concern in trying to interpret the findings from all these studies is the fact that all but one (Chaloupka and Laixuthai 1997) exclude a measure for the monetary price of marijuana. Thus, it is difficult to know whether the estimates from these models are biased and, if so, in what direction.

Most of the research just reviewed focuses on determinants of the contemporaneous demand for marijuana. Research examining changes in the trend of marijuana use over time suggests that significant predictors of contemporaneous demand cannot account for the change that we have seen in demand over time (Bachman, Johnston, and O'Malley 1998; Bachman et al. 1988). Using data from the 1976–86 MTF survey of high school seniors, Bachman et al. (1988) use multivariate analysis to examine the influence of lifestyle factors (grades, truancy, hours worked per week, weekly income, religious commitment, political conservatism, and evenings out per week), attitudes (perceived harmfulness and disapproval of regular marijuana use), and secular trends (mean marijuana use among high school seniors for that year) on variation in individual use of marijuana over time. They find that attitudinal measures are by far the most powerful predictors of change. When attitudinal measures are included in the regression, the influence of the secular trend becomes insignificant, suggesting that the secular trend can be entirely explained by measures of perceived risk or disapproval. Similarly, the influence of lifestyle factors as a group diminishes with the inclusion of the attitudinal variables, although some factors, such as truancy and evenings out, continue to have large effects. The fact that lifestyle factors alone could not diminish the influence of the secular trend on individual marijuana use suggests that attitudes and not lifestyle factors are more important in determining trends in marijuana use over time.

In a follow-up study that expanded the previous research by examining a longer time period and replicated the analysis on eighth and tenth graders, Bachman, Johnston, and O'Malley (1998) reaffirm their previous findings. Using data from the period 1976–96, they again find evidence that the influence of lifestyle variables on marijuana use occurs primarily through disapproval and perceived risk. Further, they also find that the secular trends in marijuana use can be completely explained by changes in attitudes over time.

In the light of these findings and the fact that self-reported perceived availability did not change significantly during the periods being examined, Bachman, Johnston, and O'Malley (1998) concluded that supply reduction has limited potential to influence use over time and that the focus of government efforts should be on trying to influence perceived harm and disapproval. Caulkins (1999) challenged this conclusion by arguing that the MTF indicator of availability may not be properly calibrated to detect significant changes in perceived availability. He showed that there is indeed a strong negative correlation between median national marijuana prices and high school seniors' self-reported use between 1981 and 1997. Depending on the measure of use, Caulkins found a correlation coefficient between -0.79 and -0.95, which overlaps with the simple correlation coefficients obtained between participation and perceived harm. Although this is not definitive evidence that supply factors substantially influence marijuana use by youths over time, Caulkins argued that it suggests that further analyses exploring the relative importance of supply factors over time are needed. We conduct such analyses in the remainder of this paper.

6.3   Time-Series Analysis

In this section, we focus on national trends in marijuana participation in the past year (annual participation) and in the past thirty days (thirty-day participation) by MTF high school seniors for the period from 1982 through 1998. We relate these trends to trends in the real price of marijuana, the purity of marijuana as measured by its delta-9-tetrahydro-cannabinol (THC) potency, and the perceived risk of great harm from regular marijuana use as reported by the MTF seniors.[4] Included are multiple regressions of past-year or past-month participation on the three variables just mentioned and a time trend. We begin with data for 1982 because that is the first year in which potency and prices are available.

Compared to the repeated cross-sectional analysis that follows, the national analysis has certain advantages. First, it covers a longer period of time. Second, it puts purity on equal footing with other determinants since this variable is available only at the national level. Third, we can examine whether changes in price and the perceived harm from regular marijuana use have the potential to account for a significant share of the observed changes in youth marijuana use over time.

The disadvantages of the time series are that there are a small number of observations and a considerable amount of intercorrelation among the variables. In addition, this analysis is limited by the lack of data on marijuana prices prior to 1982, particularly when comparing the contributions of price and perceived harm in predicting the downward trend in marijuana use in the 1980s. Starting in 1982 misses the early part of the downturn in use that began in 1979 and the 25 percentage point increase in the proportion of youths seeing great risk from regular marijuana use that occurred between 1978 and 1982. Any conclusions reached from these analyses must be interpreted with caution.

6.3.1 MTF Prevalence Data

The MTF survey is a nationally representative, annual school-based survey of approximately sixteen thousand high school seniors in approximately 130 public and private high schools each year. One of the main purposes of the study is to explore changes in youths' perceptions of, attitudes toward, and use of alcohol, tobacco, and other drugs. As such, great care is taken to ensure that responses pertaining to the use of each of these substances are valid and reliable. Students complete self-administered, machine-readable questionnaires in their normal classroom, so parents are not present when the students are filling out the questionnaires, nor are they informed of the students' responses. The survey was developed and is conducted by the Institute for Social Research at the University of Michigan. Detailed information pertaining to survey design and sampling methods is available in Johnston, O'Malley, and Bachman (1999). Further

---

4. The MTF data contain other measures of youth attitudes toward marijuana, including the risk of harm from occasional marijuana use, the risk of harm from experimental use, and disapproval of regular, occasional, or daily use. Given the length of this chapter and the complexity of the analyses that it contains, a more complete treatment of the attitudinal variables is not included. While these measures are highly correlated, the use of different attitudinal measures is likely to have some effect on the estimates reported below. Further consideration of these variables deserves high priority in future research.

information regarding the validity of these data is available in Johnston and O'Malley (1985). The University of Michigan team reports aggregate measures of use from the survey annually (Johnston, O'Malley, and Bachman [1999] is the most recent in this annual monograph series).

6.3.2 Data on Marijuana Prices and Potency

There are two sources of data on marijuana prices: the System to Retrieve Information from Drug Evidence (STRIDE) and the *Illegal Drug Price/Purity Report* (*IDPPR*). The Drug Enforcement Administration (DEA) of the U.S. Department of Justice maintains both. DEA and FBI agents and state and local police narcotics officers purchase illicit drugs on a regular basis in order to apprehend dealers. Taubman (1991) argues that DEA agents must make transactions at close to the street prices of the drugs in order to make an arrest because an atypical price can cause suspicion on the part of dealers.

Information on the date and city of the purchase, total cost, total weight in grams, and purity (as a percentage) for certain drugs is recorded in STRIDE for each of approximately 140 cities. Most of the data pertain to cocaine or heroin because DEA agents have focused their efforts on apprehending cocaine and heroin dealers since STRIDE was created in 1977. Cocaine purchases are the most numerous: approximately thirty thousand in the period from 1981 through 1998, compared to only three thousand for marijuana. No information on the purity of marijuana is recorded. In addition, no distinction is made between wholesale and retail purchases, although the latter involve smaller quantities than the former.

Given the small number of marijuana purchases, and given that almost 30 percent are made in the District of Columbia, STRIDE cannot be used to develop marijuana prices at the state or local level. Moreover, this database cannot be used to adjust price for purity and to distinguish between retail and wholesale purchases. Therefore, in the repeated cross-sectional analysis in the next section, and in the trend analysis in this section, prices are taken from the following publications of the DEA Office of Intelligence or Intelligence Division of the U.S. Department of Justice: *The Domestic Cities Report* (1982–1985:3); the *Illicit Drug Wholesale/Retail Price Report* (1985:4–1990:4); and the *Illegal Drug Price/Purity Report* (1991:1–1998:4). The publications just mentioned contain data for nineteen cities in sixteen states. In general, the prices are reported quarterly. In 1982, 1983, and 1984, a single city-specific figure is given for each of the four marijuana-price series (for more details, see below), and the quarter for which the figure pertains is not given.[5] Data for the first and third quarters of 1985, the second quarter of 1988, and the second quarter of 1996 are missing. The cities are as follows: Atlanta; Boston; Chicago; Dallas; Denver; De-

---

5. We assume that the data for 1982, 1983, and 1984 pertain to the second quarter of each year.

troit; Houston; Los Angeles; Miami; Newark, New Jersey; New Orleans; New York; Philadelphia; Phoenix; San Diego; San Francisco; Seattle; St. Louis; and the District of Columbia.

Four marijuana-price series are contained in these publications: the wholesale price (price per pound) of commercial-grade marijuana, the wholesale price of a more potent grade called *sinsemilla*, and the retail price (price per ounce) of each of these two grades. In most cases, the price range (minimum and maximum price) is reported. In some cases, a single price is quoted. The number of observations on which the price range or price is based is not reported.

For convenience, we refer to prices from the sources just described as *IDPPR* or *nineteen-cities* prices from now on. The purchases on which these prices are based are sent to a laboratory at the University of Mississippi, which distinguishes between commercial marijuana and sinsemella and ascertains the THC content of each purchase as a percentage. Annual average percentages for commercial marijuana and sinsemilla potency are published, but figures for the individual cities are not given.[6] No distinction is made between potency at the wholesale and potency at the retail levels. In our sample period, the mean potency of commercial marijuana was 4.09 percent, and the mean potency of sinsemilla was 8.39 percent, with the simple pairwise correlation coefficient between the two equal to 0.43.

We obtain four annual price series from *IDPPR* by taking the midpoint of each price range (defined as the simple average of the maximum and minimum price), converting all prices into prices per gram, and converting to real prices by dividing by the annual consumer price index for the United States as a whole (1982–84 = 1). The four prices are highly correlated. The pairwise simple correlation coefficients between them range from 0.73 in the case of the retail commercial price and the retail sinsemilla price to 0.92 in the case of the wholesale and retail sinsemilla prices. In the trend and regression analyses reported in this section, we employ the retail commercial price and the potency of commercial marijuana. The retail price is clearly the most relevant one for youth-consumption decisions. There are no data, however, to indicate whether commercial marijuana or sinsemilla is more commonly consumed by young marijuana users. Given the evidence that commercial marijuana dominates the U.S. marijuana market for the period covered by these analyses (Kleiman 1992; NNICC 1998), we suspect that commercial marijuana is likely to be the type most used by high school seniors.[7]

---

6. Information on the nineteen-cities prices and the publications that contain them were kindly supplied by Nick Mastrocinque and Mark Redding of the DEA Intelligence Division. It is not clear why the purchases on which these prices are based are not contained in STRIDE.

7. If youths are more likely to use sinsemilla rather than commercial marijuana, then an additional source of measurement error is introduced into our models. However, given the relatively high correlations between price and potency, the regression results obtained with

For the period as a whole, the average nominal price of retail commercial marijuana was $5.97 per gram, and the average nominal price of wholesale commercial marijuana was $3.15 per gram. The corresponding prices for sinsemilla were $10.41 per gram at the retail level and $6.71 per gram at the wholesale level. Since a marijuana cigarette (a joint) typically contains 0.5 grams (Rhodes, Hyatt, and Scheiman 1994), one retail commercial joint costs approximately $3.00 in nominal terms in our sample period. For comparative purposes, a six-pack (six twelve-ounce cans) of beer costs approximately $3.50. If one assumes that a joint produces the same high as two or three cans of beer, the purchase of marijuana puts at least as great a dent in a youth's budget as the purchase of beer.

6.3.3   Trends

Trends in annual marijuana participation as a percentage, thirty-day marijuana participation as a percentage, and the percentage reporting great risk of harm from regular marijuana use (termed *harm* from now on) are shown in figure 6.5. These data reveal a cycle in use in the period at issue: a contraction from 1982 through 1992 followed by an expansion from 1992 through 1998. Annual prevalence fell from 44.3 percent in 1982 to 21.9 percent in 1992 and then rose to 37.5 percent in 1998. Thirty-day prevalence followed a similar pattern. It declined from 28.5 percent in 1982 to 11.9 percent in 1992 and then grew to 22.8 percent in 1998.

The trend in the harm measure leads the trends in the two participation series. It grew from 60.4 percent in 1982 to 76.5 percent in 1992 and then shrank to 58.5 percent in 1998. This suggests that the trend in harm has the potential to help explain the differential trend in the number of users in the two subperiods 1982–92 and 1992–98. This is particularly true because the peak in harm (78.6 percent in 1991) leads the trough in annual or thirty-day participation by one year.

The real price of commercial retail marijuana and the potency of commercial marijuana are plotted in figure 6.6. These two series are more erratic than the three presented in figure 6.5 above. Their behavior during the two subperiods, however, has the potential to help explain the cycle in participation. From 1982 to 1992, price more than tripled, while potency fell by 22 percent. Since 1992, real price fell by 16 percent, and potency increased by 53 percent. Moreover, the peak in the real price of one gram of marijuana ($7.64 in 1991) leads the trough in participation by one year.

Between 1982 and 1998, the number of high school seniors using marijuana in the past year declined by 15 percent, and the number using marijuana in the past thirty days declined by 20 percent. At the same time, price almost tripled, potency increased by approximately 20 percent, and

---

alternative series are very similar to those reported in this chapter, suggesting that this is not a significant problem.

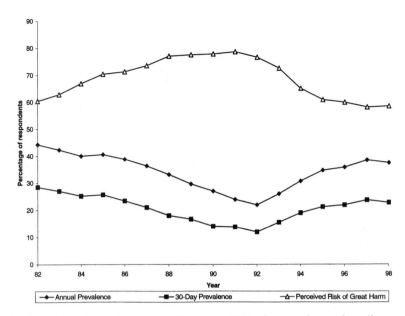

Fig. 6.5   Annual prevalence of marijuana use, thirty-day prevalence of marijuana use, and the perceived risk of great harm from regular marijuana use, 1982–98

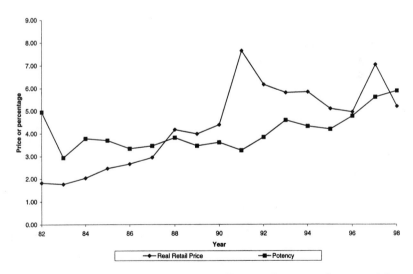

Fig. 6.6   Real retail price of commercial marijuana and potency of commercial marijuana, 1982–98

the number reporting harm from regular marijuana use fell by 3 percent. If we compare only the two end points (1982 and 1998), the price rise is consistent with the decline in the prevalence of marijuana use, but the increase in potency and the decline in perceived risk are not. In our view, however, it is misleading to focus on the end points given the considerable change within the interval. Given this change, it is much more meaningful to examine the 1982–92 contraction and the 1992–98 expansion separately.

In theory, price and potency should be positively correlated. The simple correlation between these two variables is 0.35 for the entire period, but they are negatively correlated in each of the two subperiods. This is likely to reflect the considerable measurement error in these data, particularly in the potency data (Kleiman 1992).

Limited information is available to explain trends in price and potency. Presumably, price varies over time owing, in part, to variations in resources allocated to apprehension and conviction of dealers and to crop reduction. Pacula (1998b) documents that the first factor explains differences in the price of marijuana among cities in 1987, and Grossman and Chaloupka (1998) report a similar finding in the case of cocaine prices in 1991. Crane, Rivolo, and Comfort (1997) show that increases in interdiction led to increases in the real price of cocaine in a time series for the years 1985–96. Kleiman (1989) presents evidence suggesting a positive correlation between resources allocated to enforcing marijuana laws and the real price of marijuana in the 1980s.

The DEA (1999) hypothesizes that the increase in potency over this time period can be at least partially attributed to the implementation of its Domestic Cannabis Eradication and Suppression Program in 1979. The program began as an aggressive eradication effort in just two states, Hawaii and California. By 1982, it had grown to include eradication efforts in twenty-five states. By 1985, all fifty states were receiving funding for similar eradication programs. Although the program targets both outdoor and indoor cultivation, indoor cultivation is more difficult to detect. One of the main outcomes of this program, therefore, has been the abandonment of large outdoor plots for indoor cultivating areas that are safer and easier to conceal. This movement indoors has led to the more widespread use of hydroponic cultivation, a cultivation method employing a nutrient solution instead of soil that enables growers to produce a more potent form of marijuana.

6.3.4 Conceptual Issues

Three conceptual issues need to be addressed in specifying time-series demand functions for marijuana participation. The first pertains to the appropriateness of including the harm measure in these demand functions. High school seniors' perceptions about the perceived risk of great harm from regular marijuana use are not formed in a vacuum.[8] Instead, these perceptions are likely to depend on attitudes and behaviors of parents, older siblings, and peers. If this is the case, then harm is an endogenous variable that may be correlated with the disturbance term in the structural demand function for marijuana participation that includes it. One factor is that harm may be correlated with an unmeasured characteristic, such as a thrill-seeking personality, that causes both marijuana participation and perceptions of risk. A second factor is that there may be true reverse causality from participation to risk. A youth who smokes marijuana may be less likely to report that it is a harmful behavior than a youth who does not smoke marijuana.

We term the first factor *statistical endogeneity* arising from a recursive model with correlated errors and the second factor *structural endogeneity*. Both factors cause the coefficient of harm in the demand function to be biased and inconsistent. In addition, the price coefficient is biased if it is correlated with harm. A relation between price and harm in which a reduction in the real price leads to a reduction in perceived harm is quite plausible. For example, suppose that a reduction in price encourages participation or consumption given participation by older peers. This should lower high school seniors' perception of harm and increase their participation.[9]

In principle, one could employ simultaneous-equations methods, such as two-stage least squares, to obtain consistent estimates of the structural demand function. However, we lack an instrument for harm. Since harm is endogenous, one wants to allow both for a direct effect of price on participation with harm held constant and for an indirect effect that operates through harm. In this section, we estimate demand functions with and without the harm variable by ordinary least squares. We also estimate equations that include harm but exclude price and potency. This allows us to examine the importance of price as a determinant of youth marijuana participation and to determine how the price coefficients change when harm is included or excluded from the models.

A second conceptual issue pertains to biases in the price coefficient due to measurement error and the endogeneity of this variable. It is plausible that price is subject to measurement error because only its midpoint is available. Moreover, we do not know the quantity employed to calculate the retail price of a one-gram purchase of marijuana. A distinguishing

8. Becker and Mulligan (1997) develop an economic framework that highlights the incentives of parents to make investments that raise the future orientation of their children. Clearly, these investments can also alter attitudes and perceptions governing potentially risky behaviors.
9. A positive correlation between price and harm is also possible. Suppose that an increase in price is due to an expansion in resources allocated to enforcing marijuana laws. If the expected penalty for possession of marijuana rises, and if this penalty is one of the harms associated with use, price and harm would be positively related.

characteristic of the market for illegal drugs is that the average cost of a purchase falls as the size of the purchase increases (DiNardo 1993; Caulkins 1994; Rhodes, Hyatt, and Scheiman 1994; Grossman and Chaloupka 1998). If youths typically purchase one or two grams (two or four joints) at a time and the retail price is estimated from a larger purchase, we underestimate the price actually paid by youths. Trends in the purchase size on which the *IDPPR* price is calculated or trends in the purchase size made by youths create biases due to measurement error. If the error due to these factors or to the absence of mean or median prices is random, the price coefficient is biased toward 0.

We assume that the supply function of marijuana is infinitely elastic and that price varies over time owing to variations in resources allocated to apprehension and conviction of dealers and to crop reduction. Even if the supply function is not infinitely elastic, high school seniors can be viewed as price takers if they represent a small fraction of marijuana users. If this is not the case and the supply function slopes upward, we understate the price coefficient or elasticity in the demand function in absolute value. If the supply function slopes downward owing to externalities (the greater is market consumption, the smaller is the probability of catching a given dealer), the price coefficient or elasticity in the demand function is overstated. On balance, we believe that biases due to measurement error are the most important and that the price coefficients or elasticities that we report are conservative lower-bound estimates.

The final conceptual issue deals with the incorporation of purity or potency into the demand function. Here, it is natural to view purity as an index of quality and to appeal to the literature on the demand for the quantity and quality of a good (Houthakker 1952–53; Theil 1952–53; Rosen 1974). The simplest model in this literature is one in which consumers demand quality-adjusted quantity and base consumption decisions on quality-adjusted price. In our context, quality-adjusted quantity is given by $Q = mq$, where m is the number of marijuana cigarettes smoked, and q is quality or potency as measured by THC content. Quality-adjusted price is given by $p^* = p/q$, where p is the price of a joint. This model suggests a conditional demand function for m by marijuana users whose arguments are p and q. With p held constant, an increase in q lowers, raises, or has no effect on m as the price elasticity of demand for m is less than, greater than, or equal to 1 in absolute value.[10] The model also suggests a demand

---

10. The simplest way to prove this is to write the demand function as

$$\ln Q = \alpha - \varepsilon \ln p^*,$$

where α is a constant. Using the definitions of Q and p^* offered in the text, one can rewrite this demand function as

$$\ln m = \alpha - \varepsilon \ln p + (\varepsilon - 1)\ln q.$$

Table 6.1   **Definitions, Means, and Standard Deviations of Variables in Time-Series Regressions**

Variable	Definition	Mean	Standard Deviation
Annual marijuana participation	Percentage who used marijuana in past year	34.176	6.666
Thirty-day marijuana participation	Percentage who used marijuana in past thirty days	20.547	4.944
Price	Real retail price of one gram of commercial marijuana in 1982–84 dollars	4.349	1.840
Potency	THC potency of commercial marijuana as a percentage	4.088	.828
Harm	Percentage reporting great risk of harm from regular use of marijuana	68.676	7.550
Time	Time in years, 1982 = 1	9.000	5.050
Time squared	Square of time	105.000	93.523

function for participation in which this decision is a negative function of $p*$. Hence, participation is more likely the smaller is p and the larger is q.[11]

6.3.5   Results

Definitions, means, and standard deviations of the variables in the time-series regressions are shown in table 6.1. Tables 6.2 and 6.3 contain demand functions for annual and thirty-day marijuana participation, respectively. The t-ratios of all regression coefficients in these tables are based on Newey and West (1987) standard errors, which allow for heteroscedasticity and for autocorrelation up to and including a lag of three. Standard errors based on longer lags were very similar to those contained in the tables. The first regression in panel A of either table 6.2 or table 6.3 includes the real retail price of commercial marijuana and the potency of commercial marijuana. The second regression adds a linear time trend, and the third adds the square of time. Regressions 4–6 delete price and potency from regressions 1–3 and add the percentage of high school seniors reporting great risk of harm from regular marijuana use. Panel B of either table employs price, potency, and harm in the same models.

According to the first three models in panel A of table 6.2, price always has a negative effect on annual participation that is significant at conven-

---

11. In terms of the model specified in the preceding note, the elasticity of participation with respect to q should equal the elasticity of participation with respect to p with the sign reversed. This constraint could be imposed by employing p/q as the regressor in the demand function. We do not take this approach because our measure of q does not distinguish between wholesale and retail potency and because THC content may not be the only determinant of quality.

Table 6.2   **Annual Marijuana Participation Regressions**

A. Price and Harm Entered Separately						
	(1)	(2)	(3)	(4)	(5)	(6)
Price	−3.205	−3.167	−2.122			
	(−7.83)	(−3.27)	(−2.59)			
Potency	4.074	4.120	−.406			
	(4.04)	(2.59)	(−.37)			
Time		−.020	−3.326		−.861	−1.400
		(−.06)	(−3.10)		(−4.50)	(−1.08)
Time squared			.192			.032
			(3.30)			(.41)
Harm				−.590	−.746	−.656
				(−2.95)	(−5.91)	(−3.19)
R^2	.723	.723	.851	.446	.839	.841
F-statistic	93.54	60.70	31.96	8.70	20.27	12.03
Price elasticity[a]	−.407	−.402	−.269			

B. Price and Harm Entered Together		
	(7)	(8)	(9)
Price	−2.408	−1.595	−1.626
	(−5.81)	(−2.08)	(−2.01)
Potency	.263	.776	.411
	(.26)	(.76)	(.32)
Time		−.385	−.949
		(−1.28)	(−.79)
Time squared			.036
			(.53)
Harm	−.517	−.567	−.485
	(−4.47)	(−4.20)	(−3.55)
R^2	.866	.881	.882
F-statistic	96.74	45.94	42.38
Price elasticity[a]	−.306	−.203	−.206

Note: Newey-West (1987) t-statistics are given in parentheses. Standard errors on which they are based allow for heteroscedasticity and for autocorrelation up to and including a lag of 3. Intercepts are not shown.

[a]Evaluated at sample means.

tional levels. As expected, the regression coefficient of potency is positive and significant except in the model that includes a quadratic time trend. Evaluated at the sample means, the price elasticity of annual marijuana participation ranges between −0.27 and −0.41. In the two models in which the potency coefficient is positive, its elasticity equals 0.49. This is somewhat larger than the absolute value of the price elasticity of 0.41 in model 1 or 0.40 in model 2, but the price and potency elasticities do not differ dramatically. This gives some support to the notion that participation depends on quality-adjusted price.

Table 6.3 Thirty-Day Marijuana Participation Regressions

A. Price and Harm Entered Separately

	(1)	(2)	(3)	(4)	(5)	(6)
Price	−2.280	−2.079	−1.156			
	(−6.73)	(−2.80)	(−2.16)			
Potency	3.100	3.341	−0.657			
	(4.31)	(2.85)	(−1.04)			
Time		−.105	−3.025		−.632	−.881
		(−.38)	(−4.28)		(−5.76)	(−1.20)
Time squared			.169			.015
			(4.49)			(.34)
Harm				−.471	−.586	−.545
				(−3.32)	(−8.79)	(−4.79)
R^2	.679	.682	.863	.518	.904	.904
F-statistic	78.02	57.30	26.30	11.03	40.74	26.55
Price elasticity[a]	−.483	−.441	−.245			

B. Price and Harm Entered Together

	(7)	(8)	(9)
Price	−1.577	−.658	−.673
	(−4.47)	(−1.33)	(−1.34)
Potency	−.263	.318	.140
	(−.31)	(.52)	(.21)
Time		−.435	−.710
		(−2.15)	(−1.07)
Time squared			.017
			(.51)
Harm	−.456	−.512	−.473
	(−5.18)	(−6.04)	(−5.66)
R^2	.855	.916	.917
F-statistic	155.50	73.65	57.86
Price elasticity[a]	−.331	−.139	−.143

Note: Newey-West (1987) *t*-statistics are given in parentheses. Standard errors on which they are based allow for heteroscedasticity and for autocorrelation up to and including a lag of 3. Intercepts are not shown.

[a]Evaluated at sample means.

The regression coefficient of harm is negative and significant in the last three models in panel A of table 6.2. A 10 percentage point increase in the harm measure lowers annual participation by between 6 and 7 percentage points.

When harm is entered together with price and potency in the models in panel B of table 6.2, the price coefficient retains its negative sign and is significant at the 5 percent level on a one-tailed test. The price elasticities are reduced by between 23 and 50 percent and now range from −0.20 to −0.31. The potency effects are positive but not significant when harm is held constant. The two positive potency coefficients in panel A are much larger than the corresponding coefficients in panel B. Harm retains its significance when price and potency are held constant, but the magnitude of the effect is reduced by between 12 and 24 percent.

The results in table 6.3 are similar to those in table 6.2. The price elasticity of thirty-day participation is somewhat larger than the price elasticity of annual participation except in models that include a quadratic time trend or harm and time. But the observed differences are not substantial. The largest occurs when the only other regressor is potency: −0.48 for the price elasticity of thirty-day participation compared to −0.41 for the elasticity of annual participation.

One way in which to evaluate the nine models in each table is to see how well they predict the reduction in marijuana participation between 1982 and 1992 and the increase between 1992 and 1998. Table 6.4 contains estimates of the predicted changes in annual and thirty-day marijuana prevalence based on the estimates contained in tables 6.2 and 6.3 above. The component labeled *price* is obtained by multiplying the change in price between the initial and the terminal years by the regression coefficient of price. The *potency* and *harm* components have similar interpretations. In general, the predicted changes in participation associated with the changes in perceived risk are relatively stable across specifications, while those associated with price and potency are more sensitive to the choice of specification.

Between 1982 and 1992, annual participation declined by 22.4 percentage points. On the basis of the estimates from the specifications that include price, potency, and harm, the changes in price during this period suggest a 6.9–10.4 percentage point reduction in annual participation, while those in potency imply a reduction of 0.3–0.9 percentage points. Similarly, the changes in harm during this period suggest a 7.8–9.1 percentage point reduction in annual prevalence. Because an increase in price unadjusted for potency or a reduction in potency raises quality-adjusted price, the price and potency components can be summed to form a single, quality-adjusted price component. In the most complete specifications that control for time trends (linearly or quadratically), the quality-adjusted price changes predict a 7.5–7.8 percentage point reduction in prevalence, while the changes in harm predict a 7.8–9.1 percentage point reduction.

Similarly, in the period 1982–92, monthly participation declined by 16.6 percentage points. On the basis of the estimates from specifications that include price, potency, and harm, with or without controlling for time trends, the changes in price during this period predict a 2.8–6.8 percentage point reduction in monthly participation, while the changes in potency suggest relatively little change. The changes in harm predict a 7.3–8.2 percentage point reduction in monthly prevalence. In the specifications that include a linear or quadratic time trend, the changes in quality-adjusted

Table 6.4   **Percentage-Point Effects of Price, Potency, and Harm on Marijuana Participation**

Model	(1)	(2)	(3)	(4)	(5)	(6)	(7)	(8)	(9)
				A. Annual Participation					
			1981–92, Observed Change in Participation = 22.40						
Marijuana price	−13.88	−13.72	−9.19				−10.43	−6.91	−7.04
Marijuana potency		−4.57	.45				−.29	−.86	−.46
Harm				−9.49	−12.02	−10.57	−8.32	−9.12	−7.81
Total predicted change	−18.41	−18.29	−8.74	−9.49	−12.02	−10.57	−19.04	−16.90	−15.31
			1992–98, Observed Change in Participation = 15.60						
Marijuana price	3.10	3.06	2.05				2.33	1.54	1.57
Marijuana potency		8.40	−.83				0.54	1.58	.84
Harm				10.61	13.44	11.81	9.30	10.20	8.74
Total predicted change	11.41	11.46	1.22	10.61	13.44	11.81	12.16	13.33	11.55
				B. Thirty-Day Participation					
			1982–92, Observed Change in Participation = −16.60						
Marijuana price	−9.88	−9.01	−5.01				−6.83	−2.85	−2.91
Marijuana potency		−3.71	.73				.29	−.35	−.16
Harm				−7.59	−9.44	−8.11	−7.34	−8.25	−7.61
Total predicted change	−13.32	−12.72	−4.28	−7.59	−9.44	−8.11	−13.88	−11.45	−10.68
			1992–98, Observed Change in Participation = 10.90						
Marijuana price	2.20	2.01	1.12				1.52	.64	.65
Marijuana potency		6.82	−1.34				−.54	.65	.29
Harm				8.48	10.56	9.80	8.21	9.22	8.51
Total predicted change	8.53	8.82	−.22	8.48	10.56	9.80	9.19	10.51	9.45

Note: Estimates for annual participation are based on the specifications in table 6.2; estimates for thirty-day participation are based on the specifications in table 6.3.

price predict a 3.1–3.2 percentage point reduction in participation, while those in harm predict a 7.6–8.2 percent reduction.

Between 1992 and 1998, annual participation rose by 15.6 percentage points, while monthly participation rose by 10.9 percentage points. Focusing on models comparable to those discussed for the earlier period, the changes in the quality-adjusted price during this period predict an increase of between 2.4 and 3.1 percentage points in annual participation and an increase of between 0.9 and 1.3 percentage points in monthly participation. Similarly, the changes in harm predict increases of 8.7–10.2 percentage points in annual participation and 8.2–9.2 percentage points in monthly participation.

To summarize, the changes in quality-adjusted price and perceived risk predict much of the contraction in youth marijuana use in the period 1982–92 and the expansion in use after 1992. Both factors appear roughly equally important in accounting for the reduction in annual participation in the earlier period, with perceived risk somewhat more important in accounting for the reduction in monthly participation during this period. Changes in harm, however, appear to play a much stronger role than changes in quality-adjusted price during the more recent expansion in youth marijuana use.

6.4   Repeated Cross-Sectional Analysis of Marijuana Demand

To investigate individual demand for marijuana among youths, we use micro-level data from the 1985–96 MTF. These data allow us to incorporate more determinants than those employed in the time-series analysis. At the same time, we base estimates of the price elasticity of demand for marijuana on prices that vary among cities as well as over time in the context of a fixed-effects estimation strategy. By employing a set of dichotomous indicators for states of the United States in all models, we hold constant unmeasured variables that may be correlated with consumption and price. Finally, we include measures of cigarette and beer prices to investigate whether marijuana, cigarettes, and beer are substitutes or complements for youths. We examine two outcomes: past-year participation and past-month participation, as in the time-series analyses presented above.[12]

6.4.1   Measurement of Variables and Empirical Implementation

Table 6.5 contains definitions, means, and standard deviations of all variables. MTF survey respondents report the number of occasions in the

---

12. Additional measures of youth marijuana use, including frequency of use and participation in daily use, could be constructed from the MTF data. Given the focus of this chapter, these outcomes are not considered. A more complete analysis of these measures should be a priority for future research.

Table 6.5　　　　**Descriptive Statistics**

	Pooled Sample (N = 138,933)	
Variable	Mean	S.D.
Indicators of marijuana use		
Annual prevalence of marijuana use	.311	.463
Thirty-day prevalence of marijuana use	.184	.388
Demographics		
Male	.484	.500
Black non-Hispanic	.097	.296
Hispanic	.063	.242
Other race	.068	.251
Age	17.948	.559
Siblings: total number of siblings	2.490	1.839
Father had some high school	.115	.319
Father finished high school plus (finished high school or attended or graduated college)	.840	.367
Mother had some high school	.101	.302
Mother finished high school plus	.867	.340
Mother worked full-time	.515	.500
Mother worked part-time	.266	.442
Live alone	.006	.079
Live with father only	.035	.184
Live with mother only	.158	.364
Other living arrangement	.044	.205
City: live in a city	.591	.492
Suburb: live in a suburb	.211	.408
Lifestyle factors		
Infrequent religious service attendance	.538	.499
Frequent religious service attendance	.335	.472
Married or engaged	.075	.263
Hours worked per week	13.298	10.521
Earned income: real weekly earned income	37.299	34.221
Other income: real weekly other income	10.842	17.882
Attitudes and perceptions		
Harm: perceived risk of harm from regular marijuana use (0 = no risk, 1 = slight risk, 2 = moderate risk, 3 = great risk)	2.607	.742
Measures of peer use		
Peer marijuana use: fraction who used marijuana in past month in respondent's school	.180	.090
Price of marijuana		
Marijuana price: real retail price of one gram of commercial marijuana	3.325	1.280
Marijuana potency: THC potency of commercial marijuana as a percentage	3.856	.470
Substitute/complement prices		
Cigarette tax: real state tax on a pack of cigarettes	.180	.085
Beer tax: real state tax on case of 24 12-ounce cans of beer	.493	.498
Drinking age: state minimum legal age for purchase and consumption of beer, alcohol content 3.2 percent or less	20.812	.567

past year and in the past thirty days on which they used marijuana (grass, pot) or hashish (hash, hash oil). These are ordered categorical variables with seven outcomes: no occasions, one to two occasions, three to five occasions, six to nine occasions, ten to nineteen occasions, twenty to thirty-nine occasions, and forty or more occasions. Participants are youths who reported a positive number of occasions.[13]

Demographic characteristics included in this analysis are gender (male or female), race (white non-Hispanic, black non-Hispanic, Hispanic, and other), age, parents' education (less than a high school education, at least a high school education), total number of siblings, family structure (live alone, live with mother, live with father, both parents present, or other living arrangement), mother's work status while growing up (full-time, part-time, or stay-at-home), and place of residence (rural, suburb, city). Lifestyle factors include marital status (married or engaged vs. being single), attendance at religious services (no attendance, infrequent attendance, and frequent attendance), hours worked per week, real weekly earned income, and real weekly other income (primarily income from allowances).[14] The labels given to certain variables are somewhat arbitrary. For example, weekly earnings and other income reflect command over real resources. We use each income measure and hours of work as regressors because exposure to the work environment may affect marijuana consumption by channels other than pure income effects.

To capture youths' perceptions of and attitudes toward marijuana, we include an index of the perceived risk of harm from regular use of marijuana. This item was not included on all survey forms in all survey years, so the sample size is reduced when it is included in the analysis.[15] The indicator of perceived risk is set equal to 0 for youths who report no risk, equal to 1 for youths who report a slight risk, equal to 2 for those who report moderate risk, and equal to 3 for those who report great risk associated with regular marijuana use.

It is clear from the existing literature that peer use of substances has an important effect on the susceptibility of youths to the use of different substances. Although we do not have any direct measure of friends' use of particular substances, it is possible to construct school-level measures by

13. One-sixth of the MTF sample are asked separate questions about marijuana and hashish. These answers have been aggregated to form indicators of the use of any form of marijuana.

14. As in sec. 6.3 above, variables are converted from nominal to real dollars by deflating by the consumer price index for the United States as a whole (1982–84 = 1).

15. From 1985 to 1989, five different questionnaires were administered in each year, enabling investigators to increase the range of questions being asked without making any given questionnaire too long. From 1985 to 1988, only one form included the question on perceived risk (form 5). In 1989, a sixth questionnaire form was added to the survey, and the risk item was included on this sixth form. In 1990, the perceived-risk question was added to three of the existing forms, making it available on five of the forms. As noted above, additional attitudinal measures are contained in the MTF surveys, and the use of alternative measures could

aggregating responses to each of these questions for all youths in the same school that participated in the survey.[16] An indicator of the fraction of individuals reporting marijuana use in the past thirty days is used as a proxy for peer use of marijuana. This variable is almost certainly endogenous. Unfortunately, appropriate instruments are not available. Given this, some of the models presented below do not include the peer-marijuana-use measure.

There were originally 193,796 observations in the 1985–96 pooled sample. Approximately 28 percent of this sample is lost owing to missing observations on gender, race, age, marital status, number of siblings, parents' education, mother's work status, living arrangements, place of residence, religious participation, employment status, and income. Means of all variables except for marijuana participation and harm are based on 138,933 observations. Marijuana participation is known for 136,595 of these cases. The harm measure is available for 73,068 cases.

The commercial marijuana prices described in the last section are matched to MTF counties in which the high schools are located on the basis of an algorithm that matches each county in the United States to the three nearest cities in the nineteen-cities database. Three matches are made rather than one owing to missing data for certain cities in some years.[17] The price of marijuana in a given year is taken from the best or closest match. Since the wholesale commercial price has fewer missing values than the retail commercial price, the former price is used in the demand functions estimated in this section. All price coefficients in the tables have, however, been multiplied by 0.5—the coefficient of the retail price in a regression in which the wholesale price is the dependent variable.[18] The potency of commercial marijuana is the same variable employed in section 6.3 above and varies by time but not by city.

To capture potential cross-price effects associated with the consumption of cigarettes and alcohol, we include the real state tax on a pack of twenty cigarettes, the real state tax on a case of twenty-four twelve-ounce cans of beer, and the state minimum legal age for the purchase and consumption of beer with an alcohol content of 3.2 percent or less. The beer tax and legal drinking age are employed as measures of the cost of alcohol because beer is the beverage of choice among youths who consume alcohol. Nominal state-level cigarette taxes were obtained from the Tobacco Institute's annual *Tax Burden on Tobacco* and deflated by the national CPI (1982–

---

have some effect on the estimates presented in this chapter. However, space constraints prohibit a complete examination of all these measures. Further examination of these alternative attitudinal measures should be a high priority for future research in this area.

16. Classes are chosen within each school to be representative of the high school students within that school. This is a standard part of the multistage random-sampling procedure.

17. If the price is missing for all three matches, the observation is deleted.

18. Let r be the retail price, w be the wholesale price, and m be a measure of marijuana consumption. Then $\partial m/\partial r = (\partial m/\partial w)(\partial w/\partial r)$.

84 = 1). Since taxes are reported as of 1 November and the MTF interviews take place in the spring of each year, we use the average of the current year's tax and the last year's tax to obtain a better estimate of the tax at the time of the MTF interview. We similarly construct a measure of the average real state tax on a case of twenty-four twelve-ounce cans of beer using quarterly tax information from the Beer Institute's *Brewers' Almanac*. The real state tax in a given year is calculated as the average of the current year's first and second quarter and the previous year's third and fourth quarter.[19]

The minimum legal drinking age for beer was taken from Chaloupka, Saffer, and Grossman (1993). By July 1988, all states had minimum drinking ages of twenty-one. Many enacted grandfather clauses, however, exempting state residents of legal age prior to the increase. The drinking-age measure accounts for these clauses and does not become twenty-one in all states until 1991.[20]

The full price of consuming marijuana consists of the money price and the monetary value of the expected penalties for possession or use (the probability of apprehension and conviction multiplied by the fine or the monetary value of the prison sentence). For a variety of reasons, we have excluded measures of expected penalties for possession of marijuana from the demand functions. The marijuana decriminalization indicator discussed in section 6.2 above is a time-invariant variable during our sample period. Thus, it is perfectly collinear with the set of state dummies that are included in all models.[21]

In the case of monetary fines for possession of marijuana, Chaloupka, Grossman, and Tauras (1999) find that youths who reside in states with higher fines are less likely to consume marijuana. Their estimated effects are, however, very small and do not control for unmeasured state characteristics. Farrelly et al. (1999) find no effects when these controls are included. The fine measure assembled by Farrelly and his colleagues is missing for all states for the years 1986, 1987, and 1989. There is no trend in the real fine during the sample period. Therefore, it cannot explain the trend in marijuana use. Moreover, preliminary results for the period 1990–96 revealed that the real fine for the possession of one ounce of marijuana did not have a significant effect on participation or frequency when state fixed effects were included.

19. The benefits of adopting similar algorithms in the case of the marijuana price were outweighed by the amount of measurement error that they would create in an already "noisy" variable.

20. The drinking age is a weighted average of the daily effective drinking age in the state and takes account of the month in which the age was raised.

21. Alaska recriminalized the possession of a small quantity of marijuana in 1990, but that state does not appear in the MTF survey during the period 1985–96. Arizona decriminalized marijuana possession in 1996 but is not contained in the MTF survey after that year.

The probability of arrest for marijuana possession in an area is not observed since the number of users is not known. The arrest rate for possession (arrests divided by population) is available at the county level and could be employed as a regressor. A natural objection to this measure is that it reflects reverse causality: an increase in the number of users causes the number of arrests to rise. A somewhat more subtle analysis recognizes that, if the arrest rate replaces the probability of arrest in the demand function, the coefficient of the former variable is positive if the elasticity of the probability of use with respect to the probability of arrest is greater than 1 in absolute value. On the other hand, the arrest coefficient is negative if the elasticity just defined is less than 1 in absolute value. Nevertheless, the estimated arrest coefficient is inconsistent unless an instrumental-variables procedure is employed. This is because the arrest rate is correlated with unmeasured determinants of marijuana participation and because of reverse causality from participation to arrests.

These points are spelled out in more detail in the appendix. Here, we note that we lack a suitable instrument for the arrest rate. We also note that there is no trend in this measure during the sample period. Finally, in preliminary estimates, we included the state-specific per capita number of juveniles in custody for the years 1985, 1987, 1989, 1991, and 1993, obtained from Levitt (1998). This variable has a negative and significant effect on marijuana participation, but it results in the loss of seven of the twelve cross sections and has no trend. Moreover, it reflects the combined effect of the removal of potential users from the noninstitutional population and deterrence. Therefore, we do not employ it in the final models presented in section 6.4.2 below.

To parallel the models obtained in section 6.3 above, and to include marijuana potency as a determinant, we obtain three basic equations. The first omits a time trend, the second includes a linear trend in which 1985 = 0 and 1996 = 11, and the third includes time and time squared. All equations contain dichotomous variables for forty-five of the forty-six states in the repeat cross sections. Robust or Huber (1967) standard errors of logit coefficients are obtained. They allow for state/year clustering.

The conceptual issues raised with regard to the appropriateness of including the harm measure in the time-series demand functions in section 6.3.4 above also apply to the micro-level demand functions. This same concern applies to including the measure of peer marijuana use. The many pitfalls involved in obtaining peer effects have been discussed in detail by Manski (1993), and our estimated effects should be interpreted with caution.

6.4.2   Results

Table 6.6 contains maximum-likelihood logit equations for annual marijuana participation, and table 6.7 contains comparable estimates for

	Table 6.6	Annual Marijuana Participation Logit Equations ($N = 135{,}970$)		
		(1)	(2)	(3)
Male		.176	.177	.182
		(10.34)	(10.48)	(10.83)
Black		−.738	−.739	−.739
		(−16.58)	(−16.68)	(−17.16)
Hispanic		−.187	−.179	−.161
		(−4.11)	(−3.94)	(−3.61)
Other race		−.547	−.540	−.540
		(−11.11)	(−11.02)	(−11.43)
Age		−.026	−.022	−.021
		(−2.31)	(−1.96)	(−1.85)
Siblings		.046	.044	.043
		(11.31)	(10.93)	(10.50)
Father had some high school		.100	.100	.103
		(2.48)	(2.49)	(2.53)
Father finished high school plus		.114	.118	.120
		(3.01)	(3.09)	(3.10)
Mother had some high school		.304	.298	.305
		(6.15)	(6.06)	(6.16)
Mother finished high school plus		.370	.366	.370
		(7.79)	(7.76)	(7.83)
Mother worked part-time		.101	.101	.098
		(5.49)	(5.50)	(5.27)
Mother worked full-time		.137	.142	.137
		(8.92)	(9.23)	(8.84)
Live alone		.434	.439	.441
		(5.75)	(5.83)	(5.82)
Live with father only		.254	.256	.260
		(7.76)	(7.80)	(7.98)
Live with mother only		.176	.176	.178
		(9.87)	(9.89)	(9.99)
Other living arrangement		.335	.335	.340
		(10.93)	(10.89)	(11.06)
City		.377	.374	.375
		(14.04)	(14.00)	(14.33)
Suburb		.474	.471	.483
		(15.08)	(15.23)	(15.76)
Infrequent religious service attendance		−.190	−.194	−.193
		(−9.89)	(−9.99)	(−9.96)
Frequent religious service attendance		−.991	−.995	−1.002
		(−40.08)	(−40.35)	(−40.74)
Married or engaged		−.082	−.082	−.086
		(−3.06)	(−3.05)	(−3.18)
Hours worked per week		.011	.011	.011
		(11.31)	(11.67)	(11.77)
Earned income		.002	.002	.002
		(7.65)	(7.23)	(7.26)
Other income		.009	.009	.009
		(23.53)	(23.50)	(23.44)

Table 6.6   (continued)

	(1)	(2)	(3)
Cigarette tax	−.042	.337	.068
	(−.08)	(.69)	(.26)
Beer tax	−.679	−.416	−.198
	(−2.29)	(−1.34)	(−1.26)
Drinking age	−.129	−.063	.096
	(−3.64)	(−1.65)	(2.74)
Marijuana price	−.145	−.103	−.027
	(−7.95)	(−5.15)	(−1.77)
Marijuana potency	.181	.331	.002
	(4.80)	(6.21)	(.05)
Time		−.043	−.286
		(−3.78)	(−17.68)
Time squared			.023
			(16.52)
Pseudo-R^2	.066	.067	.071
χ^2	8,355.91	8,425.21	8,633.30
Price elasticity[a]	−.331	−.235	−.063

Note: All equations include state dummies. Asymptotic t-ratios are in parentheses. Huber (1967) or robust standard errors on which they are based allow for state/year clustering. Intercepts are not shown.

[a] Evaluated at sample means.

thirty-day marijuana participation. Three models are shown in each table. The first omits a time trend, the second includes a linear trend, and the third includes the trend and its square. The harm and peer-marijuana-use variables are excluded from the models reported in these tables.

Given the pronounced trends in the real price of marijuana, the potency of marijuana, and the minimum legal drinking age during the relatively short period at issue, the coefficients of these variables are sensitive to the exclusion or inclusion of a trend term and to the exact specification of the trend. A case can be made that the specifications with the quadratic trend represent an "overparameterization" of the data since the computations presented in section 6.3 above and those at the end of this section suggest that trends in the variables just mentioned provide plausible explanations of trends in participation. Moreover, we have reasonably good proxies for such hard-to-measure variables as attitudes (as indicated by perceived risk of harm) and peer behavior. Nevertheless, we present all three models to indicate the degree to which the estimates vary and to allow readers to make up their own minds on this issue.

The marijuana price coefficient is negative and significant in the three models in table 6.6 and in the first two models in table 6.7. Evaluated at sample means, the price elasticity of annual marijuana participation

	(1)	(2)	(3)
Table 6.7 **Thirty-Day Marijuana-Participation Logit Equations** ($N = 135{,}946$)			
Male	.280	.281	.286
	(14.89)	(15.07)	(15.49)
Black	−.659	−.660	−.658
	(−12.35)	(−12.38)	(−12.83)
Hispanic	−.197	−.189	−.169
	(−4.04)	(−3.94)	(−3.62)
Other race	−.471	−.464	−.465
	(−8.88)	(−8.78)	(−9.13)
Age	−.025	−.021	−.020
	(−1.90)	(−1.62)	(−1.51)
Siblings	.042	.041	.039
	(9.14)	(8.85)	(8.43)
Father had some high school	.134	.134	.138
	(2.64)	(2.65)	(2.71)
Father finished high school plus	.108	.111	.113
	(2.37)	(2.43)	(2.47)
Mother had some high school	.345	.339	.346
	(5.62)	(5.55)	(5.64)
Mother finished high school plus	.395	.392	.396
	(6.44)	(6.42)	(6.50)
Mother worked part-time	.077	.078	.074
	(3.37)	(3.39)	(3.17)
Mother worked full-time	.101	.106	.100
	(5.14)	(5.33)	(4.99)
Live alone	.603	.607	.611
	(6.65)	(6.70)	(6.69)
Live with father only	.229	.231	.236
	(5.94)	(5.97)	(6.15)
Live with mother only	.186	.186	.187
	(9.56)	(9.58)	(9.73)
Other living arrangement	.335	.335	.339
	(9.66)	(9.66)	(9.73)
City	.373	.371	.373
	(12.51)	(12.52)	(13.11)
Suburb	.468	.466	.481
	(12.54)	(12.67)	(13.52)
Infrequent religious service attendance	−.293	−.297	−.296
	(−13.66)	(−13.82)	(−13.82)
Frequent religious service attendance	−1.114	−1.117	−1.124
	(−39.15)	(−39.41)	(−39.77)
Married or engaged	−.185	−.185	−.189
	(−5.77)	(−5.76)	(−5.88)
Hours worked per week	.010	.010	.011
	(9.49)	(9.78)	(9.86)
Earned income	.002	.002	.002
	(6.36)	(5.99)	(5.98)
Other income	.010	.010	.010
	(24.64)	(24.59)	(24.40)

Table 6.7   (continued)

	(1)	(2)	(3)
Cigarette tax	.200	.532	.187
	(.38)	(1.08)	(.76)
Beer tax	−.523	−.281	−.021
	(−1.72)	(−.89)	(−.12)
Drinking age	−.137	−.078	.095
	(−3.71)	(−1.86)	(2.56)
Marijuana price	−.123	−.085	−.001
	(−6.15)	(−4.00)	(−.04)
Marijuana potency	.227	.364	−.010
	(5.70)	(6.22)	(−.22)
Time		−.039	−.307
		(−3.08)	(−17.18)
Time squared			.026
			(16.74)
Pseudo-R^2	.062	.063	.068
F-statistic	79.21	79.57	85.59
Price elasticity[a]	−.335	−.228	−.002

Note: All equations include state dummies. Asymptotic t-ratios are in parentheses. Huber (1967) or robust standard errors on which they are based allow for state/year clustering. Intercepts are not shown.

[a]Evaluated at sample means.

ranges from −0.33 in the equation with no trend to −0.06 in the equation with a quadratic trend. The elasticity estimates for thirty-day participation are quite similar and follow the same pattern, ranging from −0.34 in the equation with no trend to −0.002 in the equation with a quadratic trend. The estimates in tables 6.6 and 6.7 are much more sensitive to the inclusion of trend terms than are those in tables 6.2 and 6.3 above, most likely because the data in the latter span a longer period of time.

As in the time-series regressions, an increase in the potency of commercial marijuana increases participation, except when a quadratic trend is entered. The potency elasticity of 0.48 in model 1 for annual participation is fairly similar to the absolute value of the price elasticity of 0.33 in that specification. These results are consistent with the framework outlined in section 6.3 above in which participation decisions are based on quality-adjusted price. The potency elasticity of 0.88 in the second model in table 6.6 is not consistent with this framework. A similar pattern is observed for thirty-day participation.

There is some evidence from both tables that beer and marijuana are complements. All six of the beer-tax coefficients are negative, albeit generally not significant. In the annual-participation models that control for time, the beer-tax participation effects are significant at approximately the

20 percent level on a two-tailed test but not at the 10 percent level.[22] An increase in the legal drinking age has significant negative effects on annual and thirty-day participation, except in the models with the quadratic time trend. In those models, the effect is positive and significant, implying substitution rather than complementarity. This finding again suggests that it is difficult to sort out unmeasured trend effects from those of variables with significant trends.

Five of the six cigarette-tax coefficients are positive, but none are close to significant at conventional levels, suggesting that cigarettes and marijuana are neither substitutes nor complements.

Our finding of negative beer-tax effects is similar to that reported by Pacula (1998a, 1998b) and Farrelly et al. (1999). Pacula also reports an inverse relation between the drinking age and marijuana participation. Di-Nardo and Lemieux (1992) report a positive relation between these two variables, and we have no explanation of why their results differ from ours. Chaloupka et al. (1999) and Farrelly et al. (1999) contain evidence of either no relation or complementarity between cigarettes and marijuana. The former study does not, however, control for state fixed effects, and neither study includes a measure of the money price of marijuana.

The effects of the individual and family characteristics are consistent with those found in the literature and will not be discussed in any detail. Youths with more-educated parents, youths who do not live with both parents, and youths whose mothers worked full- or part-time while they grew up are more likely to have tried marijuana in the past year, while youths who are married or engaged are less likely to have done so. Similar differentials are observed for thirty-day participation.

Hours worked per week, weekly earned income, and weekly other income (primarily income from allowances) have positive coefficients in all demand functions. The earned-income effect would be larger if hours worked were omitted. As already pointed out, the effect of earnings might reflect forces associated with the workplace environment. This comment does not apply to other income, so its coefficients can be attributed to command over real resources. The other-income elasticity of annual participation equals 0.03. While this elasticity is modest, other income accounts for only 22.5 percent of total weekly income. Hence, the corresponding elasticity with respect to total income is 0.13.

On the basis of t-ratios, frequent religious-service attendance is the most important correlate of marijuana participation. The ratio of the odds of annual marijuana participation for those who attend services frequently compared to those who do not of 0.36 is dramatic. Evaluated at sample means, the probability of annual marijuana participation for a youth who

---

22. A two-tailed test is appropriate because the sign of the coefficient is ambiguous in theory.

never attends religious services is 0.41, while the probability for a youth who attends these services frequently is 0.21. A similar pattern is observed for thirty-day participation.

Since there is no cross-sectional variation in potency, we also explored a specification in which potency was deleted from the set of independent variables and dichotomous indicators for each of the twelve years from 1985 through 1996 were included. This logit equation was forced through the origin. The results (not shown) are very similar to those in the specifications with the quadratic time trend in tables 6.6 and 6.7 and produce similar elasticity estimates.

Following Moulton (1986), we regressed the coefficients of the time dummies on potency. These regressions, which contained twelve observations, were weighted by the square root of the inverse of the standard errors of the coefficients of the time dummies. The potency coefficient was positive and not significant, suggesting that the time effects cannot be explained by the trend in potency. A positive and insignificant potency effect also emerges from the model with the quadratic trend. These findings imply that the most flexible trend specification adds little to the quadratic specification.

Table 6.8 contains selected coefficients from annual- and thirty-day-participation logit equations that include the index of perceived risk of harm from the regular use of marijuana (harm) and peer marijuana use in specifications that are otherwise the same as those in tables 6.6 and 6.7 above. The sample size is reduced by approximately 50 percent when the harm index is included because it is not included on all MTF forms. When the models excluding harm and peer marijuana use in tables 6.6 and 6.7 were estimated on the smaller sample, the coefficients of the variables in the price vector were almost identical to those presented in the tables.

The models in table 6.8 show that harm and peer marijuana use are highly correlated with marijuana participation. An increase in the perceived risk of harm significantly lowers the probability of participation, while an increase in peer marijuana use significantly raises this probability. Evaluated at sample means, the marginal effect of an increase in peer marijuana use on the probability of marijuana use in the past year is approximately equal to 0.55 in each of the three models. In other words, if the fraction of peers who used marijuana rose from 0.31 (the sample mean) to 0.47 (a one-standard-deviation increase), the probability that a youth used marijuana in the past year would rise from 0.31 to 0.39. Similar effects are observed for thirty-day participation.

Not surprisingly, the significant price effects are reduced in absolute value when harm and peer marijuana use are added to the set of regressors. In discussing this phenomenon, we focus on the models without the quadratic trend term. Unlike the pseudo R^2 measures in tables 6.6 and 6.7 above, those in table 6.8 are the same (to three decimal places) in models

Table 6.8   **Selected Logit Coefficients from Marijuana Participation Equations with Harm and Peer Marijuana Use**

	(1)	(2)	(3)
A. Annual Participation (*N* = 71,452)			
Marijuana price	−.092	−.064	−.053
	(−6.80)	(−4.65)	(−3.37)
Marijuana potency	−.134	−.008	−.035
	(−6.26)	(−.26)	(−1.14)
Harm	−1.100	−1.104	−1.103
	(−65.64)	(−65.89)	(−65.92)
Peer marijuana use	4.498	4.484	4.383
	(30.59)	(30.14)	(27.97)
Pseudo R^2	.188	.188	.188
Price elasticity[a]	−.210	−.146	−.121
Market price elasticity[a]	−.466	−.322	−.260
B. Thirty-Day Participation (*N* = 71,478)			
Marijuana price	−.076	−.011	−.029
	(−2.72)	(−.38)	(−.93)
Marijuana potency	−.187	−.042	−.018
	(−8.29)	(−1.20)	(−.50)
Harm	−1.135	−1.139	−1.140
	(−71.19)	(−71.20)	(−71.24)
Peer marijuana use	5.665	5.647	5.731
	(34.22)	(34.05)	(32.40)
Pseudo R^2	.221	.222	.222
Price elasticity[a]	−.102	−.014	−.040
Market price elasticity[a]	−.694	−.093	−.292

Note: All equations include state dummies, real cigarette and beer taxes, minimum legal drinking age, and the family and individual characteristics contained in the equations in tables 6.6 and 6.7. Asymptotic *t*-ratios are given in parentheses. Huber (1967) or robust standard errors on which they are based allow for state/year clustering.

[a]Evaluated at sample means.

with and without the quadratic trend. The coefficients on the time-squared variable in model 3 are almost 90 percent smaller than the corresponding coefficients in tables 6.6 and 6.7. The coefficients of time itself in model 3 are over more than 70 percent smaller than the same coefficients in the third model in tables 6.6 and 6.7. While the inclusion of the square of time has a dramatic effect on the coefficient of time in table 6.6, it has less of an effect in the specifications contained in table 6.8. These results imply that the quadratic trend specification adds little in equations that include harm and peer marijuana use.

The price elasticities of marijuana participation in table 6.8 are smaller than those contained in tables 6.6 and 6.7. The estimates in table 6.8, however, hold peer participation constant. When the price of marijuana falls, peer participation increases. Thus, there is both a direct effect of price on participation with peer participation held constant and an indirect effect that operates through peer participation. The price elasticity of the market demand function for participation incorporates both effects.

Let ε be the price elasticity of the demand function that holds peer participation constant, and let α be the marginal effect of peer participation. Then the market price elasticity is $\varepsilon/(1 - \alpha)$. The market price elasticity in each of the models is contained in the last row of each panel in table 6.8. The annual-participation market price elasticities range from -0.466 to -0.260, while those for thirty-day participation range from -0.694 to -0.093. These estimates are larger than the corresponding values in tables 6.6 and 6.7, with the exception of the second model for thirty-day participation. They suggest that the market price elasticity may be underestimated when it is obtained by simply excluding peer participation from the demand function. This conclusion is very tentative given the likely endogeneity of the peer-marijuana-use measure.

We conclude this section by evaluating the contribution of key determinants to the reduction in marijuana participation between 1982 and 1992 and to the expansion in participation since 1992. National values of marijuana participation and the determinants considered in 1982, 1992, and 1998 are shown in table 6.9. Our analysis is based on the three models in tables 6.6–6.8 above.

Before the results are presented, a number of comments on the computations that underlie them are in order. First, the figures in table 6.10 pertain to a period that is longer than the one spanned by the repeated cross sections. Results for the 1985–92 contraction and the 1992–96 expansion are, however, very similar to those reported in table 6.10. Second, the percentage of youths who used marijuana in the past year or the past thirty days (the probability of participation multiplied by 100) are nonlinear functions of their determinants in the logit functions. Given this and our aim to isolate the contribution of specific variables, we base our computations on linear-probability-of-participation equations estimated by ordinary least squares. Marginal effects that emerge from the logit equations are very similar to the corresponding regression coefficients in the linear-

Table 6.9	National Values of Selected Variables, 1982, 1992, and 1998			
Variable		1982	1992	1998
Annual prevalence of marijuana use		44.30	21.90	37.50
Thirty-day prevalence of marijuana use		28.50	11.90	22.80
Harm		2.45	2.70	2.37
Marijuana price		1.83	6.16	5.19
Marijuana potency		4.95	3.84	5.88

Table 6.10	Percentage Point Effects of Selected Variables on Marijuana Participation					
Model Number[a]	(1)	(2)	(3)	(4)	(5)	(6)
A. Annual Participation						
1982–92, Observed Change in Participation = −22.40						
Marijuana price	−12.74	−9.18	−.22	−18.89	−13.04	−10.53
Marijuana potency	−3.92	−6.73	−.06	4.46	.32	.97
Harm				−9.85	−9.87	−9.65
Total predicted change	−16.66	−15.91	−.28	−24.28	−22.59	−19.21
1992–98, Observed Change in Participation = 15.60						
Marijuana price	2.84	2.05	.05	4.21	2.91	2.35
Marijuana potency	7.20	12.36	.10	−8.19	−.59	−1.78
Harm				13.05	13.08	12.78
Total predicted change	10.04	14.41	.15	9.07	15.40	13.35
B. Thirty-Day Participation						
1982–92, Observed Change in Participation = −16.60						
Marijuana price	−7.86	−5.54	−.04	−13.56	−.99	−7.10
Marijuana potency	−3.44	−5.56	.23	8.31	1.56	.89
Harm				−16.22	−16.23	−16.63
Total predicted change	−11.30	−11.10	.19	−21.47	−15.63	−22.84
1992–98, Observed Change in Participation = 10.90						
Marijuana price	1.75	1.24	.01	3.02	.22	1.58
Marijuana potency	6.32	10.22	−.43	−15.28	−2.86	−1.64
Harm				21.48	21.51	22.03
Total predicted change	8.07	11.46	−.42	9.22	18.87	21.97

[a]Models 1, 2, and 3 are based on the specifications in tables 6.6 and 6.7 above. These specifications exclude harm and peer marijuana use. Model 1 omits a trend. Model 2 includes a linear trend. Model 3 includes a quadratic trend. Models 4, 5, and 6 are based on the specifications in table 6.8 and on coefficients that take account of the effect of a given variable on peer marijuana use. Model 4 omits a trend. Model 5 includes a linear trend. Model 6 includes a quadratic trend.

probability equations. The same comment applies to elasticities at sample means in the logit and linear-probability models.

Third, given our focus on marijuana price, potency, and harm, we exclude the individual and family characteristics, the cigarette and beer taxes, and the minimum legal drinking age from the computations, although the regressions from which they are derived include these variables.

Finally, the computations based on regressions that include peer marijuana use employ coefficients from the market demand function. These are coefficients that hold peer participation constant divided by 1 minus the coefficient of peer participation. This is appropriate because basic determinants may have important indirect effects operating through peer participation. Moreover, at the national level, the mean value of peer participation coincides with the fraction of high school seniors who used marijuana.

Clearly, one does not want to hold this variable constant when examining national trends in participation.

Models 4, 5, and 6 in table 6.10 allow one to compare the predicted effects of changes in the real quality-adjusted price of marijuana and the perceived risk of harm from regular use on participation, holding all else constant. An average of the components in these three models suggests that changes in the quality-adjusted price predict approximately 55 percent of the 50 percent decline in the annual participation rate between 1982 and 1992. The changes in harm predict more than 40 percent of this decline. The comparable estimates for the nearly 60 percent decline in thirty-day participation during this period are 22 percent for quality-adjusted price and nearly 100 percent for harm.

With regard to the recent expansion in marijuana participation, changes in quality-adjusted price appear to have little predictive power in explaining the increases in use, largely because of the opposing effects of price and potency on participation during this period. If the effects of potency are ignored (given the insignificant effects of potency in the models including time trends), the changes in the real price of marijuana predict about 20 percent of the approximate doubling in the annual participation rate between 1992 and 1998 and approximately 15 percent of the somewhat larger increase in the thirty-day participation rate. The observed changes in harm predict over 80 percent of the growth in annual participation but imply more than double the observed increases in thirty-day participation.

We interpret these estimates as generally similar to those based on the time-series regressions in section 6.3 above. It should be kept in mind that these estimates are biased and perhaps overstated if the coefficient of the endogenous peer-marijuana-participation measure is biased upward.

One additional aspect of the results in table 6.10 is worth mentioning. The price components (not adjusted for quality) in models 1, 2, and 3, which exclude harm and peer participation, are usually smaller than the corresponding components in models 4, 5, and 6. This is not surprising and is consistent with our finding that the market price elasticity obtained from a demand function that includes peer participation is larger than the elasticity obtained by omitting peer participation as a regressor.

6.5   Discussion

Our most important contribution in this paper is to present the first estimates of the price elasticity of demand for the prevalence of marijuana use by high school seniors. Our estimates of this parameter span a fairly wide range (from -0.06 to -0.47) for annual participation and a similarly wide range (from -0.002 to -0.69) for thirty-day participation. These wide ranges can be attributed to a variety of factors. The price and potency variables are subject to considerable measurement error. Pronounced trends in price and several other key determinants make it difficult to sort out their effects from those due to unmeasured time effects. Indeed, it may be inappropriate to include trend terms since we have very good proxies for hard-to-measure variables in a short time series. Peer marijuana participation and perceptions concerning the risk of harm from regular marijuana use have large effects on the probability of participation. Yet these two variables potentially are endogenous, and their coefficients, as well as those for price, may be biased. Given these considerations, a conservative lower-bound estimate of the price elasticity of demand for marijuana participation is −0.30.

Our estimates imply that cycles in the real (inflation-adjusted) price of marijuana and in the perceived risk of harm from regular marijuana use contribute to an understanding of cycles in the number of high school seniors who use marijuana. The estimation of the relative effects of price and harm is complicated by a variety of factors. Price and potency are measured with error. Several key determinants are endogenous. Attitudinal variables other than a single indicator of perceived risk of harm from regular marijuana use and other potentially important variables that are correlated with harm and price have been omitted. In addition, analyses of different time periods could produce somewhat different estimates; the analyses contained in this paper (given the limited data available on price) begin in 1982, several years after the start of the downturn in marijuana use and the substantial rise in perceived risk that preceded it. Given these considerations, we have provided a wide range of estimates. These estimates clearly imply that changes in the real, quality-adjusted price of marijuana contributed significantly to the trends in youth marijuana use between 1982 and 1998, particularly during the contraction in use from 1982 to 1992. Similarly, changes in youth perceptions of the harms associated with regular marijuana use had a substantial effect on both the contraction in use during the period 1982–92 and the subsequent expansion in use after 1992.

As clearly described above, our estimates of the magnitudes of the price and attitudine effects are subject to significant variation and should not be considered definitive. Research that focuses on outcomes other than annual and thirty-day participation and that employs a wider range of attitudine measures, better data on price and potency, and additional measures of the full price of youth marijuana use is required to provide a more complete understanding of the relative effect of price and attitudes on youth marijuana use. Similarly, studies that construct and estimate structural models that treat peer behavior, risk perceptions, and marijuana-consumption decisions as endogenous deserve high priority in future investigations. These studies would be especially valuable if they could identify the basic forces that cause attitudes and perhaps price and potency to vary. In the absence of this research, and as a prelude to it, the main message of this paper is that it is useful to consider price in addition to more traditional determinants in any analysis of marijuana-consumption decisions made by youths.

Appendix

In this appendix, we examine problems that arise when the marijuana arrest rate (marijuana-possession arrests divided by population) replaces the probability of arrest (arrests divided by the number of marijuana users) in the demand function for the probability of marijuana participation. We assume that the probability of use of a representative individual or the number of users divided by the population (u) at the aggregate level depends on the probability of arrest (π):

(A1) $$u = u(\pi), \partial u/\partial \pi < 0.$$

Note that we do not distinguish between the probability of arrest and the probability of conviction given apprehension and ignore components of the full price of marijuana other than π.

If a is the arrest rate (arrests divided by population), then

(A2) $$a = u\pi.$$

From equation (A1),

(A3) $$\partial \ln u/\partial \ln a = (\partial \ln u/\partial \ln \pi) \times (\partial \ln \pi/\partial \ln a).$$

Define the elasticity of u with respect to π as

(A4) $$\varepsilon \equiv \partial \ln u/\partial \ln \pi.$$

Note that ε is analogous to the price elasticity of demand. As we have defined this elasticity, it is negative. From equation (A2),

(A5) $$(\partial \ln a/\partial \ln \pi) = 1 + \varepsilon.$$

An increase in the probability of arrest increases the arrest rate if ε is smaller than 1 in absolute value but decreases the arrest rate if ε exceeds 1 in absolute value. This is perfectly analogous to the effect of an increase in price on total revenue. Revenue rises if the price elasticity of demand is less than 1 in absolute value and falls if the price elasticity of demand exceeds 1 in absolute value. Of course, this is because the arrest rate corresponds to total revenue and the probability of arrest corresponds to price. The arrest rate is a *positive* correlate of the probability of arrest if $-\varepsilon < 1$, but the arrest rate is a *negative* correlate of the probability of arrest if $-\varepsilon > 1$. For $-\varepsilon = 1$, there is no relation between these two variables; an increase in π lowers u but has no effect on a.

From equations (A4) and (A5),

(A6) $$\phi \equiv (\partial \ln u / \partial \ln a) = \varepsilon/(1 + \varepsilon).$$

In other words, a regression of $\ln u$ on $\ln a$ gives an estimate of $\phi = \varepsilon/(1 + \varepsilon)$. The parameter ϕ is negative if ε is smaller than 1 in absolute value, while ϕ is positive and greater than 1 if ε is greater than 1 in absolute value.

Given ϕ, one can obtain ε from

(A7) $$\varepsilon = \phi/(1 - \phi).$$

This shows why ϕ must exceed 1 if it is positive. Given $\phi > 0$, ε is negative if and only if $\phi > 1$. Put differently, the theory places restrictions on the value of ϕ.

To explore estimation issues in more detail, consider a demand function for u that is linear in the $\ln u$ and $\ln \pi$:

(A8) $$\ln u = \varepsilon \ln \pi + x,$$

where x stands for an unobserved factor or the disturbance term in the regression. Other observed determinants are suppressed. Since $\ln \pi = \ln a - \ln u$,

(A9) $$\ln u = [\varepsilon/(1 + \varepsilon)]\ln a + [1/(1 + \varepsilon)]x.$$

With π held constant, an increase in x raises u by assumption. But, with a held constant, an increase in x raises u only if ε is smaller than 1 in absolute value. The reason is that the only way to fix a when u varies is for π to vary. Indeed, since $\ln a = \ln u + \ln \pi$,

(A10) $$\ln a = (\varepsilon + 1)\ln \pi + x.$$

With π held constant, x and a are positively related; unmeasured factors that increase use will also increase arrests. This is the intuition behind the proposition that the coefficient of $\ln a$ is biased upward because arrests are high when use is high. Arrests and x are positively related, but the coefficient of the omitted variable x is positive only if ε is smaller than 1 in absolute value. In that case, the estimate of ϕ, which is a negative parameter, is biased upward. When $-\varepsilon > 1$, the coefficient of the omitted variable x is negative. Hence, the estimate of ϕ, which now is a positive parameter that exceeds 1, is biased downward. Indeed, since the coefficient of x on $\ln a$ is normalized at 1, the expected value of the coefficient of $\ln a$ in the demand function is equal to 1 regardless of the value of ε.

So far we have assumed that π is exogenous. Now we follow Ehrlich (1973) and specify a production function for the probability of apprehension and conviction:

(A11)
$$\ln \pi = \alpha \ln g + \beta \ln u + y.$$

The new variable, g, stands for resources allocated to police and courts, and α is positive. The variable y stands for an unmeasured determinant. Ehrlich assumes that β is negative. He argues that the productivity of g is likely to be lower at higher levels of criminal activity because more offenders must then be apprehended, charged, and tried in court in order to achieve a given level of π. Thus, with g held constant, u and π might be negatively correlated, but the causality runs from u to π.

Since $\ln \pi = \ln a - \ln u$,

(A12)
$$\ln a = \alpha \ln g + (\beta + 1)\ln u + y.$$

The coefficient of $\ln u$ is positive if $-\beta < 1$ and negative if $-\beta > 1$. For $-\beta = 1$, the coefficient is 0. Consider equations (A9) and (A12) as a simultaneous system with two endogenous variables: u and a. From equation (A12), the estimate of ϕ is biased upward if $-\beta < 1$ both because of reverse causality from an increase in u to an increase in a and because of the positive correlation between x and a. When $-\beta > 1$, these two biases go in opposite directions.

References

American Psychiatric Association. 1987. *Diagnostic and statistical manual of mental disorders.* 3d ed., rev. Washington, D.C.
————. 1994. *Diagnostic and statistical manual of mental disorders.* 4th ed. Washington, D.C.
Anthony, James, and John E. Helzer. 1991. Syndromes of drug abuse and dependence. In *Psychiatric disorders in America,* ed. Lee N. Robins and Darrel A. Regier. New York: Free Press/Macmillan.
Anthony, James, Lynn Warner, and Ronald Kessler. 1994. Comparative epidemiology of dependence on tobacco, alcohol, controlled substances, and inhalants: Basic findings from the National Comorbidity Study. *Experimental and Clinical Psychopharmacology* 2:244–68.
Bachman, Jerald G., Lloyd D. Johnston, and Patrick M. O'Malley. 1981. Smoking, drinking, and drug use among American high school seniors: Correlates and trends, 1975–1979. *American Journal of Public Health* 71, no. 1:59–69.
————. 1998. Explaining recent increases in students' marijuana use: Impacts of perceived risks and disapproval, 1976 through 1996. *American Journal of Public Health* 88, no. 6:887–92.
Bachman, Jerald G., Lloyd D. Johnston, Patrick M. O'Malley, and Ronald H. Humphrey. 1988. Explaining the recent decline in marijuana use: Differentiating the effects of perceived risks, disapproval, and general lifestyle factors. *Journal of Health and Social Behavior* 29:92–112.
Becker, Gary S., and Casey B. Mulligan. 1997. The endogenous determination of time preference. *Quarterly Journal of Economics* 112, no. 3:729–58.
Beer Institute. Various issues. *Brewers' almanac.* Washington, D.C.
Bray, Jeremy W., Gary A. Zarkin, Chris Ringwalt, and Junfeng Qi. 2000. The rela-

tionship between marijuana initiation and dropping out of high school. *Health Economics* 9, no. 1:9–18.

Brook, Judith S., Elinor B. Balka, and Martin Whiteman. 1999. The risks for late adolescence of early adolescent marijuana use. *American Journal of Public Health* 89, no. 10:1549–54.

Brook, Judith S., Patricia Cohen, and L. Jeager. 1998. Developmental variations in factors related to initial and increased levels of adolescent drug involvement. *Journal of Genetic Psychology* 159, no. 2:179–94.

Brookoff, Daniel, Charles S. Cook, Charles Williams, and Calvin S. Mann. 1994. Testing reckless drivers for cocaine and marijuana. *New England Journal of Medicine* 331:518–22.

Caulkins, Jonathan P. 1994. *Developing price series for cocaine.* Santa Monica, Calif.: Rand.

———. 1999. Can supply factors suppress marijuana use by youth? *Federation of American Scientists Drug Policy Analysis Bulletin* 7:3–5.

Chaloupka, Frank J., Michael Grossman, and John A. Tauras. 1999. The demand for cocaine and marijuana by youth. In *The economic analysis of substance use and abuse: An integration of econometric and behavioral economic research,* ed. Frank J. Chaloupka, Michael Grossman, Warren K. Bickel, and Henry Saffer. Chicago: University of Chicago Press.

Chaloupka, Frank J., and Adit Laixuthai. 1997. Do youths substitute alcohol and marijuana? Some econometric evidence. *Eastern Economic Journal* 23, no. 3:253–76.

Chaloupka, Frank J., Rosalie L. Pacula, Mathew C. Farrelly, Lloyd D. Johnston, Patrick M. O'Malley, and Jeremy W. Bray. 1999. Do higher cigarette prices encourage youth to use marijuana? Working Paper no. 6938. Cambridge, Mass.: National Bureau of Economic Research.

Chaloupka, Frank J., Henry Saffer, and Michael Grossman. 1993. Alcohol-control policies and motor vehicle fatalities. *Journal of Legal Studies* 22, no. 1:161–86.

Compton, David R., William L. Dewey, and Billy R. Martin. 1990. Cannabis dependence and tolerance production. *Advances in Alcohol and Substance Abuse* 9:128–47.

Crane, Barry D., A. Rex Rivolo, and Gary C. Comfort. 1997. *An empirical investigation of counterdrug interdiction program effectiveness.* Alexandria, Va.: Institute for Defense Analysis.

DeFonseca, Fernando R., M. Rocio, A. Carrera, Miguel Navarro, George F. Koob, and Friedbert Weiss. 1997. Activation of corticotropin-releasing factor in limbic system during cannabinoid withdrawal. *Science* 276:2050–54.

DeSimone, Jeffrey. 1998. Is marijuana a gateway drug? *Eastern Economics Journal* 24, no. 2:149–64.

DiNardo, John. 1993. Law enforcement, the price of cocaine, and cocaine use. *Mathematical and Computer Modeling* 17, no. 2:53–64.

DiNardo, John, and Thomas Lemieux. 1992. Alcohol, marijuana, and American youth: The unintended effects of government regulation. Working Paper no. 4212. Cambridge, Mass.: National Bureau of Economic Research.

Drug Enforcement Administration (DEA). U.S. Department of Justice. 1999. *DEA briefing book.* Washington, D.C.: U.S. Government Printing Office.

Edwards, Griffith, Awing Arif, and R. Hadgson. 1981. Nomenclature and classification of drug- and alcohol-related problems: A WHO memorandum. *Bulletin of the World Health Organization* 59, no. 2:225–42.

Edwards, Griffith, and Milton M. Gross. 1976. Alcohol dependence: Provisional description of a clinical syndrome. *British Medical Journal* 1:1058–61.

Ehrlich, Isaac. 1973. Participation in illegitimate activities: A theoretical and empirical investigation. *Journal of Political Economy* 81, no. 3:521–65.

Ellickson, Phyllis L., Khanh Bui, Robert M. Bell, and Kimberly A. McGuigan. 1998. Does early drug use increase the risk of dropping out of high school? *Journal of Drug Issues* 28, no. 2:357–80.

Ellickson, Phyllis L., Ron D. Hays, and Robert M. Bell. 1992. Stepping through the drug use sequence: Longitudinal scalogram analysis of initiation and regular use. *Journal of Abnormal Psychology* 101, no. 3:441–51.

Ellickson, Phyllis L., and Sally Morton. In press. Identifying adolescents at risk for hard drug use: Racial/ethnic variations. *Journal of Adolescent Health.*

Farrelly, Mathew C., Jeremy W. Bray, Gary A. Zarkin, Brett W. Wendling, and Rosalie L. Pacula. 1999. The effects of prices and policies on the demand for marijuana: Evidence from the National Household Surveys on Drug Abuse. Working Paper no. 6940. Cambridge, Mass.: National Bureau of Economic Research.

Georgotas, Anastase, and Phillip Zeidenberg. 1979. Observations on the effects of four weeks of heavy marijuana smoking on group interaction and individual behavior. *Comprehensive Psychiatry* 20:427–32.

Grossman, Michael, and Frank J. Chaloupka. 1998. The demand for cocaine by young adults: A rational addiction approach. *Journal of Health Economics* 17, no. 4:427–74.

Hall, Wayne, Nadia Solowij, and Jim Lemmon. 1994. *The health and psychological consequences of cannabis use.* Monograph Series no. 25. Canberra: Australian Government Printing Office.

Heyser, Charles J., Robert E. Hampson, and Sam A. Deadwyler. 1993. Effects of delta-9-tetrahydrocannibinol on delayed match to sample performance in rats—alternations in short-term memory associated with changes in task specific firing of hippocampal cells. *Journal of Pharmacology and Experimental Therapeutics* 264, no. 1:294–307.

Houthakker, Hendrik S. 1952–53. Compensated changes in quantities and qualities consumed. *Review of Economic Studies* 19, no. 3:155–64.

Huber, P. J. 1967. The behavior of maximum likelihood estimates under nonstandard conditions. In *Proceedings of the Fifth Berkeley Symposium in Mathematical Statistics and Probability.* Berkeley: University of California Press.

Jessor, Richard, James A. Chase, and John E. Donovan. 1980. Psychosocial correlates of marijuana use and problem drinking in a national sample of adolescents. *American Journal of Public Health* 70, no. 6:604–13.

Johnston, Lloyd D. 1991. Toward a theory of drug epidemics. In *Persuasive communication and drug abuse prevention,* ed. R. Lewis Donohew, Howard E. Sypher, and William J. Bukoski. Hillsdale, N.J.: Erlbaum.

Johnston, Lloyd D., and Patrick M. O'Malley. 1985. Issues of validity and population coverage in student surveys of drug use. In *Self-report methods of estimating drug use: Meeting current challenges to validity,* ed. Beatrice A. Rouse, Nicholas J. Kozel, and Louise G. Richards. Washington, D.C.: U.S. Government Printing Office.

Johnston, Lloyd D., Patrick M. O'Malley, and Jerald G. Bachman. 1981. Marijuana decriminalization: The impact on youth, 1975–1980. Monitoring the Future Occasional Paper no. 13. Ann Arbor, Mich.: Institute for Social Research, University of Michigan.

———. 1999. *National survey results on drug use from the Monitoring the Future study, 1975–1998.* Vol. 1, *Secondary school students.* NIH Publication no. 99-4660. Rockville, Md.: National Institute on Drug Abuse.

Jones, Reese T. 1984. Marijuana: Health and treatment issues. *Psychiatric Clinics of North America* 7:703–12.

———. 1987. Drug of abuse profile: Cannabis. *Clinical Chemistry* 33:72B–81B.

———. 1992. What have we learned from nicotine, cocaine, and marijuana about addiction? In *Addictive states,* ed. Charles P. O'Brien and Jerome H. Jaffe. New York: Raven.

Jones, Reese T., and Neal Benowitz. 1976. The 30-day trip—clinical studies of cannabis tolerance and dependence. In *Pharmacology of marijuana,* ed. Monique Braude and Stephen Szara (vol. 2). New York: Academic.

Kandel, Denise B. 1975. Stages in adolescent involvement in drug use. *Science* 190:912–24.

———. 1985. On processes of peer influences in adolescent drug use: A development perspective. *Advances in Alcohol and Substance Abuse* 4, no. 3:139–63.

Kandel, Denise B., and Mark Davies. 1992. Progression to regular marijuana involvement: Phenomenology and risk factors for near daily use. In *Vulnerability to drug abuse,* ed. Meyer Glantz and Roy Pickens. Washington, D.C.: American Psychological Association.

Kandel, Denise B., Mark Davies, Daniel Karus, and Kazuo Yamaguchi. 1986. The consequences in young adulthood of adolescent drug involvement. *Archives of General Psychiatry* 43:746–54.

Kandel, Denise B., Ronald C. Kessler, and Rebecca Z. Margulies. 1978. Antecedents of adolescent initiation into stages of drug use: A developmental analysis. *Journal of Youth and Adolescence* 7, no. 1:13–40.

Kandel, Denise B., Kazuo Yamaguchi, and Kevin Chen. 1992. Stages of progression in drug involvement from adolescence to adulthood: Further evidence for the gateway theory. *Journal of Studies on Alcohol* 53, no. 5:447–57.

Kaplan, John. 1970. *Marijuana: The new prohibition.* New York: World.

Kleiman, Mark A. R. 1989. *Marijuana: Costs of abuse, costs of control.* New York: Greenwood.

———. 1992. *Against excess: Drug policy for results.* New York: Basic.

Levitt, Steven D. 1998. Juvenile crime and punishment. *Journal of Political Economy* 106, no. 6:1156–85.

MacCoun, Robert J., Peter Reuter, and Thomas Schelling. 1996. Assessing alternative drug control regimes. *Journal of Policy Analysis and Management* 15:330–52.

Manski, Charles F. 1993. Identification of endogenous social effects: The reflection problem. *Review of Economic Studies* 60:531–42.

Matsuda, Lisa A., Tom I. Bonner, and Stephen J. Lolait. 1993. Localization of cannabinoid receptor messenger RNA in rat brain. *Journal of Comparative Neurology* 327, no. 4:535–50.

Mensch, Barbara S., and Denise B. Kandel. 1988. Dropping out of high school and drug involvement. *Sociology of Education* 61:95–113.

Ministry of Foreign Affairs, Ministry of Health, Welfare, and Sport, Ministry of Justice, and Ministry of the Interior. 1995. *Drug policy in the Netherlands: Continuity and change.* Rijswijk.

Model, Karyn E. 1993. The effect of marijuana decriminalization on hospital emergency room drug episodes: 1975–1978. *Journal of the American Statistical Association* 88, no. 423:737–47.

Moulton, Brent R. 1986. Random group effects and the precision of regression estimates. *Journal of Econometrics* 32, no. 3:385–97.

Nahas, Gabriel, and Colette Latour. 1992. The human toxicity of marijuana. *Medical Journal of Australia* 156, no. 7:495–97.

National Institute on Drug Abuse (NIDA). 1995. *National conference on marijuana use: Prevention, treatment, and research: Conference Summary.* Rockville, Md.: U.S. Department of Health and Human Services. Available at http://www. NIDA.NID.gov.

National Institute on Drug Abuse (NIDA) and National Institute on Alcohol

Abuse and Alcoholism (NIAAA). 1998. *The economic costs of alcohol and drug abuse in the United States, 1992.* Rockville, Md.: U.S. Department of Health and Human Services.

National Narcotics Intelligence Consumer Committee (NNICC). 1998. *The NNICC report, 1997: The supply of illicit drugs to the United States.* Washington, D.C.: Drug Enforcement Administration.

Newcomb, Michael D., and Peter M. Bentler. 1988. *Consequences of adolescent drug use: Impact on young adults.* Newbury Park, Calif.: Sage.

Newey, Whitney K., and Kenneth D. West. 1987. A simple positive semi-definite heteroscedasticity and autocorrelation consistent covariance matrix. *Econometrica* 55, no. 3:703–8.

Nisbet, Charles T., and Firouz Vakil. 1972. Some estimates of price and expenditure elasticities of demand for marijuana among U.C.L.A. students. *Review of Economics and Statistics* 54, no. 4:473–75.

Office of National Drug Control Policy (ONDCP). 1999. *1999 national drug control strategy.* Washington, D.C.: U.S. Government Printing Office.

Osgood, D. Wayne, Lloyd D. Johnston, Patrick M. O'Malley, and Jerald G. Bachman. 1988. The generality of deviance in late adolescence and early adulthood. *American Sociological Review* 53:81–93.

Pacula, Rosalie L. 1998a. Adolescent alcohol and marijuana consumption: Is there really a gateway effect? Working Paper no. 6348. Cambridge, Mass.: National Bureau of Economic Research.

———. 1998b. Does increasing the beer tax reduce marijuana consumption? *Journal of Health Economics* 17, no. 5:557–86.

Polen, Michael R., Stephen Sidney, Irene S. Tekawa, Marianne Sadler, and Gary D. Friedman. 1993. Health care use by frequent marijuana smokers who do not smoke tobacco. *Western Journal of Medicine* 158:596–601.

Rhodes, William, Raymond Hyatt, and Paul Scheiman. 1994. The price of cocaine, heroin, and marijuana, 1981–1993. *Journal of Drug Issues* 24, no. 3:383–402.

Robbe, Hindrik W. J., and James F. O'Hanlon. 1993. *Marijuana and actual driving performance.* Washington, D.C.: U.S. Department of Transportation.

———. 1999. *Marijuana, alcohol, and actual driving performance.* DOT HS 808 939. Washington, D.C.: National Highway Traffic Safety Administration, U.S. Department of Transportation.

Rosen, Sherwin. 1974. Hedonic prices and implicit markets: Product differentiation in pure competition. *Journal of Political Economy* 82, no. 1:34–55.

Saffer, Henry, and Frank J. Chaloupka. 1999. The demand for illicit drugs. *Economic Inquiry* 37, no. 3:401–11.

Smiley, Alison. 1986. Marijuana: On-road and driving simulator studies. *Alcohol, Drugs, and Driving: Abstracts and Reviews* 2:121–34.

Spunt, Barry, Paul Goldstein, Henry Brownstein, and Michael Fendrich. 1994. The role of marijuana in homicide. *International Journal of the Addictions* 29, no. 2:195–213.

Stephens, Robert S., and Roger A. Roffman. 1993. Adult marijuana dependence. In *Addictive behaviors across the life span: Prevention, treatment, and policy issues,* ed. John S. Baer, G. Alan Marlatt, and Robert J. MacMahon. Newbury Park, Calif.: Sage.

Substance Abuse and Mental Health Services Administration (SAMHSA). Office of Applied Studies. 1996. *Preliminary estimates from the 1995 National Household Survey on Drug Abuse.* Rockville, Md.: U.S. Department of Health and Human Services.

———. 1998a. *Analyses of substance abuse and treatment need issues.* Analytic Series A-7. Rockville, Md.: U.S. Department of Health and Human Services.

————. 1998b. *Driving after drug or alcohol use: Findings from the 1996 National Household Survey on Drug Abuse.* Analytic Series A-8. Rockville, Md.: U.S. Department of Health and Human Services.

————. 1999. *1998 National Household Survey on Drug Abuse, fact sheet.* Rockville, Md.: U.S. Department of Health and Human Services.

Tanda, Gianluigi, Francesco E. Pontieri, and Gaetano DiChiara. 1997. Cannabinoid and heroin activation of mesolimbic dopamine transmission by common u1 opioid receptor mechanism. *Science* 276:2048–50.

Tashkin, Donald P., Suzanne Fligiel, Tzu-Cin Wu, Henry Gong, Richard G. Barbers, Anne H. Coulson, Michael S. Simmons, and Theodore F. Beals. 1990. Effects of habitual use of marijuana and/or cocaine on the lung. In *Research findings on smoking of abused substances,* ed. C. Nora Chiang and Richard L. Hawks. National Institute on Drug Abuse Research Monograph no. 99. Rockville, Md.: U.S. Department of Health and Human Services.

Taubman, Paul. 1991. Externalities and decriminalization of drugs. In *Searching for alternatives: Drug-control policy in the United States,* ed. Melvyn B. Krauss and Edward B. Lazear. Stanford, Calif.: Hoover Institution Press.

Theil, Henri. 1952–53. Qualities, prices, and budget enquiries. *Review of Economic Studies* 19, no. 3:129–47.

Thies, Clifford F., and Charles A. Register. 1993. Decriminalization of marijuana and the demand for alcohol, marijuana, and cocaine. *Social Science Journal* 30, no. 4:385–99.

Tobacco Institute. Annual. *Tax burden on tobacco.* Washington, D.C.

Tommasello, Anthony C. 1982. Marijuana effects on sperm and testosterone. *Pharmalert* 13, no. 1:1–4.

U.S. Department of Justice. Drug Enforcement Agency. Various years. *Domestic cities report.* Washington, D.C.: U.S. Government Printing Office.

————. Various years. *Illegal drug wholesale/retail report.* Washington, D.C.: U.S. Government Printing Office.

U.S. Department of Justice. Strategic Intelligence Section. Drug Enforcement Agency. Various years. *Illegal drug price/purity report.* Washington, D.C.: U.S. Government Printing Office.

Weller, Ronald A., and James Halikas. 1982. Changes in effects of marijuana: A five- to six-year follow-up. *Journal of Clinical Psychiatry* 43:362–65.

Yamada, Tetsuji, Michael Kendix, and Tadashi Yamada. 1996. The impact of alcohol consumption and marijuana use on high school graduation. *Health Economics* 5, no. 1:77–92.

7

The Determinants
of Juvenile Crime

Steven D. Levitt and Lance Lochner

Criminal involvement in the United States rises sharply with the onset of adolescence, peaking in the late teenage years before dropping steadily thereafter. An eighteen-year-old is five times more likely to be arrested for a property crime than is a thirty-five-year-old; for violent crime the corresponding ratio is two to one. In 1997, those aged fifteen to nineteen constituted roughly 7 percent of the overall population but accounted for over 20 percent of arrests for violent offenses and roughly one-third of all property-crime arrests.

This essay examines the issue of youth crime. We begin by laying out the basic facts and trends relevant to youth crime over the last thirty years. We then consider both the social costs of youth crime and the personal risks and costs borne by the criminals themselves. After reviewing the various hypotheses as to the determinants of crime identified in the previous literature, we present three new sets of estimates that shed light on the issue. The first set of regressions uses the National Longitudinal Survey of Youth (NLSY) to explore the correlates of crime at the individual level. The second analysis focuses on census-tract-level homicide data for the city of Chicago over a thirty-year period. These data provide a means of better understanding the influence of social factors and local labor market conditions on youth crime. The final data set is a state-level panel covering

Steven D. Levitt is professor of economics at the University of Chicago, a research fellow of the American Bar Foundation, and a research associate of the National Bureau of Economic Research. Lance Lochner is assistant professor of economics at the University of Rochester.

The authors thank Richard Freeman, Edward Glaeser, Jonathan Gruber, and conference participants for extremely helpful comments on and discussions of earlier drafts of this paper. All remaining errors are solely the responsibility of the authors. Financial support of the National Science Foundation is gratefully acknowledged.

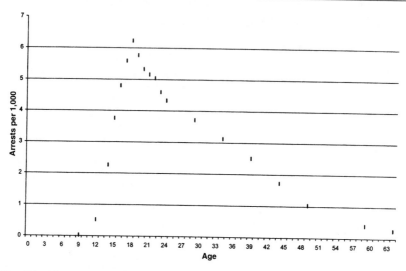

Fig. 7.1   Violent arrest rate by age, 1998

fifteen years. The state-level analysis is ideal for examining the effect of the criminal-justice system (and, to a lesser extent, economic factors). We use these three sets of estimates to determine the extent to which observed fluctuations in the correlates of crime can explain the time-series pattern of juvenile crime over the last three decades.

7.1   Youth-Crime Facts and Trends

Figures 7.1–7.3 present snapshots of criminal involvement by age in 1998, as reflected in arrest rates per capita for violent crime, property crime (excluding larceny), and murder.[1] Violent crime rises sharply in adolescence to a peak at age eighteen, before steadily declining thereafter. Property-crime offenses peak at age sixteen and drop off more quickly. The pattern for murders is similar to that of violent crime more generally.

Figures 7.1–7.3 represent a cross section of different cohorts at a fixed point in time. Following a particular cohort through the life cycle yields a generally similar pattern. Wolfgang, Figlio, and Sellin (1972) show a steeply rising and then declining pattern of arrests for their sample of ten thousand boys born in Philadelphia in 1945. Interestingly, for that cohort,

---

1. We adopt the standard Uniform Crime Reports definitions throughout the paper. Violent crime includes homicide, rape, robbery, and aggravated assault. Property crime includes burglary, larceny, and auto theft. Violent crime and property crime represent a limited subset of all crime. Fewer than 20 percent of all arrests are covered by these categories. Omitted from these categories are all drug offenses, other assaults, white-collar crimes, vandalism, and public-order offenses. Our focus on violent and property offenses is motivated by both the high social costs associated with such crimes and the lack of available data on other crimes.

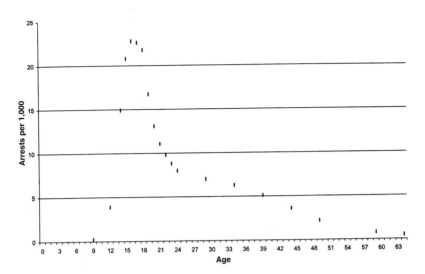

Fig. 7.2   Property arrest rate by age, 1998

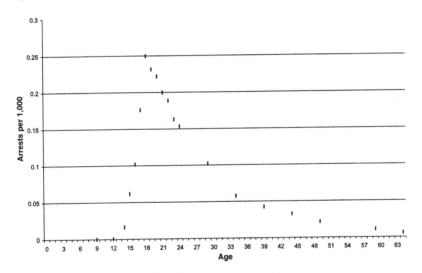

Fig. 7.3   Murder arrest rate by age, 1998

the peak in arrests occurs at age sixteen, earlier than as indicated in the more recent cross-sectional results.

Youth arrest rates vary dramatically by gender and race, as reported in table 7.1.[2] The more serious the offense, the greater the disparity across

2. Arrest rates are the only widely available measure of criminal involvement that is disaggregated by offender characteristics. To the extent that there are differences across groups in the likelihood of arrest conditional on committing a crime (e.g., owing to discrimination in arrests or differences in the mix of crimes), focusing on arrest rates may be misleading.

Table 7.1   Juvenile Arrest Rates per 1,000 by Sex and Race, 1997

Crime Category	Male	Female	White	Black
Violent crime arrests	1.9	.4	.8	3.5
Property crime arrests	9.2	3.7	6.2	12.1
Total arrests (excluding traffic offenses)	37.4	14.0	25.2	48.3

Sources: FBI, Uniform Crime Reports (various editions); and U.S. Bureau of the Census, Statistical Abstract of the United States (annual editions).

Note: Arrest rates per 1,000 individuals under the age of 18.

groups. Males under age eighteen are five times more likely to be arrested for violent crime than are females; for property crime the ratio is less than three to one. Black arrest rates are four times those of whites for violent crime and two times higher for other crimes.

An alternative measure of criminal involvement is self-reported data. Given that many crimes are not reported to the police and that most reported crimes do not lead to an arrest, criminal participation is likely to be much more prevalent than naively implied by arrest data.[3] A special supplement to the NLSY in 1980 asked respondents about self-reported crime activity, including such crimes as theft, fighting, causing injury to someone, use of force to acquire something, and drug dealing. Roughly 40 percent of fifteen- to nineteen-year-old males and 20 percent of fifteen- to nineteen-year-old females report committing at least two different categories of criminal offense in the preceding year.

There have been dramatic fluctuations in overall crime rates in recent decades; youth crime is no exception. Changes in police recording over this period make consistent comparisons difficult (Donohue and Siegelman 1994). The data on homicide rates are likely to be most reliable. Following Blumstein and Rosenfeld (1998) and Cook and Laub (1998), figure 7.4 presents homicide victimization rates per 100,000 for various age groups over the years.[4] Homicide victimization for fourteen- to seventeen-year-olds fluctuated within a relatively narrow range from 1976 to 1987 (between 4.3 and 5.8 per 100,000). Coincident with the onset of the crack epidemic, the homicide rate for that group more than doubled at its peak in 1993. The increases among black youths were especially pronounced, more than tripling from the early 1980s to the peak in 1993. White youth-homicide rates rose "only" 50 percent. Since the peak, homicide rates among youths have fallen 40 percent but are still well above those of the 1970s and 1980s. As was the case with the increase, the decline was great-

3. For example, according to the National Crime Victimization Survey (NCVS), fewer than 50 percent of violent crimes and roughly one-third of property crimes are reported to police. Approximately 50 percent of violent crimes and fewer than 20 percent of property crimes reported to the police lead to an arrest.

4. Offender ages, of course, are known only when the murder is solved. Cook and Laub (1998) demonstrate that the ages of offenders and victims tend to be similar in those instances in which an offender is identified.

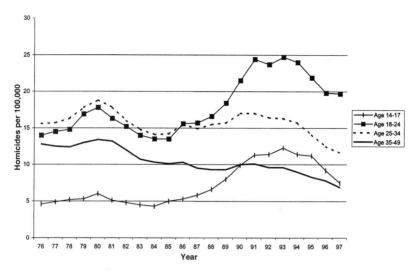

Fig. 7.4   Homicide victimization rates by age, 1976–97

est for black youths. The time series for eighteen- to twenty-four-year-olds is similar but with homicide rates two to three times higher throughout the entire period. In stark contrast, the homicide victimization rate of thirty-five- to forty-nine-year-olds has fallen almost continuously over the last two decades, with 1997 levels less than 60 percent as high as 1976 levels.

Levitt (1998) demonstrates that the differential trends for juveniles and adults are also present for violent crime more generally, although not as pronounced as for homicide. Youth property crime, on the other hand, has not substantially deviated from adult property crime.

7.2   Consequences of Youth-Crime Involvement

The social costs of crime in the United States are enormous. Estimates of the overall costs of crime range from roughly $300 billion in current dollars (Miller, Cohen, and Rossman 1993) to over $1 trillion (Anderson 1999), although estimates at the high end stretch credulity.[5] Teenagers are responsible for 20–30 percent of all crime. If the crimes committed by teenagers are representative of crime more generally, the social cost of youth crime could be between $60 and $300 billion annually.[6] The teenage criminals themselves bear only a small fraction of the social costs that

---

5. Government expenditures on anticrime measures, police, prisons, and courts total to $100 billion. In reaching the $1 trillion estimate, Anderson (1999) includes the total estimated value of all expenditures on drug trafficking ($160 billion) and, on the basis of a $6 million value of life, obtains over $400 billion in social costs associated with murder.
6. Greenwood (1995) presents evidence that the typical teenage crime is less serious than that of adults, even within relatively narrow crime categories. Consequently, the upper limit of this estimate is likely to overstate the true costs of youth crime.

they generate (e.g., through time incarcerated, forgone future earnings, or increased death probabilities); the overwhelming majority of this $60–$300 billion cost is an externality.

A very different question is the extent to which "crime pays" for the youths who engage in it. In terms of the overall amount of income generated by criminal activity, the values generally appear to be modest. Fagan and Freeman (1999) summarize estimates of the returns to street crime from a wide range of previous studies, with a typical estimate of average annual illegal income of this kind at or below $5,000. The estimated returns to drug selling vary widely depending on one's role in the drug trade. Among independent sellers who act as entrepreneurs, Reuter, MacCoun, and Murphy (1990) report an hourly wage of $30. These individuals, however, are likely to be highly skilled and occupy a relatively privileged position among drug dealers. Average wages derived from the financial records of a drug-selling gang analyzed by Levitt and Venkatesh (in press), however, range only from $6 to $11 per hour over the four years of the study. These numbers may be more representative of the typical drug-trade participant. The street-level sellers who essentially work for an hourly wage (the job held by most teenagers in the gang) earned less than the minimum wage for most of the study.

In order to make a meaningful comparison between the returns to legitimate work and street crime, the risk of incarceration needs to be included. Although the data required to perform a precise evaluation of the risks and rewards of crime are not available, there is sufficient information to generate a well-informed back-of-the-envelope calculation. In what follows, we attempt to determine the expected income from a single crime as well as the expected time spent incarcerated per crime.

The risk-return trade-off appears to be most favorable for property crimes, such as burglary, auto theft, and larceny. Victims of serious property crimes in the National Crime Victimization Survey (NCVS) report a median economic loss of approximately $100. The distribution of losses, however, is quite skewed, with the result that the mean loss (which is not reported and cannot be calculated given the data provided) is substantially higher. On the other hand, an individual criminal is unlikely to reap the full benefit of the stolen property for a number of reasons: juveniles often perform crime in groups, and the spoils of the crime need to be divided among the participants; criminals often sell stolen goods on the black market at significantly discounted prices; and property is often destroyed during a theft (e.g., a few parts are stripped from a stolen automobile, and the remainder of the car is burned to make identification more difficult). Balancing these factors, we estimate that the average return to a criminal per property crime is perhaps $200. Assuming that juvenile and adult arrests for property crime are proportional to rates of offending, juveniles commit approximately 3 million property crimes each year that are reported to the police. Victimization surveys suggest that only 30 percent of such crimes are reported to the police, implying a total of roughly 10 million property crimes annually by juveniles. At any given point in time, roughly seventeen thousand juveniles are incarcerated for serious property offenses, which translates into 6.2 million person-days of incarceration of juveniles for such crimes annually, or roughly 0.6 days of incarceration per property offense on average. For many juveniles, the trade-off between 0.6 days incarcerated and $200 per crime might look attractive. As an aside, it is worth noting that similar calculations for adults yield expected punishments at least five times greater per crime. Focusing solely on prison time served, adults receive an average of 2.6 days behind bars per property crime. If jail time were also included, the estimates would be substantially greater. The differential penalties for juveniles and adults are revisited in section 7.5 below.

The trade-off for robbery—in which the criminal uses violence or the threat of violence—is far less favorable to the criminal. Expected returns from robbery, based on the NCVS, are similar to those from property crime. Victims are much more likely to report robberies to the police, arrests are much more likely to result, and punishments are more severe. As a consequence, we estimate that juveniles serve 12.6 days incarcerated per robbery on average, or more than twenty times more than for the typical property crime. Thus, the returns to robbery appear quite low; working a minimum-wage job eight hours per day for 12.6 days would yield over $550, far more than a robbery is likely to provide, although the robbery income is untaxed.[7]

In contrast to property crime and robbery, for which the risks of injury or death are fairly small, the physical risks associated with drug dealing are immense. Previous studies have reported violent death rates between 2 and 7 percent per person-year (Kennedy, Piehl, and Braga 1996; Levitt and Venkatesh, in press) for those engaged in gang-related drug distribution. Levitt and Venkatesh (in press) report a variety of approaches to measuring the implied value of life for the gang members; none of the estimates are greater than $100,000 per statistical life, which is an order of magnitude lower than the typical estimate obtained for the general population.

7.3   Factors Affecting Criminal Involvement

There is an enormous previous literature on the determinants of criminal involvement. We do not attempt to survey this literature systematically here (for excellent surveys of various aspects of the literature, see Wilson

---

7. Our calculations suggest that adults serve approximately sixty days in prison per robbery. The low returns to robbery are consistent with the fact that property crimes such as burglary and auto theft require skill and planning, whereas robbery is often an impulsive act.

and Petersilia [1995]). Rather, we focus our discussion on identifying the handful of factors that are most likely to be both important empirically and testable (at least in a crude manner) given the available data. For purposes of exposition, we adopt a four-part classification scheme: biological; social; criminal justice; and economic. Although this framework is necessarily imperfect, it serves as a useful organizing device for what follows. The four categories are discussed in turn.

7.3.1   Biological Factors

There is little doubt that the single best predictor of crime is gender. In virtually every society for which there are records, the prevalence of violence is greater among males (Wilson and Herrnstein 1985). The pervasiveness of this pattern suggests a biological underpinning.

The consistency of the age profile of crime across time and place (first documented by Quetelet in nineteenth-century France and later noted by Blumstein et al. [1986]) also suggests an important biological component, although social, economic (Grogger 1998; Lochner 1999), and criminal-justice (Levitt 1998) factors may also provide a partial explanation for the postadolescent drop in crime in the United States.

Wilson and Herrnstein (1985) also argue that low intelligence and high discount rates are predictors of crime. To the extent that these traits are partially determined by heredity, they represent an additional biological component of crime, which may interact with other social and economic factors.

7.3.2   Social Factors

Without question, social factors exert an enormous influence on crime. There are a number of channels through which social factors might affect crime. Perhaps the most important of these is the quality of parenting. Research has demonstrated a strong link between erratic/harsh discipline, lack of adequate supervision, and rejection by the mother and later criminal involvement (Daag 1991; Sampson and Laub 1993). As Donohue and Siegelman (1994) note, the interventions that have been most successful in reducing crime have been those aimed early in life and requiring the parents' involvement (e.g., the Perry Preschool project). Empirically, the number of female-headed households is often one of the strongest predictors of city crime rates (Glaeser, Sacerdote, and Scheinkman 1996). Donohue and Levitt (1999) provide indirect evidence in support of the importance of parental factors in reducing crime rates. Their results suggest that crime is 10–15 percent lower as a consequence of legalized abortion. Levine et al. (1996) demonstrate that legalized abortion disproportionately reduces the fertility rates of teenagers and single women. Gruber, Levine, and Staiger (1999) show that children on the margin for abortion are much more likely to have been born into households on welfare, to be low birth weight, and to die in infancy.

Outside the family, the degree of "social control" exerted by a community is hypothesized to reduce crime (e.g., Hirschi 1969; Sampson 1985). For example, a willingness of other adults in a neighborhood to discipline youths, positive role models, and limited amounts of unsupervised youth activity are hypothesized to reduce crime (Wilson 1987). Positive peer-group interactions have also been shown to be important predictors of criminal activity (Case and Katz 1991).

7.3.3 Criminal-Justice System

The economic model of crime (Becker 1968) is based on the idea that crime can be deterred through punishment. While there is strong evidence that increased levels of policing (Corman and Mocan, in press; Levitt 1997; Marvell and Moody 1996) and imprisonment (Spelman 1994; Marvell and Moody 1994; Levitt 1996) reduce the *overall* level of crime, there has been surprisingly little work analyzing the response of youth crime to sanctions. Levitt (1998) presents results suggesting that increases in punishment affect juveniles as strongly as adults and also finds sharp behavioral changes concurrent with the passage from the juvenile to the adult justice systems in states where there are big differences in the relative punitiveness of the two systems.

There is a larger body of research focused on the efficacy of different criminal-justice strategies. Kennedy, Piehl, and Braga (1996) document a particularly successful antigang program implemented in Boston. Greenwood (1995) surveys the literature on various approaches to treating youths in custody (e.g., drug-abuse treatment, boot camps, etc.). The most noteworthy of these studies is a metastudy analysis conducted by Lipsey (1991), who concludes that various treatment interventions appear to be associated with reduced recidivism, although the gains are often modest—perhaps a 10 percent reduction in recidivism relative to control groups.

7.3.4 Economic Factors

Economic factors influence crime by affecting the attractiveness of alternatives to crime. Grogger (1998) argues that increased labor market attachment with age can explain a substantial fraction of the age-crime profile. Lochner (1999) expands on this, arguing that differential skill requirements across different types of crime can explain why some crimes peak earlier and decline more quickly with age than others. The fact that many criminals are employed in the legitimate sector (Freeman 1992, 1995) suggests that there may be substitution on the margin between criminal and noncriminal activities.

On the other hand, there is little evidence that public job-training programs have a lasting effect on criminal involvement (Donohue and Siegelman 1994), although this is not surprising given the minimal effects on earnings and employment typically observed for these programs. Furthermore, most empirical analyses of the link between crime and macroeconomic variables such as the unemployment rate or low-skilled wages have found no effect on violent crime and relatively weak effects on property crime (e.g., Levitt 1997; Machin and Meghir 2000).[8]

An alternative manner in which economic factors may affect crime is via income inequality. "Strain theory" argues that increased inequality generates frustration among lower-class youths, leading to increased crime (e.g., Cloward and Ohlin 1960). Although the U.S. evidence on the link between income inequality and crime is mixed, international comparisons have repeatedly found a strong link between income inequality and crime rates (Soares 1999).

7.4   Individual-Level Correlates of Youth Crime

Studying youth crime at the individual level poses a number of challenges. The most severe limitation of such an exercise is the reliance on self-reported data on criminal involvement (e.g., Grogger 1998; Lochner 1999; Mocan and Rees 1999).[9] Comparisons between crime self-reports and official arrest data generally find a strong correspondence between the two (e.g., Farrington 1973). There do, however, appear to be important discrepancies between official data and self-reports by race. Blacks are greatly overrepresented in official data but not in self-reports, although much of this racial discrepancy can be reconciled by using self-report measures that carefully account for the frequency of criminal activity among the most active offenders (Elliott and Ageton 1980; Farrington 1973; Hindelang, Hirschi, and Weis 1979).

The available crime data in recent micro data sets is generally limited.[10] The data set most frequently used to study individual-level youth-crime involvement is the NLSY. The major advantage of the NLSY is its abundance of measures of neighborhood, family, and individual background, including tests of cognitive ability. While individuals in the NLSY have been surveyed annually since 1979 (biannually since 1994), only the 1980 supplement contains self-reported information on criminal involvement. Thus, only cross-sectional comparisons from 1980 data can be used in determining criminal participation. However, we exploit the panel struc-

8. Ruhm (1996) finds murder to be strongly procyclic. Gould, Weinberg, and Mustard (1997) find that the wage rates of unskilled laborers, rather than their unemployment rates, better predict cross-sectional variation in crime rates.

9. A few individual-level studies have used official arrest records (e.g., Tauchen, Witte, and Griesinger 1994). Arrest data are also problematic because they reflect only the small subset of criminal activities that lead to arrest. For example, fewer than one in ten burglary victimizations yield an arrest.

10. Two older data sets—Glueck and Glueck (1950), which follows individuals born in the 1920s and 1930s, and Wolfgang, Figlio, and Sellin (1972), which follows a sample born in Philadelphia in 1945—contain much more detailed information. For the purposes of this paper, however, the experiences of these earlier cohorts are of only indirect relevance.

ture of the NLSY to explore the correlation between youth crime and outcomes later in life.

Another micro data set useful for studying crime, the National Longitudinal Study of Adolescent Health (NLSAH), has recently become available. The greatest advantage of the NLSAH is its large sample size (over twenty thousand adolescents interviewed) and an extensive set of questions on criminal activity. Relative to the NLSY, however, it has a more limited set of demographic and family variables and no measure of cognitive ability. Furthermore, geographic identifiers are not available, although individuals can be matched to characteristics of their county of residence. Mocan and Rees (1999) use these data to analyze the correlates of youth crime.

In this paper, we present new results using the NLSY. We also discuss the similarities of and differences between our NLSY-based findings and those of Mocan and Rees (1999).

The NLSY includes a wide range of questions relevant to criminal activity, including theft, drug sales, use of force, causing injury to someone, causing property damage, hitting someone, and fighting. For the purposes of this paper, we focus on property crimes that are likely to be economically motivated and crimes of violence. Individuals who either steal something worth more than $50 or sell hard drugs are categorized as property criminals, and individuals who either injure someone or use force to get something are categorized as violent criminals. A number of less serious criminal actions are reported in the NLSY, actions that we categorize as minor property and minor violent crimes. An individual is classified as a minor property criminal if he steals something worth less than $50 or causes property damage, while he is classified a minor violent criminal if he reports hitting someone or fighting. Our sample includes the random cross-sectional samples in the NLSY, supplemented with the oversamples of blacks and Hispanics (using the appropriate population weights in all calculations).

Table 7.2 reports our measures of criminal involvement by gender and age. Seventy-four percent of all males aged fifteen to nineteen do not report a (major) violent or property crime as defined above. While our measures reveal higher participation in violent crimes than in property crimes (20 vs. 11 percent among all young males), this does not imply that overall violent-crime rates among youths are higher than property crime rates. The ratio of property crime to violent crime rates will depend on both the severity of measured crimes and the number of types of crimes included in each category. Participation in less severe property and violent crimes is much more prevalent, as seen in the final two columns of the table. Drug dealing is also common among male youths with an average participation rate of 17 percent. Property crime peaks at age sixteen among males. Violent-crime participation rates are fairly stable across the late teenage years for males. Comparing crime rates for males and females, we observe

Table 7.2   Criminal Status by Age and Sex, 1980 NLSY (%)

Age	Noncriminals	Property Criminals[a]	Violent Criminals[b]	Violent & Property Criminals[c]	Sell Marijuana or Hard Drugs	Minor Property Criminals[d]	Minor Violent Criminals[e]
A. Males							
15	72.2	9.6	21.8	27.8	11.5	48.1	71.8
16	73.0	13.5	19.3	27.0	15.6	49.1	68.6
17	74.7	10.8	19.5	25.3	18.1	42.9	67.9
18	75.7	10.7	19.8	24.3	19.7	45.9	60.6
19	76.3	10.5	18.5	23.7	18.0	41.9	55.7
All	74.4	11.2	19.7	25.6	16.8	45.6	64.7
B. Females							
15	89.7	3.0	8.4	10.3	4.6	21.0	38.1
16	90.0	2.9	7.9	10.0	9.5	25.5	39.5
17	89.7	3.6	7.4	10.3	10.3	21.3	37.3
18	88.6	4.5	7.9	11.4	11.1	23.4	34.4
19	92.4	2.3	5.8	7.6	8.9	21.4	29.3
All	90.1	3.3	7.4	9.9	9.1	22.6	35.6

[a] Property criminals include individuals who either steal something worth more than $50 or sell hard drugs.

[b] Violent criminals include individuals who either injure someone or use force to get something.

[c] Violent and property criminals include individuals who commit a property crime as defined in n. a above and a violent crime as defined in n. b above.

[d] Minor property criminals include individuals who reported stealing something worth less than $50 or causing property damage.

[e] Minor violent criminals include individuals who reported hitting someone or fighting.

similar age patterns but substantially lower levels among females (especially among more substantial property crimes).

Youth engaged in one criminal activity are also likely to be engaged in a wide variety of others. Table 7.3 reports correlations in criminal involvement for the self-report measures available in the NLSY. The upper-right triangle of the table reports correlations for males and the lower left for females. All correlations are positive (statistically significant in all but one case for females). The first three entries correspond to the property-crime and violent-crime measures used throughout this section. Not surprisingly, there is a high correlation within such broad crime classifications as property, violent, or drug crimes. But there is also a high degree of correlation between crimes of different natures. While causing property damage may often represent minor delinquency among youths, it is highly correlated with more serious crimes like theft, use of force, and injuring someone.

Table 7.4 presents summary statistics for a wide range of variables, shown separately by gender for each major crime category. Individuals who commit multiple types of offenses are included in all relevant columns. Violent criminals are more likely to be black than is the average noncriminal. When compared with noncriminals, both violent and property criminals are of lower average ability (as measured by their percentile rank for the Armed Forces Qualifying Test [AFQT]) and less likely to have graduated from high school (if age eighteen or older). They are also likely to live in a standard metropolitan statistical area (SMSA) and live in a worse family environment—families with lower income, a teenage mother, less-educated parents, a nonworking adult male in the home, or a broken home (at least one natural parent absent) at age fourteen. Male and female property criminals are likely to live in states with fewer juvenile criminals in prison per crime committed. These patterns suggest an important role for ability, education, and a positive family environment in determining adolescent criminal behavior for both males and females.

To explore individual determinants of criminal behavior further, tables 7.5 and 7.6 report regression results for male and female criminal participation. For each crime category, we report two specifications. The first specification limits the covariates to those that are likely to be exogenous and available for nearly all respondents. The second specification includes some potentially less exogenous covariates (like high school graduation) and variables that are missing for a substantial fraction of the sample (such as parents' education and family income). We report OLS estimates for linear-probability models, although probits evaluated at the sample means yield similar conclusions.

Among male adolescents aged fifteen to nineteen, blacks and Hispanics report less involvement in property crime after controlling for other factors. Violent-crime rates are not substantially different for blacks and whites, however. Living in a broken home at age fourteen raises the

Table 7.3   Correlations in Criminal Behavior (Males and Females Aged 15–19 in the 1980 NLSY)

Males

	A, Property Crimes[a]	B, Violent Crimes[b]	C, Property & Violent Crimes[c]	D, Steal Something Worth More Than $50	E, Steal Something Worth Less Than $50	F, Shoplifting	G, Sell Hard Drugs	H, Sell Marijuana	I, Cause Property Damage	J, Injure Someone	K, Use Force to Get Something	L, Hit Someone	M, Fight
Females:													
A		.260	.600	.888	.345	.256	.547	.353	.276	.236	.248	.165	.194
B	.132		.855	.236	.198	.211	.179	.232	.279	.853	.608	.315	.333
C	.560	.855		.532	.301	.262	.328	.315	.322	.730	.520	.324	.344
D	.702	.129	.394		.342	.253	.214	.254	.274	.232	.216	.173	.193
E	.155	.098	.138	.280		.360	.158	.303	.380	.172	.165	.169	.186
F	.175	.115	.175	.125	.280		.120	.287	.405	.198	.155	.227	.272
G	.716	.069	.401	.028	.103	.127		.352	.128	.135	.231	.078	.096
H	.291	.152	.275	.097	.192	.263	.320		.300	.208	.199	.177	.197
I	.093	.151	.153	.104	.270	.247	.041	.182		.261	.203	.277	.282
J	.107	.881	.753	.080	.065	.124	.080	.151	.132		.254	.313	.313
K	.127	.535	.457	.193	.085	.033	.001	.043	.125	.156		.313	.171
L	.098	.318	.304	.078	.130	.161	.066	.218	.215	.287	.175		.319
M	.072	.229	.220	.089	.076	.154	.017	.100	.177	.214	.137	.319	

Note: Correlations for males are reported in the upper right half of the table, correlations for females in the lower left.

[a]Property crimes include either stealing something worth more than $50 or selling hard drugs.

[b]Violent crimes include either injuring someone or using force to get something.

[c]Property and violent crimes include individuals who commit a property crime as defined in n. a above and a violent crime as defined in n. b above.

Table 7.4   NLSY Summary Statistics by Sex and Criminal Status, Ages 15–19

	Males				Females			
Variable	Noncriminals	Property Criminals[a]	Violent Criminals[b]	Violent & Property Criminals[c]	Noncriminals	Property Criminals[a]	Violent Criminals[b]	Violent & Property Criminals[c]
Age (in months)	211.020	210.340	209.957	209.757*	211.271	210.225	209.495*	209.835
	(.337)	(.817)	(.618)	(.552)	(.309)	(1.441)	(.956)	(.835)
Black	.138	.149	.179**	.161	.136	.110	.238**	.206**
	(.007)	(.018)	(.015)	(.013)	(.006)	(.030)	(.026)	(.022)
Hispanic	.069	.062	.060	.061	.065	.065	.059	.058
	(.005)	(.012)	(.009)	(.008)	(.005)	(.024)	(.014)	(.012)
AFQT	48.091	36.173**	38.180**	38.539**	46.276	41.934*	34.042**	36.777**
	(.612)	(1.311)	(1.055)	(.923)	(.510)	(2.450)	(1.464)	(1.325)
Teenage mother	.187	.236**	.245**	.235**	.206	.233	.294**	.269**
	(.008)	(.022)	(.017)	(.015)	(.008)	(.041)	(.028)	(.024)
Living in SMSA	.706	.774**	.750**	.756**	.731	.853**	.726	.759
	(.009)	(.022)	(.017)	(.015)	(.008)	(.035)	(.027)	(.023)
Intact family when age 14	.760	.655**	.653**	.668**	.743	.542**	.617**	.585**
	(.009)	(.024)	(.018)	(.016)	(.008)	(.048)	(.029)	(.026)
Local unemployment rate	7.078	7.131	7.007	7.061	6.977	7.090	6.918	6.912
	(.047)	(.130)	(.092)	(.083)	(.042)	(.240)	(.141)	(.127)
High school graduate (ages 18+)	.592	.334**	.375**	.406**	.681	.346**	.402**	.374**
	(.016)	(.038)	(.029)	(.026)	(.013)	(.075)	(.048)	(.041)
Family income	23.558	20.884**	21.810**	21.800**	22.616	20.522	19.311**	19.511**
	(.346)	(.779)	(.602)	(.545)	(.312)	(1.810)	(1.007)	(.884)

(continued)

Table 7.4   (continued)

Variable	Males				Females			
	Noncriminals	Property Criminals[a]	Violent Criminals[b]	Violent & Property Criminals[c]	Noncriminals	Property Criminals[a]	Violent Criminals[b]	Violent & Property Criminals[c]
Highest grade completed (father)	12.067	11.562**	11.580**	11.649**	11.839	11.860	11.277**	11.481*
	(.079)	(.185)	(.146)	(.127)	(.072)	(.339)	(.221)	(.195)
Highest grade completed (mother)	11.670	11.362**	11.505	11.531	11.625	11.782	10.912**	11.154**
	(.060)	(.134)	(.098)	(.088)	(.053)	(.230)	(.147)	(.132)
Adult female working when age 14	.543	.526	.573	.552	.563	.579	.537	.561
	(.010)	(.026)	(.019)	(.017)	(.009)	(.048)	(.030)	(.027)
Adult male working when age 14	.941	.896**	.933	.925	.935	.908	.858**	.885**
	(.005)	(.018)	(.011)	(.010)	(.005)	(.034)	(.025)	(.021)
Juvenile punishment rate	.374	.335**	.362	.350*	.368	.298**	.400	.378
	(.007)	(.014)	(.013)	(.011)	(.006)	(.025)	(.022)	(.018)
Sample size	2,380	381	676	851	2,841	109	278	352

[a]Property criminals include individuals who either steal something worth more than $50 or sell hard drugs.
[b]Violent criminals include individuals who either injure someone or use force to get something.
[c]Violent and property criminals include individuals who commit a property crime as defined in n. a above and a violent crime as defined in n. b above.
*Statistically different from noncriminals at the 10 percent level.
**Statistically different from noncriminals at the 5 percent level.

Table 7.5   OLS Estimates (S.E.s) of Criminal Participation (males aged 15–19 in the 1980 NLSY)

Variable	Property Crimes[a]		Violent Crimes[b]		Violent & Property Crimes[c]	
Intercept	.1650**	.1992**	.3392**	.2699**	.4198**	.3474**
	(.0345)	(.0765)	(.0437)	(.0943)	(.0480)	(.1044)
Age 16	.0421**	.0454*	-.0134	-.0394	.0065	-.0118
	(.0180)	(.0241)	(.0227)	(.0297)	(.0250)	(.0329)
Age 17	.0267	.0313	-.0113	-.0187	-.0042	-.0075
	(.0186)	(.0247)	(.0235)	(.0304)	(.0259)	(.0337)
Age 18	.0223	.0668**	-.0031	.0539	-.0085	.0673*
	(.0186)	(.0269)	(.0235)	(.0333)	(.0259)	(.0367)
Age 19	.0113	.0993**	-.0295	.1096**	-.0324	.1352**
	(.0189)	(.0321)	(.0239)	(.0396)	(.0263)	(.0438)
Black	-.0418**	-.0429	-.0125	.0081	-.0466*	-.0318
	(.0180)	(.0293)	(.0227)	(.0361)	(.0251)	(.0399)
Hispanic	-.0575**	-.0390	-.0691**	-.0496	-.0970**	-.0676
	(.0232)	(.0350)	(.0294)	(.0432)	(.0324)	(.0478)
Intact family when age 14	-.0279**	-.0467*	-.0679**	-.0865**	-.0700**	-.0728**
	(.0135)	(.0255)	(.0169)	(.0315)	(.0187)	(.0347)
Teenage mother	.0092	.0199	.0382**	.0330	.0314	.0447*
	(.0143)	(.0193)	(.0180)	(.0238)	(.0198)	(.0263)
South	-.0602**	-.0447*	-.0340	.0226	-.0698**	-.0230
	(.0180)	(.0249)	(.0227)	(.0307)	(.0250)	(.0340)
Northeast	-.0454**	-.0329	-.0282	.0303	-.0366	.0213
	(.0187)	(.0256)	(.0237)	(.0317)	(.0260)	(.0349)

(continued)

Table 7.5   (continued)

Variable	Property Crimes[a]		Violent Crimes[b]		Violent & Property Crimes[c]	
North Central	-.0537**	-.0426*	-.0159	.0326	-.0397	-.0104
	(.0176)	(.0230)	(.0223)	(.0284)	(.0245)	(.0314)
Living in SMSA	.0406**	.0543**	.0328*	.0399*	.0548**	.0628**
	(.0139)	(.0190)	(.0176)	(.0235)	(.0193)	(.0259)
Local unemployment rate	.0036	.0072**	-.0016	-.0020	.0011	.0025
	(.0027)	(.0036)	(.0035)	(.0044)	(.0038)	(.0049)
AFQT	-.0013**		-.0017**		-.0023**	
	(.0002)		(.0003)		(.0003)	
Math test score		-.0028**		-.0068**		-.0077**
		(.0009)		(.0011)		(.0012)
English test score		-.0011		.0036**		.0016
		(.0013)		(.0016)		(.0018)
Mechanical-information test score		.0023**		.0025**		.0042**
		(.0009)		(.0011)		(.0013)
High school graduate (age 18+)		-.0934**		-.1704**		-.1876**
		(.0262)		(.0324)		(.0357)
Family income $10,000–$25,000		.0139		.0216		.0282
		(.0247)		(.0304)		(.0337)
Family income $25,000–$50,000		.0094		.0001		-.0077
		(.0263)		(.0325)		(.0359)

Family income $50,000–$75,000	-.0382 (.0385)		-.0298 (.0477)		-.0361 (.0525)	
Family income > $75,000	.0503 (.0748)		-.0457 (.0927)		.0216 (.1021)	
Highest grade completed (mother)	.0018 (.0040)		-.0008 (.0049)		.0027 (.0054)	
Highest grade completed (father)	.0010 (.0030)		-.0008 (.0037)		.0000 (.0041)	
Adult female working when age 14	.0027 (.0152)		-.0002 (.0187)		-.0042 (.0207)	
Adult male working when age 14	-.1483** (.0342)		-.0386 (.0418)		-.1286** (.0464)	
Juvenile punishment rate	-.0166 (.0279)		-.0201 (.0344)		-.0189 (.0380)	
Sample size	3,045	1,693	3,080	1,707	3,050	1,695
R^2	.0252	.0523	.0293	.0614	.0383	.0707

[a] Property crimes include either stealing something worth more than $50 or selling hard drugs.

[b] Violent crimes include either injuring someone or using force to get something.

[c] Property and violent crimes include individuals who commit a property crime as defined in n. a above and a violent crime as defined in n. b above.

*Statistically significant at the 10 percent level.

**Statistically significant at the 5 percent level.

Table 7.6 OLS Estimates (S.E.s) of Criminal Participation (females aged 15–19 in the 1980 NLSY)

Variable	Property Crimes[a]		Violent Crimes[b]		Violent & Property Crimes[c]	
Intercept	.0409**	.0191	.1590**	.1780**	.1925**	.1882**
	(.0198)	(.0390)	(.0294)	(.0593)	(.0335)	(.0675)
Age 16	-.0043	-.0137	-.0091	-.0027	-.0086	-.0134
	(.0105)	(.0130)	(.0155)	(.0198)	(.0177)	(.0225)
Age 17	.0072	.0005	-.0118	-.0174	-.0007	-.0187
	(.0106)	(.0133)	(.0157)	(.0202)	(.0179)	(.0230)
Age 18	.0149	.0257*	-.0039	.0041	.0134	.0227
	(.0106)	(.0155)	(.0157)	(.0235)	(.0179)	(.0268)
Age 19	-.0024	.0087	-.0237	-.0013	-.0210	-.0012
	(.0106)	(.0177)	(.0157)	(.0270)	(.0179)	(.0307)
Black	-.0216**	-.0180	.0241	.0429*	.0054	.0225
	(.0101)	(.0149)	(.0150)	(.0227)	(.0172)	(.0259)
Hispanic	-.0039	.0057	-.0242	-.0166	-.0311	-.0133
	(.0136)	(.0178)	(.0201)	(.0270)	(.0230)	(.0308)
Intact family when age 14	-.0392**	-.0155	-.0230**	.0235	-.0606**	.0003
	(.0076)	(.0135)	(.0112)	(.0205)	(.0128)	(.0233)
Teenage mother	-.0037	-.0149	.0190	.0345**	.0114	.0200
	(.0079)	(.0099)	(.0116)	(.0151)	(.0133)	(.0172)
South	-.0012	.0009	-.0064	-.0153	-.0036	-.0112
	(.0101)	(.0124)	(.0149)	(.0189)	(.0170)	(.0216)
Northeast	-.0095	-.0241*	-.0260	-.0332	-.0358*	-.0542**
	(.0110)	(.0138)	(.0162)	(.0210)	(.0185)	(.0238)
North Central	.0113	.0104	-.0007	.0142	.0022	.0156
	(.0103)	(.0124)	(.0153)	(.0189)	(.0174)	(.0215)
Living in SMSA	.0223**	.0142	.0013	-.0077	.0192	.0075
	(.0079)	(.0100)	(.0117)	(.0152)	(.0134)	(.0173)
Local unemployment rate	.0012	-.0008	-.0025	-.0009	-.0020	-.0023
	(.0016)	(.0019)	(.0023)	(.0029)	(.0027)	(.0033)
AFQT	-.0001		-.0009**		-.0009**	
	(.0001)		(.0002)		(.0002)	

	(1)	(2)	(3)
Math test score	−.0002 (.0005)	.0000 (.0008)	−.0004 (.0009)
English test score	−.0017** (.0007)	−.0037** (.0011)	−.0041** (.0012)
Mechanical-information test score	.0018** (.0007)	.0013 (.0010)	.0023** (.0011)
High school graduate (age 18+)	−.0178 (.0141)	−.0245 (.0215)	−.0354 (.0245)
Family income $10,000–$25,000	.0012 (.0127)	.0234 (.0192)	.0191 (.0219)
Family income $25,000–$50,000	−.0154 (.0136)	.0328 (.0207)	.0130 (.0236)
Family income $50,000–$75,000	−.0184 (.0208)	.0240 (.0317)	.0058 (.0361)
Family income > $75,000	.0114 (.0308)	.0927** (.0469)	.0556 (.0533)
Highest grade completed (mother)	.0039* (.0020)	−.0058* (.0031)	−.0028 (.0035)
Highest grade completed (father)	.0002 (.0015)	.0056** (.0023)	.0056** (.0026)
Adult female working when age 14	.0063 (.0079)	−.0159 (.0120)	−.0081 (.0137)
Adult male working when age 14	−.0035 (.0171)	−.0458* (.0260)	−.0322 (.0296)
Juvenile punishment rate	−.0210 (.0144)	.0144 (.0218)	−.0027 (.0249)
Sample size	3,086	3,098	3,080
R^2	.0160	.0204	.0242
Sample size	1,699	1,705	1,697
R^2	.0268	.0338	.0281

[a] Property criminals include either stealing something worth more than $50 or selling hard drugs.

[b] Violent crimes include either injuring someone or using force to get something.

[c] Property and violent crimes include individuals who commit a property crime as defined in n. a above and a violent crime as defined in n. b above.

*Statistically significant at the 10 percent level.

**Statistically significant at the 5 percent level.

probability of involvement in property crime by 3–5 percent and the rate of participation in violent crime by 7–9 percent. Being born to a teenage mother has small and generally insignificant effects on adolescent crime after controlling for other factors. Having a working adult male in the family substantially reduces involvement in property crime but has little effect on violent crime. Parents' education and family income have, perhaps surprisingly, no effect on either property- or violent-crime rates. Geographically, youths from the West (the omitted category) and living in an SMSA are significantly more likely to be engaged in crime. Higher local unemployment rates also appear to raise participation rates for property crimes. A measure of state-level punitiveness of the juvenile justice system (Levitt 1998) does not reduce participation in either crime type. Despite our focus on the most severe self-reported offenses, most of these crimes are nonetheless fairly minor and unlikely to bring about substantial punishments in any state. Education substantially reduces the probability that an adolescent male participates in crime, as evinced by the coefficient on high school graduation (interacted with a dummy for those at least age eighteen). High school graduates are 9 percent less likely to engage in property crime and 17 percent less likely to commit a violent crime. These results are consistent with those of Lochner (1999), who finds an important effect of high school graduation on older cohorts in the NLSY.

Measures of ability are also important determinants of criminal involvement. A one-quartile increase in an individual's AFQT score reduces his probability of committing a property or violent crime by about 3–4 percent. The AFQT score represents a weighted average of test scores related to verbal and math abilities. However, youths surveyed in the NLSY took a much larger battery of skill and ability tests (including mathematics, verbal skills, general science, speed and accuracy in coding and numerical operations, and mechanical knowledge). Our more general specifications include separate measures of test scores for math (mathematics knowledge and arithmetic reasoning tests), English (paragraph comprehension and word knowledge), and mechanical information (auto and shop information and electronics information). While male youths with higher mathematics test scores were less likely to participate in violent or property crime, youths with higher scores on the mechanical-information tests had higher criminal participation rates. Test scores on English were less important, but they did show positive correlation with violent criminal behavior. These findings are consistent with an environment in which math skills are relatively more important in the labor market while mechanical knowledge (and its associated abilities) may improve one's chances in the criminal world.[11]

---

11. Using AFQT percentiles rather than the individual test measures yields statistically significant negative effects of AFQT on both property and violent crime even after controlling for the larger set of covariates.

Table 7.6 reports analogous regression results for females. The findings are generally consistent with those for young males, especially for more important determinants such as living in an SMSA and an intact family at age fourteen. The most striking difference between males and females can be seen in the effects of high school graduation. While graduation substantially reduces crime among males, it has no effect on female crime rates. A working adult male in the home also has no effect on property crime among females, while it had an important influence on male property crime. Most variables, including AFQT, have less effect on female crime rates. Two exceptions are family income and parents' education. Females from families with incomes greater than $75,000 are significantly more likely to commit a violent crime. Those with more-educated mothers committed fewer violent crimes but more property crimes, although the magnitude of these effects is quite small. A more-educated father was also positively correlated with violent crime rates among female teenagers. Higher English test scores resulted in lower participation rates among females, and, as with males, higher mechanical-information scores actually increased criminal participation.

A few important conclusions can be drawn from these linear-probability regressions. First, family background matters. Adolescents raised in families where both parents are present are much less likely to engage in crime. Mother's age and parents' education have ambiguous effects on criminal involvement, but a working adult male in the home substantially lowers property-crime rates among adolescent males and reduces involvement in violent crime among teenage women. Second, ability and education are also important determinants of criminal involvement. While math appears to be a more important factor in reducing crime among males, English helps reduce crime among females. High scores on mechanical-knowledge tests are associated with higher crime rates among all youths. High school graduation substantially reduces crime among male adolescents, while it has little effect on female crime rates. Finally, the local environment also affects criminal participation. Youths living in an SMSA are more involved in crime, and property-crime rates are higher among males living in areas with high unemployment rates.

Given these conclusions, it is worth noting that none of the regressions can explain more than 7 percent of the variation in criminal participation. Among females, the R^2 values are all less than 0.04. Explaining individual differences in criminal participation is difficult, even with an abundance of family-background, geographic, and ability measures.

We have focused on some of the more severe property and violent crimes reported in the NLSY. For the most part, the results are robust to other measures of criminal involvement, which should not be surprising given the high correlations across crimes evident in table 7.3 above. Regression results for adolescent male participation in drug crimes (marijuana or hard-drug dealing), minor property crimes (stealing something worth less than $50 or causing property damage), and minor violent crimes (hitting someone or fighting) are shown in table 7.7. Living in an SMSA and high math scores are also important determinants of all three of these crime categories. The AFQT and an intact family are negatively correlated with drug crimes and minor violent crimes. High school graduation and lower local unemployment rates reduce drug dealing. Family income and juvenile punishment rates have little effect on any of the crime categories that we examine. A few differences between the more severe crimes reported in table 7.5 above and minor property and violent crimes are worth noting, however. Blacks and Hispanics report substantially less involvement in minor crimes than whites after controlling for other factors, while there was little difference across races for the more severe measures. For minor property crimes, father's education and a working adult female in the home raise participation. A teenage mother also substantially raises minor-property-and violent-crime rates. In general, determinants of drug crimes closely match those for the more severe property crimes reported in table 7.5. Minor violent crimes respond much like more severe violent and property crimes to most variables. Only regressions for minor property crimes reveal notable differences from those reported above. Ability and high school graduation appear to be more important predictors of severe violent and property crimes than of minor property crimes. Adolescent males with a young mother or a mother who is working (and less likely to be at home) are more likely to engage in minor property crimes but not more severe crimes. For adolescent females, similar regressions yield few covariates that are statistically significant, as with the more severe property and violent crimes in table 7.6 above.[12]

The effects of background, locality, and ability on criminal participation do not disappear with age. As seen in table 7.8, identical regressions for the oldest male cohorts in the NLSY (aged twenty to twenty-three at the time of the crime survey in 1980) show remarkably similar effects of race, family composition, AFQT and math test scores, and high school graduation. For older cohorts, a teenage mother is more positively correlated with violent-crime rates, while living in an SMSA is less associated with violent and property crime. Higher family income lowers crime rates among older cohorts, while it has little effect on the younger males. Finally, an analogous measure of the punitiveness of the criminal-justice system for adults (from Levitt 1998) substantially reduces adult participation in both property and violent crimes. Results for women mirror those for the younger females reported above, except that adult punishment reduces violent crime rates among older women. In general, these findings are consistent

---

12. Glaeser and Sacerdote (1999) explore the determinants of minor thefts (less than $50) in the full NLSY sample (ages fifteen to twenty-three) in their study of crime in cities. For the most part, their findings are consistent with our results for minor property crimes.

Table 7.7   OLS Estimates (S.E.s) of Criminal Participation for Minor Crimes (males aged 15–19 in the 1980 NLSY)

Variable	Drug Crimes[a]		Minor Property Crimes[b]		Minor Violent Crimes[c]	
Intercept	.0381	.1504**	.4788**	.11132**	.7587**	.8699**
	(.0893)	(.0410)	(.0554)	(.1234)	(.0523)	(.1170)
Age 16	.0343	.0488**	.0101	-.0017	-.0275	-.0265
	(.0280)	(.0213)	(.0288)	(.0390)	(.0272)	(.0370)
Age 17	.0853**	.0864**	-.0541*	-.0467	-.0260	-.0163
	(.0287)	(.0220)	(.0298)	(.0400)	(.0281)	(.0379)
Age 18	.1455**	.0993**	-.0153	-.0140*	-.0856**	-.1187*
	(.0314)	(.0220)	(.0298)	(.0436)	(.0282)	(.0414)
Age 19	.1466**	.0636**	-.0857**	-.0497	-.1574**	-.1773**
	(.0376)	(.0224)	(.0303)	(.0520)	(.0286)	(.0492)
Black	-.0608*	-.0839**	-.1008**	-.0428	-.1149**	-.1146**
	(.0341)	(.0214)	(.0287)	(.0473)	(.0272)	(.0450)
Hispanic	-.1002**	-.1173**	-.0291	.0365	-.1016**	-.0977*
	(.0412)	(.0276)	(.0372)	(.0567)	(.0351)	(.0537)
Intact family when age 14	-.1030**	-.0618**	-.0179	-.0373	-.0397*	-.0831**
	(.0297)	(.0160)	(.0215)	(.0412)	(.0203)	(.0393)
Teenage mother	-.0369	-.0208	.0622**	.0840**	.0499**	.0858**
	(.0225)	(.0169)	(.0228)	(.0312)	(.0216)	(.0297)
South	-.0578**	-.0744**	-.1106**	-.0885**	.0207	.0516
	(.0290)	(.0213)	(.0288)	(.0402)	(.0272)	(.0381)
Northeast	-.0196	-.0211	-.0262	.0191	-.0283	.0205
	(.0299)	(.0222)	(.0300)	(.0415)	(.0272)	(.0394)
North Central	-.0266	-.0456**	-.0266	.0135	-.0248	-.0014
	(.0268)	(.0209)	(.0283)	(.0373)	(.0267)	(.0354)

(continued)

Table 7.7 (continued)

Variable	Drug Crimes[a]	Minor Property Crimes[b]	Minor Violent Crimes[c]
Living in SMSA	.0820**	.0498**	.0828**
	(.0165)	(.0223)	(.0211)
Local unemployment rate	.0089**	.0021	.0086**
	(.0032)	(.0044)	(.0042)
AFQT	-.0013**	.0004	-.0027**
	(.0003)	(.0003)	(.0003)
Math test score	-.0062**	-.0064**	-.0095**
	(.0011)	(.0015)	(.0014)
English test score	.0021	.0059**	.0062**
	(.0016)	(.0021)	(.0020)
Mechanical- information test score	.0014	.0038**	.0008
	(.0011)	(.0015)	(.0014)
High school graduate (age 18+)	-.0995**	-.0636	-.0173
	(.0307)	(.0424)	(.0402)
Family income $10,000–$25,000	-.0567**	.0176	.0003
	(.0288)	(.0398)	(.0379)
Family income $25,000–$50,000	-.0237	-.0213	-.0180
	(.0307)	(.0426)	(.0404)

Family income $50,000–$75,000	−.0245 (.0449)	.0017 (.0624)	.0494 (.0593)
Family income > $75,000	−.0641 (.0873)	.0965 (.1214)	−.1834 (.1154)
Highest grade completed (mother)	.0001 (.0046)	−.0019 (.0064)	.0022 (.0061)
Highest grade completed (father)	.0071** (.0035)	.0114** (.0048)	−.0096** (.0046)
Adult female working when age 14	.0442** (.0177)	.0590** (.0245)	−.0099 (.0233)
Adult male working when age 14	.0071 (.0403)	−.0283 (.0547)	.0157 (.0519)
Juvenile punishment rate	.0132 (.0325)	.0308 (.0450)	−.05672 (.0428)
Sample size	3,034	3,072	3,087
R^2	.0383	.0261	.0535
Sample size	1,690	1,705	1,709
R^2	.0758	.0498	.0812

[a]Drug crimes include selling marijuana or hard drugs.
[b]Minor property crimes include stealing something worth less than $50 or causing property damage.
[c]Minor violent crimes include hitting someone or fighting.
*Statistically significant at the 10 percent level.
**Statistically significant at the 5 percent level.

Table 7.8   OLS Estimates (S.E.s) of Criminal Participation (men aged 20–23 in the 1980 NLSY)

Variable	Property Crimes[a]		Violent Crimes[b]		Violent & Property Crimes[c]	
Intercept	.3058** (.0473)	.3404** (.0987)	.2508** (.0579)	.3913** (.1282)	.4186** (.0654)	.4939** (.1417)
Age 21	-.0270 (.0192)	-.0116 (.0229)	-.0075 (.0234)	-.0214 (.0297)	-.0492* (.0264)	-.0578* (.0329)
Age 22	-.0166 (.0194)	-.0486** (.0234)	-.0210 (.0238)	-.0389 (.0302)	-.0415 (.0268)	-.0853** (.0335)
Age 23	-.0280 (.0315)	-.0456 (.0359)	-.0509 (.0387)	-.0342 (.0466)	-.0736* (.0435)	-.0869 (.0515)
Black	-.0493* (.0268)	-.0660 (.0402)	-.0116 (.0328)	.0155 (.0524)	-.0469 (.0370)	.0069 (.0578)
Hispanic	-.0509 (.0357)	-.0505 (.0470)	-.0698 (.0436)	-.1158* (.0607)	-.1013** (.0492)	-.1143* (.0674)
Intact family when age 14	-.0817** (.0204)	-.0523 (.0369)	-.0709** (.0250)	-.1121** (.0480)	-.1229** (.0282)	-.1048** (.0530)
Teenage mother	.0073 (.0206)	.0010 (.0250)	.0341 (.0252)	.0679** (.0322)	.0204 (.0285)	.0490 (.0359)
South	-.0652** (.0244)	-.0026 (.0340)	.0065 (.0299)	.0295 (.0441)	-.0273 (.0337)	.0218 (.0488)
Northeast	-.0216 (.0260)	-.0001 (.0322)	.0128 (.0318)	-.0309 (.0418)	-.0133 (.0359)	-.0305 (.0462)
North Central	-.0395 (.0243)	.0132 (.0312)	-.0438 (.0298)	-.0350 (.0405)	-.0608* (.0336)	-.0131 (.0447)
Living in SMSA	-.0045 (.0190)	-.0042 (.0231)	-.0118 (.0233)	-.0196 (.0299)	.0219 (.0263)	.0210 (.0331)
Local unemployment rate	-.0027 (.0038)	.0008 (.0044)	.0086* (.0047)	.0117** (.0057)	.0086 (.0053)	.0140** (.0064)
AFQT	-.0011** (.0003)		-.0012** (.0003)		-.0019** (.0004)	

	(1)	(2)	(3)	(4)	(5)	(6)
Math test score		−.0036**		−.0045**		−.0064**
		(.0011)		(.0015)		(.0016)
English test score		.0019		.0022		.0023
		(.0017)		(.0022)		(.0024)
Mechanical-information test score		−.0001		.0016		.0027
		(.0012)		(.0015)		(.0017)
High school graduate		−.0617**		−.0454		−.0666
		(.0292)		(.0380)		(.0419)
Family income $10,000–$25,000		−.0464*		−.0319		−.0626*
		(.0246)		(.0319)		(.0353)
Family income $25,000–$50,000		−.0621**		−.0334		−.0778**
		(.0260)		(.0336)		(.0372)
Family income $50,000–$75,000		−.0474		−.0800		−.0857
		(.0400)		(.0514)		(.0574)
Family income > $75,000		−.1179**		−.0800		−.1474*
		(.0582)		(.0757)		(.0836)
Highest grade completed (mother)		−.0041		−.0036		−.0048
		(.0049)		(.0064)		(.0070)
Highest grade completed (father)		.0055		.0031		.0039
		(.0034)		(.0044)		(.0048)
Adult female working when age 14		.0341*		.0238		.0487*
		(.0184)		(.0238)		(.0264)
Adult male working when age 14		−.0148		−.0607		−.0761
		(.0504)		(.0656)		(.0724)
Adult punishment rate		−.1574*		−.1958*		−.2539**
		(.0869)		(.1130)		(.1247)
Sample size	1,477	903	1,489	907	1,480	903
R^2	.0292	.0565	.0297	.0632	.0436	.0780

[a] Property crimes include either stealing something worth more than $50 or selling hard drugs.

[b] Violent crimes include either injuring someone or using force to get something.

[c] Property and violent crimes include individuals who commit a property crime as defined in n. a above and a violent crime as defined in n. b above.

*Statistically significant at the 10 percent level.

**Statistically significant at the 5 percent level.

with those of Lochner (1999), who explores the effects of education and the juvenile justice system on self-reported criminal behavior among older cohorts of the NLSY.

Given the low level of explanatory power of the regressions, it is perhaps not surprising that the coefficients obtained in these regressions are unable effectively to account for the observed time-series patterns of juvenile crime. For instance, between 1978 and 1993, juvenile arrest rates for violent crime rose 79 percent. Over that same time period, the fraction of children in single-parent families rose approximately 8 percentage points, the fraction of children with teenage mothers fell about 2 percentage points, high school graduation rates rose 2 percentage points, and the fraction of the population living in SMSAs rose 5 percentage points. Using the coefficients from the violent-crime regression in table 7.5 above, the changes in children in single-parent families, teenage mothers, high school graduates, and living in SMSAs imply (respectively) a 3.5, -0.3, -1.7, and 1.0 percent change in male juvenile violent-crime participation over the period 1978–93.[13] Combined, these factors imply a 2.5 percent increase in violent crime, compared to an observed increase in juvenile violent-crime arrests of 79 percent. Thus, these variables are able to account for only a minuscule fraction of the observed crime increase. Similarly, these variables cannot explain the sharp reductions in crime observed since 1993. It is important to note, however, that our estimates are for participation, not intensity of criminal activity, an alternative margin on which these demographic factors could also be operating.

As noted earlier, Mocan and Rees (1999) have undertaken an analysis similar to that discussed above but using NLSAH data. While they do not include measures of cognitive ability, family-income variables, high school graduation, or teenage mother in their specifications, they do include a number of variables that we do not, such as religion and a number of county-level variables (per capita welfare spending, racial composition, presidential voting, and per capita police spending). It is nonetheless useful to compare and contrast their results with ours. For the crime category theft, Mocan and Rees (1999) find statistically significantly higher rates among males who report no religion or have a parent on welfare. (Controlling for religious attachment does not change our results and yields a negative correlation between attachment and criminal participation.) Those who live in rural counties have lower crime rates. Broken families are associated with lower theft rates. Male assault rates (the category that corresponds most closely with our violent-crime measure) are higher for blacks, those whose fathers have low education attainment or who live in broken

---

13. These estimates are obtained by multiplying the OLS coefficient times the overall change in the variable and then dividing by the baseline violent-crime participation rate for males (0.197). In other words, the 3.5 percent change due to more children in single-parent families represents an increase from 0.197 to 0.204 in violent-crime participation.

families, or those residing in counties with high per capita welfare spending and high voting rates for Ross Perot in the 1996 presidential election. High rates of arrests per violent crime in the county reduce assaults, as does being Catholic or born-again Christian. Thus, while some differences emerge in the two sets of results, there is also a substantial degree of consistency across the samples.

The most recent cohorts of the National Longitudinal Surveys (NLSY97) began following a new cohort of youths aged twelve to sixteen in 1997. Unlike the original NLSY, this new survey will include repeated observations on criminal activity as well as new questions on gang activity. To date, however, only the results from the 1997 survey have been released. Because the new cohorts are currently so young, self-reported criminal activity is generally low and concentrated in very minor offenses. Preliminary analyses of these data yield results that are consistent with the results presented above. In particular, the presence of both parents is an important factor in reducing crime, as are higher mathematics achievement scores (AFQT scores are not yet available).

7.4.1 Outcomes at Age Thirty

One of the main advantages of the NLSY is its long panel structure. All respondents have been surveyed annually since 1979 (biannually since 1994), so we can examine how later outcomes in life are correlated with criminal participation during late teenage years. Table 7.9 reports education outcomes, labor market outcomes, and family measures at age thirty on the basis of criminal participation status in 1980. The first column reports the average outcome for the entire sample. For each criminal category, we report the raw difference in each outcome as well as the remaining difference after controlling for race, AFQT, whether the youth lived with both natural parents at age fourteen, and the youth's highest grade completed (highest grade completed was not controlled for when examining education measures, for obvious reasons). Since we do not have an instrumental variable for criminal participation (punishment measures were not sufficiently correlated with participation to yield reliable instrumental-variables estimates), our results are merely suggestive and should not be interpreted causally without further study. Despite this caveat, the results are interesting and informing.

Raw differences in education attainment are substantial regardless of the measure. Even after controlling for other factors, differences in education attainment between noncriminals and property criminals are large and statistically significant. Wage rates and income levels at age thirty are virtually identical across adolescent criminal backgrounds after controlling for background and ability. Hours worked are slightly lower among those reporting property crimes during adolescence but not among violent youth offenders. Unemployment rates are about 2 percent higher among

Table 7.9   Outcomes at Age 30 by Youth Criminal Status in 1980

Outcome at age 30	Outcome Mean	Property Crimes		Violent Crimes		Both Crimes	
		Raw Difference	Difference after Controlling for background[a]	Raw Difference	Difference after Controlling for background[a]	Raw Difference	Difference after Controlling for background[a]
			A. Males Aged 15–19				
Highest grade completed[b]	13.1347	−1.6263*	−.8571*	−.7553*	−.1515	−1.1193*	−.3896*
	(.0499)	(.2169)	(.1633)	(.1764)	(.1321)	(.1587)	(.1206)
High school graduate[b]	.7957	−.2468*	−.1625*	−.1010*	−.0374	−.1513*	−.0745*
	(.0078)	(.0330)	(.0296)	(.0269)	(.0240)	(.0243)	(.0219)
College graduate[b]	.2462	−.2136*	−.1112*	−.1148*	−.0319	−.1712*	−.0720*
	(.0083)	(.0357)	(.0297)	(.0287)	(.0237)	(.0259)	(.0218)
Log wage rate	2.5364	−.0730	.0142	−.0871*	−.0027	−.0760*	.0130
	(.0122)	(.0423)	(.0396)	(.0331)	(.0309)	(.0299)	(.0281)
Log wage income	10.1212	−.1154	−.0244	−.1216*	−.0201	−.1252*	−.0246
	(.0174)	(.0534)	(.0501)	(.0418)	(.0392)	(.0377)	(.0356)
Hours worked	2000.96	−126.63*	−117.38*	−33.59	−6.21	−85.67*	−66.16
	(17.18)	(48.56)	(48.68)	(38.11)	(38.13)	(34.70)	(34.62)
Unemployed	.0431	.0150	.0063	.0246*	.0186	.0265*	.0202*
	(.0039)	(.0141)	(.0142)	(.0112)	(.0112)	(.0101)	(.0101)
Married (not separated)	.5439	−.0066	−.0006	−.0025	.0190	−.0114	.0046
	(.0096)	(.0365)	(.0366)	(.0286)	(.0286)	(.0258)	(.0260)
Never married	.3257	.0061	.0327	.0028	.0044	.0167	.0286
	(.0090)	(.0342)	(.0342)	(.0268)	(.0268)	(.0242)	(.0244)
Divorced	.0915	.0106	−.0129	.0028	−.0119	.0020	−.0169
	(.0055)	(.0208)	(.0209)	(.0162)	(.0163)	(.0147)	(.0148)
Number of children	1.0098	.2512*	.0967	.2625*	.1401*	.2010*	.0627
	(.0218)	(.0798)	(.0764)	(.0624)	(.0597)	(.0564)	(.0544)

B. Females Aged 15–19

Highest grade completed[b]	13.2442	-1.3158*	-1.0148*	-.8992*	-.3087	-1.0020*	-.5024*
	(.0489)	(.3762)	(.3028)	(.2555)	(.2083)	(.2244)	(.1828)
High school graduate[b]	.8391	-.1777*	-.1428*	-.0678*	-.0155	-.0829*	-.0357
	(.0075)	(.0536)	(.0498)	(.0364)	(.0342)	(.0320)	(.0300)
College graduate[b]	.2483	-.1853*	-.1399*	-.1231*	-.0283	-.1519*	-.0725*
	(.0089)	(.0641)	(.0548)	(.0436)	(.0377)	(.0383)	(.0330)
Log wage rate	2.3275	.0702	.1346	-.0124	.1026*	-.0139	.0950*
	(.0140)	(.0829)	(.0766)	(.0550)	(.0511)	(.0487)	(.0453)
Log wage income	9.6756	-.0015	.0883	-.0805	.0706	-.0942	.0473
	(.0224)	(.1220)	(.1144)	(.0808)	(.0763)	(.0716)	(.0677)
Hours worked	1459.45	-139.87	-95.91	-98.19	-54.31	-122.11*	-79.57
	(18.55)	(93.08)	(91.79)	(61.75)	(61.28)	(54.63)	(54.31)
Unemployed	.0378	.0685*	.0688*	.0532*	.0466*	.0508*	.0461*
	(.0036)	(.0240)	(.0240)	(.0161)	(.0162)	(.0141)	(.0142)
Married (not separated)	.6046	-.0052	-.0145	-.0739	-.0405	-.0425	-.0166
	(.0093)	(.0667)	(.0659)	(.0442)	(.0439)	(.0391)	(.0390)
Never married	.2138	-.0573	-.0191	.0358	.0320	-.0036	.0026
	(.0078)	(.0563)	(.0552)	(.0373)	(.0368)	(.0331)	(.0327)
Divorced	.1267	.1046*	.0799	.0514	.0330	.0683*	.0464
	(.0063)	(.0452)	(.0447)	(.0299)	(.0298)	(.0265)	(.0327)
Number of children	1.3434	-.1010	-.2458	.2111*	.0274	.1666	-.0195
	(.0235)	(.1504)	(.1398)	(.0994)	(.0932)	(.0882)	(.0828)

[a]Controls for race (black and Hispanic), AFQT, and whether the youth lived with both parents at age 14 were included in all regressions. Highest grade completed was also included for all but the 3 education outcome measures.

[b]All 3 education outcomes only used samples of youths aged fifteen to seventeen in 1980.

*Significant at the 0.05 level.

thirty-year-old males (and 5 percent higher for women) reporting both property and violent crimes during their teenage years. No differences in marriage or divorce patterns by age thirty had emerged for youth criminals and noncriminals after controlling for background factors; however, men who reported violent criminal behavior during adolescence had significantly more children by age thirty. Women who engaged in crime during their youth did not report having more children.

On the basis of these correlations, it would be difficult to argue that criminal participation among most youths has severe consequences later in life. There is little correlation between youth crime and adult marriage or divorce decisions. Only a small negative correlation between adult work and youth crime exists, which might easily be explained by unobserved heterogeneity. While youth crime has a strong negative correlation with education attainment, neither variable is exogenous. As discussed in Lochner (1999), individuals likely to commit many crimes have little need for education, and individuals who receive little education are likely to find crime an attractive alternative to work. Causality runs both ways. For most adolescent offenders, the consequences of youth crime are likely to be small ten years later unless their involvement is so great that it leads to repeated arrest, conviction, harm, or death.

7.5   Analysis of Chicago Homicides by Census Tract

Official data on homicide provide a stark contrast to individual self-report data for studying the determinants of juvenile crime. Homicide data have both advantages and disadvantages. Among the advantages, homicides are always reported, and basic information about the victims (e.g., age, sex, and race) and the location of the crime is recorded. Furthermore, unlike the petty crimes that dominate self-reports, homicide has large social costs. The primary disadvantage of using homicide data is that homicides are extremely rare, necessitating substantial aggregation of the data. Also, detailed information on victims, such as income, education, etc., is not available. Even less is known about offenders since roughly one-third of murders are not solved.

In this paper, we use a unique homicide data set compiled by Block, Block, and ICJIA (1998) in cooperation with the Chicago Police Department. These data allow us to determine the race and age of Chicago homicide victims for a number of decades as well as the census tract in which the homicide occurred.[14]

We link the homicide data to census-tract-level data from the 1980 and

---

14. The content of the data reported in Block, Block, and ICJIA (1998) is similar to the more widely available Supplementary Homicide Reports compiled by the FBI, with the exception that the smallest unit of analysis in the latter data set is a city as opposed to a census tract.

1990 Censuses of Housing and Population in order to analyze the relation between homicide rates and local neighborhood characteristics. Because of the infrequency of homicides, we aggregate homicides by census tract over ten-year periods. Homicides for the period 1975–85 are linked to 1980 census data, and homicides for the period 1985–95 are linked to the 1990 census.

Census data provide a wide range of economic and social variables for inclusion in the analysis. Economic variables include median household income within the tract, percentage of children below the poverty level, and measures of income inequality within the tract. Social controls include the percentage of households in owner-occupied housing, the racial composition of the tract, and the fraction of the population aged sixteen to nineteen that is neither working nor enrolled in school.[15] Because all the tracts are within the city of Chicago, there is no obvious variation across tracts in either criminal-justice measures, macroeconomic variables, or gun-ownership proxies to exploit.

We eliminate from the sample roughly eighty census tracts (out of almost nine hundred) with residential populations under five hundred. These sparsely populated tracts tend to be areas of manufacturing or commerce. Thus, residential population is a poor proxy for the amount of activity in the area. Since crime statistics are tallied by place of occurrence, victimization rates per residential population are likely to be greatly inflated. For example, the central business district (known as the Loop) has very few residents despite an enormous daytime population.

Summary statistics for the remaining census tracts are provided in table 7.10. Our measure of juvenile crime is the annual homicide victimization rate per 100,000 juveniles aged fifteen to nineteen.[16] The age of victims is used rather than the age of assailants because the latter is known only when an arrest is made. Cook and Laub (1998) demonstrate that the ages of victims and killers tend to be similar in most cases. We present summary statistics for 1980, 1990, and the change between 1980 and 1990. Homicide victimization rates almost double for youths between 1980 and 1990. More than one-fourth of the children live in poverty, and this fraction rises slightly in 1990. The number of adults with less than a high school degree falls substantially between 1980 and 1990. We construct a measure of income inequality within the tract that reflects (roughly) the fraction of all income that would need to be transferred among tract residents in order to equalize incomes. This measure is not exact because of top coding of

15. There are many other potential variables available from the census, including unemployment rates, median rents, households headed by single parents, female labor force participation, etc. There is a high level of multicollinearity between many of the variables, both those that are included in our specifications and those that are left out. For that reason, caution must be exercised in interpreting the coefficients.

16. Although we report annual rates, these are averaged over ten-year periods.

Table 7.10   Summary Statistics for Chicago Census-Tract-Level Analysis

Variable	1980	1990	Change from 1980 to 1990
Annual homicide victimization rate for 15–19-year-olds (per 100,000)	37.4	69.7	33.5
	(65.3)	(99.0)	(108.7)
% of children in poverty	27.6	30.6	3.5
	(21.0)	(24.2)	(14.5)
% of adults with no high school diploma	48.3	38.1	−10.0
	(17.4)	(17.3)	(8.3)
Income inequality within tract (% of total income redistribution required to equalize incomes within tract)	20.4	19.2	−1.2
	(6.5)	(7.4)	(7.9)
% black	39.8	41.9	3.0
	(44.9)	(44.5)	(10.2)
% owner-occupied housing	38.3	40.5	1.7
	(24.3)	(24.4)	(6.0)
% of 16–19-year-olds neither working nor in school	19.0	16.0	−2.7
	(13.1)	(13.7)	(15.5)
Median household income (1990 dollars)	25,110	25,110	584
	(9,307)	(11,079)	(5,992)
No. of observations	801	803	792
No. of observations with zero homicides	408	344	235

Note: Column labeled 1980 gives homicide averages for the period 1976–85; column labeled 1990 gives averages for the period 1986–95. All other variables are taken from the decennial census in the named year. The income inequality measure is the estimated fraction of total census-tract income that would need to be redistributed to equalize income within the tract. Census tracts with fewer than 500 residents are omitted from the analysis. Standard errors are given in parentheses. Both means and standard errors are population weighted.

the income categories and because precise incomes are reported not at the tract level but, rather, by the number of residents falling within various income ranges. Income inequality remains relatively constant on average within census tracts over the sample period, although within a particular tract there is a great deal of variation. Roughly 40 percent of the sample is black, and almost the same fraction own their own home. A substantial fraction (almost 20 percent) of youths report neither working nor attending school.

Table 7.11 presents regression results for the tract-level analysis. We show cross-sectional results for 1980 and 1990 in the first four columns and estimates in first-differences in the last four columns. Because many census tracts did not experience a single youth homicide even when we aggregate homicides over a ten-year period, tobit estimates are presented.[17] In all

17. OLS estimates yield similar signs but are generally less statistically significant. The signs on the coefficients are generally robust to OLS estimation only including the census tracts where at least one homicide took place or using a dependent variable equal to 1 if any positive number of homicides occurred or 0 otherwise.

Table 7.11   Census-Tract-Level Determinants of Juvenile homicide Victimization in Chicago

| | Cross-Sectional Estimates (tobit) | | | | First-Difference Estimates | | | |
| | 1980 | | 1990 | | All Census Tracts | | Tracts with 1+ Homicides | |
Variable	(1)	(2)	(3)	(4)	(5)	(6)	(7)	(8)
% of children in poverty	1.43	1.12	1.20	.99	.93	.58	.95	.47
	(.20)	(.31)	(.21)	(.31)	(.24)	(.26)	(.32)	(.34)
% of adults with no high school diploma	.76	.83	1.68	2.07	1.37	.83	1.67	.91
	(.20)	(.23)	(.24)	(.30)	(.40)	(.41)	(.54)	(.57)
Income inequality within tract	1.01	.74	1.46	1.75	.04	-.42	.53	.08
	(.42)	(.45)	(.50)	(.53)	(.40)	(.42)	(.54)	(.55)
% black	.19	.24	1.01	1.14	.55	.57	.48	.57
	(.07)	(.08)	(.09)	(.10)	(.25)	(.25)	(.17)	(.32)
% owner-occupied housing	...	-.48	...	-.69	...	1.06	...	2.11
		(.23)		(.22)		(.60)		(.90)
% of 16–19-year-olds neither working nor in school	...	.73	...	.21	...	.14	...	.45
		(.27)		(.31)		(.21)		(.29)
Median household income	...	.0011	...	.0016	...	-.0026	...	-.0038
		(.0008)		(.0008)		(.0006)		(.0009)
Constant	-94.9	-109.8	-131.6	-166.4	35.9	31.9	48.7	41.7
	(12.6)	(32.5)	(14.7)	(35.7)	(4.8)	(4.9)	(6.5)	(6.7)
Ancillary parameter	62.9	61.5	77.7	77.3	...	...	...	...
	(2.3)	(2.2)	(2.6)	(2.6)				
(Pseudo-)R^2	.047	.051	.075	.077	.051	.076	.047	.084
No. of observations	801	798	803	801	792	788	557	556
No. of censored observations	408	406	344	342	...	...	...	...

Note: The dependent variable is the annual homicide victimization rate for 15–19-year-olds in the census tract. Columns labeled 1980 are homicide averages for the period 1976–85; columns labeled 1990 are averages for the period 1986–95. In all cases, the explanatory variables are taken from the decennial census. The income-inequality measure is the estimated fraction of total census-tract income that would need to be redistributed to equalize income within the tract. Census tracts with fewer than 500 residents are omitted from the analysis. All regressions are population weighted. For the tobit specifications, pseudo-R^2 values are reported.

cases, regression results are weighted by census-tract residential population. In the cross-sectional estimates, homicide victimization rates are positively related to the fraction of children in poverty, the fraction of adults with no high school diploma, and income inequality within the tract. More owner-occupied housing is associated with fewer homicides. In almost every instance, all these coefficients are statistically significant at the .05 level in both the 1980 and the 1990 specifications. Number of idle teens and median income are both positively related to homicide rates but are of only borderline statistical significance.

The coefficients are relatively stable across the 1980 and 1990 periods, with a few notable exceptions.[18] The fraction of adults with no high school degree becomes more important in 1990, as does the income-inequality measure and the percentage black. Given the sharp divergence between white and black homicide rates between 1980 and 1990, it is not surprising that the coefficient on percentage black increases substantially in the 1990 tobit.

The implied effect of the explanatory variables on homicide rates is substantial. For instance, a 10 percentage point increase in the number of children in poverty increases the juvenile homicide rate by six to eight per 100,000 across the various cross-sectional regressions—a substantial change relative to the baseline homicide rates of 37.4 in 1980 and 69.7 in 1990.[19] A 10 percentage point increase in the fraction of adults with high school diplomas or a 10 percentage point reduction in income inequality reduces homicide rates by four to five in 1980 and by ten to thirteen in 1990.

When doing cross-sectional estimates of this kind, an important concern is the presence of omitted-variables bias. In particular, when using census-tract-level data, there is a high degree of multicollinearity between the variables included in the regression and other potential covariates, such as single-parent families, local labor market conditions, family size, etc. Thus, the particular variables included in the regressions, in all likelihood, are proxying for other social and economic factors. First-difference estimates provide one check on the plausibility of the specification. To the extent that changes in the named variables affect changes in homicide rates in a manner similar to that in which the levels of the variables influence homicide rates in the cross section, our confidence in the coefficients is enhanced. We present first-difference estimates in columns 5–8 of table 7.11.

---

18. It is also the case that there is less censoring in the 1990 sample. When calculating the overall effect of a given change in an explanatory variable, the raw coefficient reported in the table must be corrected to account for the degree of censoring. In practice, the correction is nearly proportional to the fraction of observations that are censored (about 50 percent in 1980 and about 40 percent in 1990).

19. These calculations take into account the correction required because of censoring in the dependent variable.

In columns 5 and 6, all census tracts are included; in the final two columns, only those census tracts in which at least one youth homicide occurred over the period 1975–95 are in the sample. The coefficients on children in poverty, adults without high school degrees, and the percentage black are all robust to estimation in first differences, although, in all cases, standard errors rise. The degree of income inequality appears less robust. Owner-occupied housing and median household income actually reverse signs, making us very cautious about drawing any conclusions for these variables.

Given the dramatic increase in homicide among youths in Chicago between the years 1980 and 1990, it is worth examining the extent to which changes in the observed variables can account for this time-series pattern. The percentage of children in poverty rose 3.5 percent in Chicago between 1980 and 1990. Using the median estimate across the eight specifications in table 7.11, this increase in poverty can explain a rise of two to three homicides per 100,000, or roughly 6–10 percent of the overall increase. The dramatic increase in the number of adults with high school diplomas over this period actually works in the wrong direction, implying an expected decrease in crime of eight to nine per 100,000. Increases in the percentage black (a 3.0 percentage point rise overall in Chicago) would be predicted to increase homicide rates by only 1.5 per 100,000. Thus, on net, the three factors that are consistently linked to higher crime across the different specifications actually worked to *lower* crime between 1980 and 1990 and thus do not provide a plausible explanation for crime's increase.

7.6 State-Level Panel-Data Analysis of the Effect of the Criminal-Justice System

The final set of estimates presented use a state-level panel-data set for the period 1978–93.[20] Unlike the analyses presented in previous sections, this approach is ideal for studying the effect of the justice system on juvenile criminal behavior since crime and criminal-justice data (such as the number of juveniles in custody) are available exclusively at the state level.

Data limitations present substantial challenges for examining juvenile delinquency at the state level. First, criminal involvement by age of perpetrator is not directly observed since, for many crimes, the age of the criminal is unknown. Arrest data, which are collected by age of offender and type of crime, must therefore be used as a proxy.[21] Second, the data on juveniles in custody are more limited than the corresponding data on adults. Censuses of public and private juvenile facilities were conducted

---

20. This section draws heavily on the analysis of Levitt (1998).

21. As Greenwood (1995) notes, however, juveniles and adults may be arrested at different rates for a given crime. For instance, juveniles are more likely to commit crimes in groups, potentially leading to more arrests per crime.

roughly every two years between 1977 and 1993. Third, in some of these censuses, delinquents are not separately identified from status offenders (e.g., runaways and truants) and neglected children.[22]

Using this state-level panel data, Levitt (1998) analyzes the responsiveness of juvenile crime to juvenile punishment. Two different measures of juvenile punishment are used: juveniles in custody as a fraction of the total juvenile population and juveniles in custody per juvenile violent crime committed. In addition to the punishment variables, controls for percentage black, percentage living in metropolitan areas, the unemployment rate, drinking-age dummies, age-distribution measures, state fixed effects, and year dummies were included. In some specifications, state-level trends were also included. For both violent crime and property crime, more severe juvenile punishments are always associated with lower juvenile crime. The magnitude of the crime decrease is consistent with the response of adult crime to punishment (Levitt 1998) as well as with previous estimates of adult responsiveness (Marvell and Moody 1994; Levitt 1996). A 1 percentage point increase in the unemployment rate increases juvenile property crime by 1–2 percent but has no consistent effect on violent crime by juveniles. The estimated effect of unemployment on adult crime is very similar to that on juvenile crime.

Perhaps more interesting than these panel regressions is the unique opportunity afforded by the sharp changes in expected punishment that accompany the transition from the juvenile to the adult criminal-justice system. Prior to reaching the "age of majority," jurisdiction falls to the juvenile courts, which operate almost wholly independently of the adult courts.[23] On reaching the age of majority, the adult courts take over. In states where juvenile and adult punishments differ substantially, the age of majority represents an abrupt change in the costs associated with committing crime. If juveniles respond to the incentives of the criminal-justice system, an abrupt change in criminal behavior should be observed. For the sake of this analysis, it is fortunate that there is an enormous amount of variation in the "relative punitiveness" of the juvenile and the adult justice systems across states. Some states (e.g., Illinois and Massachusetts) are extremely lenient toward juveniles relative to adults. In other states (e.g., California), the treatment of juveniles is quite severe—perhaps even more so than that of adults (Harris 1993).

Although the logic of this analysis is straightforward, some difficulties are present. First, there is strong evidence that criminal involvement varies markedly over the life cycle (e.g., Blumstein et al. 1986). Therefore, one

22. Levitt (1998) demonstrates an algorithm—based on the number of juveniles held in public vs. private detention facilities—that appears to provide close estimates of the number of juvenile delinquents in custody.
23. In a small fraction of cases, typically the most severe offenses or those involving juveniles very close to the age of majority, jurisdiction of cases is transferred to the adult courts.

cannot simply compare crime rates in a state before and after the age of majority. Rather, one must employ a "differences-in-differences" approach, looking at crime patterns in states that have the same age of majority but in which the change in punishment on reaching adulthood varies. Second, it is difficult to make a direct comparison of the punitiveness of juvenile and adult punishments. Juvenile institutions are qualitatively different than adult institutions (typically, the former are much safer and more pleasant). Since juvenile records are sealed, the long-term financial effect of juvenile convictions may be less than that of adult convictions. On the other hand, being institutionalized may simply involve a higher psychic cost for a fourteen-year-old than for a twenty-four-year-old. For this reason, the analysis focuses on what we term the *relative punitiveness* of state juvenile and adult criminal-justice systems, defined as follows:

$$\text{relative punitiveness} = \frac{(\text{adult prisoners/adult violent crime})}{(\text{juvenile delinquents/juvenile violent crime})}.$$

The harsher are adult punishments relative to juvenile punishments, the greater is the measure of relative punitiveness, and, consequently, the greater is the predicted decrease in criminal involvement associated with the transition to adult court.[24]

The results of this analysis are presented in table 7.12.[25] The left side of the table reports results for states in which the age of majority is eighteen (the most common age of majority in the United States). Columns 1–3 divide states into three groups according to the relative punitiveness of the adult and juvenile courts. Column 1 contains those state-year pairs where the transition to adult court is associated with the greatest increase in punishment (a ratio greater than 2). Column 2 captures state-year pairs with moderate increases in punitiveness with the onset of adult status. Column 3 reflects those cases with apparent decreases (or, possibly, the smallest increases) in the severity of punishment.[26] The mean percentage change in crimes committed annually by cohort from age fifteen to age nineteen is presented for both violent crime and property crime. The boxed observations represent the age at which an individual passes from the juvenile court to the adult court.

The top row of the first column in table 7.12 shows that, in those states

---

24. To the extent that this measure of punitiveness is not perfectly capturing true differences in punishment across states (e.g., because the living conditions of juveniles in custody in one state are more pleasant than those in another state), there will be misclassification errors that should attenuate any measured differences across states, making it more difficult to find significant results.

25. Levitt (1998) demonstrates that the simple differences-in-differences results presented here are robust to the inclusion of a wide range of other controls.

26. Although the observations reported in col. 3 have relative punitiveness ratios less than 1, this does not necessarily imply that actual punishment is lower in the adult court for the reasons discussed earlier in this section.

Table 7.12 **Changes in Crime Rates and the Transition from the Juvenile Court to the Adult Court**

Year to Year % Change in Crime for Cohort	Relative Punitiveness of Adult versus Juvenile Court in States Where Age of Majority Is 18				Relative Punitiveness in States Where Age of Majority Is 17		
	Most Punitive (N = 61) (1)	Intermediate (N = 115) (2)	Least Punitive (N = 102) (3)	Difference of (1) − (3) (4)	Most Punitive (N = 29) (5)	Least Punitive (N = 29) (6)	Difference of (5) − (6) (7)
Violent Crime							
15–16	40.6	37.5	39.9	0.7	51.2	37.1	14.1
	(3.8)	(2.6)	(3.8)	(5.4)	(5.4)	(5.0)	(7.2)
16–17	25.1	28.4	24.8	0.3	**13.0**	**39.4**	**−26.4**
	(3.1)	(2.4)	(3.2)	(4.5)	(4.4)	(6.7)	(8.0)
17–18	**−3.8**	**10.2**	**23.1**	**−26.9**	26.3	29.7	−3.4
	(3.6)	(3.1)	(3.4)	(5.0)	(6.1)	(3.6)	(7.1)
18–19	.5	3.8	5.9	−5.4	−3.8	.5	−4.3
	(2.4)	(1.8)	(1.6)	(2.9)	(2.7)	(2.5)	(3.7)
Property Crime							
15–16	8.4	8.4	6.3	2.1	13.2	9.6	3.6
	(1.5)	(1.0)	(1.0)	(1.8)	(2.1)	(3.0)	(3.7)
16–17	−1.9	−1.8	−5.4	3.5	**−6.7**	**7.1**	**−13.8**
	(1.5)	(1.0)	(.9)	(1.7)	(2.6)	(3.4)	(4.3)
17–18	**−20.5**	**−12.8**	**−9.2**	**−11.3**	−2.6	4.0	−6.6
	(1.7)	(1.7)	(1.5)	(2.3)	(3.2)	(3.2)	(4.5)
18–19	−19.4	−16.2	−15.9	−3.5	−21.3	−20.9	−0.4
	(1.3)	(1.0)	(.9)	(1.6)	(1.8)	(1.4)	(2.2)

Note: Values in the table are state-population weighted means of the percentage change in crime committed by the named cohort from last year to this year. Standard deviations are given in parentheses. Values printed in boldface type reflect passage from the juvenile to the adult court. The number of observations listed at the top of the table is the number of state-year pairs in the category. The ranges in cols. 1, 2, and 3 are > 2, 1–2, and < 1, respectively. The cutoff separating cols. 5 and 6 is 1.5.

where the transition to the adult court is the harshest, sixteen-year-olds commit 40.6 percent more violent crime than that same cohort of adolescents committed as fifteen-year-olds. This large increase—mirrored in columns 2 and 3—reflects the natural age profile of violent crime. Similar results are obtained for the second row: seventeen-year-olds commit about 25 percent more crime than sixteen-year-olds. This is true across all the first three columns. For eighteen-year-olds, the age at which the adult court gains jurisdiction in these states, a starkly different pattern emerges. In the states where punishments increase the most with the adult court (col. 1), violent crime rates fall by 3.8 percent for eighteen-year-olds. In contrast, where the transition to the adult court is most lenient, violent crime committed by eighteen-year-olds increases 23.1 percent. Where the rise in sanctions with adult court is intermediate, the rise in violent crime is also intermediate: 10.2 percent. A similar but less extreme pattern also emerges in property crime (the lower-left-hand panel of the table), where the states with the harshest transition see 20.5 percent decreases in crime at age eighteen, compared to 12.8 and 9.2 percent decreases in the moderate and most lenient states, respectively.

Column 4 of table 7.12 calculates mean differences between the values in column 1 and those in column 3, along with standard errors on these differences. For violent crime, the differences are small before the transition to the adult court. For eighteen-year-olds, who have just come under the jurisdiction of the adult court, the 27 percent difference in violent-crime rates in column 4 is highly statistically significant. Crime continues to fall faster in the most punitive states for nineteen-year-olds. The identical pattern is also observed for property crime.[27]

Columns 5 and 6 present parallel estimates for states where the age of majority is seventeen. Owing to the smaller number of states falling into this classification, observations are assigned to two groups rather than three, with a punitiveness ratio of 1.5 as the dividing line. Column 7 presents the difference between column 5 and column 6. Once again, the percentage changes in both violent- and property-crime rates are slightly higher prior to the transition, dramatically lower in the year of transition, and slightly lower in the ensuing years. The magnitude of the differences across columns, displayed in column 7, is very similar to the results for states with an age of majority equal to eighteen.[28]

---

27. Bearing in mind that the estimated crime rate by cohort is not a direct measure of crime involvement but rather derived from the number of arrests by cohort, an alternative explanation for the patterns observed would be that the police are more hesitant to arrest those who have passed the age of majority because the sanctions that they will face are so severe. Anecdotal evidence, however, suggests just the opposite: that the police are less likely to arrest juveniles because punishments are so slight that it is not worth the effort.

28. It is also interesting to compare the patterns observed in states where the age of majority is eighteen to those where it is seventeen. For both crime categories, the change in crime is smaller for eighteen-year-olds becoming adults (cols. 1–3) than for eighteen-year-olds who

The results presented in table 7.12 are noteworthy for two reasons. First, they provide strong evidence that juvenile crime is responsive to punishment. This, however, is not particularly surprising given the existing literature on adult responses to increased punishments. What is more remarkable about the findings presented above is that they provide some of the most compelling empirical evidence to date of deterrence (as opposed to incapacitation). The economic model of crime revolves around the concept of deterrence (i.e., a behavioral response of potential criminals to the incentives that they face). In practice, however, it is extremely difficult empirically to differentiate between deterrence and incapacitation (i.e., a mechanical reduction in crime that occurs because criminals are unable to commit crime while incarcerated). Because the fall in crime associated with reaching the age of majority occurs so quickly, and because juvenile criminal records are sealed, leading to very low incarceration rates for those just beyond the age of majority, the results presented in table 7.12 strongly suggest a large deterrent effect.

Although the results presented in table 7.12 cannot be directly used for the purpose of calculating the extent to which criminal-justice factors can explain the time-series pattern of crime observed over the last two periods, other results reported in Levitt (1998) are useful for that purpose. Over the period 1978–93, punishment per crime fell by 20 percent for juveniles, which can account for an 8 percentage point increase in juvenile violent crime, or only about 10 percent of the total observed change. Increases in juvenile punishment since 1993 are likewise too small to explain the recent declines in crime. On the other hand, it is worth noting that the gap between juvenile and adult crime trends is relatively well explained by the differential trends in punishment. Between 1978 and 1993, adult punishments rose 60 percent, and juvenile punishments fell 20 percent. Over half the gap between juvenile and adult violent-crime growth rates (i.e., the difference between the 79 percent increase for juveniles and the 31 percent increase for adults) can be attributed to the differences in punishment. In other words, there appears to have been an unexplained upward trend in both juvenile and adult crime over the period, but, once that trend is removed, criminal penalties are quite important in explaining the residual differences between juveniles and adults.

---

were previously treated as adults (cols. 5 and 6). This suggests that, even in states where the relative punitiveness of the adult court is the least, the adult court is more severe than the juvenile court. Looking at seventeen-year-olds, however, yields a somewhat different result. In states where seventeen-year-olds are treated as adults and adults are punished severely (col. 5), crime growth rates for seventeen-year-olds are lower than they are in states where seventeen-year-olds remain juveniles (cols. 1–3). On the other hand, when seventeen-year-olds are treated leniently as adults (col. 6), crime increases are even greater than they are in states where seventeen-year-olds are considered juveniles.

7.7 Conclusion

Using three different data sets, this paper has analyzed the determinants of juvenile crime. Individual-level analysis using the NLSY highlights the importance of such factors as gender, family environment, and cognitive ability in predicting criminal involvement. Census-tract-level panel data from Chicago also point to the criminogenic effect of unstable homes as well as identifying an important role for high concentrations of children in poverty and local income inequality. State-level panel data demonstrate the importance of the criminal-justice system in restraining criminality. Coincident with the transition from juvenile to adult court, crime drops sharply in those states where adults are punished more heavily. None of these determinants of crime, however, do a particularly good job of explaining the time-series pattern of juvenile crime over the last two decades.

References

Anderson, James. 1999. The aggregrate burden of crime. *Journal of Law and Economics* 42, no. 2:611–42.

Becker, Gary. 1968. Crime and punishment: An economic approach. *Journal of Political Economy* 76:169–217.

Block, Carolyn Rebecca, Richard L. Block, and the Illinois Criminal Justice Information Authority (ICJIA). 1998. Homicides in Chicago, 1965–1995. 4th ICPSR version. Chicago: Illinois Criminal Justice Information Authority (producer). Ann Arbor, Mich.: Inter-University Consortium for Political and Social Research (distributor).

Blumstein, Alfred, Jacqueline Cohen, Jeffrey Roth, and Christy Visher, eds. 1986. *Criminal careers and "career criminals."* Washington, D.C.: National Academy of Sciences.

Blumstein, Alfred, and Richard Rosenfeld. 1998. Explaining recent trends in U.S. homicide rates. *Journal of Criminal Law and Criminology* 88:1175–1216.

Case, Anne, and Lawrence Katz. 1991. The company you keep: The effects of family and neighborhood on disadvantaged youths. Working Paper no. 3705. Cambridge, Mass.: National Bureau of Economic Research.

Cloward, R. A., and L. E. Ohlin. 1960. *Delinquency and opportunity.* New York: Free Press.

Cook, Philip, and John Laub. 1998. The social ecology of youth violence. In *Youth violence (Crime and justice: A review of research,* vol. 24), ed. Michael Tonry and Mike Moore. Chicago: University of Chicago Press.

Corman, Hope, and Naci Mocan. In press. A time-series analysis of crime and drug use in New York City. *American Economic Review.*

Dagg, P. K. 1991. The psychological sequelae of therapeutic abortion—denied and completed. *American Journal of Psychiatry* 148, no. 5 (May): 578–85.

Donohue, John, and Steven Levitt. 1999. Legalized abortion and crime. University of Chicago. Typescript.

Donohue, John, and Peter Siegelman. 1994. Is the United States at the optimal rate of crime? Chicago: American Bar Foundation. Mimeo.

Elliott, D., and S. Ageton. 1980. Reconciling race and class differences in self-reported and official estimates of delinquency. *American Sociological Review* 45:95–110.

Fagan, Jeffrey, and Richard Freeman. 1999. Crime and work. Columbia University. Typescript.

Farrington, D. 1973. Self-reports of deviant behavior: Predictive and stable. *Journal of Criminal Law and Criminology* 64, no. 1:99–110.

Federal Bureau of Investigation (FBI). Various editions. *Uniform crime reports.* Washington, D.C.

Freeman, Richard. 1992. Crime and the employment of disadvantaged youths. In *Urban labor markets and job opportunity,* ed. George Peterson and Wayne Vroman. Washington, D.C.: Urban Institute Press.

———. 1995. The labor market. In *Crime,* ed. James Q. Wilson and Joan Petersilia. San Francisco: ICS.

Glaeser, Edward, and Bruce Sacerdote. 1999. Why is there more crime in cities? *Journal of Political Economy* 107:S225–S258.

Glaeser, Edward, Bruce Sacerdote, and Jose Scheinkman. 1996. Crime and social interactions. *Quarterly Journal of Economics* 111:507–48.

Glueck, Sheldon, and Eleanor Glueck. 1950. *Unraveling juvenile delinquency.* New York: Commonwealth Fund.

Gould, Eric, Bruce Weinberg, and David Mustard. 1997. Crime rates and local labor market opportunities in the United States: 1979–1991. Working paper. University of Georgia.

Greenwood, Peter. 1995. Juvenile crime and juvenile justice. In *Crime,* ed. James Q. Wilson and Joan Petersilia. San Francisco: ICS.

Grogger, Jeffrey. 1998. Market wages and youth crime. *Journal of Labor Economics* 16, no. 4:756–91.

Gruber, Jonathan, Philip Levine, and Douglas Staiger. 1999. Abortion legalization and child living circumstances: Who is the "marginal child?" *Quarterly Journal of Economics* 114:263–91.

Harris, Ron. 1993. A nation's children in lockup. *Los Angeles Times,* 22 August, A1.

Hindelang, M., T. Hirschi, and J. Weis. 1979. Correlates of delinquency: The illusion of discrepancy between self-report and official measures. *American Sociological Review* 44:995–1014.

Hirschi, Travis. 1969. *Causes of delinquency.* Berkeley: University of California Press.

Kennedy, David, Anne Piehl, and Anthony Braga. 1996. Youth violence in Boston: Gun markets, serious youth offenders, and a use-reduction strategy. *Law and Contemporary Problems* 59:147–83.

Levine, Philip, Douglas Staiger, Thomas Kane, and David Zimmerman. 1996. *Roe v. Wade* and american fertility. Working Paper no. 5615. Cambridge, Mass.: National Bureau of Economic Research, June.

Levitt, Steven. 1996. The effect of prison population size on crime rates: Evidence from prison overcrowding litigation. *Quarterly Journal of Economics* 111:319–51.

———. 1997. Using electoral cycles in police hiring to estimate the effect of police on crime. *American Economic Review* 87, no. 3:270–90.

———. 1998. Juvenile crime and punishment. *Journal of Political Economy* 106 (December): 1156–85.

Levitt, Steven, and Sudhir Venkatesh. In press. An economic analysis of a drug-selling gang's finances. *Quarterly Journal of Economics.*

Lipsey, Mark. 1991. Juvenile delinquency treatment: A meta-analysis inquiry into the variability of effects. In *Meta-analysis for explanation: A casebook,* ed. Thomas D. Cook. Beverly Hills, Calif.: Sage.

Lochner, Lance. 1999. Education, work, and crime: Theory and evidence. Working Paper no. 465. Rochester Center for Economic Research.

Machin, Stephen, and Costas Meghir. 2000. Crime and economic incentives. University College, London. Typescript.

Marvell, Thomas, and Carlisle Moody. 1994. Prison population growth and crime reduction. *Journal of Quantitative Criminology* 10:109–40.

———. 1996. Specification problems, police levels, and crime rates. *Criminology* 34:609–46.

Miller, Ted, Mark Cohen, and Shelli Rossman. 1993. Victim costs of violent crime and resulting injuries. *Health Affairs* 12:186–97.

Mocan, H. Naci, and Daniel Rees. 1999. Economic conditions, deterrence, and juvenile crime: Evidence from micro data. University of Colorado, Denver. Typescript.

Reuter, Peter, Robert MacCoun, and Patrick Murphy. 1990. *Money from crime.* Santa Monica, Calif.: Rand Drug Policy Research Center.

Ruhm, Christopher. 1996. Are recessions good for your health? Working Paper no. 5570. Cambridge, Mass.: National Bureau of Economic Research.

Sampson, Robert. 1985. Neighborhood and crime: The structural determinants of personal victimization. *Journal of Research in Crime and Delinquency* 22:7–40.

Sampson, Robert, and John Laub. 1993. *Crime in the making: Pathways and turning points through life.* Cambridge, Mass.: Harvard University Press.

Soares, Rodrigo. 1999. Development, crime, and punishment: Accounting for the international differences in crime rates. University of Chicago, Department of Economics. Typescript.

Spelman, William. 1994. *Criminal incapacitation.* New York: Plenum.

Tauchen, Helen, Anne Witte, and Harriet Griesinger. 1994. Criminal deterrence: Revisiting the issue with a birth cohort. *Review of Economics and Statistics* 76:399–412.

U.S. Bureau of the Census. Annual. *Statistical abstract of the United States.* Washington, D.C.

Wilson, James Q., and Richard Herrnstein. 1985. *Crime and human nature.* New York: Simon & Schuster.

Wilson, James Q., and Joan Petersilia, eds. 1995. *Crime.* San Francisco: ICS.

Wilson, William Julius. 1987. *The truly disadvantaged: The inner city, the underclass, and public policy.* Chicago: University of Chicago Press.

Wolfgang, Marvin, Robert F. Figlio, and Torstein Sellin. 1972. *Delinquency in a birth cohort.* Chicago: University of Chicago Press.

8

Environment and Persistence
in Youthful Drinking Patterns

Philip J. Cook and Michael J. Moore

Excess drinking is associated with lost productivity, traumatic injury, early death, crime and violence, and neglect of family responsibilities. These and related concerns have long engendered public support for government regulation of the production, sale, and use of alcoholic beverages. Drinking by youths is a particular concern. Every state bans the sale of alcohol to those under age twenty-one.

Despite this age-based prohibition, drinking is widespread among teenagers. According to a national survey of high school students, Monitoring the Future (MTF), the thirty-day prevalence of drinking in 1998 among twelfth graders was 52 percent, and over half those (33 percent of the total) said that they had gotten drunk in the previous month; the thirty-day drinking prevalence for tenth graders was 39 percent, for eighth graders 23 percent. These alcohol-use rates are higher than use rates for other abused substances, including tobacco and marijuana (www.isr.umich.edu/src/mtf/data). Indeed, alcohol is the illicit drug most widely used by teenagers.

Philip J. Cook is the ITT/Sanford Professor of Public Policy at the Sanford Institute of Public Policy, Duke University, and a research associate of the National Bureau of Economic Research. Michael J. Moore is associate professor at the Fuqua School of Business, Duke University, a visiting professor at the University of Chicago, and a research associate of the National Bureau of Economic Research.

The authors' contributions to this effort are equal. This paper owes a great deal to Jonathan Gruber's suggestions and to helpful comments by John Mullahy, Will Manning, and participants in three NBER conferences as well as seminars at the University of Wisconsin and the University of Chicago. The authors thank Bob Malme and Zhu Wei for their very able assistance in statistical programming and in preparing figures and tables. Moore acknowledges the support of the Olin Foundation and the Stigler Center at the University of Chicago. The views expressed herein are those of the authors and not necessarily those of the National Bureau of Economic Research or any other organization.

The concern with this widespread use and misuse stems primarily from the dangers of youthful inebriation, including an increased chance of motor-vehicle accident or other type of injury, unwanted sex, criminal victimization, and other problems stemming from clumsiness, distorted perception, and cognitive deficit. But there is another type of concern as well: a teenage drinker who escapes the immediate hazards may still be burdened with longer-term deleterious effects and, in particular, a taste for alcohol that may lead to heavy drinking in later years as well as a deficit in human-capital acquisition (Mullahy and Sindelar 1989, 1991).

The public response to youthful drinking includes efforts directed at both the demand for alcohol among and the supply of alcohol to young people. For the most part, the relevant economics literature has focused on supply-side interventions, especially the minimum purchase age (MPA) and alcohol excise taxes (Cook and Moore, in press; Grossman et al. 1994; Sloan, Stout, and Whetten-Goldstein 1999). These evaluations have provided evidence that alcohol-control policies reduce the prevalence of drinking and bingeing (having a large number of drinks on a single occasion), and the immediate consequences thereof, for youths and, in the case of excise taxes, adults as well. But the scholarly consensus on the public-health benefits of alcohol excise taxes appears to have broken down in recent years. Two notable papers (Dee 1999; Mast, Benson, and Rasmussen 1999) conclude that estimates of the influence of beer excise taxes on drinking, heavy drinking, and motor-vehicle fatality rates are not robust against alternative specifications or time periods and that the true effects may be considerably smaller than suggested in the previous literature.

In this paper, we provide further evidence on the influence of the MPA and the beer excise tax on youthful drinking, using data from the National Longitudinal Survey of Youth (NLSY) for 1982–85 and 1988–89. While we, too, find that the estimated effects of excise taxes are sensitive to specification, our results are compatible with the view that increasing these taxes would reduce the prevalence of binge drinking.

Given the habitual nature of alcohol use and abuse, it is also important to understand the dynamic effects of control policies. Here, we utilize the NLSY data to assess the extent to which alcohol-control measures at age fourteen influence how much people drink later in life. Our results suggest that adolescents growing up in states with a low MPA were relatively likely to binge in later years. These results are relevant, not only to evaluating alcohol-control measures, but also (and more fundamentally) to providing evidence on the extent to which youthful drinking is habit-forming.

Government taxes and regulations are not the only features of the drinking "environment" that influence youthful consumption patterns. Sociological research, not to mention personal experience, suggests that drinking is a social activity (Skog 1980, 1985). In a "wet" environment, where most adults drink and alcohol is included in a wide variety of social occasions, adults will tend to drink more than they otherwise would, and adolescents may be initiated into drinking relatively early. In what follows, we attempt to capture the influence of social context by introducing per capita ethanol consumption as a covariate.[1] It is strongly positively associated with youthful drinking, but the proper interpretation of this result is ambiguous.

Our presentation is organized as follows. Section 8.1 presents some descriptive statistics on how much American adolescents drink and how their use of alcohol compares with that of their counterparts in other countries. Section 8.2 analyzes the twenty-five-year trend in drinking and bingeing prevalence by high school seniors in America. The similarity between this teen-drinking time profile and the time profile of adult per capita alcohol consumption suggests that the drinking decisions of teens are influenced by adult drinking behavior or, in any event, that they share a common set of determinants. Section 8.3 presents our results on the determinants of drinking by young adults, with a particular focus on the conflicts in the literature concerning the influence of the alcohol excise tax on alcohol abuse. Results on the persistence of youthful drinking are described in section 8.4, together with findings that suggest that alcohol availability at age fourteen influences the likelihood of bingeing as an adult. Section 8.5 summarizes.

8.1 Adolescent Drinking in an International Context

While American adolescents drink far more than their elders would like, they are less likely to drink or drink heavily than adolescents in some other prosperous countries. The primary source of data for such international comparisons is a series of surveys conducted under the auspices of the World Health Organization (WHO) Regional Office for Europe, known as the Health Behaviour in School-Aged Children Study (HBSC). Since 1985, surveys have been conducted at four-year intervals in a growing number of countries. In the 1997–98 survey, twenty-six European countries or regions, Canada, and, for the first time, the United States participated (Currie et al. 2000, 8). The target population in this survey was youths aged eleven, thirteen, and fifteen. The surveys were administered in school to nationally representative samples of classrooms; with a few exceptions, fifteen hundred or more students from each age group participated in each of the countries.

Table 8.1 summarizes the results for young Americans and indicates how they rank in comparison to youths in the other twenty-seven nations/regions included in the survey. A majority of Americans have had at least

1. For a general introduction to the influence of social context, see Coleman (1990) and Becker (1996).

Table 8.1   Drinking by American Adolescents: Findings for the United States from the HBSC

Indicator of Drinking	Age 11	Age 13	Age 15
Ever had a drink:			
Boys (%)	62	74	88
Girls (%)	58	78	87
Rank among 28 countries	12	6	5
Drink at least weekly:			
Boys (%)	8	10	23
Girls (%)	7	11	15
Rank among 28 countries	22	18	11
Drunk twice or more in life:			
Boys (%)	3	12	34
Girls (%)	3	11	28
Rank among 28 countries	13	18	10

Source: HBSC (Currie et al. 2000).

Note: The rankings are from the lowest (rank = 1) to the highest (rank = 28) among the countries and regions included in the survey.

one drink by age eleven, and almost everyone has been "initiated" by age fifteen; in this respect, Americans are no different than youths in other countries. (The country with the largest number of lifetime abstainers at age fifteen is Israel, but, even there, 70 percent have had at least one drink.)

With respect to two other measures—*drinks at least weekly* and *reported being drunk at least twice in lifetime*—the prevalence for Americans and youths from other countries is quite low at ages eleven and thirteen, increasing somewhat at age fifteen. By that age, 19 percent of Americans say that they drink weekly, and almost one-third indicate that they have been drunk a couple of times or more. Fifteen-year-olds from most other countries have higher prevalence rates on both measures. In particular, youths from Denmark, Britain, Ireland, Greece, and much of Central Europe are more likely to be regular drinkers; the prevalence of such frequent drinking in the Nordic and Baltic countries is somewhat less than that in the United States.[2]

Thus, we see that there is nothing unusual about the amount of drinking done by American adolescents when it is compared to that done in other countries.

2. It is interesting to note in this context that the minimum age for purchasing alcoholic beverages is lower elsewhere than it is in the United States. In Europe, the MPA differs among countries and, in some cases, differs with the type of beverage and whether the purchase is on premise or off. Youths as young as sixteen or eighteen may legally purchase beer or wine in most countries (Rossi 1992). We do not attempt here to relate international differences in MPA to youth drinking.

8.2   Trends in Teenage Drinking

It is also somewhat reassuring to place recent drinking by American teenagers in historical context; as prevalent as it is now, it was still more so a generation ago. A widely used source of information on trends in drug use by American teenagers is Monitoring the Future (MTF), conducted at the University of Michigan's Institute for Social Research. Data have been collected from fifteen to twenty thousand seniors at 130-or-so high schools by a survey administered every spring since 1975. The questionnaire includes items on the respondents' use of a variety of drugs. In particular, respondents are asked whether they have ever used alcohol and, if so, whether they have used it in the last year and the last thirty days. They are then asked whether they have consumed five or more drinks in a row any time in the last two weeks (the MTF definition of *bingeing*) and whether they have been drunk in the last month.

The accuracy of responses to such questions is difficult to calibrate. One effort to do so compared the responses of the MTF seniors in 1982 with seniors included in the National Longitudinal Survey of Youth (NLSY) in that year (Cook, Moore, and Pacula 1993). The thirty-day prevalence from MTF respondents was substantially higher than the corresponding figure from the NLSY. One possible explanation is that the NLSY survey is conducted at home while the MTF is conducted in school. The latter may be a setting more conducive to confession (or even bragging) about drinking.

Figure 8.1 depicts the thirty-day prevalence of drinking and the prevalence of bingeing during the previous two weeks since 1976 for twelfth graders aged seventeen to nineteen.[3] Both series peak in the early 1980s and then decline, first gradually, then rapidly, until 1992 or so. The thirty-day prevalence dropped 22 percentage points (from 72 percent), the binge prevalence by 15 percentage points (from 42 percent), during this time. Both series have a slight upward trend in recent years.

What explains the sharp reduction in drinking during the 1980s? The obvious answer does not apply. The price of alcoholic beverages (relative to the overall consumer price index) was essentially flat during the period 1980–90, as shown by the bars in figure 8.1. (The upward blip in 1991 was the result of an increase in federal excise taxes.) If prices had not been declining so rapidly before 1981, the reduction in drinking would presumably have started sooner. It is true that the effective price for high school seniors probably increased during the early 1980s since over half the states raised their MPA during this period. But the observed reductions in prevalence are much larger than could plausibly be associated with a change in the MPA (cf. the estimates presented in sec. 8.3 below).

---

3. The results presented here are based on our calculations from the micro data.

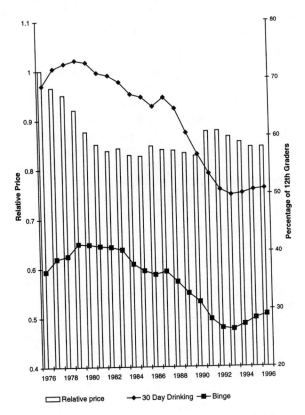

Fig. 8.1   Trend in youth drinking, twelfth graders, MTF 1976–96

Since price movement and MPA shifts cannot account for the downward shift in youth drinking during the 1980s, we consider other possibilities. One is the changing composition of the twelfth-grade population. For example, we know that minority youths are less likely to report drinking than are whites and that minorities are an increasing proportion of the high school population during this period. To check whether these and other changes in population composition can account for the observed trend, we estimated 1986 cross-sectional linear-probability models of drinking and bingeing. The independent variables are the indicators of socioeconomic characteristics of the respondent included in the public-use MTF data files. (The results are reported in app. tables 8A.2 and 8A.4.) We used the resulting equation to simulate the prevalence of drinking and bingeing, substituting into the equation mean values for the covariates for each of the other years in turn. We repeated this exercise using a fuller set of covariates that included a number of variables reflecting choices made by the respondent: smoking, drug use, school attendance, work, marriage, and so forth (tables 8A.3 and 8A.5). The results of these simulations are shown in figures 8.2 and 8.3. As it turns out, the values from the simulations do not track the trend in drinking prevalence; for bingeing prevalence, the "long-form" values predict a portion of the decline but still leave much of it unexplained.

Since the estimated model for the 1986 cross section yields biased predictions for other years, it must be true that the OLS weights on these independent variables have changed over time. We follow Gruber and Zinman (chap. 2 in this volume) in estimating the same model for other years and testing for changes in the magnitudes of corresponding coefficients (reported in the appendix). The results from the long form of the bingeing equations are perhaps most interesting: they suggest that, between 1976 and 1996, binge drinking has become less closely associated with gender, race, grades in school, and marijuana use (although all these variables remain important); at the same time, binge drinking has become much more strongly associated with smoking. The underlying causal mechanism is not revealed by this exercise.

Figure 8.4 depicts the drinking and bingeing series after converting them to indexes, with the means for the entire period set to 100. We add a third

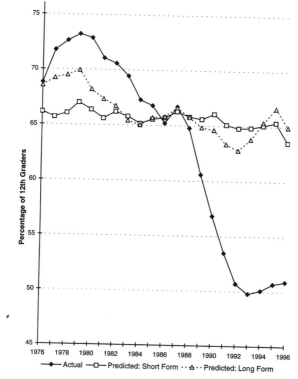

Fig. 8.2   30-day drinking prevalence, twelfth graders, actual vs. predicted

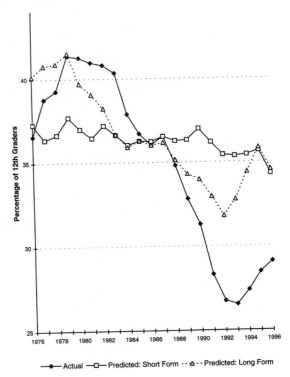

Fig. 8.3   Binge drinking, twelfth graders, actual vs. predicted

line to this chart representing an index for adult per capita consumption of ethanol, a series calculated from tax-paid sales data. (At its peak, per capita consumption was 2.8 gallons of pure alcohol per adult age fifteen and over.)[4] It is interesting that all three series follow roughly the same pattern, with perhaps the main difference being that the prevalence series turns up a bit in 1992 while the per capita consumption series continues to decline.

While the similar patterns for these series may be coincidence, Occam's razor suggests that we seek a common explanation. Having ruled out price and changes in population composition, it seems reasonable to consider changes in other alcohol-control measures next. The 1980s were a time of increased public concern about drinking, especially in connection with driving under the influence (DUI). Mothers Against Drunk Driving (MADD), an organization that was particularly effective during this pe-

4. This series is taken from the Beer Institute's *Brewer's Almanac* for various years. The method for estimating per capita consumption starts with data on the volumes of tax-paid wholesale shipments of wine, beer, and liquor. The volume of ethanol that these shipments contained is estimated by using standard estimates of the average ethanol content of each type of beverage.

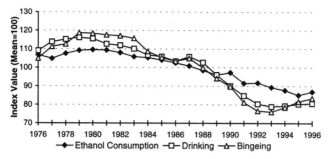

Fig. 8.4   Trend in adult (*ethanol*) consumption and twelfth-grade drinking and bingeing prevalence, MTF 1976–96

riod, opened its first chapter in 1981 and by 1986 had 395 chapters nationwide (Evans, Neville, and Graham 1991). A variety of legislation designed to increase the likelihood and severity of punishment for DUI was enacted during the 1980s (Evans, Neville, and Graham 1991). These changes may have had some influence on the prevalence of heavy drinking by initiating the era of the designated driver and making barhopping a less attractive activity. It may also be true that this legislation and the downward trend in alcohol consumption both reflect a shift in the public or private value placed on safety and health. That such a shift occurred is suggested by the fact that smoking and marijuana use were declining at the same time.

The close link between adult per capita consumption and youthful drinking provides further clues about drinking trends. The downward trend in both youthful and adult drinking may be due to a common cause (such as an increased value placed on health by adults and eighteen-year-olds alike), but it is also plausible that youthful drinking decisions are influenced by adult drinking practices. We return to that subject in section 8.4 below.

8.3   The Importance of the MPA, the Excise Tax, and the Drinking Environment

Alcoholic beverages have long been subject to government regulation and special taxes, beginning with the first domestic revenue measure of the U.S. Congress, an excise tax on liquor enacted in 1791 (Cook and Moore 1993b), and reaching the most extreme form with Prohibition. Since repeal in 1933, prohibition has (with a few local exceptions) been limited to youths; the MPA was set between eighteen and twenty-one in every state. During the 1980s, the states with lower MPAs all raised them to twenty-one, many in response to federal pressure authorized in the Uniform Drinking Age Act of 1984. No such uniformity has emerged with alcohol excise taxes. In addition to the large federal excise taxes on beer, wine, and liquor, the states have enacted widely differing rates and changed them from time to time in response to revenue needs. For example, the federal beer tax is set at $18 per barrel ($0.581 per gallon), increased from $9 per barrel in 1991, while the state rates ranged from $0.02 to $0.77 per gallon in 1999.[5]

Table 8.2 lists the changes in MPA and the beer excise tax between 1982 and 1989. As can be seen, few states enacted tax changes over this period, and the changes that did occur were rather small. That fact makes the task of identifying the effects of beer taxes on consumption difficult. Changes in the MPA, on the other hand, are more frequent, especially during the early 1980s.

An extensive literature has documented the effects of the MPA on drinking and some of its consequences (Cook and Tauchen 1984; Males 1986; Ruhm 1995, 1996; Chesson, Harrison, and Kassler 2000). The published findings are consistent in establishing the effectiveness of the MPA in reducing heavy drinking by and vehicle fatalities involving youths as well as some other alcohol-related problems. The beneficial influence of the excise tax in reducing alcohol abuse and its consequences has also been well established (Cook 1981; Cook and Tauchen 1982; Grossman et al. 1994; Grossman, Coate, and Arluck 1987; Saffer and Grossman 1987a, 1987b; Coate and Grossman 1988; Kenkel 1993; Cook and Moore 1994; Ruhm 1996; Markowitz and Grossman 1998).

This consensus on the potent effect of the excise tax has been challenged of late by two articles (Mast, Benson, and Rasmussen 1999; Dee 1999), both of which concluded from their regression analyses that, while the MPA effects on drinking are robust to different specifications, the estimated effects of the alcohol excise tax are not.

The Mast, Benson, and Rasmussen article does not focus on youth drinking but rather uses state beer sales as the dependent variable. The authors utilized a nine-year panel of forty-eight states, finding that the beer tax has a significant negative effect on beer sales per capita (in gallons) when they control for fixed state and year effects as well as income, the percentage of eighteen- to twenty-year-olds for whom drinking is legal, and several other variables; however, this tax effect disappears when they also control for the percentages of the state population who are Mormon, Southern Baptist, Protestant, and Roman Catholic. Since data for these religious-affiliation variables were available for only two years out of their nine-year series, the authors were forced to assume linear time trends in affiliation to create a complete series. The fact that the excise tax did not

5. Our source for the federal tax rate is the Bureau of Alcohol, Tobacco, and Firearms (BATF) downloaded from www.atf.treas.gov/alcohol/info/faq/subpages/atftaxes.htm on 21 March 2000. Historical tax rates are from BATF historical tax rates spreadsheet 94A1_1&2.WK1 downloaded from www.atf.treas.gov/alcohol/stats/historical.htm on 21 March 2000. State tax rates are from Federation of Tax Administrators, State Tax Rates on Beer, February 2000, downloaded from www.taxadmin.org/fta/rate/tax_stru.html on 21 March 2000.

Table 8.2 **Change in Nominal Beer Tax, MPA, and Per Capita Consumption, 1982–85, 1988–89, by State**

State	Δ Tax 1982–85 (cents/can)	Δ Tax 1985–89 (cents/can)	Δ MPA 1982–85 (years)	Δ PC Ethanol 1982–85 (gallons)	Δ PC Ethanol 1985–89 (gallons)
Alabama	−2.3	0	1	.02	−.02
Alaska	22.5	0	2	−.19	−.37
Arizona	18.0	0	3	−.05	−1.03
Arkansas	0	17.6	0	.01	.02
California	0	0	0	−.08	−.27
Colorado	0	0	0	−.14	−.34
Connecticut	3.8	9.4	2	.10	−.26
Delaware	0	0	1	−.01	−.23
DC	0	0	0	−.33	−.68
Florida	18.0	0	1	−.05	−.16
Georgia	0	0	0	.09	−.08
Hawaii	. . .	0	0	−.40	−.08
Idaho	0	0	0	−.11	−.13
Illinois	0	0	0	−.08	−.12
Indiana	0	0	0	−.01	−.11
Iowa	0	11.3	0	−.06	−.10
Kansas	0	0	1	−.07	−.13
Kentucky	0	0	0	−.12	−.07
Louisiana	0	0	0	−.21	−.07
Maine	0	11.3	1	−.07	−.08
Maryland	0	0	2	−.11	−.21
Massachusetts	0	0	1	−.18	−.11
Michigan	0	0	0	−.00	−.16
Minnesota	0	4.4	0	−.04	−.19
Mississippi	5.6	−5.6	0	−.03	.01
Missouri	0	0	0	.04	−.07
Montana	1.1	1.1	0	−.26	−.17
Nebraska	3.4	16.9	1	−.13	−.14
Nevada	6.8	0	0	−.12	−.17
New Hampshire	27	0	1	−.04	−.28
New Jersey	0	0	2	−.03	−.19
New Mexico	20.3	0	0	−.03	−.19
New York	2.4	8.2	1	−.16	−.24
North Carolina	0	0	1	.02	−.06
North Dakota	0	0	0	−.25	−.05
Ohio	0	0	1	−.03	−.12
Oklahoma	0	9.1	3	−.22	−.12
Oregon	0	0	0	−.10	−.11
Pennsylvania	0	0	0	−.09	−.11
Rhode Island	0	3.6	1	.01	−.23
South Carolina	0	0	2	.08	−.02
South Dakota	0	0	1	−.08	−.17
Tennessee	0	0	2	.01	−.03
Texas	0	0	0	−.14	−.21
Utah	49.9	0	0	−.09	−.09
Vermont	0	0	0	−.04	−.23
Virginia	0	0	1	−.04	−.04
Washington	.8	8.5	0	−.03	−.22
West Virginia	0	0	1	−.08	−.03
Wisconsin	0	0	1	−.15	−.23
Wyoming	0	0	0	−.28	−.30

Source: Tax rates and per capita consumption from the Beer Institute's *Brewer's Almanac* (various years).

survive this addition to the list of covariates does not, to our mind, constitute a serious challenge to the importance of taxes in influencing consumption.

The second article (Dee 1999) does focus on youth drinking, utilizing MTF data for the period 1977–92. Dee constructed 3,941 observations from the micro data, one for each group of high school seniors in the MTF sample defined by state, year, sex, and race. His dependent variables are drinkers (percentage of the group that had taken a drink in the preceding month), moderate drinkers (percentage who reported having ten or more drinks in the preceding month), and heavy drinkers (percentage who reported drinking five or more drinks on a single occasion within the preceding two weeks). Using weighted least squares, Dee estimates a model that includes indicators of race, gender, age, and year, together with two alcohol-policy variables: the state excise tax on beer and an indicator of whether the MPA was eighteen. Each equation was estimated with and without state fixed effects. The results for all three dependent variables (prevalence of drinkers, moderate drinkers, and heavy drinkers) follow the same pattern. The MPA variable remains positive and significant and of a magnitude to suggest that an MPA of eighteen increased the prevalence of each of the three drinking categories by at least 2 or 3 percentage points. On the other hand, the beer-tax coefficients, which are negative and significant when state fixed effects are left out, become negligible when they are included. On this basis, Dee concludes that "beer taxes have relatively small and statistically insignificant effects on teen drinking" (p. 289). It should be noted that, owing to the limitations of the MTF data, this conclusion is based on a very sparse specification, something that we are able to remedy using NLSY data in what follows.

Both papers also analyze the effect of excise taxes on vehicle fatalities, which is beyond the scope of our paper (see Dee and Evans, chap. 3 in this volume). But there is a logical relation: if excise taxes reduce vehicle-fatality rates, it is most likely through the mechanism of reducing the frequency of heavy drinking.

8.3.1 The Data

The NLSY was initiated in 1979 and has interviewed the sample of 12,686 youths (aged fourteen to twenty-two in 1979) annually since then, albeit with some attrition. In addition to extensive information on the sample youths' labor market experiences, education, family composition, and personal characteristics, the NLSY asked a series of questions about drinking behavior in the years 1982–85 and 1988–89. Among other items, NLSY respondents were asked whether they had consumed alcohol in the thirty-day period before the interview and, if so, were asked a series of questions concerning the quantities that they had consumed on drinking occasions during that period. From these items, we define two binary variables, *drinks* and *binges*. *Drinks* equals 1 if the respondent reports having consumed at least one drink in the previous thirty days. *Binges* equals 1 if the respondent reports having consumed at least six drinks on four or more occasions in the previous month.[6] For the six years of the NLSY survey that included these items, the overall prevalence of *drinks* is 70 percent and of *binges* is 14 percent.

We estimated a series of probit regressions on these two variables to determine the influence of alcohol-control measures and drinking environment on individual drinking decisions. In line with our earlier research on drinking (Cook and Moore 1993a, 1994), we use two specifications throughout this exercise. The "short form" includes predetermined covariates: indicators of sex, race, primary ethnic identification, birth cohort, age, cognitive ability (as measured by the Armed Forces Qualifying Test [AFQT] percentile score), parents' education, and several descriptors of the respondent's family when he or she was fourteen (family composition, whether the parents worked, religion, and size of place). The "long form" adds to this list a number of variables that reflect choices made by the respondent (and hence are quite possibly endogenous in the sense of being influenced by drinking history): weight, years of school completed, marital status, number of children in the household, school and employment status, income, and education aspirations. The long form also includes indicators of whether the respondent's parents had a drinking problem, based on items included in the 1988 survey. Table 8.3 provides definitions and means.

Before discussing the estimates for the alcohol-control variables, we first review some of the interesting findings on the association between socio-economic (SES) characteristics and self-reported drinking.

8.3.2 Results for SES Variables

Table 8.4 presents complete results for the short and long forms on both the *drinks* and the *binges* variables. The coefficients reported here are the marginal effects on the probability, calculated from the estimated coefficients in probit regressions and evaluated at the sample means. Thus, the prevalence of bingeing is 14 percentage points higher for males than for females (or, in the long form, 12 percentage points), other things equal. The estimated standard errors are cluster corrected to take account of the fact that there are up to six observations on each respondent[7] and corrected for general heteroskedasticity using the Huber/White/Sandwich estimator.

---

6. This definition is more stringent than that of the binge variable from the MTF, which required only one occasion of five or more drinks in the preceding two weeks. Unfortunately, that item cannot be estimated from the NLSY.

7. We estimated versions of each model that imposed an AR(1) structure on the within-person correlations. The results suggested that the unstructured clustering correction performed better; the pattern of correlations across years was more consistent with a permanent effect than an AR(1). As a separate matter, we tested for bias in the estimated standard errors due to clustering at the state level and found it to be inconsequential—approximately 5 percent.

Table 8.3	Variable Means and Definitions from NLSY, 1982–85, 1988–89 ($N = 68{,}377$)	
Variable	Mean (S.D.)	Definition
Drinks	.703	Dummy variable (d.v.): 1 if respondent drank any alcohol in the past 30 days, 0 otherwise
Binges	.143	D.v.: 1 if respondent drank 6 or more drinks containing alcohol at least 4 times in the past month
Beer tax	59.62 (63.19)	State excise tax on beer per case of 24 12-ounce cans in constant cents (1993)
MPA binding	.097	D.v.: 1 if respondent's age is currently less than his or her state's MPA
Per capita ethanol	2.06 (.39)	Average state per capita consumption of ethanol matched to respondent by state and year (computed from *Brewers Almanac* data on consumption of beer, wine, and spirits)
Age less than 21	.185	D.v.: 1 if respondent age younger than 21
Male	.509	D.v.: 1 if respondent is male
Black	.140	D.v.: 1 if respondent is black non-Hispanic
Hispanic	.064	D.v.: 1 if respondent is Hispanic
Year dummies (each)	.167	D.v.: indicators for each year, 1983, 1984, 1985, 1988, 1989
Cohort indicators:		D.v.s: 1 for each age (15–22) in 1979
Age 15	.128	
Age 16	.121	
Age 17	.124	
Age 18	.126	
Age 19	.129	
Age 20	.124	
Age 21	.128	
Age 22	.031	
Parents' education:		
Mother's education	10.99 (3.76)	Highest grade completed
Missing data, mother's education	.053	D.v.
Father's education	10.63 (4.96)	Highest grade completed
Missing data, father's education	.102	D.v.
Family history:		
Lived with mother at age 14	.942	D.v.
Lived with father at age 14	.776	D.v.
Mother worked when respondent was 14	.526	D.v.
Father worked when respondent was 14	.814	D.v.
Lived with both biological parents until age 18	.657	D.v.
AFQT percentile score	45.89 (29.93)	
Missing data, AFQT percentile score	.046	D.v.

Table 8.3   (continued)

Variable	Mean (S.D.)	Definition
Primary ethnic identification (excludes black, Hispanic, "American"):		
Asian	.010	D.v.
United Kingdom	.272	D.v.
French	.066	D.v.
German	.198	D.v.
Other European	.014	D.v.
American Indian	.042	D.v.
Irish	.062	D.v.
Italian	.030	D.v.
Polish	.016	D.v.
Other ethnic group	.046	D.v.
Religion in which respondent was raised:		
None	.040	D.v.
Protestant	.272	D.v.: excludes Baptist
Baptist	.239	D.v.
Jewish	.013	D.v.
Roman Catholic	.326	D.v.
Other Religion	.108	D.v.
Location of respondent's residence:		
Not in SMSA	.211	D.v.
In SMSA, not central city	.564	D.v.
Central city	.137	D.v.
Highest grade that respondent completed by survey year:[a]		
Less than 12	.207	D.v.
12 (high school degree)	.401	D.v.
1–3 years of college	.243	D.v.
At least 4 years of college	.149	D.v.
Employment status at time of survey:		
Out of labor force	.184	D.v.
Employed	.701	D.v.
Unemployed	.084	D.v.
Armed forces	.031	D.v.
Current school status:		
In school	.184	D.v.
Any relatives been alcoholics or problem drinkers? (asked in 1988):		
Mother	.044	D.v.: biological only
Father	.178	D.v.: biological only
Children in household under 18:		
One	.160	D.v.
Two	.114	D.v.
Three or more	.046	D.v.

(*continued*)

Table 8.3   (continued)

Variable	Mean (S.D.)	Definition
Current living arrangements:		
Lives by self	.650	D.v.
Lives in military barracks	.015	D.v.
Lives in dormitory	.030	D.v. includes living in fraternity or sorority
Lives with others	.013	D.v.
Wage and salary income	9,761.58	Past calendar year
	(15,248.80)	
Weight	154.93	Pounds
	(47.92)	
Marital status:		
Married	.382	D.v.
Single	.539	D.v.
Separated/divorced/widowed	.079	D.v.
Education aspirations	14.50	Highest grade respondent would like to complete (asked in 1982)
	(2.23)	

[a]Variables reported below this point are included in long-form regressions only. SMSA = standard metropolitan statistical area.

Race and ethnicity effects are remarkably strong. Blacks and Hispanics are less likely to drink or binge than are non-Hispanic whites. Among whites, those who identify themselves as being from Irish, Polish, German, or French stock are disproportionately represented among the drinkers and bingers. Relatedly, childhood religion is important; compared with Roman Catholics (the omitted category), all other groups are less likely to binge drink, and all but Jews are less likely to drink at all.

The AFQT results are particularly interesting. The percentile score is strongly *positively* associated with drinking but *negatively* related to bingeing participation. Most of that negative effect is dissipated in the long form, perhaps because in the short form the AFQT acts as a proxy for schooling (which is not included in the short form).

In the long form, we see that the prevalence of drinking and the prevalence of bingeing are inversely related to years of school completed at the time of the survey and to education aspirations (in 1982) and are lower for those in school than for those who are not. Different living arrangements are associated with dramatically different participation rates: compared with those who live with their parents (the omitted category), those who live in a dormitory or a fraternity/sorority house are far more likely to binge (9 percentage points). Marriage and children both reduce drinking and bingeing.

The likelihood of bingeing (but not drinking) increases with body weight. This may be an artifact of our definition of *bingeing,* which we define as weekly bouts of six or more drinks; ideally, we would tailor the definition so that the drink count was proportional to body weight. Six drinks

Table 8.4 Probit Regression Results, NLSY, 1982–85, 1988–89, Drinking and Bingeing (× 100)

Variable (omitted category in brackets)	Drink in Last 30 Days		Binge	
	(1)	(2)	(3)	(4)
Beer tax	-2.137***	-2.404***	-.254	-.153
	(.532)	(.542)	(.324)	(.316)
MPA binding	-5.516***	-5.477***	-2.536***	-2.610***
	(1.100)	(1.141)	(.573)	(.551)
Under 21	-4.826***	-4.146***	-.436	-.733
	(.829)	(.866)	(.517)	(.500)
Male	17.323***	15.517***	14.278***	11.859***
	(.677)	(.835)	(.434)	(5.051)
Race [other]: Black	-.379	-1.594	-4.043***	-4.040***
	(1.475)	(1.560)	(.792)	(.780)
Hispanic	-2.651*	-2.121	-2.348***	-1.438*
	(1.550)	(1.580)	(.808)	(.812)
Year [1982]: 1983	-.331	-.406	-.782**	-.664*
	(.537)	(.577)	(.333)	(.337)
1984	2.184***	2.193***	-.971**	-.584
	(.688)	(.644)	(.370)	(.381)
1985	-1.622**	-3.682***	-6.137***	-3.184***
	(.651)	(1.244)	(.327)	(.606)
1988	-1.663**	-.628	-2.526***	-.941*
	(.701)	(.883)	(.405)	(.499)
1989	-6.092***	-5.051***	-3.821***	-2.061***
	(.724)	(.949)	(.380)	(.483)

(continued)

Table 8.4   (continued)

Variable (omitted category in brackets)	Drink in Last 30 Days		Binge	
	(1)	(2)	(3)	(4)
Cohort indicators [age 14]:				
Age 15	.836	.479	.434	.200
	(1.386)	(1.397)	(.867)	(.822)
Age 16	1.987	1.851	.700	.631
	(1.404)	(1.423)	(.898)	(.872)
Age 17	1.064	.736	.004	−.093
	(1.479)	(1.514)	(.888)	(.865)
Age 18	1.929	2.181	.624	8.202
	(1.500)	(1.545)	(.939)	(.934)
Age 19	.758	.579	.486	1.194
	(1.543)	(1.621)	(.964)	(.994)
Age 20	.535	1.094	−1.021	−.145
	(1.615)	(1.686)	(.904)	(.949)
Age 21	−.761	.016	−.679	.935
	(1.607)	(1.679)	(.935)	(1.022)
Age 22	−3.350	−2.829	−2.804**	−1.495
	(2.587)	(2.704)	(1.195)	(1.334)
Parent's education:				
Mother's education	.308**	.325**	.030	.137
	(.151)	(.156)	(.085)	(.084)
Missing data, mother's education	4.051*	4.679**	2.294*	3.216**
	(2.024)	(2.093)	(1.361)	(1.454)
Father's education	.833***	.842***	.113	.198***
	(.125)	(.130)	(.073)	(.073)
Missing data, father's education	6.172***	5.690***	−.078	.393
	(1.511)	(1.578)	(.945)	(.971)

Family history:				
Lived with mother at age 14	2.916*	2.958*	.058	−.780
	(1.605)	(1.643)	(.886)	(.914)
Lived with father at age 14	−1.232	−.626	−1.435**	−1.059
	(1.172)	(1.208)	(.706)	(.687)
Mother worked when respondent was 14	1.646**	1.357*	.532	.505
	(.711)	(.730)	(.411)	(.402)
Father worked when respondent was 14	2.302**	2.158**	−.021	.007
	(1.038)	(1.066)	(.604)	(.587)
Lived with both biological parents until 18	−1.983**	−2.032**	−.350	.469
	(.930)	(.969)	(.532)	(.525)
AFQT percentile score	.180***	.160***	−.081***	−.022**
	(.016)	(.019)	(.009)	(.010)
Missing data, AFQT score	−1.143	−.954	−4.856***	−2.436**
	(1.896)	(2.347)	(.725)	(1.018)
Primary ethnic identification [black, Hispanic, or "American"]:				
Asian	−5.098	−3.649	−4.904**	−4.469**
	(3.562)	(3.468)	(1.596)	(1.490)
United Kingdom	4.088***	3.688**	2.295**	1.583*
	(1.417)	(1.448)	(.991)	(.943)
French	7.604***	6.985***	3.358***	2.806**
	(1.760)	(1.795)	(1.405)	(1.339)
German	7.615***	7.661***	3.475***	3.047***
	(1.466)	(1.490)	(1.109)	(1.075)
Other European	−.589	−.877	−1.121	−1.287
	(2.811)	(3.000)	(1.597)	(1.522)
American Indian	−1.704	−2.663	1.971	1.008
	(2.101)	(2.200)	(1.370)	(1.280)

(continued)

Table 8.4 (continued)

Variable (omitted category in brackets)	Drink in Last 30 Days		Binge	
	(1)	(2)	(3)	(4)
Irish	8.389***	8.193***	5.047***	4.992***
	(1.826)	(1.879)	(1.454)	(1.433)
Italian	9.324***	8.671***	.288	.273
	(2.332)	(2.374)	(1.569)	(1.492)
Polish	6.224*	6.527*	4.700**	4.248**
	(3.496)	(3.453)	(2.493)	(2.342)
Other ethnic group	5.021**	3.982*	.866	.388
	(2.205)	(2.303)	(1.377)	(1.324)
Religion in which respondent was raised [Roman Catholic]:				
None	−9.333***	−9.267***	−2.366**	−2.497***
	(2.010)	(2.088)	(.844)	(.799)
Protestant	−5.978***	−6.132***	−1.951***	−1.878***
	(1.157)	(1.184)	(.570)	(.550)
Baptist	−10.951***	−10.624***	−3.781***	−3.305***
	(1.196)	(1.226)	(.581)	(.571)
Jewish	6.903*	8.719**	−3.094	−2.864
	(3.744)	(3.830)	(1.659)	(1.572)
Other religion	−18.526***	−18.560***	−5.890***	−5.384***
	(1.479)	(1.531)	(.537)	(.525)
Location of respondent's residence [not in SMSA]:				
In SMSA, not in central city	6.271***	5.157***	.665	.590
	(.742)	(1.026)	(.437)	(.426)
In central city	4.568***	2.577**	.006	−.258
	(.966)	(1.026)	(.593)	(.569)

Highest grade that respondent completed in survey year [12 years]:		
Less than 12	2.199**	2.743***
	(.913)	(.569)
1–3 years of college	.274	−1.221**
	(.985)	(.527)
At least 4 years of college	−.618	−4.886***
	(1.423)	(−.578)
Current employment status [employed]:		
Outside labor force	−10.066***	−1.289***
	(.775)	(.432)
Unemployed	.930	1.451***
	(.802)	(.504)
Current school status:		
In school	−5.939***	−3.221***
	(.867)	(.425)
Any relatives been problem drinkers?		
Mother	1.775	.597
	(1.827)	(1.018)
Father	3.684***	2.324***
	(.898)	(.548)
Number of children under 18 in household [none]:		
One	−3.173***	−1.451***
	(.886)	(.504)
Two	−3.738***	−1.601***
	(1.079)	(.582)
Three or more	−4.574***	−1.384
	(1.547)	(.823)

(continued)

Table 8.4   (continued)

Variable (omitted category in brackets)	Drink in Last 30 Days		Binge	
	(1)	(2)	(3)	(4)
Living arrangements [lives with parents]:				
By self		7.724***		1.703***
		(.744)		(.390)
Military barracks		1.749		2.565
		(9.916)		(5.969)
Dormitory		6.735***		9.132***
		(1.658)		(1.465)
With others		−34.386***		−5.739***
		(2.156)		(.689)
Wage and salary income		.0000738**		.0000122
		(.0000336)		(.0000149)
Weight		−.025**		.0300***
		(.012)		(.0063)
Marital status [single]:				
Married		−14.981***		−7.511***
		(.903)		(.436)
Separated/divorced/widowed		1.059		.602
		(1.198)		(.675)
Education aspirations		−.055		−.454***
		(.219)		(.122)

Note: Estimated using 1982–85 and 1988–89 NLSY data: $N \geq 49,674$. Marginal effects are computed at full sample means. Cluster-corrected robust standard errors are given in parentheses.

***Statistically significant at the 1 percent level.

**Statistically significant at the 5 percent level.

*Statistically significant at the 10 percent level.

typically have a less intoxicating effect on a man weighing two hundred pounds than three drinks do on a woman weighing one hundred pounds.

Tables 8.5 and 8.6 present the results of estimating the same specification for males and females separately. The patterns that are evident in the results from the combined sample survive this decomposition. One interesting exception is that, while women are decidedly less likely to binge drink when they have children, that is not true for men. Both men and women binge less when married, but divorced men end up bingeing *more* than their single brethren.

In summary, it appears that binge drinking is most prevalent among those who are non-Hispanic white, left school early or are in school but live in a dormitory, are currently unmarried, have low cognitive ability, grew up in a Roman Catholic home, and have roots in Ireland or Poland.

8.3.3   Tax and MPA Effects

At the top of tables 8.4–8.6 are the estimates of the effects of the beer excise tax and MPA variable, for both the short and the long form, for both *drinks* and *binges*. Beginning with the combined-sample results in table 8.4, we see that a binding MPA is associated with a reduction of the prevalence of drinking (which is 70 percent overall) by about 5.5 percentage points and a reduction of the prevalence of bingeing (14 percent overall) by 2.5 percentage points. These results are highly significant and little affected by the addition of the long-form covariates. The estimated effect of the beer excise tax on drinking prevalence is statistically significant and quite important: a dollar increase per case reduces prevalence by over 2 percentage points. On the other hand, the effect of the tax on the prevalence of bingeing is much smaller and insignificantly different from 0. From tables 8.5 and 8.6, we see that the results for males and females are similar, the main difference being that MPA binding reduces male bingeing prevalence by 4 percentage points and female bingeing prevalence by just 1.5 percentage points, in line with the sexes' very different baseline rates.

The excise tax has negligible effects on bingeing in these specifications; if correct, then it is logical to suppose that it will have little effect on motor-vehicle-injury rates either. That conclusion is in line with the revisionists, including Dee (1999), Mast, Benson, and Rasmussen (1999), and Dee and Evans (chap. 3 in this volume). In our view, there remains the possibility that the excise tax does reduce bingeing prevalence among youths but that the effect is masked by other state-level policies or characteristics. We experiment with two approaches to exploring this possibility: controlling for state fixed effects and including a measure of how wet the state drinking environment is, namely, per capita ethanol consumption.[8]

---

8. This variable is calculated from data on wholesale shipments of wine, beer, and liquor. The ethanol content of each type of beverage is estimated using standard percentages. The total ethanol is then divided by the state's population aged fourteen and older to get the annual state per capita ethanol consumption.

Table 8.5   Probit Regression Results, NLSY, 1982–85, 1988–89, Drinking and Bingeing (× 100)—Males

Variable (omitted category in brackets)	Drink in Last 30 Days		Binge	
	(1)	(2)	(3)	(4)
Beer tax	-1.859***	-2.306***	-.410	-.373
	(.681)	(.701)	(.608)	(.620)
MPA binding	-4.911***	-4.711***	-3.980***	-4.069***
	(1.446)	(1.493)	(1.116)	(1.133)
Age less than 21	-5.239***	-4.619***	-.582	-.925
	(1.091)	(1.129)	(.976)	(.989)
Race [other]:				
Black	-.119	.349	-6.945***	-6.622***
	(1.900)	(2.020)	(1.511)	(1.591)
Hispanic	-1.994	-1.660	-3.213*	-1.889
	(2.099)	(2.159)	(1.612)	(1.692)
Year [1982]:				
1983	.583	.283	-.470	-.743
	(.667)	(.715)	(.643)	(.667)
1984	3.036***	2.076**	-.510	-.392
	(.727)	(.801)	(.714)	(.756)
1985	-.346	1.780	-8.868***	-3.421**
	(.841)	(1.800)	(.677)	(1.485)
1988	-.678	-1.954*	-3.258***	-2.170**
	(.911)	(1.176)	(.788)	(.975)
1989	-4.015***	-5.309***	-5.137***	-3.614***
	(.950)	(1.280)	(.753)	(.970)

Cohort indicators [age 14]:				
Age 15	1.167 (1.721)	.259 (1.760)	−.546 (1.558)	−1.223 (1.543)
Age 16	2.904 (1.735)	1.318 (1.821)	2.035 (1.700)	1.118 (1.696)
Age 17	.660 (1.879)	−1.493 (2.001)	−.424 (1.661)	−1.601 (1.654)
Age 18	1.850 (1.890)	−.594 (2.068)	.990 (1.741)	.333 (1.781)
Age 19	.266 (2.009)	−2.281 (2.240)	1.180 (1.830)	1.236 (1.901)
Age 20	1.906 (2.055)	−.777 (2.275)	−.786 (1.786)	−1.012 (1.871)
Age 21	−.431 (2.156)	−2.703 (2.381)	−.606 (1.824)	.444 (1.965)
Age 22	−.672 (3.365)	−4.454 (3.788)	−2.753 (2.503)	−2.462 (2.639)
Parent's education:				
Mother's education	−.138 (.197)	−.035 (.206)	.042 (.163)	.203 (.168)
Missing data, mother's education	1.327 (2.629)	1.787 (2.740)	3.279 (2.485)	3.561 (2.639)
Father's education	.626*** (.169)	.722*** (.176)	.018 (.142)	2.175 (.147)
Missing data, father's education	2.272 (2.065)	2.791 (2.141)	−.843 (1.807)	.619 (1.950)

(*continued*)

Table 8.5 (continued)

Variable (omitted category in brackets)	Drink in Last 30 Days		Binge	
	(1)	(2)	(3)	(4)
Family history:				
Lived with mother at age 14	2.377	2.187	1.025	−.347
	(2.100)	(2.186)	(1.718)	(1.812)
Lived with father at age 14	−3.012**	−3.256**	−2.889**	−2.600*
	(1.508)	(1.555)	(1.381)	(1.408)
Mother worked when respondent was 14	−.075	−.496	1.224	1.063
	(.946)	(.975)	(.798)	(.814)
Father worked when respondent was 14	3.608***	3.677**	1.312	1.462
	(1.398)	(1.453)	(1.157)	(1.175)
Lived with both biological parents until 18	−.105	−.495	−1.278	−.412
	(1.231)	(1.297)	(1.034)	(1.068)
AFQT percentile score	.129***	.131***	−.116***	−.029
	(.021)	(.026)	(.017)	(.021)
Missing data, AFQT score	−2.749	−.725	−8.111***	−4.415**
	(2.363)	(2.832)	(1.420)	(1.986)
Primary ethnic identification [black, Hispanic, or "American"]:				
Asian	−6.296	−3.521	−11.341***	−11.367***
	(4.623)	(4.449)	(2.361)	(2.103)
United Kingdom	2.080	1.122	2.503	1.770
	(1.874)	(1.963)	(1.789)	(1.820)
French	4.318*	3.824	3.444	3.501
	(2.424)	(2.507)	(2.502)	(2.553)
German	5.712***	5.813***	4.821**	4.372**
	(1.941)	(1.988)	(2.010)	(2.058)

Other European	5.023	4.006	1.745	.869
	(3.730)	(4.003)	(3.675)	(3.656)
American Indian	−.200	−1.258	1.346	.377
	(2.830)	(3.058)	(2.354)	(2.350)
Irish	4.910**	4.900*	5.676**	5.997**
	(2.319)	(2.371)	(2.403)	(2.481)
Italian	7.431**	6.516**	−1.660	−.683
	(2.736)	(2.823)	(2.655)	(2.752)
Polish	1.943	2.102	6.414	6.149
	(4.502)	(4.471)	(4.243)	(4.184)
Other ethnic group	1.308	.473	−.422	−.887
	(3.042)	(3.256)	(2.469)	(2.531)
Religion in which respondent was raised [Roman Catholic]:				
None	−9.044***	−9.072***	−4.043**	−4.582**
	(2.631)	(2.745)	(1.652)	(1.632)
Protestant	−5.291***	−5.614***	−3.218***	−3.193***
	(1.602)	(1.668)	(1.136)	(1.149)
Baptist	−9.391***	−8.993***	−6.494***	−5.764***
	(1.666)	(1.729)	(1.170)	(1.199)
Jewish	5.113	7.269*	−6.582*	−5.513
	(4.335)	(3.847)	(3.300)	(3.474)
Other religion	−19.826***	−19.809***	−10.403***	−10.000***
	(2.229)	(2.340)	(1.103)	(1.132)
Location of respondent's residence [not in SMSA]:				
In SMSA, not in central city	4.842***	3.834***	1.479*	1.425*
	(.991)	(1.033)	(.831)	(.851)
In central city	.712	−.798	−.669	−.626
	(1.298)	(1.389)	(1.090)	(1.114)

(continued)

Table 8.5   (continued)

Variable (omitted category in brackets)	Drink in Last 30 Days		Binge	
	(1)	(2)	(3)	(4)
Highest grade that respondent completed in survey year [12 years]:				
Less than 12		2.156*		2.976***
		(1.167)		(1.059)
1–3 years of college		.719		-1.426
		(1.352)		(1.119)
At least 4 years of college		.001		-7.888***
		(1.961)		(1.279)
Current employment status [employed]:				
Outside labor force		-9.228***		-.800
		(1.270)		(1.037)
Unemployed		.041		2.168**
		(.991)		(.955)
Current school status:				
In school		-7.811***		-5.981***
		(1.202)		(.875)
Any relatives been problem drinkers?				
Mother		-.266		-2.068
		(2.678)		(2.114)
Father		1.943		3.723***
		(1.277)		(1.159)
Number of children under 18 in household [none]:				
One		.099		.493
		(1.260)		(1.223)

Two	−.789	1.791
	(1.619)	(1.533)
Three or more	−1.591	.775
	(2.360)	(2.059)
Living arrangements [lives with parents]:		
By self	5.880***	2.587***
	(.929)	(.789)
Military barracks	1.757	5.474
	(9.500)	(9.805)
Dormitory	7.880***	10.914***
	(1.783)	(2.321)
With others	−40.468***	−10.542***
	(2.511)	(1.335)
Wage and salary income	.000023	−.000021
	(.000030)	(.000029)
Weight	.031*	.058***
	(.017)	(.014)
Marital status [single]:		
Married	−10.336***	−11.314***
	(1.337)	(.926)
Separated/divorced/widowed	1.751	2.486*
	(1.660)	(1.468)
Education aspirations	−.127	−.750***
	(.286)	(.239)

Note: Estimated using 1982–85 and 1988–89 NLSY data: $N \geq 49{,}674$. Marginal effects are computed at full sample means. Cluster-corrected robust standard errors are given in parentheses.

***Statistically significant at the 1 percent level.

**Statistically significant at the 5 percent level.

*Statistically significant at the 10 percent level.

Table 8.6   Probit Regression Results, NLSY, 1982–85, 1988–89, Drinking and Bingeing (× 100)—Females

Variable (omitted category in brackets)	Drink in Last 30 Days		Binge	
	(1)	(2)	(3)	(4)
Beer tax	-2.375***	-2.337***	-.133	.095
	(.787)	(.793)	(.321)	(.280)
MPA binding	-5.933***	-6.122***	-1.523***	-1.541***
	(1.559)	(1.633)	(.536)	(.452)
Age younger than 21	-4.047***	-3.552***	-.333	-.692
	(1.196)	(1.257)	(.504)	(.434)
Race [other]:				
Black	.040	-2.433	-1.722**	-1.813**
	(2.162)	(2.253)	(.819)	(.686)
Hispanic	-2.329	-1.911	-1.546*	-.978
	(2.176)	(2.205)	(.766)	(.676)
Year [1982]:				
1983	-1.266	-1.100	-.924***	-.487
	(.802)	(.869)	(.311)	(.300)
1984	1.231	2.272**	-1.189***	-.521
	(.883)	(.971)	(.341)	(.341)
1985	-2.804***	-7.198***	-4.006***	-2.464***
	(.943)	(1.645)	(.288)	(.392)
1988	-2.517**	.758*	-1.871***	.299
	(1.016)	(1.271)	(.380)	(.512)
1989	-7.799***	-4.458***	-2.695***	-.580
	(1.033)	(1.344)	(.353)	(.476)

	(1)	(2)	(3)	(4)
Cohort indicators [age 14]:				
Age 15	.997	1.123	1.239	1.300*
	(2.070)	(2.071)	(.960)	(.851)
Age 16	1.844	2.719	-.145	.428
	(2.086)	(2.097)	(.861)	(.811)
Age 17	2.034	3.417	.261	.995
	(2.172)	(2.187)	(.902)	(.873)
Age 18	2.350	5.104**	.261	1.139
	(2.213)	(2.230)	(.935)	(.923)
Age 19	1.922	3.775	-.003	1.205
	(2.220)	(2.280)	(.930)	(.970)
Age 20	-.303	3.066	-1.216	.569
	(2.347)	(2.419)	(.808)	(.902)
Age 21	-.388	2.705	-.691	1.446
	(2.273)	(2.348)	(.876)	(1.020)
Age 22	-5.019	-.719	-2.839**	-.981
	(3.625)	(3.745)	(.899)	(1.226)
Parent's education:				
Mother's education	.777***	.676***	.040	.092
	(.219)	(.225)	(.081)	(.073)
Missing data, mother's education	6.224**	7.007**	1.671	3.153**
	(3.078)	(3.157)	(1.427)	(1.567)
Father's education	1.010***	.910***	.172**	.158**
	(.175)	(.182)	(.069)	(.064)
Missing data, father's education	9.589***	8.013***	.300	.069
	(2.168)	(2.270)	(.928)	(.830)

(*continued*)

Table 8.6 (continued)

Variable (omitted category in brackets)	Drink in Last 30 Days		Binge	
	(1)	(2)	(3)	(4)
Family history:				
Lived with mother at age 14	3.030	3.297	-.700	-1.039
	(2.350)	(2.371)	(.859)	(.836)
Lived with father at age 14	1.084	2.378	-.383	-.136
	(1.702)	(1.741)	(.636)	(.561)
Mother worked when respondent was 14	3.277***	3.101***	-.012	.154
	(1.009)	(1.033)	(.384)	(.340)
Father worked when respondent was 14	.588	.445	-1.064*	-.942*
	(1.483)	(1.504)	(.590)	(.511)
Lived with both biological parents until 18	-4.111***	-3.975***	.380	1.025**
	(1.332)	(1.376)	(.496)	(.438)
AFQT percentile score	.227***	.194***	-.056***	-.016
	(.024)	(.027)	(.009)	(.010)
Missing data, AFQT score	.413	-1.265	-2.638***	-.848
	(2.922)	(3.617)	(.738)	(1.034)
Primary ethnic identification [black, Hispanic, or "American"]:				
Asian	-3.311	-2.808	.222	.526
	(5.135)	(4.892)	(2.390)	(2.033)
United Kingdom	6.216***	6.351***	2.357**	1.589*
	(2.044)	(2.053)	(1.091)	(.906)
French	10.301***	9.819***	3.484***	2.479**
	(2.517)	(2.628)	(1.577)	(1.324)
German	9.239***	9.305***	2.709***	2.150**
	(2.128)	(2.150)	(1.190)	(1.026)

	(1)	(2)	(3)	(4)
Other European	-1.970	-3.759	-2.415*	-1.744
	(3.969)	(4.215)	(1.003)	(.933)
American Indian	-2.999	-3.473	2.863**	1.947
	(2.955)	(3.038)	(1.661)	(1.430)
Irish	11.798***	11.392***	5.156***	4.529***
	(2.758)	(2.868)	(1.854)	(1.671)
Italian	11.691***	11.636***	2.676	1.275
	(3.652)	(3.711)	(2.140)	(1.601)
Polish	11.534**	11.167**	3.444	2.940
	(5.020)	(4.964)	(2.910)	(2.311)
Other ethnic group	10.006***	8.836***	2.566*	1.678
	(2.946)	(3.015)	(1.648)	(1.402)
Religion in which respondent was raised [Roman Catholic]:				
None	-9.159***	-8.569***	-.943	-.833
	(2.946)	(3.053)	(.851)	(.726)
Protestant	-6.012***	-6.055***	-.888	-.813*
	(1.582)	(1.607)	(.530)	(.456)
Baptist	-11.677***	-11.572***	-1.696***	-1.469***
	(1.637)	(1.670)	(.530)	(.467)
Jewish	8.167	10.378	-.500	-1.038
	(5.781)	(6.857)	(1.610)	(1.203)
Other religion	-16.451***	-16.564	-2.691***	-2.282***
	(1.909)	(1.956)	(.503)	(.435)
Location of respondent's residence:				
In SMSA, not in central city	7.272***	6.278***	.065	.084
	(1.056)	(1.089)	(.423)	(.368)
In central city	8.391***	5.959***	.625	.221
	(1.387)	(1.459)	(.619)	(.523)

(continued)

Table 8.6 (continued)

Variable (omitted category in brackets)	Drink in Last 30 Days		Binge	
	(1)	(2)	(3)	(4)
Highest grade that respondent completed in survey year [12 years]:				
Less than 12		1.543		2.243***
		(1.371)		(.561)
1–3 years of college		.491		−.956**
		(1.387)		(.418)
At least 4 years of college		−1.904		−2.485***
		(1.971)		(.457)
Current employment status [employed]:				
Outside labor force		−7.969***		−.602*
		(.986)		(.346)
Unemployed		2.430**		.870**
		(1.220)		(.470)
Current school status:				
In school		−4.392***		−1.604***
		(1.201)		(.359)
Any relatives been problem drinkers?				
Mother		2.802		1.433*
		(2.479)		(.852)
Father		4.767***		1.418***
		(1.255)		(.443)
Number of children under 18 in household [none]:				
One		−5.491***		−1.992***
		(1.223)		(.363)

Two	-5.690***	-2.454***
	(1.477)	(.374)
Three or more	-6.286***	-2.084***
	(2.098)	(.512)
Living arrangements [lives with parents]:		
By self	9.301***	.995***
	(1.085)	(.331)
Military barracks	1.865	(Dropped)
	(21.641)	
Dormitory	3.482	6.126***
	(2.734)	(1.565)
With others	-6.247	-1.220
	(5.182)	(1.476)
Wage and salary income	.0000715	-.0000796***
	(.0000462)	(.0000255)
Weight	-.0767***	.0084
	(.0183)	(.0052)
Marital status [single]:		
Married	-19.450***	-5.121***
	(1.204)	(.383)
Separated/divorced/widowed	.242	.0004
	(1.667)	(.5262)
Educational aspirations	.122	-.246*
	(.318)	(.109)

Note: Estimated using 1982–85 and 1988–89 NLSY data: $N \geq 49{,}674$. Marginal effects are computed at full sample means. Cluster-corrected standard errors are given in parentheses.

***Statistically significant at the 1 percent level.

**Statistically significant at the 5 percent level.

*Statistically significant at the 10 percent level.

The inclusion of state fixed effects ensures that all permanent characteristics of the state relevant to youthful drinking are accounted for, a virtue that comes at the cost of reducing the relevant variation in the tax variable. The state ethanol-consumption variable arguably provides an efficient control for all state-level factors that might influence drinking, including state licensing and liability rules that may influence alcohol availability, as well as the local drinking culture.

Table 8.7 summarizes the results of these experiments. *Drinking* results are in panel A and *bingeing* results in panel B. The top row of both panels of this table repeats the results with respect to tax and MPA from table 8.4 above. The next row reports the result of adding per capita ethanol consumption: this has a large effect on youthful drinking in its own right, but its inclusion does not undermine the estimated effects of MPA and tax. In the binge equations, the ethanol variable is not influential either directly or indirectly.

The results of including state fixed effects is another story. While there is little change in the MPA results, the estimated tax effects are increased dramatically, to levels that in some cases strain credulity. For example, it is difficult to believe that a dollar increase in the beer tax (the equivalent of $0.25 per six-pack) would reduce the prevalence of drinking by 15 percentage points. This strange result may argue for inclusion of the per capita ethanol variable since the beer tax retains a more modest (and somewhat more credible) effect in fixed-effects specifications that include that variable. Turning to the results on binge prevalence, we see that the fixed-effects specification inflates the estimated influence of tax to such an extent as to make it statistically significant in several specifications. Again, the most reasonable tax effects are found when per capita ethanol is included: a dollar increase (1993 dollars) in the tax reduces the prevalence of bingeing by 3.9 percentage points (short form) or 2.5 percentage points (long form). Our corresponding estimates for the effect of a binding MPA are 2.2 or 2.4 percentage points.

So what is to be concluded about the influence of the beer excise tax on youthful drinking? The picture remains cloudy, in part, no doubt, because the changes in excise taxes between 1981 and 1988 were too few and too small to provide the basis for precise estimates of their effects (see table 8.2 above).[9] It would surely be inappropriate to rule out a role for excise taxes as a control on alcohol abuse since our favored specification, which controls for state fixed effects and overall drinking, suggests that even modest changes in the state beer taxes have had a discernible influence on the prevalence of youthful bingeing.

---

9. To test whether our results reflect the coincidence of a tax increase with an unusual change in drinking in some state, we reestimated our models a number of times, excluding in each case data from one of the states that experienced a tax increase. None of these exclusions had much effect on our estimates.

Table 8.7

Probit Regression Results, NLSY 1982–85, 1988–89, Estimated Coefficients (S.E.s), Policy Variables Only

	Beer Tax	MPA Binding	State per Capita Ethanol Use
A. Drink in Last 30 Days (× 100)			
No state fixed effects:			
Short form	−2.137***	−5.516***	
	(.532)	(1.100)	
Long form	−2.404***	−5.477***	
	(.542)	(1.141)	
Short form	−1.566***	−5.432***	5.658***
	(.542)	(1.098)	(.952)
Long form	−1.882***	−5.419***	4.941***
	(.553)	(1.141)	(.976)
With state fixed effects:			
Short form	−16.867***	−6.412***	
	(3.021)	(1.112)	
Long form	−13.970***	−6.303***	
	(3.159)	(1.166)	
Short form	−5.210*	−6.017***	12.011***
	(3.054)	(1.109)	(2.566)
Long form	−2.265	−5.907***	11.862***
	(3.233)	(1.162)	(2.636)
B. Binge (× 100)			
No state fixed effects:			
Short form	−.254	−2.536***	
	(.324)	(.573)	
Long form	−.153	−2.610***	
	(.316)	(.551)	
Short form	−.154	−2.529***	.811
	(.329)	(.573)	(.510)
Long form	−.111	−2.605***	.355
	(.321)	(.551)	(.511)
With state fixed effects:			
Short form	−9.244***	−2.369***	
	(1.841)	(.573)	
Long form	−7.167***	−2.490***	
	(1.836)	(.553)	
Short form	−3.878*	−2.213***	5.474***
	(1.987)	(.578)	(1.523)
Long form	−2.465	−2.352***	4.707***
	(1.995)	(.559)	(1.474)

Note: Estimated using 1982–85, 1988–89 NLSY data: $N \geq 50{,}000$. Marginal effects are computed at full sample means. Cluster-corrected robust standard errors are given in parentheses. All equations included indicators for sex, race, ethnicity, age in 1979, residence in SMSA, parents' education, family structure at age 14, AFQT percentile, and family religion. The long-form equations also include schooling, employment status, income, current school enrollment, weight, marital status, whether either parent was a problem drinker, number of children under 18 in household, living arrangements, and education aspirations in 1982.
***Statistically significant at the 1 percent level.
**Statistically significant at the 5 percent level.
*Statistically significant at the 10 percent level.

Our results in this respect are in accord with much of the literature but contrast with those reported in Dee (1999). His analysis of panel data on bingeing by high school seniors finds that the estimated effect of the beer excise tax switches from statistically significant and negative to insignificant and positive when he enters state fixed effects into the regression specification. His data and specification are different than ours in several potentially important respects, and we will not speculate on why his results appear to contradict ours. We do note, however, that Dee's estimate for the effect of the beer excise tax on bingeing (with state fixed effects included) is not significantly different from ours at the 5 percent level.

8.3.4 Social Influence

The proper interpretation of the strong results on per capita ethanol consumption deserves further discussion. Drinking is a social activity, in the sense that the utility of taking a drink at a particular time and place depends in part on the social setting. For many people, drinking with others is more enjoyable than drinking alone; if one associates with those who are not drinking or who disapprove of drinking, the natural inclination would be to substitute another type of beverage. Of course, the social setting may also influence drinking decisions directly, by determining the availability of drinks. Given these mechanisms of social influence, it seems reasonable to presume that individual drinking is influenced by how wet the social environment is.

If individual drinking decisions are positively linked to the drinking practices of others, then there will be a social multiplier in the response of aggregate alcohol consumption to prices, income, and other external influences; social influence will amplify the direct effects of such variables. This mechanism may be particularly important for initiation into drinking. Indeed, the assumption that peers are central to adolescent alcohol and drug use is reflected in the social-influence paradigm underlying many prevention programs (Bauman and Ennett 1996).

One type of evidence supporting this view is that adolescents whose friends drink are far more likely to drink themselves. For example, Norton, Lindrooth, and Ennett (1998) studied drinking in thirty-six schools, finding that adolescents in schools with a high prevalence of drinking were more likely to drink themselves. This result holds after controlling for various individual, household, and neighborhood characteristics. Indeed, the estimated effect is very large, suggesting that an increase of 10 percentage points in group drinking is associated with a equal increase in the likelihood of individual drinking.

But this result is compatible with several other mechanisms besides social influence (Manski 1995). First, it may be the result of an endogenous selection process, where some parents consider the behavior of the local adolescents in deciding where to live. Second, it may reflect a "contextual" effect, where the individual's drinking behavior is influenced by other characteristics of the group (commitment to getting a good education) but not by the group's drinking per se. Third, it may be true that youths within the same group share some important but unobserved aspect of the environment, such as whether local merchants are willing sell alcohol to youths.

Of these three mechanisms, we are inclined to rule out the first in interpreting our results since the choice of state in which to live (as opposed to neighborhood) is not likely to be much affected by a concern for drinking practices. That leaves several possible interpretations for the estimated effect of the per capita consumption variable: it could be a proxy for unobserved dimensions of alcohol regulation and availability; it could be a proxy for local cultural values that are relevant to drinking, such as the value of higher education or starting a family; and it could be directly relevant to youth drinking through a process of social contagion. This variable arguably belongs in the equation regardless of the correct interpretation, but the interpretation matters in evaluating the policy implications of our results. In particular, if social contagion is the right explanation, then the excise tax will have an indirect effect on youth drinking through its effect on per capita consumption; if, on the other hand, the per capita-consumption variable is only a proxy for other factors, then there will be no indirect effect.

8.4   Drinking Persistence and Habit

Alcohol-control measures that promote moderation or abstinence will produce contemporaneous public-health benefits, such as reduced injury rates. To the extent that drinking is habit-forming, there will also be delayed benefits. The belief that teenage drinking is habit-forming is plausible but perhaps not so well established as the notion that tobacco, heroin, and some other drugs are habit-forming. In what follows, we document the high degree of autocorrelation in youth drinking and provide evidence that the autocorrelation may in part reflect habit formation.

The NLSY provides four consecutive years of data on drinking, 1982–85. The intertemporal pattern for *drinks* and *binges* is displayed in probability-tree diagrams in figures 8.5 and 8.6. The patterns of response suggest a heterogeneous population, including the full range of possibilities from persistent abstainers to persistent drinkers. The probability of drinking in 1985, given three successive years of drinking, equals 0.90 and that of abstaining, given three previous years of abstinence, equals 0.84.

Such heterogeneous patterns presumably reflect an underlying heterogeneity, both in individuals' tastes for alcohol and in the contexts in which they make drinking decisions. But these patterns also suggest habit forma-

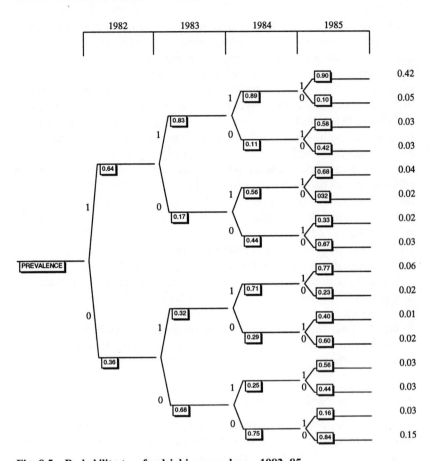

Fig. 8.5   Probability tree for drinking prevalence, 1982–85
Note: 1 = consumed alcohol in past 30 days; 0 = did not consume any alcohol in past 30 days.

tion, where persistence results from a process whereby experience with alcohol strengthens subsequent taste for alcohol.[10]

The economics literature offers a number of analogous inquiries where the econometric challenge is to distinguish between state dependence and heterogeneity (Heckman 1981). An individual who was unemployed last period is relatively likely to be unemployed this period. Does past unemployment therefore cause future unemployment, or does unemployment in each period simply act as a proxy for some unobserved traits that render the individual more prone to unemployment (Ellwood 1982)? Labor force

10. On the dynamics of habitual consumption in general, see Becker (1992, 1996) and Becker and Murphy (1988). Empirical studies of habituation and addiction include Becker, Grossman, and Murphy (1991), Chaloupka and Wechsler (1996), Grossman, Chaloupka, and Sirtalan (1998), and Moore and Cook (1995).

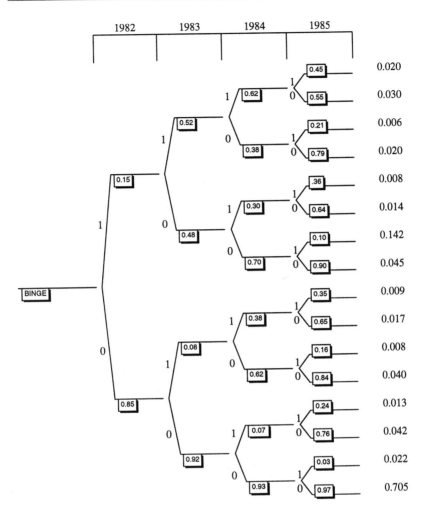

Fig. 8.6   Probability tree for bingeing, 1982–85
Note: 1 = binge drinking; 0 = did not binge drink.

participation patterns of married women (Heckman and Willis 1977) and a wide range of other behaviors that are strongly autocorrelated give rise to the same question of interpretation. If the event experienced in time $t - 1$ somehow alters preferences or opportunities in such a way that the likelihood of experiencing the event in period t is altered, the observed correlation reflects a structural relation or true state dependence (Heckman 1981).[11] If the event is more likely to be experienced by a given indi-

---

11. There is sometimes a distinction made in the literature between habit formation and state dependence, habit formation relating to persistence in continuous outcomes (quantities)

vidual only because he or she possesses some permanent trait or characteristic that renders the event more likely, such as unobserved tastes, abilities, or motivation, spurious state dependence results, and the observed correlation of events has no structural interpretation. It is also possible that serial correlation in other unobservables, such as environment, will give rise to spurious state dependence.

In distinguishing between habit and heterogeneity, only habit clearly predicts that more recent behavior should have greater weight in generating that prediction. Table 8.8 presents the results of probit estimates based on an autoregressive specification for the six years for which the NLSY includes drinking items. The predicted probability that a respondent reports drinking in 1989 is analyzed as the weighted sum of previous indicators (with controls for race, sex, and age), where the weights, calculated from the probit coefficient estimates, are reported in the table. The weights are always positive, as would be expected from both the heterogeneity and the habit models: the fact that they tend to decline as the lag increases is some evidence of habit formation, although that evidence is far from definitive.[12]

In an effort to bypass this last problem, we now turn to a reduced-form version of the habit-formation model, where past consumption is replaced by variables that act as proxies for the availability of alcohol in the youth's early environment.[13] As shown by Chamberlain (1984), this model allows us to test for the presence of habit formation in a straightforward manner (Hsiao 1986).

8.4.1   Reduced-Form Estimation

We seek to determine whether the association between current drinking and past drinking reflects the habit-forming properties of alcohol (true state dependence) or the influence of some unobserved dynamic feature in the environments in which drinking decisions are made. This distinction is illuminated by specifying a conceptual experiment. Suppose that a sample of youths is randomly assigned to one of two groups, designated *Wet* and *Dry*. The Wets are frequently offered drinks, while the Dries are somehow kept in an alcohol-free environment. The outcomes of this experiment would be measured by the subsequent differences in quantity and patterns of alcohol consumption. If the Wets drink more in later years, we could then conclude that drinking history has a direct effect on current drinking choices.

---

and state dependence describing persistence in discrete outcomes. We will use the concepts interchangeably as descriptions of the same phenomenon.

12. One of many alternative interpretations is that environment is heterogeneous but changes from time to time.

13. This model is not, strictly speaking, a true reduced form. Rather, we eliminate potentially endogenous right-hand-side drinking variables by substituting measures of the early drinking environment. See Moore and Cook (1995) for the first application of this procedure to the habit-formation problem.

Table 8.8   Autoregressive Drinking Equations, Reduced-Form Probit Models, Marginal Effects, Selected Coefficients (S.E.s)

Variable	pr(drinks = 1/1989)	pr(binges = 1/1989)	pr(drinks = 1/1985)	pr(binges = 1/1985)
30-day indicator, 1988	.430***	.249***		
	(.012)	(.015)		
30-day indicator, 1985	.151***	.052***		
	(.014)	(.011)		
30-day indicator, 1984	.123***	.071***	.369***	.149***
	(.015)	(.010)	(.012)	(.012)
30-day indicator, 1983	.081***	.062***	.243***	.068***
	(.015)	(.010)	(.013)	(.010)
30-day indicator, 1982	.098***	.039***	.176***	.045***
	(.014)	(.009)	(.012)	(.008)
Male	.091***	.054***	.078***	.056***
	(.011)	(.006)	(.010)	(.005)
Black	−.025	.027***	−.028***	−.020***
	(.013)	(.007)	(.012)	(.005)

Note: Estimated using 1982–85 and 1988–89 NLSY data: $N > 9,600$. Marginal effects are computed at full sample means. All equations include age indicators for each year of age (not shown). The 30-day indicator is defined as the *drinks* or *binges* in correspondence with the dependent variable. Cluster-corrected standard errors are given in parentheses.

***Statistically significant at the 1 percent level.

While we cannot literally create this experimental setup, we can mimic it with the NLSY data, which include information on the respondent's state of residence at age fourteen. From this item, we are able to say something about the alcohol availability that prevailed in that time and place. While individuals in the NLSY sample are not randomly assigned to this alcohol-availability condition, as in our hypothetical experiment, it is true that fourteen-year-olds rarely have any influence on which state they live in. In that sense, the assignment is exogenous.

Knowing the state of residence at age fourteen allows us to impute for each respondent the MPA, the beer excise tax, and the per capita sales of alcoholic beverages relevant to the individual at that age. We include this sales variable as an indicator of how wet that state's environment was at that time, on the assumption that the fourteen-year-old would have more opportunities to drink—and perhaps more inclination—in an environment where drinking was more common, for given prices and MPA restriction.

8.4.2   Results

Table 8.9 presents estimated effects of contemporaneous and age-fourteen levels of the key variables for both *drinks* (panel A) and *binges* (panel B) for various specifications. Each row of this table is extracted from a different regression. For the contemporaneous variables, the results are much the same as those reported in table 8.7 above and discussed above. The new results are for the age-fourteen variables. They have no discernible effect on the prevalence of drinking, but the bingeing results (presented in panel B of table 8.9) are a different story: the estimated effects of the MPA variable on bingeing are fairly consistent across specifications and offer an indication of habit formation. In particular, respondents who at age fourteen lived in a state where the MPA was eighteen are more likely to binge drink in subsequent years than are respondents who lived in states with a higher minimum age. The effect is not large—about 1 percentage point—but statistically significant in most specifications. The estimated effects for the other age-fourteen variables have the wrong sign but are small and, with one minor exception, not discernibly different than 0.

The result on MPA at fourteen provides some indication that availability of alcohol during adolescence may have an effect on the likelihood of alcohol abuse years later. That is, the persistence that we observed in binge drinking appears at least in part to be the result of habit formation. Since the MPA at fourteen does not have a discernible effect on drinking per se, we speculate that adolescent experience may have a greater long-term effect on the style of drinking (bingeing or moderation) than on whether one drinks at all.

Table 8.9   Probit Regression Results, NLSY 1982–85, 1988–89, Estimated Coefficients (S.E.s), Policy Variables Only

	Beer Tax	MPA Binding	State per Capita Ethanol Use	Beer Tax at Age 14	MPA at Age 14 Was 18	State per Capita Ethanol Use at Age 14
		A. Drink in Last 30 Days (× 100), including Age 14 Variables				
No state fixed effects:						
Short form	-2.581*** (.838)	-5.618*** (1.101)		.243 (.448)	.293 (.760)	
Long form	-2.518*** (.865)	-5.836*** (1.149)		.0787 (.462)	-.167 (.778)	
Short form	-2.056** (.853)	-5.674*** (1.101)	6.658*** (1.360)	.289 (.466)	-.031 (.761)	-1.007 (1.235)
Long form	-2.109** (.882)	-5.900*** (1.151)	5.408*** (1.427)	.173 (.482)	-.447 (.780)	-.307 (1.309)
State fixed effects:						
Short form	-17.233*** (3.032)	-6.730*** (1.119)		.0004 (.4650)	-.139 (1.026)	
Long form	-14.222*** (3.172)	-6.773*** (1.175)		-.080 (.481)	-.956 (1.056)	
Short form	-5.551* (3.073)	-6.335*** (1.116)	12.070*** (2.648)	.054 (.481)	-.160 (1.029)	.133 (1.284)
Long form	-2.474 (3.258)	-6.403*** (1.171)	11.367*** (2.726)	.078 (.500)	-1.000 (1.058)	.728 (1.350)

(continued)

Table 8.9 (continued)

B. Binge (× 100), including Age 14 Variables

	Beer Tax	MPA Binding	State per Capita Ethanol Use	Beer Tax at Age 14	MPA at Age 14 Was 18	State per Capita Ethanol Use at Age 14
No state fixed effects:						
Short form	-.898*	-2.179***		.332	1.301***	
	(.488)	(.599)		(.262)	(.430)	
Long form	-.610	-2.321***		.215	1.086***	
	(.478)	(.576)		(.257)	(.421)	
Short form	-.751	-2.162***	1.656**	.264	1.259***	-1.011
	(.491)	(.600)	(.672)	(.270)	(.429)	(.627)
Long form	-.485	-2.293***	1.271*	.119	1.075**	-1.120*
	(.481)	(.577)	(.683)	(.265)	(.420)	(.637)
State fixed effects:						
Short form	-9.525***	-2.342***		.259	1.120*	
	(1.871)	(.586)		(.261)	(.575)	
Long form	-7.276***	-2.467***		.149	.906	
	(1.867)	(.565)		(.258)	(.573)	
Short form	-3.988**	-2.179***	5.954***	.229	1.071*	-.645
	(2.027)	(.591)	(1.579)	(.272)	(.574)	(.717)
Long form	-2.478	-2.324***	5.189***	.096	.869	-.797
	(2.032)	(.571)	(1.522)	(.203)	(.572)	(.720)

Note: Estimated using 1982–85 and 1988–89 NLSY data: $N \geq 50{,}692$. Marginal effects are computed at full sample means. Cluster-corrected robust standard errors are given in parentheses. All equations included indicators for sex, race, ethnicity, age in 1979, residence in SMSA, parents' education, family structure at age 14, AFQT percentile, and family religion. The long-form equations also include schooling, employment status, income, current school enrollment, weight, marital status, whether either parent was a problem drinker, number of children under 18 in household, living arrangements, and education aspirations in 1982.

***Statistically significant at the 1 percent level.
**Statistically significant at the 5 percent level.
*Statistically significant at the 10 percent level.

8.5 Discussion

The results presented above further establish the importance of the MPA as a deterrent to drinking and bingeing by those who are young enough to be governed by it. The effects are substantial and hold up well over a variety of specifications. We also present evidence that the minimum age has an effect on the likelihood of binge drinking years after the youth is no longer directly affected: youths who are exposed at age fourteen to a lower drinking age appear to be more likely to acquire a habit of heavy drinking. That evidence is relevant to judging, not only the importance of the MPA, but also the habit-forming potential of youthful drinking and, consequently, the importance of early intervention.

The beer excise tax also appears to be an effective deterrent to youthful drinking and bingeing, although the evidence is not as consistent as in the case of the MPA. A clearer resolution to the controversy in the literature may have to await a more powerful experiment than that provided by the small and infrequent changes in state excise taxes.

Finally, we note that per capita ethanol consumption has a consistent and important estimated effect on youthful drinking and bingeing, even after controlling for tax, MPA, state fixed effects, and a long list of individual characteristics. Clearly, youthful drinking decisions are closely linked to overall consumption; whether that link is the result of direct influence or shared but unmeasured determinants is an important issue for future research.

Appendix

Table 8A.1 **Variable Means and Definitions from the MTF ($N = 367,043$)**

Variable	Mean (S.D.)	Definition
Drinks	.626	Dummy variable (d.v.): 1 if respondent drank any alcohol in the past 30 days, 0 otherwise
Number of drinks[a]	8.38 (11.52)	
Binges	.351	D.v.: 1 if respondent drank 5 or more drinks containing alcohol in a row in past 30 days
Number of times bingeing[a]	3.48 (3.43)	
Black	.124	D.v.: 1 if respondent is black
Other race	.160	D.v.: 1 if respondent is Hispanic
Male	.490	D.v.: 1 if respondent is male
Age 17	.017	D.v.: age 17
Age 19	.246	D.v.: age 19
Both parents	.716	D.v.: both parents live in household
Parents' education:		D.v.: highest grade completed
Mother:		
12 years	.386	
13–15	.187	
16 or more	.263	
Father		
12 years	.303	
13–15	.168	
16 or more	.336	
Mother working when growing up?		D.v.
Sometimes	.277	
Most of the time	.177	
Always	.282	
Location of respondent's residence		D.v.
In SMSA	.774	
Region:		D.v.
Northeast	.231	
North Central	.271	
South	.309	

Table 8A.1   (continued)

Variable	Mean (S.D.)	Definition
Environment grew up in:		D.v.
Rural area	.147	
Town	.258	
City	.287	
Marital status:		D.v.
Married	.020	
Engaged	.062	
Divorce/separated	.006	
Current employment status:		
Working	.770	D.v.: 1 if working
Hours of work	14.966 (13.367)	
Income from work	7.731 (14.615)	
Income from other sources	6.664 (10.192)	
GPA	5.800 (1.944)	
High school type:		
College prep	.510	D.v.
Vocational/technical	.122	
Religiosity:		
Frequency of attending services	1.561 (1.819)	Number of times attend religious services each month
Religion is important	.590	D.v.
Number of school days missed	2.688 (4.208)	
Other drug use:		
Used marijuana in past 30 days	.252	D.v.
Used other drugs in past 30 days	.224	D.v.
Smoker	.312	D.v.: 1 if currently smokes
Education aspirations: going to college?		D.v.
Definitely no	.182	
Probably no	.152	
Probably yes	.228	

[a]Conditional on those who report drinking/bingeing only.

Table 8A.2   **30-Day Drinking Participation, Short Form, Age 17–19 Only, Coefficient Stability, MTF 1976, 1986, 1996**

Variables	1996	1986	1976	1996–86	1986–76	1996–76
Black	-.225***	-.311***	-.200***	.086***	-.111***	-.025
	(.014)	(.015)	(.017)	(.020)	(.022)	(.022)
Other race	-.088***	-.170***	-.079***	.082***	-.091***	-.009
	(.012)	(.013)	(.016)	(.018)	(.021)	(.020)
Male	.067***	.061***	.114***	.006	-.053***	-.047***
	(.009)	(.008)	(.009)	(.012)	(.012)	(.012)
Age 17	-.084**	-.075**	-.039	-.009	-.036	-.045
	(.037)	(.034)	(.026)	(.050)	(.043)	(.046)
Age 19	.030***	-.002	.0004	.032**	-.001	.031**
	(.010)	(.010)	(.011)	(.014)	(.014)	(.014)
Both parents	-.053***	-.045***	-.038***	-.008	-.007	-.015
	(.010)	(.010)	(.011)	(.014)	(.015)	(.015)
Mother's education:						
12 years	.017	.015	.037***	.003	-.022	-.020
	(.015)	(.013)	(.012)	(.020)	(.018)	(.020)
13–15	.020	.018	.004	.001	.015	.016
	(.016)	(.015)	(.016)	(.022)	(.022)	(.023)
16 or more	.014	.019	.031**	-.005	-.013	-.018
	(.016)	(.015)	(.016)	(.022)	(.022)	(.023)
Father's education:						
12 years	.015	-.005	-.006	.020	.001	.021
	(.014)	(.013)	(.012)	(.019)	(.017)	(.018)
13–15	.035**	-.013	-.024	.048**	.011	.059***
	(.016)	(.015)	(.015)	(.022)	(.021)	(.022)
16 or more	.043***	.006	.002	.037*	.004	.041**
	(.015)	(.014)	(.014)	(.020)	(.020)	(.020)

	(1)	(2)	(3)	(4)	(5)	(6)
Mother worked when growing up:						
Sometimes	.053***	.004	.004	.050***	.0001	.050***
	(.014)	(.011)	(.010)	(.018)	(.015)	(.017)
Most time	.051***	.024*	.025*	.026	-.001	.026
	(.015)	(.013)	(.014)	(.019)	(.018)	(.020)
Always	.082***	.032***	.030**	.050***	.002	.052***
	(.013)	(.012)	(.013)	(.017)	(.018)	(.018)
SMSA	.003	.009	.012	-.006	-.003	-.008
	(.012)	(.011)	(.012)	(.016)	(.016)	(.016)
Northeast	.079***	.055***	.140***	.024	-.085***	-.062***
	(.014)	(.013)	(.013)	(.019)	(.019)	(.019)
North Central	.036**	.072***	.085***	-.036*	-.013	-.049**
	(.015)	(.012)	(.013)	(.019)	(.018)	(.019)
South	.035**	-.005	-.004	.041**	-.002	.039**
	(.014)	(.012)	(.013)	(.018)	(.018)	(.019)
Environment grew up in:						
Rural	-.071***	-.054***	-.050***	-.018	-.004	-.021
	(.015)	(.014)	(.015)	(.021)	(.020)	(.021)
Town	-.020	-.022***	-.013	.001	-.009	-.008
	(.013)	(.011)	(.012)	(.017)	(.017)	(.017)
City	-.020*	.009	-.012	-.030*	.021	-.008
	(.012)	(.011)	(.011)	(.016)	(.016)	(.016)
Constant	.440***	.666***	.617***	-.226***	.049	-.177***
	(.025)	(.023)	(.023)	(.034)	(.033)	(.034)
N	12,768	12,979	10,857			
Adjusted R^2	.039	.059	.053			

Note: OLS estimates (standard errors in parentheses).

***Statistically significant at the 1 percent level.

**Statistically significant at the 5 percent level.

*Statistically significant at the 10 percent level.

Table 8A.3　　30-Day Drinking Participation, Long Form, Age 17–19 Only, Coefficient Stability, MTF 1976, 1986, 1996

Variables	1996	1986	1976	1996–86	1986–76	1996–76
Black	-.110***	-.222***	-.163***	.112***	-.060***	.052**
	(.014)	(.015)	(.017)	(.021)	(.023)	(.022)
Other race	-.028**	-.134***	-.089***	.106***	-.045**	.061***
	(.012)	(.013)	(.016)	(.018)	(.021)	(.020)
Male	.032***	.035***	.059***	-.002	-.024**	-.027**
	(.008)	(.008)	(.009)	(.012)	(.012)	(.012)
Age 17	-.054	-.062*	-.057**	.008	-.005	.003
	(.034)	(.032)	(.026)	(.047)	(.041)	(.043)
Age 19	.028***	-.004	.007	.031**	-.010	.021
	(.009)	(.009)	(.010)	(.013)	(.014)	(.014)
Both parents	.003	-.006	.003	.010	-.009	.001
	(.009)	(.010)	(.011)	(.014)	(.015)	(.015)
Mother's education:						
12 years	.005	.033**	.041***	-.028	-.008	-.036*
	(.014)	(.013)	(.012)	(.019)	(.017)	(.018)
13–15	.003	.039**	.006	-.036*	.032	-.004
	(.015)	(.015)	(.015)	(.021)	(.021)	(.022)
16 or more	.019	.046***	.050***	-.027	-.004	-.031
	(.015)	(.015)	(.015)	(.021)	(.021)	(.022)
Father's education:						
12 years	.013	-.009	.009	.022	-.017	.005
	(.013)	(.013)	(.011)	(.018)	(.017)	(.017)
13–15	.033**	-.014	.0004	.047**	-.014	.033
	(.014)	(.014)	(.014)	(.020)	(.020)	(.020)
16 or more	.043***	.005	.010	.038**	-.005	.033**
	(.014)	(.014)	(.014)	(.019)	(.019)	(.019)

Mother worked when growing up:						
Sometimes	.029**	−.015	−.016	.044***	.001	.045***
	(.013)	(.010)	(.010)	(.017)	(.014)	(.016)
Most time	.015	−.001	−.008	.016	.006	.022
	(.014)	(.012)	(.013)	(.018)	(.018)	(.019)
Always	.043***	−.002	.006	.045***	−.007	.038**
	(.012)	(.011)	(.013)	(.016)	(.017)	(.017)
SMSA	−.013	.001	.002	−.013	−.001	−.015
	(.011)	(.011)	(.011)	(.015)	(.015)	(.015)
Northeast	.039***	.036***	.118***	.003	−.082***	−.079***
	(.013)	(.013)	(.013)	(.018)	(.018)	(.018)
North Central	.003	.074***	.072***	−.071***	.002	−.069***
	(.014)	(.012)	(.012)	(.018)	(.017)	(.018)
South	.027**	.026**	.012	.002	.013	.015
	(.013)	(.012)	(.013)	(.017)	(.018)	(.018)
Environment grew up in:						
Rural	−.042***	−.015	−.012	−.027	−.003	−.030
	(.014)	(.014)	(.014)	(.020)	(.020)	(.020)
Town	−.005	−.002	−.003	−.003	.001	−.002
	(.012)	(.011)	(.012)	(.016)	(.016)	(.016)
City	−.016	.013	−.005	−.029*	.018	−.011
	(.011)	(.010)	(.011)	(.015)	(.015)	(.015)
Marital status:						
Married	−.038	−.044	−.029	.006	−.014	−.008
	(.031)	(.030)	(.032)	(.043)	(.044)	(.044)
Engaged	−.038**	−.092***	−.043***	.054**	−.048**	.006
	(.018)	(.017)	(.017)	(.025)	(.024)	(.025)
Divorced/separated	−.054	−.034	.015	−.020	−.048	−.068
	(.054)	(.054)	(.074)	(.076)	(.091)	(.091)

(continued)

Table 8A.3   (continued)

Variables	1996	1986	1976	1996–86	1986–76	1996–76
Currently working	.039***	.059***	.010	−.019	.049***	.030
	(.013)	(.013)	(.013)	(.018)	(.018)	(.019)
Hours worked	.001**	.001***	.002***	−.001	.0003	−.001
	(.0004)	(.0003)	(.0004)	(.001)	(.0006)	(.001)
Income from work	.0002	.0004	.0006**	−.001	.0002	−.0009**
	(.0003)	(.0003)	(.0003)	(.0007)	(.0004)	(.0004)
Income from other sources	.002***	.002***	.001*	.0007	.001	.0013***
	(.0003)	(.0003)	(.001)	(.001)	(.0008)	(.0007)
GPA	−.009***	−.011***	.0002	.002	−.011***	−.009
	(.002)	(.002)	(.003)	(.003)	(.004)	(.004)
Type of high school:						
College prep	.007	.021**	.016	−.015	.006	−.009
	(.010)	(.010)	(.011)	(.014)	(.015)	(.015)
Vocational	−.011	−.021	.010	.010	−.031	−.021
	(.016)	(.014)	(.013)	(.021)	(.019)	(.021)
Frequency attending religious services	−.019***	−.017***	−.021***	−.002	.004	.001
	(.003)	(.003)	(.003)	(.004)	(.004)	(.004)
Religion is important	−.017*	−.033***	−.055***	.016	.022*	.038***
	(.010)	(.009)	(.010)	(.013)	(.013)	(.014)
Number of days missed school	.005***	.007***	.003***	−.001	.004**	.002
	(.001)	(.001)	(.001)	(.001)	(.002)	(.001)

Used marijuana in past 30 days	.287***	.229***	.243***	.058***	-.014	.044***
	(.011)	(.011)	(.010)	(.016)	(.015)	(.015)
Used other drug in past 30 days	.025***	.017***	.003	.008	.014*	.022***
	(.006)	(.006)	(.006)	(.009)	(.008)	(.008)
Current smoker	.291***	.179***	.177***	.112***	.002	.114***
	(.010)	(.010)	(.010)	(.014)	(.014)	(.014)
Planning to go to college?						
No plan	-.023	-.029**	-.022	.006	-.006	.0002
	(.016)	(.014)	(.014)	(.021)	(.019)	(.021)
Probably will not	-.018	-.020	-.014	.002	-.007	-.005
	(.015)	(.013)	(.014)	(.020)	(.019)	(.020)
Probably will	-.022**	-.014	-.005	-.008	-.009	-.016
	(.011)	(.010)	(.011)	(.015)	(.015)	(.016)
Constant	.301***	.528***	.473***	-.227***	.055	-.171***
	(.030)	(.030)	(.033)	(.043)	(.044)	(.045)
N	11,593	11,867	9,655			
Adjusted R^2	.269	.205	.232			

Note: OLS estimates (standard errors in parentheses).

***Statistically significant at the 1 percent level.

**Statistically significant at the 5 percent level.

*Statistically significant at the 10 percent level.

Table 8A.4   Binge Drinking: Participation, Short Form, Age 17–19 Only, Coefficient Stability, MTF 1976, 1986, 1996

Variables	1996	1986	1976	1996–86	1986–76	1996–76
Black	-.211***	-.267***	-.183***	.056***	-.084***	-.028
	(.013)	(.015)	(.017)	(.019)	(.023)	(.021)
Other race	-.090***	-.126***	-.032*	.036**	-.094***	-.058***
	(.011)	(.014)	(.017)	(.018)	(.022)	(.020)
Male	.121***	.170***	.210***	-.049***	-.040***	-.089***
	(.008)	(.008)	(.009)	(.011)	(.012)	(.012)
Age 17	-.099***	-.082**	-.058**	-.017	-.023	-.041
	(.033)	(.034)	(.027)	(.048)	(.044)	(.043)
Age 19	.030***	.008	.015	.022*	-.006	.015
	(.009)	(.010)	(.011)	(.013)	(.015)	(.014)
Both parents	-.037***	-.049***	-.040***	.013	-.010	.003
	(.009)	(.010)	(.012)	(.013)	(.015)	(.015)
Mother's education:						
12 years	.005	.016	.026**	-.012	-.010	-.021
	(.014)	(.013)	(.012)	(.019)	(.018)	(.019)
13–15	.005	-.012	-.018	.018	.006	.024
	(.015)	(.016)	(.017)	(.021)	(.023)	(.022)
16 or more	.008	-.003	-.012	.011	.009	.021
	(.015)	(.015)	(.016)	(.021)	(.023)	(.022)
Father's education:						
12 years	.008	-.003	-.003	.011	.0004	.011
	(.013)	(.013)	(.012)	(.018)	(.018)	(.018)
13–15	.014	-.016	-.012	.030	-.004	.026
	(.014)	(.015)	(.016)	(.021)	(.022)	(.021)
16 or more	.025*	-.011	-.017	.036*	.006	.042**
	(.013)	(.014)	(.015)	(.019)	(.020)	(.020)

Mother worked when growing up:						
Sometimes	.019	.033***	.017	−.014	.016	.001
	(.013)	(.011)	(.011)	(.017)	(.015)	(.017)
Most time	.022*	.022*	.037***	.0001	−.015	−.015
	(.013)	(.013)	(.014)	(.018)	(.019)	(.019)
Always	.041***	.045***	.033**	−.004	.012	.008
	(.012)	(.012)	(.014)	(.017)	(.018)	(.018)
SMSA	.025**	−.010	−.006	.035**	−.004	.031
	(.011)	(.011)	(.012)	(.016)	(.017)	(.016)
Northeast	.051***	.032**	.095***	.019	−.062***	−.043**
	(.013)	(.013)	(.014)	(.018)	(.019)	(.019)
North Central	.032**	.068***	.085***	−.036*	−.018	−.054***
	(.013)	(.012)	(.013)	(.018)	(.018)	(.019)
South	.019	−.003	.003	.022	−.006	.016
	(.012)	(.013)	(.014)	(.018)	(.019)	(.019)
Environment grew up in:						
Rural	−.019	−.033**	−.004	.014	−.029	−.015
	(.014)	(.015)	(.015)	(.020)	(.021)	(.020)
Town	−.001	−.024**	.031**	.023	−.055***	−.032*
	(.011)	(.011)	(.013)	(.016)	(.017)	(.017)
City	−.015	.006	−.007	−.021	.013	−.008
	(.010)	(.011)	(.012)	(.015)	(.016)	(.016)
Constant	.217***	.334***	.253***	−.116***	.080**	−.036
	(.023)	(.023)	(.024)	(.033)	(.034)	(.033)
N	12,790	13,010	10,928			
Adjusted R^2	.052	.068	.073			

Note: OLS estimates (standard errors in parentheses).

***Statistically significant at the 1 percent level.

**Statistically significant at the 5 percent level.

*Statistically significant at the 10 percent level.

Table 8A.5   Binge Drinking: Participation, Long Form, Age 17–19 Only, Coefficient Stability, MTF 1976, 1986, 1996

Variables	1996	1986	1976	1996–86	1986–76	1996–76
Black	-.116***	-.187***	-.163***	.071***	-.024	.046**
	(.013)	(.015)	(.018)	(.019)	(.023)	(.022)
Other race	-.049***	-.086***	-.052***	.037**	-.034*	.003
	(.011)	(.013)	(.016)	(.017)	(.021)	(.019)
Male	.089***	.136***	.148***	-.047***	-.012	-.059***
	(.008)	(.008)	(.009)	(.011)	(.012)	(.012)
Age 17	-.078***	-.067**	-.054**	-.010	-.013	-.024
	(.031)	(.032)	(.026)	(.044)	(.041)	(.040)
Age 19	.027***	-.004	.015	.031**	-.018	.013
	(.008)	(.009)	(.010)	(.012)	(.014)	(.013)
Both parents	.008	.004	.008	.004	-.004	.0001
	(.009)	(.009)	(.011)	(.013)	(.015)	(.014)
Mother's education:						
12 years	-.004	.036***	.036***	-.040**	.0005	-.040**
	(.013)	(.013)	(.012)	(.018)	(.017)	(.018)
13–15	-.006	.015	-.003	-.022	.019	-.003
	(.014)	(.015)	(.015)	(.020)	(.021)	(.021)
16 or more	.011	.027*	.021	-.016	.006	-.011
	(.014)	(.015)	(.015)	(.020)	(.021)	(.021)
Father's education:						
12 years	.006	-.007	.015	.013	-.022	-.008
	(.012)	(.012)	(.011)	(.017)	(.017)	(.017)
13–15	.014	-.011	.019	.025	-.030	-.005
	(.013)	(.014)	(.015)	(.019)	(.020)	(.020)
16 or more	.021*	.0003	.007	.022	-.007	.015
	(.012)	(.014)	(.014)	(.018)	(.019)	(.019)

	(1)	(2)	(3)	(4)	(5)	(6)
Mother worked when growing up:						
Sometimes	−.001	.014	−.001	−.015	.015	.0006
	(.012)	(.010)	(.010)	(.016)	(.014)	(.015)
Most time	−.008	−.002	−.004	−.006	.002	−.004
	(.012)	(.012)	(.013)	(.017)	(.018)	(.018)
Always	.015	.015	.001	.0002	.014	.013
	(.011)	(.011)	(.013)	(.015)	(.017)	(.017)
SMSA	.014	−.018*	−.025**	.033**	.007	.040***
	(.010)	(.011)	(.011)	(.015)	(.015)	(.015)
Northeast	.024**	.012	.065***	.011	−.053***	−.042**
	(.012)	(.013)	(.013)	(.017)	(.018)	(.018)
North Central	.011	.070***	.068***	−.060***	.003	−.057***
	(.012)	(.012)	(.012)	(.017)	(.017)	(.017)
South	.015	.029**	.016	−.014	.014	−.001
	(.011)	(.012)	(.013)	(.016)	(.018)	(.017)
Environment grew up in:						
Rural	.008	.004	.025*	.004	−.021	−.017
	(.013)	(.014)	(.014)	(.019)	(.020)	(.019)
Town	.013	−.004	.036***	.017	−.040**	−.023
	(.010)	(.011)	(.012)	(.015)	(.016)	(.016)
City	−.006	.006	.004	−.012	.002	−.010
	(.010)	(.010)	(.011)	(.014)	(.015)	(.015)
Marital status:						
Married	−.031	−.054*	−.093***	.023	.039	.062
	(.028)	(.030)	(.032)	(.041)	(.044)	(.043)
Engaged	−.073***	−.101***	−.043***	.029	−.059**	−.030
	(.017)	(.017)	(.017)	(.024)	(.024)	(.024)
Divorced/separated	−.002	.032	.087	−.034	−.055	−.089
	(.048)	(.053)	(.074)	(.072)	(.091)	(.089)

(continued)

Table 8A.5 (continued)

Variables	1996	1986	1976	1996–86	1986–76	1996–76
Currently working	−.004	.06	.007	−.010	−.001	−.011
	(.012)	(.013)	(.013)	(.017)	(.018)	(.018)
Hours worked	.001***	.001***	.001***	.0002	.0002	.0003
	(.0003)	(.0004)	(.0003)	(.0005)	(.0005)	(.0006)
Income from work	.0004	.0002	.0003	.0001	.0006	.0007*
	(.0003)	(.0003)	(.0002)	(.0004)	(.0004)	(.0004)
Income from other sources	.002***	.002***	.001**	.0002	.0005	.0003
	(.0003)	(.0003)	(.001)	(.0005)	(.0008)	(.0007)
GPA	−.008***	−.016***	−.018***	.008**	.002	.010**
	(.002)	(.002)	(.003)	(.003)	(.004)	(.003)
Type of high school:						
College prep	−.008	.012	−.002	−.021	.014	−.007
	(.009)	(.010)	(.011)	(.013)	(.015)	(.014)
Vocational	−.034**	−.019	−.005	−.015	−.015	−.030
	(.015)	(.014)	(.013)	(.020)	(.019)	(.020)
Frequency attending religious services	−.007***	−.014***	−.008***	.007*	−.006	.001
	(.002)	(.002)	(.003)	(.003)	(.004)	(.004)
Religion is important	−.009	−.004	−.034***	−.006	.030**	.024*
	(.009)	(.009)	(.010)	(.013)	(.013)	(.013)
Number of days missed school	.006***	.007***	.006***	−.0007	.0006	.0001
	(.001)	(.001)	(.001)	(.001)	(.002)	(.001)

	(1)	(2)	(3)	(4)	(5)	(6)
Used marijuana in past 30 days	.259***	.288***	.283***	−.029*	.005	−.024*
	(.010)	(.011)	(.010)	(.015)	(.015)	(.015)
Used other drug in past 30 days	.057***	.063***	.048***	−.006	.015*	.010
	(.006)	(.006)	(.006)	(.008)	(.008)	(.008)
Current smoker	.229***	.169***	.170***	.060***	−.001	.059***
	(.009)	(.010)	(.010)	(.013)	(.014)	(.013)
Planning to go to college?						
No plan	−.021	−.011	.007	−.010	−.018	−.028
	(.014)	(.013)	(.014)	(.020)	(.019)	(.020)
Probably will not	−.037***	−.003	.013	−.033*	−.016	−.050**
	(.014)	(.013)	(.014)	(.019)	(.019)	(.020)
Probably will	−.017*	.001	.007	−.018	−.006	−.024
	(.010)	(.010)	(.011)	(.014)	(.015)	(.015)
Constant	.110***	.210***	.165***	−.100***	.045	−.055
	(.028)	(.029)	(.033)	(.040)	(.044)	(.043)
N	11,589	11,866	9,664			
Adjusted R^2	.264	.258	.294			

Note: OLS estimates (standard errors in parentheses).

***Statistically significant at the 1 percent level.

**Statistically significant at the 5 percent level.

*Statistically significant at the 10 percent level.

References

Bauman, K. E., and S. T. Ennett. 1996. On the importance of peer influence for adolescent drug use: Commonly neglected considerations. *Addiction* 91, no. 2: 185–98.

Becker, G. S. 1992. Habits, addictions, and traditions. *Kyklos* 45:327–46.

———. 1996. *Accounting for tastes.* Cambridge, Mass.: Harvard University Press.

Becker, G. S., M. Grossman, and K. M. Murphy. 1991. Rational addiction and the effect of price on consumption. *American Economic Review* 81, no. 2:237–41.

Becker, G. S., and K. M. Murphy. 1988. A theory of rational addiction. *Journal of Political Economy* 96, no. 4:675–700.

Beer Institute. Various years. *Brewer's almanac.* Washington, D.C.

Chaloupka, F. J., and H. Wechsler. 1996. Binge drinking in college: The impact of price. *Contemporary Economic Policy* 14, no. 4:112–24.

Chamberlain, G. 1984. Panel data. In *Handbook of econometrics,* ed. Z. Grilliches and M. Intrilligator. New York: North-Holland.

Chesson, H. W., P. Harrison, and W. J. Kassler. 2000. Sex under the influence: The effect of alcohol policy on sexually transmitted disease rates in the United States. *Journal of Law and Economics* 43, no. 1:215–38.

Coate, D., and M. Grossman. 1988. Effects of alcoholic beverage prices and legal drinking ages on youth alcohol use. *Journal of Law and Economics* 31, no. 1:145–71.

Coleman, J. S. 1990. *Foundations of social theory.* Cambridge, Mass.: Harvard University Press.

Cook, P. J. 1981. The effect of liquor taxes on drinking, cirrhosis, and auto fatalities. In *Alcohol and public policy: Beyond the shadow of Prohibition,* ed. Mark Moore and Dean Gerstein. Washington, D.C.: National Academy of Sciences.

———. 1993b. Taxation of alcoholic beverages. In *Economic research on the prevention of alcohol-related problems* (NIH Publication no. 93–3513), ed. M. Hilton and G. Bloss. Rockville, Md.: National Institute on Alcohol Abuse and Alcoholism.

Cook, P. J., and M. J. Moore. 1993a. Drinking and schooling. *Journal of Health Economics* 12:411–29.

———. 1994. This tax's for you. *National Tax Journal* 47, no. 3 (September): 559–73.

———. In press. Alcohol. In *Handbook of health economics,* ed. J. P. Newhouse and A. Culyer. New York: North-Holland.

Cook, P. J., M. J. Moore, and R. Pacula. 1993. Drinking by young adults: Part 1, Demographics. Working paper. Sanford Institute of Public Policy. Duke University, November.

Cook, P. J., and G. Tauchen. 1982. The effect of liquor taxes on heavy drinking. *Bell Journal of Economics* 13, no. 2:379–90.

———. 1984. The effect of minimum drinking age legislation on youthful auto fatalities, 1970–77. *Journal of Legal Studies* 13:169–90.

Currie, C., K. Hurrelmann, W. Settertobulte, R. Smith, and J. Todd. 2000. *Health and health behaviour among young people.* Copenhagen: World Health Organization, Regional Office for Europe.

Dee, T. S. 1999. State alcohol policies, teen drinking, and traffic fatalities. *Journal of Public Economics* 72:289–315.

Ellwood, D. T. 1982. Teenage unemployment: Permanent scars or temporary blemishes. In *The youth labor market problem: Its nature, causes, and consequences,* ed. Richard B. Freeman and David A. Wise. Chicago: University of Chicago Press.

Evans, W. N., D. Neville, and J. D. Graham. 1991. General deterrence of drunk driving: Evaluation of recent American policies. *Risk Analysis* 11, no. 2:279–89.

Grossman, M., F. J. Chaloupka, H. Saffer, and A. Laixuthai. 1994. Effects of alcohol price policy on youth: A summary of economic research. *Journal of Research on Adolescence* 4:347–64.

Grossman, M., F. J. Chaloupka, and I. Sirtalan. 1998. An empirical analysis of alcohol addiction: Results from the Monitoring the Future panels. *Economic Inquiry* 36:39–48.

Grossman, M., D. Coate, and G. M. Arluck. 1987. Price sensitivity of alcoholic beverages in the United States: Youth alcohol consumption. In *Control issues in alcohol abuse prevention: Strategies for states and communities,* ed. H. Holder. Greenwich, Conn.: JAI.

Heckman, J. J. 1981. Heterogeneity and state dependence. In *Studies in labor markets,* ed. S. Rosen. Chicago: University of Chicago Press.

Heckman, J. J., and R. Willis. 1977. A beta-logistic model for the analysis of sequential labor force participation of married women. *Journal of Political Economy* 85, no. 1:27–58.

Hsiao, C. 1986. *Analysis of panel data.* New York: Cambridge University Press.

Kenkel, D. S. 1993. Drinking, driving, and deterrence: The effectiveness and social costs of alternative policies. *Journal of Law and Economics* 36:877–913.

Males, M. A. 1986. The minimum purchase age for alcohol and young-driver fatal crashes: A long-term view. *Journal of Legal Studies* 15, no. 1:181–211.

Manski, C. F. 1995. *Identification problems in the social sciences.* Cambridge, Mass.: Harvard University Press.

Markowitz, S., and M. Grossman. 1998. Alcohol regulation and domestic violence towards children. *Contemporary Economic Policy* 16, no. 3:309–20.

Mast, B. D., B. L. Benson, and D. W. Rasmussen. 1999. Beer taxation and alcohol-related traffic fatalities. *Southern Economic Journal* 66, no. 2:214–49.

Moore, M. J., and P. J. Cook. 1995. Habit and heterogeneity in the youthful demand for alcohol. Working Paper no. 5152. Cambridge, Mass.: National Bureau of Economic Research.

Mullahy, J., and J. L. Sindelar. 1989. Life cycle effects of alcoholism on education, earnings, and occupation. *Inquiry* 26:272–82.

———. 1991. Gender differences in labor market effects of alcoholism. *American Economic Review* 81, no. 2:161–65.

Norton, E. C., R. C. Lindroth, and S. T. Ennett. 1998. Controlling for the endogeneity of peer substance use on adolescent alcohol and tobacco use. *Health Economics* 7, no. 5:439–53.

Rossi, D. 1992. *Alcohol: Consumi e politiche in Europa* (Alcohol: Consumption and policy in Europe). Rome: Permanent Observatory on Youth and Alcohol.

Ruhm, C. J. 1995. Economic conditions and alcohol problems. *Journal of Health Economics* 14, no. 5:583–603.

———. 1996. Alcohol policies and highway vehicle fatalities. *Journal of Health Economics* 15:435–54.

Saffer, H., and M. Grossman. 1987a. Beer taxes, the legal drinking age, and youth motor vehicle fatalities. *Journal of Legal Studies* 16:351–74.

———. 1987b. Drinking age laws and highway mortality rates: Cause and effect. *Economic Inquiry* 25, no. 3:403–17.

Skog, O. J. 1980. Social interaction and the distribution of alcohol consumption. *Journal of Drug Issues* 10, no. 1 (winter): 71–92.

———. 1985. The collectivity of drinking cultures: A theory of the distribution of alcohol consumption. *British Journal of Addiction* 80:83–99.

Sloan, F. A., E. Stout, and K. Whetten-Goldstein. 1999. *Drinkers, drivers, and bartenders: Balancing private choices and public accountability.* Chicago: University of Chicago Press.

9

Dropout and Enrollment Trends in the Postwar Period
What Went Wrong in the 1970s?

David Card and Thomas Lemieux

Over most of the last century, successive cohorts of children had rising en-rollment rates and increasing educational attainment. This trend stopped abruptly with cohorts that entered high school in the late 1960s. Young men's high school completion rates drifted down over the 1970s, while their college entrance rates plummeted. Young women's high school graduation and college entry rates were stagnant. As a consequence, men and women born in the 1960s had about the same high school graduation rates, *and lower four-year college graduation rates,* than men and women born a de-cade earlier. Even by the late 1990s, college entry rates of young men were no higher than they were thirty years earlier. This lack of intergenerational progress stands in marked contrast to earlier trends and poses a major puzzle: What went wrong in the 1970s?

Any slowdown in the rate of growth of educational attainment is a cause of obvious concern. Apart from the fact that better-educated workers earn more and experience a range of other benefits, including lower unemploy-ment, better health, and longer life expectancy (Haveman and Wolfe 1984), a slowdown in the rate of human-capital accumulation will lead ultimately to slower economic growth for the economy as a whole and is likely to cause continuing upward pressure on the earnings differentials between more- and less-educated workers (Katz and Murphy 1992; Topel 1997).

David Card is the Class of 1950 Professor of Economics at the University of California, Berkeley, and a research associate of the National Bureau of Economic Research. Thomas Lemieux is professor of economics at the University of British Columbia and a research associate of the National Bureau of Economic Research.

The authors are grateful to Ethan Lewis and Jesse Rothstein for outstanding research assistance and to Jonathan Gruber for helpful discussions in formulating their research. This project was funded in part by the Center for Labor Economics at the University of California, Berkeley, and by a National Science Foundation grant to Card.

In this paper, we use a variety of data sources to document trends in school enrollment and completed schooling attainment and to attempt to understand the underlying sources of these trends. In particular, drawing on the human-capital-investment model (Becker 1967; Mincer 1974), we focus on the role of various demand-side factors affecting the decision of when to leave school. These include changes in the expected economic return to an additional year of education, the level of real interest rates, tuition costs, and cyclic labor market conditions. We also highlight the role of a specific supply-side variable—the relative size of the cohort currently in school—that may be particularly relevant for understanding education outcomes of the baby-boom generation.

A major difficulty confronting any analysis of long-run trends in education outcomes is the absence of micro-level data sets that include information on family-background factors, geographic location, and schooling outcomes for a broad range of cohorts. Conventional micro data sets such as the Current Population Survey and the decennial censuses lack any family-background data. On the other hand, specialized education data sets such as High School and Beyond cover only a narrow range of cohorts. To sidestep this problem, we pursue a multilevel estimation strategy. We begin by using individual micro data from the General Social Survey to examine the contribution of changing family-background factors to intercohort trends in high school and college graduation. Next, we turn to an analysis of average enrollment and completed-schooling outcomes for individuals in specific cohorts and states. Here, we focus on the effects of three local-level variables: state unemployment rates, tuition levels at state colleges and universities, and the relative size of the high school cohort in the state. Finally, we use time-series models to analyze the role of purely aggregate explanatory variables, including the real interest rate and the rate of return to education for young workers.

We also use data from the National Longitudinal Survey of Youth to show that dropping out of school is, by and large, a once-for-all decision since only a small fraction of dropouts eventually return to school. This interpretation of the data is confirmed by later results that variables such as the unemployment rate have quantitatively similar effects on enrollment and completed education. These results suggest that enrollment and completed education can be used as comparable measures of trends in educational achievement.

Although family-background factors are important determinants of individual schooling outcomes, we conclude that they cannot explain the slowdown in enrollment or educational attainment for post-1950 cohorts. Likewise, tuition costs and local unemployment rates do not move in the right direction to explain longer-run trends in enrollment. Cohort size is a more promising explanation for the slowdown in education among post-1950 birth cohorts, although our preferred estimates imply only a modest aggregate effect associated with the baby boom's passage through the education system. Changes in the return to education for young workers are highly correlated with the enrollment rates of college-age youths, and this variable, coupled with cohort size and trend factors, can explain the changes in male and female college-age enrollment rates over the period 1968–96 fairly well. For women, our results imply that the slow growth in enrollment in the 1970s was largely a temporary phenomenon, driven by low returns to education and the size of the baby-boom cohort. For men, however, the decline and slow rebound in enrollment seem to reflect a combination of adverse temporary factors (a large cohort and low returns to education) coupled with a virtual collapse in the long-run trend in educational attainment.

9.1 Trends in Dropout Behavior and Educational Attainment

This section provides a descriptive overview of basic trends in enrollment, dropout behavior, and completed education in the United States over the past several decades. We begin by examining data on enrollment and dropout rates derived from the School Enrollment Supplements of the 1968–96 Current Population Surveys (CPS). A key limitation of this analysis is the absence of CPS micro data prior to 1968. To provide a longer time-series context, we turn to cohort-level data on high school and college completion rates. Patterns of enrollment and completed education among children in the National Longitudinal Survey of Youth (NLSY) confirm that there is a relatively tight link between teenage enrollment and completed education later in life. In the light of this, we use information on completed education for adults in the 1960–90 decennial censuses and recent Current Population Surveys to measure intercohort trends in educational attainment for cohorts born from 1920 to 1970. These longer-term trends provide a valuable historical context for evaluating changes in enrollment and completed education among more recent cohorts.

9.1.1 Time-Series Patterns in Enrollment

Figure 9.1 graphs enrollment rates of young men and women by age over the period 1968–96. The underlying data are drawn from the October CPS and pertain to school enrollment (full-time and part-time) as of mid-October. An examination of the figures suggests that enrollment rates of sixteen-year-old men and women have been quite stable over the period 1968–96 while seventeen-year-olds experienced a slight dip in enrollment in the late 1960s, followed by modest rises in the late 1980s and the 1990s.[1]

---

1. Published tabulations of the October CPS data, available for 1945–67, show that enrollment rates of fourteen- to seventeen-year-olds rose from just under 80 percent at the end of World War II to around 92 percent by the late 1960s and have been relatively stable ever since (U.S. Department of Education 1997, table 6).

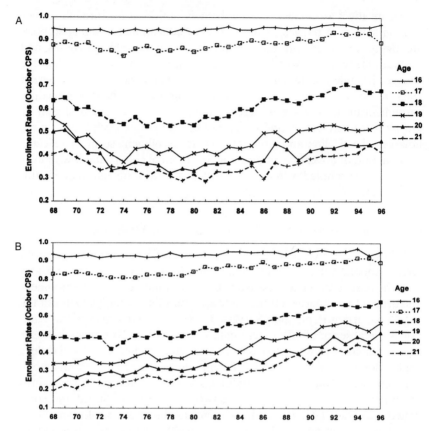

Fig. 9.1   Enrollment rates of young men and women by age, 1968–96: *A*, **young men;** *B*, **young women**

More remarkable are the patterns for college-age youths—particularly men. The enrollment rates of eighteen- to twenty-one-year-old men declined from the late 1960s to the mid-1970s, stabilized over the late 1970s, and then rose in the 1980s and 1990s. Despite recent gains, the fraction of eighteen- to twenty-one-year-old men in school today is not much higher than it was in the late 1960s. Enrollment rates of eighteen- to twenty-one-year-old women held steady during the 1970s and then began rising. As a consequence, the fraction of eighteen- to twenty-one-year-old women in school is much higher in the late 1990s than it was in the late 1960s, and the enrollment rate of nineteen-year-old women is now above the rate for comparable men.

One potentially important aspect of enrollment behavior among college-age youths (i.e., those age nineteen and older) is the fraction enrolled in two-year versus four-year colleges (see, e.g., Rouse 1994). Information on type of college attended by enrolled students has been collected in the CPS since 1976 and shows a slight rise in the relative share of two-year colleges over the past two decades. Specifically, the fraction of nineteen- to twenty-one-year-old men who were enrolled in two-year versus four-year colleges rose from 23.9 percent in 1976 to 25.7 percent in 1986 and to 26.5 percent in 1996. Among nineteen- to twenty-one-year-old enrolled women, the fraction in two-year colleges was 22.3 percent in 1976 and rose to 27.9 percent in 1986 before falling back slightly to 27.3 percent in 1996.[2] These figures point to a modest shift in the nature of college enrollment—especially for women—that should be kept in mind in interpreting overall enrollment trends. In particular, a rise in the fraction of enrollment at two-year colleges implies that traditional college graduation rates (based on four years of college) will not rise as quickly as college-age enrollment.

Another factor that has some possible effect on the trends in enrollment shown in figure 9.1 is the changing racial composition of the population. Over the past thirty years, the fraction of nonwhites in the teenage population (ages sixteen to nineteen) has risen from 13.6 percent in 1968 to 21.2 percent in 1996. To the extent that nonwhites have systematically lower or higher enrollment rates than whites, this change would be expected to cause some trend in average enrollment rates. As it turns out, however, the gap in enrollment rates between nonwhite and white teenagers varies: in 1968, nonwhites had 3.3 percent *lower* enrollment rates than comparable whites, while, in 1976, nonwhites had 2.8 percent *higher* enrollment rates than whites. During the later 1980s and the 1990s, the gap was typically negative but small in absolute value. These changing patterns are illustrated in figure 9.2, which graphs enrollment rates for eighteen-year-olds by race and gender. Black enrollment rates were below those of whites in the late 1960s and early 1970s, then surged between 1973 and 1976, and remained above white rates until the early 1980s, when whites caught up. We are unsure of the reasons for the relative enrollment gains of blacks in the mid-1970s. One hypothesis is that the early wave of affirmative-action programs in higher education led to a rise in black enrollment rates that reversed with the scaling back of these programs in the early 1980s.[3]

We have also examined the implications of the rising fraction of Hispanic youths on trends in average enrollment rates. CPS data on Hispanic ethnicity are available from 1973 on and show a steady rise in the proportion of Hispanic teenagers from 5.2 percent in 1973 to 13.0 percent in 1996. On average, Hispanics have lower enrollment rates than do non-Hispanics—about 6 percentage points lower at age sixteen and 10–12 percentage points lower at ages seventeen, eighteen, and nineteen. Thus, the

2. The gain in share for women from 1976 to 1996 is statistically significant (gain of 5.0 percentage points, standard error of 1.9 percent), while the gain for men is not (gain of 2.6 percentage points, standard error of 2.0 percent).

3. See the discussion in Bowen and Bok (1998, 7–10).

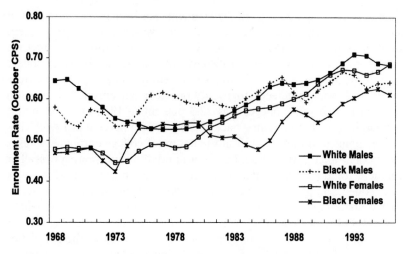

Fig. 9.2   Enrollment rates of 18-year-olds by race and gender, 1968–96

rising fraction of Hispanic youths has contributed to a modest downward trend in average enrollment rates. Among seventeen- to nineteen-year-olds, for example, the rise in the proportion of Hispanics has probably led to a 1 percentage point drop in average enrollment rates for all youths over the period 1973–96.

The lower enrollment rate of Hispanic youths can be attributed to several factors. Perhaps most important, many young Hispanics are immigrants from Mexico and Central America, and many others are "second-generation" children of poorly educated immigrants. Data from the 1995 October CPS suggest that 30 percent of Hispanic teenagers are immigrants and that another 26 percent are native born with an immigrant mother. The enrollment rate of Hispanic immigrant teenagers in 1995 was relatively low (57 percent on average, compared to 73 percent for Hispanic natives and 79 percent for non-Hispanics) and even lower among the roughly half who have arrived in the United States within the last five years (47 percent). Interestingly, however, the enrollment rate among second-generation Hispanic teenagers is higher than that for Hispanic teenagers whose mothers were born in the United States (76 vs. 70 percent).[4]

A final factor that may complicate the interpretation of age-specific enrollment rates is a change in the grade distribution of enrolled students. Many students presumably stay in school until they reach a target grade (rather than a target age). Thus, a shift in the grade distribution of students can lead to a change in enrollment propensities at each age without necessarily signaling a change in the desired level of completed schooling. One important source of such shifts is a change in the fraction of students who

4. Card, DiNardo, and Estes (2000) find that second-generation individuals typically have relatively high education levels, controlling for parents' education.

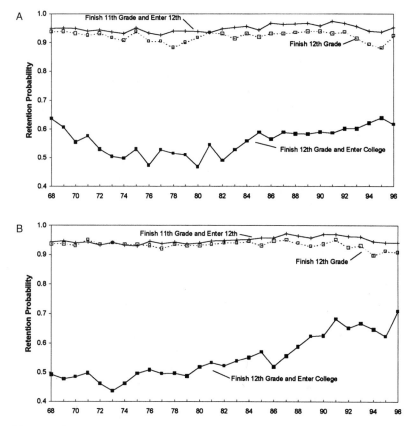

Fig. 9.3   Grade retention rates for young men and women, 1968–96: *A*, young men; *B*, young women

have been held back a year (or who started school late). In fact, there is evidence of a modest decline in the average grade attended by a given age group over the past thirty years that may account for some rise in age-specific enrollment rates.[5]

An alternative to studying the enrollment rate for a given age group is to examine the rate at which students move to higher levels of the education system. Figure 9.3 shows data from 1968 to 1996 for three such transition rates: the probability that a student who was enrolled in the eleventh

5. A regression of current grade on race and gender dummies (interacted) and year dummies using data on enrolled students in the 1968–96 CPS files shows a fall of about 0.1 in the mean grade attended over the past thirty years. The drop is similar for students aged seventeen, eighteen, and nineteen. A look at the distribution of grades attended by a given group leads to the same conclusion. In 1968, e.g., 20 percent of enrolled seventeen-year-old men were in the eleventh grade, 63 percent were in the twelfth grade, and the remainder were in other grades. By 1996, the fraction in the eleventh grade had risen to 30 percent, while the fraction in the twelfth grade had fallen to 58 percent.

grade last October is enrolled in the twelfth grade this October (i.e., the probability of finishing the eleventh grade and entering the twelfth with no interruption); the probability that a student who was enrolled in the twelfth grade last October has obtained a high school diploma by this October (i.e., the probability of high school graduation, conditional on attending the eleventh grade last year); and the probability that a student who was enrolled in the twelfth grade last October is enrolled in college this October (i.e., the college entry rate for those who were high school seniors).[6]

As might be expected from the trends in enrollment rates for sixteen- and seventeen-year-olds shown in figure 9.1 above, the retention rates from the eleventh grade to the twelfth for both men and women are very stable over the period 1968–96, averaging about 95 percent. Rates of high school completion (conditional on having been enrolled in the eleventh grade) are also fairly stable, at around 92–94 percent, although in the last few years the rates seem to have slipped. For both men and women, the college entry rate (for those who were in the twelfth grade last year) follows a pattern similar to that of the enrollment rate of eighteen-year-olds. This is not too surprising since eighteen-year-olds typically either are just finishing their last year of high school or have recently graduated from high school. Given the stability of the transition rate from the eleventh grade to the twelfth, most of the variation in the enrollment rate of eighteen-year-olds arises from changes in the college entry rate. Interestingly, the college matriculation rate of young men is no higher in the late 1990s than it was in 1968, while the rate for young women has risen about 18 percentage points over the past thirty years.

9.1.2   Intercohort Trends in Completed Education

Preliminary Issues

On the basis of the data presented in figures 9.1–9.3, it is difficult to assess the significance of the decline in male enrollment during the 1970s or of the recent gains for women. Depending on how enrollment rates were moving prior to 1968, these changes may represent a sharp departure from historical patterns or a continuation of preexisting trends. Unfortunately, pre-1968 CPS micro data are not available.[7] To provide a historical context

6. The October CPS supplement asks individuals whether they were enrolled last year and when they obtained a high school diploma. We assume that all those enrolled in the twelfth grade were enrolled in the eleventh grade in the previous year.

7. The decennial censuses also report school enrollment, although the question pertains to the census week (1 April). Comparisons of enrollment in the 1970 census and the 1969–70 October CPS suggest that the timing of the question significantly affects age-specific enrollment rates since the census-based estimates are quite different from the October CPS numbers. Published tabulations of CPS enrollment data are available for 1945–67. Data on the enrollment of eighteen- to nineteen-year-old men and women show a roughly constant trend from 1945 to 1968.

for the post-1968 trends in enrollment behavior, we decided to use the decennial censuses and the Current Population Surveys to construct data on completed education by birth cohort. The key assumption underlying this exercise is that changes in youth enrollment rates will be reflected in differences in completed education rates for the same birth cohorts. Under this assumption, a comparison of the completed education of men born in 1945 with that of those born in 1955 will allow us to infer the trend in male enrollment rates between 1963 and 1973. Of course, one might argue that completed education is the main outcome of the education process: thus, intercohort comparisons of educational attainment are interesting in their own right as well as for any insight that they provide on school enrollment behavior.

As a check on the assumption that completed educational attainment is highly correlated with enrollment behavior during ages sixteen to twenty-four, we analyzed a sample of men and women in the NLSY who can be followed from their teenage years to their early thirties. Specifically, we selected individuals aged fourteen to sixteen in the first (1979) NLSY interview who missed no more than two interviews between 1980 and 1990. We used retrospective enrollment data collected in each wave of the survey to construct a series of fall-enrollment indicators.[8] Table 9.1 summarizes the enrollment histories of this sample, focusing on the question of how often people who drop out of school as teenagers ever return to continue their schooling.[9] For example, the first row of the table pertains to the 20 percent of the NLSY sample who were out of school in the fall after their sixteenth birthday. Of these, 75 percent never enrolled again in the fall term over the next ten years. (A very small number were enrolled in the spring or for fewer than three months in some later fall.) Among the one-quarter who subsequently reenrolled, 56.3 percent were enrolled in only one term. Thus, a majority of those who ever returned to school obtained *at most* one additional year of formal schooling. Looking down the rows of the table, the fraction of those who drop out and never return at different ages is fairly stable, at around 75 percent (for all but those who first drop out in the fall of their twentieth year), and the relative fraction of reenrollees who attend for only a year or less is also fairly stable. Although some dropouts eventually return to school, the majority do not, and only a very few get much additional schooling.

Nevertheless, the *measured* educational attainment of early dropouts is somewhat higher than their formal schooling would suggest because of the acquisition of high school equivalency degrees (i.e., GEDs, or general

8. After much experimentation, we settled on a fairly tight definition of *fall enrollment:* we coded an individual as enrolled if he or she reported being enrolled in school for at least three months between August and December.

9. These tabulations are unweighted and overrepresent the experiences of relatively disadvantaged youths.

Table 9.1   Fall Enrollment Histories for NLSY Sample Members Age 14–16 in 1979

	% Who First Drop Out	% of Dropouts Who:		% of Those Who Return for 1 Term Only	% Who Get GED	Years of Education in 1996
		Never Return	Return			
Fall after age 16 or earlier	20.0	75.5	24.5	56.3	34.0	11.0
Fall after age 17	27.9	75.0	25.0	46.2	13.1	12.4
Fall after age 18	22.9	74.0	26.0	45.3	7.6	12.6
Fall after age 19	9.0	74.3	25.7	34.5	8.6	13.1
Fall after age 20	4.2	55.1	44.9	37.1	3.9	14.6
Fall after age 21	6.0	72.1	27.9	54.0	. . .	15.8
Fall after age 22	5.0	72.7	27.3	51.0	. . .	16.5
Fall after age 23	2.6	83.5	16.5	68.8	. . .	16.6
Fall after age 24	1.1	90.7	9.3	. . .	. . .	16.9
Fall after age 25	.7	100.0	. . .	. . .	. . .	17.8
Still enrolled in fall after age 26	.6	. . .	. . .	. . .	. . .	19.2

Note: Sample contains 3,745 men and women in the NLSY who were 14–16 in 1979 and missed no more than 2 subsequent interviews. Individuals are classified as enrolled in the fall if they were enrolled 3 or more months from August to December. Tabulations are unweighted. Individuals are followed only until age 26: thus, reenrollment rates do not account for any schooling after age 26. Measured years of education in 1996 counts GED as high school.

equivalency diplomas).[10] As shown in the fifth column of table 9.1, about one-third of those who were not in school in the fall after their sixteenth birthday obtained a GED over the next ten years, and a significant fraction of later dropouts also obtain GED certificates. Evidence in Cameron and Heckman (1993, fig. 1) suggests that the incidence of GED certification rose rapidly in the 1960s and 1970s: thus, GED acquisition rates for dropouts in earlier cohorts may be only 10–20 percent as high as the rates for the NLSY sample are. To the extent that a GED certificate is *not* equivalent to a regular high school diploma[11] and GED holders are coded as regular high school graduates, the rising incidence of GED certification poses a problem for intercohort comparisons of completed education. A full consideration of this problem is beyond the scope of our analysis here. It should be kept in mind, however, in interpreting trends in high school graduation rates of more recent cohorts.

10. A GED is obtained by writing a test (see Cameron and Heckman 1993). Census Bureau coding procedures assume that a GED is equivalent to a regular high school diploma: thus, the decennial censuses and the CPS do not separately identify GED holders from regular high school graduates. The NLSY uses a similar rule.

11. Cameron and Heckman (1993) argue that GED recipients are much closer to high school dropouts than to high school graduates, although Tyler, Murnane, and Willett (2000) find that the GED has some effect on wage outcomes.

Educational Attainment by Cohort

We use data from the 1960–90 decennial censuses and the 1996–99 March CPS to estimate measures of completed education by year of birth for native men and women born from 1920 to 1965. We begin by assuming that the educational attainment of an individual (indexed by i) who was born in year c and observed at age j in year t ($t = j + c$) follows a simple model of the form:

$$E_{icj} = a_c + f(j) + d_t + e_{icj},$$

where E_{icj} is the measure of education (e.g., years of completed schooling), a_c represents a birth-cohort effect, $f(j)$ is a *fixed* age profile (normalized so that $f[j] = 0$ at some standard age), d_t is a year effect associated with any specific features of the measurement system used in year t, and e_{icj} represents a combination of sampling error and any specification error. The age profile is included to capture the fact that educational attainment tends to rise with age.[12] Thus, unless all cohorts are observed at exactly the same age, it is necessary to adjust the data for differences in age at observation.

We fit this equation to data on individuals who were ages twenty-four to sixty-five (and born between 1920 and 1965) in the public-use samples of the 1960–90 censuses and the pooled 1996–99 March CPS.[13] We included a quartic polynomial in age (normalized to equal 0 at age forty), year dummies for observations from the 1990 census and the 1996–99 CPS (to reflect differences in the education questions in these surveys relative to the earlier censuses), and a full set of year-of-birth dummies. We used two key measures of educational attainment: an indicator for having completed high school and an indicator for having a college degree. The cohort effects associated with these outcomes are plotted in figure 9.4.[14]

The intercohort trends in these two measures of completed education are quite consistent with the enrollment trends reported in figure 9.1 above. For example, the stability of the enrollment rates of sixteen- and seventeen-year-old men and women after 1968 suggests that high school graduation rates have been relatively stable for cohorts born after 1950: this is confirmed by the patterns shown in figure 9.4*A*. On the other hand, the decline

---

12. For example, in 1970, the average years of education reported by native men who were born in 1940 is 12.26. In 1980, the average for the same cohort of men is 12.85 years. Comparable means for the 1940 cohort of women are 11.91 average years of schooling in 1970 and 12.37 in 1980.

13. Our 1960 and 1970 samples include 1 percent of the population, our 1980 and 1990 samples include 5 percent of the population, and our pooled CPS sample includes (approximately) 0.14 percent of the population. Our models are weighted to reflect the varying sampling probabilities.

14. We estimated the cohort effects relative to a reference group of people born in 1950. For purposes of the graphs, we then estimated the average outcomes of the reference group in 1990 (when they were age forty) and added these to the relative cohort effects.

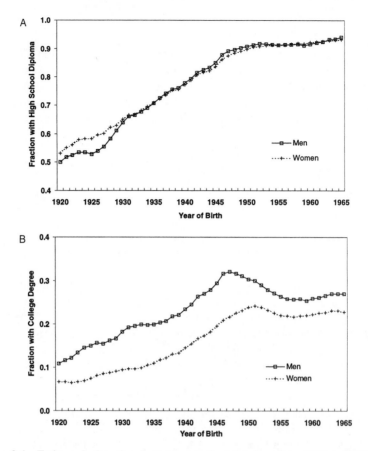

Fig. 9.4   Estimated educational attainment of cohorts born from 1920 to 1965: *A*, fraction of cohort with high school diploma by age 40; *B*, fraction of cohort with college degree by age 40

in enrollment rates of men aged eighteen to twenty-one from 1968 to 1975 suggests that men born in 1957 (who were eighteen in 1975) were less likely to complete a college degree than were men born in 1950 (who were eighteen in 1968). The data presented in figure 9.4*B* confirm that there is indeed a sizable drop in the fraction of men with a college degree between the cohort born in 1950 and that born in 1957.

The most interesting feature of figure 9.4 is the relative stagnation in educational attainment for post-1950 cohorts. This lack of progress is especially remarkable in the light of the steady intercohort trend in high school and college graduation rates for earlier cohorts. Even among women, there is almost no indication of a rise in college completion rates for cohorts born after 1945. At first glance, the relative stability of the college graduation rate for women may seem inconsistent with the rising college entry rates for women shown in figure 9.2*B* above and with the rising enrollment rates of eighteen- to twenty-one-year-old women shown in figure 9.1*B* above. We believe that the discrepancy can be attributed to two factors. First, the fraction of women with some college (i.e., thirteen to fifteen years of completed education) shows some growth after the 1950 cohort.[15] Second, much of the rise in female enrollment rates observed in figure 9.1*B* occurs after 1985 and presumably will be reflected in the completed education levels of cohorts born after 1965.

Another feature of the college graduation rates shown in figure 9.4*B* is the divergence in trends between men and women for cohorts born from 1945 to 1950. Men in this cohort graduated at slightly higher rates than would be predicted on the basis of earlier trends, while women's graduation rates followed the existing trend rather closely. The relative gain for men was quickly reversed with the 1950–55 cohort, as men's graduation rates fell and women's continued to rise.[16] One explanation for the divergence is draft-avoidance behavior associated with the Vietnam War. Throughout most of the war, college deferments were available that allowed enrolled students to delay the final determination of their draft status and potentially avoid compulsory military service.[17] The relative rise in men's college graduation rates for the 1945–50 cohort—who were at high risk of induction but eligible for education deferments—is consistent with the view that draft-avoidance behavior raised college enrollment and graduation rates.

To summarize, the available evidence suggests the following conclusions regarding trends in enrollment and completed education: (1) High school completion rates rose steadily for cohorts born from 1920 to 1950 (at a rate of about 12–14 percentage points per decade) but were relatively stable for 1950–65 cohorts, at about 90 percent. (2) Enrollment rates of sixteen- to seventeen-year-old men and women have risen slightly over the past thirty years, while the fraction of eleventh graders who complete high school by the next fall has been roughly constant. Over the period 1970–96, the rising fraction of Hispanics has lowered the average enrollment rate of sixteen- to seventeen-year-olds by 0.5–1.0 percentage points. (3) In the NLSY sample, only a quarter of school-leavers ever return to formal schooling,

15. Relative to the 1950 birth cohort (49 percent of whom had some college by age forty), those born in 1960 have a 1.7 percentage point higher rate of completing some college, and those born in 1965 have a 4.5 percentage point higher rate of completing some college. Among men, however, rates of completing some college fell from 57 percent for the 1950 cohort to 50 percent for the 1960 cohort and 53 percent for the 1965 cohort.

16. Notice that the relative decline in male college graduation rates from the 1945 to the 1955 cohorts is consistent with the relative decline in enrollment rates of college-age men from 1968 to 1974 observed in fig. 9.1 above.

17. The draft was operated by local draft boards, which had considerable discretion in the use of deferrals. Deferrals were also available for certain occupations and for those with dependent family members.

and those who do return typically do so for a year or less. However, many early dropouts (up to one-third of those who drop out before age seventeen) eventually obtain a GED. The presence of GEDs leads to some overestimation of the educational attainment of recent cohorts. (4) College graduation rates of men and women trended steadily upward for cohorts born from 1920 to 1945 (at a rate of 6–7 percentage points per decade). The male college graduation rate declined by about 5 percentage points for cohorts born from 1945 to 1955 and has risen slightly for later cohorts. The female college graduation rate was relatively stable for cohorts born from 1950 to 1965. (5) The college entrance rate of male high school seniors fell from 1968 to 1980, then rose in the 1980s back to its earlier level. The rate has been relatively stable over the 1990s, at about 62–65 percent. The college entry of female high school seniors was roughly constant from 1968 to 1980 but has subsequently risen to a level as high as or slightly higher than the male rate. (6) The fraction of nineteen- to twenty-one-year-old men in two-year versus four-year colleges has been relatively stable since 1976, at about 25 percent. The corresponding fraction for women has risen from 22 to 27 percent.

9.2   A Theoretical Framework

In this section, we present a simple version of the human-capital-investment model and summarize some of its key implications for the determination of individual schooling outcomes (for more in-depth surveys, see Rosen [1977] and Willis [1986]). Our main focus is on the insights that the model provides for explaining the time-series and intercohort trends documented in the previous section.

Assume that individuals have an infinite planning horizon that begins at the minimum school-leaving age ($t = 0$) and that each individual chooses a level of schooling to maximize the discounted present value of lifetime earnings, net of education costs. Education is measured in years of school attended: an individual with S years of postcompulsory schooling has real earnings of $y(S, t)$ in period t ($t \geq S \geq 0$). A student who is attending school at age t with S years of education can earn $p(S, t)$ in part-time earnings and must pay tuition costs of $T(S)$. If people can make only a single, once-for-all decision on when to leave school, the appropriate objective function is

$$(1) \qquad V(S) = \int_0^S [p(t,t) - T(t)]e^{-rt}\,dt + \int_S^\infty y(S,t)e^{-rt}\,dt,$$

where r is an individual-specific discount rate. The acquisition of an additional unit of schooling leads to a marginal cost of

(2a) $MC(S) = y(S, S) - p(S, S) + T(S)$

(measured in period S dollars), which includes two components: a net opportunity cost $y(S, S) - p(S, S)$ and an out-of-pocket cost $T(S)$. On the other hand, a delay in school-leaving leads to a marginal benefit (measured in period S dollars) of

(2b) $MB(S) = \int_S^\infty dy(S,t)/dSe^{-r(t-S)}dt = \int_0^\infty dy(S, S + \tau)/dSe^{-r\tau}d\tau,$

where $dy(S, t)/dS$ is the derivative of the earnings function with respect to schooling. If log earnings are additively separable in education and years of postschooling experience (as assumed by Mincer 1974) $y(S, t)$ can be written as $y(S, t) = g(S) h(t - S)$, the marginal benefit of an added unit of schooling is

$$MB(S) = g'(S) \int_0^\infty h(\tau)e^{-r\tau}d\tau = g'(S)H(r),$$

where $H(r)$ is a decreasing function of the interest rate. Assuming that the marginal cost of additional schooling rises faster than the marginal benefit, the criterion function $V(S)$ is concave, and the individual's schooling choice is determined by the condition $MC(S) = MB(S)$.[18] This gives an optimal schooling choice that depends on the discount rate, tuition costs, the relative level of earnings for part-time-enrolled students versus recent school-leavers, and the characteristics of the life-cycle earnings function.

As a basis case, assume that earnings are independent of age or experience, with

$$\log y(S,t) = a + bS - \frac{1}{2}kS^2, \quad \text{for } k \geq 0.$$

This specification assumes that the "marginal return to schooling" (i.e., the derivative of log earnings with respect to an additional year of schooling) is linear in years of completed schooling, with a strictly declining marginal return when $k > 0$. Under these assumptions, $MB(S) = 1/r \times (b - kS)y(S, S)$, and the optimal schooling choice satisfies the condition

(3) $b - kS = r[1 - \alpha(S)] + rT(S)/y(S, S),$

where $\alpha(S) = p(S, S)/y(S, S)$ is the ratio of part-time student earnings to full-time earnings for a person with S years of completed education. If

---

18. Note that $V'(S) = e^{-rS}[MB(S) - MC(S)]$. For the case of an additively separable log earnings function, $MB(S)$ is decreasing in S if $g(S)$ is concave. If $V(S)$ is concave, people who leave school will never want to return, so the assumption of a once-for-all dropout decision can be relaxed.

students earn nothing while in school and tuition is free, then this equation leads to the familiar rule that an optimal level of schooling equates the marginal return on the last unit of schooling (the left-hand side of [3]) with the discount rate (e.g., Willis 1986). In such a "stripped-down" model, $S = (b - r)/k$, and variation in schooling outcomes arises from two sources: differences in the return to education and differences in discount rates. People with higher returns to education (i.e., a higher individual value of b) will leave school at a later age. Likewise, cohorts that anticipate relatively high returns to education (i.e., a higher average value of b) are likely to choose to extend their schooling relative to cohorts that perceive relatively low returns to education. On the other hand, people who have more restricted access to credit markets (i.e., a higher individual value of r) or who are in their teenage years during a period of high real interest rates (i.e., a higher average value of r for the cohort) are likely to choose lower levels of schooling.

More generally, the optimal schooling choice also depends on part-time/full-time relative earnings and differences in tuition costs. Assuming that $k > 0$, a rise in part-time earnings for students, holding constant the earnings of school-leavers, will lead to higher levels of optimal schooling, while a rise in tuition will lead to a lower level of schooling.

The model presented so far builds in an assumption that people are indifferent between attending school and working. In this case, individuals with access to a perfect capital market can maximize lifetime utility by maximizing the discounted present value of earnings net of schooling costs. More generally, however, school attendance may require more or less effort than full-time work. Let $c(t)$ denote the level of consumption in period t (measured in real period-t dollars), and assume that an individual receives utility $u[c(t)]$ if he or she is out of school and working in period t (where $u[\cdot]$ is some increasing concave function) and utility $u[c(t)] - \phi(t)$ if he or she is attending school in period t. The function $\phi(t)$ measures the relative disutility of school versus work for the tth year of schooling and may be positive or negative. Finally, assume that individuals choose schooling and consumption to maximize

$$\int_0^S \{u[c(t)] - \phi(t)\}e^{-\rho t}dt + \int_S^\infty u[c(t)]e^{-\rho t}dt,$$

where ρ is a subjective discount rate, subject to the constraint that the discounted present value of consumption (discounted at the interest rate r) is equal to the discounted present value of earnings minus discounted tuition costs. Under these assumptions, it is readily shown that the marginal cost of the Sth year of schooling includes the terms in equation (2a) plus an added component:

$$1/\lambda e^{-(\rho-r)S}\phi(S),$$

where λ is the marginal utility of wealth in the planning period.[19] This extra term is simply the dollar equivalent of the relative disutility of schooling in period S. As in the simpler case where $\phi(t) = 0$, if the marginal costs of schooling are rising faster than the marginal benefits, an optimal schooling choice will equate the marginal cost of the last unit of schooling with the marginal benefit.[20]

Consideration of the relative disutility of schooling suggests an important route by which individual-specific factors—particularly family-background variables—may influence schooling outcomes. Children of better-educated parents may be able to succeed more easily at higher levels of schooling or may have stronger preferences for attending school versus working. Either way, such children will have a lower marginal cost of schooling and would be expected to acquire more schooling.

A long-standing idea in the education literature is that students tend to stay in school longer in a temporarily depressed labor market (see, e.g., Gustman and Steinmeier 1981; and Light 1995). Returning to the simplified model represented by equations (1)–(3), assume that "normal" earnings $y(S, t)$ are temporarily depressed by a fraction δ and that this condition is expected to persist for Δ periods into the future, where $\delta\Delta$ is small.[21] During the recession, the optimal schooling choice for a student will (approximately) satisfy the equation

$$(3') \qquad b - kS = r[1 - \alpha(S)](1 - \delta) + rT(S)/y(S, S),$$

leading to a higher level of schooling than under normal conditions ($\delta = 0$). Of course, a temporary drop in earnings will raise the optimal school-leaving age only for students who would otherwise have dropped out during the recession.

At first glance, the case of a temporary labor market boom appears to be symmetrical: a boom causes a rise in the opportunity cost of schooling that may lead some students to drop out earlier than they would in a stationary environment. The effect of a temporary boom is more complicated, however, because the second-order condition for an optimal schooling choice may fail if earnings of young workers are expected to fall in the near future. Under the assumption that individuals make a once-for-all school-leaving decision, dropping out today closes off the option of future schooling. A simple comparison of the current marginal costs and benefits of schooling is sufficient only to characterize the optimal schooling choice

---

19. As in eq. (2a), this is measured in period-S dollars.

20. The derivative of lifetime utility with respect to schooling is $\lambda e^{-rS}\{MB(S) - MC(S)\}$, where $MB(S)$ is the same as in eq. (2b) and $MC(S)$ is the same as in eq. (2a), with the addition of the disutility-of-effort term.

21. Specifically, the earnings of an individual who is still in school at age $t = S$ are $y(S, t)(1 - \delta)$ for t in the interval from $t = S$ to $t = S + \Delta$ and will return to the normal level $y(S, t)$ for $t > S + \Delta$.

when marginal costs are expected to rise faster than marginal benefits, in which case the option value of staying in school is zero whenever the *current* marginal cost exceeds the current marginal benefit. If marginal costs are expected to fall soon, it may be worthwhile to remain in school even if the current marginal cost is high. This line of reasoning suggests that the effect of a temporary boom will be to accelerate the school-leaving rates of those who were close to completing their optimal schooling, with little or no effect on those who would otherwise have completed substantially more education.

So far we have been assuming that individuals make a once-for-all school-leaving decision. As noted in the discussion of table 9.1 above, this seems like a valid assumption for most youths, although a significant minority of dropouts eventually return to formal schooling. The preceding model can be extended to allow for the possibility of interrupted schooling. Analytically, such a model is equivalent to a dynamic investment model with irreversible investment (see, e.g., Dixit and Pindyck 1994). A general property of these models is that current school-enrollment decisions will be more sensitive to variation in the current marginal cost of schooling than they are in models with a once-for-all schooling decision because dropping out does not foreclose the option of returning to school when marginal costs are lower. In particular, a short-term boom is likely to lead more students to drop out of school when reenrollment is feasible than when it is not. The extent of such "intertemporal substitution" in the timing of schooling is presumably limited by various institutional hurdles and by the start-up costs associated with returning to school when the boom is over.[22]

It is an open question whether children who drop out of school and return later have chosen to interrupt their schooling to take advantage of short-term fluctuations in the opportunity cost of schooling or whether their behavior reflects other factors outside the realm of the simple model that we have presented. For example, in a more realistic model with credit constraints, liquidity-constrained youths may drop out of school for a few years and return when they have better access to credit or less pressing income needs. Another explanation for reenrollment is that individuals have changing preferences—particularly with respect to the relative value of current versus future income. It is sometimes argued that youthful decision makers tend to undervalue the future: in the schooling context, this may lead some children to leave school "too early." If time preferences change between adolescence and adulthood, some people who dropped out early may ultimately decide to return to school. Finally, reenrollment behavior may be attributable to mistakes or unexpected changes in the economy. For example, a teenager deciding on an optimal level of school-

---

22. For example, most high schools will not allow students to reenroll after a certain age: thus, students who leave high school may have to return to "adult school."

ing in the late 1970s may have (mistakenly) assumed that the earnings differentials across education groups at that time would persist into the future. Within a few years, the payoffs to education were much higher, and some dropouts may have returned to school to take advantage of the new information.

9.3   Decomposing Trends in Enrollment and Completed Schooling

9.3.1   Framework

The human-capital-investment model suggests that desired schooling attainment depends on a number of factors, including the expected return to an additional year of education, the discount rate, tuition costs, the relative level of part-time earnings for students in school, the disutility of school versus work, and cyclic fluctuations that differentially affect earnings opportunities today versus expected earnings in the future. Some of these factors are common to all individuals in a given cohort (such as the general level of returns to education), some are shared by all members of a cohort who grew up in the same geographic area (such as the strength of the local labor market or the cost of attending a nearby public college), and some are purely idiosyncratic (such as tastes or aptitude for schooling). In order to evaluate the potential contribution of these factors to the time-series trends in enrollment and completed education, we posit a simple behavioral equation that relates the optimal schooling choice S_{ijc} for the ith individual born in cohort c and raised in geographic region j to a vector of observable factors X_{ijc}, a set of cohort effects (α_c), a set of permanent location effects (γ_j), and a random component:

$$(4) \qquad S_{ijc} = X_{ijc}\beta + \alpha_c + \gamma_j + \varepsilon_{ijc}.$$

This can be interpreted as a linear approximation to the solution for an optimal schooling choice as determined by an equation such as (3) or (3′). Subdivide $X_{ijc} = \{F_{ijc}, Z_{jc}, m_c\}$, where F_{ijc} includes individual-level variables such as parents' education and other family-background characteristics, Z_{jc} includes cohort- and location-specific variables, such as tuition rates and the local unemployment rate, and m_c includes variables that are common to everyone in a cohort, such as the interest rate or the expected return to education. Assuming that (4) is correct, the average level of schooling for individuals in cohort c from region j satisfies the equality

$$(5a) \qquad S_{jc} = F_{jc}\beta_F + Z_{jc}\beta_Z + m_c\beta_m + \alpha_c + \gamma_j,$$

where F_{jc} is the mean level of the individual characteristics for the group. Similarly, the average level of schooling for all individuals in the cohort satisfies the equality

(5b) $$S_c = F_c \beta_F + Z_c \beta_Z + m_c \beta_m + \alpha_c,$$

where F_c and Z_c represent the mean values of the family-background and regional variables for all those in cohort c. Equation (5b) implies that the growth in average educational attainment between any two cohorts (e.g., 1 and 2) can be decomposed as

(6) $$S_2 - S_1 = (F_2 - F_1)\beta_F + (Z_2 - Z_1)\beta_Z + (m_2 - m_1)\beta_m + (\alpha_2 - \alpha_1).$$

If estimates of the coefficient vector $(\beta_F, \beta_Z, \beta_m)$ and of the cohort-specific means (F_c, Z_c, m_c) are available, this equation can be used to compare the actual intercohort change in completed education with the change predicted by trends in individual and family-background characteristics, local conditions, and the aggregate variables m_c. A similar approach can be used to decompose trends in enrollment or dropout rates. For example, assuming that desired schooling is determined by equation (4), the probability of being enrolled in the kth year of education is $P(S_{ijc} > k)$, which can be approximated by a logistic regression model that includes X_{ijc} as well as region and cohort effects. Trends in average enrollment rates between cohorts can then be decomposed by simulating the change in average enrollment rates if there is no change in the mean characteristics and comparing this with the actual change.

There are two key problems in estimating the components of a decomposition such as (6). The first is that the coefficients associated with the aggregate-level variables (the β_c's) cannot be identified in models such as equation (4) that include unrestricted cohort effects. The causal effects of aggregate variables (such as the interest rate or the average return to schooling) can be identified only through their time-series correlations with cohort-average schooling outcomes. Given the short samples available, this is a relatively weak source of identification. A second and even more serious problem is the absence of micro-level data sets that include information on family-background factors, geographic location, and schooling outcomes for a broad range of cohorts. CPS micro data files are available only starting in 1968 and lack any family-background information for youths who are no longer living with their parents. Similarly, the decennial censuses have no information on such family-background variables as parents' education and only very limited geographic information (place of residence and state of birth). On the other hand, the data sets that are conventionally used to study the micro-level determinants of education, such as the NLSY or High School and Beyond, cover a very narrow range of cohorts.

In the light of these problems, we pursue a mixed estimation strategy in trying to evaluate the determinants of the trends in enrollment and school attainment. We begin by using individual micro data from the General Social Survey (GSS) to examine the contribution of changing family-background factors to intercohort trends in high school and college graduation. Next, we turn to an analysis based on average enrollment and completed schooling outcomes for individuals in specific cohorts and states. We focus on the effects of three local-level variables: state unemployment rates, tuition rates at state colleges and universities, and the relative size of the high school cohort in the state. Finally, we use aggregate time-series data to examine the role of two key aggregate explanatory variables: the rate of return to education and the real interest rate at the time when a cohort is just finishing high school. Taken as a whole, these three levels of analysis provide, we believe, a fairly comprehensive assessment of the empirical content of the human-capital-investment model and its ability to explain the trends in school enrollment and educational attainment documented in section 9.1 above.

9.3.2 The Contribution of Trends in Family Background

There is a substantial literature documenting the powerful effect of family-background variables on individual education outcomes (for overviews, see Card [1999] and Solon [1999]). Typically, parents' education explains 20–25 percent of the cross-sectional variation in completed education, while such factors as race, ethnicity, family size, and location provide additional explanatory power.[23] Despite the importance of family background in explaining individual education outcomes, changes in family-background variables are not a strong candidate to explain the U-shaped pattern of male enrollment rates observed in figure 9.1*A* above or the break in the intercohort trend in educational attainment observed for post-1950 cohorts in figure 9.4 above. The reason is that demographic, family-structure, and family-location variables tend to evolve smoothly over time. Moreover, average parents' education is essentially a lagged value of average individual education. Given the rising education levels of cohorts born from 1920 to 1950, one would expect average parents' education levels to have continued rising relatively smoothly for cohorts born until the mid-1970s. Thus, it is unlikely that a shift in the trend in parents' education can explain the slowdown in the rate of growth of educational attainment for cohorts born after 1950.

A full evaluation of the role of family-background factors requires information on schooling outcomes and family-background characteristics for a broad range of cohorts. One of the few available sources of such data is the GSS, which has surveyed one to two thousand adults annually since

23. For example, in the NLSY sample used in table 9.1 above, a regression of completed education (as of 1996) on race and Hispanic ethnicity dummies, mother's and father's education, number of siblings, presence of a father in the home at age fourteen, region of residence at age fourteen, and an indicator for urban residence at age fourteen has an R^2 coefficient of just over 25 percent. The parents' education variables by themselves explain about 24 percent of the variance in completed education.

Table 9.2   Estimated Models for Probability of Obtaining High School Diploma and College
                   Degree and for Years of Completed Education: GSS Data

	Men			Women		
	High School (1)	College (2)	Years School (3)	High School (4)	College (5)	Years School (6)
Mother's education	.013	.019	.174	.021	.028	.200
	(.001)	(.002)	(.010)	(.001)	(.002)	(.008)
Father's education	.014	.032	.199	.017	.025	.172
	(.001)	(.002)	(.010)	(.001)	(.001)	(.007)
Single mother (at age 16)	−.069	−.067	−.470	−.091	−.074	−.565
	(.009)	(.018)	(.086)	(.010)	(.013)	(.061)
Number siblings	−.005	−.011	−.046	−.004	−.012	−.039
	(.001)	(.002)	(.006)	(.001)	(.002)	(.004)
Black	−.028	−.129	−.629	.000	−.007	.070
	(.009)	(.022)	(.088)	(.010)	(.014)	(.062)
Live in South (at age 16)	−.039	−.018	−.394	−.049	.016	−.189
	(.009)	(.016)	(.080)	(.010)	(.012)	(.061)
Life on farm (at age 16)	−.056	−.160	−1.209	−.035	.004	−.423
	(.009)	(.018)	(.080)	(.010)	(.014)	(.063)
Live in small town (at age 16)	−.016	−.072	−.484	.001	−.019	−.192
	(.007)	(.011)	(.059)	(.008)	(.008)	(.044)
No. of observations	10,687	10,687	10,687	13,344	13,344	13,344

Note: Standard errors are given in parentheses. Entries in cols. 1, 2, 4, and 5 are normalized logistic regression coefficients (multiplied by $p[1 - p]$ where p is the average probability of the education outcome for individuals born in 1945–49). Entries in cols. 3 and 6 are OLS regression coefficients. Models are estimated on sample of adults age 24–70 in pooled 1972–96 GSS. Models include a cubic in age at time of survey, unrestricted cohort dummies (for 5-year birth cohorts), dummies for living in the Northeast and Midwest at age 16, and a dummy for having imputed father's education (for imputation method, see the text). Sample includes only people who report their own education and their mother's education.

1972 and asked a range of family-background questions. We used the pooled GSS sample for 1972–96 to estimate a series of models for completed educational attainment among adults (ages twenty-four to seventy) who were born between 1900 and 1970. Given the relatively small number of individuals in this data set, we defined cohorts using five-year birth intervals. These models are reported in table 9.2 and include a cubic function of age at the time of the survey and unrestricted cohort effects as well as the covariates shown in the table.[24] The effects of the family-background variables in the GSS sample are generally similar to those obtained in other data sets. For example, comparing the models in columns 3 and 6 of table 9.2 to a comparable model for the completed education of men and

24. The cubic in age is included to account for the age profile in educational attainment. The estimated coefficients reported in table 9.2 are very similar to the results from models that exclude the cohort effects.

women in the NLSY, we find very similar effects of parents' education in the two data sets: about 0.2 years of education per year of either parent's education.

To evaluate the effects of changing family-background characteristics on intercohort trends in educational attainment, we began by fitting a second series of models (not shown in table 9.2) that include only the cohort dummies and the polynomial in age at the time of the survey. The estimated cohort effects from these models are plotted in figures 9.5 and 9.6 as the "unadjusted" fractions of men and women with a high school diploma or college degree by age thirty. Assuming that the GSS sample of household heads is representative of the adult population, these unadjusted series should track the cohort effects plotted in figure 9.4 above, and, indeed, they show trends that are similar to the estimates based on

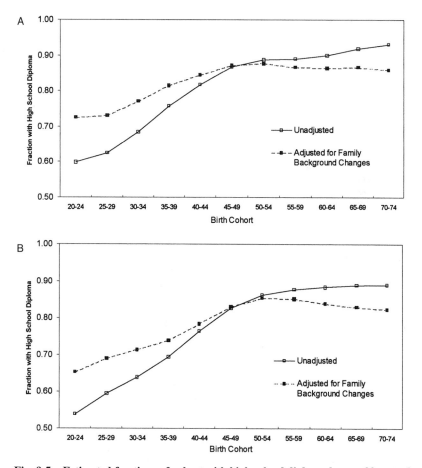

Fig. 9.5 Estimated fractions of cohort with high school diploma by age 30, actual vs. adjusted: *A*, men; *B*, women

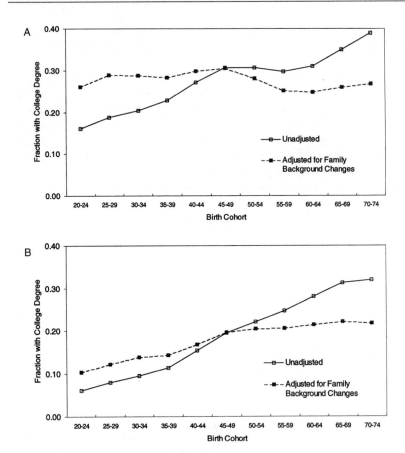

Fig. 9.6   Estimated fractions of cohort with college degree by age 30, actual vs. adjusted: *A*, men; *B*, women

census and CPS data. In particular, the unadjusted GSS data show relatively stable high school graduation rates for men and women born after 1950 and relatively stable college graduation rates for cohorts of men born between 1950 and 1965.[25] Unlike the census/CPS data, however, the GSS data show continued gains in college graduation rates for women born from 1950 to 1965, relative to the 1945–49 cohort. We are unsure of the reason for the divergence. Given the much larger samples in the census and CPS data sets and the rather large sampling errors for the GSS-based estimates, we believe that the census/CPS estimates should be treated as definitive.

25. The college graduation rates of individuals born in the 1965–69 and 1970–74 cohorts are imprecisely estimated since we observe only a relatively small number of these individuals as adults in later waves of the GSS.

In a second step, we used the models presented in table 9.2 above to calculate the predicted fractions of men and women in each cohort with a high school or college degree, under the assumption that the average values of the covariates were held constant for each cohort at the means for the 1945–49 birth cohort. These predicted attainment levels are plotted in figures 9.5 and 9.6 as "adjusted" fractions of each cohort with a high school or college degree and exhibit two interesting features. First, the adjusted graduation rates for the older (pre-1945) cohorts are uniformly above the unadjusted rates but below the rates for the benchmark 1945–49 cohort. This configuration means that some fraction of the intercohort trend in educational attainment for pre-1945 cohorts can be attributed to improving family-background characteristics. Second, the adjusted graduation rates for the post-1950 cohorts are uniformly below the unadjusted rates and below the graduation rates of the benchmark 1945–49 cohort in three of four cases. The implication is that changing family-background characteristics can "explain" larger increases in high school and college graduation rates than actually occurred among the post-1950 cohorts (for three of the four cases).

These findings are summarized in table 9.3. Panel A shows the estimated fractions of high school and college graduates in three cohorts: an early cohort (born 1920–24); the benchmark 1945–49 cohort; and a late cohort (born 1965–69). Panel B shows the actual intercohort changes in gradua-

Table 9.3	Decomposition of Intercohort Trends in Educational Attainment			
	Men		Women	
	High School Diploma	College Degree	High School Diploma	College Degree
A. Estimated % with Education Level by Age 30				
1920–24 cohort	62.1	16.9	53.5	5.3
1945–49 cohort	88.0	32.4	83.9	20.9
1965–69 cohort	92.1	34.8	89.3	33.5
B. Intercohort Changes				
1920–24 to 1945–49 cohort:				
Actual change	25.9	15.5	30.5	15.5
Change explained by changes in family background	12.8	10.5	11.1	3.5
1945–49 to 1965–69 cohort:				
Actual change	4.0	2.3	5.4	12.6
Change explained by changes in family background	4.5	8.3	6.1	10.1

Note: Based on logit models in table 9.2 above. Family background variables used to explain changes in educational attainment include mother's and father's education, single mother at age 16, number of siblings, race, and measures of family location at age 16 (region of residence, farm residence, small-town residence).

tion rates and the predicted changes that can be attributed to changing family-background characteristics. Comparing the 1920–24 and the 1945–49 cohorts, the relative magnitudes of the predicted and actual changes suggest that improving family-background characteristics can explain 20–60 percent of the rise in high school and college graduation rates. Comparing the 1965–69 cohort to the 1945–49 cohort, however, the actual changes are smaller than the predicted changes in three of four cases. Only the fraction of women with a college degree rose faster than predicted by changing family-background characteristics, although, as noted, the GSS sample seems to overstate the rise in the college graduation rate of women among post-1950 cohorts. On the basis of the results in this table, we conclude that the rapid growth in educational attainment by men and women born prior to 1950 can be partially explained by improving family-background characteristics, whereas the post-1950 slowdown is *even more* of a puzzle once changes in family-background characteristics are taken into account.

9.3.3   The Effect of Local Variables

Having eliminated changes in family background as a possible explanation for the stagnation in enrollment and completed education among post-1950 cohorts, we turn to a second set of explanations, which are based on factors that potentially affect the education choices of individuals from the same cohort and location. The discussion in section 9.2 above suggests two potential variables of this type: the level of tuition at local colleges and universities and cyclic conditions in the local labor market. Average tuition costs (adjusted for inflation) at state colleges and universities declined by about 18 percent over the 1970s, then began to rise fairly rapidly in the 1980s, with a 60 percent average increase between 1980 and 1992.[26] These national trends suggest that, even if college entry rates are highly sensitive to tuition costs, tuition costs cannot explain the stagnation in enrollment rates over the 1970s and the rebound in the 1980s. The overall effect of trends in labor market conditions is similarly unclear. Average unemployment rates trended up in the 1970s, peaked in the early 1980s, and trended down in the 1980s and 1990s (with an interruption during the 1990–92 recession). Other things equal, this pattern might have led to a rising incentive for enrollment in the 1970s and a declining incentive in the 1980s and 1990s. However, the discussion around equation (3′) focused on the effect of *transitory* labor market shocks, and it is unclear whether to interpret longer-run shifts in unemployment rates in this manner.

A third and more promising "local" variable that may have some effect

---

26. These comparisons are based on a population-weighted average of tuition levels at state colleges and universities. The tuition data were originally assembled by the University of Washington as part of a fee-monitoring project and were generously provided to us by Thomas Kane (for a further description, see Kane 1994).

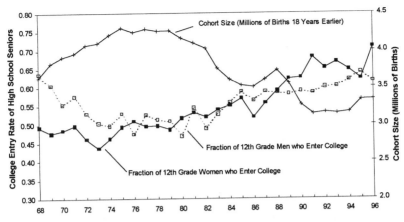

Fig. 9.7   College entry rates of high school seniors vs. cohort size, 1968–96

on school enrollment and completed education is cohort size. While the standard human-capital-investment model focuses on factors that affect individual or per capita demand for education, a broader view of the education system suggests that shifts in population size may affect the per capita *supply* of education resources and, ultimately, the amount of education acquired by members of smaller versus larger cohorts. In particular, students in larger cohorts may be "crowded out" of college if the capacity of the education system does not expand as rapidly as the student-age population or if the system only partially adjusts to a temporary bulge in enrollment.[27]

At the national level, trends in enrollment are highly negatively correlated with the relative number of college-age youths. This is illustrated in figure 9.7, which plots relative cohort size (measured by the number of births eighteen years earlier) and the college entry rates of male and female high school seniors over the period from 1968 to 1996. Cohort size increased rapidly from 1968 to 1975 (corresponding to the "baby boom" in births between 1950 and 1957) and then remained relatively stable until 1982, before falling precipitously in the "baby-bust" era (i.e., for cohorts born after 1964).[28] These swings were matched by opposing movements in

27. School quality may also be lower for larger cohorts, leading to a decline in the perceived benefit of school attendance and a decline in enrollment rates. We examined this hypothesis using state-level pupil-teacher ratios for 1946–96 and found a significant positive effect of cohort size on the pupil-teacher ratio.

28. The negative effect of cohort size on school enrollment suggested by the data presented in fig. 9.7 is the opposite of what one might have predicted by focusing on the role of labor market conditions in the school-enrollment decision. For example, it is widely believed (e.g., Welch 1979) that larger cohorts depress the youth labor market (although, for opposing evidence, see Shimer [1999]), leading to a fall in the opportunity cost of staying in school that could potentially lead to a rise in enrollment. The negative correlation between cohort size

the college entry rate, suggesting that cohort size may provide at least a partial explanation for the aggregate trends in enrollment and educational attainment noted in section 9.1 above.

To evaluate the effects of tuition, local labor market conditions, and cohort size on school-enrollment rates, we fit the models summarized in table 9.4 to data on average enrollment rates by state and year for four different age groups. These models take the form

$$(7) \qquad P_{jt} = X_{jt}\beta + \gamma_j + \upsilon_t + e_{jt},$$

where P_{jt} is the average enrollment rate for a specific age group in state j in year t, X_{jt} includes state- and year-specific determinants of enrollment behavior as well as the average characteristics of the school-age population in state s in year t, γ_j represents a set of fixed state effects, υ_t represents a set of fixed year effects, and e_{jt} represents a combination of sampling error and unobserved factors that also influence enrollment outcomes.[29] The dependent variables are estimated from the October CPS files for 1968–96. A limitation of these files is that only a subset of states is individually identified before 1977. Consequently, our sample contains observations for all the individually identified states in the years from 1968 to 1976 plus observations for all fifty states and the District of Columbia for 1977–96. The models are estimated by weighted least squares, using as a weight the number of people in the state/year/age-group cell for whom the dependent variable is measured.

The three key independent variables are the unemployment rate of prime-age men (age twenty-five to fifty-four) in the state in year t, the log of the relative number of people born in state s and in the age group relevant for the particular enrollment outcome, and the log of average tuition at public colleges and universities in the state. The unemployment rates are estimated by pooling data for each year from the March and October CPS files.[30] The tuition data pertain to rates for in-state students at the "lower-level" state college and university systems in each state and are available only for 1972–92.[31] The cohort-size variables are constructed from population counts by state and year of birth from the public-use samples of the 1960, 1970, 1980, and 1990 censuses. Specifically, we calculated the number of people born in each year in each state in each census and then fit a model to the pooled set of population counts that expresses

---

and college entry rates suggests that the baby boom had a bigger effect on the education system than it did on the labor market.

29. Note that the inclusion of year effects is equivalent to the inclusion of cohort effects.

30. We pooled the two samples to reduce the effect of sampling errors. On the basis of the correlations of the state-level unemployment estimates from the two months, we estimate that the (weighted) reliability of the average of the unemployment rates is over 0.8.

31. We follow Kane (1994) and Moretti (1999) in using tuition data at the "upper-level" state universities for Alaska, Delaware, Hawaii, and Wyoming.

Table 9.4   Effects of Unemployment, Cohort Size, and College Tuition Rates on Enrollment Probabilities: Pooled State-Year Data for 1968–96

| | Both Sexes Ages 15–16 (fraction enrolled) | | Both Sexes Age 17 (fraction enrolled) | | Both Sexes Age 18 | | | | Men Age 19–21 (fraction in college) | | Women Age 19–21 (fraction in college) | |
| | | | | | Fraction Enrolled | | Fraction in College | | | | | |
	(1)	(2)	(3)	(4)	(5)	(6)	(7)	(8)	(9)	(10)	(11)	(12)
Mean of dependent variable	.964	.963	.873	.870	.581	.569	.380	.376	.378	.362	.350	.344
Coefficients:												
Unemployment rate	.090	.141	.324	.397	−.138	.106	−.225	−.085	−.053	.016	−.224	−.109
	(.048)	(.053)	(.117)	(.135)	(.180)	(.203)	(.185)	(.214)	(.152)	(.171)	(.153)	(.170)
Log cohort size	−.005	.010	−.006	.041	−.101	−.104	−.086	−.079	−.111	−.122	−.121	−.125
	(.006)	(.010)	(.016)	(.025)	(.025)	(.039)	(.026)	(.041)	(.023)	(.036)	(.022)	(.035)
Log tuition	⋯	−.014	⋯	−.025	⋯	−.036	⋯	−.036	⋯	−.011	⋯	−.038
		(.005)		(.013)		(.019)		(.020)		(.015)		(.015)
R^2	.335	.339	.460	.442	.545	.523	.386	.384	.578	.544	.653	.605
No. of observations	1,167	866	1,167	866	1,167	866	1,167	866	1,167	866	1,167	866

Note: Standard errors are given in parentheses. All models include unrestricted state and year effects as well as controls for the fraction of nonwhites, the fraction of females, and (in cols. 9–12) the average age of the group. Models are fit by weighted OLS, using the number of observations in the state-year cell as a weight. Unemployment rate is the average unemployment rate of men age 25–54 in the state in March and October of the calendar year. Cohort size is estimated number of people born in the state in the indicated age group, based on data from the 1960, 1970, 1980, and 1990 censuses (see the text). Tuition is the average amount of tuition and fees for state colleges and universities (see the text). Sample includes individually identified states in the CPS from 1968 to 1996 (19 states in 1968–72 [including the District of Columbia], 13 states in 1973–76, and 51 states in 1977–96). Tuition data are available for 1972–92 only for 50 states (excluding the District of Columbia).

the log of the observed count for each state and year of birth in each census as a function of the cohort's age (a cubic in age) and unrestricted cohort × year-of-birth effects. We use the latter as "smoothed" estimates of cohort size for a particular year of birth and state of birth.

The models in columns 1 and 2 of table 9.4 pertain to the enrollment rate of fifteen- and sixteen-year-olds. Virtually no one this age has completed high school: thus, nonenrollment for this group is tantamount to having dropped out of high school. The coefficient estimates show a modest positive effect of higher unemployment on enrollment, with a stronger effect in the period 1972–92, for which tuition data are also available, than over the entire sample. Cohort size has no effect on the enrollment behavior of these relatively young teenagers, while tuition levels have a small but significantly negative effect. Since college tuition rates presumably have no direct effect on the cost of attending school for fifteen- and sixteen-year-olds, the finding of a significant tuition effect may seem anomalous. One interpretation of the estimate is that teenagers are more likely to stay in high school when college is expected to be less costly.

The dependent variable in columns 3–4 is the enrollment rate of seventeen-year-olds. The vast majority of children this age are enrolled in the eleventh or the twelfth grade: thus, shifts in the enrollment of seventeen-year-olds reflect shifts in high school completion rates. Overall enrollment is positively affected by unemployment, suggesting that students who are nearly finished high school are more likely to stay in school if unemployment is higher. The effect size is modest, however. A rise in the prime-age male unemployment rate from 0.035 to 0.065 is predicted to raise enrollment of seventeen-year-olds by about 1 percentage point. As for the fifteen- to sixteen-year-olds, the enrollment of seventeen-year-olds is unaffected by state-specific cohort size but is significantly negatively related to tuition levels at local public colleges.

Columns 5–8 present results for eighteen-year-olds. About two-thirds of enrolled eighteen-year-olds are in college, while most of the rest are high school seniors. Unlike the results for younger students, the estimated effects of unemployment on this age group are weak and variable in sign, with some indication of a negative effect on college enrollment rates. A possible explanation for this result is that college attendance rates are negatively affected by rises in the opportunity cost of school and positively affected by rises in parents' income (perhaps because of borrowing constraints). A rise in unemployment causes both variables to fall, with a small net effect on college enrollment. Unlike the models for younger teenagers, the results for eighteen-year-olds show a significant negative effect of cohort size on enrollment. The coefficient estimates imply that a 10 percent larger birth cohort in a state is associated with about a 1 percentage point lower enrollment rate among eighteen-year-olds, holding constant national trends and permanent state effects. The estimated effects of college tuition are negative and significant but, again, relatively modest in size. For example, a twenty-five-log-point increase in tuition is estimated to lower enrollment rates of eighteen-year-olds by about 1 percentage point.

Finally, in columns 9–12, we present results for nineteen- to twenty-one-year-olds, with separate results by gender. The unemployment effects for this older age group show an interesting pattern, with very small effects for young men but more negative effects for young women. It is possible that this difference arises because young men's earnings are more cyclically sensitive than are young women's, whereas their parents' incomes are equally responsive to local unemployment fluctuations. In this case, poor labor market conditions affect young women mainly through their parents' incomes, while young men are affected both through an opportunity-cost channel and a parents'-income channel, with offsetting effects. Cohort size has somewhat larger effects on nineteen- to twenty-one-year-olds than on eighteen-year-olds, with comparable magnitudes for men and women. Finally, higher tuition exerts a small negative effect on the enrollment rate of nineteen- to twenty-one-year-old men but a substantially larger negative effect on women. We are uncertain of the reasons for the gender differential, although it may be driven in part by differences in choice of college program and/or by differences in the resources of young women relative to young men.[32]

As noted in section 9.1 above, the October CPS data can be used to examine dropout or retention rates at specific grade levels as well as enrollment rates at a given age. Table 9.5 presents a series of models fit to state × year average probabilities of finishing the eleventh grade and starting the twelfth, finishing the twelfth grade, and finishing the twelfth grade and starting college.[33] The sample sizes available for calculating these grade-specific retention probabilities are quite small for some of the smaller states. Thus, the dependent variables in table 9.5 are somewhat "noisier" than the ones in table 9.4 above. On the whole, however, the results are quite consistent with the results in table 9.4: higher unemployment leads to higher probabilities of attending and finishing the last year of high school, while larger cohort size and higher college tuition lead to a reduced probability of attending college.

Our final set of results, presented in table 9.6, pertains to completed education by state of birth and year of birth. In this table, the dependent variable consists of observations on mean educational attainment for individual state × year-of-birth cells in the 1960, 1970, 1980, and 1990 cen-

32. As noted in sec. 9.1 above, women are slightly more likely to attend junior (two- or three-year) colleges than are men. Young women are also less likely to live with their parents (Card and Lemieux 2000).

33. The probability of finishing the eleventh grade is estimated by the fraction of people in the October CPS who are enrolled in the twelfth grade, conditional on being enrolled in the eleventh grade the previous year. The other retention rates are estimated similarly.

Table 9.5   Effects of Unemployment, Cohort Size, and College Tuition Rates on Retention Probabilities: Pooled State-Year Data for 1968–96

	Finish 11th and Start 12th Grade		Finish 12th Grade		Finish 12th Grade and Start College	
	(1)	(2)	(3)	(4)	(5)	(6)
Mean of Dependent Variable	.949	.949	.929	.930	.549	.535
Coefficients						
Unemployment rate	.054	.137	.055	.178	−.074	.167
	(.079)	(.090)	(.106)	(.119)	(.211)	(.242)
Log cohort size	.002	.027	−.021	.015	−.099	−.034
	(.011)	(.012)	(.015)	(.023)	(.029)	(.047)
Log tuition	...	.008	...	.006	...	−.036
		(.008)		(.011)		(.023)
R^2	.249	.269	.211	.208	.498	.481
No. of observations	1,115	816	1,116	816	1,116	816

Note: See notes to table 9.3 above. All models include unrestricted state and year effects and controls for the fraction of nonwhites and females and the average age of the risk group. In cols. 1 and 2, retentions are defined over the set of people who were enrolled in the eleventh grade in the previous October. In cols. 3–6, retentions are defined over the set of people who were enrolled in the twelfth grade in the previous October.

suses. (Observations are included only for groups that are between the ages of twenty-four and sixty-five at the time of the census.) The models have the form

$$(8) \qquad S_{jc\tau} = X_{jc}\beta + h(\text{age}_{c\tau}) + \alpha_c + \gamma_j + d_\tau + e_{jc\tau},$$

where $S_{jc\tau}$ is the average years of education among individuals born in state j in cohort c and observed in census year τ (or the fraction of the state-of-birth and cohort group with a certain level of education), X_{jc} represents a set of state- and cohort-specific determinants of completed education, $h(\text{age}_{c\tau})$ represents a polynomial function of the age of cohort c in census year τ, α_c represents an unrestricted cohort effect, γ_j represents a state effect, d_τ is a dummy for the specific census year (restricted to be the same for all years except 1990, when the census introduced a new education question), and $e_{jc\tau}$ represents a combination of sampling errors and other unobserved factors that influence completed education outcomes. The key covariates of interest are cohort size, the unemployment rate experienced by the cohort × state group at age seventeen, and the level of tuition for the cohort × state group at age eighteen.[34]

Not all individuals who were born in a given state actually lived there

34. We use the state average unemployment rate over the calendar year as our measure of unemployment.

Table 9.6 Effects of Unemployment, Cohort Size, and College Tuition Rates on Completed Educational Attainment: Pooled Data by State of Birth and Year of Birth

	Years of Education			High School Graduate			Complete Some College			College Graduate		
	All Cohorts (1)	1940–64 (2)	1954–64 (3)	All Cohorts (4)	1940–64 (5)	1954–64 (6)	All Cohorts (7)	1940–64 (8)	1954–64 (9)	All Cohorts (10)	1940–64 (11)	1954–64 (12)
A. Men:												
Log cohort size	−.644	−.899	−.506	−.100	−.098	−.062	−.025	−.097	−.088	−.037	−.080	−.044
	(.026)	(.039)	(.071)	(.003)	(.005)	(.010)	(.002)	(.005)	(.016)	(.002)	(.005)	(.011)
Unemployment rate age 17	⋯	⋯	.847	⋯	⋯	.167	⋯	⋯	.133	⋯	⋯	−.010
			(.322)			(.044)			(.070)			(.051)
Log tuition age 18	⋯	⋯	.119	⋯	⋯	.010	⋯	⋯	.015	⋯	⋯	.015
			(.035)			(.005)			(.008)			(.006)
R^2	.938	.938	.970	.948	.934	.968	.955	.958	.963	.901	.926	.951
B. Women:												
Log cohort size	−.508	−.592	−.363	−.098	−.089	−.041	−.016	−.070	−.085	−.032	−.057	−.027
	(.022)	(.029)	(.061)	(.003)	(.005)	(.009)	(.002)	(.015)	(.014)	(.002)	(.004)	(.011)
Unemployment rate age 17	⋯	⋯	.842	⋯	⋯	.176	⋯	⋯	.200	⋯	⋯	−.034
			(.273)			(.043)			(.065)			(.048)
Log tuition age 18	⋯	⋯	.027	⋯	⋯	.006	⋯	⋯	.001	⋯	⋯	−.008
			(.030)			(.005)			(.007)			(.005)
R^2	.937	.951	.972	.931	.928	.960	.954	.967	.970	.890	.908	.948

Note: Standard errors are given in parentheses. Dependent variable is average educational attainment for men by state of birth and year of birth, as measured in the 1960, 1970, 1980, and 1990 censuses. State-of-birth/year-of-birth cells are included only for groups aged 24–65 at the time of the census. All models include unrestricted state and year effects as well as a cubic function of the age at which education is observed and a dummy for observations from the 1990 census. Models are fit by weighted OLS, using the average size of the state birth cohorts from 1930 to 1960 as a weight. Unemployment rate is the average state unemployment rate in the calendar year the cohort was age 17. Cohort size is estimated number of people born in the state in the indicated age group, based on data from the 1960, 1970, 1980, and 1990 censuses (see the text). Tuition is the average amount of tuition and fees for state colleges and universities for the state of birth in the year the cohort was age 18 (see the text).

during their teenage years. Thus, relative to a specification in which each individual's education outcome is associated with the specific unemployment rate and tuition level that he or she actually faced, estimates from specification (8) are likely to be attenuated by a factor that varies with the probability that an individual who was born in state j actually lived there during high school and the transition to college.[35] Since 75–85 percent of teenagers live in their state of birth, we suspect that the attenuation factor is on the order of 10–25 percent.

For each of the education outcomes, estimates are presented for three samples: a "maximum-possible" sample that includes all cohorts born from 1910 to 1964; a "post-1940" sample that includes only cohorts born from 1940 to 1964; and a sample for which tuition data are also available (individuals born after 1954). Results for men are presented in the upper panel of the table, results for women in the lower panel. As in tables 9.4 and 9.5 above, a larger cohort is associated with lower schooling, whereas a higher unemployment rate at age seventeen leads to higher schooling. Contrary to the findings in tables 9.4 and 9.5, however, there is no evidence of a negative effect of tuition on educational attainment. This may be due to the limited range of cohorts for which we have both completed education and tuition data: the samples in columns 3, 6, 9, and 12 are limited to only eleven birth cohorts.

A comparison of the relative effect of unemployment at age seventeen on enrollment rates and completed education suggests that rises in unemployment have roughly consistent effects on the two. Specifically, the estimates in columns 1–4 of table 9.4 imply that the total number of years of enrollment between the ages of fifteen and seventeen is raised by about 0.005–0.007 per point increase in the prime-age male unemployment rate.[36] By comparison, the estimates in table 9.6 imply that a one-point rise in the overall unemployment rate at age seventeen leads to about a $+.008$ increase in completed education. Given the sampling errors involved and the potential attenuation biases, we regard these effects as roughly comparable. Interestingly, the results in tables 9.4 and 9.6 both indicate that most of this effect is concentrated on the probability of finishing high school.

These results are consistent with the view that individuals make a once-for-all school-leaving decision, as suggested by the NLSY results reported in table 9.1 above. If, instead, youths took advantage of a temporary boom by dropping out and returning to school later, the effect of the unemployment rate on enrollment should be larger than its effect on completed education. One possibility is that youths drop out of school thinking that they

35. A similar argument is made by Card and Krueger (1992) in their analysis of the effect of school quality on returns to education.

36. To calculate this effect, we add the coefficient for the probability of enrollment at age seventeen plus two times the coefficient for the probability of enrollment at ages fifteen to sixteen.

will eventually return but never do so because of unexpected institutional hurdles or start-up costs associated with returning to school. If this is the case, lower unemployment will have a long-term unintended consequence on completed education because youths drop out "too early" when economic times are good. The evidence suggests that these effects are relatively small, however, given the modest estimated effects of local unemployment rates on enrollment and completed education.

The effects of cohort size on enrollment and completed education are also comparable. The estimates in table 9.4 imply that total years of enrollment between ages eighteen and twenty-one fall by about 0.044 per 0.1 increase in log cohort size, while the estimates in table 9.6 imply a 0.04–0.06 reduction in total years of completed education and a 0.5 percentage point reduction in the probability of completing a college degree.

Taken as a whole, the results shown in tables 9.4–9.6 point to two main findings that are relevant for understanding the long-run trends in enrollment and completed education presented in section 9.1 above. First, cohort size has a modest negative effect on college enrollment and college completion that works in the right direction to explain some of the post-1950 slowdown in the intercohort trend in schooling attainment. To understand the implications of the estimates, consider the comparison between the 1946 and the 1956 birth cohorts. Relative to the 1946 cohort, the 1956 cohort was 27 percent larger. The coefficients in table 9.4 suggest that this rise in cohort size contributed to a 3 percentage point fall in the enrollment rate of nineteen- to twenty-one-year-olds between 1966 and 1976 (about one-fifth of the decline that actually occurred for men), while the estimates in table 9.6 suggest that size effects led to a 1.4 percentage point lower college graduation rate for the 1956 cohort relative to the 1946 cohort (a modest change relative to the trend shifts evident in fig. 9.4*B* above). Second, changes in cyclic conditions and tuition levels probably had little or no effect on longer-run trends in enrollment or completed education. This is a reflection both of the very small coefficient estimates associated with these variables and the fact that trends in unemployment and tuition move in the wrong direction to explain a slowdown in enrollment rates in the 1970s relative to earlier trends or a rebound in college enrollment growth in the 1980s.

9.3.4   The Effect of Aggregate Variables

In this section, we evaluate a third set of explanations for long-run trends in enrollment and completed schooling, associated with changes in aggregate-level variables. Specifically, we examine the effects of changes in the average return to education and changes in interest rates. Recall that, in a simple human-capital-investment model, the marginal benefit of additional schooling is just the discounted present value of the incremental gain in earnings. Under the assumption that log earnings are additively separable in years of education and postschooling experience (x), the marginal benefit has the form

$$MB(S) = d \log y_{sx}(S, x)/dS \times y_{sx}(S, 0) \times H(r),$$

where $y_{sx}(S, x)$ denotes earnings as a function of schooling and experience, and $H(r)$ is a decreasing function of the interest rate, with $H(r) = 1/r$ in the simplified case of a flat experience profile.[37] Since a rise in $MB(S)$ will lead to higher schooling, this expression implies that people will invest in additional education if they perceive that their marginal returns ($d \log y_{sx}(S, x)/dS$) are higher or if they face a lower discount rate.

Freeman (1976) and subsequent authors (e.g., Topel 1997) have argued that teenagers use information on the current wage gap between recent college and high school graduates to gauge the size of their own future returns to schooling. Following this idea, we used information on the weekly earnings of full-time full-year workers in the March CPS to estimate the college–high school wage gap for men and women with three to seven years of postschooling experience. We refer to this wage gap (divided by 4) as the *return to education* for young workers in a given year.

Despite the symmetrical roles played by returns to education and interest rates in the human-capital-investment model, few previous studies have focused on the link between interest rates and schooling decisions. Part of the difficulty may be in finding a relevant real interest rate for students who are considering borrowing money to finance an additional year of schooling. Many existing student-loan programs use an interest rate that is linked to either the three-month Treasury-bill rate or the prime rate. The federally subsidized and unsubsidized Stafford loan programs and the Parent Loan for Undergraduate Students (PLUS) program both use an interest rate that is linked to the three-month Treasury-bill rate, while many private bank loans are linked to the prime rate.[38] Since these two rates move together very closely, we decided to use the prime rate as a nominal interest rate. We then subtracted the annual percentage change in the consumer price index to obtain a real interest rate.[39]

Figure 9.8 plots the return to college for young men, the real interest

---

37. Using the notation from sec. 9.2 above, assume that $y(S, t) = g(S) h(t - S) = g(S) h(x)$, with $h(0) = 1$. The marginal benefit of schooling is $MB(S) = g'(S) \int_0^\infty h(\tau)e^{-r\tau}d\tau = g'(S) H(r) = \partial \log y_{sx}(S, x)\partial S \times y_{sx}(S, 0) \times H(r)$. If $h(x) = 1$, then $H(r) = 1/r$.

38. The subsidized Stafford loans use an interest rate equal to the three-month Treasury-bill rate plus 2.3 points. The PLUS program uses the Treasury-bill rate plus 3.1 points. A search of financial websites offering student loans suggests that many banks and similar institutions charge the prime rate plus a small premium.

39. We used the CPI-U-X1 for 1967–83 and the CPI-U for later years as a price index. Our real interest rate for year t is $r(t) = i(t) - 100 \times [P(t) - P(t - 1)]/P(t - 1)$, where $i(t)$ is the annual average prime rate, and $P(t)$ is the annual average CPI in year t. We experimented with several different inflation adjustments and found that the resulting real-interest-rate series all had roughly similar effects on enrollment.

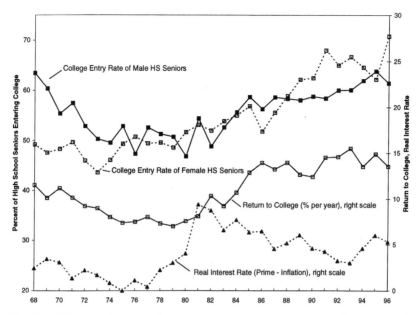

Fig. 9.8   College entry rates of young men and women, returns to college, and real interest rates

rate, and the college entry rates of male and female high school seniors over the period 1968–96. (The return to college for young women follows a path that is fairly similar to that for the return for men and is omitted in the interests of clarity.) The college entry rate of young men is strongly positively correlated with the return to college (correlation coefficient = 0.80), while the correlation is a little weaker for young women (correlation = 0.74). On the other hand, there is no obvious negative connection between college entry rates and real interest rates. Indeed, the steep rise in real interest rates between 1979 and 1982 coincided with a modest upturn in college entry rates.

Table 9.7 presents a series of simple regression models fit to annual data on the college entry rate (cols. 1–4) and the average enrollment rate of nineteen- to twenty-one-year-olds (cols. 5–8) for the period 1968–96. All the models include a linear trend and are fit separately by gender with gender-specific returns to education, the real interest rate, and aggregate cohort size as the other independent variables. The results in columns 1 and 5 confirm that college entry and enrollment rates are strongly related to changes in the average returns to college for young workers, even after controlling for trends. The models in columns 2 and 6 add our estimate of the real interest rate: this variable has a negative effect but is statistically insignificant in three of four cases. Although we do not show them in the table, we also fit a set of models that included the *difference* between the

Table 9.7   Estimated Time-Series Models for College Entry Rate and Average Enrollment Rate of 19–21-Year-Olds, 1968–96

	College Entry Rate of High School Seniors				Average Enrollment of 19–21-Year-Olds			
	(1)	(2)	(3)	(4)	(5)	(6)	(7)	(8)
A. Men:								
Return to college (% per year)	1.73	1.73	.83	1.37	1.83	1.83	.72	1.46
	(.28)	(.29)	(.48)	(.27)	(.28)	(.27)	(.44)	(.22)
Real interest rate (prime inflation)	...	−.06	...	...	...	−.33	...	...
		(.25)				(.24)		
Log cohort size	...	...	−.29	−.12	...	...	−.36	−.12
			(.13)	(...)			(.12)	(...)
Trend (× 100)	−.14	−.13	−.21	−.17	−.25	−.21	−.35	−.29
	(.09)	(.10)	(.09)	(.09)	(.09)	(.09)	(.08)	(.08)
R^2	.68	.68	.73	.56	.66	.69	.75	.56
B. Women:								
Return to college (% per year)	.83	.79	−.11	.45	.56	.48	.29	.17
	(.29)	(.29)	(.49)	(.27)	(.18)	(.17)	(.33)	(.18)
Real interest rate (prime inflation)	...	−.19	...	...	...	−.35	...	...
		(.25)				(.14)		
Log cohort size	...	...	−.29	−.12	...	...	−.08	−.12
			(.13)	(...)			(.08)	(...)
Trend (× 100)	.65	.68	.54	.60	.75	.81	.72	.70
	(.08)	(.09)	(.09)	(.07)	(.05)	(.05)	(.06)	(.05)
R^2	.87	.88	.90	.85	.95	.96	.95	.94

Note: Standard errors are given in parentheses. Models are estimated on 29 annual observations for national average data. Return to college is estimated difference in mean log wages for full-time full-year workers with 16 and 12 years of education, divided by 4. Returns are estimated separately for men and women using March CPS data. Real interest rate is difference between the prime rate and the percentage increase in the annual average CPI between the previous and the current calendar year. Cohort size is number of births 18 years previously. In cols. 4 and 8, the coefficient of log cohort size is constrained to equal −0.12 (see the text).

return to college and the real interest rate as an explanatory variable. This specification is motivated by an elementary version of the human-capital model that assumes linearly declining returns to education, a flat experience profile, and no tuition costs or earnings while in school (see eq. [3] above). Under these assumptions, the optimal schooling level for an individual is $S = (b - r)/k$, where b is the individual's marginal return to education at the minimum level of schooling, and r is a person-specific interest rate. This model predicts that average schooling outcomes for a cohort will depend on the difference between the average return to education anticipated by the cohort and the average real interest rate faced by the cohort during the teen years. As suggested by the results in table 9.7, however, this specification fits much worse than one that simply ignores interest rates, so we decided to ignore real interest rates in the remainder of our analysis.

We noted in the discussion of figure 9.7 above that the decline in college entry rates between the late 1960s and the late 1970s coincided with a rapid increase in the size of the college-age population. Moreover, the findings in tables 9.4–9.6 above confirm that larger cohorts at the state level are associated with lower college enrollment. The models in columns 3 and 7 of table 9.7 include the log of aggregate cohort size as an additional explanatory variable for aggregate enrollment trends. The inclusion of cohort size substantially reduces the size and estimated significance of the returns to college variable. In fact, in none of the four models in the table is the returns-to-college variable statistically significant once cohort size is included. A problem with the specifications, however, is that, in three of the cases, the estimated effect of log cohort size is substantially bigger (in magnitude) than the estimates obtained using state $\times$ year data with unrestricted year effects. Indeed, in specifications not reported in the table that include only cohort size and a trend, the coefficient of log cohort size is about -0.50 in the models for male college entry and enrollment and about -0.25 in the models for female college entry and enrollment. These are two to four times bigger than the coefficients obtained in table 9.4 using state $\times$ year data.

The facts that the aggregate models yield estimates of the cohort-size effect that are "too big" and that cohort size is actually a better predictor of enrollment trends than are changes in the returns to education are causes for concern. The root of the problem is that returns to college vary nationally: thus, any inferences must be based on aggregate time-series correlations over a relatively short sample period.[40] Unfortunately, given that March CPS data are available on a consistent basis only from 1968

---

40. There is some variation in returns to college across regions. However, an initial look at the data suggested that most of this is permanent. Moreover, recent college graduates are highly mobile, and it may be unwise to assume that college entry decisions are made only on the basis of local returns to college.

on, we are unable to extend our estimates of the returns to education for young workers back in time. Thus, there is no way to use the data on completed educational attainment for earlier cohorts to build a longer sample of data on schooling decisions and returns to schooling observed at ages eighteen to twenty-one.

If one believes that estimates based on the variation in enrollment outcomes at the state level provide more reliable information on the causal effect of cohort size (as we do), then a valid approach is to *impose* the estimates from the disaggregated approach on the aggregate data. The results of this exercise are reported in columns 4 and 8 of table 9.7. Drawing on the results in table 9.4 above, we use an estimate of −0.12 as the effect of log cohort size on college entry and enrollment. The specifications for men yield estimates of the effect of the returns to college that are slightly smaller than the estimates from models that ignore cohort size, but not too different. In the models for women, on the other hand, the estimated effect of changing returns to college is substantially attenuated.

An important feature of the models in table 9.7 is the sharp discrepancy between the estimated trends for women versus men. For women, the estimated trend growth rates range from 6 to 7 percentage points per decade. This is fairly similar to the intercohort trend in college graduation rates for women born between 1920 and 1950 (6 percentage points per decade) and suggests that there was no permanent slowdown in the rate of growth of educational attainment for women. Rather, the relative stagnation of enrollment rates in the 1970s can be attributed to the temporary decline in the returns to college for young women coupled with a cohort-size effect. For men, on the other hand, the estimated trends are all negative and in the range of from −1 to −3 percentage points per decade. This range represents a substantial departure from the very strong intercohort trend in male college graduation rates among pre-1950 cohorts (7 percentage points per decade) and suggests that the dip in educational attainment among post-1950 cohorts is not simply a result of low returns to college in the 1970s but rather a combination of temporary factors (low returns to college and large cohort size) and a permanent trend shift.

Table 9.8 summarizes the implications of the models in table 9.7 for aggregate trends in college entry and enrollment over the period 1968–96. The upper panel of table 9.8 shows average college entry rates and college-age enrollment rates in 1968, 1978, 1988, and 1996 for men and women along with contemporaneous values of the returns to college and cohort size. The middle panel of the table shows the ten-year changes in the variables. Of particular interest are the 1968–78 and 1978–88 changes. Over the period 1968–78, returns to college dropped, cohort size rose, male enrollment rates fell dramatically, and female enrollment rates were fairly stable. Over the period 1978–88, returns to college rebounded, cohort size shrunk, men's enrollment rates recovered somewhat, and women's enrollment rates grew rapidly. The bottom panel of the table shows the predicted

Table 9.8 **Contribution of Changes in Returns to College and Cohort Size to Changes in College Entry Rate and Average Enrollment Rate of 19–21-Year-Olds**

	Men		Women		Returns to College (per year)		Log of Cohort Size
	College Entry Rate	Enrollment Rate	College Entry Rate	Enrollment Rate	Men	Women	
1968	63.5	49.0	49.3	25.8	.115	.120	1.290
1978	51.3	35.3	49.6	31.0	.073	.081	1.450
1988	58.4	41.5	58.9	42.3	.140	.116	1.320
1996	61.5	47.3	70.8	48.9	.136	.151	1.200
			Actual Changes				
1968–78	−12.2	−13.7	.3	5.2	−.042	−.039	.160
1978–88	7.1	6.2	9.3	11.3	.067	.035	−.130
1988–96	3.1	5.8	11.9	6.6	−.004	.035	−.120
		Changes Explained by Changes in Returns to College and Cohort Size					
1968–78	−7.8	−8.1	−3.6	−2.7			
1978–88	10.9	11.4	3.1	2.3			
1988–96	.9	.9	3.0	2.2			

Note: College entry rate is fraction of youth in college among those who were enrolled in the twelfth grade in the previous fall. Enrollment rate is average enrollment rate of 19–21-year-olds. Explained changes use coefficient estimates from cols. 4 and 8 of table 9.7 above (see the text).

changes in the schooling variables, changes based on the observed shifts in returns to college and cohort size and the coefficient estimates in columns 4 and 8 of table 9.7. The actual and predicted changes for men over the period 1968–88 track each other reasonably well. The correspondence is less obvious for women, although, if one takes account of a steady upward trend in female enrollment rates, the predicted and actual changes are fairly close. In particular, factoring in a 6 percentage point per decade upward trend in female college enrollment rates, female enrollment rates were predicted to rise 2–3 percent between 1968 and 1978 and 8–9 percent between 1978 and 1988. These are fairly similar to the actual changes. Over the period 1988–96, the models do less well in predicting the continuing rise in male enrollment but a better job in predicting changes for women.

The results presented in tables 9.7 and 9.8 point to two key conclusions. First, for women, changes in returns to education, coupled with cohort-size effects and a strong underlying upward trend, provide a relatively good model for enrollment trends for college-age youths over the period 1968–96. Moreover, the estimated trend is comparable to the intercohort trend in college completion rates for women born before 1950. Second, although changes in returns to education and cohort size also do a reasonably good job of predicting enrollment trends of young men over the period 1968–96, the underlying trend in college entry rates over this period is 0 or even slightly negative. By contrast, among cohorts born from 1920 to 1950, college graduation rates rose by about 6 percentage points per decade. Thus, even after accounting for the effect of changes in returns to education and cohort size, the dramatic trend shift in the intercohort rate of growth of college graduation for men evident in figure 9.4*B* above is essentially unexplained.

9.4   Conclusions

This paper begins by documenting trends in enrollment rates over the past thirty years and trends in completed education for cohorts of U.S. children born from 1920 to 1965. Although earlier cohorts of children had rising enrollment rates and rising educational attainment, this trend stopped with the cohorts born after 1950, who began entering college in the late 1960s. The enrollment rate of eighteen- to twenty-four-year-old men declined sharply in the 1970s, while the rate for women stagnated, with the net effect that cohorts born from 1950 to 1965 experienced little or no net growth in educational attainment. Enrollment rates began to rise again in the early 1980s and have trended upward since then, but even today the fraction of male high school seniors who enter college immediately after graduation is not much higher than it was in 1968.

We then proceed to examine potential explanations for the slowdown in enrollment and educational attainment in the 1970s. Motivated by a human-capital-investment framework, we consider three sets of explanatory variables: individual-level variables such as family background and location; market-level variables such as local unemployment rates, state-level tuition costs, and local cohort size; and aggregate-level variables such as interest rates and the wage gap between recent college and high school graduates. An analysis of micro data from the General Social Survey suggests that improving family-background characteristics can explain some of the rising trend in educational attainment for cohorts born prior to 1950 but none of the post-1950 slowdown. Indeed, controlling for family background, the stagnant growth in educational attainment among later cohorts is even more of a puzzle. Next, we moved to an analysis of education outcomes at the state level, focusing on the effects of three key market-level variables: unemployment, tuition costs, and cohort size. We find that higher unemployment rates lead to a rise in high school completion rates while larger cohorts (at the state level) lead to lower college enrollment and completion. Cohort size moves in the right direction to help explain the slowdown in enrollment and completed education among post-1950 cohorts, but the size of the effect is small. In particular, our estimates from the state-level analysis imply that the size of the baby boom potentially accounts for about one-fifth of the national decline in enrollment rates over the 1970s.

Finally, in the third stage of our analysis, we examine the role of two purely aggregate variables: real interest rates and the college–high school wage gap for young workers. A simple time-series analysis suggests that college entry rates and college-age enrollment rates are positively correlated with the returns to college for young workers. A caveat to this conclusion is that enrollment rates are even more highly correlated with aggregate cohort size and that the latter dominates the former in a multivariate model. Nevertheless, if we impose the cohort-size effects estimated from our analysis of state-level enrollment, we find that models that include an underlying trend, cohort effects, and changes in the returns to education can explain the patterns of college entry and college-age enrollment observed over the period 1968–96 reasonably well. For women, the implied trends over the period 1968–96 are comparable to the intercohort trend in college graduation estimated for pre-1950 cohorts. For men, however, the implied trends over the period 1968–96 are 0 or slightly negative—much different than the steady upward trend in college graduation observed among pre-1950 cohorts.

In terms of "what happened" to college-age enrollment rates and educational attainment in the 1970s, the available evidence suggests different explanations for women and for men. For women, the slowdown in enrollment growth rates in the 1970s appears to have been a temporary phenomenon, driven by low returns to education and the size of the baby-boom cohort. For men, however, the slowdown seems to reflect a combination of adverse transitory shocks (a large cohort and low returns to education) coupled with a discrete downward trend shift. Unless the underlying trend can be restored, our findings point to a pessimistic view of future rises in educational attainment, at least for young men. In addition, the relatively slow growth in educational attainment for cohorts born in the 1950s and 1960s may well have an "echo effect" on those cohorts' children, slowing down the rate of growth of human capital in the U.S. economy for decades into the future.

References

Becker, Gary S. 1967. *Human capital and the personal distribution of income.* Ann Arbor: University of Michigan Press.

Bowen, William G., and Derek Bok. 1998. *The shape of the river.* Princeton, N.J.: Princeton University Press.

Cameron, Stephen V., and James J. Heckman. 1993. The non-equivalence of high school equivalents. *Journal of Labor Economics* 11 (January): 1–47.

Card, David. 1999. The causal effect of education on earnings. In *Handbook of labor economics,* vol. 3A, ed. Orley Ashenfelter and David Card. Amsterdam: Elsevier.

Card, David, John DiNardo, and Eugena Estes. 2000. The more things change: Immigrants and the children of immigrants in the 1940s, the 1970s, and the 1990s. In *Issues in the economics of immigration,* ed. George J. Borjas. Chicago: University of Chicago Press.

Card, David, and Alan B. Krueger. 1992. Does school quality matter? Returns to education and the characteristics of public schools in the United States. *Journal of Political Economy* 100 (February): 1–41.

Card, David, and Thomas Lemieux. 2000. Adapting to circumstances: The evolution of work, school, and living arrangements among North American youth. In *Youth employment and joblessness in advanced countries,* ed. David Blanchflower and Richard Freeman. Chicago: University of Chicago Press.

Dixit, Avinash K., and Robert S. Pindyck. 1994. *Investment under uncertainty.* Princeton, N.J.: Princeton University Press.

Freeman, Richard B. 1976. *The overeducated American.* San Diego, Calif.: Academic.

Gustman, Alan, and Thomas Steinmeier. 1981. The impact of wages and unemployment on youth enrollment and labor supply. *Review of Economics and Statistics* 63:553–60.

Haveman, Robert H., and Barbara L. Wolfe. 1984. Schooling and economic well-being: The role of nonmarket factors. *Journal of Human Resources* 19:377–407.

Kane, Thomas. 1994. College entry by blacks since 1970: The role of college costs, family background, and the returns to education. *Journal of Political Economy* 102:878–911.

Katz, Lawrence F., and Kevin M. Murphy. 1992. Changes in relative wages, 1963–1987: Supply and demand factors. *Quarterly Journal of Economics* 107:35–78.

Light, Audrey. 1995. Hazard model estimates of the decision to re-enroll in school. *Labour Economics* 2:381–406.

Mincer, Jacob. 1974. *Schooling, experience, and earnings.* New York: Columbia University Press.

Moretti, Enrico. 1999. Estimating the social return to education: Evidence from repeated cross sectional and longitudinal data. Working Paper no. 22. Center for Labor Economics, University of California, Berkeley, October.

Rosen, Sherwin. 1977. Human capital: A survey of empirical research. In *Research in labor economics,* vol. 1, ed. Ronald Ehrenberg. Greenwich, Conn.: JAI.

Rouse, Cecilia E. 1994. What to do after high school? The two-year vs. four-year college enrollment decision. In *Contemporary policy issues in education,* ed. Ronald Ehrenberg. Ithaca, N.Y.: ILR.

Shimer, Robert. 1999. The impact of young workers on the aggregate labor market. Working Paper no. 7306. Cambridge, Mass.: National Bureau of Economic Research, August.

Solon, Gary. 1999. Intergenerational mobility in the labor market. In *Handbook of labor economics,* vol. 3A, ed. Orley Ashenfelter and David Card. Amsterdam: Elsevier.

Topel, Robert H. 1997. Factor proportions and relative wages: The supply side determinants of wage inequality. *Journal of Economic Perspectives* 11:55–74.

Tyler, John H., Richard J. Murnane, and John B. Willett. 2000. Estimating the labor market signalling value of the GED. *Quarterly Journal of Economics* 115 (May): 431–68.

U.S. Department of Education. 1997. *Digest of education statistics.* Washington, D.C.: U.S. Government Printing Office.

Welch, Finis. 1979. Effects of cohort size on earnings: The baby boom babies' financial bust. *Journal of Political Economy* 87 (October): S65–S97.

Willis, Robert J. 1986. Wage determinants: A survey and reinterpretation of human capital earnings functions. In *Handbook of labor economics,* vol. 1, ed. Orley Ashenfelter and Richard Layard. Amsterdam: Elsevier.

10

Youths at Nutrition Risk
Malnourished or Misnourished?

Jay Bhattacharya and Janet Currie

The words *youth malnutrition* conjure up images of gaunt, starving waifs. Fortunately, such extreme nutrition deprivation is rare in the United States and in other developed countries. Nevertheless, as we will show, many American youths are "misnourished." The nutrition problems prevalent in the West are generally due to the composition of the diet—many youths underconsume important nutrients while overconsuming calories and high-fat foods. This pattern is linked to the increasing prevalence of obesity, which has important long-term health consequences. Poor diet quality (e.g., overconsumption of fats and underconsumption of foods such as fruits and vegetables) has also been increasingly linked to the development of leading killers such as cancer and heart disease in later life.

Standard human-capital theory suggests that youths (or their parents) choose diets in order to maximize utility, subject to two sets of constraints. The first constraint is the information that they have available about the link between food inputs and health outcomes that they care about. The second constraint is the household budget. This formulation leads naturally to the question of whether misnourished youths lack information about the relation between nutrition and health or whether they lack re-

Jay Bhattacharya is associate economist at the Rand Corp. in Santa Monica, Calif., and visiting professor in the Department of Economics at the University of California, Los Angeles. Janet Currie is professor of economics at the University of California, Los Angeles. She is a consultant with the Labor and Population group at Rand, a research associate of the National Bureau of Economic Research and a member of the NBER's Children and Families programs, and a faculty associate at the Chicago/Northwestern Poverty Center.

The authors thank Jon Gruber, Sara McLanahan, Don Kenkel, and conference participants for helpful comments. Currie is grateful for support from the Canadian Institute for Advanced Research, from the National Institutes of Health, and from the National Science Foundation. Matthew Neidell provided excellent research assistance.

sources (which would imply that nutrition problems are heavily concentrated among the poor)?

U.S. public policies concerning nutrition are generally predicated on the notion that resource constraints are of paramount importance. In order to assess this hypothesis, we focus on an array of outcome measures, including various nutrition deficiencies, obesity and high cholesterol, measures of overall dietary quality, and food insecurity.

Food insecurity is the most commonly used measure of nutrition status. It can be thought of as uncertainty about where one's next meal is coming from. We find that, while poor youths are more likely to suffer from food insecurity, they are also more likely to be obese than are other youths. Yet they are no more likely to suffer vitamin deficiencies, and the overall quality of their diets is no worse than that of other youths.

Thus, resource constraints alone cannot explain the patterns that we see. On the other hand, proxies for information are very important. Youths in households with more-educated heads are less likely to be obese, eat healthier diets, and are less likely to suffer from food insecurity, other things being equal. We also find that school-meals programs have positive effects on the quality of the diet, which is likely due to the fact that they are mandated to follow particular meal patterns.

These findings all suggest that policies designed to alter the composition of the diet are likely to address the nutrition problems of American youths more effectively than are those policies (such as food stamps) that merely seek to increase the quantity of food consumed.

The rest of the paper is laid out as follows. In section 10.1, we discuss important background information related to the measures of nutrition status that we examine. In section 10.2, we provide an overview of the human-capital theory underlying our approach. Section 10.3 provides an overview of the data, while section 10.4 presents our main results. Section 10.5 concludes.

10.1   Background

10.1.1   Measures of Nutrition Status

As discussed above, measures of nutrition status can be grouped into four broad categories: food insecurity, dietary quality (measured using dietary intake surveys), and measures of nutrition deficiency and obesity that are based on physical examinations. This section discusses the pros and cons of the different measures.

Food Insecurity

The most commonly used measure of nutrition status in the United States is *food insecurity,* which is often defined as missing a meal because there was no food in the house or because there was no money to buy food. More simply, respondents may be asked if there is "enough food to eat, sometimes not enough to eat, or often not enough to eat," as they are in NHANES (National Health and Nutrition Examination Survey) III. A recent USDA report (Nord, Jemison, and Bickel 1999) found that one in ten U.S. children suffer from food insecurity.[1] This estimate is almost double our estimate (5.5 percent) for adolescents.

The link between food insecurity and actual nutrition deficiencies is, however, unclear. In the USDA study, only 3.5 percent of households had food insecurity severe enough that one or more household members were hungry at some point during the year. Rose and Oliveira (1997) use data from the longitudinal 1989–91 Continuing Survey of Food Intake by Individuals and find a negative relation between food insecurity and nutrient intakes among young women and the elderly but not among children. Wilde (1997) and Wilde and Ranney (1997) use data from the Consumer Expenditure Survey and find that, while adults in families using food stamps frequently eat less during the fourth week of the month (the benefits are issued monthly), children do not. These findings suggest that parents are largely successful in shielding their children from the nutritional effects of food insecurity, although such insecurity could well have negative psychosocial consequences. As we will show below, we also find little relation between food insecurity and measures of nutrition deficiencies.[2]

Dietary Recall

A second common source of information about nutrition is dietary-recall data. Respondents are typically asked to keep a food diary for lengths of time varying from one or two days to up to one week. In NHANES III, respondents were asked how many times they ate various foods in the past month. Nutrient values are then calculated on the basis of the respondent's account of the types of foods and the amounts that were eaten. Since food intakes vary a great deal from day to day, food intakes measured over longer periods are considered more accurate (see Beaton, Burema, and Ritenbaugh 1997).

Because dietary recalls are self-reported, there is a possibility of system-

1. The definition used in this study includes those who answered yes to questions ranging from "We worried whether our food would run out before we got money to buy more" to "In the last 12 months did any of the children ever not eat for a whole day because there wasn't enough money for food?"

2. Still, some would dispute this assessment. For example, Neuhauser, Disbrow, and Margen (1995) estimate that 2 million children in California alone go hungry because their parents do not have the resources to buy food. They obtain this estimate by comparing estimates of total family income less other necessities with the amount necessary to purchase an adequate diet. However, their estimates are much higher than those obtained from surveys of the poor, probably because they underestimate the total resources available to households. Frank et al. (1996) show that the fraction of emergency-room visits accounted for by children who are small for their age rises during the winter months in a Boston hospital. They attribute this to a "heat-or-eat" effect, but it could also be due to selection if small children are more susceptible to illness.

Table 10.1   Components of the HEI

Component	Criteria for Score of 10	Criteria for Score of 0
1. Grains	6–11 servings[a]	0 servings
2. Vegetables	3–5 servings	0 servings
3. Fruits	2–4 servings	0 servings
4. Milk	2–3 servings	0 servings
5. Meat	2–3 servings	0 servings
6. Total fat	< 31% calories from fat	> 46% calories from fat
7. Saturated fat (s.f.)	< 10% calories from s.f.	> 14% calories from s.f.
8. Cholesterol	< 300 mg	> 449 mg
9. Sodium	< 2,400 mg	> 4,800 mg
10. Variety	> 16 different categories	< 7 different categories

[a] These criteria refer to the number of servings consumed daily. Recommended numbers of servings vary with the energy needs of the individual.

atic bias. For example, Briefel et al. (1997) compare the self-reported energy-intake information derived from NHANES III with a measure of basal metabolic rate for sedentary individuals derived from fundamental principles of energy physiology (Goldberg, Black, and Jebb 1991). They find that 18 percent of men and 28 percent of women underreport their consumption of energy. Underreporting is greatest among overweight individuals and among those trying to lose weight.

Nevertheless, food-frequency questionnaires provide useful information for researchers. Studies generally report moderate to high correlations between the dietary information gleaned from food-frequency questionnaires and methods that rely on direct observation (see Rockett and Colditz 1997). Since extensive food diaries and direct observation place considerable burdens on researchers and subjects, and since the act of observation may by itself alter the diets of subjects, food-frequency questionnaires are an indispensable tool for nutrition researchers.

We have adopted the USDA's Healthy Eating Index (HEI) as a way of summarizing the food-diary information available in NHANES III (Kennedy et al. 1995).[3] The USDA uses the HEI to assess overall diet quality. The index has ten components, and each component is scored between 0 and 10. The components and the scoring algorithms are shown in table 10.1. Intakes that fall between the criteria for scores of 0 and 10 are scored proportionally.

Perhaps surprisingly, the index does not penalize those with a high sugar

3. We use a slightly modified version of the HEI. Kennedy et al. (1995) define the *variety* component of the HEI using a survey that asks about food intake over the past several days, whereas NHANES asks about intake over the past month. We redefined the top and bottom *variety* criteria in such a way that the same proportion of people received a score of 0 and 10 in NHANES as Kennedy et al. (1995) report for their sample. The cutoffs that we use are more than thirty-three different food items (for a score of 10) and fewer than fourteen different food items (for a score of 0).

intake, which could well contribute to the consumption of excessive numbers of calories. Hence, we will look separately at the determinants of high sweets consumption, where *high sweets* is a variable set equal to 1 if the person consumed more than thirty sweets per month.

Measures Based on Physical Examinations

Measures based on physical examinations are likely to be the most accurate of the three types of measures, although their interpretation is not without controversy. In what follows, we focus on measures based on body-mass index (BMI) (a measure of obesity)[4] and on measures of blood cholesterol and of vitamin and iron deficiencies based on blood and urine samples.

BMI is defined as weight in grams/(height in meters)^2. Adults with a BMI over 30 are considered to be obese. Gauging obesity among adolescents is complicated by the fact that adolescents undergo growth spurts that change their weights and heights disproportionately. One commonly used measure (see Himes and Dietz 1994) is BMI over the eighty-fifth percentile for sex and half-year of age. This measure results in fewer false positives than alternatives based on measures such as skin-fold fat or waist-hip ratios. However, a conceptual difficulty that arises with this definition is that, in any given data set, 15 percent of adolescents would always be found to be obese. A second problem is that the NHANES surveys used to calculate the cutoffs yield relatively small sample sizes and cutoffs that bounce around from one age to the next. For example, rather than being smooth, the National Center for Health Statistics (NCHS) growth curves, which are based on NHANES I and two earlier surveys, show ninetieth percentile cutoffs that rise from 21.9 to 23 between the ages of 13.75 and 14.25 and then fall again to 22.4 by age 14.75 (U.S. DHEW 1977). These cutoffs are old and are due to be updated by the NCHS in the very near future.

In this paper, we use a fixed cutoff for obesity, which is BMI over 27.3 for females and BMI over 27.8 for males. These cutoffs are the eighty-fifth percentiles of BMI for young adults between twenty and twenty-nine, calculated from NHANES II, which was fielded between 1976 and 1980. While one would expect young adults to be heavier than teens (i.e., that these are conservative cutoffs to use for a sample of teens), we will see below that, in NHANES III 10 percent of teens still exceed these cutoffs.

Blood or urine tests are used to assess the existence and extent of specific micronutrient deficiencies, such as essential vitamins and minerals.

---

4. In an earlier version of this paper, we also considered determinants of anorexia. We defined a person as anorexic using a BMI cutoff of the fifteenth percentile for the person's age and gender in addition to indicators of negative body image (the individual considered herself to be overweight or was trying to lose weight). However, in samples of this size, few people are anorexic, and we had little success in modeling the prevalence of this condition.

The relation between micronutrient intake and blood levels of these nutrients is complicated. Because the body can store some vitamins and minerals for a long time, it is not anomalous to find a respondent who has not recently consumed the recommended amount of some vitamin yet does not have a deficiency in that vitamin according to blood tests. For example, it can take between three and six years for a deficiency in vitamin B_{12} to become clinically evident (Middleman, Emans, and Cox 1996). Nevertheless, blood tests can provide solid, objective evidence of micronutrient malnutrition when properly interpreted.

The appendix presents the cutoff values that we use to determine vitamin and mineral deficiencies in this paper. These cutoffs, which are taken from a pediatrics textbook (DeAngelis et al. 1999), typically represent blood levels below which the nutrient deficiencies manifest themselves clinically. When possible, the cutoffs used are specific to adolescents.

In addition to providing the information necessary to assess the extent of anemia, NHANES III allows us to assess the determinants of shortages of essential vitamins A, C, and E.[5] We will focus on a measure that is equal to 1 if the person is short any of these vitamins and 0 otherwise. Finally, we can examine the level of cholesterol in the blood (serum-cholesterol levels). This measure is linked to obesity and provides an alternative to measuring this important threat to health using BMI.

10.1.2 Long-Term Effects of Poor Nutrition in Adolescents

The nutrition habits of adolescents are important for at least two reasons. First, poor nutrition habits are hard to unlearn as an adult (as the model of O'Donoghue and Rabin [chap. 1 in this volume] would predict). Second, poor nutrition can immediately damage a young person's health, and the effects can persist into adulthood. The literature on the long-term effects of poor nutrition is large, and a comprehensive review is beyond the scope of this paper. Hence, we will focus on some of the most important health consequences of adolescent obesity, high cholesterol, and micronutrient deficiencies below. It is not known whether food insecurity has any negative long-term effects, other things being equal.

The long-term effects of obesity among children are relatively well documented. While the majority of obese adults were not obese children, obese children are much more likely to become obese adults. For example, Charney et al. (1976) followed children born between 1945 and 1955 and found that, of the children who were at the ninetieth percentile of the weight distribution for their sex and age, 36 percent became obese adults, compared to only 14 percent of average or lighter-weight children. Obese adults are known to be at increased risk of many diseases, such as diabetes and heart

---

5. We found little evidence of any shortages of vitamin B_{12} or of calcium, so we do not examine these outcomes.

disease. Moreover, the negative effects of childhood obesity may persist even in adults who are no longer obese. Lauer, Lee, and Clark (1989) found in a sample of Iowan children that childhood obesity was linked to an increased risk of high cholesterol as an adult.[6]

The long-term effects of micronutrient deficiencies vary considerably, depending on the vitamin or mineral in question. Interested readers can find a good review from a clinical perspective in any standard pediatrics text, such as DeAngelis et al. (1999). Iron-deficiency anemia is a particularly pernicious condition since it can have devastating effects on the school outcomes of children and youths. Even mild iron deficiency is associated with fatigue, shortened attention span, decreased work capacity, reduced resistance to infection, and impaired intellectual performance (CDC 1996). About 8 percent of black Americans carry the sickle-cell trait, which places them at much higher risk of anemia than they would face otherwise (Wilson et al. 1991).

Recently, attention has been focused on the possibly beneficial effects of diets rich in the micronutrients found in fruits and vegetables rather than on the harmful effects of deficiencies. Epidemiological evidence links diets rich in fruits and vegetables to reductions in the risk of stroke, cardiovascular disease, asthma, osteoporosis, and many specific types of cancer (see Joshipura et al. 1999; Lampe 1999; Butland, Strachan, and Anderson 1999; Palace et al. 1999). While the mechanisms for these effects are not well understood, there are many plausible biological reasons that eating fruits and vegetables has positive effects. These include stimulation of the immune system, reduction of platelet aggregation, modulation of cholesterol synthesis and hormone metabolism, reduction of blood pressure, and antioxidant, antibacterial, and antiviral effects (Lampe 1999).

10.1.3   Trends over Time in the United States

A number of authors have documented an increase in the proportion of U.S. children and adolescents who are obese, although the exact trends depend on the definition of *obesity* used.[7] Figure 10.1 shows our analysis of trends in obesity using data from NHANES I, II, and III. NHANES I covers the period 1971–74, NHANES II the period 1976–80, and

---

6. Anorexia can also have severe long-term consequences on the health of patients, even if they receive appropriate care. The most severe consequence is death (usually due to starvation or suicide), which occurs in 6 percent of patients. Long-term follow-up studies of surviving anorexics find that about half the patients reach normal weight, 20 percent remain underweight, 20 percent continue to be anorexic, and about 5 percent become obese (Foster 1991).

7. Gortmaker et al. (1987) compare measurements of skin-fold thicknesses (a standard measure of the amount of body fat) in NHANES I and NHANES II. They report a 39 percent increase in the proportion of obese children over the interval of time spanned by these two data sets (from 1971 to 1980). Ogden et al. (1997) compare data from NHANES I and NHANES III and find that the proportion of obese preschoolers grew from 5 to 10 percent. The NCHS reports a similar finding for older children (CDC 1999).

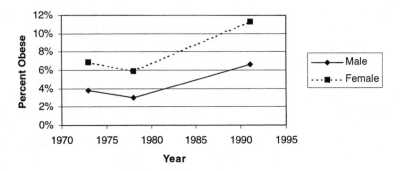

Fig. 10.1   Trends in obesity by sex
Note: Data are plotted at midpoint of year range.

NHANES III the period 1988–94. For both boys and girls (aged twelve to sixteen), the proportion obese decreased slightly between NHANES I and NHANES II but increased greatly between NHANES II and NHANES III. Figures 10.2 and 10.3 show changes in obesity by race for boys and girls, respectively. The time trends are similar for all six race and gender groups, but the much higher incidence of obesity among Hispanic men is striking, as is the increasing divergence between whites and either blacks or Hispanics.

One interesting hypothesis is that an increase in television watching is behind the increase in obesity among young people (Gortmaker et al. 1996).[8] More generally, Philipson and Posner (1999) conjecture that technological change is responsible for the increase in obesity. They argue that the number of calories consumed has been relatively constant over time but that technology has led to a reduction in the number of calories expended. Philipson and Posner dismiss the role of information in combating obesity, arguing that everyone knows how to lose weight. Thus, it will be interesting to ask whether such proxies for information as the education and age of the household head have an effect independent of income in the models of obesity estimated below.

Relatively few studies attempt to examine trends in vitamin deficiencies, primarily because relatively few American adolescents suffer from them (see Devaney, Gordon, and Burghardt 1995). For example, one recent study (Middleman, Emans, and Cox 1996) found only one reported case of vitamin B_{12} deficiency due to inadequate dietary intakes among adolescents (that of a fourteen-year-old female on a strict vegetarian diet). On average, U.S. adolescents consume more than the U.S. recommended daily allowances of all vitamins. Nevertheless, as we will show below, there are

---

8. The prevalence of anorexia has also been increasing over time (CDC 1996) but remains low, at 0.5–1 percent of adolescent girls.

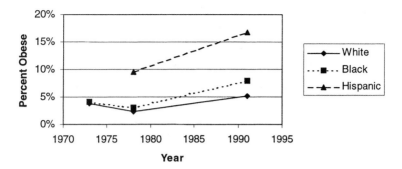

Fig. 10.2   Male trends in obesity by race
Note: Data are plotted at midpoint of year range.

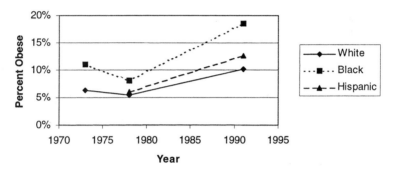

Fig. 10.3   Female trends in obesity by race
Note: Data are plotted at midpoint of year range.

significant numbers of U.S. adolescents who suffer from deficiencies of vitamins A, C, and/or E.[9]

A second reason for the paucity of information about trends in nutrition deficiencies is that the NHANES surveys, which are the main U.S. source of information about nutrition status, have changed the laboratory methods used to track deficiencies. For example, the methods used to evaluate white- and red-cell counts, serum folate, and serum vitamin C levels were updated in NHANES III, so it is difficult to infer time trends from these surveys (see Raiten and Fisher 1995; and Wright et al. 1998).

Data from other sources suggest that iron-deficiency anemia has declined significantly since the late 1960s, when several studies found that a

---

9. Researchers have also noted declines in calcium intakes among adolescents, which are associated with decreases in the consumption of milk (see Albertson, Tobelmann, and Marquart [1997], which examines changes between 1980 and 1992). These declines are of concern given that most adolescent girls consume less than 100 percent of the USDA-recommended daily allowance of calcium. However, we found little evidence of inadequate blood-calcium levels in our NHANES III sample.

large number of Americans (especially infants and young females) were iron deficient (see Committee on Iron Deficiency 1968; and Stockman 1987). However, Looker et al. (1997) conduct a careful assessment of trends in anemia using data from NHANES II (1976–80) and NHANES III (1988–94), adjusting for differences in the way anemia was measured in these two surveys, and find no change in the incidence of anemia. This study suggests that even trained observers may have difficulty using the NHANES surveys to detect trends in many outcomes.

Data on nutrient intakes and food insecurity have not been collected consistently either.[10] In view of these data problems, we will confine our own analysis of trends to an examination of obesity since that can be measured in the same way using data from NHANES I, II, and III.

10.1.4 U.S. Public Policy and Nutrition

Food and Nutrition Programs

The U.S. government operates a wide variety of food and nutrition programs (FANPs), including the Food Stamp Program (FSP), the National School Lunch Program (NSLP), and the School Breakfast Program (SBP), among others.[11] Most FANPs were developed with the goal of increasing food consumption among populations deemed likely to lack food. For example, the NSLP was established in 1946 in response to nutrition-deficiency-related health problems identified among young men being drafted during World War II.

The FSP provides coupons that can be redeemed for food to households with incomes less than 130 percent of the federal poverty line. There are few restrictions on the types of foods that can be purchased. The NLSP and SBP programs provide free or reduced-price meals to children with incomes less than 130 percent or 185 percent of poverty, respectively. Meals are designed to offer one-third of the USDA recommended daily allowances of specified nutrients.

However, as we have discussed, the nature of nutrition risk has changed in the United States from a situation in which significant numbers of people suffered food shortages to one in which obesity is prevalent even among the homeless—Luder et al. (1990) examined a sample of homeless-shelter users in New York City and found that 39 percent were obese.

---

10. In NHANES III, youths were asked about how many times they had consumed a particular type of food (e.g., broccoli) in the past month. In NHANES II, youths were asked about more general categories of food intakes (e.g., fruits and vegetables) and could report consumption in the last day, week, or month (however the person chose to respond). One might expect that asking about detailed categories of foods would lead to higher reported consumption while asking about foods consumed over the past month would lead to lower reported consumption. Hence, it is not clear a priori how the reported food intakes would be expected to differ between the two surveys.

11. For an overview of U.S. FANPs, see Currie (2000).

This observation raises the question of whether supplying meals (or food coupons) is the most effective way to address the nutrition risks facing the majority of FANP recipients.

In particular, school nutrition programs were roundly criticized in the early 1990s for providing meals that were high in fat and sodium and low in carbohydrates relative to the recommendations included in the *Dietary Guidelines for Americans* (USDA/U.S. DHHS 1995) (see Gordon, Devaney, and Burghardt 1995). These criticisms led to the Healthy Meals for Healthy Americans Act in November 1994, which mandated implementation of the dietary guidelines in school nutrition programs. Unfortunately, the data available do not allow us to assess the effects of these changes, although NHANES IV (which is currently in the field) will allow such analyses.

Whether or not FANPs improve the quality of the diet, one would expect the availability of these programs to reduce the probability of suffering from food insecurity. Yet, to our knowledge, no studies have been conducted of this issue. We will attempt to fill this gap in the literature in our analyses below.

Educational Interventions

Several studies have looked directly at the question of whether the provision of information through education programs can affect eating patterns. The existing evidence suggests that a wide variety of interventions can successfully improve young children's eating patterns. For example, Harrell et al. (1996) find that both classroom and individual nutrition education had positive effects on third- and fourth-grade children in terms of reducing blood cholesterol levels. Glenny et al. (1997) report similar results for family therapy and other interventions aimed at lifestyle modification.

Evaluations of the federal Nutrition Education and Training Program (NET), which provides grants to states that implement nutrition-education programs in their schools, have found that it is much easier to improve nutrition knowledge than it is to affect behavior. However, some evaluations of school-based programs have shown that children's willingness to try new foods offered in school lunches and the quality of snacks chosen away from home improved and that children were more likely to consume fruits, vegetables, protein foods, and foods with vitamin A. Poor children have been shown to be more likely to consume dairy products and foods with vitamin C as a result of school nutrition-education programs. Longer programs (e.g., fifty classroom hours or more) have been found to have greater effects on behavior (Contento, Manning, and Shannon 1992).

The Personal Responsibility and Work Opportunity Reconciliation Act of 1996 beefed up the nutrition-education component of the FSP considerably. Nutrition-education spending increased from $32.7 million in fiscal year 1997 to a projected $75 million in fiscal year 1999. In response to the

Healthy Meals for Healthy Americans Act, the USDA has also implemented the School Meals Initiative for Healthy Children to provide nutrition education to both children and food-service staff (Hamilton and Fox 2000).

Thus, public investments in nutrition education have grown considerably in the past few years, and it would be useful to know whether these investments can be expected to "pay off" in the form of improved eating habits. These investments can be contrasted with alternative approaches designed to promote the provision of nutrition information by the private sector.

A number of studies by Pauline Ippolito and Alan Mathios (1990, 1995, 1996) have examined the effects of attempts by both the government and advertisers to inform the public about the health benefits of diets low in fat and high in fiber. They argue that government efforts to get this message out during the 1970s were relatively unsuccessful (perhaps because they were underfunded?). But, in the mid-1980s, the Federal Trade Commission and the Food and Drug Administration relaxed rules that had prevented food manufacturers from making health claims for their products. Ippolito and Mathios show that, after declining very slowly between 1977 and 1985, the consumption of fats and cholesterol fell dramatically between 1985 and 1990 while the consumption of cereals rich in fiber increased. The Nutrition Labeling and Education Act of 1990 is apparently also influencing consumer choices (Ippolito and Mathios 1993).

10.1.5   International Comparisons

The evidence on the negative long-term effects of obesity is international in scope. For example, Mossberg (1989) reports the results of a forty-year follow-up of a sample of Swedes who were obese as children. Forty-seven percent of this sample remained obese. Power, Lake, and Cole (1997) provide an overview of similar evidence for the United Kingdom. Both studies also find an elevated mortality risk among adults who were obese as children, even among those who later slimmed down. Similarly, Post et al. (1997) report that Dutch children with a high fat diet were more likely to develop high cholesterol as adults, regardless of whether they remained obese. Gonzalez-Requejo et al. (1995) report that, in a sample of Spanish children, those with high-fat diets had higher blood cholesterol and lipid levels, which themselves can cause heart damage over time.

Similarly, the available evidence suggests that the increase in the prevalence of obesity over time is not an exclusively U.S. phenomena. Similar findings have been reported in England, particularly in the twenty-seven-year-old National Study of Health and Growth (Rona 1995). For example, Hughes et al. (1997) report that triceps skin-fold measurements from samples of five- to eleven-year-old English and Scottish children increased by 7–8 percent between 1972 and 1994. This problem is especially acute for minority populations within England, except for Caribbean blacks (Chinn, Hughes, and Rona 1998). As in the United States, there is concern that adolescents eat too much junk food: "The average 11–12 year old consumes three portions of crisps, six cans of soft drink, seven bars of chocolate or other biscuits and seven puddings every week" (Shepard and Dennison 1996, 347).

Other countries have similar problems with increasing trends in child obesity. Barth et al. (1997) report that, between 1985 and 1995, the ninetieth percentile of BMI for children taken from a sample of German pediatric hospitals increased by 5 kilograms per meter squared for males and 2.5 kilograms per meter squared for females, a dramatic rise. Seidell (1995) reports that increasing obesity is a problem throughout Europe, but especially in the Southern and Eastern European countries. Even in China, where the trend has been toward improving the nutrition status of children, there have been recent increases in obesity prevalence among adolescents (Wang, Popkin, and Zhai 1998).[12]

As in the United States, it is rare to find vitamin deficiencies in most European countries. For example, de Bree et al. (1997) review studies of vitamin B_{12} and folate deficiency in Europe and find that mean intake levels of these nutrients meet or exceed recommended levels in most European countries. However, just as in the United States, there is concern that some pregnant women may not be getting enough extra folate (found in green leafy vegetables) to prevent neural-tube defects in their babies.

In Europe, as in the United States, there is evidence that a substantial number of women may be iron deficient. Hallberg (1995) reviews the literature on the iron-deficiency status of Europeans. He reports that, in Europe, estimates of the prevalence of iron deficiency among menstruating females range between 11 and 45 percent, depending on the country and also on the particular measure of iron-deficiency status used in the study. In general, studies that focus on younger age groups tend to find higher prevalence rates. If these studies are accurate, they indicate that iron deficiency is a much greater problem in Europe than it is in the United States.[13]

12. Anorexia nervosa is apparently less prevalent in Europe than it is in the United States. For example, using the British General Practice Research Database, Turnbull et al. (1996) estimate that the prevalence of anorexia in England is 4.2 cases per 100,000 population. In a study of nearly twenty-five hundred Austrian, German, and Hungarian college students, Szabo and Tury (1995) report that not one person met the DSM-III-R (APA 1987) criteria for a diagnosis of anorexia nervosa (DSM-III-R is the predecessor to DSM-IV [APA 1994]). Not surprisingly, then, anorexia nervosa has not enjoyed the scholarly interest in Europe that it has in the United States.

13. However, Hallberg (1995) points out that some of the prevalence studies are methodologically flawed because they do not account for the fact that measurements of iron deficiency spuriously rise if subjects have a cold (or other insults to the immune system). Accounting for this, he reduces the prevalence estimate of one of the studies that he reviews by half.

10.2   Nutrition as an Investment in Human-Capital Formation

Grossman (1972) offers a model of health as a form of human capital that is "produced" by investing in certain activities. Health is treated as a durable-stock variable that depreciates with age and that can be improved by investing in health-producing activities, such as adopting a healthy diet. In his model, a consumer's utility depends on the stock of health rather than on the consumption of any of the investment goods per se. However, this restriction can easily be relaxed to allow consumers to obtain utility from the consumption of "investment" goods (e.g., hamburgers) as well as from health outcomes.

Consumers choose a stream of health investments with the aim of maximizing lifetime utility. In making these choices, they are constrained both by what they know about the production of health capital (the human-capital production function) and by their budget constraints. The key equilibrium condition in Grossman's model is that consumers choose their stream of investments to equate the marginal cost of the investment (which includes the lost utility from choosing carrots over cookies) with the present value of the marginal benefit of that investment.

Grossman's model generates an important prediction about patterns of health stocks and investments over the life cycle. If the rate of depreciation of health stocks increases with age, then health investments will increase with age, as long as the elasticity of the marginal efficiency of health investment is less than 1.[14] Since children and adolescents have the highest stock of health capital and the lowest rates of depreciation, the model predicts that, conditional on the resources and information available to them, they will be less likely than adults to choose a healthy diet. As a practical matter, the food choices of young children may be determined largely by what their parents provide for them to eat. Thus, one might well expect adolescents, who enjoy increasing autonomy from their parents, to make the worst food choices.

Of course, poor food choices in adolescents are a matter of concern largely because they may forecast a lifetime of poor eating habits. An explanation for the persistence of poor eating habits that is consistent with the Grossman model is that food choices are determined largely by information and resource constraints rather than by health depreciation rates and that these constraints show persistence over the life cycle (i.e., the children of the poor and uneducated are more likely to be poor and uneducated). A second possible explanation (see O'Donahue and Rabin, chap. 1 in this volume) is that teenagers rationally decide that they can afford to subsist on hamburgers and french fries for the moment but underestimate how difficult it will be to lose their taste for these foods later on.

---

14. That is, a 10 percent increase in health investment improves health by less than 10 percent.

These considerations suggest estimation of an input demand function, or health outcome function, of the following form:

(1) $\text{OUTCOME} = a_0 + a_1\text{INFO} + a_2\text{RESOURCE} + a_3 X + e,$

where INFO represents variables that affect the information available to the decision maker, RESOURCE is a vector of variables affecting resource constraints, X is a variable of other variables that may affect the outcome in question (such as gender), and e is an error term that is assumed to be uncorrelated with the other right-hand-side variables in the model.

10.3 Data

Our main source of data is NHANES III. This nationally representative survey was conducted between October 1988 and October 1994 and over-sampled blacks and Mexican Americans. NHANES is unique in that it combines demographic information, data from a standard clinical exam conducted by doctors (including blood and urine tests), questions about dietary intakes, information about participation in the FSP, the NLSP, and the SBP, and questions on food insecurity. Our sample includes all those who were aged twelve to sixteen at the time of the survey and who had nonmissing explanatory variables.[15] These restrictions yield a sample of 1,358 youths.

Means of the outcome variables that we consider are given in table 10.2, for everyone and by gender, race, and ethnicity. Precise definitions of these variables are given in the appendix. These means indicate that, as discussed above, anemia is rare and is found primarily among black girls. However, vitamin deficiencies are surprisingly common, affecting 9 percent of the sample. It is interesting that Hispanics are less likely than blacks or whites to suffer from these deficiencies. Obesity is also common, especially among blacks and Hispanics. In the table, we show 100 minus the HEI (so that high numbers for any of our outcomes are always "bad"). This measure of the composition of the diet indicates that blacks have worse diets than whites or Hispanics on average but that the differences are not large. Blacks are also more likely than are whites to have high sweets consumption, while Hispanics are less likely. Finally, blacks and Hispanics are much more likely than are whites to report that they suffer from food insecurity: the fractions are 4, 12, and 9 percent for whites, blacks, and Hispanics, respectively.

The second half of table 10.2 examines the relations between these variables. If, for example, it was true that those with vitamin deficiencies also

---

15. Unfortunately, older adolescents were asked somewhat different questions (they completed the adult questionnaire rather than the youth questionnaire), and it proved impossible to integrate them into the sample. For example, questions about food frequencies were asked only of the twelve- to sixteen-year-old sample.

Table 10.2   Means of Outcome Variables and Fraction with One Problem Who Also Have Another

A. Means

	All	Male	Female	White	Black	Hispanic
Anemia	.035	.005	.069	.019	.122	.019
Short any vitamin (A, C, E)	.089	.100	.078	.093	.107	.063
High blood cholesterol	.048	.032	.065	.032	.075	.099
Obese	.089	.066	.113	.075	.134	.146
100—Healthy Eating Index	40.3	44.5	35.7	39.9	43.8	38.8
	(.420)	(.563)	(.563)	(.780)	(.670)	(.864)
High sweets	.243	.239	.248	.232	.324	.147
Food insecure	.055	.062	.048	.038	.115	.092
No. of observations	1,358	622	736	371	527	402

B. Fraction with One Problem Who Also Have Another

	Anemic	Short Vitamins	High Cholesterol	Obese	100 HEI	High Sweets	Food Insecure
Anemic	1	.096	.053	.104	39.4	.241	.089
Short vitamins	.038	1	.016	.102	43.5	.283	.062
High blood cholesterol	.039	.030	1	.183	39.3	.168	.121
High BMI	.041	.103	.098	1	41.5	.111	.110
HEI ≤ 25th percentile	.032	.110	.032	.103	60.9	.235	.083
High sweets	.035	.104	.033	.040	38.1	1	.069
Food insecure	.057	.100	.105	.176	43.8	.302	1
No. of observations	100	150	81	172	341	353	133

Note: Standard errors are given in parentheses. Means are calculated using sampling weights.

usually suffered from food insecurity, then it would not be necessary to examine the two measures separately. Instead, table 10.2 shows that, while there are nutrition problems that tend to be found together, our measures of nutrition quality do seem to measure different dimensions of "misnutrition." Moreover, measures of deficiencies and food insecurity are often related to overconsumption of calories and sweets. For example, among those who are short vitamins, 4 percent are anemic, and 6 percent are food insecure, but 10 percent are obese, and a surprising 28 percent consume too many sweets. Thus, for many youths, being vitamin deficient is less a matter of consuming too little food than a matter of consuming the wrong types of food. The results for food insecurity are also striking. Of youths suffering from food insecurity, 10 percent have high blood-cholesterol levels, 18 percent are obese, and 30 percent consume too many sweets. Thus, although these youths do not always know where their next meal is coming from, on average they are consuming too much sugar and fat and too many calories overall.

Means of the explanatory variables that we consider are shown in table 10.3, arranged by whether respondents had one of four types of nutrition problem. Of the potential explanatory variables that we observe, education of the head is the most obvious indicator of the extent of nutrition information that is likely to be available to the household. The age of the head may also be important if there are cohort effects in the ability of household heads to assimilate new information and pass it on to their children. Immigrant parents may also bring with them different information about foods than native-born parents do. Urban residents may have greater exposure to new information as well as to a wider array of products.[16]

An additional measure that we consider is the youth's exposure to television, measured by the number of hours of television that he or she watched on the previous day. While the decision to watch television is clearly an endogenous choice, it also affects the youth's store of nutrition information via passive exposure to advertising messages. These messages generally promote the consumption of sweet, high-fat food and drink. And, evidently, television watching will reduce the number of calories expended if it takes the place of less sedentary activities.

The most natural measure of resources is household income, and an

16. On the other hand, a large literature on urban food prices argues that people in poor inner-city neighborhoods pay more for food than do those in more affluent neighborhoods. This literature suggests that people in poor urban neighborhoods may find things like fresh fruits and vegetables prohibitively expensive. Hayes (1999) reviews this literature and argues that most of it is flawed by the use of "samples of convenience" rather than random samples. Using data from a stratified random sample of stores in New York City, he finds no differences in food prices between the inner city and other areas. The USDA recently reported that 90 percent of the poverty population lives in an area with at least one supermarket and that supermarkets in poor areas do not charge more than those in other areas (Mantovani et al. 1997).

Table 10.3 Means of Explanatory Variables

	Short Vitamins		Obese		100 HEI		Food Insecure	
	No	Yes	No	Yes	< 25	> 75	No	Yes
Education head	12.6	11.95	12.6	11.1	12.0	12.8	12.6	10.1
	(.086)	(.217)	(.086)	(.195)	(.144)	(.178)	(.083)	(.282)
Age head	40.4	39.0	40.4	39.3	39.6	40.9	40.4	37.9
	(.205)	(.619)	(.203)	(.666)	(.406)	(.363)	(.207)	(.457)
Urban	.486	.347	.470	.515	.394	.554	.473	.484
	(.014)	(.039)	(.014)	(.038)	(.027)	(.027)	(.014)	(.043)
Immigrant	.149	.127	.148	.137	.148	.170	.147	.142
	(.102)	(.027)	(.010)	(.026)	(.019)	(.020)	(.010)	(.030)
Income less than 1.3 times poverty line	.288	.382	.276	.498	.333	.241	.266	.811
	(.013)	(.040)	(.013)	(.038)	(.026)	(.023)	(.0126)	(.034)
Female head	.210	.287	.202	.367	.250	.178	.190	.671
	(.012)	(.037)	(.012)	(.037)	(.023)	(.021)	(.011)	(.041)
Household size	4.68	4.46	4.68	4.44	4.60	4.80	4.64	4.98
	(.044)	(.125)	(.044)	(.118)	(.094)	(.077)	(.043)	(.150)
Mother's BMI	25.7	26.9	25.6	28.1	26.3	24.6	25.7	26.5
	(.160)	(.502)	(.158)	(.522)	(.298)	(.288)	(.160)	(.520)
Hours television viewing	2.91	3.32	2.87	3.71	3.06	2.55	2.94	3.01
	(.052)	(.154)	(.053)	(.143)	(.103)	(.098)	(.052)	(.162)
Food stamps	.158	.209	.148	.312	.163	.121	.152	.341
	(.010)	(.033)	(.010)	(.035)	(.020)	(.018)	(.010)	(.041)
No. of times school lunch/week	3.14	3.56	3.16	3.39	3.56	2.92	3.17	3.42
	(.063)	(.167)	(.063)	(.161)	(.114)	(.119)	(.062)	(.177)
No. of times school breakfast/week	.484	.508	.451	.840	.533	.419	.462	.895
	(.040)	(.113)	(.039)	(.134)	(.077)	(.069)	(.039)	(.156)
No. of observations	1,208	150	−1,186	172	341	340	1,225	133

Note: Standard errors are given in parentheses. Means are computed using sample weights.

indicator equal to 1 if the household's income is below 1.3 times the poverty line is included in table 10.3. This is the cutoff for free school meals and for participation in the FSP. Additional indicators of household resources include whether the family is female headed and indicators for household size. Participation in food and nutrition programs can also be expected to increase the resources available to the household. However, because the families who select into these programs are likely to differ from families who do not, one may well find that participation is associated with poorer nutrition outcomes, even if the programs have positive effects. Finally, we have included mother's BMI as an indicator of the parent's health status (and thus of the child's endowment).[17]

Table 10.3 provides an initial look at whether these explanatory variables appear to be related to nutrition outcomes. Youths with poorer nutrition outcomes come, on average, from households with poorer, younger, less-educated, and often female heads. These differences are particularly large when we compare youths who suffer from food insecurity with other youths. Misnourished youths also tend to watch more television than others. For example, obese youths typically watched almost one hour more of television in the previous evening than did other youths. Compared to youths from other households, youths from households that use food stamps are more likely to be short vitamins, to be obese, and to suffer food insecurity. However, they do score better on the HEI. The (unconditional) differences in the use of school nutrition programs show similar patterns. Thus, although participation in food and nutrition programs may narrow gaps in nutrition outcomes between participants and nonparticipants, it does not appear to close them.

10.4 Results

10.4.1 Baseline Estimates

Estimates from baseline models of the form (1) appear in table 10.4. Increased education of the head is associated with a reduced incidence of obesity, better overall diet quality, and lower sweets consumption as well as with a reduced probability of food insecurity. The estimates indicate, for example, that youths in households with college-educated heads would be 4 percentage points less likely to be obese than are those in households with high-school–educated heads. There is little evidence of cohort effects, although older heads are somewhat less likely to be food insecure. Being urban reduces the probability of being short vitamins but also increases

17. In earlier work, we also included father's BMI as well as indicators equal to 1 if either parent had high blood pressure, stroke, or diabetes. We found that it was difficult to sort out the separate effects of these variables as they were all positively correlated. An additional problem was that father's BMI is often missing. Hence, we focus only on mother's BMI.

Table 10.4 **Baseline Estimates**

	Anemia (1)	Short Vitamins (2)	High Cholesterol (3)	Obese (4)	100 HEI (5)	High Sweets (6)	Food Insecure (7)
Education head	-.0003 (.144)	-.004 (1.496)	.002 (.761)	-.010 (3.48)	-.518 (3.39)	-.013 (2.801)	-.007 (2.93)
Age head	.001 (1.395)	-.002 (1.536)	-.0002 (.256)	-.001 (1.28)	-.089 (1.56)	-.0006 (.385)	-.002 (1.85)
Urban	.004 (.418)	-.033 (1.994)	-.002 (.201)	.036 (2.29)	-2.02 (2.40)	-.024 (.965)	.006 (.486)
Immigrant	-.004 (.203)	.026 (.903)	.038 (1.748)	-.031 (1.08)	-2.95 (1.98)	.048 (1.01)	-.029 (1.29)
Income less than 1.3 times poverty line	-.003 (.214)	.020 (.939)	.059 (3.804)	.034 (1.65)	1.60 (1.49)	-.047 (1.49)	.071 (4.45)
Female head	.004 (.278)	.013 (.556)	-.014 (.848)	.022 (.976)	.120 (.103)	-.011 (.337)	.113 (6.50)
Household size	.002 (.618)	-.005 (.942)	-.007 (1.619)	-.011 (2.14)	-.294 (1.05)	.009 (1.07)	.014 (3.24)
Mother's BMI	.001 (.101)	.025 (1.75)	.005 (.434)	.055 (4.01)	2.43 (3.37)	-.064 (3.02)	-.007 (.681)
Male	-.061 (6.22)	.019 (1.20)	-.031 (2.726)	-.046 (3.02)	8.93 (11.24)	-.012 (.516)	.002 (1.85)
Black	.098 (6.46)	-.005 (.198)	.026 (1.445)	.007 (.313)	2.99 (2.45)	.109 (3.04)	.002 (.090)
Hispanic	-.005 (.279)	-.055 (1.85)	.033 (1.526)	.032 (1.09)	-.420 (.278)	-.113 (2.57)	.011 (.504)
Other	.018 (.710)	-.047 (1.16)	-.002 (.073)	-.032 (.808)	3.98 (1.95)	.097 (1.61)	-.001 (.038)
Constant	.003 (.058)	.176 (2.32)	.044 (.781)	.175 (2.36)	41.09 (10.57)	.567 (4.98)	.099 (1.72)
R^2	.069	.021	.033	.058	.130	.032	.121

Note: *t*-statistics are given in parentheses. There were 1,358 observations in all regressions.

the probability of being obese. Children of immigrants are more likely to have high blood cholesterol but also have healthier diets overall, as measured by the HEI.[18]

It is striking that, while poverty is associated both with higher blood-cholesterol levels and obesity, it is not a significant determinant of either of our deficiency measures (short vitamins or anemia). Poverty is associated with food insecurity, however, as is female headship and a larger household size. Mother's obesity is associated with adolescent obesity, a higher probability of being short vitamins, and poorer overall diet quality, as one might expect. However, it may be surprising to see that youths with obese mothers consume fewer sweets, perhaps in an attempt to avoid obesity themselves.

There are also some significant differences by race, gender, and ethnicity that are generally consistent with the differences shown in table 10.2 above. Males have worse overall diet quality than do females and are more likely to report food insecurity. However, females are more likely to suffer from anemia, high blood cholesterol, and obesity. Blacks have poorer-quality diets and consume more sweets. Hispanics have better diet quality and are less likely to be short vitamins. They also consume fewer sweets. There are many potential explanations for these differences, including differences in teenage metabolism between boys and girls and differences in socioeconomic status. These racial and ethnic differences are explored in further detail in table 10.7 below.

In summary, if we group our dependent variables into those representing deprivation, obesity, and overall diet quality, table 10.4 supports the following generalizations. First, both education and income have important effects on our outcome measures. The effects of education are always positive (where they are significant), while effects of poverty are always negative. Second, education affects some outcomes that do not seem to be sensitive to income, and vice versa. To be more specific, measures of household resources are important determinants of food insecurity but have little effect on actual nutrition deficiencies, such as anemia and vitamin deficiencies. Information, as proxied by the education of the household head, plays an important role in the determination of overall diet quality, the prevention of obesity, and the reduction of food insecurity. Other variables, such as urbanicity, immigrant status, and mother's BMI, also play significant roles in the determination of some nutrition outcomes, but it is difficult to determine whether this reflects information or resource effects, or both.

---

18. The finding on immigrant status complements the conclusions of a recent National Research Council/Institute of Medicine (1998) report on the health status of immigrant children, which concluded that, despite poorer economic status, the health of immigrant children tends to be better than that of native-born children and to decline with assimilation.

10.4.2   Effects of Television and of Food and Nutrition Programs

The estimated effects of two sets of potentially endogenous explanatory variables are shown in table 10.5. Panels A and B report estimates from two separate sets of regression. In the first panel, the variables representing hours of television watched were added to models identical to those shown in table 10.4 above, while, in the second panel, variables indicating participation in food and nutrition programs were added to these models. For the sake of brevity, only the coefficients on the added variables are shown.

Effects of Television

Excessive television watching is associated with some very negative effects on diet quality. While we found no statistically significant effects among youths who reported watching two to four hours of television the previous evening, those who had watched five or more hours were more likely to be short vitamins, had poorer overall diet quality, and had a higher BMI than other youths. On the other hand, these youths consumed fewer sweets (although this effect is only marginally statistically significant) and were less likely to report food insecurity.

These observations are consistent with those of Gortmaker et al. (1996). There are many ways in which television watching can affect obesity. It is possible that the information content of the programming and especially of the advertising plays a role, by enticing people to eat junk food. Alternatively, one can view advances in television technology as something that makes this sedentary form of recreation more attractive than other, more active ways in which people could spend their leisure hours.

Of course, the correlations that we find do not prove that television watching causes poor dietary habits or obesity. It is possible that both are caused by some third, unobserved factor, such as a low value attached to health or a lack of information about healthy lifestyles. Without an exogenous source of variation in the data, it will be difficult to demonstrate a causal linkage.

Effects of Food and Nutrition Programs

The second panel of table 10.5 contains initial estimates of the effects of participation in food and nutrition programs on nutrition outcomes. These estimates may also be biased by unobserved variables. For example, if youths in observationally similar nonparticipating households are actually less needy, then these estimates may be biased toward finding negative or nil effects of participation. On the other hand, if youths in observationally similar households do not participate because they lack information about the programs or because their parents place less value on good nutrition, then these estimates will overstate the positive effects of the programs.

Table 10.5   Effects of Television and Nutrition Programs

	Anemia (1)	Short Vitamins (2)	High Cholesterol (3)	Obese (4)	100 HEI (5)	High Sweets (6)	Food Insecure (7)
			A. Television Watching				
2–4 hours yesterday	.008	.007	−.007	.015	.489	−.001	−.018
	(.752)	(.427)	(.549)	(.919)	(.568)	(.043)	(1.38)
Over 5 hours yesterday	−.014	.077	.001	.086	3.92	−.071	−.051
	(.838)	(2.93)	(.026)	(3.36)	(2.92)	(1.79)	(2.58)
R^2	.070	.027	.034	.066	.135	.034	.125
			B. Food and Nutrition Programs				
Food stamps	.001	−.009	.018	.034	−1.04	−.069	−.064
	(.059)	(.327)	(.942)	(1.32)	(.770)	(1.73)	(3.18)
School breakfast 1–4 times/week	−.021	.036	−.003	.036	−2.98	.025	.033
	(.928)	(.984)	(.109)	(1.03)	(1.62)	(.456)	(1.21)
School breakfast 5 times/week	.015	−.027	.057	.051	−3.48	.044	−.0002
	(.739)	(.843)	(2.39)	(1.61)	(2.10)	(.905)	(.010)
School lunch 1–4 times/week	−.045	.007	.039	−.011	−1.42	.015	.007
	(3.08)	(.303)	(2.27)	(.464)	(1.20)	(.443)	(.403)
School lunch 5 times/week	−.020	.013	−.020	−.003	−.581	.007	−.019
	(1.62)	(.669)	(1.34)	(.160)	(.569)	(.236)	(1.29)
R^2	.077	.023	.047	.051	.136	.034	.131

*Note: t-*statistics are given in parentheses. All models include all the variables listed in table 10.4 above and 1,358 observations.

In any case, the estimates suggest that the FSP has little effect on measures of deficiencies, obesity, or dietary quality, although it is associated with reductions in food insecurity. School lunch is associated with a lower prevalence of anemia, which is encouraging given that these meals aim to provide iron. School breakfast and lunch are, however, both associated with higher cholesterol levels, although school breakfast is also associated with slightly better overall diet quality.

Table 10.6 lays out the results of an attempt to address the endogeneity of school nutrition program participation using difference-in-difference methods. The identification in panels A and B comes from the fact that, while children may be income eligible for school meals year-round, the meals are provided only while school is in session.[19] Thus, after controlling for the main effects of eligibility and of school being in session, the interaction term can be interpreted as measuring "exposure" to school meals. Panel A measures exposure to free school meals by defining the eligible as those with incomes less than or equal to 1.3 times the federal poverty line. Panel B measures exposure to free or reduced-price meals by using 1.85 times the federal poverty line as the income eligibility cutoff.

Panel A suggests that exposure to free school meals improves the overall quality of the diet, although it has no significant effect on our measures of deficiencies (anemia and being short vitamins), obesity, or food insecurity. The magnitude of the improvement is enough to offset the negative effect of simple eligibility (i.e., poverty) on diet quality. Panel B indicates that, in addition to improving overall diet quality, exposure to free or reduced-price school meals reduces blood cholesterol (which is increased by poverty) and sweets consumption. Since the difference between panel A and panel B is that the latter includes children with incomes between 1.3 and 1.85 times the federal poverty line in the eligible group, these results suggest that the reduction in cholesterol and sweets intake is concentrated in this group. These generally positive results of exposure to school meals suggest that, despite the fact that these meals have been found to be high in cholesterol and sodium, they are healthier than the meals that youths would eat in the absence of school meal programs.

10.4.3   Differences by Race and Ethnicity

As noted above, we estimated all our models separately by race and ethnicity. These estimates are shown in table 10.7. Note that, since blacks and Hispanics were oversampled in NHANES III, we actually have larger

19. Some youths may participate in the Summer Food Service Program, which provides meals similar to those of the NLSP or the SBP during the summer months and is often run through the schools. However, the caseload is small relative to the NLSP or the SBP. In the summer of 1998, the program served 2.3 million children per day, compared to the 14.7 million children per day who participated in the NLSP and the 6.8 million who participated in the SBP during the 1997–98 school year.

Table 10.6   Difference-in-Differences Evaluations of the Effects of School Nutrition Programs

	Anemia (1)	Short Vitamins (2)	High Cholesterol (3)	Obese (4)	100 HEI (5)	High Sweets (6)	Food Insecure (7)
A. Eligible for Free School Meals							
Eligible	−.019	−.004	.090	.050	5.82	.019	.086
	(.847)	(.099)	(.027)	(1.39)	(3.12)	(3.51)	(3.11)
School in session	−.033	.010	−.022	−.021	1.83	.086	.006
	(2.39)	(.477)	(1.39)	(.972)	(1.64)	(2.64)	(.352)
Eligible × in session	.025	.026	−.038	−.020	−5.94	−.090	−.023
	(.988)	(.627)	(1.25)	(.496)	(2.86)	(1.47)	(.728)
R^2	.073	.020	.038	.061	.133	.037	.122
B. Eligible for Reduced-Price School Meals							
Eligible	−.010	−.008	.096	.028	2.83	.068	.078
	(.465)	(.237)	(3.99)	(.857)	(1.70)	(1.40)	(3.16)
School in session	−.050	.011	−.010	−.024	1.46	.128	.006
	(1.99)	(.458)	(.535)	(1.03)	(1.18)	(3.54)	(.332)
Eligible × in session	.011	.015	−.054	−.004	−3.09	−.159	−.014
	(.472)	(.407)	(1.99)	(.124)	(1.64)	(2.90)	(.515)
R^2	.073	.020	.040	.059	.128	.042	.122

Note: See table 10.5 above. These models did not include the indicator for income < 1.3 and poverty since this is the same as eligibility.

Table 10.7   Differences in the Effects of Information and Resources by Race and Ethnicity

	Anemia (1)	Short Vitamins (2)	High Cholesterol (3)	Obese (4)	100 HEI (5)	High Sweets (6)	Food Insecure (7)
White							
Education head	.002	-.002	.002	-.016	-.950	-.011	-.004
	(.554)	(.257)	(.431)	(2.97)	(3.14)	(1.22)	(.969)
Age head	.001	-.004	-.001	-.003	-.137	-.002	-.001
	(1.08)	(1.46)	(.926)	(1.20)	(1.19)	(.640)	(.810)
Urban	-.012	-.045	-.020	.042	-2.52	-.033	.006
	(.820)	(1.38)	(1.03)	(1.50)	(1.63)	(.703)	(.319)
Immigrant	.033	.145	.009	-.088	-2.70	.014	-.034
	(.904)	(1.86)	(.189)	(1.31)	(.729)	(.127)	(.733)
Income less than 1.3 times poverty line	.0002	.048	.045	.119	.372	-.038	.027
	(.013)	(1.07)	(1.64)	(3.08)	(1.75)	(.576)	(1.01)
Female head	.001	-.020	-.010	-.056	-1.22	.019	.209
	(.041)	(.394)	(.326)	(1.27)	(.507)	(.253)	(6.86)
Household size	.004	-.012	.005	-.022	-.651	.024	-.020
	(.685)	(1.02)	(.629)	(2.09)	(1.12)	(1.37)	(2.77)
Mother's BMI	-.001	.002	.000	.006	.268	-.007	-.001
	(.914)	(.742)	(.086)	(2.26)	(1.90)	(1.63)	(.329)
Male	-.040	.023	-.018	-.057	8.73	-.039	.015
	(2.79)	(.762)	(.955)	(2.15)	(5.98)	(.864)	(.818)
Constant	-.012	.250	.048	.344	49.72	.577	.010
	(.165)	(1.61)	(.508)	(2.55)	(6.72)	(2.54)	(.107)
R^2	.033	.035	.020	.105	.178	.021	.186

Black

	(1)	(2)	(3)	(4)	(5)	(6)	(7)
Education head	−.006	−.002	−.0004	.002	−.150	−.015	.001
	(1.01)	(.369)	(.076)	(.352)	(.490)	(1.61)	(.200)
Age head	.0004	.002	.0004	.001	−.037	.002	−.001
	(.252)	(1.27)	(.278)	(.663)	(.480)	(.643)	(−.775)
Urban	.072	.045	.005	.042	.317	−.008	−.016
	(2.52)	(1.63)	(.198)	(1.41)	(.231)	(.186)	(.574)
Immigrant	−.050	−.027	−.026	−.045	−6.04	−.060	.089
	(.944)	(.515)	(.576)	(.800)	(2.34)	(.752)	(1.69)
Income less than 1.3 times poverty line	.015	.019	.010	−.042	−.229	−.025	.150
	(.489)	(.625)	(.394)	(1.27)	(.152)	(.535)	(4.87)
Female head	.023	.070	−.032	.065	−2.37	−.002	−.033
	(.742)	(2.34)	(1.26)	(2.03)	(1.60)	(.037)	(1.09)
Household size	−.001	−.001	−.005	.007	.066	.001	−.005
	(.095)	(.129)	(.788)	(.861)	(.166)	(.050)	(.616)
Mother's BMI	.001	−.000	.004	.010	.016	−.003	.001
	(.364)	(.016)	(2.51)	(4.57)	(.164)	(.925)	(.570)
Male	−.166	.022	−.061	−.102	4.58	.055	.003
	(5.98)	(.800)	(2.66)	(3.53)	(3.42)	(1.33)	(.116)
Constant	.188	−.020	.010	−.226	45.72	.511	.073
	(1.30)	(.142)	(.086)	(1.50)	(6.56)	(2.38)	(.511)
R^2	.084	.026	.031	.077	.036	.014	.060

(continued)

Table 10.7 (continued)

	Anemia (1)	Short Vitamins (2)	High Cholesterol (3)	Obese (4)	100 HEI (5)	High Sweets (6)	Food Insecure (7)
Hispanic							
Education head	−.003	−.008	.009	−.005	−.025	−.006	−.020
	(1.61)	(2.03)	(2.00)	(.971)	(.106)	(1.19)	(4.86)
Age head	−.001	−.002	.006	−.002	−.052	.006	−.004
	(1.19)	(1.06)	(3.33)	(.772)	(.507)	(2.66)	(2.54)
Urban	−.006	.048	.039	.051	−3.08	−.050	.015
	(.391)	(1.83)	(1.26)	(1.35)	(1.85)	(1.33)	(.508)
Immigrant	−.019	−.028	.092	.066	−3.92	−.007	−.140
	(1.22)	(1.04)	(2.84)	(1.69)	(2.27)	(.186)	(.473)
Income less than 1.3 times poverty line	−.017	−.004	.089	−.115	2.09	−.039	.090
	(1.08)	(.147)	(2.65)	(2.83)	(1.17)	(.952)	(2.94)
Female head	−.013	−.011	.089	.172	7.01	−.060	.054
	(.677)	(.334)	(2.30)	(3.65)	(3.38)	(1.28)	(1.51)
Household size	.007	.014	−.026	−.005	−1.15	.029	.019
	(1.35)	(1.64)	(2.53)	(.367)	(2.09)	(2.35)	(2.04)
Mother's BMI	.000	.003	−.002	−.002	.650	−.007	−.005
	(.004)	(1.54)	(.645)	(.512)	(4.73)	(2.28)	(2.27)
Male	−.031	−.007	−.030	.017	12.30	.080	.137
	(2.21)	(.265)	(1.03)	(.473)	(7.77)	(2.22)	(5.06)
Constant	.105	.104	−.206	.135	25.06	.045	.467
	(1.48)	(.827)	(1.38)	(.745)	(3.16)	(.249)	(3.43)
R^2	.039	.050	.117	.067	.252	.073	.215

Note: t-statistics are given in parentheses. There are 371 whites, 527 blacks, and 402 Hispanics.

samples of these groups than we do of whites. The effects of information and resources differ substantially between the three groups. For example, among whites, education reduces the incidence of obesity and improves the overall quality of the diet. Among Hispanics, education reduces the probability of being short vitamins and of being food insecure but has a small positive effect on the incidence of high blood cholesterol. Among blacks, education of the head has no statistically significant effects. Similarly, we find evidence of cohort effects only for Hispanics—for them, increases in the age of the household head are associated with higher cholesterol and sweets intake but also with a lower probability of food insecurity. Urban residence is associated with a higher probability of anemia among blacks but with lower probabilities of being short vitamins and higher overall diet quality among Hispanics. Being an immigrant is associated with higher-quality diets among blacks and Hispanics (although Hispanic immigrants are also more likely to have high cholesterol and to be obese) but with vitamin deficiencies among whites.

Turning to the effects of resource constraints, poverty increases the probability of high cholesterol and obesity among whites and is associated with worse overall diet quality. Among Hispanics, poverty is also associated with high cholesterol as well as with food insecurity. However, poverty is actually associated with a lower probability of obesity among Hispanics. Remarkably, among blacks, poverty has no effect on any outcome except food insecurity.

The contrast between the effects of income on BMI among whites and Hispanics is suggestive of the Jeffrey et al. (1991) result that obesity tends to rise with income in poor countries and to fall with income in rich countries. A possible explanation is that, in rich countries, where most jobs are sedentary, it takes money and leisure to exercise, so thinness becomes a status symbol. In poor countries, where many people engage in manual labor, fatness is the status symbol. Many Hispanics may have brought this attitude with them from their countries of origin.

Among both blacks and Hispanics, female headedness is an important predictor of problem diets—black youths in these households are more likely to be short vitamins and also to be obese. Hispanics in these households are more likely to be obese, to have high cholesterol, and to have diets of worse overall quality. Among whites, female headedness predicts food insecurity but is not related to the other outcome measures. Finally, it is interesting that larger white households are less likely to experience food insecurity while larger Hispanic households are more likely to be food insecure.

To summarize, the main conclusion to be drawn from table 10.7 is that most of our explanatory variables have quite different effects on whites, blacks, and Hispanics. Differences between whites and Hispanics in the effects of education and income are particularly striking. Essentially, education of the head appears to improve diet quality and to lower BMI only among whites. Among Hispanics, education is associated with less deprivation but also with less healthy diets. Similarly, poverty increases BMI among whites but decreases it among Hispanics. Education and income have no significant effect on deficiencies or quality of diet among blacks, although poverty does affect food security.

10.4.4 Differences by Gender

Table 10.8 shows the results of regressions similar to those of table 10.4 above except that they are estimated separately for boys and girls. There is some evidence that both information and resources are needed to explain the pattern of outcomes. Increased education of the household head improves diet quality for both boys and girls but reduces the proportion obese among girls only. For boys, increased education of the household head reduces sweets consumption and food insecurity. Girls from poor families have higher blood cholesterol, worse diet quality, and a higher probability of food insecurity than girls from richer families. Among boys, poverty is associated with a higher incidence of vitamin deficiencies and obesity but not with worse diet quality. Overall, this pattern of results suggests that, while there are some differences in the effect of these covariates for boys and girls, education generally improves nutrition status and poverty decreases it. Since the covariates do not differ markedly among boys and girls and the effects of these covariates on nutrition outcomes also do not differ markedly, the most plausible explanation for differences in outcomes across gender are biological and metabolic differences in the rate of maturation in adolescence for boys and girls.

10.4.5 Determinants of Trends in Obesity over Time

Using NHANES I, II, and III, separately, table 10.9 compares coefficients from a regression of obesity status (high BMI) on a limited set of covariates that are available in all three data sets. For all three data sets, increasing education of the household head is correlated with lower obesity prevalence, but the effect is largest in NHANES III, the most recent data set. Urban children are 3 percentage points more likely to be obese in NHANES III but not in the other data sets. Immigrant children are less likely to be obese in NHANES II and III but not in NHANES I. These patterns on the effect of urbanity and immigration status are likely due to demographic shifts in these populations over time. Larger households tend to have lower obesity prevalence in all three data sets, with the largest absolute effect in NHANES III. Children from poor households are more likely to be obese than are children from other household in NHANES III but not in NHANES I and II. Females are 3–4 percentage points more likely to be obese than are males in all three data sets, with a 1 percentage point increase in the gap in NHANES III over the other two time points.

Table 10.8   Differences in the Effects of Information and Resources by Sex

	Anemia (1)	Short Vitamins (2)	High Cholesterol (3)	Obese (4)	100 HEI (5)	High Sweets (6)	Food Insecure (7)
Females							
Education head	.0004	−.003	.003	−.016	−.57	−.0010	−.001
	(.105)	(.836)	(.840)	(3.85)	(2.78)	(1.65)	(.368)
Age head	.002	−.000	.001	−.002	−.072	.002	−.003
	(1.68)	(.227)	(.503)	(1.31)	(.937)	(1.05)	(2.44)
Urban	.008	−.008	−.014	.037	−1.06	.028	−.008
	(.417)	(.395)	(.738)	(1.52)	(.914)	(.834)	(.474)
Immigrant	−.0002	−.016	.081	−.089	−4.55	.027	.008
	(.004)	(.403)	(2.31)	(1.99)	(2.11)	(.437)	(.268)
Income less than 1.3 times poverty line	−.004	−.032	.061	−.013	2.93	−.043	.079
	(.158)	(1.21)	(2.53)	(.422)	(1.99)	(1.03)	(3.45)
Female head	.009	.032	−.053	.041	−1.93	−.012	.056
	(.339)	(1.14)	(2.05)	(1.24)	(1.21)	(.266)	(2.53)
Household size	.007	.005	−.016	−.015	−.851	.012	.010
	(1.08)	(.710)	(2.40)	(1.80)	(2.14)	(1.07)	(1.87)
Mother's BMI	.0001	.007	.004	.005	.527	−.011	−.001
	(.056)	(3.99)	(2.08)	(2.54)	(5.05)	(3.71)	(.409)
Constant	−.090	−.075	−.038	.317	36.24	.507	.099
	(1.01)	(.781)	(.426)	(2.84)	(6.72)	(3.30)	(1.32)
R^2	.062	.028	.047	.065	.107	.048	.082

(*continued*)

Table 10.8 (continued)

	Anemia (1)	Short Vitamins (2)	High Cholesterol (3)	Obese (4)	100 HEI (5)	High Sweets (6)	Food Insecure (7)
Males							
Education head	-.0001	-.005	.001	-.004	-.465	-.014	-.013
	(.096)	(.979)	(.520)	(.985)	(2.01)	(2.02)	(3.63)
Age head	-.0001	-.002	-.001	-.001	-.080	-.003	.000
	(.339)	(1.40)	(.561)	(.625)	(.963)	(1.32)	(.037)
Urban	.002	-.061	.003	.023	-3.39	-.070	.012
	(.368)	(2.27)	(1.65)	(1.06)	(2.69)	(1.83)	(.603)
Immigrant	-.007	.085	.008	.010	-1.57	.052	-.071
	(.645)	(1.92)	(.309)	(.284)	(.752)	(.814)	(2.14)
Income less than 1.3 times poverty line	.002	.069	.046	.089	-.164	-.024	.058
	(.265)	(2.07)	(2.34)	(3.24)	(.104)	(.512)	(2.34)
Female head	.0002	-.007	.027	-.004	2.08	-.005	.170
	(.019)	(.182)	(1.27)	(.148)	(1.20)	(.096)	(6.21)
Household size	-.0002	-.015	.003	-.009	.269	.005	.016
	(.087)	(1.73)	(.543)	(1.24)	(.669)	(.402)	(2.50)
Mother's BMI	-.0000	-.001	-.002	.006	-.029	-.002	-.001
	(.093)	(.647)	(1.47)	(3.17)	(.284)	(.628)	(.427)
Constant	.0080	.378	.049	.010	53.95	.587	.124
	(3.84)	(3.13)	(.690)	(.098)	(9.52)	(3.41)	(1.39)
R^2	.032	.045	.040	.068	.038	.044	.186

Note: t-statistics are given in parentheses. Regressions also include race dummies.

Table 10.9   **Trends in BMI Regression Results—NHANES, I, II, and III**

	NHANES I (1)	NHANES II (2)	NHANES III (3)
Education head	−.0036	−.0028	−.012
	(3.6)	(1.5)	(4.0)
Age head	.00024	.0016	−.0012
	(.33)	(2.2)	(1.1)
Urban	−.012	−.0037	.030
	(.99)	(.28)	(1.9)
Immigrant	.0053	−.053	−.039
	(.26)	(2.4)	(1.4)
Income less than 1.3	−.014	.013	.043
times poverty line	(.92)	(.86)	(2.1)
Female head	.0073	.0021	.018
	(.42)	(.13)	(.81)
Household size	−.0066	−.003	−.011
	(2.2)	(.90)	(2.1)
Male	−.030	−.032	−.044
	(2.7)	(3.0)	(2.9)
Black	.028	.0062	.017
	(1.6)	(.36)	(.73)
Hispanic	—	.056	.018
		(2.2)	(.67)
Constant	.22	.040	.33
	(4.1)	(.85)	(5.0)
R^2	.0194	.0191	.0445
N	1,697	1,509	1,358

Note: *t*-statistics are given in parentheses. Non-English language spoken at home is used as a proxy for immigration status in the NHANES I sample.

Finally, despite the racial differences present in figures 10.2 and 10.3 above in obesity prevalence, the regressions reveal no significant differences by race, except for Hispanics in NHANES II.

Overall, these results suggest that a structural break in the relation between the covariates and obesity prevalence occurred between NHANES II and NHANES III. In particular, the importance of both information (education of household head) and resources (poverty) in predicting obesity increased in NHANES III over the other two data points.

10.5   Conclusions

We find that, although many youths suffer from nutrient deficiencies (either anemia or vitamin deficiencies), these conditions are not generally sensitive to measures of resource constraints and hence are unlikely to be due solely to a lack of food. The only exception is in black female-headed households, where youths are more likely to be vitamin deficient. Hence, as discussed in the introduction, most U.S. youths who suffer nutrition deficiencies are "misnourished" rather than malnourished and in fact often consume too many rather than too few calories.

These results suggest that such programs as the FSP that provide additional access to food but do not attempt to alter the composition of the diet may have smaller effects on important nutrition outcomes such as overall diet quality than do school meal programs, which offer specific types of food. Our difference-in-difference estimates do in fact suggest that school nutrition programs lead to healthier diets than would otherwise be consumed. The recent reforms to the program are likely to enhance this effect.

A second noteworthy finding is that the determinants of food insecurity appear to be quite different than the determinants of nutrition deficiencies, obesity, or diet quality. In particular, resource constraints are more strongly linked to food insecurity than to the other nutrition outcomes that we examine. It is also remarkable that we find little evidence that access to school nutrition programs relieves food insecurity, at least in our difference-in-difference models. These findings suggest that it is somewhat simplistic to equate food insecurity with hunger, as is often done. Food insecurity appears to be a more complex problem, with strong relations to such social phenomena as female headedness. More generally, our results suggest that it is worthwhile to examine a range of indicators that capture different aspects of nutrition status.

Although it is difficult directly to test the hypothesis that information or technology matters, we find several pieces of evidence consistent with this idea. First, education of the head has a consistently beneficial effect in models of obesity, diet quality, and food insecurity. It is worth noting, however, that we find these effects predominantly among whites. Second, the age of the head matters in Hispanic families, with families with older heads having poorer-quality diets. This type of cohort effect is consistent with a slow diffusion of new information about nutrition through the population over time, with younger heads being more receptive to new ideas than older heads. Indeed, we find that the effect of the household head's education level on obesity prevalence increases in size in the most recent data set that we examine. Third, we find that television viewing has consistently negative effects on all our outcome measures. This could be due either to the content of the programming and advertising (i.e., advertisements for soft drinks and potato chips) or to the fact that television technology encourages people to spend their leisure hours in sedentary activity.

While the preceding summary emphasizes instances in which our explanatory variables have statistically significant effects, it is striking that, in many cases, our models have relatively little explanatory power. This finding suggests that poor nutrition is a problem for American youths regardless of family background. The very pervasiveness of the problem suggests that it is unlikely to be entirely due to a lack of household resources and that broadly based policies designed to alter the composition of the diet, either through the provision of information (e.g., through nutrition labeling) or through the direct provision of healthy food (as in the revised school lunch program), should be encouraged.

Appendix
Definitions of Outcome Variables

Sufficient Food

When asked whether they had "enough food to eat, sometimes not enough to eat, or often not enough to eat," respondents answered that they had enough food to eat.

Dietary Intakes

Healthy Eating Index. Described in text.
High sweets. Reported consuming more than thirty sweets per month.

Measures Based on Physical Examination and Laboratory Measures

Anemia. For age twelve, cutoffs were hemoglobin 11.5 g/dL and hematocrit lt 35 percent. For over twelve years, cutoffs were hemoglobin 12 g/dL and hematocrit lt 37 percent.
High blood cholesterol. Serum cholesterol gt 5.44 nmol/L.
Short vitamin C. 11.4 mmol/L.
Short vitamin A. 1.05 umol/L.
Short vitamin E. 11.6 umol/L.
Obese. 27.3 for females and 27.8 for males.

References

Albertson, A. M., R. C. Tobelmann, and L. Marquart. 1997. Estimated dietary calcium intake and food sources for adolescent females: 1980–92. *Journal of Adolescent Health* 20, no. 1:20–26.
American Psychiatric Association (APA). 1987. *Diagnostic and statistical manual of mental disorders.* 3d ed., rev. Washington, D.C.
————. 1994. *Diagnostic and statistical manual of mental disorders.* 4th ed. Washington, D.C.
Barth, N., A. Ziegler, G. W. Himmelmann, H. Coners, et al. 1997. Significant weight gains in a clinical sample of obese children and adolescents between 1985

and 1995. *International Journal of Obesity and Related Metabolic Disorders* 21, no. 2:122–26.

Beaton, G. H., J. Burema, and C. Ritenbaugh. 1997. Errors in the interpretation of dietary assessment. *American Journal of Clinical Nutrition* 65, suppl.: 1100S–1107S.

Briefel, R. R., C. T. Sempos, M. A. McDowell, S. C. Y. Chien, and K. Alaimo. 1997. Dietary methods research in the third NHANES: Underreporting of energy intake. *American Journal of Clinical Nutrition* 65, suppl.:1203S–1209S.

Butland, B. K., D. P. Strachan, and H. R. Anderson. 1999. Fresh fruit intake and asthma symptoms in young British adults: Confounding or effect modification by smoking? *European Respiratory Journal* 13, no. 4:744–50.

Centers for Disease Control (CDC). 1996. Guidelines for school programs to promote lifelong healthy eating. *Morbidity and Mortality Weekly Report* 45, no. RR-9:1–41.

———. National Health Examination Surveys. Division for Health Examination Statistics. 1999. Table 71: Overweight children and adolescents 6–17 years of age according to sex, age, race, and Hispanic origin: United States, selected years, 1963–65 and 1988–94. http://www.cdc.gov/nchs/fastats/pdf/hus98t71.pdf.

Charney, E., H. C. Goodman, M. McBride, B. Lyon, and R. Pratt. 1976. Childhood antecedents of adult obesity: Do chubby infants become obese adults? *New England Journal of Medicine* 295, no. 1:6–9.

Chinn, S., J. M. Hughes, and R. J. Rona. 1998. Trends in growth and obesity in ethnic groups in Britain. *Archives of Disease in Childhood* 78, no. 6:513–17.

Committee on Iron Deficiency. 1968. Iron deficiency in the United States. *Journal of the American Medical Association* 203:119–24.

Contento, I. R., A. D. Manning, and B. Shannon. 1992. Research perspectives on school-based nutrition education. *Journal of Nutrition Education* 24, no. 5: 247–60.

Currie, J. 2000. U.S. food and nutrition programs. University of California, Los Angeles. Working paper.

DeAngelis, C. D., R. D. Feigin, J. B. Warshaw, and J. A. McMillan. 1999. *Oski's pediatrics: Principles and practice.* 3d ed. Philadelphia: Lippincott, Williams, & Wilkins.

de Bree, A., M. van Dusseldorp, I. A. Brouwer, K. H. van het Hof, and R. P. M. Steegers-Theunissen. 1997. Folate intake in Europe: Recommended, actual, and desired intake. *European Journal of Clinical Nutrition* 51:643–60.

Devaney, B. L., A. R. Gordon, and J. A. Burghardt. 1995. Dietary intakes of students. *American Journal of Clinical Nutrition,* no. 1, suppl.205S–212S.

Foster, D. W. 1991. Anorexia nervosa and bulimia. In *Harrison's principles of internal medicine* (12th ed.), ed. J. D. Wilson, E. Braunwald, K. J. Isselbacher, R. G. Petersdorf, et al. New York: McGraw-Hill.

Frank, D. A., N. Roos, A. Meyers, M. Napoleone, et al. 1996. Seasonal variation in weight-for-age in a pediatric emergency room. *Public Health Reports* 111, no. 4:366–71.

Glenny, A. M., S. O'Meara, A. Melville, T. A. Sheldon, and C. Wilson. 1997. The treatment and prevention of obesity: A systematic review of the literature. *International Journal of Obesity and Related Metabolic Disorders* 21, no. 9:715–37.

Goldberg, G. R., A. E. Black, and S. A. Jebb. 1991. Critical evaluation of energy intake data using fundamental principles of energy physiology: 1. Derivation of cut-off limits to identify underrecording. *European Journal of Clinical Nutrition* 45:569–81.

Gonzalez-Requejo, A., M. Sanchez-Bayle, J. Baeza, P. Arnaiz, S. Vila, J. Asensio, and C. Ruiz-Jarabo. 1995. Relations between nutrient intake and serum lipid and apolipoprotein levels. *Journal of Pediatrics* 127, no. 1:53–57.

Gordon, A. R., B. L. Devaney, and J. A. Burghardt. 1995. Dietary effects of the national school lunch program and the school breakfast program. *American Journal of Clinical Nutrition* 61, no. 1:221S–231S.

Gortmaker, S. L., W. H. Dietz Jr., A. M. Sobol, and C. A. Wehler. 1987. Increasing pediatric obesity in the United States. *American Journal of Diseases of Children* 14, no. 5:535–40.

Gortmaker, S. L., A. Must, A. M. Sobol, K. Peterson, et al. 1996. Television viewing as a cause of increasing obesity among children in the United States, 1986–1990. *Archives of Pediatrics and Adolescent Medicine* 150, no. 4:356–62.

Grossman, M. 1972. On the concept of health capital and the demand for health. *Journal of Political Economy* 80, no. 2:223–55.

Hallberg, L. 1995. Results of surveys to assess iron status in Europe. *Nutrition Reviews* 53, no. 11:314–22.

Hamilton, W. and M. K. Fox. 2000. *Nutrition and health outcomes study, final report.* Cambridge Mass.: Abt.

Harrell, J. S., R. G. McMurray, S. I. Bangdiwala, A. C. Frauman, S. A. Gansky, and C. B. Bradley. 1996. Effects of a school-based intervention to reduce cardiovascular disease risk factors in elementary-school children: The Cardiovascular Health in Children (CHIC) study. *Journal of Pediatrics* 128, no. 6:797–805.

Hayes, L. 1999. Are prices higher for the poor in New York City? Working Paper no. 423. Princeton University, Industrial Relations Section, September.

Himes, J. H., and W. H. Dietz. 1994. Guidelines for overweight in adolescent preventive services: Recommendations from an expert committee, the Expert Committee on Clinical Guidelines for Overweight in Adolescent Preventive Services. *American Journal of Clinical Nutrition* 59, no. 2:307–16.

Hughes, J. M., L. Li, S. Chinn, and R. J. Rona. 1997. Trends in growth in England and Scotland, 1972 to 1994. *Archives of Disease in Childhood* 76, no. 3:152–89.

Ippolito, P., and A. Mathios. 1990. Information, advertising and health: A study of the cereal market. *Rand Journal of Economics* 21, no. 3:459–80.

———. 1993. New food labeling regulations and the flow of nutrition information to consumers. *Journal of Public Policy and Marketing* 12:188–205.

———. 1995. Information and advertising: The case of fat consumption in the United States. *American Economic Review* 85, no. 2:91–95.

———. 1996. Information and advertising policy: A study of fat and cholesterol consumption in the United States, 1977–1990. Bureau of Economics Staff Report. Washington, D.C. Federal Trade Commission.

Jeffrey, R. W., S. A. French, J. L. Forster, and V. M. Spry. 1991. Socioeconomic status differences in health behaviors related to obesity: The healthy worker project. *International Journal of Obesity* 15:689–96.

Joshipura, K. J., A. Ascherio, J. E. Manson, M. J. Stampfer, et al. 1999. Fruit and vegetable intake in relation to risk of ischemic stroke. *Journal of the American Medical Association* 282, no. 13:1233–39.

Kennedy, E., J. Ohls, S. Carlson, and K. Fleming. 1995. The Healthy Eating Index: Design and Applications. *Journal of the American Dietetic Association* 95, no. 10 (October): 1103–8.

Lampe, J. W., 1999. Health effects of vegetables and fruit: Assessing mechanisms of action in human experimental studies. *American Journal of Clinical Nutrition* 70, no. 3, suppl.:475S–490S.

Lauer, R. M., J. Lee, and W. R. Clarke. 1989. Predicting adult cholesterol levels from measurements in childhood and adolescence: The muscatine study. *Bulletin of the New York Academy of Medicine* 65, no. 10:1127–42.

Looker, A. C., P. R. Dallman, M. D. Carroll, E. W. Gunter, and C. L. Johnson. 1997. Prevalence of iron deficiency in the United States. *Journal of the American Medical Association* 277, no. 12:973–96.

Luder, E., E. Ceysens-Okada, A. Loren-Roth, et al. 1990. Health and nutrition surveys in a group of urban homeless adults. *Journal of the American Dietetic Association* 90:1387–92.

Mantovani, R. E., L. Daft, T. Macaluso, and K. Hoffman. 1997. *Food retailers in the food stamp program: Characteristics and service to participants.* Washington D.C.: Food and Nutrition Service, U.S. Department of Agriculture, February.

Middleman, A. B., S. J. Emans, and J. Cox. 1996. Nutritional vitamin B_{12} deficiency and folate deficiency in an adolescent patient presenting with anemia, weight loss, and poor school performance. *Journal of Adolescent Health* 19: 76–79.

Mossberg, H. O. 1989. 40-year follow-up of overweight children. *Lancet* 2, no. 8661:491–93.

National Research Council and Institute of Medicine. 1998. *From generation to generation: The health and well-being of children in immigrant families.* Edited by Donald Hernandez and Evan Charney. Washington D.C.: National Academy Press.

Neuhauser, L., D. Disbrow, and S. Margen. 1995. Hunger and food insecurity in California. Technical Assistance Program Report. California Policy Seminar, University of California.

Nord, M., K. Jemison, and G. Bickel. 1999. Prevalence of food insecurity and hunger by state, 1996–1998. Food and Rural Economics Division, Economic Research Service, USDA, Food Assistance and Nutrition Research Report no. 2. Washington, D.C., September.

Ogden, C. L., R. P. Troiano, R. R. Briefel, R. J. Kuczmarski, K. M. Flegal, and C. L. Johnson. 1997. Prevalence of overweight among preschool children in the United States, 1971 through 1994. *Pediatrics* 99, no. 4:E1.

Palace, V. P., N. Khaper, O. Qin, and P. K. Singal. 1999. Antioxidant potentials of vitamin A and carotenoids and their relevance to heart disease. *Free Radical Biology and Medicine* 26, nos. 5–6:746–61.

Philipson, T. and R. Posner. 1999. The long-run growth in obesity as a function of technological change. Working Paper no. 7423. Cambridge, Mass.: National Bureau of Economic Research, November.

Post, G. B., H. C. Kemper, J. Twisk, and W. van Mechelen. 1997. The association between dietary patterns and cardiovascular disease risk indicators in healthy youngsters: Results covering fifteen years of longitudinal development. *European Journal of Clinical Nutrition* 51, no. 6:387–93.

Power, C., J. K. Lake, and T. J. Cole. 1997. Body mass index and height from childhood to adulthood in the 1958 British born cohort. *American Journal of Clinical Nutrition* 66, no. 5:1094–1101.

Raiten, D. J., and K. D. Fisher, eds. 1995. Assessment of folate methodology used in the Third National Health and Nutrition Examination Survey (NHANES III, 1988–1994). *Journal of Nutrition* 125:1371S–1398S.

Rockett, H. R. H., and G. A. Colditz. 1997. Assessing diets of children and adolescents. *American Journal of Clinical Nutrition* 65, suppl.:1116S–1122S.

Rona, R. J. 1995. The National Study of Health and Growth (NSHG): 23 years on the road. *International Journal of Epidemiology* 24, suppl. 1:S69–S74.

Rose, D., and V. Oliveira. 1997. Nutrient intakes of individuals from food-insufficient households in the United States. *American Journal of Public Health* 87, no. 12:1956–61.

Seidell, J. C. 1995. Obesity in Europe: Scaling an epidemic. *International Journal of Obesity and Related Metabolic Disorders* 19, suppl. 3:S1–S4.

Shepard, R., and C. M. Dennison. 1996. Influences on adolescent food choice. *Proceedings of the Nutrition Society* 55:345–57.

Stockman, J. A. 1987. Iron deficiency anemia: Have we come far enough? *Journal of the American Medical Association* 258:1645–47.

Szabo, P., and F. Tury. 1995. Prevalence of clinical and subclinical forms of anorexia and bulimia nervosa among working females and males. *Orvosi Hetilap* 136, no. 34:1829–35.

Turnbull, S., A. Ward, J. Treasure, H. Jick, and L. Derby. 1996. The demand for eating disorder care: An epidemiological study using the general practice research database. *British Journal of Psychiatry* 169, no. 6:705–12.

U.S. Department of Agriculture (USDA) and U.S. Department of Health and Human Services (DHHS). 1995. *Nutrition and your health: Dietary guidelines for Americans.* Home and Garden Bulletin no. 232. 4th ed. Washington D.C.: U.S. Government Printing Office.

U.S. Department of Health, Education, and Welfare (DHEW). 1977. *NCHS growth curves for children: Birth–18 years.* Publication no. 78–1650. Hyattsville, Md..

Wang, Y., B. Popkin, and F. Zhai. 1998. The nutritional status and dietary pattern of Chinese adolescents, 1991 and 1993. *European Journal of Clinical Nutrition* 52, no. 12:908–16.

Wilde, P. 1997. A monthly cycle in food use by food stamp recipients. Paper presented at research briefing, Board on Children, Youth, and Families. Cornell University, 19–20 May.

Wilde, P., and C. Ranney. 1997. A monthly cycle in food expenditure and intake by participants in the U.S. food stamp program. Working Paper no. 97-04. Department of Agricultural, Resource, and Managerial Economics, Cornell University.

Wilson, J. D., E. Braunwald, K. J. Isselbacher, R. G. Petersdorf, J. B. Martin, A. S. Fauci, and R. K. Root, eds. *Harrison's principles of internal medicine.* 1991. New York: McGraw-Hill.

Wright, J. D., K. Bialostosky, E. W. Gunter, M. D. Carroll, M. F. Najjar, B. A. Bowman, and C. L. Johnson. 1998. Blood folate and vitamin B12: United States, 1988–94. *Vital and Health Statistics. Series 11: Data from the National Health Survey* 243 (December):1–78.

Contributors

Jay Bhattacharya
RAND
1700 Main Street
P.O. Box 2138
Santa Monica, CA 90407

David Card
Department of Economics
University of California, Berkeley
549 Evans Hall #3880
Berkeley, CA 94720

Frank J. Chaloupka
Department of Economics
College of Business Administration
University of Illinois
601 S. Morgan Street, Room 2103
Chicago, IL 60607

Philip J. Cook
Terry Sanford Institute of Public
 Policy
Box 90245
Duke University
Durham, NC 27708

Janet Currie
Economics Department
UCLA
405 Hilgard Avenue
Los Angeles, CA 90095

David M. Cutler
Department of Economics
Harvard University
Cambridge, MA 02138

Thomas S. Dee
Department of Economics
Swarthmore College
500 College Avenue
Swarthmore, PA 19081

William N. Evans
Department of Economics
University of Maryland
College Park, MD 20742

Matthew C. Farrelly
Research Triangle Institute
P.O. 12194
Research Triangle Park, NC 27709

Edward L. Glaeser
Department of Economics
327 Littauer Center
Harvard University
Cambridge, MA 02138

Michael Grossman
National Bureau of Economic
 Research
365 Fifth Avenue, 5th Floor
New York, NY 10016-4309

Jonathan Gruber
Department of Economics, E52-355
Massachusetts Institute of Technology
50 Memorial Drive
Cambridge, MA 02142-1347

Lloyd D. Johnston
Institute for Social Research
University of Michigan
426 Thompson Street
Ann Arbor, MI 48104-2321

Thomas Lemieux
Department of Economics
University of British Columbia
997-1873 East Mall
Vancouver, BC V6T 1Z1
CANADA

Phillip B. Levine
Department of Economics
Wellesley College
Wellesley, MA 02481

Steven D. Levitt
Department of Economics
University of Chicago
1126 East 59th Street
Chicago, IL 60637

Lance Lochner
Department of Economics
University of Rochester
Rochester, NY 14627

Michael J. Moore
Graduate School of Business
University of Chicago
1101 East 58th Street
Chicago, IL 60637

Karen E. Norberg
Department of Child and Adolescent
  Psychiatry
Boston Medical Center
818 Harrison Avenue
Boston, MA 02118

Ted O'Donoghue
Department of Economics
Cornell University
464 Uris Hall
Ithaca, NY 14853-7601

Patrick M. O'Malley
Institute for Social Research
University of Michigan
426 Thompson Street
Ann Arbor, MI 48104-2321

Rosalie Liccardo Pacula
Associate Economist
RAND
1700 Main Street
P.O. Box 2138
Santa Monica, CA 90407-2138

Matthew Rabin
Department of Economics
549 Evans Hall #3880
University of California
Berkeley, CA 94720-3880

Jonathan Zinman
Department of Economics
Massachusetts Institute of Technology
50 Memorial Drive
Cambridge, MA 02142-1347

Author Index

Subject Index

Abortion: effect of laws on teen motherhood, 211; effect of restrictions on teen sexual activity, 205; rates for teens (1972–98), 169–74

Accident rates, motor-vehicle: for passenger-car occupants (1988–97), 133–34, 138; teen involvement and survivability, 133–42; tow-away accidents for passenger-car occupants, 134–35, 138

Accidents, motor vehicle: characteristics of passenger-vehicle occupants, 138–39; Fatal Accident Reporting System (FARS), 123, 127, 135, 139, 153

Addiction: to marijuana, 280–81; rational-addiction model, 3–4

Affective development, 4

Air bags, 141–42

Alcohol-control policies: influence of excise taxes on, 376, 384; minimum legal drinking age (MLDA), 136, 149; minimum purchase age (MPA), 375–76; Uniform Drinking Age Act (1984), 383

Alcohol (ethyl alcohol): consumption per capita, 410, 411t; effect of beer tax and MPA on consumption of, 410, 411t; involvement in fatal crashes by time of day, 135–36; social influences on teen consumption of, 412–13. *See also* Bingeing, teen; Driving behavior; Drunk-driving policies; Excise taxes

Antismoking policies: advertising restrictions, 93; clean-air regulation, 92, 97, 103–4, 117–19; counteradvertising, 93; licensing of retailers, 93; penalties on tobacco purchases by minors, 93; youth-access restrictions, 92–93, 97, 103–4, 117–19

Armed Forces Qualifying Test (AFQT), 339, 349–50, 387

Automobiles: crashworthiness, 138–42; incidence of teens' travel by, 130–32. *See also* Driving behavior; Fatalities, motor vehicle

Beer tax. *See* Excise taxes

Behavioral economics, 31–32, 63–65

Beliefs: about future behavior, 42–43; irrational, false, or exaggerated, 58–60; not affecting behavior, 43

Bingeing, teen: probability of persistence and habit, 413–16; social influences, 412–13

Birth control. *See* Contraception

Birth rates: to teen mothers (1972–98), 169–74; to teens by race and ethnicity (1988–98), 170–71, 173

BMI. *See* Obesity

Clinton administration: on increasing price of cigarettes, 2; tobacco regulation bill, 69

DEMCO